Professor Robert Merton of Harvard described the past, present, and future of finance with an analogy to boom boxes. Prior to the advent of stereo sound, mono sound was produced by gramophones. After stereo technology was developed, stereo sound was produced and packaged in the form of consoles. Then, in the 1960's and 1970's, radio and phonograph makers began selling the components of sound separately. Consumers would buy a tuner, a turntable, an amplifier, a tape deck, an equalizer, and a set of speakers. Consumers purchased their preferred configuration, buying tuners from a manufacturer specializing in tuners, speakers from another known for quality speaker construction, and so forth.

But all did not work so well. It was complicated for some to properly configure a sound system. The wiring became even more complicated when compact disc players, reverb units, and remote control operators were added. The exploding numbers of permutations and combinations of brands and components became confusing and frustrating to consumers.

After two decades of this componentization phase, vendors got the message, and in the 1980's, they created the "boom box," which had all components properly matched, integrated, and combined in a single portable unit complete with lightweight earphones. The result is a single unit with higher quality sound reproduction than most of the expensive console cabinets of earlier years.

The history of financial instruments is much the same, but with a time offset of about 10 years. Until the 1970's, financial instruments were sold in fairly simple "plain vanilla" packages known as stocks, bonds, whole loans, mortgages, and futures. It later became apparent that each instrument was really comprised of some combination of more fundamental components.

Wall Street investment bankers got the idea of slicing and dicing the prevalent securities and selling their components. Investors could then purchase these components and combine them in a way to satisfy their needs. Repackaging of components produced numerous new securities with features that behaved in ways quite different from their underlying securities.

With the proliferation of derivative securities came a lot of confusion for investors. It seemed that in some cases, investor knowledge was not keeping up with the pace of innovation. Today, the finance community is getting the message. Consumers and investors want a few basic results from their investment. They may wish to provide for a certain standard of living upon retirement, or to generate sufficient funds to send a son or daughter to college, or to fund their anticipated lavish weddings or kitchen renovations. In essence, consumers want a finance boom box. Most consumers and investors do not have the time, aptitude, training, or patience to do this for themselves. They would prefer that someone else package the options, futures, stocks, bonds, and derivatives into a portfolio that meets their needs. Whether this vision of the future is accurate remains to be seen, but it sounds right to us.

Boom Boxes and the Evolution of Finance

Financial Markets, Instruments, and Institutions

Anthony M. Santomero
David F. Babbel
both of The Wharton School, University of Pennsylvania

IRWIN

Chicago • Bogotá • Boston • Buenos Aires • Caracas
London • Madrid • Mexico City • Sydney • Toronto

Irwin Book Team

Publisher: *Michael W. Junior*
Sponsoring editor: *Gina M. Huck*
Senior development editor: *Jane T. Ducham*
Marketing manager: *Katie Rose*
Senior project supervisor: *Jean Lou Hess*
Production supervisor: *Pat Frederickson*
Designer: *Crispin Prebys*
Prepress Buyer: *Charlene R. Perez*
Compositor: *Shepard Poorman Communications Corp.*
Typeface: *10/12 Times Roman*
Printer: *R. R. Donnelley & Sons Company*

Library of Congress Cataloging-in-Publication Data

Santomero, Anthony M.
    Financial markets, instruments, and institutions / Anthony M.
Santomero, David F. Babbel.
      p.   cm. — (The Irwin series in finance, insurance, and real
estate)
    Includes bibliographical references and index.
    ISBN 0-256-16626-9
    1. Finance.   2. Financial services industry.   I. Babbel, David
F., 1949–   . II. Title. III. Series.
    HG173.S523   1997
    332.63—dc20   96–38961

Printed the United States of America
1 2 3 4 5 6 7 8 9 0 DOC 3 2 1 0 9 8 7 6

Preface

Financial markets, instruments, and institutions have undergone substantial change over the last decade. There has been a proliferation of financial instruments as well as an explosion in trading volume. The once staid institutions involved in the creation and trading of financial assets have transformed themselves in response to these changes. In light of this revolution in the financial market, teachers of this material constantly have had to modify and adapt their course outlines. To aid in this process of change, the present volume attempts to update the textbooks in this area in order to respond to the dynamics of the financial markets. It develops more fully the approaches used to price financial instruments; it presents a more up-to-date description of the markets; and offers more current insight into the evolution of financial sector institutions.

The Underlying Philosophy

The study of financial markets has traditionally been taught either as a money and banking course or as an institutionally based money and capital markets course. The former begins with the role of money in society and moves to the macroeconomic implications of diversified financial markets. It does not address the wide range of individual financial instruments, nor does it examine the structure of financial markets and institutions in any detail. The latter avoids issues of valuation and pricing methodologies in favor of descriptive material with an institutional focus.

In today's dynamic financial environment, the knowledgeable participant requires a more firm grounding in financial theory, a greater exposure to the diversity of financial instruments, and an appreciation of the role of institutions within these markets. Choosing to concentrate strictly on the monetary sector or the descriptive elements of the market does not allow the student to appreciate the key concepts of theory and how they are incorporated into financial markets. Rather than forcing the instructor to choose between these two approaches, the current textbook offers a perspective that centers more on the function, pricing, and institutional structure of the financial markets. While neglecting macroeconomic apparatus, it develops more fully the pricing of various financial instruments and the differences between instruments and institutions that operate in the financial markets.

Organization of the Text

In Section I the textbook opens with a discussion of financial markets' role in the economy. It integrates both the markets and institutions into an overall view of how the economy works and how its activity is measured.

Section II begins with a discussion of the determination of financial market interest rates. It explains both the level of interest rates and reasons for interest rate movements over time. Next, it uses current market interest rates to value cash flows of different kinds. Starting from simple present value, it develops the more modern techniques that are currently in use in financial markets.

Section III explores the main instruments of the money and capital markets. Starting from short-term money market instruments, it explores the bond, mortgage, and equity markets. It then introduces futures and options, floating rate securities, and other more esoteric derivatives. In each case, the institutional features of the market are presented, key characteristics of the instrument reviewed, and the valuation techniques developed in Section II employed to determine market prices for the instrument in question.

Section IV has two parts. In the first three chapters (17, 18 and 19), the nature of markets is reviewed and the role of markets in facilitating new issues and ownership transfer discussed. Next, this section reviews the major institutions in the financial markets. The section ends with a discussion of financial structure changes and how these institutions use the techniques developed in this textbook to manage their own financial performance.

The textbook concludes with Section V, where the role of the Federal Reserve and the money supply is discussed. Given the important role that the money supply plays in the financial sector, these chapters review how the Federal Reserve affects this quantity and how it interrelates with other parts of the financial markets.

Intended Audience

This textbook is designed for a one-semester course in money and capital markets taught within a finance department of a business school. By design, the course does not require nor does it overlap with monetary economics or finance topics taught elsewhere in the curriculum. It is designed to be used in the first financial markets course. After completing this course, students will be well prepared for the more advanced material in courses such as investments, speculative markets, international finance, and fixed income. On the other hand, if the student chooses to take no further courses in finance, the textbook can be used to offer a broad overview of financial markets, pricing, and institutions.

Ancillary Support

The following supplementary materials are available for instructors who use this book to support them in their teaching efforts:

Instructor's Manual/Test Bank

The manual for this textbook includes solutions to all end-of-chapter review questions. These are supplemented by additional questions and problems that can be used as a test bank for each of the 27 chapters. In addition, the Instructor's Manual includes chapter outlines/transparency masters designed to assist in the chapter-by-chapter presentation of the material. In these outlines, key subjects are indicated and pertinent formulas presented for in-class discussion.

Acknowledgments

We are indebted to the many colleagues who gave us their insight and guidance while we were writing this textbook. Their careful work was a major factor in our creating a book that is current, accurate, and fresh in its approach. Among all who helped in this endeavor:

Zolton Acs	University of Baltimore
Nasser Arshadi	University of Missouri
Maureen Burton	California State Polytechnic University, Pomona
Alexander E. Cassuto	California State University-Hayward
Robert A. Connolly	University of North Carolina at Chapel Hill
David R. Durst	University of Akron
Peter Eisemann	Georgia State University
Sid Gautum	Methodist College
Erika W. Gilbert	Illinois State University
Peter Gomori	St. Francis College
Owen Gregory	University of Illinois, Chicago
Sam Ramsey Hakim	University of Nebraska at Omaha
Charles Haywood	University of Kentucky
Dan Himarios	University of Texas at Arlington
William E. Jackson, III	University of North Carolina at Chapel Hill

Richard LeCompte	Wichita State University
Marvin Margolis	University of Pennsylvania at Millersville
Thomas McGahagan	University of Pittsburgh
Robert W. McLeod	University of Alabama
W. Douglas McMillin	Louisiana State University
Charles Meiburg	University of Virginia
Craig Merrill	Brigham Young University
Paul Natke	Central Michigan University
Coleen C. Pantalone	Northeastern University
David Pyle	University of California at Berkeley
Ganas K. Rakes	Ohio University
Nanda Rangan	Southern Illinois University at Carbondale
Eugene Sarver	Pace University
Lester Seigel	World Bank
Robert Schweitzer	University of Delaware
Tom Varghese	James Madison University
James Verbrugge	University of Georgia
Mike Walker	University of Cincinnati
Sam Webb	Wichita State University
Mark Witte	Northwestern University

Special thanks are due to Paul Hoffman, Daniel Klim, and Anthony Ng, who helped us prepare the manuscript for final submission to the publisher by securing permissions, updating exhibits, and proofreading. Their hard work has helped make this book accurate and as current as possible. Finally, we thank the Richard D. Irwin staff, especially Gina Huck, Sponsoring Editor; Jane Ducham, Senior Development Editor; Jean Lou Hess, Senior Project Supervisor; Mike Junior, Publisher; and Crispin Prebys, Designer, without whom this book could not have been developed and published.

We welcome any comments and suggestions for enhancement. Please let us know of your experience with this text, either through Irwin or at our E-mail addresses below.

Anthony M. Santomero
santo@wharton.upenn.edu

David F. Babbel
babbel@wharton.upenn.edu

About the Authors

Anthony M. Santomero

Anthony M. Santomero is the Richard K. Mellon Professor and Director of the Wharton Financial Institutions Center at the Wharton School, where he has been since 1972. He has published extensively in the academic journals and is currently an Associate Editor of the *Journal of Banking and Finance*, the *Journal of Money, Credit and Banking, Journal of Financial Services Research*, and *European Finance Review*. He serves on the editorial boards of the *Journal of Economics and Business, Open Economies Review, European Financial Management*, and *Advances in Finance, Investments, and Banking*.

As a consultant for leading financial institutions in the United States and abroad, Dr. Santomero has addressed issues of financial risk management procedures, the pricing of risks of various kinds, and credit risk evaluation and management. He has advised the Federal Reserve Board of Governors, the FDIC, and the General Accounting Office on a wide range of issues relating to capital regulation and structural reform. Internationally, he has been a consultant to the Europen Economic Community in Brussels, the Inter-American Development Bank, the Kingdom of Sweden, the Ministry of Finance of Japan, the Treasury of New Zealand, the Bank of Israel, the National Housing Bank of India, the Saudi Arabian Monetary Agency, and the Capital Markets Board of Turkey. In addition, he currently serves as a permanent advisor to the Swedish Central Bank.

Dr. Santomero holds an A.B. in Economics from Fordham University, a Ph.D. in Economics from Brown University, and also received an honorary doctorate from the Stockholm School of Economics in 1992.

David F. Babbel

David F. Babbel joined the Wharton School faculty in 1984 and currently is Associate Professor of Insurance and Finance. He teaches in the graduate program primarily in the areas of insurance finance and investment management. Prior to joining Wharton, he was on the finance faculty for seven years at the University of California at Berkeley, where he taught principally in the areas of international financial management, corporate finance, and investments.

A former vice president and director of research in the Pension and Insurance Department at Goldman, Sachs & Co., and economist at the World Bank, Dr. Babbel is a financial consultant for several of the largest financial institutions. He has published prolifically in academic and professional literature on asset/liability management, insurance, fixed income investments, and foreign exchange risk management. He is coauthor of a 1996 monograph entitled *Valuation of Interest-Sensitive Financial Instruments.*

He received his undergraduate training in economics at Brigham Young University, and his graduate training at the University of Florida in finance. His postdoctoral education in insurance was undertaken at the University of Pennsylvania's Wharton School.

Brief Contents

PART IV

MARKETS AND INSTITUTIONS

PART V

THE IMPORTANT ROLE OF BANKS

Contents

PART **III**

INSTRUMENTS IN THE MARKET

PART V

THE IMPORTANT ROLE OF BANKS

PART I

Ground Rules and Reasons for Study

Introduction: Functions Performed by Financial Markets

Chapter Outline

Intermediating Savings and Investing
Financial Markets as a Venue for Trade
    The Need for Trading Capability
    The Nature of Secondary Market Transactions
    Institutions as an Alternative to the Secondary Market
The Effect of Efficient Financial Markets on the Economy
Aggregate Totals in the Financial Markets

This chapter presents an overview of the fundamental services provided by the financial structure of the real economy. Through financial markets and institutions, the current savings of one sector are funneled into the investments of another. In addition, these markets and institutions provide a marketplace for the trading of securities that are the result of previous saving and investment decisions. In combination, the various parts of the financial markets permit a developed economic system to allocate money to its highest and best use and therefore facilitate high per capita income and better use of an economy's scarce resources.

An important part of any modern economy is its **financial structure,** the combination of its financial markets and institutions. These two parts of any financial system allow a highly complex, specialized economy to function in a decentralized manner. The financial structure brings borrowers and lenders together and fosters economic efficiency and a better use of society's resources, which, in general, results in a higher capital stock for the economy as a whole and a better standard of living for its inhabitants.

Without a developed financial system, institutions, firms, and households would be forced to operate as self-contained economies. As a result, they could not save without deploying their resources somewhere, and they could not invest without saving from their own current output. A financial system allows trade between individuals to accomplish both of these ends. It allows savers to defer consumption and obtain a return for waiting. Likewise, it permits investors to deploy resources in excess of those that they have available from their own wealth in order to gain the productivity that such investment yields. The economy also gains from the financial system, as both households and firms advance the economy, total output, and economic growth.

However, the complexity of a developed financial system often obscures its function. Observers frequently become lost in the details of the system's markets and institutions and miss the purpose and function of those elements. Yet, it is important to understand the role that a financial market plays in any developed economy. It is equally important to understand the intricacies of this market, its institutions, and its instruments. It is our goal here to explain both the forest and the trees.

Intermediating Savings and Investing

There are two primary functions of any financial market. The first of these functions is to trade claims on output between economic agents that have different timing needs for consumption. Some economic agents wish to transfer current resources to the future, while others need access to current output for current period consumption. The financial markets facilitate such trades. The second function performed by these markets is to provide liquidity for the exchange of the financial claims created to transfer purchasing power across time. This allows trading in financial assets between agents that wish to buy and sell them before maturity.

The first of these activities is the central role performed by financial markets in affecting current output and economic activity. The system of institutions and markets allows **economic agents** to deploy their economic resources to best advantage. Economic agents are the participants in the economy and include households, corporations, and the government itself. Some economic agents have more resources than they wish to use during the current period; others have too little. Economic agents, in the first group, are said to be **surplus economic units.** They wish to save part of current income for future consumption. Economic agents in the second group, known as **deficit economic units,** wish to gain access to current income for use either for current consumption beyond existing income sources or for investment and its future expected return.

To see how this is accomplished in the financial markets, consider a simple economy with both individuals or households and business firms. The households receive income or wages for their productive activity at the firms. While most of this income is consumed, some of it is saved to be used later. Households may save in two ways. They may buy goods that will last over several periods, or they may

Exhibit 1.1

The financial system

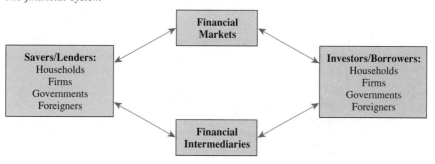

buy financial assets issued by firms, which, in turn, use current output for such things as plant and equipment or inventory investment. In practical terms, the household must choose between buying an inventory of consumption goods, such as consumer durables like washing machines or automobiles, or using its income to enter into an investment transaction in the financial markets. The last of these is referred to as a **financial investment** because the household surrenders its current output for a paper claim to the future output of another part of the economy.

Firms, on the other hand, issue financial claims in order to invest in their inventory of both finished and unfinished goods, as well as in the plant and equipment that they use and require for production. They do so in an effort to profit from the increased quantity of output they produce or from the reduced cost of production associated with the efficiency gains achieved as a result of the investment. To expand, these firms must obtain resources from the household sector in order to meet the required financial commitments that result from their real investment in their business venture.

Resources change hands in the financial system in one of two ways. As Exhibit 1.1 illustrates, borrowers either transact directly with savers in a financial market or work through intermediaries, financial institutions, to obtain their needed resources. Savers will transact directly with borrowers whenever they feel comfortable doing so. This will be the case when the borrower's reputation is good, the project to be undertaken is clear, and the investor's rights and obligations are understood.

If these conditions are not met, the investor/saver will generally employ the services of a **financial intermediary.** Financial intermediaries are institutions that assist both sides of the market by providing a host of services to facilitate the financial transaction. Among other services, financial intermediaries may provide assistance in evaluating investment proposals, offer diversified investments in a large number of projects for their investor clients, or monitor such projects on an ongoing basis. As is evident in Exhibit 1.1, financial intermediaries are competitors to direct lenders, but they are complements to the lending process. They provide services that range from information and quality evaluation to divisibility of assets. In all, these intermediary institutions increase the ability of both sides of the transaction to participate in the market and thereby increase the amount of saving and potential investment in the economy as a whole.

Thus far, borrowers have been referred to as firms who are seeking to expand their business through capital investment. However, borrowers may also be households seeking credit to purchase consumer durables, including the largest durable of all, their homes, through the mortgage market. In addition, the government may borrow funds if it chooses to spend more than its tax and user fee revenues. Borrowers may be domestic firms, households, or governments, but they may also be foreign nationals, firms, or governments. To the investor, this distinction will matter little. In any case, borrowers enter the marketplace offering claims on future output in exchange for current income. As will be discussed below, these offers include a complex array of promises and prices, all of which aim to attract savers—surplus economic units—to the particular financial asset.

Investors in these financial instruments come from several sectors as well. The first and largest of these is the household sector discussed above. However, other participants are also present in the marketplace. Firms with excess cash accumulate these funds in anticipation of future investment. In the interim, they offer these funds to other firms or to financial institutions seeking short-term resources. Governments, too, enter the market, procuring funds for special purposes such as housing or education. In addition, governments will regularly enter the market when tax revenues do not coincide with spending patterns. Moreover, the internationalization of the financial markets in recent years has resulted in foreign households, firms, and governments increasingly investing their resources in markets outside their own countries.

Financial Markets as a Venue for Trade

The Need for Trading Capability

As noted at the outset, financial markets and institutions provide two separate functions to the economy. The first of these was discussed above and is commonly referred to as **primary market** activity. In addition to this role of transferring funds between savers and investors, financial markets and institutions allow for the trading of preexisting assets. This activity is so intense, visible, and institutionalized that it frequently overshadows the first function of financial markets. However, it is important to recognize that both functions are important.

To make financial instruments attractive, surplus units must be able to dispose of financial investments once they are purchased. This trading of existing financial assets is generally done in a **secondary market** in which buyers and sellers of preexisting securities meet to trade. Obviously, the more efficient that secondary transactions can become, the more likely investors are to devote their resources to financial investments.

The Nature of Secondary Market Transactions

The exchange of financial assets between two individuals takes place in a secondary market. It is, in essence, a market for "used" or "previously owned" securities. In this market, individuals or institutions that have securities try to find buyers. This process can be informal or highly structured. It may take place over the phone or in organized exchanges with sophisticated systems and rigid trading rules and regulations.

The simplest of such secondary markets is sometimes referred to as the private placement market, which will be discussed in a later chapter. The most complex secondary markets include the organized exchanges such as the New York Stock Exchange and the Chicago Mercantile Exchange, which will also be detailed later in this book. Regardless of the complexity of the secondary market, the process is the same. The individuals, either directly or through brokers, enter the market to buy or sell a preexisting security. They negotiate the price based upon the value of that security to both the buyer and the seller.

Secondary markets are often referred to as good or bad, using a fairly precise notion of what market participants want. A well-functioning financial market is generally thought to possess three desirable attributes. The market should be **efficient** in the sense that transactions occur with ease and at prices that closely correspond to the true value of the instrument being traded. Markets are considered **inefficient** if these conditions are lacking. Markets are said to be **liquid** when assets are easily transferable at a price that accurately and fairly represents the value of the future cash flow they represent. Markets are **illiquid** to the extent that they do not permit this easy transfer at a fair price. Markets are called **deep** if there are many buyers and sellers and **shallow** or **thin** if there are relatively few. This latter characterization refers to the ability of the market to facilitate a large volume of trades with small price swings.

An efficient, liquid, and deep market facilitates the trading of assets and the initiation of new assets. This is because, in this market environment, purchasers of new securities know that their decision is reversible. If the buyer wishes to sell, he may enter the secondary market and easily dispose of any financial instrument.

Institutions as an Alternative to the Secondary Market

Some instruments are not directly traded with other buyers; instead, they are turned in at financial institutions, which then reissue them to other savers. In these cases, the institution serves as an alternative to a secondary market as it stands ready to redeem the institution's debt or equity claims at a prespecified price or time. This redemption service is one of the roles performed by financial institutions. Instances of institutions providing this important service to their constituents are easy to find. For example, some mutual funds redeem their shares at open market value, and banks allow depositors to reclaim their investment either on demand or at fixed intervals.

In some cases, these institutions merely decline in size when investors choose to withdraw their funds. In other cases, they find other investors to replace those wishing to redeem their assets. In any case, the intermediary sector provides some of the same services as a secondary market.

The Effect of Efficient Financial Markets on the Economy

Efficient financial markets have a substantial effect on the real economy. From the point of view of savers, efficient financial markets provide them with an opportunity to increase future consumption by allowing others to use their surplus current income. The yield that savers obtain from the financial asset means higher consumption tomorrow. In addition, it encourages thrift by allowing individuals to defer current consumption and build wealth in the future.

At the same time, investors benefit from the access to real resources that an efficient financial market permits. By providing resources necessary for increasing plant and equipment and, hence, productivity, an efficient financial market enables the business sector to invest in the future. To the extent that resources are readily available, investment is high, and the firm can finance expansion and exploit profitable opportunities.

For the economy as a whole, an efficient financial market means a better standard of living. Higher consumption is made possible by greater capital intensity and greater output. Unlike the stereotypical view of financial markets as a wasteful activity without a real resource effect, financial markets are an integral part of a developed economy. They allow specialization and a complex flow of resources between borrowers and lenders. Very specialized projects are financed through the financial markets and their institutions, as the expertise of specialists is tapped to funnel funds into their most efficient use. In fact, no developed economy can maintain a high level of consumption and growth without a sophisticated financial system.

Aggregate Totals in the Financial Markets

Before an extensive treatment of the pricing and characteristics of financial instruments is presented, it is appropriate to look at the level of activity in financial markets. From an aggregate point of view, world financial markets are substantial in size. The U.S. market, a major part of this global market, is equally dazzling in size and complexity. This can be seen in any number of ways.

Looking only at total borrowing by the domestic nonfinancial sector, the Federal Reserve estimates that the U.S. economy raised $819.6 billion in 1995. Exhibit 1.2 indicates that of this total, $193.6 billion was absorbed by the government sector, while the private sector borrowed an additional $626.0 billion. At the same time, foreign net borrowing in the United States during 1995 is estimated to have been $36.0 billion, indicating that a total of $855.6 billion was raised. However, nonfinancial firms were contracting corporate equity. For 1995, it is estimated that corporate buy-backs of equity exceeded new issues by $73.2 billion. More will be said of this trend in subsequent chapters.

EXHIBIT 1.2   **Funds Raised in U.S. Credit Markets**
($ Billions Quarterly Data at Seasonally Adjusted Annual Rates)

Nonfinancial Sector						
	1990	*1991*	*1992*	*1993*	*1994*	*1995(2Q)*
Total net borrowing by domestic nonfinancial sectors	**635.3**	**478.7**	**540.6**	**618.5**	**602.4**	**819.6**
By sector and instrument						
U.S. government	246.9	278.2	304.0	256.1	155.9	193.6
Treasury securities	238.7	292.0	303.8	248.3	155.7	192.0
Budget agency issues and mortgages	8.2	−13.8	0.2	7.8	0.2	1.6
Private	388.4	200.4	236.7	362.4	446.6	626.0
By instrument						
Tax-exempt obligation	48.7	68.7	31.1	75.5	−29.9	−20.3
Corporate bonds	47.1	78.8	67.6	75.2	22.0	119.5
Mortgages	199.5	161.4	123.9	155.7	187.2	163.2
Home mortgages	185.6	163.8	179.5	183.9	195.2	153.3
Multifamily residential	4.8	−3.1	−11.2	−6.0	1.7	8.0
Commercial	9.3	0.4	−45.5	−22.6	−11.4	−1.9
Farm	−0.3	0.4	1.1	0.5	1.8	3.9
Consumer credit	15.6	−14.8	7.3	58.9	121.2	147.9
Bank loans n.e.c.	0.4	−40.9	−13.8	4.8	71.4	102.2
Commercial paper	9.7	−18.4	8.6	10.0	21.4	44.8
Other loans	67.5	−34.4	11.9	−17.7	53.2	68.6
By borrowing sector						
Household	218.5	171.1	214.2	280.9	353.5	324.7
Nonfinancial business	123.9	−33.3	0.8	18.5	137.1	328.8
Farm	2.3	2.1	1.0	2.0	2.8	6.8
Nonfarm noncorporate	10.1	−27.9	−43.5	−24.6	15.5	32.0
Corporate	111.4	−7.4	43.2	41.1	118.8	289.9
State and local government	46.0	62.6	21.7	63.0	−44.0	−27.5
Foreign net borrowing in United States	23.9	14.8	22.6	68.8	−20.3	36.0
Bonds	21.4	15.0	15.7	81.3	7.1	46.7
Bank loans n.e.c.	−2.9	3.1	2.3	0.7	1.4	5.6
Commercial paper	12.3	6.4	5.2	−9.0	−27.3	−9.6
U.S. government and other loans	−7.0	−9.8	−0.6	−4.2	−1.6	−6.7
Total domestic plus foreign	**659.2**	**493.4**	**563.3**	**687.3**	**582.1**	**855.6**
Financial Sector						
Total net borrowing by financial sectors	202.6	151.7	239.2	289.5	456.3	381.7
By instrument						
U.S. government–related	167.4	145.7	155.8	164.2	284.3	186.1
Government-sponsored enterprises securities	17.1	9.2	40.3	80.6	176.9	127.2
Mortgage pool securities	150.3	136.6	115.6	83.6	112.1	59.0
Loans from U.S. government	−0.1	0.0	0.0	0.0	−4.8	0.0
Private	35.3	6.0	83.4	125.3	172.1	195.6
Corporate bonds	46.0	66.8	80.5	118.6	110.2	145.3
Mortgages	0.6	0.5	0.6	3.6	9.8	4.8
Bank loans n.e.c.	4.7	8.8	2.2	−14.0	−12.3	10.1

(continued)

EXHIBIT 1.2   (concluded)

Financial Sector

	1990	1991	1992	1993	1994	1995(2Q)
Open market paper	8.6	−32.0	−0.7	−6.2	41.6	33.3
Loans from Federal Home Loan Banks	−24.7	−38.0	0.8	23.3	22.8	2.2
By borrowing sector						
Government-sponsored enterprises	17.0	9.1	40.2	80.6	172.1	127.2
Federally related mortgage pools	150.3	136.6	115.6	83.6	112.1	59.0
Private	35.3	6.0	83.4	125.3	172.1	195.6
Commercial banks	−0.7	−11.7	8.8	5.6	10.0	18.4
Bank holding companies	−27.7	−2.5	2.3	8.8	10.3	20.3
Funding companies	15.4	−6.5	13.2	2.9	24.2	10.4
Savings institutions	−30.2	−44.5	−6.7	11.1	12.8	−6.9
Credit unions	0.0	0.0	0.0	0.2	0.2	−0.1
Life insurance companies	0.0	0.0	0.0	0.2	0.3	0.1
Finance companies	23.8	17.7	−1.6	0.2	50.2	61.1
Mortgage companies	0.0	−2.4	8.0	−1.0	−11.5	1.2
Real estate investment trusts (REITs)	0.8	1.2	0.3	3.4	13.7	6.4
Brokers and dealers	1.5	3.7	2.7	12.0	0.5	−0.1
Issuers of asset-backed securities (ABSs)	52.3	51.0	56.3	81.8	61.2	84.7

All Sectors

	1990	1991	1992	1993	1994	1995(2Q)
Total net borrowing, all sectors	**861.8**	**645.2**	**802.5**	**976.8**	**1,038.4**	**1,237.3**
U.S. government securities	414.4	424.0	459.8	420.3	444.9	379.8
Tax-exempt securities	48.7	68.7	31.1	75.5	−29.9	−20.3
Corporate and foreign bonds	114.5	160.6	163.8	275.1	139.3	311.5
Mortgages	200.1	161.9	124.5	159.2	197.0	168.0
Consumer credit	15.6	−14.8	7.3	58.9	121.2	147.9
Bank loans n.e.c.	2.2	−29.1	−9.4	−8.5	60.6	117.9
Open market paper	30.7	−44.0	13.1	−5.1	35.7	68.5
Other loans	35.8	−82.2	12.1	1.3	69.6	64.1

Funds Raised through Mututal Funds and Corporate Equities

	1990	1991	1992	1993	1994	1995(2Q)
Total net share issues	**19.7**	**215.4**	**296.0**	**440.1**	**162.1**	**146.6**
Mutual funds	65.3	151.5	211.9	320.0	138.3	178.5
Corporate equities	−45.6	64.0	84.1	120.1	23.7	−31.9
Nonfinancial corporations	−63.0	18.3	27.0	21.3	−44.9	−73.2
Financial corporations	10.0	15.1	26.4	38.3	26.0	5.6
Foreign share purchased in United States	7.4	30.7	30.7	60.5	42.7	35.7

Source: *Federal Reserve Bulletin*, January 1996, p. A40.

In any case, the net primary market activity of any sector is only a small part of the total story, as indicated above. If one were to look at total outstanding debt, the number would be substantially larger—$17.667 trillion. Exhibit 1.3 indicates that looking at total credit market debt, both domestic and foreign, substantially increases the perceived level of this activity. Total credit

EXHIBIT 1.3   Summary of Credit Market Debt Outstanding
($ Billions; End of Period)

	Nonfinancial Sector					
	1990	*1991*	*1992*	*1993*	*1994*	*1995(2Q)*
Total credit market debt owed by domestic nonfinancial sectors	**10,692.0**	**11,184.1**	**11,727.9**	**12,368.3**	**12,970.5**	**13,343.2**
By lending sector and instrument						
U.S. government	2,498.1	2,776.4	3,080.3	3,336.5	3,492.3	3,583.5
Treasury securities	2,465.8	2,757.8	3,061.6	3,309.9	3,456.6	3,556.7
Budget agency issues and mortgages	32.4	18.6	18.8	26.6	26.7	26.8
Private	8,193.9	8,407.7	8,647.6	9.031.8	9,478.2	9,759.7
By instrument						
Tax-exempt obligations	1,062.1	1,108.6	1,139.7	1,215.2	1,185.2	1,164.6
Corporate bonds	1,008.2	1,086.9	1,154.5	1,229.7	1,251.7	1,292.0
Mortgages	3,715.4	3.920.0	1,043.9	4,220.6	4,407.9	4,505.9
Home mortgages	2,580.6	2,780.0	2,959.6	3,149.6	3,344.8	3,431.8
Multifamily residential	305.5	304.8	293.6	289.0	290.7	293.6
Commercial	750.8	755.8	710.3	700.8	689.4	696.1
Farm	78.4	79.3	80.4	81.2	83.0	84.4
Consumer credit	813.0	797.2	804.6	863.5	984.7	1,026.6
Bank loans n.e.c.	747.8	686.0	672.1	677.0	748.3	807.9
Commercial paper	116.9	98.5	107.1	117.8	139.2	162.5
Other loans	730.6	710.6	725.7	707.9	761.1	800.3
By borrowing sector						
Household	3,594.8	3,784.5	3,998.7	4,285.8	4,638.9	4,780.1
Nonfinancial business	3,728.5	3,712.1	3,716.1	3,750.1	3,887.5	4,050.0
Farm	134.9	135.0	136.0	138.3	141.2	143.4
Nonfarm noncorporate	1,219.0	1,116.9	1,075.0	1,050.4	1,065.8	1,091.5
Corporate	2,374.6	2,460.2	2,505.1	2,561.5	2,680.5	2,815.1
State and local government	870.5	911.1	932.8	995.9	951.8	929.6
Foreign credit market debt held in United States	**285.1**	**299.7**	**313.1**	**381.9**	**361.6**	**387.1**
Bonds	115.4	130.5	146.2	227.4	234.6	249.6
Bank loans	18.5	21.6	23.9	24.6	26.1	29.6
Commercial paper	75.3	81.8	77.7	68.7	41.4	48.5
U.S. government and other loans	75.8	65.9	65.3	61.1	59.6	59.5
Total credit market debt owed by nonfinancial sectors, domestic and foreign	**10,997.1**	**11,483.8**	**12,041.0**	**12,750.2**	**13,332.3**	**13,730.4**

	Financial Sector					
Total credit market debt owed by nonfinancial sectors	**2,559.4**	**2,751.0**	**3,005.7**	**3,300.6**	**3,762.2**	**3,936.3**
By instrument						
U.S. government–related	1,418.4	1,564.2	1,720.0	1,884.1	2,168.4	2,245.0
Government-sponsored enterprises and securities	393.7	402.9	443.1	523.7	700.6	748.1
Mortgage pool securities	1,019.9	1,156.5	1,272.0	1,355.6	1,467.8	1,496.9
Loans from U.S. government	4.9	4.8	4.8	4.8	0.0	4.8

(continued)

EXHIBIT 1.3   (concluded)

	Financial Sector					
	1990	*1991*	*1992*	*1993*	*1994*	*1995(2Q)*
Private	1,140.9	1,186.6	1,285.8	1,416.5	1,593.8	1,691.3
Corporate bonds	549.9	638.9	725.8	844.4	952.1	1,027.3
Mortgages	4.3	4.8	5.4	8.9	18.7	21.2
Bank loans n.e.c.	52.0	78.4	80.5	66.5	54.3	59.4
Open market paper	417.7	385.7	394.3	393.5	442.8	462.8
Loans from Federal Home Loan Banks	117.1	79.1	79.9	103.1	125.9	120.5
By borrowing sector						
Government-sponsored enterprises	398.5	407.7	447.9	528.5	700.6	748.1
Federally related mortgage pools	1,019.9	1,156.5	1,272.0	1,355.6	1,467.8	1,496.9
Private	1,140.9	1,186.8	1,285.8	1,416.5	1,593.8	1,691.3
Commercial banks	76.7	65.0	73.8	79.5	89.5	95.4
Bank holding companies	114.8	112.3	114.6	123.4	133.6	142.0
Funding corporations	137.9	139.1	161.6	169.9	199.3	229.1
Savings institutions	139.1	94.6	87.8	99.0	111.7	105.2
Credit unions	0.0	0.0	0.0	0.2	0.5	0.3
Life insurance companies	0.0	0.0	0.0	0.2	0.6	0.6
Finance companies	374.4	391.9	390.4	390.5	440.7	467.3
Mortgage companies	7.3	22.2	30.2	29.2	17.8	20.1
Real estate investment trusts (REITs)	12.4	13.6	13.9	17.4	31.1	34.4
Brokers and dealers		19.0	21.7	33.7	34.3	26.8
Issuers of asset-backed securities (ABSs)	278.3	329.1	391.7	473.5	534.7	570.0
	All Sectors					
Total credit market debt, domestic and foreign	**13,536.5**	**14,234.8**	**15,046.7**	**16,050.7**	**17,094.3**	**17,666.7**
U.S. government securities	3,911.7	4,335.7	4,795.5	5,215.8	5,660.7	5,828.5
Tax-exempt securities	1,062.1	1,108.6	1,139.7	1,215.2	1,185.2	1,164.6
Corporate and foreign bonds	1,673.5	1,856.3	2,026.4	2,301.5	2,438.4	2,568.9
Mortgages	3,719.7	3,924.8	4,049.3	4,229.6	4,426.6	4,527.1
Consumer credit	813.0	797.2	804.6	863.5	984.7	1,026.6
Bank loans n.e.c.	818.3	785.9	776.6	768.2	828.8	896.9
Open market paper	609.9	565.9	579.0	580.0	623.5	673.8
Other loans	928.4	860.4	875.7	877.0	946.6	980.4

Source: *Federal Reserve Bulletin*, January 1996, p. A43.

market debt owed by the domestic nonfinancial sector exceeds $13 trillion, with the private sector borrowing a substantially greater amount than the government, as conveyed by the data. Notice also that the inclusion of the financial sector transactions substantially inflates the data. Total credit market debt owed by the financial sector is nearly $4 trillion, or almost five times the net new borrowing indicated in Exhibit 1.2. The bottom of Exhibit 1.3 also indicates the importance of consumer debt in total financial activity. Mortgages account for

---

Box 1.1

Boom Boxes and the Evolution of Finance

At the October 1995 meeting of the Financial Management Association, Professor Robert Merton of Harvard described the past, present, and future of finance with an analogy to boom boxes. Until the 1960s, stereo sound was produced and packaged in the form of consoles—large furniture cabinets known more for their beauty than for their sound quality. Then, in the Woodstock era, radio and phonograph makers got the idea of selling the components of sound separately. Thus, a consumer would buy a tuner, a turntable (for phonograph records), an amplifier, a tape deck, an equalizer, and a set of speakers. This approach allowed consumers to purchase their preferred configuration, buying tuners from a manufacturer specializing in tuners, speakers from another company known for quality speaker construction, and so forth.

But this process did not always work well. Some consumers found it too complicated to properly configure a sound system. It was easy to buy a set of speakers of the wrong impedance load relative to the capacity of the amplifier, to reverse the polarity when connecting one of the speakers (thereby producing distorted sound), and to have difficulty ensuring that all of the wires went to their proper locations. The problem worsened in the 1980s, when compact disc players, reverb units, and remote control operators were added. The exploding numbers of permutations and combinations of brands and components became confusing and frustrating to consumers. Incompatibilities and wiring became a nightmare for some.

After two decades of this componentization phase, vendors got the message, and in the 1980s they created the "boom box," which had all of the components properly matched, integrated, and combined in a single portable unit, complete with lightweight earphones. To produce the illusion of greater speaker separation, ambiance circuitry and other electronic wizardry were added. The result is a single unit with higher quality sound reproduction than most of the expensive console cabinets of earlier years.

The history of financial instruments is much the same, but with a time offset of about ten years. Until the 1970s, financial instruments were sold in fairly simple "plain vanilla" packages known as stocks, bonds, whole loans, mortgages, and futures. As more was learned about the valuation of these instruments, it became apparent that each was really composed of some combination of more fundamental units. For example, corporate bonds were really a package of zero coupon bonds, a call option, and a default option. The options themselves were found to be based on even more primitive financial instruments.

Wall Street investment bankers got the idea of slicing and dicing the prevalent securities and selling their components. Their idea was that investors could purchase these components and combine them in whatever way would satisfy their needs. The combination of components produced new securities with features that behaved in ways quite different from their underlying securities. The possibilities for creating whatever was desired seemed endless.

However, with the proliferation of derivative securities came a lot of confusion for investors. It seemed that in some cases, investor knowledge was not keeping up with the pace of innovation. Today, the finance community is getting the message. Consumers and investors want a few basic results from their investments. They may wish to provide for a certain standard of living upon retirement, or to generate sufficient funds to send a son or daughter to college, or to fund their anticipated lavish weddings, kitchen renovations, or home purchases. In essence consumers want a finance boom box. They want someone else to package the options, futures, stocks, bonds, and derivatives into a portfolio that meets their needs. Many consumers and investors do not have the time, aptitude, training, or patience to do this for themselves. Thus, the next phase of finance, during the late 1990s and into the next millennium, will be for financial engineers to take existing financial instruments and tailor products from them that are specifically designed to meet consumer and investor needs. Whether this vision of the future is accurate remains to be seen, but it sounds right to us.

more than $4 trillion, and consumer credit outstanding exceeds $1 trillion. This is pointed out only to illustrate the importance of intrasector financial transactions.

However, even these numbers understate the true volume of activity in financial markets. As pointed out above, primary market activity is only a small fraction of the total trading in financial assets. In the secondary market it is not uncommon for the daily total value of New York Stock Exchange trades of a handful of secondary market instruments to exceed the total volume of new securities created in an entire year! More will be said about this in later chapters.

Summary

The financial structure involves institutions and markets that concentrate on the creation, purchase, and resale of financial claims. The system is an essential part of the real economy. It brings together surplus units, savers, with deficit units, investors, and permits a divergence between an individual's own resources and his investment potential. As such, the financial system allocates saving to its highest and best use and encourages real investment and wealth accumulation.

Both primary and secondary markets exist in the financial system. While these can be understood separately, knowledge of their interconnection is essential to a full appreciation of the role that any financial structure plays in the economy. Primary markets marshal new resources into current period real investment. Secondary markets encourage this investment by allowing for orderly trading and disposition of assets created in the primary market.

The secondary market function is performed either directly, by financial markets, or indirectly, through alternate mechanisms established by various types of financial intermediaries. In the first situation, buyers and sellers are assembled, either in person, by phone, or electronically, to trade existing securities. A price is negotiated between buyer and seller. In an efficient market, the price obtained by each participant represents the true value of the underlying asset being traded. In this way, an efficient market facilitates future fund raising for investment purposes and encourages saving.

Institutions also facilitate the disposition of preexisting financial assets. These financial intermediaries frequently serve the role of a middleman between borrower and seller and replace those investors who wish to withdraw from the market. They may also offer investors the possibility of simple redemption at current market value. While different, both of these services function to make the claims issued by these institutions more liquid and, hence, more attractive.

The volume of activity in the financial market has grown dramatically in the 20th century. As will be discussed in later chapters, this growth is the result of increased sophistication and efficiency in financial markets, as well as technological breakthroughs in communication, which have facilitated the increased interest in various types of financial assets and transactions. In any case, the U.S. financial market has an enormous volume of activity on a daily basis. However, rather than distracting the economy from its true activity, the depth of the financial market encourages growth and increases the well-being of the economy.

Key Concepts

deep and shallow markets,   7
deficit economic units,   4
economic agents,   4
efficient and inefficient markets,   7
financial intermediary,   5
financial investment,   5

financial structure,   3
liquid and illiquid markets,   7
primary market,   6
secondary market,   6
surplus economic units,   4

Review Questions

1. In the absence of financial markets, what can a household with surplus income, a surplus economic unit, do with its excess resources?
2. In the absence of financial markets, what can a firm do if it wishes to invest in the development of a factory? How does your answer affect the level of economic activity in the economy?
3. In what way can financial intermediaries be considered as substitutes for the financial market? On the other hand, what arguments can be made to suggest that intermediaries are complements to the financial market in providing needed resources for the growth of the real economy?
4. What is the difference between the primary and the secondary financial markets? In what sense is the secondary market a complement to the primary market?
5. What are the characteristics of an efficient primary market? How does an efficient primary market help the economy reach its true potential?
6. What are the characteristics of an efficient secondary market? Why should people uninterested in financial transactions wish to have an efficient financial system?
7. Explain the importance of foreign capital flows to the domestic financial market and domestic economic activity.
8. Using Exhibits 1.2 and 1.3, discuss the relative importance of the various sectors in the financial market. Also discuss the importance of various instruments in both the primary and secondary markets.

References

Dobson, Steve W. "Development of Capital Markets in the United States?" *Business Review*, Federal Reserve Bank of Dallas, April 1976.

Downes, John, and Jordan E. Goodman. *Barron's Finance and Investment Handbook.* Woodbury, N.Y.: Barron's Educational, 1990.

Fabozzi, Frank J.; Franco Modigliani; and Michael G. Ferri. *Foundations of Financial Markets and Institutions.* Englewood Cliffs, N.J.: Prentice Hall, 1994.

Friedman, Benjamin M., et. al. *Postwar Changes in the American Financial Markets.* Reprint 150. New York: National Bureau of Economic Research, 1980.

Herring, Richard J., and Anthony M. Santomero. *The Role of the Financial Structure in Economic Performance.* Stockholm: SNS Forlag, 1991.

Kaufman, George G. *The U.S. Financial System.* 6th ed. Englewood Cliffs, N.J.: Prentice Hall, 1995.

Simpson, Thomas D. "Developments in the U.S. Financial System since the Mid-1970s." *Federal Reserve Bulletin,* January 1988.

Smith, George David, and Richard Sylla. "The Transformation of Financial Capitalism: An Essay on the History of American Capital Market." *Journal of Financial Markets, Institutions and Instruments*, May 1993.

Stigum, Marcia. *The Money Market*. 3d ed. Burr Ridge, Ill.: Irwin Professional Publishing, 1990.

Van Horne, James. *Financial Market Rates and Flows*. 4th ed. Englewood Cliffs, N.J.: Prentice Hall, 1994.

The Flow of Funds
in the Markets

This chapter analyzes the flow of funds through the financial system and its many institutional structures. It starts abstractly and moves to a discussion of the elaborate Federal Reserve system of accounts, which serves as a fundamental starting point to the understanding of financial flows. The material in this chapter also serves as a reference point for subsequent work on variations in both stocks and flows that are the result of yield differentials.

The **financial sector** of the economy is the focus of this chapter—indeed, of the entire book. To better understand the financial sector, its importance, and how it fits into the economy, it is useful to distinguish it from the **real sector.** To understand the real sector, we must first review some basic economics concepts. Because this material is contained in most introductory economics texts, we provide here only the most cursory review.

Review of Basic Definitions

A **good** is anything that has the power to satisfy a need or desire. Some goods, known as **free goods,** are useful things that exist in quantities sufficient for all who desire them and can thus be obtained without any appreciable effort. Examples are air and sunshine. **Economic goods,** on the other hand, are useful things that are in scarce supply relative to the need or desire for them. Such goods can be obtained only by expense or effort. Economic goods range from material goods, which are tangible (e.g., clothing and food), to professional or personal services, which are rendered by persons (e.g., plumbers, teachers, and entertainers) for the purpose of satisfying needs and desires.

Wealth refers to the value of economic material goods and money, which can be used to purchase goods and services. **Income,** on the other hand, is a flow of goods, services, or money received or accrued over a period of time. For economists the distinction between these concepts is important. Wealth, because it has a particular value at a given moment of time, is referred to as a **stock.** In contrast, income, as we have previously noted, is a **flow.** As we will point out later, the changes in stocks are accomplished by flows. For example, wealth, as we have defined it here, increases as income exceeds spending; the flow increases the value of the stock.

Economic goods are also sometimes classified as consumer goods and producer goods. **Consumer goods** are goods that satisfy needs or desires directly, such as furniture, automobiles, food, and televisions. **Producer goods** are goods that satisfy wants indirectly by aiding in the production of either consumer goods or more producer goods. Examples of producer goods are raw materials, machinery, and tools. Sometimes producer goods are referred to as **capital goods,** or **capital.**

The Real Sector and Gross Domestic Product

The **real sector** of the economy encompasses all economic goods and services. The total market value of all final goods and services produced in the nation's economy during a given period of time (usually a quarter or a year) is known as the **gross national product (GNP).** Another concept, called **gross domestic product (GDP),** is more frequently used. This total omits net earnings from the rest of the world and measures the output produced in the domestic economy. This distinction is not large for the United States, but it can be substantial for other countries. Accordingly, GDP has become the standard notion of total output used for international comparisons.

The term **total market value** refers to the value, in terms of current market prices, of all goods and services. The term **nation's economy** refers to the labor, land, capital, and entrepreneurial services provided by permanent residents of any country. Everything that is produced by both private business and government is included.

Methods of Measuring GDP

The gross domestic product may be measured in two ways:

1. Summing the expenditures made for the goods and services produced during the period.
2. Summing the incomes paid and other costs incurred in producing the goods and services for which the expenditures were made.

Both methods give the same total because, for the economy as a whole, total expenditures must equal total income.

GDP: The Total of Expenditures

If the first method—adding up expenditures—is used to measure gross domestic product, we calculate the total market value of what has been produced in the economy by summing the purchases of all goods and services. To avoid duplication in counting, only "final" goods are included. "Intermediate" products are excluded. For example, in making bread, wheat is grown, flour is made from wheat, and then bread is baked and sold to consumers. The value of the national output would include the full value of the bread but would not include the values of the wheat and flour that were used in producing the bread.

All purchases are placed into one of four different categories: (1) personal consumption expenditures, (2) gross private domestic investment, (3) net foreign investment, and (4) government purchases of goods and services. The total number of purchases across these four categories gives the money value of all goods and services produced, valued at market prices.

The definitions of each of these components of the GDP are sometimes at odds with simple intuition, so we must clarify these terms further.

Personal Consumption Expenditures.   This component includes the market value of all consumer goods and services purchased for direct consumption by individuals, families, and nonprofit institutions such as hospitals and schools. Food, clothing, medical services, and financial services are included. Also included are the estimated current rental values of owner-occupied residences. The purchase costs of new dwellings are included in a different category—gross private domestic investment.

Gross Private Domestic Investment.   This component encompasses the total market value of all capital goods created in the economy during the period. Any newly created capital goods produced or acquired by private business firms and nonprofit institutions are included. For example, factory, hospital, and school buildings; equipment and tools; and houses are included in this category. In addition to these new capital goods, changes in the volume of inventories of goods held by business firms between the beginning and end of the period are included. An increase or decrease in the value of inventories, when not occasioned by a change in the prices of items held in inventory, indicates an increase or decrease, respectively, in gross private domestic investment.

Note that the term *investment,* as used here, does not connote the same thing as it does in common usage. Purchasing land, acquiring stocks and bonds, or investing in goods (e.g., existing housing or classic automobiles) produced during a previous period does not result directly in the creation of new goods during the period under consideration. Therefore, these activities are not part of the investment component of gross domestic product. It is only when expenditures are made for the production of goods during the current period that investment results.

Net Foreign Investment.   Net foreign investment is measured as the difference between the flow of money (and money claims) into the economy from abroad and the flow outward. This difference may be either positive or negative. Net foreign investment measures (1) exports of our goods and services over imports from other countries; (2) the excess of the amount paid (via interest, dividends, etc.) for U.S. capital and services used in production abroad over the amount paid by U.S. residents for use of foreign capital and services; and (3) the excess of foreign cash gifts and contributions to U.S. residents over that which is given and contributed by U.S. residents to foreigners.

Government Purchases of Goods and Services.   Government expenditures for salary and benefits to employees, payments for consumption goods, outlays for government enterprises, and net purchases from abroad made by the government are all part of the category of government purchases of goods and services. Indeed, this component of gross domestic product is composed of all expenditures at all levels of government (local, state, and federal), with the following exceptions: (1) purchases by government of land and used assets (i.e., those assets produced in an earlier period); (2) transfer payments (i.e., payments for which no services are rendered currently, such as welfare payments and social security); and (3) interest on government debt.

Using these four categories, Exhibit 2.1 reports the gross domestic product of the United States, based on the most recent estimates, for the second quarter of 1995. As is evident from the exhibit, personal consumption accounts for more than two-thirds of GDP. Domestic investment, on the other hand, is approximately 15 percent. However, this total is extremely volatile and frequently exacerbates business cycle activity. The statistic for net exports is −124.7. The negative figure is evidence of the U.S. economy's continued balance of trade deficit with the rest of the world. In fact, this figure has quadrupled since 1992. The final number in the table reports the amount of government spending. It illustrates that the combination of federal, state, and local government spending exceeded $1.2 trillion in 1995 and accounted for nearly 20 percent of total spending in the U.S. economy. (Note, however, that this total excludes transfer payments, as is indicated in the definition section above.)

EXHIBIT 2.1   **Components of the Gross Domestic Product, Second Quarter 1995**
($ Billions)

Personal consumption expenditures	$4,851.0
Durable and nondurable goods	
Services	
Gross private domestic investment	1,094.1
New construction	
Producers' durable equipment	
Changes in business inventories	
Net foreign investment	−124.7
Government purchases of goods and services	1,209.6
GROSS DOMESTIC PRODUCT	$7,030.0

Source: *Federal Reserve Bulletin,* January 1996, p. A51.

GDP: The Total of Incomes to Domestic Factors of Production

The second way to compute gross output of the economy over a period of time is to total the incomes generated by the domestic **factors of production.** Because any dollar spent is a dollar received by someone else, this method gives us the same result as summing all expenditures. Therefore, we can total either the dollars spent or the dollars received and arrive at the same number.

The recipients of income are usually divided into categories that correspond to the owners of the four factors of production:

- Labor (including both physical and mental effort directed to the production of goods and services).
- Land (or natural resources).
- Entrepreneurs (who initiate and direct production and assume the risk of production).
- Capital (economic goods that are used to aid in production).

The sum of incomes to the owners of these four factors of production is known as the **national income.** Certain other items are added to national income, such as indirect business taxes and the consumption of capital associated with current production, before we arrive again at gross domestic product. Exhibit 2.2 illustrates how this approach arrives at the same value as the expenditure method.

The elements of the left-hand side of Exhibit 2.2 require some elaboration.

Compensation of Employees. This component of national income encompasses wages, salaries, tips, commissions, bonuses, and benefits (e.g., employer contributions for social and private insurance and pensions) paid for private, military, and government civilian employment. In 1995, of a GDP total of

EXHIBIT 2.2   Gross Domestic Product and Income Account, Second Quarter 1995
($ Billions)

Income to Factors of Production		*Expenditures*	
Compensation of employees	$4,183.0	Personal consumption expenditures	$4,851.0
Proprietors' and rental income	511.4	Gross private domestic investment	1,094.1
Corporate profits and inventory		Net foreign investment	−124.7
valuation adjustment	581.1	Government purchases of goods and	
Net interest	444.0	services	1,209.6
NATIONAL INCOME	5,719.4		
Other charges against GDP			
Indirect business taxes, business transfer			
payments, government subsidies less			
income of government enterprises	613.1		
Statistical discrepancies	67.0		
NET NATIONAL PRODUCT	6,265.5		
Consumption of capital	743.1		
TOTAL CHARGES AGAINST GROSS			
DOMESTIC PRODUCT	$7,030.0	**GROSS DOMESTIC PRODUCT**	$7,030.0

Note: The sum of the individual items may not correspond exactly to the totals because of rounding.
Source: *Survey of Current Business,* October 1995, Table 1.9.

$7.03 trillion, employees received compensation of $4.183 trillion, or nearly 60 percent. Therefore, this means that nearly 60 cents of each dollar of output was spent on employees.

Proprietors' and Rental Income.   This income classification consists of incomes to agricultural and professional establishments and unincorporated businesses. Examples are farmers, doctors, lawyers, small merchants, and some producers' cooperatives. When calculating the incomes of unincorporated businesses, it is necessary to adjust for any changes that may have occurred in inventories during the period. The category also includes rental income paid to individuals. In 1995, the value of this category was $511.4 billion.

Corporate Profits and Inventory Valuation Adjustment.   This income classification consists of earnings of privately owned for-profit corporations. The income is measured before federal, state, and local taxes have been deducted and does not include gains or losses from the sale of capital assets. The total of $581.1 billion, therefore, is less substantial than it appears, as it is a pretax figure. The incomes are adjusted for changes in the volume of inventories held during the period.

Interest.   The interest embraced by this category is that which is paid or accrued to persons or business firms in the United States. Interest paid by government is not included, however, because it does not arise in connection with current production. Nonetheless, interest paid by government is a part of personal income to those who receive it. The net interest, which totaled $444 billion in 1995, will be affected by the overall level of interest rates in the economy.

The total of these four items constitutes the national income during the period under consideration. National income may be linked to **personal income and savings** through the following adjustments.

Other Charges against Gross Domestic Product.   In glancing at Exhibit 2.2, it is obvious that national income does not equal gross domestic product. Several other items are listed as additional charges against total output. One category is known as *indirect business taxes and nontax liability.* Indirect business taxes are those levied on business apart from income taxes. Excise taxes on tobacco, alcoholic beverages, and cosmetics are examples. Other payments to government that are not taxes, referred to as nontax liabilities, are also part of this category. *Business transfer payments* are largely a result of bad debts and gifts from private business firms to nonprofit institutions. While these payments are not connected directly with production, they are, in a sense, a normal cost of production. *Government subsidies less surplus of government entities* is a category of increasing importance in recent years. Subsidies are given to private business firms to encourage production. These subsidies lower the costs of the firms' production and thus are a proper part of the charges against gross domestic product. Certain government entities, such as the Post Office Department and the National Park Service, generate funds that offset part or all of the expenses of running the service. If a surplus results, it is added to the national income at this point. The total of these other charges was $613.1 billion for 1995.

Obviously, in measuring gross domestic product, numerous estimations must be made, and there is much measurement error. Although the two methods for GDP measurement are supposed to produce the same final sum, they rarely do. Hence, a *statistical discrepancy* item is added as a charge against net domestic product to balance the two approaches. The statistical discrepancy totaled $67 billion in 1995, not a small sum but not bad when compared to a $7 trillion estimate. Finally, *capital consumption allowances* are added to capture the depreciation of capital goods through normal usage. This allowance, $743.1 billion in 1995, is a production cost and is normally covered in the market prices of the commodities resulting from productive efforts.

From this point forward, most of our attention will be on the savings and investment components of the gross domestic product and income accounts. As noted in Chapter 1, these are the fund flows that dominate the financial markets and institutions that are the subject of this book. However, it is important to know how these totals are obtained. Exhibit 2.3 achieves this end. Notice that national income converts to personal income after a number of adjustments are made. Corporate profits and contributions to social programs are not part of personal income, and are therefore subtracted from the national income total. On the other

EXHIBIT 2.3   **Derivation of Personal Savings from National Income, Second Quarter 1995**
($ Billions)

National Income			5,719.4
Less:	Corporate profits and inventory valuation adjustment	581.1	
	Contributions for social insurance	652.2	
Plus:	Business and government transfer payments	1,016.6	
	Net interest income	444.0	
	Dividends	208.1	
Personal Income			6,008.1
Less:	Personal tax and nontax payments (federal, state, local)	807.1	
Disposable Personal Income			5,201.0
Less:	Personal consumption expenditures	4,994.9	
Personal Savings			206.1

Source: *Survey of Current Business,* October 1995, Table 2.1.

hand, transfer payments, dividends, and interest paid by the government increase household income. Pretax personal income is converted to disposable personal income by subtracting personal tax and nontax payments of $807.1 billion. Disposable income not consumed equals personal savings that flow into the financial markets.

Simple Flow of Funds Analysis

A powerful tool has been developed to help us understand and analyze the flow of savings in the financial markets. The tool, known as the **flow of funds framework,** has several important uses.

1. It enables financial market analysts to track the movement of savings through the economy in a structured and consistent manner.
2. It provides a key to unlocking the complex interdependencies of financial claims throughout the economy.
3. It uncovers the changing patterns in the saving and borrowing behavior of households. This information can help financial institutions decide what kinds of securities and services to offer their clients.
4. It tracks changes in the sources and uses of funds within the financial institution sector. This information is useful to these institutions as they attempt to keep pace with trends among their competitors.
5. It can be used to link flows of funds over time to interest rate movements. A historical analysis of this linkage can provide insights into the dynamics of the relationship and can improve forecasts of interest rates.

The flow of funds accounts complement the national income accounts used in estimating gross domestic product. While the national income accounts focus on the real side of the economy—goods and services—the flow of funds accounts highlight the financial flows. For example, while national income accounts report the amount of savings, they give no information as to where the savings are channeled. How the savings get transmuted into investment is not revealed. Flow of funds accounts uncover the steps by which savings flow into investment.

Steps in Flow of Funds Accounting

There are three steps involved in deriving any flow of funds accounting system for an economy:

1. Partition the economy into various sectors.
2. Prepare sources and uses of funds statements for each sector.
3. Create a table or matrix in which all sector accounts are placed side by side.

Partition Economy into Sectors.   The entire economy must be divided into sectors that represent economic units of similar behavior. The number of sectors may vary from a few to several dozen or more. In theory, there could be as many sectors as there are separate individual economic units—over 100 million in the United States. There is a trade-off between the level of partitioning (i.e., number of sectors) chosen and the ability to interpret. If too few sectors are provided, many significant economic relationships will be concealed and it is less likely that the sectors will be composed of units exhibiting relatively similar economic behavior. If too many sectors are provided, our analyses of the interactions between the sectors will become unwieldy. However, in this case, it is more likely that the composition of each sector will be relatively homogeneous in terms of economic characteristics.

Other factors act to constrain the number of sectors, including the availability of data, the cost and time required to collect and organize the data, and the consistency of data measurement among economic units. Ultimately, the optimum number of sectors will depend upon the purposes of analysis and the extent of sectoring required to support the desired level of analysis.

Prepare Sources and Uses of Funds Statements.   Having divided the economy into appropriate sectors, we must then develop sources and uses of funds statements for each sector. A sources and uses of funds statement is akin to measuring the water level in a bathtub. Water enters the tub through the spout and exits through the drain. If water is entering faster than it is draining, the water level will climb. Similarly, a sources and uses statement does not measure the total flow of funds into and out of a particular sector; rather, it measures the net change. If more funds are entering a sector than are leaving it, a positive net flow of funds to that sector would be produced. To measure this net flow, we note the amounts of the balance sheet items—assets, liabilities, and net worth—for the various sectors at the beginning and end of a quarter or a year. Some of these accounts may have increased in value, while others may have decreased in value during the period. Net changes in each of these items during the time interval of measurement are computed. Increases in liabilities and net worth are treated as a source of funds; increases in assets are treated as a use of funds.

Returning to the bathtub analogy for a moment, if water swirls from one end of the tub to the other but is replaced by water from the other end, the water level is unchanged. That is, there is no net change in the amount of water in the tub. Similarly, if one business sector firm loans money to another firm in the business sector, there is no net change in the amount of funds in that sector. Because sources and uses statements record only intersectoral flows, such an intrasector transaction would not be included in the statements.

To illustrate the development of a sources and uses statement, Exhibit 2.4 presents two balance sheets for an arbitrary sector, "Sector X," measured a year apart. By noting the differences in each account across time, we can formulate a simple sources and uses of funds statement for Sector X. This statement is shown as Exhibit 2.5.

Note that in the final analysis, sources of funds always equal uses. An increase in net worth could result from either an increase in total assets, a decrease in total liabilities, or some combination of the two (as was the case for Sector X). In fact, assets and liabilities could both increase and yet result in a positive increment to net worth, provided that assets increase faster than liabilities. Similarly, assets and liabilities could both decrease, but as long as assets decrease more slowly than liabilities, a positive increment to net worth would result. In this instance, a 12% (= 6 ÷ 50) increase in net worth has occurred. This increase was due partially to an appreciation or increase in real asset holdings (+3) and a rise in money balances (+2). In addition to these contributions to net worth, there was some reduction in debt (−2) offset by lesser holdings of financial assets (−1).

The positive change in net worth in Sector X represents savings for the period. Current income was higher than expenditures. Such a sector is called a

---

EXHIBIT 2.4   Balance Sheet Changes for Sector X

Sector X Balance Sheet, 12/31/95				*Sector X Balance Sheet, 12/31/96*			
Real		Liabilities		Real		Liabilities	
assets	60		40	assets	63		38
Money	2	Net worth	50	Money	4	Net worth	56
Other				Other			
financial				financial			
assets	28			assets	27		
		Total				Total	
		liabilities &				liabilities &	
Total		net worth		Total		net worth	
assets	90		90	assets	94		94

EXHIBIT 2.5   Sector X Sources and Uses of Funds, 1996

Uses		Sources	
ΔReal assets		ΔLiabilities	
(investment or disinvestment)	+3	(borrowing or debt repayment)	−2
ΔMoney	+2	Net worth	
ΔFinancial assets (lending,		(saving or dissaving)	+6
purchase or sale of securities)	−1		
ΔTotal assets	+4	Total liabilities & net worth	+4

---

savings-surplus sector. If Sector X had increased its holdings of real assets without an equal or greater rise in net worth, it would have needed to reduce its money holdings, sell off some additional financial assets, increase its borrowings, or undertake some combination of these measures. In that case, Sector X would be called a **savings-deficit sector.**

Create a Table or Matrix.   The next step in the flow of funds system is to replicate this sources and uses of funds analysis for all remaining sectors and integrate all of the analyses into a matrix for the entire economy. Exhibit 2.6 shows an example of such a matrix for a hypothetical economy. The hypothetical economy is partitioned into five sectors: households, nonfinancial businesses, financial institutions, governments, and foreign. "U" stands for uses, and "S" stands for sources of funds.

The matrix does not give the levels of savings, investments, money, and so forth in each sector; rather, it provides information only about the changes in these levels during a period. For example, the sources side of the households' net worth category indicates that net savings for households increased during the period by 200 from the level that prevailed at the start of the period.

Some Basic Flow of Funds Relationships

There are several important items to notice in Exhibit 2.6. First, the sources and uses of funds within each sector are in balance. For example, nonfinancial businesses used 260 and received 260. The sources and uses of funds for the entire economy, which is obtained by summing the sources and uses of each sector, must also balance. This is a reflection of the self-contained construction of the matrix. Therefore, in each sector we will find the following basic relationships:

$$\text{Uses of funds} = \text{Sources of funds}$$

or

$$\Delta\text{Real assets} + \Delta\text{Financial assets} = \Delta\text{Financial liabilities} + \Delta\text{Net worth}$$

or

$$\text{Investment} + \text{Lending} = \text{Borrowing} + \text{Saving}$$

EXHIBIT 2.6   Hypothetical Flow of Funds Accounts for Calendar Year 1996

	Households		Nonfinancial Businesses		Financial Institutions		Governments		Foreign		All Sectors	
	U	*S*	*U*	*S*	*U*	*S*	*U*	*S*	*U*	*S*	*U*	*S*
Net worth (saving)		200		140		5		−50		75		370
Real assets (investment)	150		210		10		4				370	
Money	4		2			15				5	15	15
Other financial assets	96		48		170		6		130		450	
Financial liabilities (debt)		50		120		160		60		60		450
Totals	**250**	**250**	**260**	**260**	**180**	**180**	**10**	**10**	**135**	**135**	**835**	**835**
Sector surplus (deficit)	50		(70)		(5)		(50)		75		—	

Because these relationships hold true for each sector, it must be the case that four conditions are true. First, in any sector, if saving is greater than investment, then lending must be greater than borrowing. Such a sector would be considered a net funds provider to the other sectors, or a savings-surplus sector. On the other hand, if investment is greater than saving, then this investment in excess of saving must be funded by borrowing that is greater than lending. Such a sector would be considered a net borrower of funds from other sectors, or a savings-deficit sector.

In our hypothetical economy shown in Exhibit 2.6, households added $200 billion to their savings during the period. Together with a $50 billion increment to their borrowing, households used the $250 billion total for purchasing real assets (amounting to $150 billion) and for acquiring $100 billion in financial assets (higher money balances plus other financial assets). The nonfinancial business sector added $140 billion to its savings during the period. Together with net new borrowing of $120 billion, the nonfinancial business sector plowed most of the $260 billion total into investment in real assets ($210 billion), while the remainder went into financial assets.

Second, aggregate savings must equal increased investment in real assets during the period. Both were $370 billion in this example. This is true because, across all sectors, savings flows must be deployed somewhere in the economy. Therefore, by construction, savings must equal investment in this framework.

Third, total funds provided by financial institutions (and monetary authorities) must equal the total increase in cash balances held by households, governments, nonfinancial businesses, and the foreign sector. These balances include currency as well as demand deposits. Finally, the increase in financial assets must equal the increase in financial liabilities. (Both are $450 billion in this example.) The reason for this is easy to understand when it is recognized that any financial asset held by someone is a financial liability issued by someone else. For example, a bond or other debt instrument issued by a corporation will be held by an investor or bank as a financial asset.

EXHIBIT 2.7   Hypothetical Credit Flows for Calendar Year 1996
($ Billions)

Funds provided, by sector	
Households	100
Nonfinancial businesses	50
Financial Institutions	170
Governments	10
Foreign	135
Total	465
Funds acquired, by sector	
Households	50
Nonfinancial businesses	120
Financial institutions	175
Governments	60
Foreign	60
Total	465

Credit Flows: Stocks versus Flows

The sources and uses of funds statements can be modified to highlight the credit flows. To do this, we turn away from the real sector saving and investment flows and focus only on changes in financial assets and financial liabilities. At the bottom of Exhibit 2.6, we have the sector surplus or deficit information, which serves as the starting point for our analysis. Households show a surplus during the period of $50 billion (= $4 billion in cash + $96 billion in other financial assets – $50 billion in financial liabilities). The foreign sector was also in surplus during the period, contributing $75 billion. The other three sectors were net users of credit, and show deficits totaling $125 billion. Nonfinancial businesses account for the majority, at $70 billion, followed by governments ($50 billion) and financial institutions ($5 billion). The credit flows are summarized in Exhibit 2.7.

The Federal Reserve Flow of Funds System

The most widely used system of flow of funds accounting in the United States is that published by the Board of Governors of the Federal Reserve. Annual flow of funds data were first published in 1955, and beginning in 1959, quarterly data have been published regularly by the Federal Reserve System.[1]

---

[1]The *Flow of Funds Accounts* is available upon request from the Board of Governors, Federal Reserve System, Washington, D.C. 20551.

EXHIBIT 2.8   **Sector Structure in the Federal Reserve Flow of Funds Accounts**

1. Households	Households
	Personal trusts
	Nonprofit organizations
2. Nonfinancial businesses	Farm
	Nonfarm
	Noncorporate
	Corporate
3. Governments	States and local governments
	U.S. government
	Federally sponsored credit agencies
	Mortgage pools
4. Banking system	Monetary authorities
	Commercial banks
5. Nonbank finance	Savings and loan associations
	Credit unions
	Finance companies
	Real estate investment trusts
	Open-end investment companies
	Money market funds
	Security brokers and dealers
	Life insurance companies
	Other insurance companies
	Private pension funds
	State and local government retirement funds
6. Foreign	

Earlier, we mentioned that any flow of funds accounting system must start by dividing the economy into sectors. As shown in Exhibit 2.8, the Federal Reserve System of the United States supplies information on 23 sectors. This represents a useful compromise between the desires for economic homogeneity within a sector and the ability to interpret economic relationships of primary importance to the economy as a whole.

With so many sectors, the kinds of data provided are far more informative than the simple sources and uses statements we have discussed thus far. Moreover, the financial flows are broken down into still finer categories that report a wealth of information on specific credit market instruments. On the other hand, subsectors can be consolidated in a manner that fosters improved economic intuition.

For each sector or group of sectors, the flow of funds accounting system reports annual flows and changes in outstanding levels of financial instruments. For example, Exhibit 2.9 contains the flow of funds data for households and nonprofit organizations over a 13-year period. It includes the allocation of gross saving to various types of capital expenditures and net financial investment. It also includes net increases in liabilities by this sector over the same period of time.

These data can also be used to analyze total economywide activity in a particular instrument. For example, Exhibit 2.10 shows the deposit market, analyzing the changes in checkable deposits and small time deposits at various financial institutions. In essence, this report sums across all sectors to report the activity in a particular financial instrument.

Such information is invaluable in understanding the financial activity of individual sectors and the aggregate transactions in specific financial instruments. This is, in fact, the primary data used by economic forecasters to obtain insights into the financial behavior of any one sector or within any one market. For example, economists interested in household behavior construct large-scale models of consumer choice to understand why this sector shifts resources from one area of the financial market to another. Planners from various sectors eagerly await such insights, as they need a perspective on future consumer preferences and areas where growth potential is likely to be highest (see Box 2.1).

Likewise, their counterparts are most interested in how households respond to interest rate changes in any one market, such as the deposit market shown in Exhibit 2.10. Commercial bankers take notice of such things as price sensitivities and market share data that illustrate consumer preferences and changes in the attractiveness of any one of their products.

However, gaining much insight from these data is no easy task. It involves substantial energy and resources to understand financial behavior and shifts in asset allocation over time. Nonetheless, if such insights can be obtained, the flow of funds data will be the source. It is unquestionably the best data source, and for many data series, it is the only game in town.

EXHIBIT 2.9 Households and Nonprofit Organization Activity from the Flow of Funds
($ Billions)

	1982	1983	1984	1985	1986	1987	1988	1989	1990	1991	1992	1993	1994	1995 Q5
Personal Income	2,691.0	2,862.5	3,154.6	3,379.8	3,590.5	3,802.0	4,075.9	4,380.2	4,673.8	4,860.3	5,154.4	5,375.1	5701.7	6004.3
–Personal taxes and nontaxes	371.4	368.8	395.1	436.8	459.0	512.5	527.8	593.3	623.2	623.7	648.6	686.4	742.1	806.9
=Disposable personal income	2,319.6	2,493.7	2,759.5	2,943.0	3,131.5	3,289.6	3,548.2	3,787.0	4,050.6	4,236.6	4,505.8	4,688.7	4,959.6	5197.4
–Personal outlays	2,120.1	2,325.1	2,537.5	2,753.7	2,944.0	3,147.5	3,392.5	3,634.9	3,880.6	4,025.1	4,257.9	4,496.2	4,756.5	4991.2
=Personal saving, NIPA (1)	199.5	168.6	222.0	189.3	187.5	142.0	155.7	152.1	170.0	211.5	247.9	192.5	203.1	206.2
+Credit from gov't. insurance	43.6	49.4	63.5	72.5	92.8	78.9	76.0	101.3	92.0	86.8	99.0	109.9	100.5	127.0
+Net durables in consumption	22.4	50.6	81.8	95.8	111.4	102.9	112.6	109.0	90.0	52.2	62.6	88.9	114.8	127.0
+Capital consumption	285.0	298.3	313.5	339.8	364.5	393.2	423.5	463.4	493.8	525.8	566.9	583.2	625.9	651.7
=Gross saving	550.5	566.9	680.7	697.3	756.2	717.1	767.8	825.8	845.9	876.3	976.4	914.4	1044.3	1111.9
Gross investment	541.6	617.6	681.9	742.9	839.4	788.4	814.2	938.5	936.6	914.7	1,044.7	1,015.5	1008.4	1199.8
Capital expend., net of sales	344.4	429.0	497.7	537.6	604.3	631.2	675.9	701.2	696.9	666.2	765.8	808.6	890.5	911.4
Residential construction	88.8	132.4	157.1	161.5	189.6	198.5	206.8	206.8	191.5	173.1	205.5	230.2	259.6	253.3
Consumer durable goods	236.5	275.0	317.9	353.0	389.6	403.7	437.1	459.4	468.2	456.6	492.7	538.0	591.4	619.1
Nonprofit plant and equip.	19.2	21.6	22.7	23.2	25.1	29.0	32.1	35.0	37.2	36.5	37.6	40.4	39.5	38.9
Net financial investment	197.2	188.6	184.2	205.3	235.1	157.2	138.3	237.3	239.8	248.5	308.9	207.0	117.9	288.4
Net acq. of financial assets	286.4	385.3	409.8	526.5	510.9	432.3	434.3	534.9	466.0	430.5	528.5	519.4	479.5	620.6
Deposits	162.7	166.7	254.2	124.9	206.5	112.0	161.8	142.2	72.2	-43.4	-30.0	-17.8	38.4	471.8
Checkable dep. & curr.	20.8	13.2	-0.9	16.9	87.9	-4.3	19.0	-5.6	5.8	61.9	123.5	77.0	9.1	-11.6
Small time & svgs. dep.	122.4	187.2	138.2	115.3	98.6	52.5	93.9	64.0	66.3	-45.4	-64.7	-68.8	-5.8	171.4
Large time deposits	12.3	-2.5	73.6	-9.7	-15.7	41.8	33.0	7.0	-28.5	-68.6	-47.0	-19.2	16.6	27.9
Money mkt. fund shares	31.8	-31.2	43.3	2.3	35.7	22.0	15.9	76.8	28.6	8.7	-41.8	-6.9	18.5	284.0
Credit mkt. instruments	27.9	93.3	94.6	161.5	-28.1	176.2	196.7	94.7	157.0	-39.6	74.2	3.1	317.3	-157.1
U.S. govt. securities	1.5	38.6	74.9	14.9	-36.3	47.3	132.3	65.5	127.0	-34.9	100.9	-1.4	364.6	-174.9
Treasury	23.2	43.9	51.9	1.8	-20.2	4.8	68.9	19.2	114.3	-42.8	51.7	41.7	188.8	-66.0
Savings bonds	N/A	3.1	3.0	5.3	13.6	7.8	8.5	8.2	8.5	11.9	19.1	14.7	8.0	4.8
Other	N/A	40.8	48.9	-3.4	-33.7	-3.0	60.5	11.1	105.8	-54.7	32.5	27.1	180.8	-70.8
Agency	21.7	-5.3	23.0	13.1	-16.1	42.5	63.4	46.3	12.7	7.9	49.2	-43.1	175.8	-108.9
Tax-exempt securities	24.0	34.7	27.6	72.2	-15.8	80.1	39.7	55.6	17.7	34.9	-34.8	-19.7	-33.4	-48.5
Corporate & fgn. bonds	-3.8	2.5	-6.0	-0.8	33.9	18.3	-21.8	-17.2	37.8	10.4	-1.3	50.9	25.7	30.5
Mortgages	10.3	-0.4	-0.3	16.9	-4.2	27.2	15.2	-0.2	-17.2	-15.1	4.1	10.5	11.7	26.2
Open market paper	-4.1	17.9	-1.6	58.4	-5.8	3.3	31.3	-9.0	-8.3	34.8	5.2	-37.2	-51.3	9.6

EXHIBIT 2.9 (concluded)

	1982	1983	1984	1985	1986	1987	1988	1989	1990	1991	1992	1993	1994	1995 Q5
Mutual fund shares	3.8	26.9	20.2	75.5	120.0	56.9	14.1	36.0	37.7	115.1	146.5	190.0	85.9	141.3
Corporate equities	-20.7	-22.6	-66.8	-111.2	-103.9	-102.6	-92.6	109.1	-21.7	-33.8	43.8	-29.9	-96.9	-188.7
Life insurance reserves	7.2	8.0	5.2	10.7	17.5	26.0	25.3	28.8	25.7	25.7	27.3	35.2	20.1	25.3
Pension fund reserves	170.9	168.2	157.2	271.7	289.1	201.3	132.3	321.2	165.1	360.3	249.7	309.2	103.6	311.2
Inv. in bank pers. trusts	8.1	3.2	15.1	10.2	18.1	13.2	2.2	19.6	29.7	16.1	-7.1	1.6	18.8	22.3
Net inv. in noncorp. bus.	-83.7	-76.5	-72.3	-58.6	-34.6	-70.0	-23.5	-25.8	-27.1	-4.2	18.3	-11.7	-30.0	-13.1
Security credit	3.1	2.7	1.0	13.5	9.0	-5.8	1.8	12.3	9.2	24.6	-11.0	26.6	5.2	-20.6
Miscellaneous assets	7.1	15.5	1.3	28.3	17.2	25.1	16.4	14.9	18.2	9.6	17.0	13.1	17.1	28.3
Net increase in liabilities	89.2	196.7	225.5	321.2	275.8	275.1	296.1	297.6	226.2	182.0	219.7	312.5	361.4	332.2
Credit market instruments	82.8	185.3	225.7	299.1	268.1	268.1	291.4	281.6	218.5	171.1	214.2	280.9	353.5	324.7
Home mortgages	46.0	108.1	128.1	161.3	196.5	196.5	227.9	217.6	179.0	159.2	174.4	178.2	189.1	146.9
Consumer credit	1.6	48.9	81.7	82.3	57.5	57.5	50.1	45.8	15.6	-14.8	7.3	58.9	121.2	147.9
Tax-exempt debt	8.5	11.4	10.7	30.2	-2.2	-2.2	1.3	2.5	3.8	7.7	9.3	11.9	14.5	7.6
Other mortgages	2.6	13.1	7.0	5.9	8.1	8.1	9.5	19.1	15.3	12.4	12.4	17.5	9.7	13.3
Bank loans n.e.c.	1.8	0.5	-4.1	10.1	1.5	1.5	-3.9	-10.4	-6.5	-3.4	2.7	8.1	10.8	1.4
Other loans	7.4	3.3	2.9	9.3	6.6	6.6	6.5	7.1	11.2	10.1	8.1	6.2	8.2	7.5
Security credit	2.8	8.4	-2.3	18.9	6.7	6.7	1.7	-1.0	-3.7	16.3	-1.8	22.7	-1.8	-3.2
Trade debt	2.8	2.4	3.1	3.1	2.3	2.3	2.5	16.1	11.3	-4.7	7.2	8.1	9.0	9.8
Deferred life ins. premium	0.9	0.6	-1.0	0.1	-1.3	-1.3	0.4	0.8	0.1	0.7	#	0.9	0.9	0.9
Discrepancy	8.9	-50.7	-1.2	-45.6	-83.2	-83.2	-46.4	-112.7	-90.8	-38.5	-68.3	-41.1	35.9	-87.9

Source: *Flow of Funds Accounts: Flows and Outstandings, Second Quarter 1993,* Board of Governors of Federal Reserve System.

33

EXHIBIT 2.10 The Deposit Market of the Flow of Funds
($ Billions)

Checkable Deposits and Currency

	1982	1983	1984	1985	1986	1987	1988	1989	1990	1991	1992	1993	1994	1995:2
Net change in liabilities	37.7	39.5	46.9	83.8	124.4	3.9	42.7	6.4	43.6	86.3	113.5	117.3	-10.1	103.3
Monetary authority	10.2	13.0	10.3	16.6	12.4	16.7	18.1	9.5	25.2	29.2	17.6	37.1	25.3	57.0
U.S. gov't. cash & deposits	0.7	-1.3	1.7	4.1	-1.9	-2.3	3.3	-2.4	2.8	8.8	-10.3	7.2	-7.7	36.6
Foreign deposits	-0.2			0.1	-0.2	-0.1	0.1	0.2	-0.2	0.6	-0.7	0.1	-0.1	-0.7
Currency outside banks	9.7	14.3	8.6	12.4	14.4	19.0	14.7	11.7	22.6	19.8	28.7	29.8	33.1	21.1
Commercial banking	19.2	15.0	28.7	54.2	94.5	-19.7	17.1	-3.4	21.7	37.6	92.8	74.1	32.1	26.1
U.S. government deposits	6.1	-5.3	4.0	10.3	1.7	-5.8	7.3	-3.4	5.3	5.5	-5.9	12.1	-18.9	35.6
Foreign deposits	-3.4	1.6	2.1	1.4	2.9	-1.3	-0.6	-0.1	-0.1	-0.2	2.3	-0.4	4.4	-3.0
Private domestic deposits	16.5	18.8	22.6	42.6	90.0	-12.6	10.4	0.1	-16.5	34.1	96.4	62.4	-17.6	-6.5
Thrift institutions	8.3	11.5	7.9	13.0	17.5	7.0	7.5	0.2	-3.3	19.5	3.2	6.1	-3.3	19.9
Savings institutions	6.5	9.2	6.4	9.9	17.1	5.3	6.8	-1.1	-4.8	17.3	-1.4	4.4	-5.4	17.2
Credit unions	1.8	2.3	1.5	3.1	0.4	1.7	0.8	1.3	1.5	2.2	4.5	1.7	2.0	2.7
Net change in assets	37.7	39.5	46.9	83.8	124.4	3.9	42.7	6.4	43.6	86.3	113.5	117.3	-10.1	103.0
Households	20.8	13.2	-0.9	16.9	87.9	-4.3	19.0	-5.6	5.8	61.9	123.5	77.0	9.1	-11.6
Business	11.6	29.3	34.2	38.6	29.1	21.1	6.7	18.2	8.0	9.3	-3.1	6.7	6.6	15.6
Farm	0.2	0.3	0.2	0.7	1.1	-0.2	0.5	0.1	0.4	1.0	1.8	1.7	1.7	1.7
Nonfarm noncorporate	3.5	8.2	4.8	11.5	6.0	2.5	7.7	4.3	-0.5	0.1	5.5	2.0	3.7	3.0
Corporate	7.9	20.8	29.1	26.5	22.0	18.8	-1.5	13.9	8.1	8.3	-10.4	3.1	1.2	10.9
State & local governments	-1.6	-0.7	5.0	1.1	2.5	-0.7	3.0	0.4	-1.0	4.7	3.1	1.4	2.5	3.6
U.S. government	6.4	-8.3	5.3	13.0	0.4	-8.1	9.0	-14.2	4.8	27.4	16.9	20.7	-21.7	91.2
Foreign	-3.7	1.6	2.1	1.5	2.7	-1.4	-0.5	0.2	-0.3	-1.4	1.5	-0.3	4.3	-3.7
Financial sectors	5.5	0.2	2.6	10.6	11.5	-3.0	3.1	1.2	14.5	-7.0	3.1	14.4	-3.2	32.2
Gov't.-spons. enterprises	-0.2	0.2	0.6	0.8	1.5	-0.1		-1.3	-0.2	-0.9		0.9	-0.9	1.3
Commercial banking	0.5	0.2	0.5	0.4	-0.1	-0.8	-0.6	-0.4	-0.1	-0.8	-0.5	-0.3	1.6	3.5
Savings institutions	2.8	0.8	-1.2	0.8	0.5	-2.3	0.8	-0.8	-0.3	2.0	-0.6	3.1	-1.5	5.2
Credit unions	0.2	0.4	0.4	0.7	0.7		0.2	0.6		0.6	1.2	-0.1		0.6
Life insurance companies	0.3	-0.6	0.7	0.5	0.7	-0.9	-0.3	0.5	-0.1	0.5	-0.6	0.3	0.3	0.6
Other insurance companies		-0.4	0.5	1.2	1.3	-0.1	-0.1	0.6	0.5	-1.1	-0.2	-0.4		0.3
Private pension funds	-1.2	0.5	0.6	0.7	0.3	0.7	-0.5	1.2	0.1	-1.1	-0.1		-1.1	-1.4
St. & local gov't. rtr. funds	0.4	0.4	0.6	0.4	0.7	1.8	-0.4	-1.2	1.5	0.6	0.8	0.7	-0.6	-0.2
Finance companies	0.1	0.1	0.2	0.3	0.4	0.6	0.8	1.0	1.1	1.2	1.3	0.4	0.4	0.4
Mutual funds	0.3	0.6	0.4	1.7	2.6	0.5	0.3	1.3	0.2	3.6	3.8	6.5	0.6	8.7
Money market mutual funds	0.8	-0.6	-1.0	1.4	-0.2	-0.3	1.0	-0.6	11.3	-11.6	-2.5	1.5	-1.3	18.3

Exhibit 2.10 (concluded)

	1982	1983	1984	1985	1986	1987	1988	1989	1990	1991	1992	1993	1994	1995:2
Checkable Deposits and Currency														
Brokers and dealers	1.7	-0.9	0.3	2.4	2.2	-1.4	1.9	0.4	0.5	-0.1	0.2	2.0	-0.4	-5.0
Bank personal trusts	-0.3	-0.5	0.3	-0.6	0.8	-0.8	0.1	-0.1	0.1		-0.1	-0.1	-0.3	-0.1
Mail float	-1.5	4.2	-1.4	2.1	-9.5	0.4	2.5	6.2	11.8	-8.6	2.2	-2.8	-7.6	-24.3
Small Time and Savings Deposits														
Net change in liabilities	139.6	216.6	151.3	142.6	129.4	77.1	121.6	98.7	63.7	1.5	-57.2	-70.3	-40.5	134.3
Commercial banking	97.2	130.9	75.1	81.8	74.3	27.9	73.7	100.7	123.0	78.9	2.7	-11.9	-1.6	147.6
U.S. chartered banks		130.8	74.6	80.3	71.6	27.4	73.1	96.5	121.9	80.0	2.1	-10.9	-0.7	144.7
Foreign banking off. in U.S.	96.4	-0.9	0.5	1.1	2.2	0.6	0.5	3.7	-1.0	-0.1	0.2	-0.8	-1.1	2.1
Banks in U.S.-aff. areas	0.9	0.9	#	0.3	0.5	-0.1	0.3	0.5	2.1	-1.0	0.4	-0.2	0.3	0.8
Thrift institutions	42.3	85.8	76.2	60.8	55.2	49.2	48.9	-2.0	-59.3	-77.4	-60.0	-58.4	-38.9	-13.3
Savings institutions	34.1	73.1	64.9	41.4	29.0	37.9	37.6	-6.2	-73.7	-94.9	-75.5	-68.1	-44.4	-34.8
Credit unions	8.2	12.6	11.3	19.4	26.1	11.4	11.3	4.2	14.4	17.5	15.5	9.8	5.5	21.4
Net change in assets	139.6	216.6	151.3	142.6	129.4	77.1	122.8	98.7	63.7	1.5	-57.2	-70.3	-40.5	134.3
Households	122.4	187.2	138.2	115.3	98.6	52.5	93.9	64.0	66.3	45.4	-64.7	-68.8	-5.8	171.4
Nonfinancial businesses	4.8	11.1	8.9	8.4	8.0	-0.4	8.1	4.7	-0.5	-0.7	-1.3	-0.8	1.6	-0.3
Nonfarm noncorporate	2.0	8.2	8.0	6.9	6.7	-1.1	5.6	5.1	0.4	-2.0	-0.5	-1.8#		0.6
Corporate	2.8	2.9	0.9	1.5	1.3	0.7	2.5	-0.4	-0.9	1.3	-0.8	1.1		-0.9
State and local governments	1.5	5.3	-2.6	-5.4	0.2	9.2	7.1	9.9	7.3	5.8	1.0	-3.1	-10.1	-16.3
U.S. government	0.5	-0.5	0.5	#	0.2	0.2	-0.2	-0.1	0.1	0.1	-0.7	-0.1	-0.1	-0.3
Credit unions	4.9	3.2	-0.7	5.3	6.6	0.2	-2.7	-3.7	0.2	2.7	0.2	-0.7	-5.4	2.9
Private pension funds	5.3	10.0	6.9	18.7	15.4	14.9	16.2	23.8	-9.8	39.7	9.0	3.3	-20.9	-23.4
Bank personal trusts	0.1	0.2	0.1	0.3	0.4	0.5	0.4	0.1	#	-0.7	-0.8	-0.2	0.3	0.2

Source: *Flow of Funds Accounts: Flows and Outstandings, Second Quarter 1993*, Board of Governors of Federal Reserve System.

Box 2.1

In Building Household Wealth, the Shift Is One from Real Estate to Stocks

Behind the rapid run-up in stock prices in the 1990s lies a historic change: Stocks are replacing homes as the primary nest egg for many American families, according to economists and market analysts.

With the upward march of stock prices in this decade, when the Dow Jones industrial average has doubled to 5,000 and other indexes also have surged, the value of U.S. stocks held by Americans now exceeds $5 trillion, Dean Witter Reynolds chief economist Joseph Carson said. Using Federal Reserve Board statistics, Carson estimated that the equity Americans have in their homes totals $4.5 trillion.

This change also reflects the slowing of inflation in house prices and a tremendous flow of cash into mutual funds and retirement plans, which, in turn, has helped push the stock market higher.

"This is an astonishing, long-term asset shift away from residential real estate and toward stocks," said Carson, who prepared such a research report on the subject last summer.

Other economists agree.

"Households continue to put a larger percentage of assets into the stock market," said Daniel Bachman, senior economist at the Wefa Group, a Bala Cynwyd, Pa., economic forecasting firm. "This is a shift of historic proportions in that the future composition of household wealth is changing dramatically and will not return to the pattern of the 1970s and 1980s, when residential real estate was such a large part of household wealth."

There are no definitive current numbers about how many American households have more money in stocks than in real estate. Stephen Zeldes, a professor of finance at the Wharton School, said that, in 1989, one-third of households held shares either directly or indirectly, while in 1992, 40 percent did.

"I suspect the number is higher today," Zeldes said. "Mutual funds have risen in popularity in the past three years. Some of that includes people who had not previously been owners of stock."

Zeldes cautioned that, while more money is invested in stocks than in real estate, "housing . . . remains a significant fraction of household net worth."

From 1992 to 1994, the number of stock mutual fund accounts climbed 79 percent, from 33 million to 59.1 million, according to the Investment Company Institute, a trade group based in Washington.

Most of the time since World War II, Americans bought houses, saw them appreciate in price, and sold them to buy larger homes or to finance retirement. In the 1950s and 1960s, the value of stocks and bonds held by American households was about equal, with stocks taking a slight edge in the late 1960s.

In the 1970s and much of the 1980s, residential real estate prices rose sharply because of inflation and buying pressure as baby boomers entered the market.

Today, boomers are increasingly looking to the stock market, not the housing market, to build the wealth they will need in retirement, according to John Tuccillo, chief economist for the National Association of Realtors, a trade group.

The change should benefit the economy as well as Wall Street, according to Carson at Dean Witter. Successful investment in stocks has created a windfall that offsets the decline in home values that has afflicted many parts of the country in recent years, he said.

"As people become more aware of the financial resources sitting in their stock and retirement funds, they should become more confident of the future, and that should be good for consumer spending and the economy," he said.

The emphasis of stocks is expected to continue, analysts say. The Wefa Group forecast that the value of stocks held by American families will nearly double by 2001.

That assumes there is no stock market crash that reduces the value of Americans' holdings and their appetite for investing more.

Source: Brett D. Fromson, "In Building Household Wealth, the Shift Is One from Real Estate to Stocks," *The Washington Post*, January 28, 1996. © 1996 *The Washington Post*. Reprinted with permission.

Summary

In this chapter, we have dissected the economy into its real and financial sectors. For the real sector, we introduced the notion of total output as captured by gross domestic product. This aggregate statistic can be estimated using a number of different techniques, two of which are described here.

From total output, individual economic units allocate some of their resources to the purchase of financial instruments. These units are referred to as net savers. Still other economic units rely upon the financial markets to permit them to invest in greater amounts than their own resources will allow. The national income accounting system tracks real sector income and expenditures by all economic units.

The flow of funds analysis discloses the financial transactions associated with the savings and investment decisions. It also reports transactions within the financial sector by gathering information on the financial activity of various parts of the economy and within specific financial markets. The Federal Reserve system of accounts, while complex, contains important information about the evolution of the financial sector and the balance sheet of various parts of the U.S. economy.

Key Concepts

financial versus real sectors,   17
flow of funds framework,   24
free good versus economic good,   18
gross domestic product (GDP),   18
national income,   21
personal income,   23

personal savings,   23
producer goods versus consumer goods,   18
savings-deficit sector,   27
savings-surplus sector,   27
stock versus flow,   18
wealth versus income,   18

Review Questions

1. What are two approaches to measuring GDP? How do they differ? Why should, in theory, the two methods lead to the same number? Why are there often differences in the estimates?
2. What is the logic underlying the assertion that the sources of funds must equal the uses of funds? How is it central to both national income accounting and the flow of funds approach?
3. What logic underlies the relationship captured in the equation below?

$$\Delta\text{Real assets} + \Delta\text{Financial assets} = \Delta\text{Financial liabilities} + \Delta\text{Net worth}$$

4. In Exhibit 2.9, U.S. Government securities annual flow to the household and nonprofit organization sectors in 1991 is listed as −$80.5 billion. What does it mean for this number to be negative?
5. Suppose the interest rate offered to depositors by the commercial banking sector were to fall relative to interest rates offered elsewhere between 1992 and 1993. How would the flow of funds respond to this situation and how would it be reflected in the Federal Reserve statistics?

References

Board of Governors of the Federal Reserve System. *Introduction to the Flow of Funds.* Washington, D.C., February 1975.

Cohen, Jacob. "Copeland's Money Flows after Twenty-Five Years: A Survey." *Journal of Economic Literature,* March 1972.

Cohen, Jacob. *The Flow of Funds in Theory and Practice.* Norwell, Mass.: Kluwer Academic Publishers, 1987.

Dewald, Wand Mulan. "Appreciating U.S. Savings and Investment." *Business Economics,* January 1992.

Eisner, Robert. "The Total Income System of Accounts." *Survey of Current Business,* January 1985.

Goldsmith, Raymond W. *Capital Market Analysis and the Financial Accounts of the Nation.* Morristown, N.J.: General Learning Press, 1972.

National Bureau of Economic Research. *The Flow-of-Funds Approach to Social Accounting.* New York: National Bureau of Economic Research, 1962.

Ritter, Lawrence S. *The Flow of Funds Accounts: A Framework for Financial Analysis.* New York: Institute of Finance, New York University, 1968.

Webb, Roy H. *Macroeconomics Data: A Users Guide.* Federal Reserve Bank of Richmond, 1990.

PART II   Pricing Cash Flows

CHAPTER
3

Fundamentals of Interest Rate Determination

_____

Chapter Outline

This chapter introduces the role interest rates play in determining the allocation of resources by individuals and firms. It begins with a simple two-period consumption problem and a simple capital investment decision. Together, these factors form a market interest rate in the exchange market for the consumption–investment decision. The chapter then considers the effect of inefficiencies in the exchange market on the consumption–investment decision. Finally, it looks at a broader range of determinants of the market rate of interest using a loanable funds approach to interest rate determination.

In financial markets, the price of credit is referred to as the "interest rate." As with other prices, the interest rate is determined by demand and supply. However, there are some unique factors affecting the demand and supply of credit, including the fact that the interest rate is an "intertemporal" price—the price today for money that is to be returned at some future date.

In his 1930 treatise on the theory of interest,[1] famed economist Irving Fisher laid the foundations for much of modern thought on how interest rates can be

_____

[1] Irving Fisher, *The Theory of Interest* (New York: Macmillan, 1930; reprint New York: Augustus M. Kelley, 1961).

41

derived from examining the consumption and savings decisions of individuals. His theory was framed in a two-period world. To be concrete, we can think of these periods as this year and next year (or alternatively, this semester and next semester). There will be consumption opportunities for us in both periods, and we wish to determine how much to consume in each period.

There are three essential components of the two-period economic model of real interest rate determination set forth by Fisher:

1. He constructed an indifference curve for consumption across the two periods.
2. He added a set of investment opportunities to the consumer's choice.
3. He added a financial market, allowing for saving or borrowing.

In this section, we will describe each essential component of the theory in some detail. We will then merge the components, as Fisher did, to uncover an important role for financial markets and interest rates in the economy.

Consumption Time Preferences

One of the most delightful aspects of wealth or income is that it can be spent for consumer items that we need or desire. Suppose that in the two-period world of Fisher, we were each asked to indicate our preference for consuming goods and services now, relative to postponing gratification until next year and consuming goods and services at that time. Most people would require higher consumption opportunity in the future to willingly forgo current consumption. The extra amount of future consumption would serve as a reward for being patient. For each additional unit of forgone current consumption, individuals would require increasing rewards in terms of their future consumption opportunity.[2] There are all sorts of combinations of present and future consumption that would leave the individual indifferent. For example, he or she might be indifferent between the three combinations shown in Exhibit 3.1.

Combination *A1* allows the individual to achieve a certain level of satisfaction, or gratification, in each period. To sacrifice 5,000 units of current consumption (from 35,000 to 30,000), the individual might require an additional 8,000 consumption units (from 40,000 to 48,000) next year to feel as well off. To garner the consumer's willingness to forgo an additional 5,000 units of current consumption (from 30,000 to 25,000), an even greater increment to future consumption of 12,000 units might be required.

---

[2]This is a well-known result from basic microeconomics in which an individual receives increasing utility, but diminishing marginal utility, from consumption. Therefore, one must be offered increasing amounts of future consumption, each unit of which produces a lower boost to overall utility than the preceding unit, in order to induce the individual to sacrifice willingly some current consumption.

EXHIBIT 3.1   Consumption Combinations of Equal Utility

Combination	Present Consumption		Future Consumption	
A1	35,000		40,000	
		Δ–5,000		Δ +8,000
A2	30,000		48,000	
		Δ–5,000		Δ+12,000
A3	25,000		60,000	

If we plotted all of the possible consumption combinations that would make the consumer indifferent with the utility derived from the combinations in Exhibit 3.1, the plot would appear something like curve *U1* in Exhibit 3.2. This curve is called an **indifference curve** because the consumer would be equally satisfied by, or indifferent between, any combination of consumption over the two periods along this curve. The shape of the curve is a reflection of the amount of "impatience" of the individual and of the **diminishing marginal utility** for consumption in any one period. In other words, the shape reflects the fact that, other things being equal, the individual would prefer to consume now rather than later. The steeper the slope of the curve, the more impatient the individual is. The greater its bend, or curvature, the less rapidly the individual gains utility from additional units of current consumption. In general, indifference curves like those contained in Exhibit 3.2 are referred to as negatively sloped and **convex**.[3]

A second set of consumption combinations could be plotted, such as those indicated by points *B1*, *B2*, and *B3*, that would produce a higher level of utility than the first set of combinations (*A1, A2, A3*, etc.), yet leave the consumer indifferent between any of the new combinations. For any point along curve *U1* (e.g., *A1*, *A2*, or *A3*), there is a corresponding point along curve *U2* (e.g., *B1*, *B2*, or *B3*) that provides for the same amount of current consumption but higher future consumption. Hence, curve *U2* represents a curve of higher utility. Indeed, there could be a whole host of such curves for a given individual.

Curves located toward the northeast of the quadrant would produce higher utility for the individual than those located closer to the origin, because the former would allow for greater current and future consumption than the latter. Obviously, an individual would be motivated to strive for the combination of present and future consumption available to him or her that produced the highest possible utility.

---

[3]An exceptional case is a straight line with a vertical slope. This is sometimes dubbed the "Marin Curve," so named in honor of the residents of Marin County, California, whose appetite for current consumption is legendary. A CBS *60 Minutes* television documentary on Marin County, "We Want It All, And We Want It Right Now!" detailed this lifestyle.

EXHIBIT 3.2

*Time preference
for consumption*

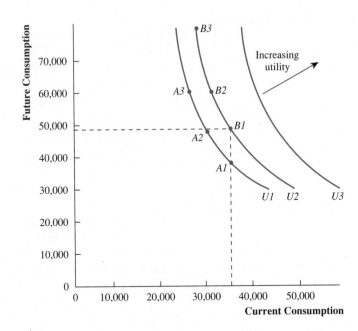

The Investment Opportunity Set

Each individual in the Fisherian two-period world must allocate present and future wealth for consumption now and later. By forgoing some amount of current consumption, the savings can be invested in productive activities that will generate greater wealth, and thus higher consumption opportunity, in the future. Fisher assumed in his model that there was no uncertainty. Thus, if an individual invested an amount of wealth at the beginning of a period, he or she would know exactly how much the investment would be worth at the end of the period.

Consider now how the individual would choose which projects to invest in today in lieu of enjoying current consumption. Being rational, he or she would first consider those projects with the highest return next period. Then, the next best project would be considered, and then the next, until all of the projects were ranked in order of efficiency or future payoff per unit of consumption forgone for its investment.

A plot of investment opportunities for a given individual, referred to as the **investment opportunity set,** is given in Exhibit 3.3. The **concave** shape of the curve exhibits the property of **diminishing marginal returns to investment.** For example, an individual may begin with 50,000 units of wealth that can be used for current consumption. By cutting current consumption to 40,000 units, and investing the 10,000 in the most productive assets, the individual can achieve an

EXHIBIT 3.3

*Investment opportunity
set*

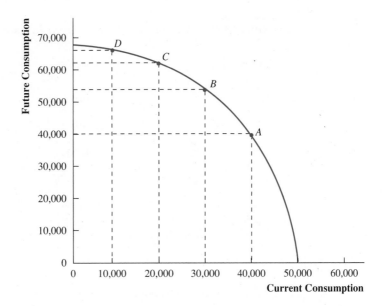

By reducing current consumption another 10,000 units, to 30,000, the individual may be able to consume 54,000 units in the next period. As is illustrated in Exhibit 3.4, further reductions in current consumption allow for additional investment and, therefore, increased future consumption.

Note in Exhibits 3.3 and 3.4 how the property of diminishing marginal returns to incremental investment translates into numbers. The slope of the curve at any given point has special significance. Its absolute value represents the return on investment over the next period of time. This is seen easily as follows. The slope of a line or curve segment is measured by the "rise over the run." The rise shows the amount of wealth available for future consumption that will be achieved by investing a given amount of wealth today. The run, in this case, is the amount of current wealth channeled away from current consumption toward investment. In other words, it represents the amount of wealth invested. If we invest one extra dollar of present wealth, and receive \$1.15 in return next period, our rate of return is 15 percent. The slope of the curve at this point would be equal to $1.15/(-1.00) = -1.15$.

The steeper slope at the lower part of the curve reflects the tendency of rational investors in a world of certainty to select first those investments with the highest possible rates of return. As those opportunities are exhausted, the investor will proceed on to the investments whose returns are almost as high. This process will continue until the investor reaches those investments that have very low, and perhaps even negative, rates of return. In general, one would not expect that a

---
Exhibit 3.4   Consumption Values Given Investment Opportunities
---

Point	Present Consumption		Future Consumption	
A	50,000		0	
		$\Delta-10{,}000$		$\Delta+40{,}000$
B	40,000		40,000	
		$\Delta-10{,}000$		$\Delta+14{,}000$
C	30,000		54,000	
		$\Delta-10{,}000$		$\Delta +8{,}000$
D	20,000		62,000	
		$\Delta-10{,}000$		$\Delta +4{,}000$
E	10,000		66,000	
		$\Delta-10{,}000$		$\Delta +1{,}000$
F	0,000		67,000	

rational person would continue to invest if he or she knew that the rate of return on further investment would be negative. (This is the case for that portion of the investment opportunity set above point *B* in Exhibit 3.3, where the absolute value of the slope is less than unity, which actually produces negative rates of return.) Unless the nature of the investable wealth is perishable, in the absence of capital markets it would be preferable for the investor simply to hold in safekeeping that portion of his wealth desired for use in the next period, thereby guaranteeing at least a zero percent rate of return, rather than to invest in a project with a known negative return.

Not ordering investments in this way will produce an investment opportunity curve that falls within the lower boundaries of the one represented in Exhibit 3.3. For example, if an investor selected the worst investments first and then proceeded toward the best ones, he or she would achieve an investment opportunity set shaped like the innermost curve of Exhibit 3.5. It is obvious that such an approach will not attain the same level of utility as the recommended strategy. Only lower indifference curves will intersect with this investment opportunity set.

In Exhibit 3.6, we place the concave investment opportunity set, ordered from best to worst investment, together with a few of the convex indifference curves. Note that the highest possible indifference curve is reached at point *A'*. To reach this point, the individual must forgo 8,000 units of current consumption *(AD)* and invest these savings, thus providing 38,000 units of future consumption *(AA')*. Indifference curve *U3* is unattainable given the investment opportunities facing the individual, and indifference curve *U1* clearly provides less utility to the individual than he or she could reach by following an optimal investment strategy in which the highest returning investments are selected first, followed by less attractive investments.

Notice that there are some important properties illustrated at point *A'* in Exhibit 3.6. At point *A'*, the indifference curve slope is equal to the investment

EXHIBIT 3.5

Investment opportunity sets

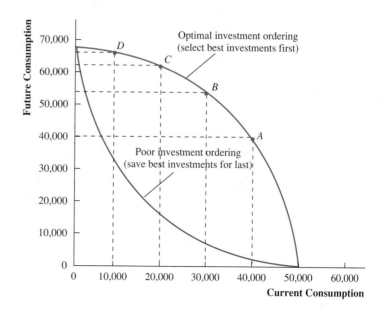

opportunity set slope. As noted above, the marginal utility of consumption today and tomorrow is defined by the slope of the indifference curve. We also know that the marginal return on investment is given by the slope of the investment opportunity set. At A', both of these are equal! The marginal utility of the next unit of forgone current consumption is exactly equal to the productivity of the last investment.

Capital Market Opportunities and Budget Lines

Up to this point, we have considered an individual who has preferences regarding current versus future consumption and who has opportunities for investment in productive assets or activities. By putting together the preferences with the opportunities, the individual was able to maximize the utility derived from consumption. However, this individual was essentially operating alone. Fisher next introduced capital markets into the two-period world. In addition to being able to invest in productive assets and activities, an individual could save money by putting it into financial assets or placing it in a financial institution. These funds would then be made available to borrowers who have investment opportunities in physical capital. Such individuals borrow money from the financial market to increase their investment in productive real assets and, perhaps, to finance higher current consumption. The increase in current consumption is financed by the high returns of the increased productive investments made possible by the funds borrowed from the financial market.

EXHIBIT 3.6

Optimal investment–consumption

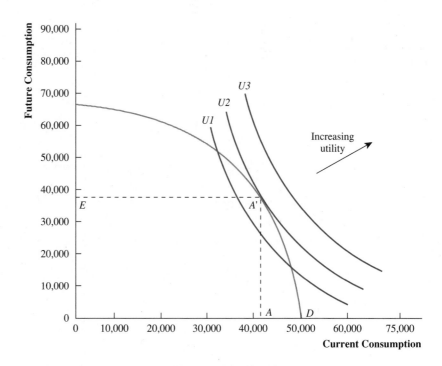

At the outset, Fisher assumed that the interest rate paid on savings was the same as the rate charged for borrowing.[4] This assumption results in a set of **capital market opportunity lines** whose identical slopes are directly related to the interest rate paid on savings or charged on loans. (See Exhibit 3.7.) With an identical borrowing and savings rate of interest, the capital market opportunity borrowing and savings lines become indistinguishable from each other. From any point along a given line, an individual may save or borrow. Moving downward and to the right entails a decrease in savings and, when savings are totally exhausted, an increase in borrowing. Moving upward and to the left represents a repayment of loans, and upon liquidation of all debts, an increase to savings.[5] The capital market opportunity lines are all perfectly straight lines, suggesting that no

---

[4]While this simplification is at odds with reality, economists typically begin their analyses with simplifying assumptions such as a single rate of interest to enable them to gain insights into the basic structure of the problem at hand. Later, they introduce complicating factors like spreads between borrowing and savings interest rates and are able to discern the importance of these factors as the resulting equilibrium solution changes.

[5]In the simple certainty model of Fisher, no one would be simultaneously a saver and a borrower. In a world of uncertainty and liquid investments, one might borrow more than he could productively invest and place the remainder of his borrowings in a savings account to provide a cushion of liquid assets against any unforeseen needs that might arise. This is related to what is sometimes referred to as the precautionary demand for cash.

EXHIBIT 3.7

*Capital market
opportunities and
budget lines*

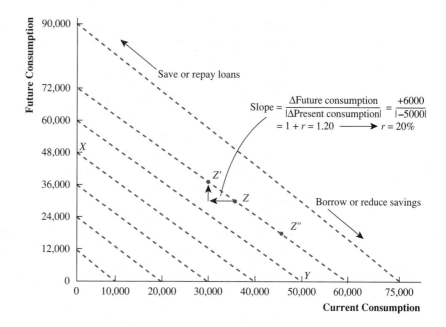

matter how much a given individual borrows or saves, the interest rate will remain
unaffected.[6]

To gain a better understanding of these market opportunity lines, consider
three individuals, whose initial wealth endowments and income opportunities are
represented by points *X, Y,* and *Z.* Individual *X* has no current wealth but will be
generating income equal to 48,000 consumption units in the future. (You may
think of individual *X* as an impoverished student who is out of the workforce until
next period.) If we assume prices are fixed, we can think of these units of consumption as being each equal in value to a dollar. Individual *X* can borrow against
her future income of $48,000 and use the funds for current consumption. If she
were to pledge all of her future income to the lender as security for her debt, she
could borrow up to $40,000, repaying $48,000 one year later. The implicit interest
rate on her borrowing is therefore [$48,000 ÷ $40,000] − 1 = 20%.

Individual *Y,* on the other hand, has current wealth of $50,000 but no future
income. (You may think of individual *Y* as a retiree who has generated considerable savings but receives no pension.) If he anticipates surviving for another year,

---

[6]In a world of certainty, the problem of insolvency is not an issue. Because there is perfect
certainty, it is known in advance whether a given individual will be solvent or insolvent at the
time a loan is due to be repaid. If it is known the individual will be unable to repay the loan,
the loan simply will not be made. Hence, no higher rate of interest is charged for riskier loans,
because in a world of certainty, no loans are risky. This simplification in the model will be
relaxed in later chapters.

individual Y may wish to put aside some of his current wealth and save it for future consumption. If individual Y were to save everything, he would have $60,000 available to him in the future, although forgoing all current consumption would probably result in his demise long before the next period arrived.

Individual Z has both present and future income. However, she need not consume it in exactly the same amounts as her income endowment pattern dictates, because the capital market allows her to alter her consumption pattern by saving or borrowing. As shown, individual Z has current income worth $35,000, and next period, she will receive additional income worth $30,000. Suppose her plans for consumption require only $30,000 now but an additional $36,000 next year. Given her earnings stream, how could she achieve this consumption pattern?

First, individual Z could save the surplus income of $5,000 during the first period and earn an interest rate of 20 percent per year. That would leave her $30,000 for the current period, exactly her desired amount. Next year, she could retrieve her $5,000 from savings, plus $1,000 in interest earnings, plus $30,000 in additional income. The total of $36,000 is just sufficient to meet her desired spending for next year. This action is shown as a northwesterly movement along the budget line, beginning at point Z and moving to Z'. Individual Z could have moved in the opposite direction by borrowing against her $30,000 in future income and increasing her current consumption beyond $35,000. For example, she could have borrowed $10,000 and consumed $45,000 during the first period. After repaying her loan (she will owe $12,000: $10,000 principal plus $2,000 interest), she will have $18,000 (= $30,000 − $12,000) left for consumption in the second period (see point Z''). Indeed, she could fund any kind of combination of first- and second-period consumption that lies along her budget line.

Each individual could be portrayed by a single point in the consumption quadrant, representing his or her claims to present and future consumption. These claims may be based on an endowment of wealth, future income, or some combination of the two. The capital market opportunity line passing through an individual's endowment/income point would then, in a sense, represent a budget line. It would show the possible combinations of current and future consumption made available to the individual through the opportunity to borrow or save at a given interest rate. The size of the budget, measured in the consumption units of either period, is given by the point at which the budget line intersects an axis. The further out from the origin this budget line intersects an axis, the larger the budget.[7]

---

[7] The "present value" of any point along a given line can be computed as the sum of the current consumption, which has a value equal to itself, and present value of future consumption, which has a present value equal to itself divided by $(1 + r)$. For example, consider individual Z. The present value of her budget is equal to $35,000 in current income plus [$30,000 ÷ (1 + interest rate)] = $35,000 + $25,000 = $60,000. The construction of the capital market line automatically performs this operation and renders the result along the horizontal axis. If her

EXHIBIT 3.8

Optimal consumption and investment with capital markets

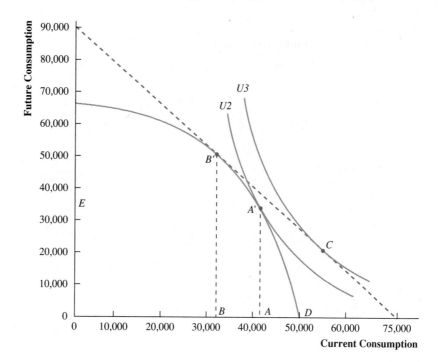

As shown in Exhibit 3.8, the three elements of the Fisher model can be blended together. In this exhibit, the individual starts with a wealth endowment of D, or $50,000, with no future income. If there were no borrowing opportunities, the highest attainable indifference curve would be $U2$, which could be obtained by investing $D - A$ of current consumption claims. However the individual can do better when borrowing and lending are possible.

To reach his highest indifference curve, the individual will invest an amount equal to $D - B$, or approximately $18,000. This will allow the individual to reach point B', representing current and future consumption claims of approximately 32,000 units and 52,000 units, respectively. He may then proceed to point C by borrowing against his future consumption claim, reaching $U3$, the highest indifference curve possible given the initial endowment, investment opportunity set, and capital market opportunity lines.

Note that, rather than borrowing, the individual could proceed back from point B' toward D by "disinvesting." However, he would sacrifice some higher returning investments in so doing, and the sacrificed return would exceed the borrowing rate. In other words, it would be cheaper for him to borrow to

consumption plans call for a combination of present and future consumption with a present value in excess of $60,000, there is nothing in the simple capital market that individual Z can do to adequately fund her consumption plan. Consequently, she will need to move to a new budget line.

EXHIBIT 3.9

*Optimal consumption
and investment with
capital markets for
individuals with
differing time
preferences*

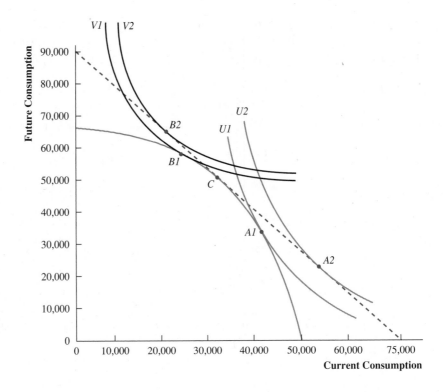

increase current consumption than to forgo investing in some profitable ventures.

Proceeding on to Exhibit 3.9, we show the indifference curves of individuals with identical investment opportunity sets and similar wealth and income endowments but with differing tastes for present versus future consumption. One individual, whose indifference curves are given by *V1* and *V2*, does not mind deferring consumption. The other individual, whose indifference curves are given by *U1* and *U2*, has a greater degree of impatience.

We can see that regardless of one's time preference for consumption, all individuals will invest up to point *C*. The patient individual, after investing up to point *C*, will then save (which earns a higher return than additional investment) up to point *B2*, reaching her indifference curve *V2*. The impatient individual, after investing up to point *C*, would borrow back to point *A2*, reaching his indifference curve *U2*.

Note that for the patient individual, the capital market will permit her to achieve a higher level of utility than if she were restricted to whatever level of consumption combinations were made available through the investment opportunity set. Her highest attainable indifference curve without capital markets would be achieved at point *B1*. Similarly, the impatient individual would achieve his highest indifference curve, *U1*, at point *A1* without the help from capital markets. The middle of the roader (the indifference curve for whom is not shown but which would be tangent to the opportunity set at point *C*) is neither helped nor hindered by the existence of capital markets. Therefore, we can say that with capital markets, everyone, regardless of their degree of impatience, is at least as well off as they would be in the absence of capital markets, and their conditions may even be improved.

Interest Rate Spreads

The conditions for all three parties are improved if the exchange is possible. However, without help, the saver might not be able to find the investor, or vice versa. To facilitate the exchange, a financial intermediary, such as a banker, might enter the scene—but only for a price. However, our model so far has assumed that borrowing and saving occur at the same interest rate. That leaves no spread for the banker. A profitable bank will lend out money at higher rates than it will pay to savers. To help the banker, we will introduce a positive spread between the lending and deposit rates. Such a situation is depicted in Exhibit 3.10.

In Exhibit 3.10, the borrowing line is steeper than the savings line, indicating that the interest charged to borrowers is higher than the rate paid to depositors. Note that the highest indifference curve possible under such circumstances is lower for all individuals (except the "middle of the roader" and the banker!) than that which was attainable with no spread in the borrowing and savings rates. The patient individual will no longer be able to reach point *B2* along indifference curve *V2*; she will have to reconcile herself with lower present and/or future consumption. Similarly, the impatient individual will no longer be able to reach point *A2* along indifference curve *U2*; he will have to endure a reduced lifestyle. Nonetheless, both individuals will be better off than with what they could attain were there no capital market. And now the banker is happy, too!

Market Equilibrium for Interest Rates

Up to this point, we have examined an individual's investment, savings, and borrowing behavior given the interest rates prevailing in the economy. We have not yet discussed how the slope—and hence, the interest rate(s)—of the capital market opportunity line is determined. To simplify our exposition, let us return for a moment to the case where borrowing and savings rates are equal to each other. We will see that the interest rate is the rate in the economy that equilibrates the aggregate desire for borrowing and the aggregate desire for saving.

To show this, consider an economy with only two individuals, as depicted in Exhibit 3.11. Individual 1 (with indifference curves labeled *V1* and *V2*) wishes to save money in order to maximize her utility, while individual 2 (with indifference

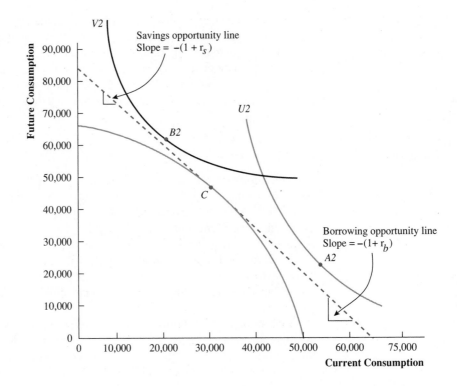

curves labeled *U1* and *U2*) desires to borrow money. Given the shape of the
investment opportunity set and the slope of the original capital market opportunity line, both individuals will invest until they reach point *C* and then either save
or borrow until reaching their highest attainable indifference curves (*V1* and *U2*),
at points *B* and *A*, respectively.

At the initial interest rate, the desired amount for borrowing far exceeds the
savings available for lending. This excess demand for funds will force interest
rates higher. In Exhibit 3.11, this is shown by the steeper new solid blue capital
market opportunity line (reflecting a higher interest rate for depositors and
borrowers). The new line will intersect a higher indifference curve (*V2*) for individual 1, due to the higher interest rate she will be earning on her savings, and a
lower indifference curve (*U1*) for individual 2, due to the higher interest rate he
will be charged for his borrowing.

Note how investment in productive (real) assets will decrease from *C* to *C'* in
this higher interest rate environment. This decrease occurs because individuals
will find that some investments no longer produce rates of return as high as those
that can be earned through savings, and as a result, they will not undertake these
marginal investments. At this lower level of investment, it appears as if the excess
demand for borrowing and the short supply of loanable funds situation has

Exhibit 3.11

Equilibrium interest rates

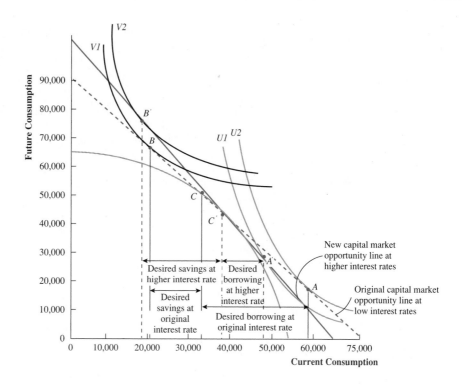

reversed itself. Now there are more loanable funds available than what are desired by borrowers at the new interest rate. Therefore, interest rates will have to decline to somewhere between the initial level and the new level before equilibrium will be reached.

By continuing to rotate the capital market opportunity line to successively higher and lower slopes, we can derive the entire demand and supply curves for borrowing and saving—or more succinctly, for loanable funds—as a function of the interest rate. Only one interest rate will balance the supply and demand.

To illustrate this aggregation process, we will return to our two individuals of the prior illustration, the patient female (individual 1) and impatient male (individual 2), and add the third individual, our "middle of the roader." Her patience lies somewhere between that of the first two individuals. Below, we list the demand and supply schedules for loanable funds for the three individuals and then aggregate them into economywide schedules.

Exhibit 3.13 illustrates these supply and demand functions in graphical form. Note that the equilibrium interest rate for this three-person economy is somewhere between 9 and 10 percent. In principle, the same process could be repeated for the entire population of a nation or group of nations to arrive at broader-based

---

Exhibit 3.12   Aggregating Supply and Demand Schedules for Loanable Funds

Interest Rate	Individual 1		Individual 2		Individual 3		Aggregate Economy	
	Supply	*Demand*	*Supply*	*Demand*	*Supply*	*Demand*	*Supply*	*Demand*
6%	100	50	10	160	40	100	150	310
8%	110	40	20	140	60	80	190	260
10%	120	30	30	120	80	60	230	210
12%	130	20	40	100	100	40	270	160
14%	140	10	50	80	120	20	310	110

---

supply and demand curves and an interest rate that reflects the time preferences of many more market participants.

While our example began with only two individuals in the economy, the same process can be used to derive the supply and demand for loanable funds for the economy as a whole. To do so, however, requires that we aggregate not just over individuals, but over all economic agents, including firms and even governments, to arrive at the total demand and supply functions for loanable funds. This includes firms, some of which are supplying resources and some of which are demanding them, and it also includes the government itself. So, deficits at both national and local levels can be seen to increase the net demand for funds and, therefore, the pressure on the price of credit. The international sector also adds to this analysis. If borrowers from abroad have demands that exceed their supply, the total supply of loanable funds shifts less than the demand from investing segments from abroad. Seen in this light, the loanable funds market includes all of the forces of society, with each sector's demand and supply of funds leading to aggregate interest rate effects. Each sector's net demand for funds in turn causes changes in the market interest rate and the quantity of total investment being undertaken. As we include more and more individuals in the economy and aggregate their individual supply and demand schedules, we will ultimately arrive at economywide supply and demand equilibrium. Where the supply and demand schedules intersect, we will have the equilibrium interest rate for the entire economy, which depends upon total household savings, firm investment levels, government deficits, and foreign capital flows. In truth, all of these factors determine the financial market equilibrium and, therefore, the price of credit—the market rate of interest.

Exhibit 3.13

Equilibrium interest rates for three-person economy

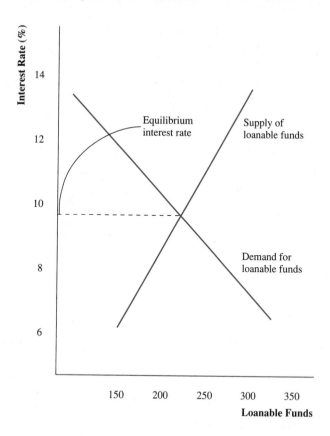

Summary

This chapter introduced the role that interest rates play in decisions to consume or save and the allocation of current resources among individuals. It began with a simple two-period consumption problem and a capital market investment decision. In this initial scenario, the individual, in isolation, trades current consumption for (greater) future consumption. While impatient to consume, the economic agent is willing to defer some consumption if the returns from investment opportunities are sufficient. Current consumption, therefore, is determined by weighing the value of potentially greater future consumption against current gratification.

The presence of a capital market improves the situation. With the ability to either borrow or save, each participant is at least as well off as he or she would have been in isolation. Impatient consumers can borrow resources from the market for consumption beyond current income. Patient consumers can supply such resources in exchange for higher consumption in the future. The ability to borrow and save adds value to all who engage in such activity.

However, not all of us can borrow and lend at the same rate. Bankers' fees, or the cost of transactions, may lead to a spread between borrowing and saving rates. This is considered here as well. Nonetheless, the presence of a capital market still adds value to its participants.

We close the chapter with a discussion of the determinants of the interest rate charged within the capital market. Using a loanable funds approach, we show how the interest rate is determined from market demand and supply for credit. The equilibrium interest rate is the price at which aggregate supply equals aggregate demand.

Key Concepts

aggregate supply and demand for loanable
  funds,   56
capital market opportunity line,   48
convex versus concave,   43–44
diminishing marginal returns to investment,   44

diminishing marginal utility of
  consumption,   43
indifference curve,   43
investment opportunity set,   44
market equilibrium interest rate,   53

Review Questions

1. If the investment opportunity set is a straight line, what does this tell us about the investment opportunities? Diminishing marginal returns?
2. When there are no capital markets, is it possible for an individual to have a different marginal utility of consumption and marginal return on investment at his optimal investment choice? Is it possible when there are capital markets?
3. If everyone had the same preferences, is it possible that the addition of capital markets would not result in an increase in utility? Does this result depend on the interest rate?
4. Suppose interest rates were to decline. Is it possible for one individual to switch from being a saver to being a borrower? Why would this occur? Is it possible for an individual to switch in the opposite direction?
5. In Exhibit 3.1, consumption, both present and future, is presented in numerical units, such as 35,000, rather than in dollar units. Why?
6. If the investment opportunity set available to an individual is a straight line, is it necessary to have a capital market?
7. Why is it impossible for the indifference curves of an individual to cross one another?
8. As capital markets become more efficient, spreads tend to decline. Using an extension of Exhibit 3.10, can you show how this will improve the welfare of both borrowers and savers?

References

DeFina, Robert H. "The Link between Savings and Interest Rates: A Key Element in the Tax Policy Debate." *Business Review,* Federal Reserve Bank of Philadelphia, Nov./Dec. 1984.

Fisher, Irving. *The Theory of Interest.* New York: Macmillan, 1930.
Friedman, Milton. "Factors Affecting the Level of Interest Rate." In *Current Issues in Monetary Theory*

and Policy, 2d ed., ed. by Thomas M. Havrilsky and John T. Boorman. Arlington Heights Ill.: Harlan Davidson, 1980.

Hirshleifer, Jack. *Investment, Interest, and Capital*. Englewood Cliffs, N.J.: Prentice Hall, 1970.

Howrey, E. P., and S. H. Hyman. "The Measurement and Determination of Loanable-Funds Saving." *Brookings Papers on Economic Activity,* 1978.

Kopcke, Richard W. "The Determinants of Investment Spending." *New England Economic Review,* Federal Reserve Bank of Boston, July/August 1985.

Mishkin, Frederic. *The Economics of Money, Banking and Financial Markets*. 2d ed. Glenview, Ill.: Scott Foresman, 1989.

Mullineaux, Donald J. "Efficient Markets, Interest Rates, and Monetary Policy." *Business Review,* Federal Reserve Bank of Philadelphia, May/June 1981.

Van Horne, J. *Financial Market Rates and Flows*. 4th ed. Englewood Cliffs, N.J.: Prentice Hall, 1994.

The Behavior of Nominal Interest Rates

Chapter Outline

Nominal versus Real Rates of Interest
Expected Inflation and Nominal Interest Rates
Empirical Evidence Regarding Inflation and Nominal Interest Rates
    Expected Real Rate and Inflation Proxies
    Extracting Estimates from Theoretical Models
    Other Problems Associated with Expected Inflation
Evidence from Several Countries

The notion of nominal versus real interest rates is developed in this chapter. Consideration is given to ex ante *estimates of inflation and their* ex post *counterparts. Review of the empirical evidence is presented, both in national and in cross-country comparisons to evaluate the importance of nominal considerations.*

In Chapters 2 and 3, we discussed elements of the national income accounts and the consumption–investment models and showed how the real rate of interest is linked to real wealth, capital productivity, and the time preferences for consumption. We introduced the flow of funds model and the loanable funds framework to show how changes in the equilibrium real rate may arise from a shift in consumer, firm, or government net demand for credit from the financial markets. These changes were said to cause changes in the price of credit, the interest rate. However, the interest rate that is actually observed in the economy is a nominal rate of interest that incorporates more than real demands for credit. In this chapter, we discuss this feature of market rates and relate the observed rate to the interest rate derived in the previous chapters. To do so, however, requires that we address another feature of financial markets, the role that inflation plays in financial pricing. This leads us to make a distinction between the real rate discussed in Chapter 3 and the market rate, which will be defined as the nominal rate of interest. In this chapter, we will develop an understanding of the nominal interest rate, its importance in the economy, and its relationship to the real rate of interest.

Nominal versus Real Rates of Interest

Consider a land in which there is only one traded commodity—wheat. A farmer lends 1,000 bushels of wheat to another farmer who promises to repay the loan in one year with 1,050 bushels of wheat of similar quality to that which was lent. We could say that the farmer providing the 1,000 bushels of wheat will earn a real rate of return (or interest) of 5 percent because he will get 50 more bushels of wheat than he lent.

Alternatively, the lender could make an equivalent loan in currency. (We will call the currency of this land "dollars.") Suppose that wheat sells for $2.00 a bushel today and is expected to remain at that price in the next period. The farmer could convert his 1,000 bushels of wheat into $2,000 and lend currency. If he charges an interest rate of 5 percent, he will receive $2,100 at the end of the period. He could then convert the cash back into bushels of wheat by buying 1,050 bushels at the going price of $2 per bushel. The farmer would be indifferent to these two methods of lending because his return in real value, i.e., bushels of wheat, will be 5 percent in both cases.

However, the above example critically depends upon the assumption that wheat will remain priced at $2.00 per bushel. If this were not the case and both farmers knew that wheat prices would be rising to $2.20 per bushel,[1] the lender would no longer be happy with the currency transaction. In this case, a change in price reduces the value of the repayment and results in a smaller number of bushels next period (954.5) than either the agreed amount of 1,050 or the 1,000 bushels lent.

To protect the lender against the decline in the buying power of the currency lent to the borrower, our farmer would require compensation for price change in the dollar contract. If he charges an interest rate of 15.5 percent per annum, he will receive $2,310 (= $2,000 × [1 + .155]) when the loan comes due a year from now. He can then take the loan proceeds and purchase 1,050 bushels (= $2,310 ÷ $2.20/ bushel). Thus, under these terms, he would be indifferent between making a commodity loan or a currency loan.

This simple example contains the essence of fundamental definitions for real interest, inflation, and nominal interest rates. The **real interest rate,** as shown in Chapter 3, is the equilibrium rate at which claims to future consumption are traded for current consumption; it is, in essence, wheat for wheat. Let Q_0 and Q_1 represent the amounts of goods and services available for consumption at time 0 and time 1, respectively. Then, the one-period real rate of interest, r, is

---

[1]The price at the end could be considered a one-year "forward price." In commodity markets, it is common to make forward contracts that lock in today the future price at which a trade will be transacted.

$$r = \frac{Q_1 - Q_0}{Q_0} = \frac{Q_1}{Q_0} - 1$$

In the case of our farmer-turned-lender, we would have

$$r = \frac{1,050 \text{ bushels}}{1,000 \text{ bushels}} - 1 = .05, \text{ or } 5\%$$

Note that the real rate of interest is defined without respect to commodity prices. When prices change, however, currency contracts relate not to quantities of goods and services available for consumption but to the prices of those goods and services. Such contracts are referred to as **nominal contracts.**

The **nominal interest rate** takes into account changes in quantities as well as changes in prices. Thus, it incorporates both the real rate of interest and the effect of price change. This result can be generalized by some additional notation and the introduction of the concept of inflation. **Inflation** is the rate of change in prices. Let P_0 represent the current aggregate price level (see Box 4.1, p. 64) and P_1 represent the price level at the end of the period. Then the nominal interest rate, R, may be expressed as

$$R = \frac{Q_1 P_1 - Q_0 P_0}{Q_0 P_0} = \frac{Q_1 P_1}{Q_0 P_0} - 1$$

By substituting the numbers from our farmer-turned-lender example, we have

$$R = \frac{1,050 \times \$2.20}{1,000 \times \$2.00} - 1 = 15.5\%$$

This can be expressed in a somewhat different way. The one-period inflation rate, π, is given by

$$\pi = \frac{P_1 - P_0}{P_0} = \frac{P_1}{P_0} - 1$$

Returning to our enterprising farmer, where the only traded good under consideration is wheat, we would have:

$$\pi = \frac{\$2.20}{\$2.00} - 1 = .10, \text{ or } 10\%$$

The above equations can be combined to show explicitly the interrelationships between the nominal interest rate, inflation rate, and real interest rate.

$$R = \frac{Q_1}{Q_0} \times \frac{P_1}{P_0} - 1$$

$$= (1 + r) \times (1 + \pi) - 1$$

$$= r + \pi + r\pi$$

Substituting from our farmer example, we can compute the nominal rate of interest to be charged as:

Box 4.1

The Consumer Price Index and Inflation Rates

In 1963, a three-course meal at McDonald's consisting of a hamburger (15¢), a milkshake (20¢), and a bag of french fries (12¢), cost 47¢. In 1993, the same meal at the same McDonald's franchise cost $2.61—a whopping increase of 455 percent! Or was the price increase really so whopping? During that same time period, the value of the dollar declined in purchasing power. The overall inflation rate was 372 percent. Therefore, if the price of a meal at McDonald's had increased just enough to exactly compensate for the erosion in the value of the dollar, the three-course meal would have to cost $2.22 [= 47¢ × (1 + 372%)]. The extra 39¢(= 17.57% over 30 years) amounts to a real price increase of only 54/100 of 1 percent per year (= $\sqrt[30]{1 + .1757} - 1$). This is not an exact rate of real price increase because the quality of the McDonald's product has undergone slight changes over the years. For example, the milkshakes are now much lower in fat content, and much to the chagrin of the author who once was a milkshake specialist, his 90¢ per hour job has been replaced by a machine that mixes the ingredients automatically, resulting in generallly fresher shakes and faster service.

In tabulating the rate of inflation for consumers, the Bureau of Labor Statistics attempts to collect prices for all categories of consumption that would reflect annual expenditures by urban consumers. An average Ameri-can consumes a variety of goods and services during any given year. A hypothetical "basket" of goods and services might include the following:

10 haircuts @ $12	$120.00
1 pair Rollerblades, slightly used @ $275	275.00
30 lbs. of potatoes @ 30¢/lb.	9.00
650 gallons of 89 octane gasoline @ $1.49 9/10/gal.	974.35
7 movie theater tickets @ $6.50 per ticket	45.50
30 oz. raisins @ 7¢ per oz.	2.10
110 oranges @ 15¢ each	16.50
3 compact discs @ $14.20 each	42.60
⋮	⋮
TOTAL (end-of-year 1995 prices)	$19,362.65

The same goods and services would then be re-priced at the end of 1996, with a new total of, say, $20,756.76. That means that it takes $1,394.11 more than it did a year earlier to buy the same amount of goods and services and that the value of the dollar is only worth 93.28 percent (= 19,362.65 ÷ 20,756.76) of what it was in 1995. Therefore, the inflation rate during the year, in terms of this representative bundle of goods and services, was 7.2 percent [= ($20,756.76 ÷ $19,362.65) − 1].

$$R = .05 + .10 + (.05 \times .10) = .155, \text{ or } 15.5\%$$

This equation allows us to answer the question: What nominal interest rate should the farmer charge to get the same real return if he makes the loan in currency instead of commodity?

We can rearrange the above equation to solve for the real rate in terms of the nominal rate and inflation rate:

$$r = \frac{1 + R}{1 + \pi} - 1 = \frac{R - \pi}{1 + \pi}$$

which in our example, gives

The Bureau of Labor Statistics does not widely publicize the aggregate prices of the representative basket of goods and services. Rather, they publicize a price index, created by dividing current prices by those of a "base year"—say 1974—and multiplying the resulting quotient by 100. For example, if the price of our hypothetical basket of goods and services was $5,314.98 in 1974, the Bureau would divide that number by itself and then multiply by 100, resulting in an index number of 100. They would also divide the 1995 figure, $19,362.65, by the 1974 basket price of $5,314.98, and multiply that quotient by 100, resulting in a price index of 364.3. Similarly, the 1996 price index would be computed as 390.5. Note that we can arrive at an inflation rate by using these index numbers just as easily as if we had used the actual basket prices. The inflation rate during 1995, using this representative basket of goods and services, would be 7.2 percent [= (390.5 ÷ 364.3) − 1].

There have been volumes written about the actual construction of price indices, but it will suffice to mention a few of the problems in passing. First, the weights of the various categories (e.g., medical care, entertainment, transportation, housing, food and beverages, and apparel) change from time to time to reflect the consumption patterns of individuals. Second, the actual composition of the items within these categories changes. For example, eight-track audiotapes are no longer included, but compact discs are now a part of the normal consumption basket. Finally, there are often quality changes in the items included, such as transistors replacing vacuum tubes in amplifiers, increasing efficiency in automobiles over time, and so forth. These and other factors make the exact determination of inflation problematic.

To address these problems, two approaches are generally taken. First, because some of those interested in inflation wish to center their attention on only certain goods, while others have different interests, several indices are routinely constructed and reported. The first of these, the Consumer Price Index (CPI), attempts to capture the inflation faced by a typical urban household. It covers all of the usual consumer items in its base, including both goods and services, but it does not include wholesale goods or government costs. The GDP Deflator measures the changes in prices of *all* goods (not just consumption goods) included in the GDP. Each component of the GDP receives a weight based on its share of total GDP. The Producer Price Index tracks changes in wholesale prices, including prices of materials used in the final production of consumer goods.

Finally, each of these indices updates both the basket of goods selected and its sampling techniques. The Commerce Department, for example, has recently updated the GDP Deflator Index procedures (see Box 4.2). In the end, however, the price inflation of any economy will always be measured with some error, and economists will always be updating their techniques.

$$r = \frac{.155 - .10}{1 + .10} = \frac{.055}{1.10} = .05, \text{ or } 5\%$$

The relationships given above between inflation and real and nominal interest rates are definitional in content. In other words, they do not depend upon any economic theory. Their focus is mostly based on the assumption we made that everybody knows and has agreed upon the future price level. In the real financial markets, however, few know the future with such precision. Inflation rates are computed and published only "after the fact." They tell us what happened to prices over the previous period. Real interest rates, under most circumstances, are also known only "after the fact," by combining a knowledge of realized nominal rates of return with realized inflation rates. The nominal rate of return on a

---

Box 4.2

Note on Calculating Output and Price Indexes

Estimation of most components of gross domestic product (GDP) consists of two broad computational stages: (1) estimation of current-dollar values, and (2) separation of the current-dollar values into a price-change element and a quantity-change element.[1]

In the first step, the current market values of spending for each component of GDP are determined from basic source data. That is, consumer spending on apples and oranges, on small appliances, on movie admissions, and on all of the other components of personal consumer expenditures is estimated using a variety of source data, such as retail sales data from the Bureau of the Census. These calculations are usually referred to as the "current-dollar" value of a component. Current-dollar values of all the GDP components always "add up" to current-dollar GDP.

Though many technical problems arise in computing current-dollar GDP and its components, it is conceptually straightforward: Current-dollar GDP is a measure of what is actually spent in the economy in a particular period. Measuring the change in current-dollar GDP is equally straightforward, conceptually, because it is the actual change in spending that occurs in the economy between two periods.

In the second step, the period-to-period change in current-dollar GDP, or in the current-dollar value of a GDP component, is separated into a price-change element and a quantity-change element. For example, a 10-percent increase in expenditures on oranges could result from (1) a 10 percent increase in the number of oranges purchased with no change in the price of oranges, (2) a 10 percent increase in the price of oranges with no change in the number purchased, or (3) some combination of price and quantity increase totaling 10 percent. The quantity-change element in a GDP component, or in GDP itself, has in the past usually been referred to as the "constant-dollar" increase in the component, or sometimes as the change in the "real" component of GDP or in "real" GDP. Calculation of the quanity-change component is usually carried out by a process known as "deflation."[2]

Though measuring the change in current-dollar GDP is conceptually straightforward, partitioning the change into price- and quantity-change elements is not. This partitioning is an analytic step, because aggregate price change and aggregate quantity change cannot be observed directly in the economy. Instead, aggregate price and quantity changes must be calculated, and the calculation method is determined by analytic requirements.

In particular, it is important to recognize that real GDP is an analytic concept. Despite the name, real GDP is not "real" in the sense that it can, even in principle, be observed or collected directly, in the same sense that current-dollar GDP can in principle be observed or collected as the sum of actual spending on final goods and services in the economy. Quantities of apples and oranges can in principle be collected, but they cannot be added to obtain the total quantity of "fruit" ouput in the economy.

[1]There are a small number of exceptions to the description in the following sections, notably where extrapolators must be used because spending data are not available on a current basis. See "Annual Revision of the U.S. National Income and Product Accounts," *Survey of Current Business* 74 (July 1994): 26–27.

[2]The quantity-change measure for GDP is probably the most widely used number from the NIPA's. For example, the first line of the monthly GDP press release reports the percentage change in real GDP.

For this reason, real GDP must be computed by valuing the various components of GDP, using the prices of some period or periods. Real GDP is simply an index number—a computation, like the consumer price index or the price index for GDP, except that real GDP is an index number that measures *quantities*. Its computation cannot be determined by reference, or by analogy, to the methods used for the construction of current-dollar GDP.

In the past, measures of real GDP change were calculated by fixing the valuations of GDP components in some period (currently, the year 1987) and holding those valuations fixed over all years and quarters for which real GDP estimates are produced. This approach can be illustrated using a hypothetical two-commodity economy (Exhibit 1) with total current-dollar spending of $5.00 in year 1 and $9.00 in year 2. If we take year 1 to be the "base" (or "weighting" or "valuation") period, then the prices in year 1 are used to value the quantities in both years and the changes in quantities from year 1 to year 2. This is shown in panel A. In the exhibit, the consumption of oranges fell in year 2 because the price of oranges rose rapidly, while the consumption of apples, whose price rose less rapidly, increased. With this calculation, the weighted-quantity-change measure for "fruit" increased by 20 percent.

There is no reason why year 1 must always be chosen as the weighting period. In the past, BEA has periodically shifted its weighting period—before December 1991, 1982 was used as the weighting year for measuring real GDP, and before December 1985, 1972 was the weighting year. Panel B shows what happens to the quantity measure if we shift the valuation, or weight year, to year 2.

If year 2 is used for valuation, the quantities in year 1 and in year 2 are calculated as before, but both sets of quantities are valued in year 2 prices, rather than year 1 prices. Using year 2 prices results in a 6

percent increase in quantities, substantially lower than the 20 percent increase that resulted from using year 1 prices.

This example illustrates a regularity that has often been observed in the calculation of real GDP. Moving the weighting period forward tends to reduce the quantity-change measure, because in general the quantities that have increased the most are those whose prices have increased, relatively, the least. To put it another way, the use of a more recent period of valuation tends to put a lower valuation on the quantities that have increased most rapidly. Thus, measuring the change in real GDP is subject to "weighting effects," because the measure is sensitive to the valuation period, the period chosen for the weights in the calculating formula.

Which calculation, panel A or panel B, is "correct"? There is no single answer to this question, because each year's prices are equally valid for valuing the changes in quantities. A commonsense approach to the weighting problem is to take an average of the panel A and panel B calculations. Economic theory

---

EXHIBIT 1

	Year 1		
	Expenditures	*Quantity*	*Price*
Oranges	$3.00	30	10¢
Apples	$2.00	10	20¢
Total fruit	$5.00		
	Year 2		
	Expenditures	*Quantity*	*Price*
Oranges	$4.00	20	20¢
Apples	$5.00	20	25¢
Total fruit	$9.00		

Panel A   Year 1 weighted quantity change
              measure for fruit
              = [(20 × 10¢) + (20 × 20¢)] ÷ [(30 ×
              10¢) + (10 × 20¢)]
              = Hypothetical expenditure on fruit in
              year 2 using year 1 prices, divided by
              actual expenditure on fruit in year 1
              = $6.00/$5.00 = 1.20

Panel B   Year 2 weighted quantity change
              measure for fruit
              = [(20 × 20¢) + (20 × 25¢)] ÷ [(30 ×
              20¢) + (10 × 25¢)]
              = Actual expenditure on fruit in
              year 2, divided by hypothetical
              expenditure on fruit in year 1
              using year 2 prices
              = $9.00/$8.50 = 1.06

---

indicates that taking a geometric mean of the two measures is the preferred form of averaging. The geometric mean can be calculated by multiplying the panel A and panel B results together and then taking the square root—that is: $\sqrt{1.20 \times 1.06} = 1.13$. In the index number literature, this geometric average calculation of quantities is known as the "Fisher Ideal" index number.

BEA has adopted geometric averaging as the new method for calculating real GDP and for calculating measures of price change in GDP and its components. This method is presently employed in calculating the "chain-type annual-weighted" measures in NIPA tables 7.1–7.3 and 8.1.

Why is BEA changing its calculation method for real GDP? What are the advantages of the new calculating method over the old one? The main advantage of the old method is its simplicity: Only one set of valuations is necessary for calculating GDP for all periods. In the past, BEA has used one set of valua-

tions (currently, those for 1987) to construct real GDP measures from the most recent period all the way back to 1929.

In addition, experience shows that the use of a single weighting period generally produces accurate measures of GDP as long as the periods being compared are close to the weighting period. The reason is that changes in relative valuations are usually small for periods close to the weighting period, so that "weighting" effects are also small.

The main disadvantage of using a single valuation period for calculating real GDP is that the measure becomes increasingly subject to "weighting effects" as the time between weighting, or valuation, period and the current period lengthens.

BEA's new method of calculating real GDP has another advantage. It permits shifting the valuations on a year-by-year basis, which means that long-term growth, past business cycles, and productivity are measured in the valuations that are appropriate to the period being studied. For example, in the present 1987-weight calculating method, change in output in both the 1980–81 recession and the 1974–75 recession is measured in 1987 prices. In the new method, output change in these recessions will be measured in the prices that prevailed at that time—that is, the 1981–82 recession will be measured in prices of the early 1980s, and the 1974–75 recession, in the prices of the mid-1970s. Experience has shown that applying a single, fixed valuation to historical time periods tends to statistically dampen economic recessions and recoveries and also distorts the picture of long-term economic growth. Cyclical fluctuations in the economy are best measured using valuations that are appropriate to the period being studied rather than valuations from some distant period.

Source: *Survey of Current Business,* July 1995.

financial asset (including distributions of any form such as interest or dividends) during a given holding period may be reasonably predictable, particularly for fixed-rate instruments like bank time deposits or bonds. However, in the cases of inflation and real interest rates, we are seldom that lucky. Only in a world of make-believe would expected and realized rates always be the same.

In many countries, where inflation-linked instruments are regularly issued and actively traded, the real interest rate can be known "before the fact."[2] In the United States, a few corporate debt issues have been inflation-linked and a U.S. government issue was planned for late 1996, but there is no active market in these securities as this book went to press.

Expected Inflation and Nominal Interest Rates

In an effort to develop some economic content from the purely definitional concept of expected real return, which is part of any nominal interest rate instrument, Irving Fisher altered the hindsight view of the nominal interest rate definition to a forward-looking view. He noted that because lenders could always convert their currency and financial assets into real assets and earn the real rate of return to capital, they must be enticed to lend by being able to charge interest rates sufficiently high to compensate them for any expected erosion in the value of the monies received in satisfaction of the loans. They must therefore be compensated at nominal interest rates that provide for an attractive real rate of return. The Fisher theory stated that in a competitive capital market, rational individuals would seek to maintain purchasing power in the face of anticipated inflation. Therefore, nominal rates of interest would be set at levels so that

$$R = r^e + \pi^e + r^e \pi^e$$

where the superscript ^{e} denotes expected, or anticipated, future rates. Because the last term of this equation usually results in only a small adjustment to nominal interest rates, it is often dropped for convenience from the relationship, thus leaving

$$R \approx r^e + \pi^e$$

or

Nominal interest rate ≈ Anticipated real interest rate + Expected inflation rate

A key element to this theory is that expected inflation is posited to be unrelated to, or independent from, real interest rates. While nominal interest rates are said to adjust to reflect fully any changes in anticipated inflation, the expected real interest rates are unaffected by these changes.

---

[2]This is only approximately true, because payments on these inflation-linked instruments usually are lagged by a month or more, leaving the value of the final payment subject to the erosion of uncertain inflation during the final period. More will be said in Chapter 12 on the subject of inflation-indexed bonds.

Some economists have argued that for a number of reasons, we should expect less than one-for-one adjustments in nominal rates to changes in expected inflation. One argument is that as inflationary expectations increase, the real rate of interest declines; therefore, nominal rates of interest rise less than the full amount of changes in inflation. Often referred to as the **Mundell effect,** the basis for this claim is that as inflation rises, money assets (coin, currency, checking deposits, etc.) depreciate in real value; hence, real wealth declines. In an effort to restore real wealth to desired levels, saving is increased, which brings downward pressure on the real rate of interest.

On the other hand, if less inflation is expected, the real rate rises, and therefore, the nominal rate falls by less than the full amount of reduction in anticipated inflation. In either the case of rising or falling inflationary expectations, the effects of the real rate will spill over into the real economy and increase or reduce, respectively, the amount of real investment.

Another school of thought is that nominal interest rates adjust more than one-for-one with changes in anticipated inflation. It is argued that due to a perverse peculiarity in the U.S. tax code (and also in the tax codes of some other countries), where taxes are levied on nominal returns rather than real returns (see Box 4.3), nominal interest rates must rise by more than any increase in expected inflation in order to leave the lender as well off in real, after-tax terms. This results in what is often called a **Darby effect.** To understand this better, let us return to our farmer example one last time.

Recall that the farmer had 1,000 bushels to lend and expected a return of 50 extra bushels for his trouble. Suppose the government were to tax returns by 40 percent. That would leave the farmer with 30 extra bushels after tax, or a 3 percent real after-tax return. The same situation would prevail if the wheat were denominated in a currency with a stable monetary value. But if the loan is denominated in an inflationary and depreciating currency, the situation worsens. The 1,000 bushels, at $2.00 per bushel, are worth $2,000 now. Recall that the $2,000 currency loan would be made at an interest rate of 15.5 percent, to reflect the 10 percent anticipated inflation and 5 percent before-tax real rate. The currency loan will therefore return $2,310 at the end of the period. The government looks at the nominal dollar gain of $310, takes $124 (or 40 percent) of it for taxes, leaving ($186 + $2,000 =) $2,186 for the farmer. At the year-end price of $2.20/bushel, the farmer can now buy only ($2,186 ÷ $2.20/bu. =) 993.6 bushels of wheat, which is less than the 1,000 bushels he had at the start. It can be shown that in order for the farmer to receive the same 3 percent after-tax real rate of return on his lending activities, the nominal rate of interest he would need to charge is 22.167%. The loan would then return $2,443.33, for a $443.33 nominal dollar profit. After subtracting the 40 percent tax on this profit, the farmer would be left with $2,266.00. This amount of cash could purchase ($2,266 ÷ $2.20/bushel =) 1,030 bushels of wheat, restoring to the farmer the 3 percent real rate of return. To maintain a given level of real, after-tax interest rates of r^*, nominal rates, R, where the marginal tax bracket is τ, will need to adjust to:

$$R = \frac{r^*(1 + \pi^e) + \pi^e}{(1 - \tau)}$$

EXHIBIT 4.1

Annual inflation and single-year interest rates, 1955–1995

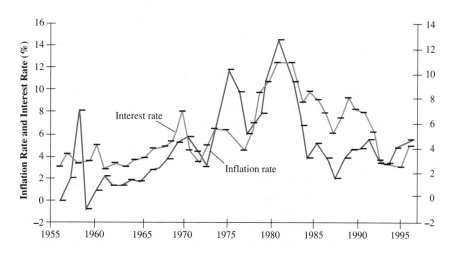

Source: *Federal Reserve Bulletin,* January 1996.

As long as expected inflation, π^e, and tax rates, τ, are positive, this will lead to a greater than one-to-one impact of inflation on nominal interest rates.

Likewise, an increase in expected inflation of 10 percent (from 0 percent to 10 percent) would cause an increase in nominal interest rates of 17.167 percent (from 5 percent to 22.167 percent), clearly a greater than one-to-one response. Thus, under this school of thought the higher the tax rate on nominal returns, the greater the response of nominal interest rates to inflation.

The three schools of thought discussed above all agree that nominal interest rates will rise if there is an increase in the rate of expected inflation. Whether changes in nominal interest rates will match changes in expected inflation, or change by less or more than one-for-one, remains a matter of theoretical dispute.

Empirical Evidence Regarding Inflation and Nominal Interest Rates

Which theory does the empirical evidence support? Let's look at the data and see. Exhibit 4.1 shows the nominal one-year interest rate and the annual inflation rate. As is evident, these two rates have moved fairly closely together over the last 40 years. However, a couple of things can be noted from this exhibit. First, the difference between the nominal rate and inflation has not been steady over the period and has been negative over several years. This clearly does not seem to be consistent with the views expressed by Fisher. Second, the movements in the inflation rate seem to lead or precede movements in the nominal interest rate over the period.

How can this be reconciled with the work of Fisher and others who argue that nominal rates are merely additions of the real rate of interest and inflation? The explanation of the differences between theory and empirical evidence results from a recognition that in testing the relationship between real and nominal rates,

Box 4.3

Income Tax or Wealth Tax?

Suppose that during the late 1970s, you had $10,000 invested in a savings account paying 6 percent per annum. At the end of a year, your savings would have climbed to $10,600 [= $10,000 × (1 + .06)]. During that same year, suppose that the value of the dollar in terms of its purchasing power fell by 15 percent. Then, your total investment (including the $600 interest) would have had a purchasing power amounting to $9,217.39 [= $10,600 ÷ (1 + .15)]. In other words, by placing your money in a savings deposit for a year, you would have actually lost $782.61 (= $10,000 − $9,217.39) in purchasing power value.

What did the U.S. national and state governments do in recognition of this real loss? They taxed you on it as if it were a gain! They focused on the $600 nominal interest gain and took approximately half of it for taxes (which was the approximate U.S. and state combined marginal tax rate at that time). That would

leave you with $10,300 nominal dollars after tax, and $8,956.52 (= 10,300 ÷ 1.15) worth of purchasing power at the end of the year, a loss of $1,043.48 (= $10,000 − $8,956.52) in real terms. Yet this accurately portrays the situation for millions of Americans during the late 1970s and early 1980s. Most economists and other fair-minded individuals recognize this tax policy for what it is. While nominally it is an income tax, in real terms it is what amounts to a wealth tax.

Many countries around the world deduct the inflation component from the nominal interest gains and tax their citizens on the "real interest" earnings. Although such a modification to our taxation system was proposed repeatedly during the administration of President Ronald Reagan, it was often branded as a "give-away to the wealthy" by Congress and was never implemented.

several problems loom. At the heart of the matter is that in the equation $R \approx r^e + \pi^e$, neither r^e nor π^e is directly observable. This fact can explain each of the two points listed above.

This observation has important implications for empirical studies of the Fisher effect. The lack of perfect correlation in the movements of the two series may be due to the difference in anticipated and realized inflation rates. The relation defined above would indicate that when the realized inflation rate equals the expected inflation rate, the distance between the lines is the expected real rate of interest. However, the expected and realized inflation rates are most likely not equal, so the distance between the lines reflects both the real rate and errors in expectation of the inflation rate.

Moreover, the tendency for movements in the inflation rate to lead movements in the nominal interest rate might be due to a time lag before the realized inflation rate becomes known so that expectations, and thus the nominal interest rate, can be adjusted accordingly.

Expected Real Rate and Inflation Proxies

The use of actual inflation and actual real rates points to the need for proxies for the expected rate of inflation. A number of tools have been used to investigate the relationship between nominal interest rates and expected inflation. First, numerous studies have used series of past inflation rates as predictors of expected future inflation rates. The weightings on past inflation rates and changes in inflation rates differ from study to study, but the idea behind this approach is that market expectations of inflation are conditioned by recent experience with inflation.

A second approach is to use survey data on inflationary expectations. There are several surveys of experts and consumers that include an assessment of inflationary expectations. The problem with the surveys is that they are based on a small sample of experts or consumers, and they are not necessarily reflective of the consensus expectations of inflation upon which market interest rates are based. Nonetheless, a direct survey approach has merit for statistical testing.

Third, some economists have advocated extracting a measure of expected inflation from movements in long-term interest rates versus movements in short-term interest rates. The idea here is that long-term interest rates tend to be most sensitive to changes in inflationary expectations, whereas changes in short-term interest rate levels are dominated by market conditions and Federal Reserve actions.

Another approach involves inflation-indexed bonds, where the index to which the payments and/or principal of the bonds are linked is a broad-based measure of inflation, such as the Consumer Price Index, the Producer Price Index, or the GDP Deflator. Comparing these yields with those on Treasury bonds will provide a rough estimate of expected inflation—rough because there can be elements in these bonds that differ from Treasury bonds apart from their inflation linkage (e.g., credit quality, callability, liquidity, etc.). In the United States, unfortunately, the inflation-indexed bonds are still few and far between, and those that are available are seldom traded, so it is difficult to get viable market prices and yields on them. This situation may soon change.

Finally, commodity-linked bonds have also been used to extract an estimate of the *ex ante* real rate of interest. A commodity-linked bond has its periodic payments and/or principal linked to the price of some commodity or group of commodities. For instance, there have been bonds linked to the prices of gold, lumber, oil, and other commodities. The yields on these bonds provide a very rough idea (because they are based on only one commodity as well as default risk) of the expected real rate of interest, and a comparison of these yields with those on Treasury bonds provides an estimate of expected inflation. Some of the earlier studies examined the expected returns on common stocks versus expected returns on bonds. The (rather debatable) idea behind this approach is that the returns on assets like common stocks tend to be expressed in real terms, whereas those on bonds tend to be expressed in nominal terms.

Extracting Estimates from Theoretical Models

As an alternative to the series of rather arbitrary attempts to extract inflationary expectations from market prices, estimates of expected inflation and real interest rates can be inferred from more comprehensive, macroeconomic models. For example, using the loanable funds framework, we know that the real rate of interest can be viewed as consisting of two components—an equilibrium real rate that equates planned savings and investment, and temporary deviations of current real rates from the equilibrium real rate. The equilibrium rate is a function of changes in real output, real income, real wealth, the federal deficit, tax rates, and risk. Deviations of current real rates from equilibrium rates may be occasioned by changes in money supply or transitory supply/demand imbalances in the money market. This approach, which essentially extracts interest rate forecasts from real macroeconomic models, has been attempted for some time. However, the results have been less than satisfactory.

Finally some investigators have tried to use the relationship between aggregate money demand and supply in this area. Here, the real rate is assumed to be related to the real stock of money and the level of real income. Models estimating money demand and supply are constructed, and implied interest rates are extracted. While conceptually sound, this approach has also failed to produce robust results and unbiased forecasts.

Other Problems Associated with Expected Inflation

In addition to the need for estimates of variables on the right-hand side of the Fisher equation, there are numerous other difficulties associated with expected inflation. While we may accept the theory that the nominal interest rate incorporates inflation, it is not at all clear which inflation rate should be used (or proxied) in our theory. Should it be based on consumer prices, producer prices, the GDP Deflator, or some other broad measure of the value of money?

Another problem arises in the "ideal case" where inflation-indexed bonds may be used. If the real rate of interest is quoted as a yield on the inflation-indexed bond, and if estimates of expected inflation are generated by subtracting this real yield from that on nominal bonds, we get into a tautology. In other words, the Fisher equation is true because we have generated our estimates of real and inflation rates based on the equation. Therefore, we will get a perfect fit every time!

Finally, the conclusions of nearly all of these studies depend upon the assumption that *ex ante* real rates of interest are either constant or move so gradually that they might as well be constant for statistical purposes. Therefore, these studies assume that any changes in nominal interest rates simply reflect changes in expected inflation. In the changing world of the second half of the 20th century, this, too, seems highly unlikely.

There have been far more studies on this subject than could be encompassed in a single volume. Hence, we will not attempt to chronicle them here. It is fair to say, however, that the empirical results have been mixed. Support can be found for nominal interest rates exhibiting smaller, equal, or larger shifts than changes in expected and/or realized inflation. The conclusions vary widely, depending on the period of study, the model employed, and the measures used for the variables under study.

Nevertheless, the preponderance of evidence supports the notion that nominal interest rates move in the same direction as expected inflation—sometimes more, sometimes less, but in the same direction. Such expectations are rarely accurate, but they are clearly important; they move financial markets and are watched closely by participants. (See Box 4.4.)

Box 4.4

Why Investors Fear Inflation

When inflation rises, so generally do interest rates. That depresses the price of stocks, as investors are willing to pay less for each dollar of corporate earnings. Figures are based on 476 monthly measurements from 1955 through the present.

Inflation rate (number of months)	Long-term bond rate	Treasury bill rate	Stock price multiple*
Less than 3% (175)	4.8%	3.5%	17.5
3% to 4% (87)	7.1	5.0	16.1
4% to 5% (62)	8.6	6.9	14.9
5% to 6% (43)	7.5	6.4	14.5
6% to 7% (33)	8.5	6.8	10.9
More than 7% (76)	9.9	9.6	9.0

*Average stock price as a multiple of pre-share earnings for stocks in Standard & Poor's 500-Stock Index

Source: Nomura Securities

Investors' Jitters on Inflation Aren't Spooking Most Advisers

The inflation bogeyman may not be at the door yet, but he's lurking in the yard.

That's what investors seem to think at the moment. On Friday, the Dow Jones Industrial Average fell more than 33 points after a worse-than-expected jump of 0.6% in one inflation measure, the Producer Price Index. Yesterday, the industrial average rose nearly 20 points as the monthly reading of another inflation gauge, the Consumer Price Index, comforted investors with a gain of just 0.3%.

Clearly, investors have inflation on their nerves. But should they act on their jitters?

Most investment experts aren't sounding the alarm yet, since they don't expect inflation to be a real problem until 1995. But others warn that waiting until next year, when the bad news is obvious to all, may be too late. Better to make a preemptive strike against inflation by adjusting your portfolio today, they say.

Some people evidently have been taking that advice. In the month through Monday, precious-metals stocks, traditionally viewed as an inflation hedge, leaped 15%. Forest products stocks, another inflation-worry favorite, rose 6%.

But not all the traditional "inflation hedges" paid off. Oil stocks, which traditionally soar in inflation scares, have remained flat for the past month.

"There's definitely going to be more inflation over the next 18 months," says William Fleckenstein, a principal of Olympic Capital Management in Seattle. He expects that by the end of next year, the recent tame pace of inflation—about 3%—will have jumped to 5% or even 6%.

Mr. Fleckenstein, for one, already has put his portfolio where his mouth is. About 12% of his holdings are in gold and silver investments, including an unusual preferred stock from Freeport-McMoRan Copper & Gold. The eventual redemption value of this oddball security is derived from the price of four ounces of silver; in the meantime it pays 4% interest. Another 15% of Mr. Fleckenstein's holdings are in energy-related stocks.

Source: John R. Dorfman, "Investors' Jitters on Inflation Aren't Spooking Most Advisers," *The Wall Street Journal,* September 15, 1994. Reprinted by permission of *The Wall Street Journal,* © 1994 Dow Jones & Company, Inc. All Rights Reserved Worldwide.

Box 4.5

Arithmetic versus Geometric Average Returns

Suppose that at the start of the year, you placed $100 in an investment that would double your money by year's end. The annual rate of return, or interest rate, on such an investment would be 100 percent. Then suppose that the next year, with your $200 proceeds and bursting confidence, you again placed your money in an investment, but over the course of that year, you lost half of your money, winding up the year with only $100. The annual rate of return on your investment that year would be −50 percent.

If you were to calculate your average investment performance over the two-year period you would rack up an impressive record: 25 percent per annum! [(+100% − 50%) ÷ 2 years = 25% per year.] Your overall average return might even attract some unsophisticated investors and entice you to become a "professional money manager," earning sizable commissions on each dollar of invested assets. The only problem is that you did not make a single dollar in investment profits over the two-year period. The

misleading 25 percent average return is engendered by the arithmetic averaging process.

To rectify the misleading nature of the arithmetic averaging process, knowledgeable investors typically look at geometric averages. To compute the geometric average of rates of return over a period of n years, we add each annual rate of return to 1, multiply the sums together, take the nth root of the resulting product, and finally, subtract 1. For example, in the case described above, we would get

$$\sqrt[2]{(1 + 100\%) \times (1 - 50\%)} - 1$$

$$= \sqrt[2]{(1 + 1) \times (1 - .5)} - 1$$

$$= \sqrt[2]{1} - 1 = 0.0\% \text{ geometric average rate of return}$$
per annum

With a track record presented in this form, the throngs of investors you had hoped to attract may take their money and go elsewhere!

Evidence from Several Countries

While the evidence on the Fisher equation is mixed for the United States, the same relationship has been tested for a number of other countries. Here, too, the evidence supports the positive relationship between inflation and interest rates but little else. However, when looked at across countries, there is overwhelming support that over time, nominal interest rates reflect changes in expected inflation. Below, we present evidence that levels of nominal interest are set consistent with inflationary experience.

Exhibit 4.2 is a scatter plot of recent 10 year geometric averages of nominal interest rates plotted against 7 year geometric averages of annual inflation rates for 12 countries. (Box 4.5 explains the significance of the geometric averaging.) The data used to construct this exhibit are contained in Exhibit 4.3. You will notice that inflation rates vary from 1.29 percent for Japan to 25.4 percent for Colombia. At the same time, interest rates varied from a low of 3.76 percent for Japan to a high of 39.24 percent for Colombia. The graphical presentation in Exhibit 4.2 shows a clear, positive relationship between the rates of inflation and

EXHIBIT 4.2

Inflation and nominal interest rates: a cross-country comparison

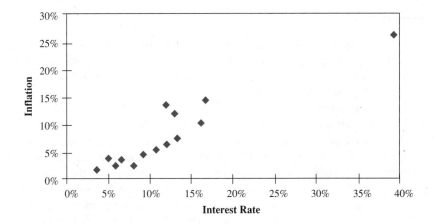

**EXHIBIT 4.3   Inflation and Nominal Interest Rates:
A Cross-Country Comparison**

	Interest rate	Inflation
Japan	3.76%	1.29%
Korea	13.10	6.25
South Africa	13.89	11.92
Philippines	16.31	10.15
Israel	13.18	13.72
Germany	6.04	2.37
United Kingdom	8.61	4.20
United States	5.22	3.54
Colombia	39.24	25.42
Canada	7.99	2.05
Greece	17.06	14.44
Italy	11.59	5.27
Sweden	10.33	4.68
Austria	6.68	3.06

Source: *International Financial Statistics,* January 1996.

nominal interest rates in these 10 arbitrarily selected countries. In fact, this exhibit makes clear that the relation between interest rates and inflation is fairly constant across countries. The positive slope of a fitted line (not shown) running through these observations upward and to the right indicates that in these countries, the nominal interest rate adjusts to the inflation rate in order for lenders to achieve an expected real rate of return. It is also interesting to note that this sample suggests a positive real interest rate below 5 percent. This is revealed in the placement of the data points slightly below a 45 degree line.

Summary

This chapter develops the distinction between real and nominal rates, an issue avoided in Chapter 3. However, in the presence of unprecedented inflation in the United States, and substantial inflation in many other countries over the last century, this distinction is crucial.

Financial investments generally carry nominal rates of return. Their real return depends upon inflation over the period. Real rates of return can be computed after the fact, but investors making current decisions must estimate future price inflation in order to evaluate the appropriateness of nominal interest rates offered in the market. However, such estimations are difficult to make and are liable to be wrong. Therefore, observed nominal rate movements often diverge substantially from changes in inflation rates, in part because of this error in forecasting future rates.

Nominal interest rates may not keep pace with inflation for other reasons as well. For example, tax rates are applied to nominal returns, and wealth can be adversely affected by inflation surprises. For these and other reasons, nominal interest rates will not exactly mirror inflation. However, over time, and for country after country, there is a clear relationship between nominal interest rates and general price inflation that cannot be ignored.

Key Concepts

Darby effect,   70
expected versus realized inflation,   69
expected versus realized real rates,   69
Mundell effect,   70

nominal contracts,   63
nominal interest rate,   63
real interest rate,   62

Review Questions

1. Many writers, in specifying the relationship between nominal interest rates and inflation, drop the interaction term ($\pi \times r$), claiming that it is of negligible importance. What would happen to the importance of this term if inflation rates were to rise to double digits again?

2. If taxes were lowered, what would you expect to happen to nominal interest rates?

3. What are some of the main problems in testing the validity of the Fisher equation?

4. Real interest rates truly reflect the opportunity forgone in terms of purchasing power. Why, then, are financial assets quoted in terms of their nominal yields?

5. Why would investors be willing to purchase assets when their expected real rate of return is negative?

6. Assume that the tax rate is 35 percent and the Darby effect is operative. The nominal interest rate is 17 percent and inflation is expected to be 8 percent. What is the expected real rate of interest?

7. What are possible reasons for a long-term shift in the real rate of interest?

References

Black, Fischer. "Interest Rates as Options." *Journal of Finance,* December 1995.

Boudoukh, Jacob; Matthew Richardson; and Robert F. Whitelaw. "Industry Returns and the Fisher Effect." *Journal of Finance,* December 1994.

Darby, Michael R. "The Financial and Tax Effects of Monetary Policy on Interest Rates." *Economic Inquiry,* 1975.

Evans, Martin D., and Karen K. Lewis. "Do Expected Shifts in Inflation Affect Estimates of the Long-Run Fisher Relation?" *Journal of Finance,* March 1995.

Fama, Eugene F. "Short Term Interest Rates as Predictors of Inflation." *American Economic Review,* June 1975.

Fama, Eugene F., and Michael R. Gibbons. "Inflation, Real Returns and Capital Investment." *Journal of Monetary Economics,* May 1982.

Feldstein, Martin. "Inflation, Income Taxes and the Rate of Inflation: A Theoretical Analysis." *American Economic Review,* December 1976.

Fisher, Irving. "Appreciation and Interest." *Publication of the American Economic Association* XI (August 1896).

Friedman, Benjamin M. "Price Inflation, Portfolio Choice and Nominal Interest Rates." *American Economic Review,* March 1980.

Gandolfi, Arthur E. "Inflation, Taxation, and Interest Rates." *Journal of Finance,* June 1982.

Garner, C. Alan. "The Yield Curve and Inflation Expectations." *Economic Review,* Federal Reserve Bank of Kansas City, September/October 1987.

Holland, A. Steven. "Real Interest Rates: What Accounts for their Recent Risk." *Review,* Federal Reserve Bank of St. Louis, December 1984.

Kandel, Shmuel; Aharon R. Ofer; and Oded Sarig. "Real Interest Rates and Inflation: An Ex-Ante Empirical Analysis." *Journal of Finance,* March 1996.

Lewis, Karen K. "Do Expected Shifts in Inflation Affect Estimates of the Long-Run Fisher Relation?" *Journal of Finance,* March 1995.

Mundell, Robert. "Inflation and Real Interest." *Journal of Political Economy,* June 1963.

Santoni, G. J., and Courtenay C. Stone. "What Really Happened to Interest Rates? A Longer Run Analysis." *Review,* Federal Reserve Bank of St. Louis, November 1981.

Taylor, Herbert. "Interest Rates: How Much Does Expected Inflation Matter?" *Business Review,* Federal Reserve Bank of Philadelphia, July/August 1982.

The Term Structure of Interest Rates

The chapter begins by introducing the concepts and terminology necessary to deal with financial assets of differing maturity. It next offers traditional theories of the term structure and their implications on yield curve shapes and movement. Finally, empirical evidence on the term structure of interest rate volatility is presented.

Imagine that you have $10,000 of extra cash in your checking account at the bank. You want to save it in an interest-bearing time deposit, or certificate of deposit (CD), which offers a prespecified rate of interest over a period of time stipulated on the certificate. If you go to your local bank officer and inquire about the rate of interest that you could earn on your savings, the response undoubtedly will be, "It depends . . ." The same bank will offer different annual rates of interest on its CDs, depending on the length of time for which you have agreed to leave the money on deposit. For example, the bank may offer an interest rate of 7 percent per annum (p.a.) on overnight deposits, 8 percent p.a. on a one-year CD, 8.75 percent p.a. on a two-year CD, 9.33 percent p.a. on a three-year CD, 9.79 percent p.a. on a four-year CD, and 10.13 percent p.a. on a five-year CD.

Now suppose you are willing to leave your money on deposit only for one year, but feel that the 8 percent one-year rate of interest is unattractive. What could you do? You might place your funds in the higher-yielding three-year CD earning 9.33 percent p.a. and then withdraw them prematurely, after only one year. Your cleverness will be rewarded with a notice from the bank that you will not receive 9.33 percent for the single year you left your money on deposit; instead, you will be assessed "a substantial interest penalty for early withdrawal" of your funds. After the penalty is deducted from your earnings, you are likely to receive less than the 8 percent you could have earned on a single-year CD. Banks are clever, too.

If the bank were not so clever, it would expose itself to a possible loss. The bank, anticipating that your money would be available for three years to invest or lend to others, presumably followed sound investment policy[1] and placed the money in a three-year investment. To get the money back from the borrower earlier than agreed so that it can return your funds after only one year, the bank may have to either offer a costly financial incentive to the borrower or sell the investment to another party, perhaps at a loss. The bank is unlikely to earn the rate that it expected, and therefore, it is not feasible for the bank to pay you 9.33 percent while maintaining any profit margin. Hence, the typical bank assesses a severe interest penalty on the early withdrawal of funds.

Spot and Forward Interest Rates and Yields to Maturity

Computing Interest Rates

In this illustration, we have the makings of an example of the differences between what are referred to as spot rates of interest and their closely related adjuncts, forward rates of interest. A **spot rate of interest** is the annual rate of interest that you could earn (or would pay if you were a borrower) on an investment (or loan) made today, which would be repaid with interest on a specified date in the future. The spot rates in our example are 7.0 percent (the overnight rate), 8.0 percent, 8.75 percent, 9.33 percent, 9.79 percent, and 10.13 percent.[2]

---

[1]To avoid the risk of changing interest rates during the period of the CD, a bank will often attempt to match the period of the deposit to the period of their investment. More will be said about this strategy in Chapter 26.

[2]The bank may report interest earnings to the Internal Revenue Service on your three-year CD even though you have not yet received it. Typically, it is merely a book entry in your account. The actual cash payment will come at the end of the three years. However, to make payment of your tax more convenient, it is often possible to collect the interest on an annual basis, even though your CD has not matured. Nonetheless, the receipt of interest does not preclude the bank

EXHIBIT 5.1

Spot versus forward rates of interest

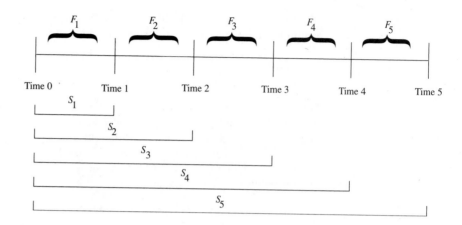

A **forward rate of interest** is the rate of interest, implicit in the quoted spot rates, that would be applicable from one point of time in the future to another point of time in the future. Forward rates are those single-period implied rates of interest that would give rise to the observed spot rates of interest.

The difference between these two concepts is more easily explained with a time line illustration. Suppose we represent the passage of time on a simple horizontal line, with today designated as Time 0. On this line, borrowing and lending for specific periods of time would be represented by an interest rate on a financial instrument, such as our CD, over a certain length of time extending from Time 0.

In Exhibit 5.1, the S_n lines below the time line are the n-year annualized spot rates of interest. These lines illustrate the time over which interest rate S_n will accrue. If money were deposited for one year, from now (Time 0) until a year from now (Time 1), it would earn 8 percent p.a. in our hypothetical example. Therefore, the line S_1 runs from Time 0 to Time 1 and would be 8 percent in our example. If it were deposited for two years (Time 0 to Time 2), S_2 would be 8.75 percent p.a., etc.

Notice that S_2, the 8.75 percent two-year spot rate, covers a period of time that overlaps with the one-year spot rate, S_1. The amount paid on this two-year instrument beyond the amount received on the one-year instrument can be computed by knowing S_1 and S_2. This second-year rate is called a forward rate of interest. Notice that it must be computed because it is not observed. Accordingly, it is sometimes referred to as the implicit forward rate. How high must it be? Obviously, it must be much higher than 8 percent for the two-year average to be 8.75 percent p.a.

---

from reducing your principal if you attempt to withdraw your funds prior to maturity. Hence, in our hypothetical example, it is not accurate to say that you really earned a 9.33 percent return during your first and second years.

To compute the implicit forward rate of interest during the second year, we can do the following. First, calculate the return from the two investments.

$10,000 @ 8.00% one year later = $10,000(1 + .08)^1 = $10,800.00

$10,000 @ 8.75% two years later = $10,000(1 + .0875)^2 = $11,826.56

You now have enough information to calculate the implied rate of interest that the bank would be paying during the second year. If you had $10,800 at the end of the first year and $11,826.56 at the end of the second, your rate of return during that second year must have been $(11,826.56 \div 10,800.00 - 1 =)$ 9.5 percent. We would call this the second-year forward rate of interest.

Similarly, we could compute the third-year forward rate of interest as follows:

$10,000 @ 8.75% two year later = $10,000(1 + .0875)^2 = $11,826.56

$10,000 @ 9.33% three years later = $10,000(1 + .0933)^3 = $13,068.27

Therefore, the third-year forward rate of interest would be ($13,068.27 $\div$ $11,826.56 - 1 =$) 10.5 percent. The same procedure would result in a fourth-year implied forward rate of interest of 11.2 percent and a fifth-year forward rate of 11.5 percent.

The implied single-year forward rates of interest can be extracted from a schedule of spot rates of interest by using the following formula:[3]

$$F_n = [(1 + S_n)^n \div (1 + S_{n-1})^{n-1}] - 1$$

This is equivalent to the procedure that we just went through to arrive at our implied forward rates. We compounded the investment (assumed to be $1 in the above formula) at 1 plus a rate of interest for the longer period, divided that product by the investment compounded at 1 plus a rate of interest for the shorter period, and then subtracted 1 from the quotient.

Applying this formula to a schedule of spot rates of interest to extract all of our implied forward rates, we would have

$$S_1 = .0800, \therefore F_1 = [(1 + .0800)^1 \div (1 + .0000)^0] - 1 = 8.0\%$$

$$S_2 = .0875, \therefore F_2 = [(1 + .0875)^2 \div (1 + .0800)^1] - 1 = 9.5\%$$

$$S_3 = .0933, \therefore F_3 = [(1 + .0933)^3 \div (1 + .0875)^2] - 1 = 10.5\%$$

$$S_4 = .0979, \therefore F_4 = [(1 + .0979)^4 \div (1 + .0933)^3] - 1 = 11.2\%$$

$$S_5 = .1013, \therefore F_5 = [(1 + .1013)^5 \div (1 + .0979)^4] - 1 = 11.5\%$$

Note that the spot rates of interest are very close to simple arithmetic averages of the forward rates of interest. For instance, the two-year spot rate of 8.75 percent is close to an average of the 8.0 percent first-year forward rate and the 9.5 percent

---

[3]Financial economists sometimes compute multiyear forward rates of interest. For instance, they may wish to know the implicit three-year forward rate extending from Time 2 to Time 5. This is easily computed as $F_{2,5} = \sqrt{[(1 + S_5)^5 \div (1 + S_2)^2]} - 1 = 11.06$ percent.

second-year forward rate. Similarly, the three-year spot rate of 9.33 percent is close to an average of the first three forward rates of interest (8.0 percent, 9.5 percent, and 10.5 percent). This arithmetic average is close, but it is not quite exact. If we had included enough digits in our computations, the discrepancy would have been apparent.[4] This is because spot rate of interest calculations implicitly assume a compounding of returns at the same spot rate for all years included in its multiyear term, rather than growing at the corresponding forward rates of interest. That is why the spot rates of interest are actually geometric averages. The precise formula for converting forward rates of interest into spot rates is given below.

$$S_n = \sqrt[n]{(1 + F_1)(1 + F_2) \cdots (1 + F_n)} - 1$$

To illustrate this formula, let us compute S_3, the three-year spot rate of interest. We compute this by substituting the three single-year forward rates of interest applicable to years 1, 2, and 3 in the above formula. Then, by taking the third root of the product, we get:

$$S_3 = \sqrt[3]{(1 + .08)(1 + .095)(1 + .105)} - 1 = 9.33\%$$

Valuation of Bonds Given Interest Rates

At this point, it is useful to introduce the concept of **zero-coupon bonds** and to distinguish them from their more ubiquitous relatives, **coupon bonds.** This will be helpful as our chapter ensues. Many investments pay interest (called coupons) at six-month intervals and return the face amount, or principal, at maturity. However, zero-coupon bonds make no periodic interest payments; they merely return the face amount at maturity. For example, a typical coupon bond may pay 8 percent of face value in semiannual coupon installments of 4%, or $40, each six months and return the **face value** of $1,000 at maturity. By contrast, a comparable zero-coupon bond would pay only the $1,000 face value at maturity. Zero-coupon bonds are therefore sold at a discount from face value so that the investor can earn a positive rate of return. In short, you pay a price below $1,000 today and receive nothing until maturity, at which time you receive the $1,000 face value. Zero-coupon bonds, which first gained popularity in the 1980s, are similar to bank CDs. With both instruments, a single payment is made to purchase them, and a single cash flow is received at maturity. The primary difference between CDs and other such bonds in terms of their structure is that the zero-coupon bond is sold at a discount and returns face value, whereas a CD is generally sold at its face value and returns face value plus interest at maturity.

For example, a three-year zero-coupon bond with a $1,000 face value may sell for $765.21. Its annual rate of return can be calculated by dividing its maturity value (what you ultimately get) by its price (what you pay) and then computing its

---

[4]A more precise calculation of the implied forward rates gives $F_1 = 8\%$, $F_2 = 9.5052\%$, $F_3 = 10.4993\%$, $F_4 = 11.1816\%$, and $F_5 = 11.5006\%$. Computing arithmetic averages of these forward rates will not correspond to the spot rates.

compounded yield. Define the price of a bond of maturity n as P_n. Since $P_n(1 + S_n)$ = \$1,000, we can see that the formula to convert from discount price to yield is

$$\sqrt[n]{\$1,000 \div P_n} - 1 = S_n$$

Using this equation for our current example results in an annual rate of return equal to

$$\sqrt[3]{\$1,000 \div \$765.21} - 1 = 9.33\%$$

The annual rate of return on the zero-coupon bond is therefore equivalent to a spot rate of interest. Consequently, many people refer to the zero-coupon Treasury yield interchangeably with the spot rate of interest. As we will show in Chapter 6, spot and forward rates of interest are fundamental factors used in determining the economic value not only of a zero-coupon bond but also of any stream of fixed cash flows.

Yield to Maturity Calculations

Another kind of interest rate, called **yield to maturity (YTM),** is often used in the financial pages of our newspapers. For the preceding example of a zero-coupon bond, the YTM is the same as the spot rate.[5] However, this is not generally the case. For coupon bonds, which feature payments throughout their lives, the YTM will depend on the spot rates of interest associated with each cash flow provided by the bond. This is because a coupon bond can be thought of as a collection of zero-coupon bonds. Each coupon payment, and the principal, can be valued as an individual zero-coupon bond. Therefore, each payment is valued by a different spot rate of interest. The bond's yield to maturity depends on the entire collection of spot rates used in valuing its cash flows.

Exactly what would the average yield be on a coupon bond? This is the question that led to the development of the concept of YTM. The yield to maturity is a complex weighted average of spot rates of interest in which the weights depend on the pattern of cash flows receivable on a particular instrument over all points in time.[6] Accordingly, it is quite specific to a particular instrument and cannot be used to estimate the fair value of other instruments.[7] Indeed, the YTM can be determined only after the market value of an instrument is already known and its payment stream has been indicated. The YTM is unique to that bond at that

---

[5]This YTM is not to be confused with the "bond equivalent yield" reported by many newspapers. The latter computes semiannual yields and then doubles (rather than compounds) them to annualize them. This results in a slight distortion.

[6]The YTM may be approximated by taking the spot rates applicable to each cash flow and applying a complex scheme of weights to them. This is discussed further in Chapters 6 and 8.

[7]An exception is the YTM on a zero-coupon bond, which is identical to the spot rate of interest. These YTMs can be used as spot rates to value other streams of fixed cash flows.

time. Nonetheless, YTM is often referred to in the press and in the marketplace, and more will be said about it in subsequent chapters.

The Term Structure of Interest Rates

As we have seen, there are different rates of interest quoted for different lengths of time. The **term structure of interest rates** is the name given to the pattern of interest rates available on instruments of a similar credit risk but with different terms to maturity. Most often among economists and market analysts, the interest rates referred to when discussing the term structure of interest are spot rates of interest applicable to the valuation of U.S. government-issued securities. This is the case because analysts want to be exact and avoid confusing the discussion with issues of different borrowers or different types of financial instruments. However, the term structure most often referred to in the popular press is based on government coupon bonds and their YTMs. In this book, unless otherwise stated, we will be referring to the spot rate term structure when we speak of term structures of interest. We will also occasionally make use of the forward term structure, but it will also be derived from the spot rates applicable to government bonds.

Exhibit 5.2 provides a sample of term structures of spot interest rates for various dates in the past. These curves, which represent the term structure, are known as **yield curves.** Several items are striking about the yield curves shown. First, the general levels of interest rates over time have undergone substantial changes. Second, the term structures exhibit varying slopes, some positive,

EXHIBIT 5.2

Spot rate term structures of interest implicit in U.S. Treasury bonds

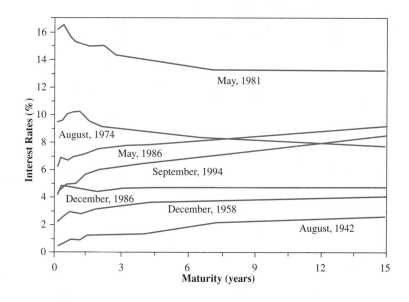

some negative, and some virtually flat across maturities. Third, there are differing levels of curvature, or bend, to the shapes of the term structures of interest. Some exhibit smooth, gradual curvature, and others demonstrate sharper, rougher bends.

Exhibit 5.3 extracts two of the spot rate term structures from Exhibit 5.2—the May 1981 and May 1986 curves—and displays them along with their corresponding forward rate curves. Two items are of particular note. First, the forward rate term structure exhibits sharper, more sudden bends than the spot rate term structure. This is because the spot rate, which is a geometric average, of sorts, of the forward rates, cannot bend as sharply because the averaging process dampens any sudden shifts in the forward rates. Second, if the forward rate curve resides above the spot rate curve, the latter will tend to rise as term is increased. Conversely, if the forward rate curve is below the spot rate curve, the latter will tend to fall as term is extended. This, again, is a simple reflection of the averaging process implicit in the conversion of forward rates of interest to spot rates. As higher forward rates are included in the geometric average, they will tend to pull the average higher, but as lower forward rates are included, they will tend to pull the average downward.

Theories of the Term Structure of Interest

A voluminous amount of research has been conducted in an attempt to gain a precise understanding of what determines the relationships among spot rates of interest for differing lengths of time and how these relationships change over time. Efforts at explaining these relationships have come to be known as theories of the term structure of interest.

We will devote the remainder of this chapter to a review of the traditional theories of the term structure of interest: the pure expectations theory, the liquidity preference theory, and the preferred habitat theory. These theories have their

EXHIBIT 5.3

Spot versus forward rates of interest

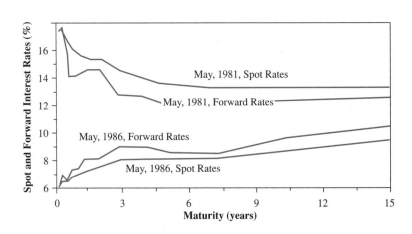

origins dating from as early as the 1890s, and they have been standards in economics since the 1960s.[8] In Chapter 7, we will follow our discussion of the traditional theories with an introduction to two highly influential strands of the recent economic literature on interest rates that allow for pathbreaking applications in the valuation of securities.

There are several questions about the relationship between short- and long-term rates and the information we can glean from the yield curve that each of these three theories purports to answer. To understand how these competing theories address these issues, the theories themselves are developed in some detail below. For each theory, we will present the assumptions embedded in its view of financial markets. These assumptions deal with market efficiency or how quickly markets react to new information, investors' objectives and attitudes toward risk, and both firms' and investors' preferences for securities of different maturities. Each of these theories presents implications based on assumptions that the world works in a particular way. We will consider the assumptions and implications of each theory in turn.

The Pure Expectations Theory

The **pure expectations theory** dates back to the early works of Irving Fisher and, today, has several variants. The main themes of the theory and its variants are described below.

Assumptions.   The theory begins with a focus on instruments that are free of default risk, which for practical purposes means Treasury securities. Market participants in the trading of these securities are presumed to be indifferent to risk. They are willing to accept investments based on only their expected return, without reference to the range of potential outcomes. In finance, we refer to such individuals as **risk neutral.** Thus, buyers are presumed not to prefer securities of one particular maturity over any other. They seek bonds with the highest expected returns, and they will not hold any bond whose expected return is less than that of a bond with a different maturity. Treasury bond markets are assumed to operate efficiently. This entails the presumption that all available information that bears on the valuation of these bonds is already incorporated into their prices. As new information is revealed, prices adjust rapidly to incorporate it. Otherwise, excess profits would be possible, and market participants would jump in to exploit them. These actions themselves would alter market prices and restore equilibrium. For example, if the price of a

---

[8]The pure expectations theory was first articulated in Irving Fisher, "Appreciation and Interest," *Publications of the American Economic Association* XI (August 1896): 23–29; and *The Theory of Interest* (New York: Macmillan, 1930). The expectations theory was further discussed and the liquidity preference theory was introduced by John R. Hicks in *Value and Capital* (London: Oxford University Press, 1946), chapters 21 and 22. The notion of a liquidity premium, which is a key element in the liquidity preference theory, dates to John M. Keynes, *The General Theory of Employment, Interest and Money* (New York: Harcourt, Brace, 1936), chapter 13. The preferred habitat theory is described by Franco Modigliani and Richard Sutch, "Innovations in Interest Rate Policy," *American Economic Review* 56 (May 1966), pp. 178–97.

particular security were judged by market participants to be too low (and its yield, therefore, higher than market conditions can support), they would purchase the security in large quantities, and its price would therefore rise (and yield would fall) until it reached a supportable level. On the other hand, if market participants judged a security to be overpriced, they would sell it (in an attempt to avoid the expected downturn in price), which would tend to depress the price. This activity by participants in the market, known as **arbitrage** across maturities, forces interest rates on different assets to conform to market expectations of future short rates.

Implications.   Numerous implications stem from the activities embodied in these assumptions. We will enumerate some of the more important ones.

1. Every Treasury security is expected to produce the same rate of return over the short run, regardless of the security's maturity. The emphasis here is on *expected*. If a security is purchased with multiple cash flows or with a single cash flow that does not coincide with the end of the current period, the *realized* rate of return may be different from the expected rate of return. Looking forward, however, no systematic gain is expected from investing in bonds of one maturity over bonds of any other maturity.

2. There is no sequence of investments in Treasury securities that is expected to produce higher rates of return than any other sequence of investments. For example, a person investing in a sequence of single-year Treasury bills should expect to receive the same amount over a period of three years as another person who invests directly in a four-year zero-coupon Treasury bond but who sells it after three years or a person who invests first in a one-year Treasury bill and, at the end of the year, invests in a two-year zero-coupon Treasury bond. Once again, this is only an expectation, as actual interest rates may well change over any particular period of time.

3. The implied forward rates of interest from today's spot rate term structure are the market's best, unbiased estimates of the interest rates that are actually expected in the future. For instance, the third-year forward rate, F_3, is the market's unbiased expectation of what the one-year spot rate of interest will be after two years have passed. On average, the actual one-year spot rate of interest at that time is just as likely to be higher as it is to be lower. Similarly, F_4 is the market's best predictor of what the one-year spot rate of interest will be after three years have passed.

4. Unobserved expected future rates of interest can be estimated from observed current spot rates and implied forward rates of interest. These estimates can be helpful to businesses in planning for the future. A methodology for extracting implied forward rates from spot rates was given earlier in this chapter.

5. Long-term interest rates are determined by market expectations of future short-term rates. Therefore, expectations account for the shape of the term structure of interest. Changes in the shape of the term structure reflect changes in market expectations of future short-term rates. If the term structure is sloped upward, the market expects short-term rates to be higher in the future than they are now. If the term structure is sloped downward, the market expects lower interest rates to prevail in the future. If the term structure is flat, it indicates that the market expects more of the same for the future.

6. Spot interest rates for securities of different maturities tend to move together. This occurs for two reasons, the first of which is simply a consequence of the math. Because long-term spot rates are merely geometric averages of shorter-term rates, when the shorter-term rates rise (or fall), the averages embedded in the longer-term rates will also tend to rise (or fall), other things being equal. The second reason is that interest rates are based on expectations. Usually, if an interest rate for a given year is expected to rise, it is a result of higher expected inflation or tighter money for that year. To the extent that the expectations for the underlying conditions spill over into other years, interest rates for those years can also be expected to move in a similar direction.

An illustration of the implications of the pure expectations theory is given in Exhibit 5.4. The second column gives the spot rates of interest for a hypothetical yield curve. It is identical to the term structure given at the outset of this chapter. The forward rates of interest implied by that set of spot rates are given in the third column. These forward rates were computed earlier. Under the pure expectations theory of interest, these same forward rates of interest would be the market's unbiased estimates of the future single-year spot rates of interest, as shown in the last column. The spot rate term structure of interest rates illustrated in the second column of Exhibit 5.4 will be used repeatedly to compare and contrast the various theories of the term structure.

Liquidity Preference Theory

The **liquidity preference theory** had its origins in the work of Keynes and Hicks, and it was often enlisted to help explain a curious and persistent phenomenon: Historically, the term structure of interest has had an upward slope more often than a flat or downward slope. Perhaps the best way to explain this theory is to use the pure expectations theory as a point of departure.

Assumptions.   Like the pure expectations theory, the liquidity preference theory also focuses on instruments that are free of default risk. Again, Treasury bond markets are assumed to operate efficiently. Market participants, however, are

---

EXHIBIT 5.4   Deriving Expected Future Rates: Pure Expectations Theory

Time Period (years)	Spot Rate Yield Curve	Forward Rates of Interest	Expected Future Single-Year Spot Rates of Interest
0	7.00%		
1	8.00	8.0%	8.0%
2	8.75	9.5	9.5
3	9.33	10.5	10.5
4	9.79	11.2	11.2
5	10.13	11.5	11.5

presumed to have a short horizon and to be **risk averse.** That is, participants prefer highly liquid investments over less liquid ones. You will recall from Chapter 1 that by "liquid" we mean that an investment can be easily and rapidly converted into cash (or liquidated) with little or no effect on its price. A long-term government bond has two things going against it in this regard. First, the difference, or "spread," between the price at which you can buy the bond from a broker (the "ask price") and the price at which you can sell the bond back to the broker (the "bid price") is often larger than that associated with short-term bonds. Thus, if you were to buy the long-term bond and immediately turn around and sell it back to the broker, you would lose more money than if you attempted to do the same thing with a shorter-term bond. Second, the price volatility of long-term bonds is considerably higher than that of shorter-term bonds. For example, a 10-year zero-coupon bond would change in price by approximately 9 percent in response to a 1 percent, or 100 basis point (hereafter b.p.), change in interest rates, whereas a 1-year zero-coupon bond would change less than 1 percent in price in response to a 100 b.p. change in interest rates. The aversion on the part of investors to wide bid–ask spreads and to volatile prices means that longer-term securities must offer a higher yield than would otherwise be the case in order to attract investors and compensate them for absorbing these risks.

Implications.   The important implications of the liquidity preference theory are as follows:

1. Treasury securities are expected to produce different rates of return over the next period, depending on the securities' liquidity. Generally, longer-term, less-liquid securities are expected to return more than short-term, liquid securities.

2. Some sequences of investments in Treasury securities are expected to produce higher rates of return than others. For example, a person investing in a sequence of single-year Treasury bills should expect to receive less over a period of three years than another person who invests directly in a three-year zero-coupon Treasury bond or a person who invests in a six-year zero-coupon Treasury bond but who liquidates it at the end of three years.

3. The implied forward rates of interest from today's spot rate term structure are the market's **upward-biased** estimates of the interest rates that are actually expected in the future. This means that on average, the actual one-year spot rate of interest at that time is likely to be lower than that implied by the forward rate. For instance, the third-year forward rate, F_3, is the market's upward-biased expectation of what the one-year spot rate of interest will be after two years have passed.

4. Long-term interest rates are determined by market expectations of future short-term rates, plus a **liquidity premium** applicable to the term and liquidity of the investment. Therefore, expectations only account for some of the shape of the term structure of interest, and the liquidity premium accounts for the rest. Changes in the shape of the term structure may reflect changes either in market expectations of future short-term rates or in the liquidity premium.

EXHIBIT 5.5   Deriving Expected Future Rates: Liquidity Preference Theory

Time Period (years)	Spot Rate Yield Curve	Liquidity Premium, in Basis Points	Spot Rate Curve Adjusted for Liquidity Premium	Expected Future Single Year Rates, Liquidity Preference	Forward Rates of Interest
0	7.00%	0 b.p.	7.00%		
1	8.00%	20 b.p.	7.80%	7.800%	8.00%
2	8.75%	50 b.p.	8.25%	8.702%	9.50%
3	9.33%	65 b.p.	8.68%	9.545%	10.50%
4	9.79%	70 b.p.	9.09%	10.329%	11.20%
5	10.13%	70 b.p.	9.43%	10.801%	11.50%

5. Unobserved expected future rates of interest can be estimated from observed current spot rates and implied forward rates of interest only if the applicable liquidity premiums embedded in these rates are known. If the term structure is sloped upward, the market may or may not expect short-term rates to be higher in the future than they are now, depending on the size of the liquidity premium embedded in the spot rates.

An illustration of the liquidity preference theory is given in Exhibits 5.5, 5.6, and 5.7. Exhibit 5.5 gives the data underlying the curves plotted in Exhibits 5.6 and 5.7. The second column of Exhibit 5.5 gives the spot rates of interest for our illustrative yield curve. The forward rates of interest implied by that set of spot rates are given in the last column. As we saw in the previous section, under the pure expectations theory of interest, these same forward rates of interest would be the market's unbiased estimates of the future single-year spot rates of interest. However, if the market charges a liquidity premium on the less-liquid instruments, as given in column three, then the expected future single-year spot rates of interest would need to be adjusted downward. For example, the one-year spot rate currently includes, and is expected to continue to include, a 20 b.p. liquidity premium,[9] while the two-year spot rate includes a 50 b.p. liquidity premium. These liquidity premia can be subtracted from the spot rates of interest to arrive at an adjusted spot rate curve, stripped of all liquidity premia. We can then use this adjusted curve to arrive at the market's expectations for the one-year future rates of interest, using the same formula we employed earlier to compute forward rates of interest. Note how these expectations differ from those given by the unadjusted forward rates in the last column of Exhibit 5.5.

In Exhibit 5.6, the liquidity premia, spot rate curve, and adjusted spot rate curve are plotted. In Exhibit 5.7, we show the differences in the implied

---

[9]Presumably, the shortest-term (overnight) rate would elicit no liquidity premium.

EXHIBIT 5.6

*Liquidity preference
theory*

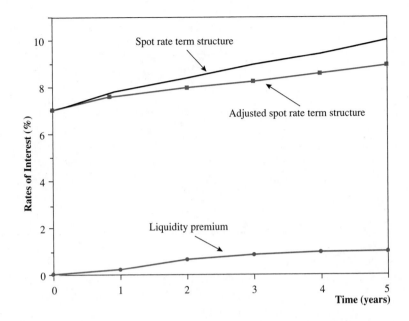

expectations for future interest rates given by the unbiased expectations theory
and the liquidity preference theory.

Preferred Habitat Theory

The **preferred habitat theory** of Modigliani and Sutch is actually a variation of
an older "market segmentation" theory presented by J. M. Culbertson.[10] It, too, is
an extension of the pure expectations theory.

Assumptions.   The theory begins with the assumption that different categories of
investors have preferences regarding the maturities of investments. These
preferences may arise naturally from the structure of their liabilities, from their risk
aversion, or from both. For example, a life insurance company typically makes long-
term promises to its policyholders and may therefore prefer to invest in securities
that offer a stable return over a long period of time. Commercial banks, on the other
hand, generally have short-term liabilities and may prefer to invest in short-term
loans and liquid securities. Depending on their needs and ability to absorb risk,
individual investors may prefer either short-term or long-term investments. In
addition to the investors in securities of various terms, issuers of debt may also have
needs to lock in a given interest rate over a period of years consistent with the
lengths of projects they are funding. Thus, the interaction of borrowers and lenders

---

[10]See J. M. Culbertson, "The Term Structure of Interest Rates," *Quarterly Journal of
Economics* (November 1957): 489–504; and Franco Modigliani and Richard C. Sutch, *op cit.*

EXHIBIT 5.7

Pure expectations versus liquidity preference expectations

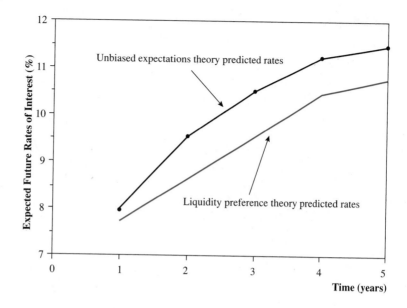

gives rise to supply and demand curves for securities of differing maturities. These supply and demand curves reflect both the market participants' expectations for the future evolution of interest rates and their preferences for participating in one segment of the market over another. It is important to note that this theory does not assume that participants are unwilling to shift or arbitrage across markets; they are merely reluctant to do so. While participants' preferences may be strong, they are willing to participate in other segments of the market, provided the interest rate incentives are sufficiently attractive. Thus, securities of differing maturities are substitutes—but imperfect substitutes—for one another.

Implications.   The important implications of the preferred habitat theory are as follows:

1. The stated rates of interest for securities of differing maturities reflect an average of short-term interest rates expected to prevail over the life of the long-term security plus a term premium that arises from market participants' preferences to participate in one segment of the market or another. Therefore, the supply and demand curves for each segment reflect both market expectations and market maturity preferences.

2. Some sequences of investments in Treasury securities are expected to produce higher rates of return than others. Those sequences expected to produce the highest rates of return would be linked to high term premia due to supply and demand conditions for securities of a particular term.

3. The implied forward rates of interest from today's spot rate term structure are biased estimates of the interest rates that are actually expected in the future.

Exhibit 5.8

Preferred habitat view of interest rates

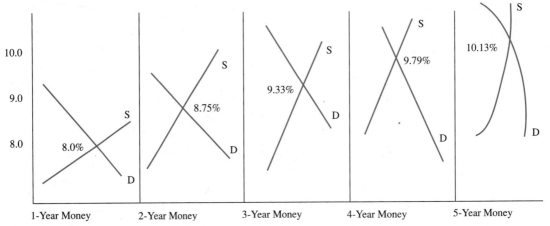

Whether the bias is upward or downward depends on supply and demand conditions for securities of various terms.

4. Due to the strong market preferences for borrowing and lending in securities of particular maturities, arbitrage across maturities will not entirely eliminate the term premia associated with securities of various terms. That is, investors cannot buy and sell different maturities so as to force prices to move to equate yields on different maturities.

5. Changes in the shape of the term structure may reflect changes in market expectations of future short-term rates or changes in the term premia arising from shifting supply and demand conditions and market preferences. For example, if the Treasury were to issue a relatively large quantity of long-term debt, the long-term interest rates would probably rise relative to short-term rates to a point where the new demand and supply curves are in equilibrium. To the extent that markets for loanable funds are not rigidly segmented, the new equilibrium point in the long-term sector would reflect changes in the supply and demand curves at other points along the term structure as well.

An illustration of the preferred habitat theory is given in Exhibit 5.8. Note that there are supplies and demands for loanable funds of various maturities. Linking the intersections of these supply and demand curves results in a term structure identical to those obtained in our examples of the pure expectations and liquidity preference theories. However, no unique expected future rate series can be obtained from the analysis, nor can a unique bias in the forward rates be defined. Variations in rates across the yield curve can only be said to be the result of both expectations of future rates and unique supply-demand conditions in each market. As such, this theory is the most difficult of the three to apply for predictive purposes. In some respects, it argues that the market worries about everything! (See Box 5.1 on page 100.)

EXHIBIT 5.9

The term structure of interest rate volatility

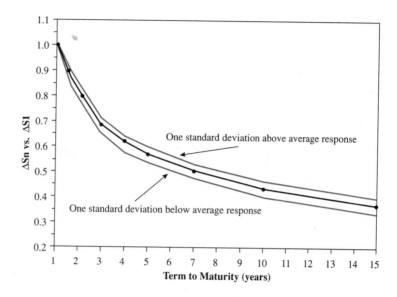

The Term Structure of Interest Rate Volatility

While there is a lot that can be said about the uncertainty in interest rates, one thing can be said with *certainty.* Interest rates change. But how? When one spot rate changes, what becomes of other spot rates? Do all rates move in lockstep, or do they change by varying degrees? This aspect of the behavior of spot rates of interest relative to one another is known as the **term structure of interest rate volatility.**[11] For example, suppose the one-year spot rate of interest changes by 100 basis points, either higher or lower. What then would likely happen to the two-year spot rate? The three-year spot rate? The *n*-year spot rate?

In Exhibit 5.9, we have regressed monthly changes in spot rates for maturities ranging from 1 year to 15 years against changes in the one-year spot rate. Our time period extends from 1941 through 1990. Note how we see a fairly smooth, declining pattern. For example, the five-year spot rate has tended to move about 57 percent as far, but in the same direction, as the one-year spot rate. Relative to the one-year spot rate, the 15-year spot rate has moved even less (approximately 34 percent). These relative movements, however, are only suggestive of what might happen. There is variation from one case to another. To capture the statistical variation around the average values, curves showing one standard deviation above and below the means are plotted alongside the curve reflecting the average responses.

---

[11]A description of this notion is given by David F. Babbel, "The Term Structure of Interest Rate Volatility," in *Innovations in Bond Portfolio Management: Duration Analysis and Immunization,* ed. G. Bierwag, G. Kaufman, and A. Toevs (New York: JAI Press, 1983).

EXHIBIT 5.10

1-year versus 15-year spot rate movements

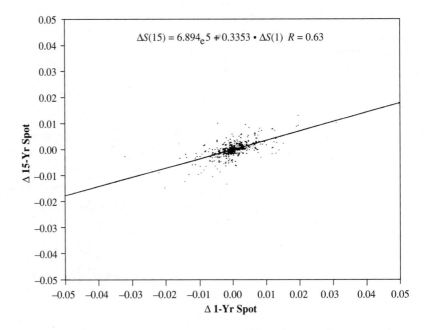

$\Delta S(15) = 6.894_e5 + 0.3353 \cdot \Delta S(1) \quad R = 0.63$

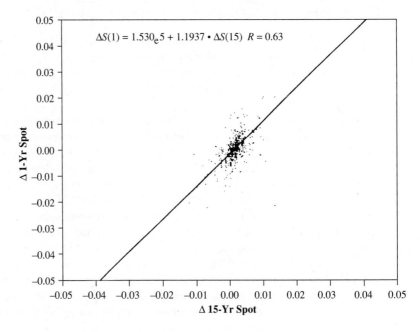

$\Delta S(1) = 1.530_e5 + 1.1937 \cdot \Delta S(15) \quad R = 0.63$

Exhibit 5.11

The term structure of interest rate volatility

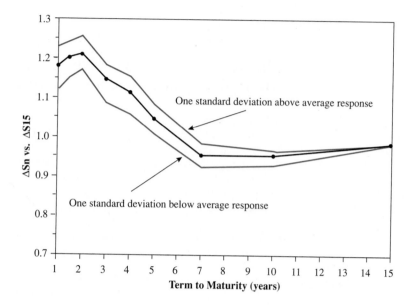

Even more indicative of the variety of responses that have been observed in relative interest rate movements are the scatter plots of the 1-year versus 15-year spot rate movements shown in Exhibit 5.10. The upper figure shows how the 15-year spot rate moved in relation to movements in the 1-year spot rate. The slope of the regression line best fitting the observations is 0.3353, meaning that the 15-year rate, on average, fluctuated about one-third as much, but generally in the same direction, as the 1-year spot rate.

Contrast this finding with that portrayed in the lower figure of Exhibit 5.10. This figure shows how the 1-year spot rate moved in relation to movements in the 15-year spot rate. The slope of the best-fitting regression line is 1.1937. This means that the 1-year spot rate tended to fluctuate by approximately the same amount (actually about 20 percent more) and in generally the same direction as the 15-year spot rate.[12] If the short- and long-term interest rates had been perfectly correlated to each other, the slope of the lower figure would have been equal to the reciprocal of the slope of the upper figure, or 2.9824.

As in Exhibit 5.9, Exhibit 5.11 shows the entire term structure of interest rate volatility. However, here we examine spot rate movements relative to the 15-year spot rate movements. Again, there are three curves, with the top and bottom curves showing one standard deviation above and below the average response curve. Note that the relationship is much flatter than that which was generated using the 1-year spot rate movements as the reference factor.

---

[12]Note that the slope of the left figure, 0.3353, when multiplied by the slope of the right figure, 1.1937, is equal to the correlation coefficients, R, of 0.6327 multiplied by each other, or R-square of 0.4002.

Box 5.1

Markets Worry about Everything: Inflation, Real Rates, and Supply

Prone to motion sickness? Avoid boats and—in coming weeks—the bond market. A collision of financial weather systems will likely roil interest rates like a rowboat in a typhoon.

The biggest disturbance is likely to be the giant storm of Treasuries slated to move through the market this week.

The Treasury Department expects to sell $44.5 billion of securities—$18.5 billion of three-year notes, $14 billion of 10-year notes, and $12 billion of 30-year bonds—its biggest quarterly debt auction ever.

On its own, such a large offering would be enough to cause bond prices and interest rates to gyrate. Nearly a third of the auction will be new supply for investors—the rest will be used to redeem maturing bonds or raise funds to pay interest due—and that likely will put downward pressure on prices.

But this time the auction also collides with what already are unsettled conditions in the bond market.

For starters, few feel confident anymore predicting how the balanced-budget debate in Washington will sort out and what its effects will be on the economy and the markets.

The recent signs bode well for a credible deal, with Congressional Democrats and Republicans meeting in an effort to find common ground on a budget that would balance by 2002.

But the investment community is wary. Lawmakers have come close to a budget deal before in nearly five months of negotiations, only to walk away from the table at the last minute amid vituperative rhetoric.

Secondly, important economic data remain suspect. January's employment report released Friday is a case in point. The Labor Department took the unusual step of renouncing the report's accuracy, saying January snowstorms along the East Coast fueled an abnormal—and unmeasurable—slowdown in business activity. It's the second month in a row that this nugget of data—perhaps the most important piece for economists' projections—has proved unusable.

Lastly, inflation signals have turned contradictory. The price of gold is skyrocketing, the February spot-month contract closing Friday at $414.70 an ounce, up $3.90, in trading on the Comex division of the New York Mercantile Exchange. That's the highest close in nearly 5½ years. Historically, rising gold prices have been a sign of pending inflation. Yet, December's consumer price index rose at an annual rate of only 2.4%, less than expected, a sign that inflation was slowing.

Source: Fred Vogelstein, "Tempest of Treasurys to Flood Market," *The Wall Street Journal*, February 5, 1996. Reprinted by permission of *The Wall Street Journal*, © 1996 Dow Jones & Company, Inc. All Rights Reserved Worldwide.

We can conclude several things from these findings. First, if we are using short-term interest rate movements as our primary factor, longer-term interest rate movements can be expected to be more subdued. But if we are using long-term interest rate movements as our reference factor, shorter-term rates can be expected to move by approximately the same amount. Second, there is good reason to believe that there are things other than the movement in one interest rate that cause the term structure to move. In technical terms, there is more than a single factor determining rate movements. **Single-factor models** assume, implicitly, that movements in all spot rates of interest are perfectly correlated.[13] This is obviously incorrect. We found, for instance, that over time, the 15-year spot rate changes explained only about 40 percent of the changes in the 1-year spot rate. Therefore, other factors must be added to explain movements in the term structure. Such models are likely to have more promise in terms of their ability to explain interest rates, changes in interest rates, and prices of fixed-income securities and their derivatives. More will be said about this in Chapter 7.

---

[13]This does not mean that they all move one-to-one with each other; rather, it means that the movement in one spot rate is perfectly correlated with the movement in another.

Summary

This chapter introduces the concepts and terminology necessary to deal with financial assets of differing maturity. It begins with the distinction between spot and forward rates of interest, which will prove essential to any understanding of multiperiod financial instruments. The derivation of forward rates from spot rates is explained and illustrated for one term structure in particular, and equations are offered that permit the derivation of forward rates from any yield curve.

However, the real fun begins when we attempt to understand the implications of any single term structure of rates. This is an area in which much work has been done but differences of opinion continue to exist. Accordingly, the three traditional theories of the term structure are presented in some detail for consideration. In each case, the assumptions and implications of the theory are presented. All three of the theories are based on the assumption that economic agents forecast future interest rates and contrast them with the forward rates implicit in current spot rates. The theories differ only to the degree that expectations have an impact upon forward rates.

The pure expectations theory argues that only expectations matter and that the forward rates are the market's best estimate of expected future spot rates. The liquidity preference theory maintains that while expectations are important, they are not the only thing that affects the term structure. Advocates of this theory argue that investors prefer liquidity and will move to longer-term investments only if induced to do so by extra yield. Accordingly, proponents of this theory argue that the forward rates are biased upward when compared to expected rates for the future. Finally, the preferred habitat school of thought goes one step further. These advocates believe that there is a balance between supply and demand for each and every maturity. Therefore, expected future spot rates cannot easily be extracted from current forward rates. While a rich theory, the preferred habitat theory offers us little insight into the value of forward rates and their predictive value regarding likely changes in the shape of the yield curve.

Nonetheless, the yield curve does change. The chapter ends with evidence of the term structure of interest rate volatility. Clearly, short rates move substantially more than long ones. However, the fluctuation of rates across the entire term structure is correlated, albeit not perfectly. We close with a recognition that there is much about the movement in interest rates that is not yet understood and is therefore not amenable to reliable forecasts.

Key Concepts

arbitrage,   90
biased versus unbiased,   92
face value versus coupon,   85
forward rate of interest,   83
liquidity preference theory,   91
liquidity premium,   92
preferred habitat theory,   94
pure expectations theory,   89
risk averse,   92

risk neutral,   89
single-factor models,   101
spot rate of interest,   82
term structure of interest rates,   87
term structure of interest rate volatility,   97
yield curve,   87
yield to maturity,   86
zero-coupon bond versus coupon bond,   85

Review Questions

1. You have the following spot rates:

   One-year spot rate: 9.5%
   Two-year spot rate: 8.8%
   Three-year spot rate: 8.5%

   Compute the corresponding forward rates of interest.

2. Referring to the previous question, is it possible for the market to expect interest rates to be increasing?

3. Using the spot rates in the text, calculate the two-year spot rates for subsequent years (i.e., the two-year rate spanning years two and three, three and four, etc.). Assume that the pure expectations theory holds.

4. Suppose that you are a firm believer in the pure expectations theory. Your discerning eye spots a bond that appears to be priced much too low. Should you buy it?

5. As the text states, compared to short-term bonds, the values of long-term bonds are much more sensitive to changes in interest rates. Why do you think this is so?

6. Under the liquidity preference theory, is it possible that forward rates could be biased downward?

7. Why would an investment company use a single-factor model to explain movements in the term structure?

8. One assumption of the pure expectations theory is that market participants are risk neutral. If this assumption is violated, will interest rates be lower or higher than the ones predicted by the theory?

References

Babbel, David F. "The Term Structure of Interest Rate Volatility." In *Innovations in Bond Portfolio Management: Duration Analysis and Immunization,* ed. G. Bierwag, G. Kaufman, and A. Toevs. New York: JAI Press, 1983.

Black, Fischer. "Interest Rates as Options." *Journal of Finance,* December 1995.

Cox, John C.; Jonathan Ingersoll, Jr.; and Stephen A. Ross. "A Reexamination of Traditional Hypotheses about the Term Structure of Interest Rates." *Journal of Finance,* September 1981.

Culbertson, John M. "The Term Structure of Interest Rates." *Quarterly Journal of Economics,* 1957.

Dobson, Steven W.; Richard C. Sutch; and David E. Vandeford. "An Evaluation of Alternative Empirical Models of the Term Structure of Interest Rates." *Journal of Finance,* September 1976.

Fama, Eugene F. "Forward Rates as Predictors of Future Spot Rates." *Journal of Financial Economics,* September 1976.

Fama, Eugene F. "The Information in the Term Structure." *Journal of Financial Economics,* December 1984.

Fisher, Irving. "Appreciation and Interest." *Publications of the American Economic Association* XI (August 1896).

Friedman, Benjamin M. "Interest Rate Expectations versus Forward Rates: Evidence from an Expectations Survey." *Journal of Finance,* September 1979.

Hicks, J. R. *Value and Capital.* 2d ed. London: Oxford University Press, 1946.

Homer, Sidney, and Martin L. Leibowitz. *Inside the Yield Book.* Engelwood Cliffs, N.J.: Prentice Hall, 1972.

Kessel, Reuben A. *The Cyclical Behavior of the Term Structure of Interest Rates.* New York: National Bureau of Economic Research, 1965.

Keynes, John M. *The General Theory of Employment, Interest and Money.* New York: Harcourt Brace, 1936.

Macaulay, Frederick R. *Some Theoretical Problems Suggested by the Movements of Interest Rates, Bond Yields, and Stock Prices in the United States Since 1856.* New York: National Bureau of Economic Research, 1938.

Malkiel, Burton G. "Expectations, Bond Prices, and the Term Structure of Interest Rates." *Quarterly Journal of Economics,* May 1962.

Meiselman, David. *The Term Structure of Interest Rates.* Engelwood Cliffs, N.J.: Prentice Hall, 1962.

Modigliani, Franco, and Richard Sutch. "Innovations in Interest Rate Policy." *American Economic Review,* May 1966.

Roley, V. Vance. "The Determinants of the Treasury Yield Curve." *Journal of Finance,* December 1981.

Roll, Richard. *The Behavior of Interest Rates: An Application of the Efficient Market Model to U.S. Treasury Bills.* New York: Basic Books, 1970.

Tuttle, Donald L., ed. *Managing Investment Portfolios.* Boston: Warren Gorham and Lamont, 1983.

Van Horne, James. *Financial Market Rates and Flows.* 4th ed. Englewood Cliffs, N.J.: Prentice Hall, 1994.

Valuing Cash Flows

The fundamental concepts of present value and discounted cash flows are presented in this chapter. By evaluating an arbitrary stream of cash flows, an entire array of valuation techniques is offered, including present value and future value for fixed cash flows. The goal is to allow the student to become comfortable with the mechanics for valuation of a stream of fixed cash flows.

In the previous chapter, we painstakingly developed the notion of spot and forward rates of interest, and potential future interest rate paths, all in connection with our discussion of the term structure of interest rates. We will now use these concepts to show how the value of a single cash flow and of a stream of many cash flows can be determined.

Valuing a Single Cash Flow

Suppose that you have $500 and wish to invest it for seven years. If the interest rate applicable to seven years (i.e., the seven-year spot rate of interest) is 10.41 percent, how much would your investment be worth at the end of that period? To compute this **future value** (*FV*), we begin with the $500 we wish to invest, which is called the **present value** (*PV*), and allow the interest to compound for seven full years. Our result would be

$$\text{Amount invested} \times (1 + \text{Interest rate})^7 = \text{Future value of investment}$$

$$\$500 \times (1.1041)^7 = \$1,000$$

In words, we would double our money in seven years at this interest rate. In general, the formula for computing the future value in *n* years of a current investment is

$$FV = PV \times (1 + S_n)^n$$

In computing future values, notice that we utilize the interest rate appropriate for the time period that the saving will be left on deposit—in this case, the *n*-year spot rate of interest, S_n. We also raise the interest rate factor, $(1 + S_n)$, to the *n*th power indicating that the initial investment is compounding at the *n*-period rate for *n* years.

This situation can be turned around. Suppose, instead, that you are going to receive $1,000 seven years from now. How much is it worth today? Because we have already determined that $500, invested today, can accumulate to $1,000 in seven years, we know that $1,000 in seven years must be worth $500 today. The general formula for computing the present value of a cash flow occurring in *n* years is obtained by recasting the earlier formula into a present value focus:

$$PV = FV \div (1 + S_n)^n$$

This equation can be used to determine the present value of any fixed, single future cash flow, such as a zero-coupon bond, described in the previous chapter. A zero-coupon bond typically returns a face value of $1,000 at maturity, so we could say that if the seven-year spot rate of interest is 10.41 percent, the price of a seven-year zero-coupon bond is $500 today.

Suppose, on the other hand, you were given both the current price and the future price of this bond. One other useful thing can be uncovered by recasting the earlier formula to focus on interest rates implied by the two given prices. The formula allows an investor to solve for the yield given the present and future values of the zero-coupon bond. The equation becomes

$$FV \div PV = (1 + S_n)^n$$

$$\Rightarrow S_n = \sqrt[n]{FV \div PV} - 1$$

For a zero-coupon bond, the future value is the face value, and the present value is the price (*P*). Thus, we can reword the equation to read

$$S_n = \sqrt[n]{FV \div P} - 1$$

In the case of our seven-year zero-coupon bond, our calculation would be

$$S_n = \sqrt[7]{\$1,000 \div \$500} - 1 = 10.41\%$$

This last version of the equation is often used to estimate the term structure of interest rates, based on the prices of a series of zero-coupon bonds having differing maturities. For example, the table below shows both the prices of zero-coupon bonds of varying maturities and the implied term structure from these prices. The prices and implied spot rates are given as follows:

Maturity	Price	Spot Rate
1 year	$915.74	9.20%
2 years	$827.80	9.91
3 years	$751.93	9.97
4 years	$683.01	10.00
5 years	$615.31	10.20
6 years	$553.82	10.35
7 years	$500.00	10.41
8 years	$456.45	10.30
9 years	$431.10	9.80
10 years	$396.22	9.70

Valuing Multiple Cash Flows

Many financial instruments have multiple cash flows. How can you calculate how much they are worth? The financial value of a series of cash flows can be determined in several different ways using the approach just described. Each method is equally correct, but each approaches the problem somewhat differently. Let's examine each in turn.

Value Additivity

First, we could rely on the principle of **value additivity.** This principle indicates that the price of a financial instrument whose payoffs are a linear combination of a series of single payoff instruments is given by the same linear combination of the prices of the single payoffs. In other words, the value of the whole is equal to the sum of the values of its parts.

For example, consider an asset with payoffs of $1,000 in each of years 3 and 5, a $333.33 payoff in year 8, and a final payoff of $5,000 at the end of year 10. If the term structure of interest rates is the same as that given in the table above, what would this asset be worth? We know from the table that the price of a zero-coupon bond with a face value of $1,000 and maturing in 3 years is $751.93. Similarly, we know the prices of other zero-coupon bonds with maturities extending up to 10 years. Therefore, we can take those prices and multiply them by the proportion of $1,000 due on each date. Our calculation would proceed as follows:

(1) Year of Cash Flow	(2) Value of Cash Flow per $1,000	(3) Number of $1,000 Cash Flows during Year	(4) (2) × (3)
3 years	$751.93/per $1,000 face	1	$ 751.93
5 years	$615.31/per $1,000 face	1	615.31
8 years	$456.45/per $1,000 face	1/3	152.15
10 years	$396.22/per $1,000 face	5	1,981.10
	SUM:		$3,500.49

Therefore, the present value of the multiple cash flows is $3,500.49, which is the combination of the present value of each cash flow.

Valuation Using Spot Rates

Second, we could use the concept of value additivity in a slightly different way. Suppose we discount each cash flow by its appropriate spot rate of interest and then add them together at the end. In this case, the formula will be

$$P_0 = \sum_{t=1}^{m} \frac{CF_t}{(1 + S_t)^t}$$

where CF_t is any cash flow occurring at time t, m is the date of the final cash flow, Σ is a summation operator, and P_0 denotes the present value or price (now, at time 0) of the stream of cash flows. This equation can be expanded into its terms. We show the first three terms below:

$$P_0 = \frac{CF_1}{(1 + S_1)^1} + \frac{CF_2}{(1 + S_2)^2} + \frac{CF_3}{(1 + S_3)^3} + \cdots$$

Applying this formula to the particular stream of cash flows considered earlier, we would have

$$P_0 = \frac{\$1,000}{(1.0997)^3} + \frac{\$1,000}{(1.102)^5} + \frac{\$333.33}{(1.103)^8} + \frac{\$5,000}{(1.097)^{10}}$$

$$= \$751.93 + \$615.31 + \$152.15 + \$1,981.10$$

$$= \underline{\$3,500.49}$$

Notice that the individual values are identical to the present values in the fourth column of the above table and that the answer that is obtained is the same as that which is derived using the additivity of the present values of each individual cash flow.

Valuation Using Forward Rates

Third, we could use what we know about forward rates to value the cash flows in our example. Since the term structure of interest rates allows us to derive the implied forward rates, we could discount each cash flow by the time-specific forward rates implied by the yield curve. After some arithmetic, it can be shown that this would result in the discounting of each cash flow by the product of the appropriate forward rates of interest. The general formula is

$$P_0 = \sum_{t=1}^{m} \frac{CF_t}{\prod_{i=1}^{t}(1 + F_i)}$$

where $\prod_{i=1}^{t}(1 + F_i)$ is a term denoting the product of 1 plus the applicable forward rates of interest, F_i. This equation also can be expanded into its terms. We show the first three terms below:

$$P_0 = \frac{CF_1}{(1 + F_1)} + \frac{CF_2}{(1 + F_1)(1 + F_2)} + \frac{CF_3}{(1 + F_1)(1 + F_2)(1 + F_3)} + \cdots$$

To apply this formula to the particular stream of cash flows considered earlier, we first would have to compute the implied forward rates of interest. Since you have already learned how to do this in Chapter 5, we will not belabor the details again. You can verify, if you wish, that we have done it properly. After computing these forward rates, we would have:

$$P_0 = \frac{\$1,000}{(1.092013)(1.106233)(1.100900)}$$

$$+ \frac{\$1,000}{(1.092013)(1.106233)(1.100900)(1.100906)(1.1110026)}$$

$$+ \frac{\$333.33}{(1.092013)(1.106233)(1.100900)(1.100906)(1.1110026)(1.111029)(1.107640)(1.095410)}$$

$$+ \frac{\$333.33}{(1.092013)(1.106233)(1.100900)(\ldots)(\ldots)(\ldots)(1.107640)(1.095410)(1.058803)(1.088032)}$$

$$= \$751.93 + \$615.31 + \$152.15 + \$1,981.10 = \underline{\$3,500.49}$$

Again, our result comes out the same! This, however, should be expected as each method relies on the same cash flows and term structure of interest rates.

Yield to Maturity Calculations

As noted in Chapter 5, there is considerable attention given to **yield to maturity** in the financial markets. In addition, this figure is frequently reported in the financial press for individual bonds. We can use our current discussion of valuing cash flows to explain how this figure is calculated, as well as what it does and does not explain.

Suppose we knew the market price of a bond, P_0, with a series of cash flows, CF_t. We could derive the yield to maturity by solving for Y in the following general formula:

$$P_0 = \sum_{t=1}^{m} \frac{CF_t}{(1 + Y)^t}$$

In fact, we could do so quite easily these days by merely asking our handy calculator to compute the YTM, or internal rate of return from the investment. Notice, however, that the yield to maturity as calculated carries no subscript. In

EXHIBIT 6.1   Valuing Cash Flows: Comparisons of Different Approaches

Approach	CF_1		CF_2		CF_3		CF_4		P_0
Value additivity	$751.93	+	$615.31	+	$152.15	+	$1,981.10	=	$3,500.49
Spot rates	$751.93	+	$615.31	+	$152.15	+	$1,981.10	=	$3,500.49
Forward rates	$751.93	+	$615.31	+	$152.15	+	$1,981.10	=	$3,500.49
Yield to maturity	$755.22	+	$626.31	+	$157.66	+	$1,961.30	=	$3,500.49

other words, it is the single "interest rate" that is used to discount all of the cash flows, irrespective of their timing. Below, we expand this equation into its first three terms:

$$P_0 = \frac{CF_1}{(1+Y)^1} + \frac{CF_2}{(1+Y)^2} + \frac{CF_3}{(1+Y)^3} + \cdots$$

If we already know the market price P_0 and the cash flows $CF_1, CF_2, CF_3, \ldots$, we can obtain the yield to maturity from this calculation. However, note that the yield to maturity can be derived only if we already know the market price. This is because we use the price to derive the yield, not vice versa.

Whereas spot and forward rates can be used to determine the value of any stream of fixed cash flows, the yield to maturity, as is shown in Box 6.1, is unique to a particular pattern of cash flows and hence is valid only for discounting the cash flows of an instrument exhibiting exactly the same pattern. On the other hand, the yield to maturity offers a simple, single number in place of the numerous yields associated with all of the cash flows. It is, in essence, a complex average of the spot rates that results from the valuation of the cash flows of the financial asset under consideration.[1]

In the example here, our trusty calculator indicates that the yield to maturity is 9.8102 percent. We can use this figure in the equation above to derive the present value of the four cash flows under consideration.

$$P_0 = \frac{\$1,000}{(1+.098102)^3} + \frac{\$1,000}{(1+.098102)^5} + \frac{\$333.333}{(1+.098102)^8} + \frac{\$5,000}{(1+.098102)^{10}}$$

$$= \$755.22 + \$626.31 + \$157.66 + \$1,961.30$$

$$= \$3,500.49$$

Note that, by construction, the appropriate YTM produces the correct present value of the entire cash flow stream. However, using YTM will not allow us to obtain the correct present value of each cash flow separately. To show this, we have repeated the final result from each of our calculation methods in Exhibit 6.1.

All of the individual cash flow values are consistent with each other except for the YTM result, which provides different present value information for each

[1]The complex weighting scheme used to develop YTM is described in Chapter 8, Box 8.2.

Box 6.1

The Uniqueness of Yield to Maturity

One of the most common uses of yield to maturity is in the pricing of bonds. Let us consider two default-free three-year bonds. Bond A offers an interest payment, called a coupon, of $40 each year, while Bond B provides a coupon of $130 each year. Both bonds have a face value of $1,000 to be repaid, along with the final coupon, at the end of the third year.

Now suppose that the spot rates of interest for one-, two-, and three-year periods are as follows: $S_1 = 5.0\%$, $S_2 = 7.0\%$, and $S_3 = 8\%$. The values of these bonds may be computed as follows:

$$P_{Bond\,A} = \frac{\$40}{(1 + .05)^1} + \frac{\$40}{(1 + .07)^2} + \frac{\$1040}{(1 + .08)^3}$$

$$= \$898.62$$

$$P_{Bond\,B} = \frac{\$130}{(1 + .05)^1} + \frac{\$130}{(1 + .07)^2} + \frac{\$1130}{(1 + .08)^3}$$

$$= \$1,134.39$$

After determining the appropriate prices, we can solve for yield to maturity by keying in the prices and cash flows and using the YTM or IRR (internal rate of return) function built into most financial calculators. For Bond A, the YTM is 7.93 percent. For Bond B, the YTM is 7.80 percent.

There are three things noteworthy in this example. First, the appropriate yield to maturity cannot be calculated until after the correct price has already been determined. Second, as long as the cash flows are fixed and free of default, we can just as easily use the schedule of spot rates of interest in the valuation of different cash flow streams. Third, each cash flow stream will be associated with a unique yield to maturity. In our example, Bond A elicited a higher yield to maturity than Bond B. The reason for this is that a yield to maturity is a complex weighted average of the spot rates of interest. In this case, Bond A has lower early cash flows, and hence a lesser weighting on the lower, shorter-term interest rates, and a relatively greater weighting on the higher, longer-term interest rates than Bond B.

of the four cash flows. When taken together, these present values produce offsetting errors by construction, thus resulting in a correct cumulative present value. It is only in the case of the valuation of a single cash flow, or zero-coupon bond, that these differences do not arise.

Valuing Consols

Having discussed the valuation of zero-coupon bonds, which pay only principal and no coupon, we next proceed to the case of multiple cash flows, which is more consistent with ordinary coupon bonds. To do this, let us begin by examining the valuation issues associated with bonds at the opposite end of the spectrum—the **consol.** Consols pay a perpetual (yes, perpetual) coupon at fixed calendar intervals, but they *never* pay principal. Never. Consols are a stream of constant coupon payments from now until forever.

What would be the value of a financial instrument that promises to make payments on a fixed, periodic schedule throughout all eternity? (After you expire, the consol will continue making payments to your heirs, and their heirs, *ad infinitum.*) If the promise is a viable one, it means that over time, you (and your heirs) will receive an infinite amount of cash. If you were to receive that infinite amount of cash all at once and today, the value of the promise would be worth an infinite amount. Instead, the money is dribbled out to you in relatively small parcels over an infinite amount of time. In this case, the instrument is clearly worth less than it would be if it paid the total amount now. But how much less?

We can obtain an answer to this question by referring back to our present value methodology. Using this approach, we can develop a simple expression for the present value or price of a consol. In general, the price would be

$$P_0 = \sum_{t=1}^{\infty} \frac{CF_t}{(1 + y)^t}$$

Note in the summation sign that t goes from 1 to ∞. If every cash flow is equal, which it is in the case of a consol, then this expression simplifies to[2]

$$P_0 = \frac{CF}{y}$$

where CF is the annual coupon and y is the single discount rate.

Suppose that you could purchase a consol that will pay back $100 per year forever and that the market interest rate for consols at the moment is 10 percent. How much would you be willing to pay for this investment? Using the above expression, we would deduce that the present value of a promise to make a fixed coupon payment forever would be

$$P_0 = \frac{\$100}{.10} = \$1,000$$

We could turn this equation around to obtain the market consol rate of interest, y, given the price or present value of a consol and its coupon:

$$y = \frac{CF}{P_0} = \frac{\$100}{\$1,000} = 10\%$$

The trick in valuing consols is in knowing what the appropriate valuation rate of interest, y, should be. For example, suppose that a consol offering $100 per year is valued using an 8 percent consol rate. Then, the value of that promise is

$$P_0 = \frac{CF}{y} = \frac{\$100}{.08} = \$1,250$$

On the other hand, if the appropriate consol rate rises to 12 percent, the consol would be worth only

$$P_0 = \frac{CF}{y} = \frac{\$100}{.12} = \$833.33$$

---

[2]This is because $P_0 = \sum_{t=1}^{\infty} \frac{CF_t}{(1 + y)^t} = CF \sum_{t=1}^{\infty} \frac{1}{(1 + y)^t} = CF \frac{1}{y} = \frac{CF}{y}.$

Clearly, the level of the interest rate used for discounting the coupon payments is of extreme importance. This is true for two distinct reasons. If the consol is to be valued accurately, the correct consol rate must be used. Small variations cause large changes in perceived value. In addition, variations in market interest rates result in substantial changes in market prices. Consols are not instruments for the faint-hearted!

How do we obtain this consol rate, which is so important to our valuation? Exactly what is this rate, and where does it come from? The consol rate is actually a complex weighted average of the spot or forward rates of interest from now into infinity. Note that we call it a consol rate rather than a yield to maturity because there is no maturity. (Accordingly, we used y instead of Y as the symbol for the discount rate.) However, in other respects the consol rate is quite similar to the yield to maturity. It is a single interest rate that discounts each coupon into the future. Unfortunately, it is difficult to find spot rates of interest that extend as far into the future as consol payments do. Usually, we cannot find spot rates beyond about 40 years. Accordingly, we cannot obtain the "appropriate" rate of interest for a consol by using the method of creating a complex weighted average of spot rates into the infinite future. However, all hope is not lost.

Suppose we return to the valuation of cash flows using the spot rates approach. A consol's value or price can be written as

$$P_0 = \sum_{t=1}^{\infty} \frac{CF_t}{(1 + S_t)^t} = \frac{CF_1}{(1 + S_1)^1} + \frac{CF_2}{(1 + S_2)^2} + \frac{CF_3}{(1 + S_3)^3} + \ \cdots$$

Notice that the present value of the coupons declines into the distant future. Beyond several decades, the value of the future coupon payment is extremely low. Exhibit 6.2 shows the incremental value associated with each consol payment through the first five decades under the assumption of a 10 percent consol rate. This pattern is roughly similar for all consols, regardless of the consol rate.

As in the yield to maturity concept, the consol rate is the single rate that equates the current price of a consol with the value of its stream of coupons. The consol rate, however, values the stream of coupons over an infinite horizon. As Exhibit 6.2 demonstrates, the earlier cash flows have a much larger influence on the total present value of the consol. Thus, the consol rate is going to be most heavily influenced by the earlier spot rates, which, fortunately, can be observed in the market. The complex weighting scheme applied to spot rates to obtain the consol rate applies extremely low—indeed, vanishing—weights to very-long-term spot rates. Thus, we can arrive at a close approximation of the appropriate consol rate by examining the underlying spot rates of interest that are available.

Exhibit 6.3 shows the weightings to be applied to spot rates of interest for the consol priced as in Exhibit 6.2 to yield a 10 percent consol rate. These are the weights that are applied to the spot rates used to discount each cash flow. In this exhibit, it is apparent that much of the weight is placed on spot rates with maturities in the lower ranges. Indeed, the cumulative weight placed on the first 40 spot rates of interest approaches 90 percent. After 50 years, the remaining weights sum

Exhibit 6.2

Present value of cash flows for a 10% consol rate

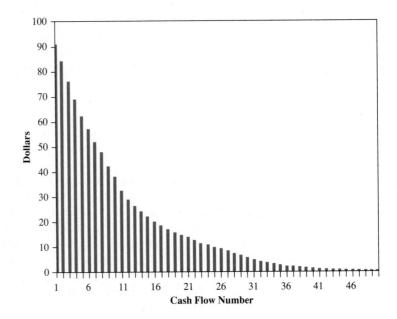

to less than 5 percent.[3] Beyond 100 years, less than .1 percent of the cumulative weight remains to be assigned.

Finally, there is another problem with this entire approach to determining the appropriate yield rate for a consol. Although we do not demonstrate at this juncture how the correct weights to be applied to the spot rates are derived, suffice it to say that, as in the computation of virtually all yields, the precise weights cannot be determined unless the price, and hence, the yield, is already known. As in the case of yield to maturity, the appropriate consol rate cannot be determined precisely unless the consol price is already known. In this case, the yield offers us no independent help in determining the correct value of the consol. However, a more fruitful way to view a consol rate is as a compact restatement of price and coupon in a single number. This restatement is useful in that it does convey a notion of the rate of return, over time, that is anticipated to be earned on the consol.

Valuing Annuities

Annuities are a lot like consols, except that they do not last as long. Annuities offer periodic payments over a number of years, and then they stop. There are two major kinds of annuities: **life annuities** and **fixed annuities.** A life annuity

---

[3]For a more precise calculation of the weights to apply to spot rates to get appropriate yields, we again refer the reader to Box 8.2 of Chapter 8.

EXHIBIT 6.3

The consol rate as a complex weighted average of underlying spot rates of interest

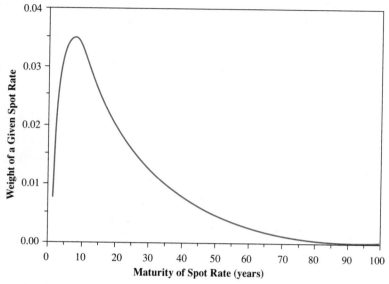

Note: Weights sum to 1.0.

makes payments as long as the annuitant (or his/her spouse, in the case of a joint survivorship annuity) is alive and ceases upon her/his death. Valuing a life annuity falls into the realm of actuarial science, as it involves the application of mortality rates to a stream of cash flows. Life annuities are the kind most often held by retirees, who need an income throughout life, but not thereafter. A fixed annuity offers periodic payments over a fixed interval of time and then ceases to make further payments. Here we will discuss the valuation of fixed annuities.

One way to value an annuity is to take the promised payment at each point in time, discount it by its respective spot rate of interest, and then sum all of the discounted cash flows.

$$PV(A_N) = \frac{CF}{(1 + S_1)^1} + \frac{CF}{(1 + S_2)^2} + \frac{CF}{(1 + S_3)^3} + \cdots + \frac{CF}{(1 + S_N)^N}$$

where $PV(A_N)$ denotes the value of an N-year annuity and CF is the cash flow associated with the annuity's annual payment. In this regard, the valuation of the annuity is no different from the valuation of a fixed stream of cash flows or a coupon bond. The previous analysis can be applied in exactly the same fashion.

Another way to value an annuity is to return to our concept of the value of a consol. A consol can be broken down into two subsets: (1) an annuity extending from Time 0 to Time N, and (2) a deferred consol offering periodic payments equal to that of the annuity but extending from Time N until eternity. Now an N-year fixed annuity can be viewed as the first part of a regular consol, that part which remains after removing the deferred consol. Stated differently, an N-year fixed annuity is a consol with its distant payments removed. Since we already know that the value of a regular consol is equal to the periodic payment divided by the consol rate, the value of the deferred consol must be equal to the value of a regular consol reduced by the time value of money for the delay period.

$$PV(\text{Regular consol}) = \frac{CF}{y}$$

$$PV(\text{Deferred consol}) = \frac{PV(\text{Regular consol})}{(1 + y)^N}$$

Thus, the value of an annuity can be given by the difference between these two consols, as follows:

$$PV(\text{Annuity}) = PV(\text{Regular consol}) - PV(\text{Deferred consol})$$

$$= \frac{CF}{y} - \frac{CF \div y}{(1 + y)^N}$$

$$= CF\{[1 - 1/(1 + y)^N] \div y\}$$

The term in braces is known as an **annuity factor.** It is used to compute the value of a stream of level payments for N years, valued at an annuity rate of y.

This last point is worth discussing further. Given that the genesis of this formula is the difference between the value of two consols, the formula is applicable only if these two consols have the same consol rate, an extremely unlikely event. What makes this formula even more difficult to use for valuation purposes is that there are seldom any consols observable and tradable in the marketplace, much less two (one of which is deferred) that coincide exactly with the periodicity of the annuity in question. Notwithstanding these real-world circumstances, annuity factors are in common usage, but they should be interpreted more as an artifact (or by-product) of an annuity value than as a determinant of it. Moreover, they do provide at least a ballpark notion of values and rates of return.

Expected Returns, Realized Returns, and Yields

Before closing this chapter on valuing cash flows and deriving various versions of interest rates prevalent in the market, it is useful for us to point out the distinction between several notions of return in investors' minds. Investors in financial instruments make decisions based on the returns they expect to receive. Their wealth, on the other hand, is enhanced by the realized returns they actually receive on their investments. Thus, the distinction between expected and realized returns is central to the investment process.

The **expected rate of return** over a period of time is measured by taking the return you expect to get by the end of the period, dividing it by what you paid for the particular investment, and subtracting one. The **realized rate of return** over a period of time, often referred to as the **holding period return,** is measured by taking the return you actually received at the end of the holding period, dividing by what you paid for it, and subtracting one. This holding period return includes any earnings you may have received prior to the expiration of the holding period, accumulated at the prevailing interest rates until the end of the holding period.

Both of these concepts are different from the **current yield.** The current yield, which is a measure applied to coupon-bearing financial instruments, is the ratio of the (annualized) coupon on a financial instrument to its market price.[4] Further, all three of these concepts are different from the yield to maturity. We have previously defined yield to maturity as that discount rate that sets the price of a financial instrument equal to its promised cash flows.

We will illustrate the concepts of expected rate of return, holding period return, and current yield with two numerical examples. In the first example, interest rates follow the paths anticipated by the forward rate term structure. In the second example, interest rates diverge from that path. Consider a two-year annuity that pays $1,000 at the end of each of the ensuing two years. Suppose that the one-year spot rate is 8 percent, and the two-year spot rate is 10 percent. This implies that the second-year forward rate is 12.03704 percent.[5] The price of this annuity may be computed as

$$P_0 = \frac{\$1,000}{(1 + .08)} + \frac{\$1,000}{(1 + .08)(1 + .1203704)} = \$1,752.37$$

Assuming that interest rates follow the path specified in the forward rate term structure, let us now compute the one-year period holding period return. To compute this rate of return, we must first determine what the annuity will be worth at the end of the first period. To accomplish this, we simply take the remaining cash flow and discount it back to the end of the first period. This number is then added to the $1,000 cash flow received at the end of the first period to arrive at the total end-of-first-period value, P_1.

$$P_1 = \frac{\$1,000}{1.1203704} + \$1,000 = \$1,892.56$$

Taking this end-of-period value, dividing it by the price paid for the annuity, and subtracting 1.0, we now have the one-period holding period return:

$$\text{One-period holding return} = \frac{\$1,892.56}{\$1,752.37} - 1 = 8.0\%$$

Next, let us compute the holding period return over two periods. To get this number, we first determine the accumulated value we will have at the end of two periods. This value is determined by taking the first coupon, accumulating it at interest for one year, and then adding that product to the second coupon:

---

[4]For example, if a bond were currently selling at $932.09 and offered an annual coupon of $70, its current yield would be $70 ÷ $932.09 = 7.51%.

[5]As has been mentioned previously, the one-year spot rate and one-year forward rate are the same. The two-year spot rate is equal to $\sqrt{1.08 \times 1.1203704} - 1 = 10\%$.

$$($1,000 \times 1.1203704) + $1,000 = $2,120.37$$

Now, by taking this end-of-second-period value and dividing it by the price paid for the annuity, taking the square root of that quotient, and then subtracting 1.0, we get the two-period holding period return:

$$\sqrt{\frac{$2,120.37}{$1,752.37}} - 1 = 10.0\%$$

Therefore, the holding period returns for one and two periods for this annuity are 8 percent and 10 percent, respectively. As we expect no surprises in this example, these returns are presumably both expected and actual returns.

Now compare these yields with the yield to maturity of this two-year investment. We can calculate the yield to maturity that solves this equation:

$$$1,752.37 = \frac{$1,000}{(1 + y)} + \frac{$1,000}{(1 + y)^2} => y = 9.283405\%$$

In this case, the yield to maturity is lower than the two-year holding period return of 10 percent but higher than the one-year return. The YTM calculation implicitly assumes that the $1,000 first coupon can not be reinvested at the YTM rate. Our findings are summarized in Exhibit 6.4.

This exhibit shows that spot rates of interest are equal to expected returns; they are also equal to realized returns, provided that interest rates follow their anticipated path. It also shows that yield to maturity equals neither expected return nor realized return but lies somewhere between the one- and two-period spot rates.

Next, as a presage to the following chapter, we will let interest rates jump in a random fashion. In particular, at the end of the first period, we let the second-period interest rate go to 11 percent rather than the 12.03704 percent anticipated by the term structure. In this case, the end-of-first-period value of the annuity will be

$$P_1 = \frac{$1,000}{1.11} + $1,000 = $1,900.90$$

Thus, the realized first period return will be 8.48 percent:

$$\text{One-period holding period return} = \frac{$1,900.90}{$1,752.37} - 1 = 8.48\%$$

EXHIBIT 6.4   Understanding Different Return Concepts: Accurate Expectations

Period	Forward Rate	Spot Rate	Holding Period	Expected Return	Realized Return	Yield to Maturity
1	8.0%	8.0%	1 period	8.0%	8.0%	9.2834%
2	12.03704%	10.0%	2 periods	10.0%	10.0%	9.2834%

EXHIBIT 6.5   **Understanding Different Return Concepts: Unexpected Rate Movements**

Period	Forward Rate	Spot Rate	Holding Period	Expected Return	Realized Return	Yield to Maturity
1	8.0%	8.0%	1 period	8.0%	8.48%	9.2834%
2	12.03704%	10.0%	2 periods	10.0%	9.73%	9.2834%

and the two-period holding period return will be 9.73 percent:

$$(\$1,000 \times 1.11) + \$1,000 = \$2,110.00$$

$$\sqrt{\frac{\$2,110.00}{\$1,752.37}} - 1 = 9.73\%$$

Our findings for the case in which interest rates exhibit this random fluctuation are summarized in Exhibit 6.5. This table shows that spot rates of interest are equal to expected returns[6] but are no longer equal to realized returns, either for one- or two-period holding periods. As before, yield to maturity is equal to neither the expected nor the realized returns.

Our findings illustrate the differences between yield to maturity, expected return, and actual returns, and they spotlight the need to appreciate the differences among these concepts. Nonetheless, all of these concepts are in popular use, and it is important to understand their limitations in order to avoid making misleading representations and basing investment decisions on erroneous information. Such mistakes are all too common these days, however. As measures proliferate and computer-generated reports become more common than the trees they replace, it is easy for the investor to become numb and almost unaware of his or her return. (See Box 6.2.) More will be said about appropriate measures of return in subsequent chapters, and it will be shown that many do have valuable uses, as long as the investor understands their true meaning.

---

[6]The calculation is based on the expected end-of-first-period value, which, in turn, is based on the second-period forward rate. In the next chapter, we will show how a rich array of random interest rate fluctuations is related to the spot rate term structure of interest.

Box 6.2

Understanding Returns

Jim Getty can tell you about investment gauges such as beta, price-earnings multiples, and earnings growth rates. But ask Mr. Getty about his investments' performance last year, and he has only a hunch.

"My return? I would say it was around 15%," he says, "But that's really just a guess."

Not that the retired engineer from Fairborn, Ohio, doesn't care about his portfolio's performance. "I just wish I knew of a neat way to figure it out," he says.

Join the crowd. "If there's one thing people increasingly want to know, it's 'How am I doing?' " says Lee Gremillion, a partner at Price Waterhouse in Boston.

Investment returns are getting big play these days, as mutual-fund companies, brokerage firms, and the media shine a spotlight on stellar figures such as last year's 37.5% gain by the Standard & Poor's 500-stock index. Yet when it comes to the performance of their own portfolios, investors are in the dark.

"Most people don't really know how their portfolio is doing," says John Markese, president of the nonprofit American Association of Individual Investors in Chicago. "Some people think they're getting these great, high returns just because they are investing in stocks versus certificates of deposit. Others forget about withdrawals they've made during the year and think their performance is lousy."

Strategy Isn't Followed

There's a saying among some money managers: Investors don't earn the published investment returns. The performance of funds and market benchmarks assumes a strict buy-and-hold strategy that isn't followed by most people. These figures also assume you reinvested all dividends and income, and never bought or sold shares in any other way during the year.

"People often ask me, 'My fund did well last year, so why didn't I?' " says Karyn Vincent, a Price Waterhouse senior manager in Portland, Oregon. "They don't know there's a difference between the returns published in the newspaper and the returns they earn in a fund."

In the real world, timing also counts. Plunk down a big sum in your mutual fund when its share price is at a peak, and you may be out of pocket at the end of year, even though the fund's published performance indicates a gain for the past 12 months. Similarly, if you gradually bought shares of a surging fund or stock, instead of investing a lump sum at the start of the year, you won't do as well as the raw performance figures indicate.

Knowing your return can help you fine-tune your goals. If you earned 10% in 1995, but you were aiming for 15%, you can make up the difference by saving more this year. You might also want to alter your mix of investments.

Alternatively, suppose you invest in stocks because you believe they'll deliver the highest returns in the long run, yet the ups and downs of the stock market roil your stomach. If your portfolio roared ahead by 20% last year, instead of the 10% you were expecting, you can probably afford to cut back on your stock holdings and increase your exposure to more stable securities, such as short-term bonds.

It's Basic Math

Individual investors should nail down the performance of their portfolios at least once a year. All it really takes are those year-end summary account statements that brokerage firms and mutual-fund companies send out and about 15 minutes doing some basic math. But first, see if there's a shortcut.

If you work with a broker, ask him or her to tell you your return. Many have software that can quickly spit out your account's performance, though they often don't tell you how you did unless you ask.

Some brokerage firms are starting to promote this as a new service. Prudential Securities, Inc., a unit of Prudential Insurance Co. of America, for one, is listing its clients' 1995 performance on their year-end account statements. Other brokerage firms may soon begin to provide similar information.

If you manage your investments by yourself, though, you're on your own. General personal-finance software can do the math for you. But that doesn't mean you'll save time. Most programs require you to enter every transaction for each security you own—a tedious task if you reinvest dividends and fund distributions.

If you're dying to know your return before and after taxes or before and after fees, you can buy a more sophisticated portfolio-management program.

Personal computers aren't your thing?

No problem. Here's a quick way suggested by Mr. Markese to make a rough estimate of your return using simple arithmetic. It isn't perfect. For one thing, it assumes that any money you added to your account during the course of a year was invested for six months; if you add a big sum to your portfolio near the start or the end of the year, your result will be slightly off. But many investors will find the answer sufficiently close to serve as a useful reality check.

First, get out your year-end account statement and find the amount you added to or removed from your account during the year. Total the new money you put in and subtract any money you took out—including checks you received for dividends or interest. (Don't forget to include among the withdrawals any checks you wrote against bond-fund accounts). Divide this number by two.

Now add the result to the beginning value of your account and subtract it from your year-end value. Divide the new adjusted ending value by the adjusted starting value.

Confused? Consider the following example. Say you invested $200 a month, or $2,400 over the course of the year, in a stock-mutual fund for your child's future college tuition. The account, worth $15,368 on Jan. 1, grew to $19,627 by year-end.

How much did you make? Start by taking half of $2,400, or $1,200, and adding this number to your beginning balance of $15,368, giving you $16,568. Next, subtract the same number, $1,200, from the year-end balance of $19,627, leaving you with $18,427.

Finally, divide $18,427 by $16,568. Result? You should end up with 1.11. To turn the number into a percentage, simply subtract 1 and multiply by 100. So in the example above, you would get about 11%.

You can also use this method to figure the return on your entire portfolio, including any money-market funds.

You should check your investments' return once a year. There's always the chance you earned more than you thought. Ted Wojnar, for one, has been lucky. He was aiming for 15% last year, but was glad to learn he made 18%.

Source: Vanessa O'Connell, "How'ya Doing? Many Investors Don't Know," *The Wall Street Journal*, February 8, 1996. Reprinted by permission of *The Wall Street Journal*, © 1996 Dow Jones & Company, Inc. All Rights Reserved Worldwide.

Summary

This chapter introduces the basic tools of valuation—present value, future value, and annuity factors. It begins with a simple single cash flow problem to illustrate how present value, future value, and the interest rate are interconnected. Given a future cash flow and a market spot rate, the present value can be computed. Likewise, the future value of a given investment is easily computed with knowledge of the spot rate applicable to the investment.

Next, multiperiod cash flows are analyzed and valued. Using value additivity, a sequence of cash flows can be valued by adding the present values of the individual payments. We offer three distinct ways to calculate the total present value and show how yield to maturity can be computed.

Next we turn to consols and annuities. These instruments represent multiple-period cash flows of an extended duration, with a consol going on into perpetuity. Valuation techniques for these instruments are merely applications of the present value formula, but they do add increasing complexity to the process.

The chapter closes with a discussion of differing return concepts to alert the reader to the ambiguities associated with the concept of yield in the financial market. While each notion of return has some use, the uninitiated often confuse them and make unfortunate investment decisions as a result.

Key Concepts

annuities,   114
annuity factor,   116
consol,   111
current yield,   117
expected rate of return,   116
future value,   106

holding period rate of return,   116
life annuity versus fixed annuity,   114
present value,   106
realized rate of return,   116
value additivity,   107
yield to maturity,   109

Review Questions

1. Calculate the present value of the following cash flows:

Year	Cash Flow	Spot Rate
1	$ 400	4%
3	−150	4.7
4	600	4.9
7	1,250	5.8
10	−575	6.3

2. Calculate the five-year term structure of spot rates and forward rates for the following table of zero-coupon bonds:

Maturity	Price
1	$923.56
2	849.31
3	776.58
4	724.23
5	674.85

3. Using the price structure in Question 2, should you purchase a risk-free agreement that pays $125 at the end of Year 1, $1,500 at the end of Year 3, and $800 at the end of Year 4? The price of the agreement is $1,800.

4. What is the yield to maturity of the series of cash flows in Question 3 if the price of the agreement is $1,500?

5. A friend has just purchased a consol that pays $2,000 annually for a price of $16,000. How much should you pay for a 20-year annuity that offers the same annual payment?

6. If you are going to retire in 10 years, which of the following investments do you prefer?

   i) $1,000 invested today at a 5 percent annual yield.

   ii) $100 invested at the beginning of each year at 8 percent.

   iii) $150 invested at the beginning of each year at 9 percent for the first five years and 7 percent for the ensuing five years.

7. A company is going to hire you and offers you two compensation plans.

   Plan A: A signing bonus of $100,000 and an annual salary of $80,000.
   Plan B: An annual salary of $88,000 with no signing bonus.

If the current rate of interest is 6 percent and the yield curve is flat, how many years would you have to work for the company to prefer Plan B to Plan A assuming no pay increases? If the yield curve were upward sloping, how would you change your answer?

References

Brealey, Richard, and Stewart C. Myers. *Principles of Corporate Finance.* 5th ed. New York: McGraw Hill, 1996.

Kaufman, George. *The U.S. Financial System: Money, Markets and Institutions.* 5th ed. Englewood Cliffs, N.J.: Prentice Hall, 1992.

Mishkin, Frederic. *The Economics of Money, Banking and Financial Markets.* 2d ed. Glenview, Ill.: Scott Foresman, 1989.

Stigum, Marcia. *Money Market Calculations: Yields, Break Evens and Arbitrage.* Burr Ridge, Ill.: Irwin Professional Publishing, 1981.

Trainer, Richard D. *The Arithmetics of Interest Rates.* Federal Reserve Bank of New York, 1980.

Recognizing the Uncertainty of Future Interest Rates

Chapter Outline

Stochastic Interest Rate Valuation Models
    Continuous-Time Approaches to the Term Structure
    Simulation Approach
    Discrete-Time Lattice Models of the Term Structure
The Importance of Interest-Sensitive Cash Flows
Valuation of Interest-Sensitive Cash Flows

This chapter introduces the newer, more advanced techniques of valuation that have developed in financial markets over the past decade. The central feature of the analysis is the recognition that interest rates move in a random fashion over time. Therefore, there is a need to consider the effect of uncertainty of future interest rates in the valuation of various financial assets and in the cash flows that are connected with many financial instruments.

In Chapter 5, we introduced three models of the term structure of interest rates. These models were used to explain the relationship between interest rates of various maturities. In Chapter 6, we saw how spot rates and implied forward rates could be used in the valuation of fixed cash flows. These chapters had two important things in common. With slight exceptions, it was always assumed that interest rates were certain and that cash flows were fixed. In Chapter 5, we asked what the current term structure implied about future rates. In Chapter 6, we used these deterministic rates to value single and multiple fixed cash flows. Only at the end of this exercise did we recognize that interest rates might not behave as expected.

    Reality rarely unfolds as planned. Financial markets are buffeted by the winds of change, and such change is the rule, not the exception. Market

125

participants recognize this and have developed ways to analyze the effects of such random disturbances on the value of assets. In fact, they have recently developed tools, called **stochastic interest rate valuation models,** that discount future cash flows by sequences of random possible future interest rates. These modern valuation models come in two basic flavors: continuous-time and discrete-time models. Both focus mainly on how to value assets in an environment where interest rates change randomly over time and where cash flows are correlated with interest rates as they evolve over time.

After presenting these two approaches, we will discuss **interest-sensitive cash flows.** This is a situation in which the cash flows themselves depend on fluctuations in the level of interest rates. These two changes to the basic approach presented in the previous two chapters—taking into account random interest rates and interest-sensitive cash flows—significantly improve the ability of market participants to value various financial assets and understand their true inherent risks. And as we will see later in this chapter and throughout the remainder of this book, most financial instruments feature cash flows that in some way vary with fluctuating interest rates. Therefore, unless you want to get stuck in the dust of forever valuing only Treasury bonds, it is essential that you grasp the essence of the modern valuation models we will present here.

Stochastic Interest Rate Valuation Models

Given the importance and relevance of interest rate movements, it is rather surprising that models that account for the random nature of interest rates did not develop sooner. This is largely because methods of analysis that could accommodate the complexity of the stochastic nature of spot interest rates and the changes in the financial markets had to be developed. These advances occurred in financial theory over the past two decades and were quickly incorporated into the fixed income literature. Over time, two approaches were used to analyze the effect of interest rate uncertainty: continuous-time models and discrete-time models.

Continuous-Time Approaches to the Term Structure

Continuous-time approaches to the term structure look at time as a continuum; things are always happening. Therefore, during any moment in time, interest rates may be moving—sometimes as expected, sometimes not. These approaches to the term structure employ sophisticated mathematical tools, such as stochastic differential equations, to model the behavior of interest rates. The simplest continuous-time models are called single-factor models because they focus on a single source of uncertainty in the economy—movements in the short-term interest rate over time.

One such model is due to three financial economists, John Cox, Jonathan Ingersoll, and Stephen Ross (hereafter CIR). The CIR model begins with assumptions about investor preferences and unforecastable changes in the economy.

Then, through some elaborate mathematical and economic arguments, they derive the nature of movements in the term structure of interest rates.

Even the most elementary version of their model gives a reasonably accurate representation of interest rate movements over time. It specifies that movements in the short-term (sometimes referred to as instantaneous) spot rate of interest, r, follow a mean-reverting process, as described by the following stochastic differential equation:

$$dr = \kappa(\theta - r)dt + \sigma \sqrt{r}dz$$

Perhaps the best way to illustrate this rather curious looking mathematical expression is with an analogy. Suppose you were at your desk job and wanted to retreat to the water cooler, where an unofficial social gathering usually takes place during working hours. As you start toward the water cooler, you no sooner take a step than the boss spots your intention and kicks you in some random direction. You then recover your bearings and head again toward the water cooler, whereupon the boss again delivers a swift kick that is strong enough to relocate you in a random direction. The kicks vary not only in direction but also in force. Some of them hardly budge you at all, while others cause a substantial relocation. If this process were to repeat itself continuously and *ad infinitum*, not only would you have a sore backside, but there is no telling where you might end up.

In the stochastic differential equation, dr represents the movement in the short-term interest rate at each instant in time, analogous in our illustration to your relocation over time. Its movements are determined by the combination of two forces—a deterministic force and a stochastic force. The first right-hand-side expression, $\kappa(\theta - r)dt$, is the deterministic component of the formula and represents the general direction in which the short rate tends to drift, analogous to your movement toward the water cooler. The second right-hand-side expression, $\sigma\sqrt{r}dz$, is the stochastic component, analogous to the boss's kicks, producing continuous, random dislocations in the movements of the short-term interest rate as it attempts to drift in its desired direction.

Let us dissect these two right-hand-side expressions further to gain a better understanding of the nature of this interest rate process. The first, or **drift,** term has four components. θ is the long-run equilibrium rate of interest toward which the short-term spot rate reverts. (θ is analogous to the fixed location of the water cooler in our illustration.) The gap between its current and long-run equilibrium level is represented by $(\theta - r)$. (This is analogous to the distance between yourself and the water cooler in our illustration.) κ is a measure of the sense of urgency exhibited in financial markets to close the gap, and it gives the speed at which the gap is reduced, where the speed is expressed in annual terms. The higher the κ, the greater the urgency, or speed. (In our illustration, κ is a measure of the intensity of physical/social thirst.) dt represents a tiny increment in time. Because θ is, in a sense, a "mean" interest rate this formulation is sometimes referred to as a "mean reversion model."

To be concrete, suppose the long-run equilibrium rate of interest, θ, is 5 percent and the current short-term rate, r, is 9 percent. This represents a gap of

−4 percent. If κ is 0.5, that would indicate that the short rate is expected to drift downward, half of the way toward its long-run equilibrium level, within a year, thereby closing the remaining gap to 2 percent. If this deterministic process were to go on unimpeded, by the end of one year the short rate would be at 7 percent, and the remaining gap of 2 percent would again be lessened by one half, or to 1 percent, by the end of the second year. The process would continue until the drift ultimately brought the two rates into convergence. Note that the wider the gap, the larger the expected absolute movements in the short rate are toward closing the gap. If the gap is negative, the short rate should drift downward. If it is positive, the short rate should drift upward toward θ.

Except for one thing. Remember the random kicks? The second right-hand-side expression represents a stochastic, random element that also influences the trajectory of the short rate. You can think of the *dz* term as a **diffusion process,** much like the one that would be followed by molecules from a drop of perfume diffusing around from the center of a classroom until they permeated the entire classroom space. (Indeed, if we opened the classroom door and a back window a crack, the slow air movement would create a natural drift to the diffusion of perfume molecules, causing them to reach one side of the room before the other.) The increments to diffusion movements must be scaled so that they correspond to units appropriate for measuring interest rate movements. This is accomplished by multiplying *dz*, which is defined as having a standard deviation of one, by $\sigma \sqrt{r}$. In essence, the randomness is introduced as if random numbers were being drawn from a standard normal distribution, and then it is scaled by a factor that makes the "kick" correspond to the standard deviation of the interest rate process. σ is a partial measure of interest rate volatility and is assumed to be constant here. However, the full measure of volatility, $\sigma \sqrt{r}$, will depend upon the level of interest rates. For example, if *r* is high, then $\sigma \sqrt{r}$ will tend to deliver a larger "kick" than if *r* is low. This is a useful feature in modeling interest rates and also accords with historical observations about their behavior. Interest rates tend to be more volatile when they are high than when they are low, as demonstrated in Exhibit 7.1.

A side benefit from employing this formulation is that as interest rates get very low, the size of the "kicks" to the interest rate tends to become extremely small. Indeed, if the short rate were ever to hit 0 percent, the $\sigma \sqrt{r}$ "kick" would also be zero, and all of the movement in the short rate would be due to the first, or drift, component of the stochastic differential equation, forcing the interest rate upward from zero. This means that the CIR model will not allow interest rates to become negative, which is a very useful property of a system that purports to properly model interest rate behavior. As interest rates drift upward from zero, the stochastic "kick" term would again exert its influence. The influence could be substantial if interest rates get very high, because $\sigma \sqrt{r}$ would gain in value. However, at very high interest rates, the influence of the downward drift pressure would again begin to dominate the stochastic kick element, because the strength of the kick grows only proportional to $\sqrt{r}$, whereas the strength of the drift is related to *r* itself, which increases more rapidly than its square root. If this were

EXHIBIT 7.1

Interest rate volatility

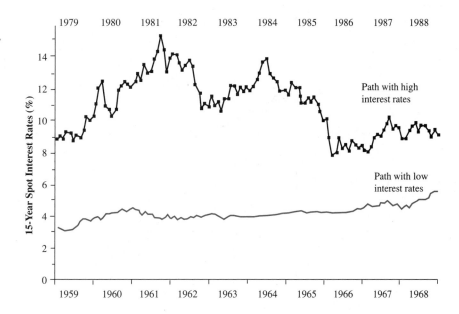

not the case, the interest rates could eventually explode to levels without bounds. Thus, this concise model of interest rate behavior has another desirable property that accords with observed behavior.

In general, the relative influence of the deterministic and stochastic components of the short-term interest rate depends on five parameters: the level of the short-term spot rate (which enters into both the deterministic and the stochastic components), the long-run mean interest rate level (which enters only into the deterministic component), the speed of mean reversion (which also enters only into the deterministic component), and the volatility scaling factor (which enters only into the stochastic component).

In Exhibit 7.2, we illustrate two possible interest rate paths that are consistent with this type of process. Initially, r is set at 9 percent, but it drifts toward θ, at 5 percent. The drift is continuously jarred by the stochastic term and thus may never cause the short-term rate to reach its equilibrium level. On the other hand, the second path shows how the interest rate may overshoot its mark and jump below θ, at which point the drift will tend to be positive. As r approaches θ, the drift term becomes very small, and its influence is easily overpowered by the stochastic term. The process creates an infinite number of these interest rate paths.

Other continuous-time processes have been suggested. Some alter the nature of the drift term, while others alter the stochastic term. For example, one model adds a liquidity preference term to the drift term, while another model changes the stochastic term to σr. Here, the level of interest rates is even more pronounced in determining the size of the "kicks."

Exhibit 7.2 .

*Cox-Ingersoll-Ross
model*

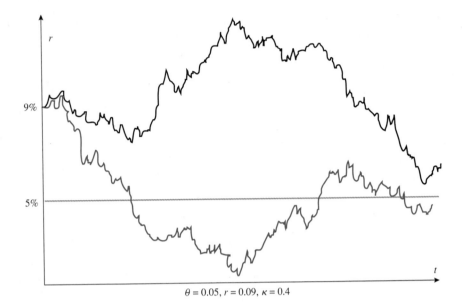

$\theta = 0.05$, $r = 0.09$, $\kappa = 0.4$

In addition, Michael Brennan and Eduardo Schwartz have introduced a popular model with added richness.[1] Their so-called **two-factor model** adds an additional element of realism, and it is able to better capture the intricate dynamics of interest rates and bond pricing. Like the previous model, Brennan and Schwartz have a short-term rate that is influenced by a deterministic and a stochastic component. The key difference is that the short-term rate reverts to the long-term rate, which itself follows a separate stochastic process that comes close to being completely random. Note that this long-term rate differs from the long-run equilibrium short rate used in the previous model. By using two factors, Brennan and Schwartz allow for different kinds of shifts in the term structure than are obtainable using one-factor models.

More elaborate three- and four-factor models have been built and are currently being used in practice. The third random factor is usually a measure of volatility. In other words, like the short-term and long-term interest rates, volatility is also allowed to follow a random process, where it tends to revert to a normal level of volatility over time but can stray from that level at any moment.[2] The

---

[1]This model was introduced in "A Continuous Time Approach to the Pricing of Bonds," *Journal of Banking and Finance*, July 1979, pp. 133–155, and has undergone various refinements since that time. A more thorough discussion of two-factor models is given in David F. Babbel and Craig B. Merrill, *Valuation of Interest-Sensitive Financial Instruments* (New Hope, Pa.: Frank J. Fabozzi Associates, 1996), chapters 6, 7, and 8.

[2]See, for example, Litterman, Scheinkman, and Weiss, "Volatility and the Yield Curve," *Financial Strategies*, Goldman Sachs, August 1988; and Litterman and Scheinkman, "Common Factors Affecting Bond Returns," *Financial Strategies*, Goldman Sachs, September 1988.

EXHIBIT 7.3   Sample Interest Rate Paths

Interest Rate Paths	1st-Year Single-Period Rate	2nd-Year Single-Period Rate	3rd-Year Single-Period Rate	4th-Year Single-Period Rate	5th-Year Single-Period Rate
Path 1:	8.00%	11.00%	13.00%	12.00%	10.10%
Path 2:	8.00	8.00	9.00	10.00	11.00
Path 3:	8.00	7.00	8.00	6.00	9.00
Path 4:	8.00	10.00	11.00	13.00	15.00
Path 5:	8.00	11.67	11.79	15.87	13.00
Simple Average	8.00%	9.53%	10.56%	11.37%	11.62%

fourth factor in these kinds of models is usually some measure of credit or default risk, which changes randomly over time. Sometimes the fourth factor is foreign exchange rates, which also fluctuate randomly over time.

One of the nicest features of the one-factor model is that it comes fully equipped with an explicit bond-pricing formula as well as the capability to estimate the term structure. While the formula is rather complex and will not be presented here, it is nonetheless useful to be able to price financial instruments with a single formula. Unfortunately, however, most of the continuous-time formulas need to be solved using discrete-time numerical methods, as they have no explicit or "closed-form" solutions. Nonetheless, the continuous-time models are valuable in providing the economic intuition that guides the development of their discrete-time analogs.

Simulation Approach

Simulation methods are employed to approximate the random paths posited in the continuous-time models by discrete-time random paths, usually by relying on monthly time intervals of interest rate observation. To see how these models are used in practice, consider the case of the five interest rate paths displayed in Exhibit 7.3, where our sampling interval is annual to facilitate the numerical exposition. Suppose that these five paths were randomly drawn from the infinite number of paths that could possibly be produced by a continuous-time model. Each path is a five-year sequence of potential single-year interest rates, where the sequence is read proceeding from left to right across each row. The five paths are depicted in graphical form in Exhibit 7.4.

These five paths were drawn from a whole set of possible interest rate paths that was consistent with the (spot rate) term structure given earlier in Exhibit 5.4, column two, and reproduced here for convenience. Here, the phrase "consistent with the term structure" means that if we were to discount cash flows occurring at various points in time by the paths of interest rates that could arise, we should get the same present values as would be achieved by computing the present values using the spot rates of interest.

Exhibit 7.4

*Simulating interest
rate paths*

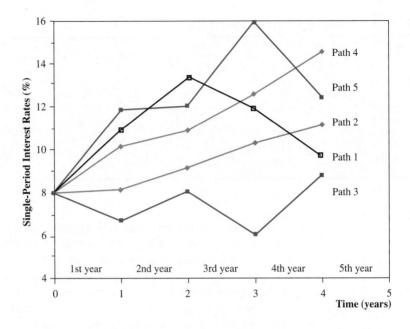

Interest Rates from Exhibit 5.4

Time Period (years)	Spot Rate Yield Curve (%)	Forward Rates of Interest (%)	Expected Future Single-Year Spot Rates of Interest (%)
0	7.00%		
1	8.00	8.0%	8.0%
2	8.75	9.5	9.5
3	9.33	10.5	10.5
4	9.79	11.2	11.2
5	10.13	11.5	11.5

To verify this claim, consider the following calculations of a single cash flow of $1,000 occurring five years into the future. First, we could compute its present value using the five-year spot rate of interest, which in this case is 10.13 percent.

$$PV = \$1,000 \div (1 + .1013)^5 = \$617.27$$

Alternatively, we could discount the $1,000 cash flow by our sample of possible interest rate paths. Using this procedure, we would compute five different values.

Path 1: $1,000 ÷ [(1.08)(1.11)(1.13)(1.12)(1.101)]   = $598.65
Path 2: $1,000 ÷ [(1.08)(1.08)(1.09)(1.10)(1.11)]   = $644.18
Path 3: $1,000 ÷ [(1.08)(1.07)(1.08)(1.06)(1.09)]   = $693.48
Path 4: $1,000 ÷ [(1.08)(1.10)(1.11)(1.13)(1.15)]   = $583.56
Path 5: $1,000 ÷ [(1.08)(1.1167)(1.1179)(1.1587)(1.13)] = $566.49

If each of these interest rate paths were drawn randomly from an accurate interest rate probability distribution, then each path would be equally likely to arise.[3] Therefore, we could sum the computed values and divide by the number of paths to get the present value.

$$PV = (\$598.65 + \$644.18 + \$693.48 + \$583.56 + \$566.49) \div 5 = \$617.27$$

To extract the five-year spot rate implicit in these interest rate paths, we take the future value of $1,000, divide it by the averaged present value of $617.27, take the fifth root, and subtract 1. Our result is 10.13 percent, which is exactly equal to the five-year spot rate given in the term structure.[4]

Next, let us see what information is contained in these interest rate paths regarding the four-year spot rate in the term structure. To extract the implicit four-year rate, we must consider a $1,000 payment that occurs one year sooner, at the end of the fourth year, and discount it by the first four single-year interest rates in each of the paths as follows:

Path 1: $1,000 $\div$ [(1.08)(1.11)(1.13)(1.12)]   = $659.11
Path 2: $1,000 $\div$ [(1.08)(1.08)(1.09)(1.10)]   = $715.04
Path 3: $1,000 $\div$ [(1.08)(1.07)(1.08)(1.06)]   = $755.90
Path 4: $1,000 $\div$ [(1.08)(1.10)(1.11)(1.13)]   = $671.09
Path 5: $1,000 $\div$ [(1.08)(1.1167)(1.1179)(1.1587)] = $640.13

Summing these possible values and dividing by the number of interest rate paths gives us $688.25. To obtain the four-year spot rate implicit in these interest rate paths, we take the future value of $1,000, divide it by the averaged present value of $688.25, take the fourth root, and subtract 1. Our result is 9.79 percent, which also is exactly equal to the four-year spot rate given in the term structure.

Similarly, we could compute the one-year, two-year, and three-year spot rates of interest implied by these interest rate paths. The final result of our efforts would be a term structure identical to that appearing in Exhibit 7.5. Note that this is exactly the same term structure of spot rates that was developed using the pure expectations, liquidity preference, and preferred habitat theories. (The reader may wish to verify our claim by computing these omitted spot rates using the five sample interest rate paths.) If our paths are based on an interest rate distribution consistent with the term structure of interest, and if we sample a sufficiently large number of paths, we should obtain a congruence between our path-driven spot

---

[3]The short rates in the paths were actually derived so that we would achieve perfect congruence with the spot rate yield curve with such a limited number of paths. A detailed description and numerical example of how to implement an interest rate simulation model in practice is given in Babbel and Merrill, *op. cit.*, chapter 8.

[4]This procedure of equal weighting also assumes risk neutrality, or a market price of risk of zero. These are areas of complexity that are beyond the scope of this textbook. A useful discussion is given in John Hull, *Options, Futures, and other Derivative Securities*, 2d ed. (Englewood Cliffs, N.J.: Prentice Hall, 1995), chapter 10; and in Babbel and Merrill, *op. cit.*, chapter 3.

Exhibit 7.5

Hypothetical term structure

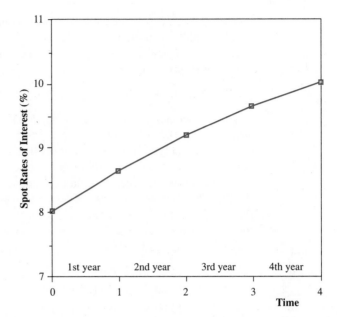

rate calculations and those obtained more directly from analyzing the values of zero-coupon bonds.[5]

In practice, Wall Street firms and other financial institutions usually sample 500 to 10,000 interest rate paths before they begin averaging discounted cash flows to obtain present values. Supercomputers and other specialized, high-speed computers are often used to enable them to make these calculations on a timely basis. The large number of paths is used to assure proper convergence to the rates of interest implicit in the term structure.

If going through this elaborate procedure of discounting cash flows by interest rate paths winds up with the same numbers obtained from the simpler procedure of computing the term structure based on zero-coupon bond prices, then why expend so much effort? The reason is that while both procedures provide similar spot rates of interest, these spot rates of interest can be used to value only cash flows whose timing and amounts are certain. Many—indeed, most—of the instruments traded in the capital market feature cash flows whose amounts and/or timing are somehow dependent on interest rate levels or paths. In such cases, we must resort to these stochastic interest rate valuation models to accurately determine fair value. Another kind of stochastic interest rate model that is often used in practice to value modern securities is called a discrete-time lattice model. This is the subject to which we now turn.

---

[5]It is no coincidence that we were able to obtain exact convergence using only five interest rate paths. Our example was "cooked." Usually, it takes many hundreds of paths before such convergence is achieved.

Discrete-Time Lattice Models of the Term Structure

Discrete-time models of the term structure of interest rates begin with a view of time that assumes that we can observe time as passing in well-defined units, such as one-hour intervals, monthly or annual intervals, or time between weekends! The techniques focus on how interest rates jump between observation points at the beginning or end of these discrete intervals of time. These models are sometimes called **lattice models.** They derive the name "lattice" because the jumps that interest rates follow are usually diagrammed on a lattice-like graph. The discrete-time intervals in these models are most often a month long, at least in practice, although any time interval is possible.

The simplest lattice models assume that interest rates move only because of a single factor, such as jumps in the short-term nominal or real interest rate. Other lattice models have two factors causing market interest rates to change. The second factor may be movements in long-term interest rates or inflation, changes in interest rate volatility, or perceived changes in default or liquidity risk.

We illustrate some of the features of these models here by introducing a popular one-factor lattice model developed by Fischer Black, Emanuel Derman, and William Toy.[6] For simplicity of exposition, we will assume time intervals of one year. The model is illustrated using the vehicle known as a **binomial tree,** or lattice. Discrete points in time are marked on the horizontal axis. The levels of current and possible future single-period interest rates are identified at each **node,** where the binomial tree forms two new branches. At each node in time, interest rates are assumed to change, either by jumping upward or downward. Assume for simplicity that jumps upward or downward are equally likely.

For example, suppose the current (at time 0) one-year spot rate is 8.0 percent but that next year it will change either to 11.41377 percent or to 7.65088 percent. If interest rates jump upward to 11.41377 percent, they could jump up to 14.96267 percent or down to 10.23239 percent the following year. However, if interest rates initially decline to 7.65088 percent, they could jump up to 10.23239 percent or down to 6.99754 percent by the start of the third period (time 2). Note how two of the branches converge to form a single node at time 2. This jumping process would continue year-by-year. Exhibit 7.6 shows the process for the first five years.

Based on our past exposition patterns, you may suspect that the jumps we have chosen were not wholly arbitrary. This suspicion is entirely correct. The Black-Derman-Toy model was carefully tuned so that jump amounts for each period would be consistent with the hypothetical spot rate term structure we have been employing throughout the previous two chapters, combined with some reasonable assumptions about the variability, or volatilities, of spot rates of interest for differing maturities. By construction, we allowed our future single-period rates, the "short rates," to have values that implied the forward rate in our example. The

---

[6]See Fischer Black, Emanuel Derman, and William Toy, "A One-Factor Model of Interest Rates and Its Application to Treasury Bond Options," *Financial Analysts Journal,* January/February 1990, pp. 33–39.

EXHIBIT 7.6

The lattice approach

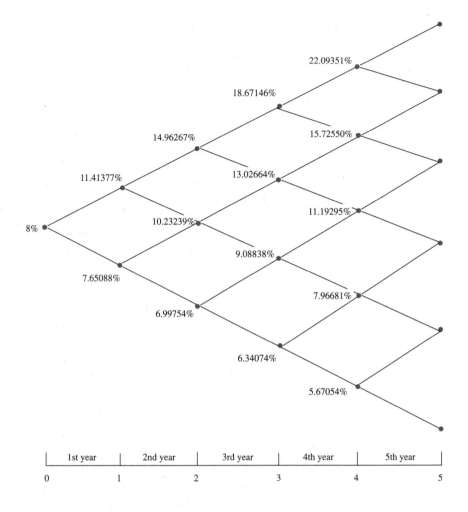

1st year	2nd year	3rd year	4th year	5th year

0　　　　　1　　　　　2　　　　　3　　　　　4　　　　　5

range over which the short rates can differ will depend on our view of how volatile rates will be in the future.[7] Here, for example, we assume that the variation in the second-year short rates will allow for a 20 percent variability in outcomes.[8]

　　To show this consistency, we will again enlist the concept of a zero-coupon Treasury bond. We will try again to match the spot rate term structure of interest

[7]The real science in these lattice models is in how to get the jumps to be consistent with currently observed market interest rates and security prices. As our purpose here is only to show that the binomial interest rate process we have chosen is indeed consistent with our hypothetical term structure of interest, our discussion will not dwell on this issue. See Black, Derman, and Toy, *op. cit.;* and John Hull and Alan White, "One-Factor Interest Rate Models and the Valuation of Interest-Rate Derivative Securities," faculty of management working paper, University of Toronto, November 1990.

[8]The volatilities assumed for the first-, second-, third-, fourth-, and fifth-year short rates of interest were 22 percent, 20 percent, 19 percent, 18 percent, and 17 percent, respectively.

used in Chapter 5 illustrations. Our binomial process starts with the assumed one-year spot rate of interest of 8 percent, which is consistent with that given by the hypothetical spot rate yield curve we have been using. In one year, however, rates will be either 7.65088 percent or 11.41377 percent with equal likelihood.

What effect will this interest rate uncertainty have on the value of a two-year zero-coupon bond and its two-period yield? The investor will receive $1,000 at maturity whether interest rates go up or down. However, its value will differ at the end of the first year, depending upon which path interest rates actually follow. Because we know the potential spot interest rates that can occur, we can discount the future cash flow by the sequences of current and potential single-year spot rates that are given in the lattice to arrive at a set of potential values at the end of two years. As there are two paths possible, we would discount the final payment of $1,000 by the interest rate sequences associated with each path. The first path that interest rates could follow in our model would be an upward jump to 11.41377 percent, and the second path would be a downward jump to 7.65088 percent. Discounting the future cash flow by the appropriate possible short rates along each path, we would then have:

First path (upward jump): $1,000 ÷ [(1.08)(1.1141377)]   = $831.07
Second path (downward jump): $1,000 ÷ [(1.08)(1.0765088)] = $860.12

Since the paths are equally likely, we can weight the possible present values equally to get the expected market value of the bond. Given that investors can compute this value as easily as we can, this must be the market price of the two-year zero-coupon bond.

$$(0.5 \times \$831.07) + (0.5 \times \$860.12) = \$845.60$$

We now have sufficient information to compute the two-year spot rate of interest implied by this lattice structure by deriving the return over the two periods from the price as we did in previous chapters.

$$\sqrt{\$1,000 \div \$845.60} - 1 = 8.75\%$$

This same approach can be extended to consider a three-year zero-coupon bond. We again must discount the $1,000 payment by the interest rate sequences associated with each possible path in the lattice. We would then have:

First path (up, up): $1,000 ÷ [(1.08)(1.1141377)(1.1496267)]   = $722.90
Second path (up, down): $1,000 ÷ [(1.08)(1.1141377)(1.1023239)]   = $753.93
Third path (down, up): $1,000 ÷ [(1.08)(1.0765088)(1.1023239)]   = $780.28
Fourth path (down, down): $1,000 ÷ [(1.08)(1.0765088)(1.0699754)] = $803.87

These choices of potential third-period short rates are driven by assumed volatility for that period. Again, the paths are equally likely, so we must weigh the possible present values equally to get the market price of the three-year zero-coupon bond.

$$(.25 \times \$722.90) + (.25 \times \$753.93) + (.25 \times \$780.28) + (.25 \times \$803.87) = \$765.25$$

This gives us sufficient information to compute the three-year spot rate of interest implicit in our lattice.

$$\sqrt[3]{\$1,000 \div \$765.25} - 1 = 9.33\%$$

Note that these first three spot rates of interest, 8.0 percent, 8.75 percent, and 9.33 percent, exactly correspond with those in our hypothetical term structure. The same procedure could be used to confirm that the four-year and five-year spot rates implicit in our lattice are 9.79 percent and 10.13 percent, respectively, which also conform to the rates given in our hypothetical term structure.

One of the features of lattice models that is highly desirable is that at each node there is an entire implicit term structure of interest. To verify this, note that we have derived an entire term structure of interest at time 0 by going through the simple procedure of discounting zero-coupon bonds by the various paths that interest rates can follow in the lattice structure, beginning with the node at time 0. From each node in the future, similar types of interest rate paths emanate right-ward. That means we should be able to follow the same simple procedure and derive implied yield curves at those nodes as well. Thus, a lattice model includes a potential term structure of interest rates at each node in the future. This feature is especially useful when attempting to place an economic value on securities whose cash flows depend, in some way, on what the future term structure may be. This will be further discussed later in the chapter.

While we have introduced the lattice approach using a popular one-factor model, there are many details that we will not discuss. Suffice it to say that a plethora of models has been developed, with single or multiple factors, and they have achieved a great deal of success in helping market participants determine what simple and complicated securities should be worth. Our presentation was deceptively simple in some ways. Yet that should not be taken as an indication that the models are without economic rigor. On the contrary, much thought and careful crafting have gone into the development of lattice models, and many are compatible with the most demanding of economic principles. Additionally, recent advances in computer technology have facilitated their use on the trading floors, as well as in the more sedate environs of academia. The most important use of these models is in the valuation of financial instruments with interest-sensitive cash flows, which is our next topic.

The Importance of Interest-Sensitive Cash Flows

Up to this point, it has been assumed that the cash flows from the bond or other financial asset were fixed and invariant to the changes in interest rates. Whether interest rates unexpectedly moved up or down was a matter of no consequence to the cash flows. Such variations affected the valuation of the bond, and the uncertainty of interest rates required additional techniques, but cash flows were not part of the discussion. Unfortunately, the world is not that simple.

Many financial instruments have **interest-sensitive cash flows.** By "interest-sensitive" we mean that the amounts and/or timing of the cash flows are related to interest rates. They may be related either contemporaneously or with a lead or lag. They may exhibit high, low, or even negative correlations with interest rates. But unless the correlations are zero, they are categorized as "interest-sensitive." This simple observation has far-reaching implications with regard to appropriate valuation technology.

To give some examples of financial instruments with interest-sensitive cash flows, consider first common stocks, particularly those of utilities and the financial sector. In fact, most companies will have some relationship between their cash flows and the rate of interest. For utilities, public regulatory agencies assure this correlation by granting rate increases in part because of a higher cost of debt. On the other hand, financial firms with assets that are longer term than their liabilities often find a negative correlation between market yields and their own net cash flow. In general, some relationship between firm cash flows and the level of interest rates is to be expected.

Bonds, too, have cash flows that change with the level of rates. Virtually all bonds other than Treasuries exhibit interest-sensitive cash flows. In some cases, this is by design, as in the case of **floating-rate instruments,** for example. The interest payments on floating-rate notes fluctuate (or float) in a prespecified way with other interest rates in the economy. The higher the market rate of interest during a given time period (e.g., month, quarter, year), the higher the interest rate payable on the floating-rate note. Other instruments have cash flows that may vary with market rates at the discretion of the issuer. **Callable** corporate and municipal bonds exhibit such interest-sensitive cash flows. They are referred to as "callable" because the issuing entity can call the bonds back from investors by paying to them the face value plus a modest, prespecified premium. Issuers of these bonds are most likely to take advantage of this callability provision when interest rates have declined, allowing the issuers to raise funds at the new, lower rates of interest. Thus, the timing of repayment of principal will be accelerated if interest rates decline enough to make it attractive for the issuer to do so. Even on noncallable corporate bonds, the actual payments received may be interest-sensitive if the probability of default is linked to market rates.[9]

Consider home mortgages. When mortgage rates decline, homeowners with older mortgages often refinance their homes by obtaining a mortgage at the new, lower interest rates. They use the funds obtained to prepay and retire the outstanding principal remaining on their old mortgages. The new mortgage will allow them to make lower monthly mortgage payments on their homes.

While we could belabor the point with other examples, we will leave their discussion to later chapters. Suffice it to say that many, and perhaps most, financial instruments traded in today's marketplace have interest-sensitive cash flows.

---

[9]See Anthony Santomero, "Fixed versus Variable Rate Loans," *Journal of Finance*, December 1983.

Accordingly, the valuation of financial assets in a world where interest rates are uncertain must recognize the fact that the cash flows themselves vary with the uncertain interest rates.

Valuation of Interest-Sensitive Cash Flows

The earlier financial models attempted to derive present values by discounting expected cash flows by spot or forward interest rates implicit in the prevailing yield curve. This is consistent with the way things have been done in financial markets for a long time. However, approximately three decades ago, Nobel laureates Kenneth Arrow and Gerard Debreu suggested a relationship between the cash payment and the "state of nature" in which the economy or the economic agent found itself. Arrow and Debreu also indicated that the value of a given cash stream may be related to this same state of the economy. For example, a given amount of cash to be received in the future would be worth far less, in terms of purchasing power, if it were received after an inflationary bout (i.e., post-inflationary state of nature) than it would be worth in a deflationary environment. Moreover, the cash flow itself may be reduced because of this same economic distrubance that caused the inflationary cycle. Their paradigm, the **state preference theory,** has served as the foundation from which much of modern valuation technology has evolved.

An application of the state preference theory is provided in Exhibit 7.7 as a continuation of our inflationary example. The top half of the exhibit portrays a riskless investment that returns $100 regardless of which state of nature transpires. The value of the dollar, the discount factor, depends, however, on whether it is received in state 1 or state 2. If it is received in state 1, it is worth 70 cents, but if it is received in state 2, it is worth 98 cents. This state-dependent value may simply be a reflection of the dollar's purchasing power in each state, or it may be the result of a combination of factors. By taking into consideration the payoff in each state, the value per dollar of payoff in each state, and the probability of each state transpiring (note here that we have assumed a 40 percent probability for state 1 and a 60 percent probability for state 2), we can calculate that the riskless investment is worth $86.80.

The lower half of Exhibit 7.7 shows the value of a risky investment whose nominal returns depend on what state of nature actually emerges. In the top panel, the cash flow was constant at $100. But in the lower panel, if state 1 occurs, $70 is received; if state 2 occurs, $120 is received. After factoring in the probabilities of the states occurring, we find that the expected nominal return on this investment is $100, which is equal to the certain return provided by the riskless investment. However, note that its present value is $90.16, which is higher than that of the riskless investment. This higher value may appear counterintuitive at first, as we traditionally associate lower values (and higher discount rates) with risky investments. However, an examination of the patterns of cash flows reveals the reason

EXHIBIT 7.7   An Example of State Preference Theory

Value of a Riskless Investment

State (i)	Return (CFi)	Probability of State(Ps)	(CFi × Ps)	Value of $1 in Alternative States (Ys)	CFi × Ps × Ys
1	$100	0.4	$ 40	0.70	$28.00
2	$100	0.6	$ 60	0.98	58.80
			$100		$86.80

Value of a Risky Investment

State (i)	Return (CFi)	Probability of State(Ps)	(CFi × Ps)	Value of $1 in Alternative States (Ys)	CFi × Ps × Ys
1	$70	0.4	$ 28	0.70	$19.60
2	$120	0.6	$ 72	0.98	70.56
			$100		$90.16

for our result. Notice that the riskier investment provides relatively more of its payoff in state 2, where money is valued more highly.

More recent models of valuation have relied on relationships analogous to the state-dependent discount rates of the Arrow-Debreu model. The pricing models outlined earlier in this chapter approach the valuation of a cash flow by discounting it with the series of interest rates that could occur in the future. In essence, the continuous- and discrete-time models were simple versions of the state preference approach.[10] In those cases, cash flows were assumed to be independent of interest rate paths. As noted, the same value could also have been derived by simply discounting the cash flow by a factor reflecting the appropriate average spot rate from the term structure of interest. However, this will only be the case when cash flows are independent of the path of future rates. When cash flows change with rates, the correspondence ceases to be valid. A series of stylized examples will illustrate in a simplified, yet concrete, way why this is the case. They will form a basis from which we can illustrate some more general issues relative to the valuation of interest-sensitive cash flows.

For our first example refer to Exhibit 7.8. In this case, the one-year interest rate (one-year spot rate) is 8.0 percent. Next year, the interest rates will change from their 8 percent level to either 12 percent or 4 percent, with equal

---

[10]There are actually several models that are variations on this theme. Some are quite complicated. Our purpose here is only to discuss the general approach at an intuitive level. A more thorough treatment is available in John Hull, *Valuation of Options and Derivative Securities* (Englewood Cliffs, N.J.: Prentice Hall, 1990).

EXHIBIT 7.8

*Discounting by
interest rate paths*

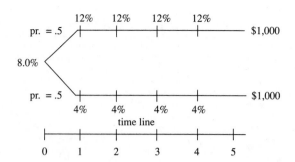

Question: What would a five-year zero-coupon bond be worth if
interest rates were to follow these kinds of paths?

$$1,000 \div \{(1.08)(1.12)(1.12)(1.12)(1.12)\} = \$588.44$$

$$1,000 \div \{(1.08)(1.04)(1.04)(1.04)(1.04)\} = \$791.49$$

$$(588.44 \times 0.5) + (791.49 \times 0.5) = \underline{\$689.96}$$

The five-year spot rate of interest would be:

$$\sqrt[5]{1,000 \div 689.96} - 1 = \underline{7.7047\%}$$

probability,[11] and they will remain at the new level throughout the remainder of
the five-year period. Suppose further that we would like to value a zero-coupon
Treasury that pays $1,000 at the end of five years and that this value is fixed and
independent of interest rates.

Modern valuation theory and practice would have us take the $1,000 future
payment and discount it by each sequence of single-period interest rates that could
prevail in the future. We call this **discounting by interest rate paths.** Under the
simplified assumptions in this case, we would discount the $1,000 by the 8 percent
and then by either the sequence of four 12 percent rates or the sequence of four
4 percent rates. Weighing the resultant path-dependent present values across the
two states will then give us the appropriate market value—$689.96 in this case. To
determine the five-year spot rate of interest, we follow the same procedures described earlier in this chapter. We simply take the promised value at maturity, divide
it by the appropriate market value just calculated, take the fifth root, and subtract 1.
Our resulting spot rate is 7.7047 percent.

We could proceed similarly to compute the value of a four-year zero-coupon
investment and the four-year spot rate of interest. To accomplish this, assume that
the $1,000 payment is received at the end of four years rather than five years. All
other conditions are as before (see Exhibit 7.9). We then discount the $1,000 by
the two somewhat shorter interest rate sequences and average the path-dependent
present values, as before, to get the market value. Then, taking the fourth root of

---

[11]The technical term used in these approaches to valuation is "risk-neutral probabilities." See
Pedersen, Shiu, and Thorlacius, "Arbitrage-Free Pricing of Interest Rate-Contingent Claims,"
Transactions of the Society of Actuaries, 1990.

EXHIBIT 7.9

Determining implied spot rates

Question: What would the entire term structure of interest rates look like under these volatility conditions?

Answer: Since we have already computed the five-year rate, we simply follow the same procedure, except that we assume the $1,000 final payment occurs earlier than the fifth year.

If the payment were to be received in four years, its market value would be computed as follows:

$$\$1,000 \div \{(1.08)(1.12)(1.12)(1.12)\} = \$659.06$$
$$\$1,000 \div \{(1.08)(1.04)(1.04)(1.04)\} = \$823.14$$
$$(659.06 \times 0.5) + (823.14 \times 0.5) = \underline{\$741.10}$$

The four-year spot rate of interest would be:

$$\sqrt[4]{1,000 \div 741.10} - 1 = \underline{7.7782\%}$$

the maturity value divided by the market value and subtracting 1, we derive the four-year spot rate.

The same process can be used to derive the entire term structure of interest (see Exhibit 7.10). Notice that the term structure is downward sloping. This is explained by the asymmetry in value changes produced by equal but opposite changes in interest rates. A decrease in interest rates produces a greater increase in value than the loss produced from an equivalent increase in interest rates. Averaging these prices together results in a higher mean value than that associated with no move in interest rates; consequently, the spot rates of interest are lower.

Note that one would obtain the same market prices for the zero-coupon bonds by estimating their value using either of two methods: (1) discounting cash flows by spot rates of interest, or (2) discounting cash flows by sequences of single-period interest rates along all interest rate paths (in this case, two paths) and averaging the resultant path-dependent present values. While the first method seems to be far simpler, the second method can actually be used under many more circumstances. In particular, this second method is adept at estimating market values of financial instruments whose cash flows exhibit interest sensitivity.

To see this, consider a situation similar to that described earlier, except that the actual size of the cash flow five years hence is dependent on the future interest rate level. If interest rates go to 12 percent, the payment is $1,500. If rates go to 4 percent, the payment is $500. (See Exhibit 7.11.) The chances of interest rates going up or down are, again, equal. Even though the expected cash flow ($1,000) is the same as that in Exhibit 7.8, and the interest rate paths and path probabilities are identical to those specified earlier, the market value of the interest-sensitive zero-coupon bond is $639.20. This is quite a bit lower than the $689.20 computed earlier. This is because the payment on the bond is contingent upon the level of interest rates. It is, as economists would say, a **state-contingent claim** or payoff.

It would be erroneous to compute the value of such an interest-sensitive investment by discounting its expected cash flow using the five-year spot rate of interest. The error in this case would be 7.94 percent in magnitude. However, having determined the appropriate price, we could compute its yield to maturity by dividing

EXHIBIT 7.10

Eliciting the term structure from prices

Continuing in a similar pattern, we would compute the entire term structure to be:

Five-year spot rate = 7.7047%
Four-year spot rate = 7.7782%
Three-year spot rate = 7.8519%
Two-year spot rate = 7.9259%
One-year spot rate = 8.0000%

Term Structure of Interest Rates

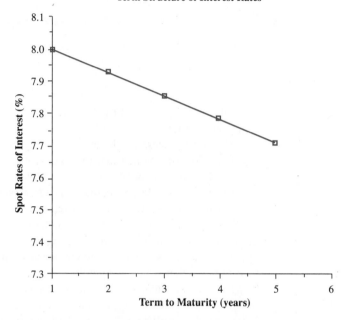

the final expected value ($1,000) by the market price ($639.20), taking the fifth root, and subtracting 1. The resulting yield to maturity would be 9.3634 percent.

Now, let's reverse the pattern of the cash flows so that the smaller payment is received if interest rates go up and the larger payment is received if they go down. (See Exhibit 7.12 on page 146.) Proceeding as before, we would estimate market value to be $740.72 and YTM to be 6.1863 percent. The estimated market value in this case, $740.72, is 7.36 percent higher than would have been estimated had we mistakenly used the five-year spot rate of interest to discount the expected cash flow of $1,000.

Notice how the two interest-sensitive zero-coupon bonds have such disparate YTMs (6.1863 percent versus 9.3634 percent) and wide-ranging market values, even though both have the same expected cash flow of $1,000 and both are valued using identical interest rate paths. The yield spread from highest to lowest is 318 basis points, and the value difference is $101.52, or 16 percent! This disparity should reinforce how dubious the common practices are of focusing on yields to maturity in comparing the attractiveness of investments and of using yields, spot rates, or forward rates of interest to value interest-sensitive cash flows.

EXHIBIT 7.11

Valuing interest-sensitive cash flows by interest rate paths

What if cash flow amounts are related to future interest rate levels?

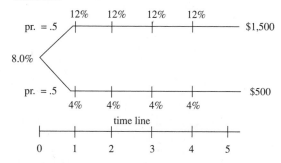

Question: What would a five-year contingent claim be worth if interest rates were to follow this kind of path?

$$1{,}500 \div \{(1.08)(1.12)(1.12)(1.12)(1.12)\} = \$882.66$$

$$500 \div \{(1.08)(1.04)(1.04)(1.04)(1.04)\} = \$395.74$$

$$(882.66 \times 0.5) + (395.74 \times 0.5) = \underline{\$639.20}$$

$$639.20 \neq 689.96 \text{ (Error is 7.94\%)}$$

The five-year implied yield would be:

$$\sqrt[5]{1{,}000 \div 639.20} - 1 = 9.3634\%$$

Having demonstrated the impact of interest sensitivity of cash flows on yields, we can go on to investigate the effect of interest rate volatility on yields. To do so, suppose we hold the maturity value at $1,000, regardless of interest rate paths. Suppose, however, that we decrease our volatility estimate by one-half. Thus, future interest rates will go either up to 10 percent or down to 6 percent, as shown in Exhibit 7.13 on page 147. Expected future interest rates remain at 8 percent. Under these circumstances, a five-year zero-coupon bond would be worth $682.92, and the five-year spot rate of interest would be 7.926 percent.

Proceeding as before, we can derive the entire term structure of interest. The results of this exercise are given in Exhibit 7.14 on page 148. Note that the lower volatility results in higher spot rates of interest along the entire term structure. This finding is consistent with the asymmetry of discounting, which was discussed earlier. However, increased volatility cannot always be assumed to lower yields, as it did with the simple "additive" interest rate process assumed above. (It is called additive because a positive or negative number of basis points is added to the initial interest rate to characterize subsequent rates.) The impact of volatility on yields will depend upon the nature of the stochastic interest rate process.[12]

---

[12]By experimenting with different starting short-term interest rates and assuming different volatilities, we can generate a whole set of possible term structure shapes and then select the one that best fits the one given by actual zero-coupon bond prices. To get better fits, economists sometimes include more parameters (e.g., nonconstant volatility, mean reversion of interest rates)

EXHIBIT 7.12

Reversing the cash flow pattern

Now, let's reverse the cash flow pattern, while maintaining the same expected value.

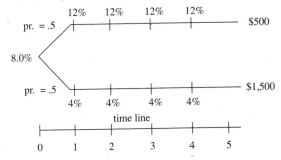

Question: What would a five-year contingent claim be worth if interest rates and cash flows were to follow this kind of pattern?

$$500 \div \{(1.08)(1.12)(1.12)(1.12)(1.12)\} = \ \$294.22$$
$$1,500 \div \{(1.08)(1.04)(1.04)(1.04)(1.04)\} = \$1,187.23$$
$$(294.22 \times 0.5) + (1,187.23 \times 0.5) = \ \underline{\$740.72}$$
$$740.72 \neq 689.96 \ (\text{Error is } 7.36\%)$$

The five-year implied yield would be:

$$\sqrt[5]{1,000 \div 740.72} - 1 = 6.1863\%$$

The preceding discussion and exhibits illustrate several important features of modern approaches to the valuation of financial assets. Our purpose here was not to derive these verities in any rigorous fashion[13] but rather to reveal them in an intuitive way and demonstrate their importance. The bottom line in the modern approaches to valuation is that interest-sensitive cash flows should be discounted by the sequences of single-period interest rates that could give rise to them, and that the resulting present values should be weighted according to the likelihood of a particular interest rate path materializing. This is true whether the size and/or timing of the flows is linked to short-term or long-term interest rates, volatility, or some other factor related to interest rates. Moreover, it doesn't hurt to apply these same approaches to the valuation of instruments whose cash flows are independent of interest rates, such as noncallable Treasury bonds. Indeed, the prices implied by the models should be just as good as those achieved by discounting the

and additional factors. But the point of this exercise is to produce a set of stochastic interest rate paths that is consistent with observable prices of highly liquid securities, and then to apply the technology to obtain prices and behavior of other assets or liabilities. Numerical procedures for implementing these kinds of models are provided by John Hull and Alan White, "Numerical Procedures for Implementing Term Structure Models" parts I and II, *Journal of Derivatives,* Fall 1994, Winter 1994. They are also described in Babbel and Merrill, *op. cit.,* chapter 5.

[13]An excellent, rigorous treatment and useful bibliography of this topic is given by Pedersen, Shiu, and Thorlacius, *op. cit.*

Exhibit 7.13

Changing volatility

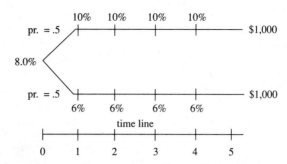

Question: What would a five-year zero-coupon bond be worth if interest rates were to follow these kinds of paths?

$$1,000 \div \{(1.08)(1.10)(1.10)(1.10)(1.10)\} = \$632.42$$
$$1,000 \div \{(1.08)(1.06)(1.06)(1.06)(1.06)\} = \$733.42$$
$$(632.42 \times 0.5) + (733.42 \times 0.5) = \underline{\$682.92}$$

The five-year spot rate of interest would be:

$$\sqrt[5]{1,000 \div 682.92} - 1 = \underline{7.9260\%}$$

cash flows with spot rates of interest. This feature often serves an important checkpoint in setting up models of stochastic interest rates.

We may say with some confidence that the stochastic interest rate models that are now the norm on Wall Street for valuation have produced significant insights into the pricing and behavior of assets and liabilities with interest-sensitive components. It is not an overstatement to say that it would be foolish in today's competitive environment for a financial institution to issue interest-sensitive liabilities or to invest in interest-sensitive assets without having gained the insights provided by these models.

EXHIBIT 7.14

*Discounting by
interest rate paths*

Continuing in a similar pattern, we would
compute the entire term structure, under
this lower volatility assumption, to be:

Five-year spot rate   = 7.9260%

Four-year spot rate   = 7.9445%

Three-year spot rate = 7.9630%

Two-year spot rate   = 7.9815%

One-year spot rate   = 8.0000%

Term Structures under Differing Volatilities

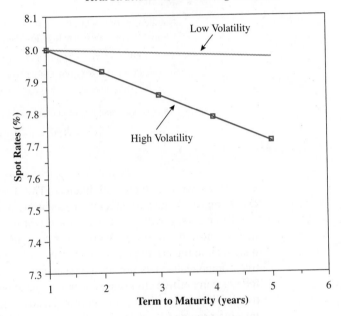

Box 7.1

Constructing a Simple Binomial Interest Rate Tree*

To demonstrate the effect of volatility on the term structure, let us consider a richer set of interest rate paths through the vehicle of a binomial tree. In this case, we will let interest rates evolve in a multiplicative fashion, asymptotically approaching a lognormal distribution. Pricing trees that use a lognormal interest rate assumption are among the most widely used models today. The exhibit below shows how the tree is constructed. Note how, instead of two simple paths, we generate an entire array of paths, whose probabilities of realization are given by something called Pascal's

triangle. For simplicity, this example assumes annual multiplicative changes in short-term interest rates, although in practice one usually assumes monthly or even shorter periods between interest rate moves.

Using the same methodology as described in Exhibits 7.8–7.10, we have computed the spot rate term structures implicit in the binomial tree for two different levels of volatility: 10 percent and 20 percent. The graph below shows what these two term structures look like. Note how the higher volatility imparts greater curvature to the term structure.

Interest Rate Binomial Tree

Yield Curves

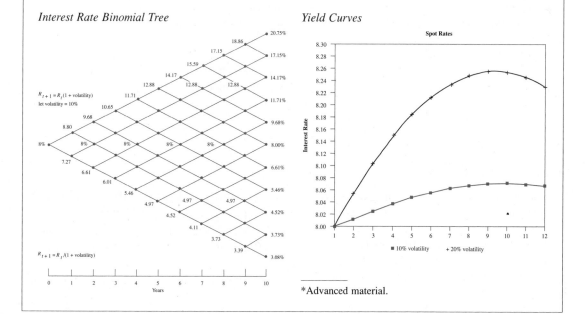

*Advanced material.

Summary

This chapter presents the newer, more advanced techniques of valuation that have developed in financial markets over the past decade. The central feature of the analysis is the recognition that inter-

est rates move in a random fashion over time. In the course of our discussion, two different approaches to this randomness in interest rates are presented. Both point to the need to consider expected and unexpected rate movements when valuing future cash flows. The latter are captured by considering a series of interest rate paths over which interest rates may evolve. When interest rates are not expected to remain stable, cash flows may be discounted by these paths that interest rates could follow, and these discounted values can be averaged to get fair market values.

If the size of cash flows is not influenced by the level of interest rates over time, one may also use the spot rate yield curve to discount the cash flows and arrive at fair market values. However, if the size of the cash flows is influenced by the level of interest rates, it is incorrect to discount cash flows by the spot term structure. The resulting calculation errors may become more sizable for higher interest rate volatility and greater variations in state-contingent payoffs. In addition, the mere addition of interest rate volatility leads to changes in the shape of the term structure, even if expected interest rates do not change.

Key Concepts

Review Questions

1. Confirm that the binomial tree in Exhibit 7.6 supports the term structure shown in Exhibit 5.4.
2. Interest rates for year 1: 10 percent. Interest rates for year 2: 12 percent (40 percent likelihood), or 7 percent (60 percent likelihood).
   What is the value of a bond with a payment of $1,000 maturing in two years?
3. What is the two-year spot rate implied by Question 2 above?
4. Assume the first three periods in the lattice of Exhibit 7.6 are as follows:

   Period 1: 10 percent.

   Period 2: 8 percent or 12.5 percent with equal probability.

   Period 3: 6.4 percent, 10 percent, 15.625 percent with equal probability.

   a. What is the value of a $1,000 zero-coupon bond maturing in Year 1? in Year 2? in Year 3?
   b. What is the implied term structure of spot rates of interest?
   c. What is the value of a three-year, $1,000 bond with a 10 percent annual coupon?
5. Finish deriving the term structure implied by Exhibit 7.8.
6. In your role as junior executive, you are given the task of comparing two projects that have the same total of net cash flows. What considerations should be contained in your evaluation of each?

7. Briefly discuss what is meant by the term "asymmetry of discounting." Try to develop an analogy to explain it to the uninitiated.

8. Looking at Exhibit 7.6, each upward interest rate jump is larger in absolute magnitude than the downward interest rate jump. Why is this? Does it introduce bias? Is it realistic?

References

Abken, Peter A. "Innovations in Modeling the Term Structure of Interest Rates." *Economic Review.* Federal Reserve Bank of Atlanta, August 1990.

Babbel, David F., and Craig B. Merrill, *Valuation of Interest-Sensitive Financial Instruments.* New Hope, Pa.: Frank J. Fabozzi Associates, 1996.

Babbel, David F. "Valuation of Interest-Sensitive Cash Flows: The Need, the Technologies and the Implications." *Record of The Society of Actuaries, 1990.*

Black, Fischer; Emanuel Derman; and William Toy. "A One-Factor Model of Interest Rates and Its Application to Treasury Bond Options." *Financial Analysts Journal,* January/February 1990.

Brennan, Michael, and Eduardo S. Schwartz. "A Continuous Time Approach to the Pricing of Bonds." *Journal of Banking and Finance,* July 1979.

Cox, John C.; Jonathan E. Ingersoll, Jr.; and Stephen A. Ross. "A Theory of the Term Structure of Interest Rates." *Econometrica, 1985.*

Fabozzi, Frank J.; T. Dessa Fabozzi; and Irving M. Pollack, eds. *The Handbook of Fixed Income Securities.* 3d ed. Burr Ridge, Ill.: Irwin Professional Publishing, 1991.

Fabozzi, Frank J., and Gifford Fong. *Advanced Fixed Income Portfolio Management: The State of the Art.* Chicago: Probus, 1994.

Heath, David; Robert Jarrow; and A. Morton. "Bond Pricing and the Term Structure of Interest Rates: A Discrete Time Approximation." *Journal of Financial and Quantitative Analysis,* 1990.

Hull, John. *Valuation of Options and Derivative Securities.* Englewood Cliffs, N.J.: Prentice Hall, 1990.

———. *Options, Futures, and Other Derivative Securities.* 2d ed. Englewood Cliffs, N.J.: Prentice Hall, 1995.

Hull, John, and Alan White. "One-Factor Interest Rate Models and the Valuation of Interest Rate Derivative Securities." Working Paper, Faculty of Management, University of Toronto, November 1990.

———. "Numerical Procedures for Implementing Term Structure Model." Parts I and II. *Journal of Derivatives,* Fall 1994, Winter 1994.

Jarrow, Robert. *Modeling Fixed Income Securities and Interest Rate Options.* New York: McGraw Hill, 1996.

Li, Anlong; Peter Ritchken; and L. Sankarasubramanian. "Lattice Models for Pricing American Interest Rate Claims." *Journal of Finance,* June 1995.

Rubinstein, Mark. "Implied Binomial Trees." *Journal of Finance,* July 1994.

Santomero, Anthony M. "Fixed versus Variable Rate Loans." *Journal of Finance,* December 1983.

Interest Rate Risk and the Value of Cash Flows

This chapter considers various aspects of interest rate risk associated with a series of cash flows and analyzes how such risks can be measured. Consideration is given to the effect of interest rate changes on present value. Interest rate risk measures such as duration and convexity are developed in an intuitive fashion.

In Chapter 5, we presented a number of traditional models of the term structure of interest. These models were used in Chapter 6 for valuing streams of cash flows. We found that spot and forward interest rates can be used in valuing fixed, default-free cash flows but not for valuing interest-sensitive, default-free cash flows. The modern stochastic interest rate valuation methods developed in Chapter 7, such as interest rate lattices and simulated interest rate paths, are acceptable for use in valuing both fixed and interest-sensitive cash flows that are not subject to default.

Interest Rate Risk: Duration Measures

In this chapter, we continue to analyze the value of future cash flows. Rather than centering our analysis on valuation of cash flows, however, we focus here on why and how much the values of future cash flows are influenced by changes in interest rates, and we develop several measures of interest rate riskiness.

Interest Rate Risk of Zero-Coupon Bonds

It has long been known that the prices of bonds with long maturities are more volatile than those of bonds with short maturities, but maturity doesn't tell us how much more volatile. However, "duration" gives us a much more precise measure. To see this, it is instructive to begin with the simplest of securities, the zero-coupon bond (Zero), and examine its **interest rate risk.** By "risk" we mean the movement in price occasioned by changes in interest rates.

Consider a 15-year Zero that pays $1,000 at maturity. What is it worth today? The value will depend on the interest rate applicable to 15-year Zeros. In Exhibit 8.1, we depict an assortment of values based on applicable interest rates ranging from 0.0 percent to 16.0 percent. This curve is known as a **value function.** Notice that the value, or price, of the Zero is always inversely related to the level of the interest rate. Highlighted is the value of the Zero under the assumption that today's applicable interest rate on such instruments is 8.0 percent. The range of possible prices for this Zero is quite wide. The price could potentially be as high as $1,000 if interest rates were to fall to 0 percent, or it could be quite low—indeed almost worthless—if interest rates were to become very high. For example, if interest rates were to skyrocket to 50 percent (not shown in graph), the value of the $1,000 15-year Zero would fall to as little as $2.28.

One measure of the price sensitivity of the zero-coupon bond to interest rate changes is the slope of the curve. This slope, measured by the change in price over the change in interest rates,[1] is often used by practitioners in assessing the risk of differing financial instruments. After reversing the sign, its value has come to be known as the **dollar duration** *(DD).*[2]

$$DD = -\frac{\text{Change in price}}{\text{Change in interest rate} \times 100} = -\text{Slope}$$

Here and in the rest of this chapter, we measure any change in interest rates in decimals. To render that difference in percentage terms, we multiply it by 100; hence, we have placed the 100 factor in the denominator of the formula above. The steeper the slope or, equivalently, the higher the dollar duration, the more

[1]This is sometimes referred to as the "rise over the run," where the vertical distance, or rise, represents the price change, and the horizontal distance, or run, refers to the change in interest rate, measured in percentage terms.

[2]The notion of "duration" implies a time element to it, and as we will show later in Exhibit 8.5, there is often a time interpretation to this measure.

EXHIBIT 8.1

Price versus interest rate, 15-year Zero

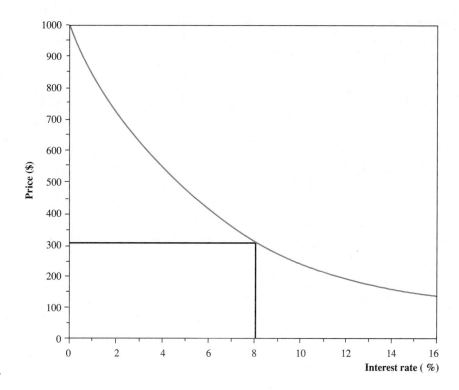

sensitive the price is to changes in interest rates. In Exhibit 8.2, we depict the slope of the curve, where the line segment is tangent to the value function at the assumed applicable current interest rate of 8.0 percent. Judging from the values on the left axis, it appears as if the dollar duration (the negative of the slope) is roughly $40. This means that a movement of 1 percent (100 b.p.) in interest rates would be accompanied by a change in the Zero's price of approximately $40. A 200 b.p. movement in interest would cause the price to change by roughly twice that amount. However, one must remember that this value change is unique to the maturity of the Zero being evaluated.

To see this, in Exhibit 8.3, we repeat the value curve for the 15-year Zero and include a value curve for a 5-year Zero. Both have a face value of $1,000. The value curve for the 5-year Zero lies above that of the 15-year Zero because the $1,000 face value will be received 10 years sooner, and hence it is of greater current value. In this exhibit, we have also drawn a tangent line to the 5-year Zero value curve at 8.0 percent interest, the slope or dollar duration of which is clearly less steep than that of the 15-year Zero. Accordingly, we may say that the 5-year Zero exhibits less interest rate risk than the 15-year Zero.

In drawing the tangent lines at the 8.0 percent interest rate, we have implicitly assumed that the appropriate discount rates for both the 5-year and 15-year Zeros are identical. It may very well be that we should use a different interest rate for the

EXHIBIT 8.2

Price versus interest rate, 15-year Zero

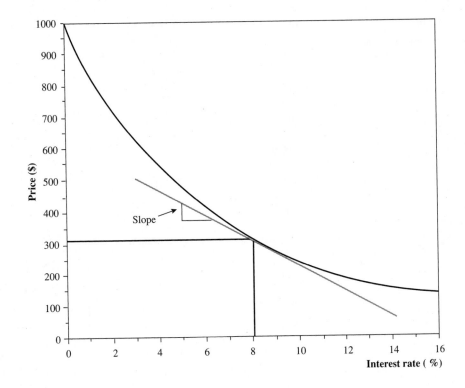

5-year Zero; in this case, we would therefore obtain a different slope. Notwithstanding this observation, it is apparent that the dollar duration of the 5-year Zero, which is near $30 when evaluated at 8 percent, is lower than that of the 15-year Zero for wide ranges of interest rates.

One problem with the dollar duration measure of price sensitivity to interest rate changes is that it measures absolute changes in bond prices without regard to the value of initial investment. For many purposes, it is desirable to find a measure of relative volatility in which the value change is related to initial investment. In these circumstances, dollar duration is a poor measure of relative volatility. For example, consider an asset with a current market price of $2 that would rise in value to $3 if interest rates declined by 100 b.p. Compared to the price rise of roughly $40 that would be experienced by the 15-year Zero, the $1 price jump appears trivial. However, we are comparing the price movement of a $2 asset versus that of an asset whose initial price is approximately $315. If we used the same $315 to purchase 157 of the $2 assets so that the investments would be roughly equivalent, we would find that the portfolio of $2 assets would rise in value by approximately $157, nearly four times more than the price movement of the 15-year Zero.

To make more meaningful comparisons between the relative volatilities of different financial instruments, another measure of interest rate risk, known as **modified duration** *(MD)*, has been developed. Modified duration measures

EXHIBIT 8.3

Prices of 15-year and 5-year Zeros versus interest rate

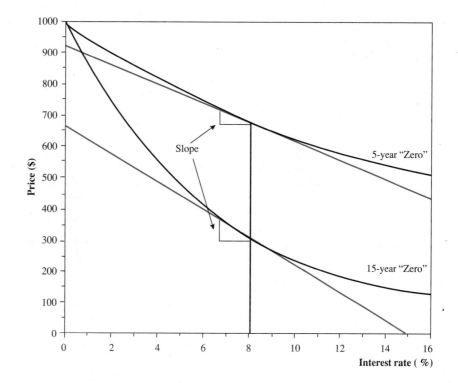

the percentage change in price associated with a 100 b.p. move in interest rates.[3] It is analogous to a price elasticity measure, but it is taken with respect to moves in interest rates. Modified duration is computed by taking the negative of the slope, or dollar duration, dividing it by the current price, and multiplying the quotient by 100 to express the measure in percentage units. Below, we display the formulas for our two duration measures together to facilitate comparison.

$$DD = -\frac{\text{Change in price}}{\text{Change in interest rate} \times 100} = -\frac{\Delta\text{Price}}{\text{Change in interest rate} \times 100}$$

$$= -\text{Slope}$$

$$MD = -\frac{\text{Percent change in price}}{\text{Change in interest rate} \times 100} = -\frac{(\Delta\text{Price} \div \text{Price}) \times 100}{\text{Change in interest rate} \times 100}$$

$$= -\frac{\text{Slope}}{\text{Price}} \times 100$$

The negative signs preceding the two ratios simply express the usual relationship, wherein prices move in the opposite direction of interest rates, in positive

---

[3]This measure is actually a modification of an earlier measure of duration known as Macaulay duration, named after Frederick Macaulay in 1938. Macaulay duration, rarely used anymore, relates the percentage change in price to a 1 percent change in the sum of 1 plus the discount rate.

EXHIBIT 8.4

Price versus interest rate, 15-year Zero

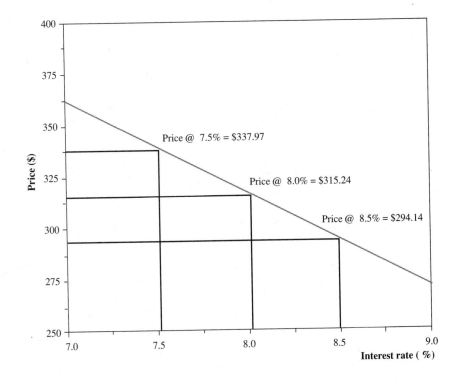

Price @ 7.5% = $337.97

Price @ 8.0% = $315.24

Price @ 8.5% = $294.14

units. An instrument whose price moves in the same direction as interest rates would have a negative dollar duration (and therefore a negative modified duration).

We can *approximate* the dollar change and percentage change in price precipitated by a change in interest rates by multiplying both equations by (change in interest rate × 100). Our approximations would be:

$$\Delta \text{Price} \approx -DD \times \text{Change in interest rate} \times 100$$

$$\% \Delta \text{Price} \approx -MD \times \text{Change in interest rate} \times 100$$

Note the emphasis on the verb "approximate." The reason for this emphasis is that the true relationship between value and interest rates is often nonlinear, as can be seen by the shapes of the value functions for the 5-year and 15-year Zeros in Exhibit 8.3. However, both of the above equations are linear. At best, they can give us an approximation of price changes only for small movements in the interest rate. Other measures are needed to capture the effects of the curvature, and these will be presented later.

To compute the duration measures in practice, the most common method is to calculate prices for interest rates slightly below and slightly above the current interest rates. These prices can then be used to estimate the slope of the curve centered at the point that gives price based on the current interest rate. In Exhibit 8.4, we have replicated a portion of our value curve from Exhibit 8.1, except that we have zoomed in on the values near the current interest rate of 8.0 percent. The customary practice is to compute prices for interest rates 50 b.p. above and below the current interest rate and to use these prices, $P_{+\Delta y}$ and $P_{-\Delta y}$, together with the initial price, P_y, for computing duration.[4] Here, the up or down shifts in interest rates are denoted $\pm\Delta r$, where r represents the reference rate of interest that is of concern to us. (This is typically a yield to maturity, but it could also be a spot rate of interest or other reference rate.) The total change in the interest rate is $2 \times \Delta r$ because the reference rate will be moved by an equal amount both upward and downward. By substituting these prices into our duration equations, we obtain the following:[5]

$$DD = - \frac{\Delta\text{Price}}{\text{Change in interest rate} \times 100} = - \frac{P_{+\Delta r} - P_{-\Delta r}}{(2 \times \Delta r) \times 100}$$

$$= - \frac{\$294.14 - \$337.97}{(2 \times .005) \times 100} = - \frac{-\$43.83}{1} = \$43.83$$

$$MD = - \frac{\%\Delta\text{Price}}{\text{Change in interest rate} \times 100} = - \frac{[(P_{+\Delta r} - P_{-\Delta r}) \div P_r]}{(2 \times \Delta r)}$$

$$= - \frac{(-\$43.83 \div \$315.24)}{(2 \times .005)} = - \frac{-.139}{.01} = 13.9$$

The interpretation of these duration numbers is as follows. For each 100 b.p. change in interest rates, the price of our 15-year Zero will change by approximately \$43.83, or 13.9 percent. Thus, a sudden 200 b.p. drop in the interest rate would be expected to produce a price increase of roughly twice as much—\$87.66, or 27.8 percent.

To practice our duration calculations once again, let us compute the duration of a 5-year Zero. At 8.0 percent, the price is \$680.58, while at 7.5 percent it is \$696.56, and at 8.5 percent it is \$665.05. Thus, our duration measures are:

$$DD = - \frac{\$665.05 - \$696.56}{(2 \times .005) \times 100} = - \frac{-\$31.51}{1} = \$31.51$$

$$MD = - \frac{(-\$31.51 \div \$680.58)}{(2 \times .005)} = - \frac{-.0463}{.01} = 4.63$$

The astute observer will recognize a pattern about the modified duration numbers. They are rather close to the maturities of the Zeros. Indeed, this observation is correct. Another way to compute the modified duration of a t-year Zero is to take its maturity, t, and divide it by 1 plus the applicable spot interest rate, S_t.[6]

---

[4]Some analysts use 1/2 or 1 b.p. shifts in their duration calculation. We prefer the 50 b.p. shifts because they produce duration measures that are more robust for large changes in interest rates. The reason to toggle the interest rates in both directions is to get a more useful bidirectional measure of slope—a measure that can be used to approximate price changes associated with interest rate moves in either direction. However, there is a calculus alternative for computing duration based on infinitesimal shifts in interest rates. (See Box 8.1.) The concept of dollar duration also links spot rates of interest to yield to maturity. (See Box 8.2.)

[5]In the modified duration formula, both the numerator and denominator are multiplied by 100, so we can drop that scaling factor.

[6]For a proof of this fact, see Box 8.1.

Box 8.1*

The Calculus Approach to Duration

To those versed in calculus, it must seem somewhat convoluted to proceed through our discussion of duration and numerical computation procedures of duration measures without resorting to the methods of calculus. After all, calculus is equipped to measure how much the value of one thing changes if the value of something else changes. This is precisely what duration measures are designed to do: measure the change in market value for a change in interest rates. Indeed, the developers of duration measures originally based their formulations on calculus. Today, the calculus approach to duration has gone out of vogue, primarily because of the computer power readily at hand, and the fact that with many of the modern interest-sensitive securities, the approach is no longer applicable. Nonetheless, it is instructive to proceed through the calculus approach to uncover the elegant genesis of duration measures.

The earliest measures of duration relied on valuation formulas based on yield to maturity. Let P represent the market price of a fixed-income security, and let CF_t denote cash flow at time t. Our symbol for yield to maturity will be Y. Then, the market price is given by:

$$P = \frac{CF_1}{(1 + Y)^1} + \frac{CF_2}{(1 + Y)^2} + \ldots = \sum_{t=1}^{m} CF_t(1 + Y)^{-t} \quad (1)$$

To determine how price will fluctuate with changes in yield, we take the derivative and move dY to the right-hand side of the formula.

$$dP = -\left\{ \sum_{t=1}^{m} t \times CF_t(1 + Y)^{-t-1} \right\} dY \quad (2)$$

Note the similarity of this formula to the dollar duration formula given in the body of the chapter:

$$\Delta P = -DD \times \Delta\text{Interest rate} \times 100$$

The term in braces of equation (2) is a mathematical expression for dollar duration, but it is in units 100 times larger than DD. Hence, dY does not need to be multiplied by 100 to get dP.

Next, to recast the formula in percentage terms, both sides are divided by price. This results in

$$\frac{dP}{P} = -\left\{ \frac{\sum_{t=1}^{m} t \times CF_t(1 + Y)^{-t}}{P} \right\} dY \quad (3)$$

Note the similarity of this formula to the modified duration formula given in the body of the chapter:

$$\%\Delta P = -MD \times \Delta\text{Interest rate} \times 100$$

The term in braces of equation (3) is a mathematical expression for modified duration, again adjusted by a factor of 100.

Finally, the interest rate sensitivity of the instrument was recast in terms of percentage fluctuations in the discount factor rather than changes in yield. This rendering was achieved by multiplying both the numerator and denominator of the term in braces by $(1 + Y)$ and rearranging the terms.

$$\frac{dP}{P} = -\left\{ \frac{\sum_{t=1}^{m} t \times CF_t(1 + Y)^{-t-1}}{P} \right\} \frac{dY}{1 + Y} \quad (4)$$

The expression in braces is a measure known as Macaulay duration (D). For over 40 years, it was the foremost measure of duration in use and in the economic literature, but it is in limited use today. Macaulay duration can be expressed more succinctly as follows:

$$\%\Delta P = -D \times \%\Delta(1 + Y), \therefore D = -\frac{\%\Delta P}{\%\Delta(1 + Y)}$$

It should be noted that in contrast to the modified duration, which equals the maturity divided by $(1 + Y)$, the Macaulay duration of a zero-coupon bond is equal to its maturity.

*Advanced material.

$$MD_{\text{15-yr. Zero}} = \frac{\text{Maturity of Zero}}{1 + S_{15}} = -\frac{15}{1.08} = 13.9$$

$$MD_{\text{5-yr. Zero}} = \frac{\text{Maturity of Zero}}{1 + S_5} = -\frac{5}{1.08} = 4.63$$

Note that both the maturity and the modified duration of the 15-year Zero are three times greater than the maturity and modified duration of the 5-year Zero. If the spot rates of interest applicable to our Zeros had not been equal to each other, however, the modified durations would have differed from each other by a factor different from that implied by their differing maturities.

Interest Rate Risk of Coupon Bonds and Other Fixed Cash Flows

While the above measures of interest rate sensitivity centered on Zeros, the application of dollar duration and modified duration is actually far wider. In earlier chapters, we pointed out that any bond, annuity, or other stream of fixed cash flows can be represented as combinations or portfolios of Zeros of varying maturities and amounts. This notion was referred to as value additivity. There is also a concept of value additivity in the case of durations, though it is somewhat more complicated than the original.

The modified durations of multiple-cash-flow fixed-income instruments can also be determined by weighting the modified duration of each individual cash flow to arrive at a duration measure for the entire series. The appropriate weight for the modified duration of a "component Zero" is the present value of that particular cash flow divided by the total present value of the entire portfolio of Zeros.

$$MD_{\text{portfolio of Zeros}} = \sum_{i=1}^{n} MD_{\text{of Zero}i} \times \frac{PV(\text{Zero}_i)}{PV(\text{Portfolio of Zeros})}$$

where n is the number of cash flows in the hypothetical instrument and PV is a present value operator.

In Exhibit 8.5 on page 164, we illustrate this formula with a concrete example. Consider a four-year, default-free noncallable bond with four annual coupon payments of $100 and a face value of $1,000. To keep things simple, we will assume for valuation purposes that the term structure in column (2) exists in the market.[7] The modified duration of the bond is given at the lower right of that exhibit.[8]

---

[7]If the term structure of interest is not flat, the most common practice is to use the yield to maturity of a bond in the discount factor to measure modified duration. Using YTM imparts a bias to the modified duration measure of interest sensitivity because it provides incorrect weightings on the modified durations of the component Zeros. This point was discussed in Chapter 6. In our example, we use the spot rates to calculate the modified durations of the individual cash flows.

[8]We have assumed this particular spot rate term structure because it will allow us to make direct comparisons of two methods for calculating duration. (See Box 8.3 on page 167.)

Box 8.2*

The Relationship between YTM and Spot Rates of Interest

With the notion of dollar duration in hand, we may now explore the relationship of yield to maturity to spot rates of interest. As we will discover, these interest rates are linked to each other through dollar duration weightings. We will demonstrate this relationship first through a simple numerical example, and then we will do so more generally with a mathematical derivation.

Suppose you were to put $2,000 in a two-bond portfolio and divide your money equally among the two bonds. One of the bonds is a 1-year Zero with a face value of $1,100, and the second bond is a 10-year Zero with a face value of $3,707.22. (These face values may appear strange at first blush, but the justification for their choice will become apparent.) Suppose also that the 1-year spot rate is 10 percent and the 10-year spot rate is 14 percent. Each Zero is then worth $1,000:

$$\$1,000 = \frac{\$1,100}{1.10^1} \text{ and } \$1,000 = \frac{\$3,707.22}{1.14^{10}}$$

Question: What is the yield to maturity on the two-bond portfolio? Since, in terms of their present values, the bonds are equally weighted in your portfolio, it is tempting to venture a guess that the portfolio yield is midway between the 10 percent and 14 percent spot rates applicable to the bonds. But a 12 percent YTM would be a wrong guess. Its actual YTM is 13.641 percent, as verified below:

$$\$2,000 = \frac{\$1,100}{1.13641^1} + \frac{\$3,707.22}{1.13641^{10}}$$

This YTM is approximated by the dollar duration (*DD*) weighted average of the spot rates. To see this, let us compute the *DD* of each zero. If we designate modified duration with *MD* and present value with *V*, we can state dollar duration as: $DD = V \times MD$. Recall that the *MD* of a Zero is its maturity divided by $(1 + Y)$, where *Y* is used to denote YTM in the equations. Accordingly, the *DD* of the first Zero is $\frac{1}{1.13641} \times 1,000 = 879.96$. The *DD* of the second Zero is $\frac{10}{1.13641} \times 1,000 = 8,799.64$. Therefore, the *DD* of the portfolio of Zeros is $879.96 + 8,799.64 = 9,679.60$. Weighing the spot rates of interest by the dollar durations of their respective Zeros relative to the portfolio dollar duration, we obtain:

$$\tfrac{879.96}{9679.60} \times 0.10 + \tfrac{8,799.64}{9679.60} \times 0.14 = 0.13636, \text{ or } 13.636\%$$

While this is only a first-order approximation of the true 13.641 percent YTM, it surely comes a lot closer than the 12 percent that market value weighting would imply.

This numerical example could be extended to approximate the yield of a portfolio having many zero-coupon bonds in it. And since a bond can be considered simply as a portfolio of Zeros, we have shown that YTMs on bonds or other portfolios are related to the dollar-duration-weighted spot rates.

Let us prove this result more generally. Consider a portfolio worth *P* dollars that is comprised of an *n*-year Zero worth P_n dollars and an *m*-year Zero worth P_m dollars. Then,

$$P = P_n + P_m \qquad\qquad (A.1)$$

A modified duration of approximately 3.24 for this bond has the same interpretation as above. For each 100 b.p. change in interest rates, the price of the bond will change by aproximately 3.24 percent.

This four-year bond will respond to interest rate changes in a manner roughly equivalent to any other instrument of similar duration. For example, a 3.5-year Zero will have a modified duration equal to 3.5 divided by 1 plus the 3.5-year spot interest rate of 8.129 percent, or $[3.5 \div (1+.08129) =]$ 3.237, very close to that of the four-year bond. Both instruments will manifest a change in price, measured in

Let CF_n denote cash flow at time n, and let S_n be the n-year spot rate. Then,

$$P_n = \frac{CF_n}{(1 + S_n)^n} \text{ and } P_m = \frac{CF_m}{(1 + S_m)^m} \quad \text{(A.2)}$$

We know from the definition of YTM that P can be restated in terms of cash flows and Y:

$$P = \frac{CF_n}{(1 + Y)^n} + \frac{CF_m}{(1 + Y)^m} \quad \text{(A.3)}$$

To simplify the derivation, we define new variables to represent the two right-hand-side expressions of (A.3). To emphasize their functional dependence on Y, we make this dependence explicit in the parentheses.

$$C_n(Y) \equiv \frac{CF_n}{(1 + Y)^n} \text{ and } C_m(Y) \equiv \frac{CF_m}{(1 + Y)^m} \quad \text{(A.3a,b,c)}$$

so that $P = C_n(Y) + C_m(Y)$.

Next, we restate the content of (A.1), but with the two new variables introduced above, adjusted to reflect the difference between YTM and spot rates. We obtain:

$$P = \{P_n\} + \{P_m\} = \left\{ C_n + \frac{\partial C_n}{\partial Y} (S_n - Y) \right\} \quad \text{(A.4)}$$
$$+ \left\{ C_m + \frac{\partial C_m}{\partial Y} (S_m - Y) \right\}$$

The expressions in braces on both sides of the second equality sign correspond to one another. In light of equation (A.3c), equation (A.4) becomes

$$0 = \frac{\partial C_n}{\partial Y}(S_n - Y) + \frac{\partial C_m}{\partial Y}(S_m - Y) \quad \text{(A.5)}$$

Earlier, we learned in Exhibit 2.4 that when applying the YTM of a portfolio, the errors in valuing of individual cash flows are exactly offsetting. In other words, the total portfolio is correctly valued, but the individual pieces are not. Equation (A.5) formalized this observation. Multiplying the partial derivatives by the expressions in parentheses and collecting terms, we have:

$$S_n \frac{\partial C_n}{\partial Y} + S_m \frac{\partial C_m}{\partial Y} = Y \left\{ \left(\frac{\partial C_n}{\partial Y} \right) + \left(\frac{\partial C_m}{\partial Y} \right) \right\} \quad \text{(A.6)}$$

Note that $\partial C_n / \partial Y$ and $\partial C_m / \partial Y$ are the *DD*s of the n-year and m-year Zeros, respectively, taken with respect to the yield of the underlying bond, and when combined, as they are in the right-hand-side term in braces, they are the *DD* of the entire bond, which is a portfolio of Zeros. Solving for y, we obtain:

$$Y = \frac{S_n \frac{\partial C_n}{\partial Y} + S_m \frac{\partial C_m}{\partial Y}}{\frac{\partial P}{\partial Y}} \quad \text{(A.7)}$$

The weights applied to the spot rates are the dollar durations of their respective Zeros relative to the dollar duration of the entire portfolio. This, of course, is only a first-order approximation of YTM. The formula holds true only in the immediate neighborhood of the partial derivatives, but it lacks precision for large absolute spreads between Y and S because it is a linear approximation to a curved function.

---

*Advanced material.

percentage terms, of about the same magnitude when interest rates fluctuate by small amounts.

However, as interest rate changes increase in size, a divergence in the price behavior of these two instruments, or of any two instruments with different cash flows but similar duration, begins to emerge. In this case, the percentage increases in the price of the bond will be greater than those of the Zero for decreases in interest, while the percentage decreases in the bond price will be less than those of the Zero for increases in interest. This is because of the difference in curvature

Exhibit 8.5   Computing Modified Duration of a Fixed Cash Flow Stream

(1) Time	(2) Spot Rates (%)	(3) MD(Zero) $= \dfrac{Time}{1+S_t}$	(4) Cash Flow ($)	(5) Present Value of Cash Flow ($)	(6) Weight of Cash Flow	(7) (3) × (6)
1	8.0000%	.9259	$ 100	$ 92.59	.08723	.08077
2	8.0567	1.8509	100	85.64	.08068	.14933
3	8.1069	2.7750	100	79.15	.07457	.20693
4	8.1502	3.6986	1,100	804.05	.75752	2.80176
			$1,400	$1,061.43	1.00000	3.23879

Modified duration ~ 3.24

between the value functions of the two bonds. The value function of the coupon bond exhibits greater curvature than that of the Zero. This curvature is referred to as **convexity** by market participants such as fixed income traders and portfolio managers, and its measurement is explained at the end of this chapter.

Because the notion of duration is most often used in the analysis and trading of bonds, we will further investigate some of the relationships between duration and bond value. However, to avoid unnecessary complications, we will do so in graphical form.[9] Exhibit 8.6 portrays the relationship between modified duration and interest rates, or in this case, bond yield to maturity. Each of the bonds depicted in this exhibit carries the same annual coupon, but they differ by maturity. Whether the bond's maturity is 5 years, 10 years, or 30 years, note that their modified durations all decline as yield is increased. The reason for this should be clear from the analysis presented above. Remember that the modified duration of a noncallable, default-free bond is a value-weighted average of the modified durations of the component Zeros. As market yields increase, the values of the longer-term Zeros decrease in value faster than those of the shorter-term Zeros, thereby eliciting smaller relative weights in the modified duration calculation. This results in a decline in the modified duration of the bond as a whole. The relative slopes in the exhibit are the result of the same feature of duration. The 30-year bond responds to a greater degree than either the 10- or 5-year instruments.

Exhibit 8.7 shows the effect of coupon rate on modified duration. In this exhibit, the market interest rate is held constant, and only the coupon rate for each of the three bonds is altered. Note that the higher the coupon, the lower the modified duration. Why is this the case? Again, recall that the modified duration calculation is based on the portfolio of Zeros concept. Therefore, with higher coupons, more of the value will be received in the near term, and greater weight is

---

[9]The bonds depicted in these exhibits provide semiannual coupon payments, and the yield follows bond market conventions—that is, it is not a true effective annual interest rate but merely a semiannual rate that has been doubled. A more thorough treatment of duration is available in G. O. Bierwag, *Duration Analysis: Managing Interest Rate Risk* (Boston: Ballinger, 1987).

EXHIBIT 8.6

Duration versus yield (8.5% coupon)

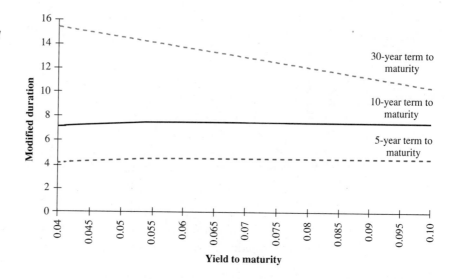

EXHIBIT 8.7

Modified duration versus coupon (8.5% yield to maturity)

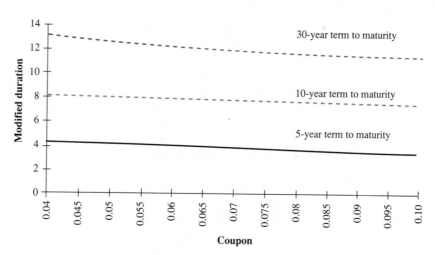

placed on the shorter-term Zeros. This shift in relative weighting implies that the modified duration must decline as coupon values increase. At the other extreme, if the coupon rate were 0.0 percent, the modified duration of the bond would be similar to that of any other Zero of equal maturity.

Next, Exhibit 8.8 shows the effect of term to maturity on modified duration for bonds of low, medium, and high coupon rates. Note that as term to maturity lengthens, modified duration increases, but at a slower rate than maturity. For the low-coupon bond, which sells at a substantial discount, modified duration even declines beyond some distant point as maturity continues to lengthen. Most bonds do not possess a maturity long enough to ever observe this rare phenomenon.

EXHIBIT 8.8

Modified duration versus term to maturity (8.5% to yield to maturity)

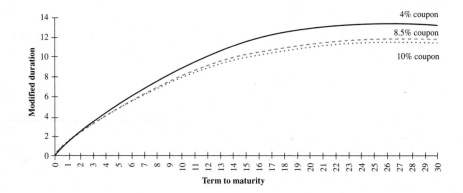

Therefore, for practical purposes, we may say that bond duration increases with term to maturity, but at a diminishing rate.

Callable Bonds and Other Interest-Sensitive Cash Flow Streams

As discussed in Chapter 7, many traded securities and nontraded financial instruments have cash flows that differ in amount and/or timing, depending on interest rate levels and/or paths over time. For example, the call provision of callable bonds will be exercised only if interest rate levels make it profitable for the issuer to do so. Instruments like these, with interest-sensitive cash flows, must be valued using modern valuation models such as interest rate lattices and simulations. In this way, the interest rate sensitivity of the cash flows is captured and taken into account in the valuation procedure. Duration measures based on these valuation methods are called **effective dollar duration** (*EDD*) and **effective duration** (*ED*).

In order to compute the effective duration of these instruments, we must use both the knowledge of the dependence of cash flows on interest rates and the concept of discounting by paths. In reality, however, the procedure is really quite simple. If you already are adept at using the lattice or simulation techniques, then all that is required to get effective duration measures is to perform the valuation procedure three times. The first time, you use that lattice or those paths that are consistent with current pricing. The next time, you add 50 b.p. to each node in the valuation lattice or to each time-point along each path in the simulation and compute price. Finally, you subtract 50 b.p. from each node in the initial valuation lattice or from each time-point along each path in the initial simulation, again computing its price under the scenarios. With the three resulting prices, we can compute effective dollar duration and effective duration in a way analogous to the computation of dollar duration and modified duration:

$$EDD = -\frac{\Delta\text{Price}}{\text{Change in short rates} \times 100} = -\frac{P_{+\Delta r} - P_{-\Delta r}}{(2 \times \Delta r) \times 100}$$

$$ED = -\frac{\%\Delta\text{Price}}{\text{Change in short rates} \times 100} = -\frac{[(P_{+\Delta r} - P_{-\Delta r}) \div P_r]}{(2 \times \Delta r)}$$

Box 8.3

Effective Duration Estimation Using Lattices

We will calculate the effective duration using the lattice technique on our example of the four-period bond from earlier in the chapter. The first step is to construct an interest rate lattice that is consistent with the spot rate term structure in the market. In the case of our previous example, the term structure is consistent with a lattice similar to the one in Box 7.1 (p. 149) where the volatility parameter is set at 20 percent throughout the lattice. The initial one-year spot rate of 8.0 percent becomes the first node of the lattice, and each successive node is generated by multiplying the interest rate by (1 + volatility) for up movements and by dividing the interest rate by (1 + volatility) for down movements. For our example, this generates the following lattice.

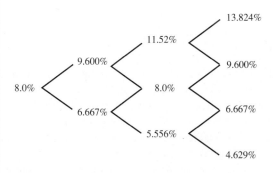

Using these interest rate paths, the present value or price of each cash flow can be calculated. The sum of those prices is the price of the whole instrument. For example, the first cash flow of $100 would be divided by (1+ .08) to get a present value of $92.59. Interest rates can go up or down with equal likelihood in the second period. To calculate the price of the second cash flow, we discount by each possible path of short rates and average the results to get a price of $85.64.

$$100 \div (1.08 \times 1.096) \qquad = 84.48$$
$$100 \div (1.08 \times 1.06667) \qquad = 86.80$$
$$(84.48 \times 0.5) + (86.80 \times 0.5) = 85.64$$

Similarly, the prices of cash flows receivable in years three and four could be calculated to be $79.15 and $804.05, respectively. Thus, the price of the whole four-period bond would be $1,061.44.

To calculate $P_{+ \, 50 \, b.p.}$, add 50 b.p., or 0.005, to each node and recalculate the price. It will be $1,044.43. Similarly for $P_{-50 \, b.p.}$, subtract 50 b.p. from each node and once again calculate the price. It will be $1,078.82. Using these three prices, we can now compute effective duration.

$$ED = -\frac{\%\Delta\text{Price}}{\Delta\text{Short rates} \times 100}$$

$$= -\frac{[(P_{r+50 \, b.p.} - P_{r-50 \, b.p.}) \div P_r] \times 100}{(.01) \times 100}$$

$$= -\frac{[(\$1,044.43 - \$1,078.82) \div \$1,061.44] \times 100}{(.01) \times 100}$$

$$= -\frac{-3.24}{1} = 3.24$$

The right-hand sides of these formulas look identical to those given for dollar duration and modified duration, except that the reference "interest rates" are now "short rates." Here, we change each of the short rates used in the valuations, both upward and downward, by an amount Δr. The main difference is that the prices used for calculating Δprice and %Δprice are computed using arrays of possible short rates rather than vectors of spot interest rates or yields to maturity. Box 8.3 illustrates the three valuations that need to be performed in order to compute effective duration measures.

In these situations, care must be taken to ensure that the cash flows being considered completely incorporate their interest sensitivity under each price scenario. For example, as interest rates decline, a callable bond or a mortgage will experience accelerated repayment of principal. This interest sensitivity changes the resultant calculations of duration. If you ignore it, you may end up with useless duration measures that have little to do with true interest rate risk. Therefore, effective duration measures have supplanted the older modified duration measures for applications involving financial instruments that exhibit interest-sensitive cash flows.

Naturally, the same approaches used for calculating duration of interest-sensitive cash flows also can be used to compute the durations of fixed-cash-flow financial instruments. In this case, the calculations should converge to the same duration values that would be obtained using the "portfolio of Zeros approach" described earlier. (Compare Exhibit 8.5 to Box 8.3.)

In later chapters, when we examine financial instruments by class, we will occasionally revisit these duration measures and show how they can be used to characterize and compare different instruments. Most references from here on in the text will be to modified duration, but it should be recognized that the same principles could be illustrated with effective duration measures. Again, the only differences are in the procedure used to value the financial instrument in question and in the reference rates of interest.

Interest Rate Risk: Convexity

As indicated earlier, the relation between price and the level of interest rates across a span of interest rates is nonlinear. While duration measures can be used to give a rough idea of how prices change in the face of shifting interest rates, they fail to account for some of the movement in price, particularly for large changes in interest rates. To help us better capture and catalog these nonlinearities in a single index-like number, a measure known as **gain from convexity** has been developed. The concept is illustrated in Exhibit 8.9. The error associated with using only duration-based measures of interest rate risk is illustrated by the shaded area of this exhibit. Notice that, in this example, the error increases at an increasing rate as interest rate shifts grow. Note also in this particular example that the error occurs regardless of which way interest rates shift. This value difference is referred to as the gain from convexity because of the value function's shape. As can be seen from Exhibit 8.9, the bondholder is better off because of this convexity, whether interest rates rise or fall, than what would be suggested by dollar duration alone.

Measuring Convexity

To measure this gain from convexity, we must retrieve the three prices—current price and the prices for upward and downward interest rates shifts of 50 b.p. that we already computed to come up with our duration measures—and apply some

EXHIBIT 8.9

Interest rate sensitivity

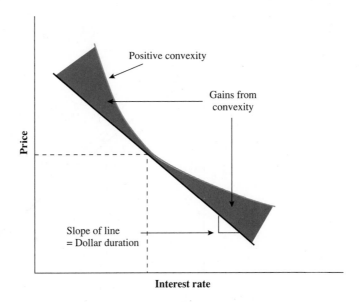

geometry.[10] In Exhibit 8.10, the point estimate of the dollar duration measure is given by the slope of the line tangent to the point on the value curve that relates current price to current interest rate, as discussed earlier. In this exhibit, we also show the prices for interest rates 50 b.p. higher and lower than the current interest rate level. If we join the points that relate to these two prices, we get a line segment that, in this case, lies above the dollar duration line. The vertical distance between these two lines gives the dollar amount that would have been our error in estimating the price change occasioned by a 50 b.p. move in interest rates if we had based our estimation solely on dollar duration.

To compute this vertical distance, we first find the midpoint of the upper line segment, which is determined by taking the two extreme prices and averaging them. Next, we plot this point above the point denoting current price at current interest rate. We then determine vertical distance by subtracting the current price from the averaged price. Provided that the two lines are approximately parallel, this distance will provide a reasonable estimate of the error that would result from using dollar-duration-based measures of price changes associated with 50 b.p. interest moves in either direction. To scale this measure, we must divide this dollar figure by 100 times the square of the one-sided change (50 b.p.) in interest rates, or $(\Delta r)^2 \times 100$. The reason for dividing by this product is that the error worsens in proportion to the square of the one-sided change in interest, as shown in Exhibit 8.11.

While the procedure described above gives the **dollar gain from convexity, (*DGFC*)**, another measure gives the **gain from convexity in percentage terms**

---

[10]Note that depending on how we derive the prices, the convexity measures can be designed for fixed or interest-sensitive cash flows.

EXHIBIT **8.10**

*Dollar gain
from convexity*

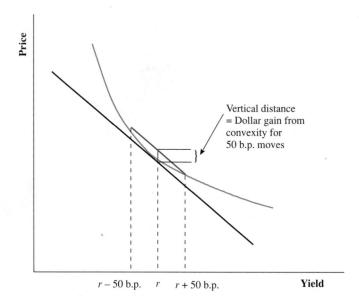

EXHIBIT **8.11**

*DGFC for two
different changes in
interest rates*

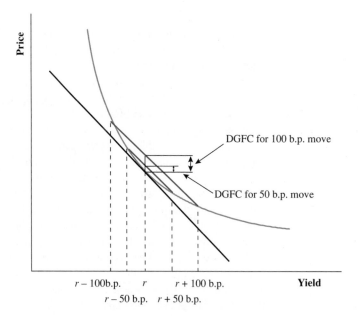

(*GFC*). These two measures are analogous to dollar duration and modified duration. The latter convexity measure is actually used more in practice. Below, we
provide formulas based on changes in interest rates, Δr, above and below the
current rate of r. Because we take the square of interest rate changes expressed in
decimals, we multiply them by the square of 100, or 10,000, to return the measures to units of dollars and percentages.

$$DGFC = \frac{[(P_{+\Delta r} + P_{-\Delta r}) \div 2] - P_r}{(\Delta r)^2 \times 10{,}000}$$

$$GFC = \frac{\dfrac{[(P_{+\Delta r} + P_{-\Delta r}) \div 2] - P_r}{P_r} \times 100}{(\Delta r)^2 \times 10{,}000}$$

To illustrate the application of these formulas, let us return to our 15-year Zero. The necessary inputs to derive the convexity measures are prices at 8.0 percent, as well as prices at interest rates 50 b.p. above and below that level. These prices are:

at 7.5 percent: $1,000 \div (1.075)^{15} = \$337.97$

at 8.0 percent: $1,000 \div (1.080)^{15} = \$315.24$

at 8.5 percent: $1,000 \div (1.085)^{15} = \$294.14$

Using these prices and substituting them into our convexity formulas, we obtain

$$DGFC = \frac{[(294.14 + 337.97) \div 2] - \$315.24}{(.005)^2 \times 10{,}000} = \$3.26$$

$$GFC = \frac{\dfrac{[(294.14 + 337.97) \div 2] - \$315.24}{\$315.24} \times 100}{(.005)^2 \times 10{,}000} = 1.03$$

These numbers have a straightforward interpretation. The *DGFC* number of $3.26 means that for a shift in interest rates in either direction of 100 b.p., the price is going to change by an amount given by the dollar duration formula (recall that the *DD* of a 15-year Zero is $43.83) plus an additional $3.26. Thus, if interest rates were to increase by 100 b.p., the Zero's price change implied by its dollar duration and dollar gain from convexity would be (−$43.83 + $3.26 =) −$40.57. On the other hand, if interest were to move the other direction by 100 b.p., *DD* and *DGFC* would imply a price change of ($43.83 + $3.26 =) $47.09.

Let us see how well we did in estimating the price changes using these dollar duration and dollar convexity measures. We will compare the price movements implied by these measures versus the actual price movements that would transpire if interest rates were to move suddenly by 100 b.p. in either direction. The true amount of the movement will be determined by recomputing the price with discount rates of 7.0 percent, 8.0 percent, and 9.0 percent.

Drop in Interest by 100 b.p.		Rise in Interest by 100 b.p.	
True Price Change	*DD and DGFC Implied Price Change*	*True Price Change*	*DD and DGFC Implied Price Change*
+$47.20	+$47.09	−$40.70	−$40.57

As can be seen, our dollar duration and dollar gain from convexity measures were not exactly on target in estimating the price change. When interest rates dropped, our measures underestimated the price rise by 11¢, and when interest rates rose, our measures underestimated the price drop by 13¢. Nonetheless, the measures together produced much more accurate estimated price changes than what would have been implied by duration alone. The duration-implied price change of $43.83 would have been off by several dollars.

The *GFC* number also lends itself to a straightforward interpretation. While modified duration would suggest that a 100 b.p. change in interest rates would produce a (15 ÷ 1.08 =) 13.89 percent change in price, the gain from convexity number would imply that the change in price would be "improved" by 1.03 percent from that suggested only by modified duration. In other words, if interest dropped by 100 b.p., price would change by (+13.89% + 1.03% =) +14.92 percent. On the other hand, if interest rose by 100 b.p., price would change by (−13.89% + 1.03% =) −12.86 percent. The true percentage changes, for comparison sake, are +14.97 percent and −12.91 percent, respectively. Clearly, these estimated percentage price changes using modified duration and gain from convexity in concert are much closer to the truth than those implied by modified duration alone.

Drop in Interest by 100 b.p.		Rise in Interest by 100 b.p.	
True %Price Change	*MD and GFC Implied %Price Change*	*True %Price Change*	*MD and GFC Implied %Price Change*
+14.97%	+14.92%	−12.91%	−12.86%

It is worth noting that the convexity formulas are robust. They are equally applicable for estimating the convexity of fixed cash flow streams or interest-sensitive cash flow streams, provided that appropriate valuation models are used in each case.

Putting It All Together

We have seen how duration and convexity measures help quantify the interest rate risk of streams of cash flows. General formulas have been developed to quantify the way in which duration and convexity measures work in concert. They are:

$$\Delta P \approx -DD \times \Delta \text{Interest rate} \times 100 + DGFC \times (\Delta \text{Interest rate})^2 \times 10{,}000$$

$$\%\Delta P \approx -MD \times \Delta \text{Interest rate} \times 100 + GFC \times (\Delta \text{Interest rate})^2 \times 10{,}000$$

It is noteworthy in these two equations that the convexity term is multiplied by a factor that changes with the square of interest rate shifts. This can result in a very powerful effect as interest rate changes get larger. For example, a bond with a modified duration of 10 and a gain from convexity of 2 will increase in price

Exhibit 8.12

Gains from convexity versus modified duration

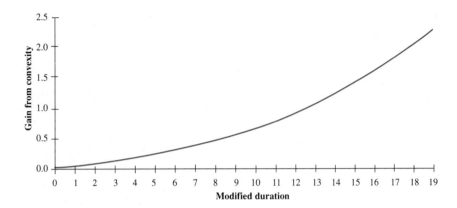

by approximately 12 percent [= −10 × (−.01) × 100 + 2 × 0.0001 × 10,000 = 10% + 2%] in the face of a 100 b.p. decline in interest. For a 200 b.p. decline, price would increase by about 28 percent [= −10 × (−.02) × 100 + 2 × 0.0004 × 10,000 = 20% + 8%]. A 300 b.p. decline in interest would cause price to rise 48 percent [= −10 × (−.03) × 100 + 2 × 0.0009 × 10,000 = 30% + 18%]. Had interest rates gone the other way and risen by 300 b.p., the price decline would have been only 12 percent (= −10 × 0.03 × 100 + 2 × 0.0009 × 10,000 = −30% + 18%). Note how as interest rate changes get larger, gain from convexity accounts for an increasing portion of the total percentage price change relative to that portion occasioned by duration.

In Exhibit 8.12, we plot the modified durations and gains from convexity for zero-coupon bonds of varying maturities, where all calculations are based on an 8.0 percent interest rate. Note that gain from convexity increases at an increasing rate as duration rises. This is a useful characteristic. It means that by combining zero-coupon bonds of varying maturities, we can manufacture financial instruments that will exhibit similar durations yet possess different convexity characteristics. For example, a Zero with a modified duration of 5.0 will have a different convexity from a weighted portfolio of equal value consisting of two Zeros having modified durations of 0.0 and 10.0. Both portfolios have a modified duration of 5.0, yet the portfolio, whose convexity is given by the halfway point along the chord linking the 0- and 10-year Zeros, will feature a greater convexity than the single Zero with a duration of 5.0.

Indeed, the curve showing the modified durations and gains from convexity for zero-coupon bonds of varying maturities forms a lower boundary, of sorts, on the convexity of fixed-cash-flow instruments. Any portfolio of zero-coupon bonds or its equivalent, such as a standard coupon-bearing bond, will feature a higher convexity than a single Zero with a duration equal to that of the portfolio. As we will show later in the book, these relationships are important considerations for investors and financial intermediaries who are attempting to structure a portfolio of financial instruments with desirable characteristics.

Exhibit 8.13

Interest rate sensitivity

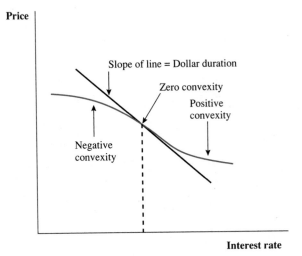

Limits to Interest Rate Risk Measures

Before we get too euphoric about the power of the duration and convexity measures, it is useful to recall that they are based on simple patterns of yield curve shifts—typically parallel. Even with such simple shifting patterns, we found that duration and convexity measures applied in concert were unable to specify fully the exact shift in prices, although they were reasonably close. However, this error may be more pronounced when there are asymmetries in the value curve. For example, a value curve for a callable bond is given in Exhibit 8.13. If we were to measure duration and convexity, we would get a duration number that was useful only for very small changes in interest rates, and the convexity number we would obtain would be close to zero. Clearly, duration and convexity measures alone are not always able to give us a very good idea of what the behavior of this financial instrument would be like in the face of changing interest rates.

Another problem occurs if the world does not operate in accordance with our assumptions. The entire discussion of rate movements was predicated on a parallel yield curve shift. However, we learned at the end of Chapter 5 that when the 1-year spot rate of interest rate shifts by 100 basis points, the 15-year spot rate is likely to change on average by only 34 basis points. Happily, other duration and convexity measures have been developed that incorporate nonparallel shifts in the term structure.[11] These more robust measures do require, however, that we specify or predict relative volatility for interest rates of differing terms.

[11]See, for example, John C. Cox, Jonathan E. Ingersoll, Jr., and Stephen A. Ross, "Duration and the Measurement of Basis Risk," *Journal of Business,* January 1979; and David F. Babbel, "The Term Structure of Interest Rate Volatility," Jeff Nelson and Stephen Schaefer, "The Dynamics of the Term Structure and Alternative Portfolio Immunization Strategies," in *Innovations in Bond Portfolio Analysis: Duration and Immunization,* ed. G. Bierwag, G. Kaufman, and A. Toevs (Greenwich, Conn.: JAI Press, 1983).

Finally, what about the possibility that an issuer of debt will default on the required payments? To the extent that this is expected and related to the level of interest rates, one could argue that this is just another application of interest-sensitive cash flow valuation. However, more will be said about this subject in the next chapter.

Notwithstanding the reservations offered above, we must stress that the simple measures of effective duration and convexity described in this chapter continue to be used most often in practice. In fact, they are heavily used in all aspects of the financial market. (Traditional measures of interest rate risk, such as Macaulay duration and modified duration, are on the wane because they do not properly take into account the impact of interest-sensitive cash flows.) More will be said about how the effective duration and convexity measures are employed by investors as we examine specific capital market instruments and discuss the management of financial institutions in subsequent chapters.

Summary

This chapter considers various aspects of interest rate risk associated with the change in value of a cash flow in response to a change in interest rates. The notion of duration is developed and proves central to our understanding of this risk. However, duration does not completely capture all of its subtlety. Dollar duration, effective dollar duration, modified duration, and effective duration are all linear measures that must be augmented by measures of convexity to achieve a more accurate estimate of the value change in the face of interest rate movements. Applying this technology to fixed payment streams is rather straightforward. Applying it to interest-sensitive cash flows is somewhat more complicated, but it is still manageable.

We end the chapter with a discussion of the imperfect nature of our techniques. All of these measures presume parallel term structure shifts and downplay borrower default. In spite of their weaknesses, however, they are a fairly efficient technology that is widely employed in modern financial markets.

Key Concepts

convexity,   164
dollar duration,   154
dollar gain from convexity,   169
effective dollar duration,   166
effective duration,   166

gain from convexity,   168
interest rate risk,   154
modified duration,   156
value function,   154

Review Questions

1. Why is a long-term zero-coupon bond more sensitive to interest rates than a short-term one?
2. In the example within the chapter, it was found that a 100 b.p. change in interest rates would cause a 13.9 percent change in the price of a 15-year Zero. It was then stated that a 200 b.p. change would result in a 27.8 percent change in price. Why must we be careful with an extrapolation of this type?
3. Given the knowledge that you have acquired on the shape of the term structure of interest and on relative movements in short-term versus long-term interest rates, what is the likelihood that the relationship of Zeros is linear vis-a-vis maturity modified duration?
4. Calculate the duration of a bond that pays $100 annually and also returns a face value of

$1,000 at the end of the fifth year. The applicable spot rates are:

Year 1: 6.1726 percent
Year 2: 6.0344 percent
Year 3: 5.9457 percent
Year 4: 5.8966 percent
Year 5: 5.8631 percent

5. Currently, there are several Treasury bonds with 10 years remaining to maturity that feature coupons at various levels, ranging from 7.25 to 13.75 percent. These differences arise from the fact that they were issued at different times in the past. Which of these bonds is likely to have the lowest sensitivity to movements in interest rates? Assume that coupons are paid annually and that the current yield curve is flat at 9 percent. How large is the difference between the durations of the most and least interest-sensitive of these bonds?

References

Babbel, David F. "The Term Structure of Interest Rate Volatility." In *Innovations in Bond Portfolio Analysis: Duration and Immunization,* ed. G. Bierwag, G. Kaufman, and A. Toevs. Greenwich, Conn.: JAI Press, 1983.

Bierwag, G. O. *Duration Analysis: Managing Interest Rate Risk.* Boston: Ballinger, 1987.

Bierwag, G. O.; George G. Kaufman; and Cynthia M. Latta. "Duration Models: A Taxonomy." *Journal of Portfolio Management,* Summer 1988.

Bierwag, G. O.; George G. Kaufman; Robert Sweitzer; and Alden L. Toevs. "The Art of Risk Management in Bond Portfolios." In *Innovations in Bond Portfolio Management,* ed. G. Bierwag, G. Kaufman, and A. Toevs. Greenwich, Conn.: JAI Press, 1983.

Bierwag, G. O.; George G. Kaufman; and Alden L. Toevs. "Duration: Its Development and Use in Bond Portfolio Management." *Financial Analysts Journal,* July/August 1983.

―――. Eds. *Duration: Its Development and Use in Bond Portfolio Management.* Greenwich, Conn.: JAI Press, 1982.

Brennan, Michael J., and Eduardo S. Schwartz, "Duration, Bond Pricing and Portfolio Management." In *Innovations in Bond Portfolio Management,* ed. G. Bierwag, G. Kaufman, and A. Toevs. Greenwich, Conn.: JAI Press, 1983.

Cox, John C.; Jonathan E. Ingersoll, Jr.; and Stephen A. Ross. "Duration and the Measurement of Basis Risk." *Journal of Business,* January 1979.

―――. "A Theory of the Term Structure of Interest Rates." *Econometrica,* 1985.

Ingersoll, Jonathan E., Jr.; Jeffrey Skelton; and Roman L. Weil. "Duration Forty Years Later." *Journal of Financial and Quantitative Analysis,* November 1978.

Leibowitz, Martin L., and Alfred Weinberger. "The Uses of Contingent Immunization." *Journal of Portfolio Management,* Fall 1981.

Nawalkha, S. K.; N. J. Lacey; and T. Schneeweis. "Closed-Form Solutions of Convexity and M-Squared." *Financial Analysts Journal,* 1990.

Nelson, Jeff, and Stephen Schaefer. "The Dynamics of the Term Structure and Alternative Portfolio Im-munization Strategies." In *Innovations in Bond Portfolio Management: Duration Analysis and Immunization,* ed. G. Bierwag, G. Kaufman, and A. Toevs. Greenwich, Conn.: JAI Press, 1983.

Chapter 9

Other Risks and the Value of Cash Flows

Chapter Outline

This chapter considers the various aspects of risk, apart from interest rate movement, that are associated with a series of cash flows and evaluates how such risks can be measured and priced. Consideration is given to the effect on present value of borrower default, illiquidity, taxes, and shifts in payment timing. In each case the additional risk factor is described in some detail, and methods of pricing this added uncertainty are developed.

In Chapters 6 and 7, we discussed valuation of cash flows and presented several methods for assessing value. Different valuation methods were shown to be applicable to cash flows having differing characteristics. Then, in Chapter 8, we explored the volatility of the market values of cash flows in the face of changing interest rates. Two measures—duration and convexity—were developed and estimated using the different valuation techniques.

Up to this point, several assumptions have been explicit or implicit in our presentation of the valuation of cash flows. First, we have assumed zero default risk. Second, we have assumed that securities, which are composed of bundles of cash flows of varying amounts and timing, are traded in a liquid, efficient market. Third, we have ignored tax considerations. Fourth, we have assumed that the amounts and timing of cash flows are known in advance. Cash flows are either fixed or related to interest rates in a deterministic way, with no uncertainty apart from that embedded in interest rate fluctuations.

In this chapter, we relax these assumptions, one by one, and see their effects on yields and valuation of cash flows. Then, together with a knowledge of the term structure of interest rates and of interest rate risk, we will have all of the basic analytical tools needed to understand fixed income instruments. The end result of our discussion should be a better understanding of why yields differ from one financial instrument to another, how the values of two instruments exhibiting ostensibly similar cash flow streams can differ, and how the values of these instruments are likely to change in the face of changing economic conditions. The next chapter, which introduces foreign exchange risk to the analysis, concludes the valuation section of this book.

In Part III of this book, a variety of financial instruments will be described and compared, one with another, in terms of the attributes and risks we have discussed. We will show how every financial security can be considered as a bundle of risks and promised cash flows that have been packaged together, much in the same way that a chef takes a set of ingredients in varying quantities and produces different kinds of food. Then, in Part IV of this book, we will describe financial institutions, their functions, and how they manage the risks inherent in the financial instruments described in Part III.

Default Risk

With many financial obligations, there is some chance that the borrower will not be able to make the promised payments, either on time or in full. This risk is known as **default risk.** Instruments exhibiting this risk must promise higher interest payments to compensate investors for the possibility of default. The difference in promised interest rates, or yields, between an obligation subject to default risk and an otherwise identical,[1] default-free security is known as a **credit spread.**

Measuring Default Risk

There are two types of measures of default risk. One is based on financial **analysts' assessments.** The other is a **market-based measure.** Each of these types of risk measures, in turn, has several variations. We will discuss them only in summary fashion. More detailed treatments are available in virtually any investments textbook.[2]

---

[1] By "identical," we mean that the promised timing of interest payments and repayment of principal from two financial instruments are the same. While the interest payments may differ from one instrument to the other, their face values are identical.

[2] See, for example, Zvi Bodie, Alex Kane, and Alan Marcus, *Investments,* 3d ed. (Burr Ridge, Ill.: Richard D. Irwin, 1995).

Analysts' Assessments.   Good financial analysts do not simply assume that the promises of a borrower will always be fulfilled. Rather, they attempt to measure the likelihood that promises will be kept. They do this by analyzing in depth the financial statements and future economic prospects of a borrower. An examination of the financial statements can show the borrower's historical level of profitability, current balance sheet state, and ability to sustain unexpected changes in market conditions. An analysis of past performance and credit relationships will also shed light on the borrower's history in keeping past promises, the evolution of creditworthiness over time, the variability of earnings over time, and which of the borrower's debts has the highest legal priority for repayment in the event of insolvency. An analyst, therefore, can glean quite a lot from the historical record. In Chapter 12, we outline in greater detail the precise numbers and ratios employed to capture this information. For the moment, however, suffice it to say that the analyst analyzes information from history and the current state of the balance sheet to determine the likelihood that promised payments can be made.

When looking ahead, particular attention is paid to how changes in the economic environment will affect the firm's ability to pay. To analyze this, particular attention is given to the degree of operating and financial leverage of the borrower. **Operating leverage** refers to the cost structure of a business and the degree to which fixed costs versus variable costs dominate the enterprise. The greater the fixed cost portion of total costs, the higher the operating leverage and the more vulnerable the enterprise is to a fluctuation in revenues. **Financial leverage** refers to the degree to which a firm is funded by debt versus equity. The greater the debt portion of total funding, the higher the financial leverage and the more vulnerable the enterprise is to fluctuations in earnings (before interest and taxes). An analysis of its economic prospects will focus on the competitive environment of the borrower, the nature of its product or service or revenue base, and how changes in the market will affect the firm's ability to pay the debt holder.

Analysts' assessments are sometimes summarized by a formal credit rating when the analysis is conducted by a credit rating agency. Four well-known rating agencies are Moody's, Standard & Poor's, Duff and Phelps, and Fitch. These agencies rate the creditworthiness of borrowers into categories and report their results to the general financial community. While they are best known for their ratings of bond issuers, rating agencies also rate other dimensions of creditworthiness, such as the claims-paying ability of insurance companies, the capacity of commercial paper issuers to repay their debts, and so forth. Exhibit 9.1 provides a listing and description of the bond rating categories used by Moody's and Standard & Poor's.

The top four grades granted by both Moody's and Standard & Poor's are often considered to be "investment grade" ratings by regulatory authorities and governmental agencies, and financial instruments carrying investment grade ratings are generally authorized by these bodies as suitable investments. Grades Ba or BB and below are referred to as "speculative grade," "below investment grade," "high-yield," or "junk bonds," and they are often considered by such regulatory and supervisory agencies to be unsuitable for prudent investing.

EXHIBIT 9.1   Credit Ratings by Investment Agencies

Moody's		Standard & Poor's	
Aaa	Best quality	AAA	Highest grade
Aa	High quality	AA	High grade
A	Upper medium grade	A	Upper medium grade
Baa	Medium grade	BBB	Medium grade
	⇧ investment grade ⇧		⇧ investment grade ⇧
	⇩ below investment grade ⇩		⇩ below investment grade ⇩
Ba	Possess speculative elements	BB	Lower medium grade
B	Generally lack characteristics of desirable investment	B	Speculative
Caa	Poor standing; may be in default	CCC	Outright speculation
Ca	Speculative in a high degree; often in default	CC	Outright speculation
C	Lowest grade; very poor prospects	C	Reserved for income bonds
		DDD–D	In default, with rating indicating relative salvage value

Note: Moody's uses a modifier of 1, 2, or 3 to indicate relative quality within a category. 1 means the security is at the higher end of the category; 3 signifies the lower end.

Note: Standard & Poor's uses a modifier of +, no notation, or – to indicate relative quality within a category. A plus indicates the higher end of a category; a minus indicates the lower end.

While Moody's and Standard & Poor's ratings differ slightly in symbols and definition, there is broad agreement between these two agencies in their credit assessments, and widely divergent ratings attract much attention.[3] Moody's and Standard & Poor's review their ratings periodically, especially during times of turmoil or new issues of debt obligations.

It is rare for an investment grade bond to go into default. One reason is that the credit agencies generally do a reasonable job of credit assessment. Another reason is that, through periodic updates, a bond is likely to be downgraded to speculative grades prior to default. Thus, the credit agencies are seldom caught in the embarrassing position of having one of their highly rated bonds go into default. In Exhibit 9.2 we see some evidence for this. Within categories AAA through B, we find that fewer and fewer of the bonds that go into default are assigned these ratings as default nears. However, within categories CCC through C, we find that the number of bonds with these ratings increases as default nears. The percentage of bonds in

---
[3]An example of a wide divergence in rankings occurred during the mid-1980s, when S&P assigned a AAA rating to Executive Life Insurance Company, while Moody's assigned an A3 (lowest subcategory of the A class) to the same company. Such a large discrepancy between the two ratings is extremely rare. Although S&P maintained the AAA rating until shortly before Executive Life became insolvent, the marketplace was doubtful of the rating, and debt backed by Executive Life (called Muni-GICS) traded at yields typical of lower grade debt.

EXHIBIT 9.2   Rating Distribution of Defaulted Issues at Various Points Prior to Default

(1971–1995)

	Original Rating (%)	*Rating One Year Prior to Default (%)*	*Rating Six Months Prior to Default (%)*
AAA	0.7%	0.0%	0.0%
AA	3.7	0.0	0.0
A	9.8	0.9	0.3
Total investment grade	24.8%	8.8%	6.9%
BB	10.8%	10.8%	7.2%
B	49.8	48.4	39.5
CCC	14.0	29.0	38.5
CC	0.6	2.1	6.9
C	0.0	0.9	1.0
Total noninvestment grade	75.2%	91.2%	93.1%

Note: This information is based on Standard & Poor's bond ratings.

Source: Edward I. Altman and Vellore Kishore, "Defaults and Returns on High Yield Bonds: Analysis through 1995," *Special Report,* New York University Salomon Center, January 1996.

default for a given rating should not be indicative of the default probabilities because many of the bonds included within each category have been issued only a year or two earlier and may ultimately wind up in default prior to their maturity. This observation notwithstanding, it is clear that most bonds that default are from the lower-rated categories, particularly as they near the time of default.

Skeptics find that the deck is thereby stacked in favor of vindicating the agencies' ratings. They argue that it is akin to assessing the accuracy of a dry weather forecast made by a meteorologist who then changes the forecast to rain as dark clouds appear on the horizon. The latent accuracy of the meteorologist is of little consolation to people who had planned a picnic based on earlier forecasts. In the case of bonds, by the time a poor credit rating is given, the price of the security is already likely to reflect the worsened economic prospects, thus making it difficult for an investor to liquidate his or her holdings of the security without incurring substantial loss. Moreover, there is an element of self-fulfilling prophecy here. The downgrading of a bond may accelerate the deterioration of credit by causing a decline in the price of outstanding debt and a perceived decline in the creditworthiness of the issuer, as fewer investors will be able to invest in the firm, thus making it more difficult for the struggling enterprise to raise needed funds to alleviate its financial problems.

Market-Based Measures of Default.   Dissatisfied with the lags inherent in the agency ratings of credit quality, many economists and market participants prefer using market-based measures of creditworthiness. This approach measures the market's perception of credit risk as is evidenced through market prices and yield differentials. The advantages in using a market-based approach are that all publicly available information (and perhaps even insider information) is presumably impounded in the observed prices of traded securities. In addition, the information and prices are updated continually by interested market participants.

One popular market-based measure of credit risk is the ratio of a security's price or yield to that of a default-free **synthetic Treasury** security.[4] The synthetic Treasury security is a hypothetical security that has cash flows exactly matched to the promised cash flow pattern of the risky security but priced according to the Treasury term structure of interest.

To illustrate this measure and its relation to default, we will compare the simplest of all securities, zero-coupon bonds. We consider two issuers of debt: the federal government, which we will regard as riskless (since they can always print money to repay debt, although as we saw in 1996, Congress can vote not to appropriate the funds necessary to pay it); and a corporation subject to default. Suppose that there are only two possible future outcomes for the corporate debt: (1) the issuer of the risky debt is solvent and debts are paid, or (2) the issuer defaults and the debt is worthless. Of course, there are more than two possible outcomes. It is an extremely unlikely outcome for a defaulting obligation to have a zero value. One should therefore think of this example as a simple version of the real world in which many outcomes and recovery rates are possible.[5]

To illustrate this market-based measure of credit risk, consider an investor wishing to lend money for a year. She may either give the government 93¢ today in exchange for a sure dollar one year from today, or she may give the corporation 92.6¢ in exchange for a promise to pay a dollar one year from today. The 0.4¢ per dollar difference in prices represents the market price of the default risk for the corporate Zero. Let's assume that investors are willing to invest in either investment opportunity based only upon its expected return. For the same expected return to prevail from holding either of the two Zeros, the following relationship must hold true:[6]

$$\left(\frac{F}{P_R}\right) \times \text{Prob}_{\text{solvency}} + \left(\frac{DF}{P_R}\right) \times \text{Prob}_{\text{default}} = \left(\frac{F}{P_T}\right)$$

where P_R is the price of the risky corporate debt, P_T is the price of the synthetic Treasury, F is the face value of the debt at maturity, and DF is the payment in default, which here is assumed to be zero. This formula allows us to solve for the

---

[4]An example of the application of this credit risk measure is given by Babbel, Merrill, and Panning, "Default Risk and the Effective Duration of Bonds," *Financial Analysts Journal,* 1996. In this article, the synthetic Treasury is found useful in adjusting bond duration estimations for the relatively lower volatility of risky bond yields to that of Treasury yields.

[5]Indeed, as noted by Litterman and Iben, the price of the corporate zero will reflect a probability-weighted present value across all possible future outcomes. (See Robert Litterman and Thomas Iben, "Corporate Bond Valuation and the Term Structure of Credit Spreads," in *Fixed Income Research* [New York: Goldman Sachs, November 1988].)

[6]To make this argument rigorous, we would have to make additional assumptions, such as the fact that the corporate defaults are uncorrelated with changes in interest rates. Also, the probabilities obtained are not literally the likelihood of the default occurring in the real world; they reflect both the actual default probabilities and investors' aversion toward default risk.

probability of solvency, $Prob_{solvency}$, and probability of default, $Prob_{default}$, from observed market prices. For the solvency probability, we obtain

$$Prob_{solvency} = \frac{P_R}{P_T}$$

Because the risky bond will either be solvent or default, it follows that

$$Prob_{default} = 1 - Prob_{solvency}$$

Therefore, the probability of default for the above example is given by

$$Prob_{default} = 1 - \frac{P_R}{P_T}$$

$$= 1 - \frac{.926}{.930}$$

$$= 0.0043$$

One could also use the observed market prices to derive the yield differential inherent in the two instruments. The difference in stated interest rates on these two securities can be computed as follows:

$$\text{Effective annual riskless interest rate} = \frac{1.00}{.930} - 1 = 7.53\%$$

$$\text{Promised annual risky interest rate} = \frac{1.00}{.926} - 1 = 7.99\%$$

$$\text{Spread} = 7.99\% - 7.53\% = 46 \text{ basis points}^7$$

Accordingly, the promised yield on the risky Zero must be 46 basis points higher than that on the riskless Zero in order to compensate just for the prospect of default.

Applying this approach to financial assets is somewhat more difficult than it may appear. This is because it is extremely difficult, and time-consuming, to construct the relevant synthetic Treasury bond that is essential for this methodology. There are many factors that complicate real world assets that make the matching a challenging activity. One such complicating factor is that most bonds are multiperiod, with periodic coupon payments. Another is that most risky bonds have call features, making the effective maturity uncertain. Furthermore, most bonds that do default pay a sizable portion of their face value to the bondholders. As illustrated in Exhibit 9.3, this payoff percentage is a function of perceived quality before default. As quality lessens, a lower percentage of face value is usually recovered.

Nonetheless, the ratio of risky to riskless bond prices or yields is a useful market indicator of default risk. However, it also entangles market risk aversion into the ratio, because aversion to default risk will be impounded into the bond prices in the form of an additional discount and, consequently, an increase in yields.

---

[7] Using the bond equivalent yield convention, wherein semiannual effective interest rates are doubled to obtain annual yields, the difference in yields would be 45 b.p.

EXHIBIT 9.3   Payoff Percentages of Defaulting Bonds

Bond Rating	1971–1995*	1912–1943†
AAA	78	60
AA	77	52
A	57	42
BBB	53	34
BB	42	34
B	35	35
CCC	33	
C	10	
NR	31	48

*Based on original issue rating. See Edward I. Altman and Vellore Kishore, "Defaults and Returns on High Yield Bonds: Analysis through 1995," *Special Report,* New York University Salomon Center, January 1996. Note that the payoff percentages on bonds rated C and NR (nonrated) were not reported in that study; payoff percentage for these bonds reflect the period 1968–1988, the data for which is reported in Edward I. Altman, "Measuring Corporate Bond Mortality and Performance," *Journal of Finance,* September 1989.

†Based on rating five years prior to default. See W. Braddock Hickman, *Corporate Bond Quality and Investor Experience* (Princeton, N.J.: National Bureau of Economic Research, 1958).

However, from an investor's point of view, the main problem with this approach is that it provides no measure of credit risk independent of market forces. As a result, investors are unable to profitably exploit this measure of default. The measure assumes that market prices adjust rapidly to new information. Therefore, a worsening ratio already coincides with a reduced price of the risky security and is indicative of reduced creditworthiness. It does not indicate that price will decline further, however. Still, investors like to use the measure to infer what the market assessments of credit risk are.

Historical Default Experience

Exhibit 9.4 portrays the default experience of U.S. publicly traded corporate bonds for the period from 1900–1995. Default rates are expressed as a percentage of the face amount of total debt outstanding. It is clear from the exhibit that from 1940 through the mid-1980s, defaults were relatively low for the market as a whole. With over 45 years of such good experience, euphoria was beginning to infect certain investors. Some, having concluded that market-based measures of default overestimated risk, were led into riskier investment portfolios. For these investors, the defaults of the late 1980s were an unpleasant reminder that there is a good reason for risky bonds to feature higher promised yields. It's unwise to ignore the pricing signals given in the open market.[8]

[8]Bond defaults, as a percentage of all corporate bonds outstanding, reached the 2.3 to 3.3 percent range from 1989 to 1991. However, default rates measured as percentage of below-investment-grade bonds outstanding were more than three times higher and reached 10.7 percent in 1991.

EXHIBIT 9.4

Default experience of publicly traded straight corporate bonds (1900–1995)

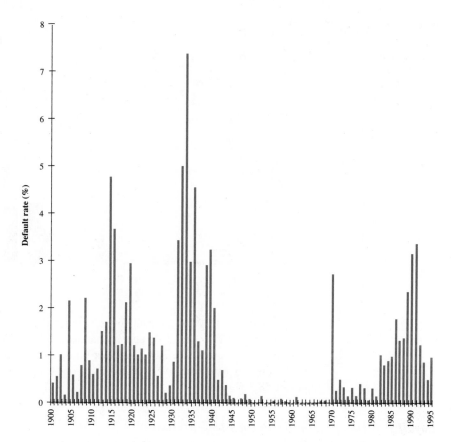

However, to decipher the market's message, it is necessary to analyze the evidence properly. This requires that default be viewed on a cumulative basis. Thus, the long-run performance of bonds issued with a given rating must be examined. Analysts prefer this method over the single-year default rates because it gives a more accurate feel of how a fixed portfolio of bonds purchased at a given moment in time can be expected to perform over the ensuing years. With single-year default rates newly issued bonds are always entering into the calculations, so the seasoning effect is less apparent.

To facilitate this analysis, Moody's forms "cohorts" of all Moody's-rated issuers with debt outstanding at the beginning of each year. These cohorts, which would include newly issued debt as well as seasoned debt, are then followed through time in each rating category that was assigned at the outset of the cohort formation. The longer a cohort is followed, the greater the accumulated percentage of bonds within the cohort that default. This holds true regardless of the rating of the bond. This is seen clearly in Exhibit 9.5, which covers cohorts of bonds formed from 1970 through 1995, with ratings spanning from Aaa to B. For example, average default rates for five-year holding periods climb from 0.13 percent for

EXHIBIT 9.5

*5-, 10-, 15-, and
20-year cumulative
default rates
(1970–1995)*

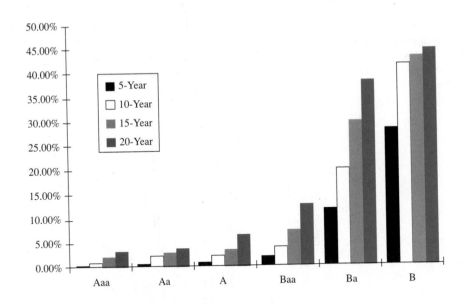

EXHIBIT 9.5

5-, 10-, 15-, and 20-year cumulative default rates (1970–1995)

issuers rated Aaa to 28.87 percent for issuers rated B. After 20 years, the Aaa cohort averaged 2.2 percent defaults, whereas the B cohort averaged 20 times more, or 45.55 percent, defaults. Another study showed that CCC-rated bonds (S&P rating) experienced 5-year default rates of 44.5 percent and 10-year default rates of 58.3 percent.[9]

Payoff Percentages and Breakeven Default Rates

Risky bonds incorporate a spread over Treasury yields to compensate investors for the default risk reported above. (See Exhibits 9.6 and 9.7.) Whether this spread is sufficient to compensate investors depends on the magnitude of default risk and the level of market risk aversion. The **breakeven default rate** is the percentage of the value of outstanding risky debt that must default in order to equalize the total realized returns of risky and riskless bond portfolios.[10] The concept is most useful in a bond portfolio mutual fund context because it neglects such things as changes in the credit spread over time and the lack of diversification that a small bond portfolio might face.[11]

In order to compensate investors for substantial downside risk, the market usually expects the actual default rate to be less than the breakeven default rate. If

---

[9]See Altman and Kishore, *op. cit.* Although this study, spanning the period from 1971 through 1995, uses a different methodology from the Moody's study in that it forms cohorts of only newly issued bonds of a given rating and follows them over the years, the results for similarly rated bonds are quite close.

[10]Our presentation in this section is based on Peter Niculescu, "Breakeven Default Rates," *Fixed Income Research,* Goldman Sachs, November 1990.

[11]This is sometimes referred to as "basis risk," which is the risk that spreads between risky and riskless bonds will change over time.

EXHIBIT 9.6   Annual Yields, Returns, and Spreads on Ten-Year Treasury and High-Yield Bonds
(1978–1995)

	Promised Yield (%)			Return (%)		
Year	High-Yield	Treasury	Spread	High-Yield	Treasury	Spread
1978	10.92%	8.11%	2.81%	7.57%	−1.11%	8.68%
1979	12.07	9.13	2.94	3.69	−0.86	4.55
1980	13.46	10.23	3.23	−1.00	−2.96	1.96
1981	15.97	12.08	3.89	7.56	0.48	7.08
1982	17.84	13.86	3.98	32.45	42.08	−9.63
1983	15.75	10.70	5.05	21.80	2.23	19.57
1984	14.97	11.87	3.10	8.50	14.82	−6.32
1985	15.40	11.65	3.75	22.51	31.54	−9.03
1986	14.45	9.55	4.90	16.09	24.08	−7.99
1987	12.66	8.75	3.91	4.67	−2.67	7.34
1988	13.95	9.00	4.95	13.47	9.20	4.27
1989	15.41	7.93	7.48	1.62	15.99	−14.37
1990	17.58	8.83	8.75	−4.36	6.88	−11.24
1991	13.11	6.70	6.41	34.58	17.18	17.40
1992	11.28	6.69	4.59	18.16	6.50	11.66
1993	9.61	5.80	3.81	17.18	12.08	5.10
1994	11.27	7.83	3.44	−1.17	−8.29	7.12
1995	9.70	5.58	4.12	19.91	23.58	−3.67
Arithmetic Annual Average:						
78–95	13.63%	9.13%	4.51%	12.40%	10.60%	1.81%
Compound Annual Average:						
78–95				11.88%	9.86%	2.01%

Source: Edward I. Altman and Vellore Kishore, "Defaults and Returns on High Yield Bonds: Analysis through 1995," *Special Report,* New York University Salomon Center, January, 1996.

an *investor* projects a default rate above the breakeven rate, risky debt would be relatively unattractive to that investor. If the *market* projects default rates above breakeven rates, risky debt would fall in price until yields were sufficiently attractive to restore equilibrium in debt markets.

To illustrate how to compute breakeven default rates, let us consider two bond portfolios, one consisting of Treasury bonds and the other of risky bonds. Consider a time horizon of four years for investing and assume that all semiannual coupon payments during that period are reinvested in their respective portfolios. Both portfolios consist of bonds with four-year maturities.[12] Suppose the risky portfolio offers yields 150 basis points above the 8.5 percent yield provided by the Treasury portfolio. If the risky bonds do not default, then the risky bond would

---

[12]The assumption that maturities are equal is not strictly necessary to compute breakeven default rates; it is only necessary that both portfolios have the same interest rate risk.

EXHIBIT 9.7

*Promised yields
and spreads on
10-year treasury
and high-yield bonds*

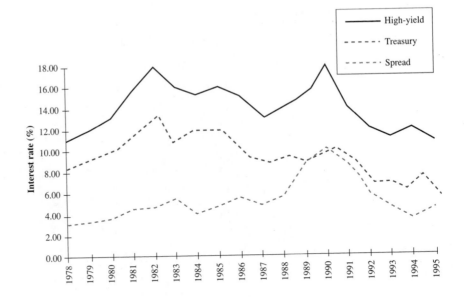

have a semiannual coupon of $50 (= $100 ÷ 2) per $1,000 of face value, whereas
the Treasury bond would have a semiannual coupon of $42.50 (= $85 ÷ 2) per
$1,000 of face value. Compounding these coupons at the portfolios' respective
semiannual reinvestment rates of 5 percent and 4.25 percent, and recognizing that
face value will be returned at maturity, the total cumulative returns are

For the risky bond: $\sum_{t=1}^{8} \$50 \times (1 + 0.05)^{t-1} + \$1,000 = \$1,477.46$

For the riskless bond: $\sum_{t=1}^{8} \$42.50 \times (1 + 0.0425)^{t-1} + \$1,000 = \$1,395.11$

Dividing these cumulative returns by the initial investment of $1,000 provides the
cumulative return of 47.75 percent on the risky portfolio, compared with a 39.51
percent return on the Treasury portfolio. These returns can be computed by using
the device of a representative bond. Note the $t-1$ exponent in the equation. While
there are eight coupons during the four-year period, the first coupon is received
after six months and the final coupon is received at maturity; thus, the compounding of interest is for $t-1$ periods. The difference in returns of 8.24 percent
means that 8.24 percent of the risky bonds could default at maturity, paying only
their coupon but returning no principal, and the cumulative rates of return would
be equal to each other. Thus, 8.24 percent is the breakeven default rate.

Exhibit 9.8 shows the breakeven default rates for 150 b.p. spreads under the
same assumptions but with different bond maturities. Clearly, the longer the elapsed
time before default, the higher the breakeven default rate. Of course, if the defaulting bonds have positive payoffs, the breakeven default rate will be much higher. On
the other hand, if bond defaults occur prior to maturity, the breakeven default rate
will be lower. The example can be extended to different spreads, different
investment horizons, different default timing (other than at maturity), and nonzero

EXHIBIT 9.8   Breakeven Default Rates for Different Maturities

Bond Portfolio Maturities	Cumulative Risky Rate of Return (%)	Cumulative Riskless Rate of Return (%)	Breakeven Default Rate (%)
1 year	10.25%	8.68%	1.57%
2 years	21.55	18.12	3.43
3 years	34.01	28.37	5.64
4 years	47.75	39.51	8.24
5 years	62.89	51.62	11.27
6 years	79.59	64.78	14.81
7 years	97.99	79.09	18.90
8 years	118.29	94.63	23.66
9 years	140.66	111.53	29.13
10 years	165.33	129.89	35.44

default bond payoffs to better enable an investor to assess the risk-return relationship. Some analysts turn the above analysis around and, assuming a particular default rate, compute breakeven yields.

To provide an idea of how important credit spreads are in establishing the breakeven default rate, we have performed the calculations below for spreads of 100 b.p., 300 b.p., and 500 b.p., assuming an 8.5 percent annual yield on the riskless portfolio, for representative bond portfolios of four- and seven-year maturities.

Bond Portfolio Maturities	100 Basis Points Spread	300 Basis Points Spread	500 Basis Points Spread
4 years	5.44%	16.89%	29.12%
7 years	12.40%	39.65%	70.46%

To put these breakeven default rates into perspective, in recent years, bonds of low speculative grades, sometimes referred to as "junk bonds," have often offered yields 500 b.p. or more higher than riskless bonds. (Refer back to Exhibit 9.6 and see Box 9.1.) If the junk bonds were able to pay coupons on time and in full for seven years, as much as 70.46 percent of these bonds could default at maturity with zero payoffs and the investor still would receive a cumulative return equal to that on the Treasury portfolio! Realistically, these defaulting bonds would provide some payoff at maturity, so the breakeven default rate could be even higher. Contrariwise, to the extent that bonds default prior to maturity, the breakeven default rate would decline.

In any case, all of this highlights the importance of default rates when considering an investment in a risky bond portfolio. Remember, however, that if the investment is in a single risky bond, the beneficial diversification effect of a portfolio default rate will be lost, substantially increasing the riskiness to the investor.

Box 9.1

Night of the Living Zombie Bonds

Two years ago, *Forbes* suggested that investors gamble on zombie bonds—unsecured debt of savings and loans on the brink of seizure by the federal government (April 3, 1989). These bonds traded at such deep discounts that buyers could recoup their money with just one semiannual interest payment—if the zombies lived that long. If buyers couldn't sell before the feds stepped in, the notes would become worthless.

That's just what happened. One of the eight zombies, Santa Barbara Savings, did pay off—making two interest payments before it was taken over by the feds in April 1990. But all the other zombies *Forbes* looked at got buried by the feds before paying any interest. Bondholders are suing a couple of the thrifts, hoping to recover some cash, but the dead are unlikely to awaken.

Source: Christopher Palmeri, *Forbes,* June 24, 1991. Reprinted by permission of *Forbes* magazine © Forbes Inc., 1991.

Zero-Coupon and Par-Spread Curves

The credit spreads discussed above differ across the yield curve. How these spreads differ is of considerable interest both to issuers of risky debt and to their investors. Through sophisticated econometric techniques, analysts are able to extract the term structure of credit spreads applicable to risky debt securities from market prices of securities. There are two ways in which this is usually presented. First, the spreads are related to zero-coupon Treasury bond yields with the use of **Zero-Spread Curves.** Different spread curves are applicable to different credit qualities. An example of these curves is provided in Exhibit 9.9. With this information at hand, analysts will be able to value an instrument that has a cash flow pattern unmatched by an existing security, because they will have an adjusted discount rate applicable to every maturity.

The second way in which credit spreads are usually presented is in terms of **par Treasury bond yields.** The par Treasury bond yield curve is actually a plot of yields to maturity on bonds that are selling at close to face value. The credit spreads are those that would need to be added to a risky bond's coupon rate in order for the bond to sell at a price near its face value. Exhibit 9.10 maps these credit spreads above the par Treasury bond yields. Obviously, these curves are of less use to investors, since they are applicable only to newly issued risky bonds or bonds selling near par value. Nonetheless, they are indicative of the market price for credit risk, and they are of particular value to new issuers.

The appropriate spreads for risky bonds change over time as market conditions and the risk aversion and perceptions of investors change. Exhibits 9.11 and 9.12 show how the par spreads fluctuated over an interesting three-year period of time that spanned the securities market crash of October 1987; the exhibits illustrate how these spreads were related to the maturities of the risky bonds

EXHIBIT 9.9

Generic zero-spread curves for financial corporations (November 4, 1988)

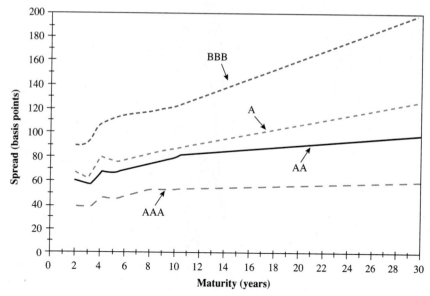

Source: Goldman Sachs.

EXHIBIT 9.10

Generic par-spread curves for financial corporations (November 4, 1988)

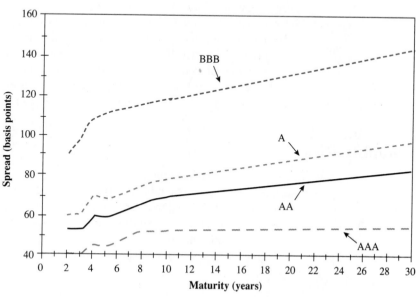

Source: Goldman Sachs.

EXHIBIT 9.11

*Historical corporate
spreads by maturity
(average of all sectors
and ratings)*

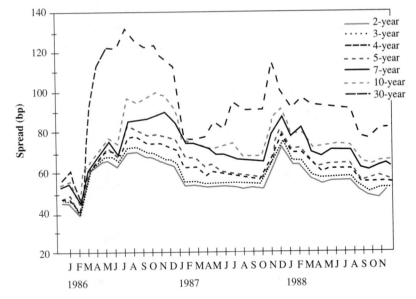

Source: Goldman Sachs.

(Exhibit 9.11) and their ratings (Exhibit 9.12). The spreads widened abruptly following the securities market crash.

The ranges of these credit spreads during the 1986–1988 period are given according to maturity and rating in Exhibit 9.13. Notice the relatively wide range over which this spread moves. Relative to its mean, the range is nearly 100 percent over the recent past. Notice also how this spread expands with maturity, with a range of nearly 100 b.p. for the 30-year bond credit spread.

In all, the data tell an interesting story. Reasonably small yield spreads represent fairly substantial breakeven default rates. This is even more pronounced for longer bonds and for situations in which problems can occur in the distant future.

Illiquidity Risk

A liquid financial instrument is one that can be converted quickly to cash in sizable volume without influencing the price of the instrument appreciably.[13] Based on this definition, there are a plethora of financial instruments that can be deemed liquid. Checking deposits are an obvious candidate. Treasury bills and many other money market instruments are also liquid. Even some Treasury bonds and certain common stocks share the attributes of liquidity.

---

[13]Although it is not inherent in the definition, a second characteristic is sometimes linked to liquidity: the investment can be converted to cash at near to its par value. See Chapter 1 for a discussion of various definitions of an efficient financial market.

EXHIBIT 9.12

Historical corporate spreads by rating (average of all sectors and maturities)

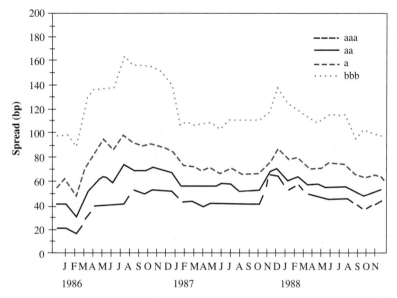

Source: Goldman Sachs.

Financial instruments exhibiting high liquidity are often priced higher than others or, conversely, have lower yields. For example, cash, the most liquid of all financial instruments, provides zero yield. Travelers' checks and most checking deposits also fall into this category.

On the other hand, many investments have low liquidity. In legal proceedings that require the valuation of illiquid financial securities, courts have been known to reduce the estimated value attached to such securities by as much as 30–80 percent relative to a liquid asset with a similar cash flow. This shows how important liquidity is in the valuation of financial instruments.

One indication of high liquidity is a very narrow bid-ask spread quoted by a dealer on a financial security.[14] Most dealers will transact only a limited volume on a quotation. Nonetheless, on highly liquid securities, the dealer will quote both a narrow spread and a high volume limit.

In a study that compares spreads and yields on T-bills and Treasury notes with less than six months to maturity, Yakov Amihud and Haim Mendelson[15] find results consistent with the above statements. Exhibit 9.14 summarizes their findings for a sample of T-notes and two samples of T-bills. Notice that the mean spread between bid and ask differs substantially between T-bills and T-notes, with the latter four

---

[14]Recall from Chapter 5 that the bid price is the price the dealer is willing to pay if you sell him the security; the ask price is the price you will have to pay if you wish to purchase the security from him.

[15]Yakov Amihud and H. Mendelson, "Liquidity, Maturity and the Yields on U.S. Treasury Securities," *Journal of Finance,* September 1991, pp. 1411–25.

EXHIBIT 9.13

*Historical ranges
for par spreads**
(basis points)

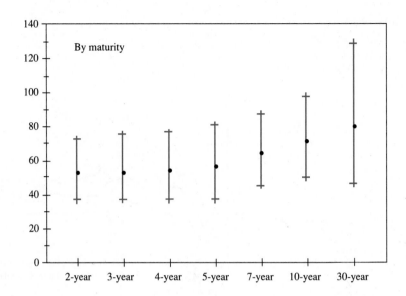

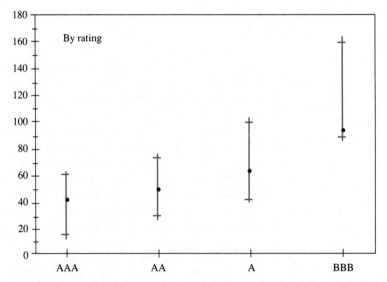

*The vertical lines designate historical ranges of par spreads for January 1986 through November 1988. A black dot (•) indicates the current par spread (as of November 4, 1988).

Source: Goldman Sachs.

times wider than the former. Even though these issues are close substitutes in many respects, such as in issue and maturity, the liquidity of the Treasury bill market is demonstrably greater than the liquidity of Treasury notes. Imagine, if you can, how wide this spread must be for assets that are highly illiquid, such as thinly traded securities or, more frightening, commercial real estate!

EXHIBIT 9.14   Bills and Notes Spreads

		Days to Maturity	Relative Spread*	Annual Yield (%)
Notes				
	Mean	97.41	0.0303	6.523%
	St. dev.	51.44	0.0004	0.607
Bill 1				
	Mean	94.69	0.00761	6.039
	St. dev.	51.53	0.00557	0.756
Bill 2				
	Mean	100.95	0.00801	6.137
	St. dev.	51.79	0.00664	0.677

* Relative spread is the spread divided by trade price.

When it comes to Treasury bonds, the most liquid are usually those bonds that were most recently issued. Traders refer to these bonds as "on-the-run" bonds. Typically, you may find on-the-run bonds in each maturity series issued by the Treasury. The on-the-run 30-year U.S. Treasury bond is one of the most closely watched and highly traded of the Treasury bonds. Other on-the-run bonds may be found with maturities of 2, 3, 5, 7, and 10 years. When comparing their yields to those of seasoned Treasury bonds with similar maturities, we often find that the on-the-run bonds are more expensive and yield as much as 10 b.p. less than their seasoned counterparts. This difference is due to the extra liquidity associated with the recently issued bonds. In the case of Japan, a similar phenomenon exists. The Japanese government officially designates certain "benchmark" bonds, which garner over 90 percent of the trading volume in Japanese government bonds. These highly liquid securities often exhibit yields from 70–100 b.p. lower than other Japanese government bonds with similar coupons and maturities.[16]

To further illustrate the relationship between liquidity and spread, consider Exhibit 9.15. Each vertical bar represents the trading activity of an individual stock traded on the NYSE or the AMEX for October 18, 1991. The stocks are sorted from most to least actively traded going from left to right. Notice that the average relative spread tends to be lower for the more actively traded stocks and that the range of relative spreads observed tends to be wider for the less actively

---

[16]See, for example, Jacob Boudoukh and Robert F. Whitelaw, "Liquidity as a Choice Variable: A Lesson from the Japanese Government Bond Market," *Review of Financial Studies* 6, no. 2 (1993). See also Leland Crabbe and Christopher Turner, "Does the Liquidity of a Debt Issue Increase with Its Size? Evidence from the Corporate Bond and Medium-Term Notes Markets," *Journal of Finance,* December 1995; Yakov Amihud and H. Mendelson, "Liquidity, Maturity and the Yields on U.S. Treasury Securities," *Journal of Finance,* September 1991; and Gregory Kadlek and John McConnell, "The Effect of Market Segmentation and Illiquidity on Asset Prices: Evidence from Exchange Listings," *Journal of Finance,* June 1994.

Exhibit 9.15

Spread versus trading activity for 14 stocks listed on NYSE or AMEX (October 18, 1991)

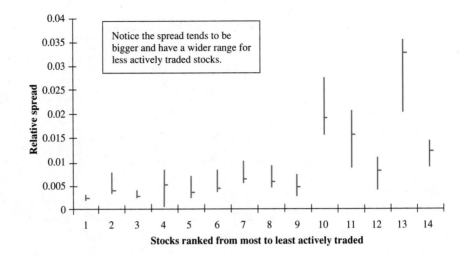

traded stocks. As the exhibit shows, however, the relationship is not simple, nor is it even clearly positive across all assets. Nonetheless, the message is clear. Liquidity has value for investors and traders alike. Illiquid assets cost investors through wider bid-ask spreads. They require issuers to increase the promised yields to investors in such instruments to offset this clearly undesirable attribute of some financial assets.[17]

Tax Rate Risk

On March 1, 1996, the 7-1/8 percent coupon U.S. Treasury bond maturing on February 15, 2023, was priced to yield 6.63 percent. New York City had an outstanding revenue bond maturing that same year but offering a lower 5-1/2 percent coupon and yielding only 5.85 percent. This is in spite of the fact that the New York City debt is subject to default risk and the city had defaulted before on other debt (because unlike the U.S. Treasury, New York City is unauthorized to print money, much to its chagrin). In addition, New York City debt is far less liquid and is subject to call risk (discussed in the next section). How can New York issue debt at rates lower than the riskless U.S. Treasury rates? The reason is the tax treatment of state and local debt. The interest income on the New York City debt is exempt from federal taxes as well as New York City and New York State taxes, while the interest on U.S. Treasury debt is exempt from state and municipal taxes, but it is subject to federal tax.

---

[17]The relationship between liquidity and price is not always this simple. For example, there exist intraday patterns of liquidity and pronounced effects of anticipated earnings announcements on bid-ask spreads. See Charles Lee, Belinda Mucklow, and Mark J. Ready, "Spreads, Depths, and the Impact of Earnings Information: An Intraday Analysis," *Review of Financial Studies* 6, no. 2 (1993).

Debt issues of state and local governments are often referred to as munis (a short form for municipal bonds). Munis may be issued against general tax revenues, sometimes called general obligation debt, or against revenues from a specific project, referred to as revenue bonds. In any case, such issues are exempt from federal taxation on interest income. Capital gains associated with buying tax-exempt debt at a discount or selling at a premium are taxable, however. The tax-exempt status of municipal debt results in yields that are generally lower than the comparable yield on both Treasury and corporate issues.

How much lower can their yield be? This question is difficult to answer because the answer will depend not only on the tax rate but also on the bond's coupon level, call risk, liquidity risk, and default risk. Let us compare the yields by abstracting from these other risks to view the tax effect in isolation. If T represents the marginal federal tax rate of an investor and the taxable and tax-exempt yields are denoted by y_t and y_{te}, the investor will need a taxable interest rate, y_t, of $y_{te} \div (1 - T)$ to achieve the same after-tax rate of return from both bonds. For example, if the federal tax rate applicable to an investor is 31 percent, a tax-exempt bond will need to provide an interest rate of 5.52 percent [$= 8\% \times (1 - .31)$] in order to provide the same after-tax return from an 8 percent taxable bond. On an after-tax basis, the investor would be indifferent between these two bonds.

This preferred tax status of municipal debt is reflected in the marketplace. As evidenced by the data reported in Exhibit 9.16A, substantial differences exist between the yields on taxable and tax-exempt investments. This difference will vary over time and will also vary across maturity. Either way, it is always quite substantial. Exhibit 9.16B shows the ratio of municipal bond yields to Treasury yields. This ratio has also fluctuated over time, but usually within a fairly narrow range between tax law changes or anticipated changes. For example, with the lower marginal tax rates of the Reagan-Bush years, the ratio increased, as would be expected. Notice that the ratio of yields is typically higher than would be suggested by the highest marginal federal income tax bracket. There are four reasons for this. First, we are comparing yields on municipal and state bonds versus Treasury bonds. Only the Treasury, of course, has the ability to print money to repay debt, so its credit rating is presumably higher than that of most states. Second, the prices and yields of bonds are determined by the marginal, not the average, investor, and the marginal investor may not be in the highest marginal tax bracket. Third, there are occasionally rumors about politicians doing away with the tax-exempt status of these bonds, which engender caution among investors. Fourth, alternative minimum tax provisions place limits on the tax benefits accorded to municipal bond investors and thereby limit demand.

Tax-exempt investing does have its risks. There are two key factors that affect the desirability of specific tax-exempt investment decisions. First, as mentioned above, the tax rate may be changed by the government from time to time. For example, the highest marginal tax rates in the United States for individual taxpayers used to be as high as 90 percent in the early 1960s. Later, they were reduced to 70 percent, and then they were reduced again to 46 percent. More recently, they were reduced to 31 percent, but then they were revised again to

Exhibit 9.16a

State bonds versus Treasuries (10-year maturity)

39.6 percent. Each time this or any marginal tax rate changes, it influences the effective after-tax yield on these investments. To see the impact of this on muni yields, suppose that during an entire period, Treasuries could be sold at par by offering 10 percent yields. Then, to appeal to people in the highest tax brackets, the muni yields, ignoring call, default, and liquidity risks, would need to have been 1 percent [= 10% × (1−.90)] when federal taxes topped off at 90 percent, 3 percent [= 10% × (1−.70)] when they were reduced to 70 percent, 5.4 percent [= 10% × (1−.46)] when they dropped to 46 percent, 6.9 percent [= 10% × (1−.31)] when they were reduced to 31 percent, and 6.04 percent [= 10% × (1 − .396)] when they were raised to 39.6 percent. Imagine what would happen to the price of muni debt and the holding period yield of this debt for those who purchased it at a time when federal tax rates were 70 percent. Just to remain competitive, the yield on the muni would be forced to rise, relative to that on taxable bonds; muni prices would drop; and the total return on the portfolio would have performed very poorly.[18]

There is another dimension of tax preference that influences the after-tax yield. As noted above, while muni interest payments may be exempt from federal tax, capital gains from investing in munis are taxed at the federal capital gains tax rates. Therefore, as either interest rates or tax rates change, the price movement associated with such variations may be subject to federal tax. It is in fact true that even

---

[18]Of course, if tax rates were to change, it might affect the taxable interest rate as well, so these comments are valid on a comparative basis and not necessarily on an absolute basis. For example, a drop in federal tax rates could precipitate a drop in taxable interest rates. If the drop in taxable interest rates is steep enough, muni rates may not even rise in absolute terms, although the spread between Treasuries and munis would narrow.

Exhibit 9.16b

Ratio of state bond versus Treasuries yield (10-year maturity)

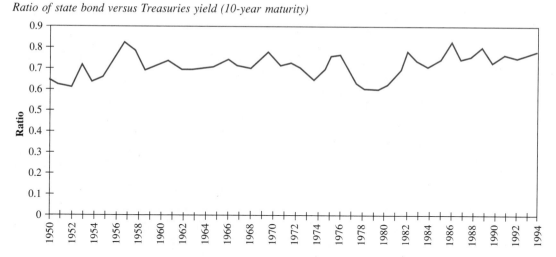

tax-exempt issues are affected by changes in the marginal tax rate. It is also true that, because of their favored tax status, the yields on munis often change by less than the yields on Treasury bonds of similar maturity for a given tax structure.[19]

Some financial instruments have certain tax preferences, and in this sense, munis are not unique. These tax preferences will be described in Part III of this book, when specific financial instruments are described in more detail. At this point, suffice it to say that tax rates and tax status are important considerations in portfolio investment, even for tax-exempt bonds.

Timing of Cash Flow Risk

In Chapter 7, we described interest-sensitive cash flows and introduced two techniques that are used to value them—lattices and simulations. We treated the interest sensitivity as a deterministic process in our previous examples, so that cash flows were related with certainty to interest rates. Often, however, cash flows exhibit a looser, even stochastic, relationship to interest rates.

In fact, many financial instruments provide cash flows of uncertain amounts and timing. At times, this uncertainty isn't even related to the level of interest rates. Consider the case of a bank that makes automobile loans. The bank does not

---

[19]For example, suppose that the tax rate is 40 percent. If taxable interest rates are 10 percent, investors will require only a 6 percent yield on tax-exempt securities of similar credit risk. However, if taxable yields increase to 11 percent, then tax-exempt securities will increase in yield to 6.6 percent. Note that the yields on tax exempts increase by only 60 percent of the increase in taxable bond yields.

EXHIBIT 9.17

Monthly conditional prepayment rate versus (GNMA coupon rate) − (10-year treasury note rate) percentage

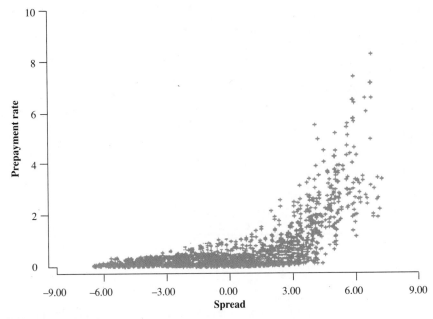

Source: *Financial Management,* Autumn 1987, p. 10.

know exactly how many of its borrowers will pay off these loans on time or exactly when they will choose to trade in their car for a new model. Any particular loan has a good deal of uncertainty associated with it. On the other hand, when a bank makes a large number of loans, they have a large pool of similar risks. The bank can therefore make some reasonable approximations.

Many financial contracts have similar characteristics. As a general statement, investors will require a higher expected rate of return for such instruments in exchange for accepting this uncertainty.

Of particular importance to investors is one subclass of financial securities that exhibit cash flow timing uncertainty in which the uncertainty is characterized by a variability in interest-sensitive cash flows. Here, the precise timing and amount of cash flows are uncertain but related to the evolution of interest rates over time.

Consider the case of callable corporate bonds, for example. A corporate bond issuer may choose either to call or not call its bond back prior to maturity, depending on subsequent interest rate levels and a host of other factors. While we may estimate the firm's tendency to call a bond based on past experience of corporate issuers in similar circumstances or based on other economic analysis, we can never be certain that the corporation's behavior will actually be consistent with our analysis.

Another example of an interest-sensitive security is that of a home mortgage. The mortgagor may have an incentive to refinance his home when new mortgage rates drop 2 percent below his existing mortgage, yet we cannot be sure that he will refinance. In fact, as shown in Exhibit 9.17, mortgage prepayments increase rapidly among mortgagors as interest rates decline below initial levels, yet the relationship is far from deterministic. The exhibit reveals a tendency to refinance at lower interest rates, but it also shows some stochastic behavior surrounding that tendency.

Investors, therefore, will be subject to uncertainty in their cash flows even if they fully analyze the cash flows under different rate environments using the most sophisticated techniques available. To encourage investors to hold such instruments, the yield must adjust to compensate for the uncertainty contained in the underlying cash flows. In short, yields must be higher on such assets. But how much higher, and how can we capture the yield differential that is embedded in market rates on such financial instruments? This is the subject to which we now turn.

Financial market participants have developed an approach to deal with cash flow uncertainty. The concept is referred to as the **option-adjusted spread** (OAS), which is a single number, based upon market observed prices, that indicates the additional yield offered to investors for bearing such risk. The OAS represents an average of the extra compensation per period that investors expect to earn by investing in a security with cash flow uncertainty.

To see how the OAS is estimated, let us begin where Chapter 7 ended. To value securities with stochastic, interest-sensitive cash flows, the lattice and simulation methods described earlier are still used, although expected cash flows, rather than deterministic cash flows, are linked to interest rate levels and paths. The OAS is a number, expressed in basis points, added to the short rate at each point along all paths that they might follow, that will correctly price the financial instrument.[20] It is the manifest price that investors in these securities require on this investment to compensate them for this uncertainty.

To illustrate how this measure is obtained, consider an investment that is free of default but which has stochastic interest sensitivity in its cash flows. We will consider only three representative interest rate paths, each equally likely to unfold. The investment provides an $80.00 cash flow annually until maturity, at which time the face value of $1,000 is also returned. However, the issuer of this debt instrument has the option to call back the debt at par value (plus accrued interest) prior to maturity. Assume that he is likely to do so if interest rates sink below 7.0 percent. The three interest rate paths are given below.

Path	Time 0	Time 1	Time 2
1	7.0%	9.0%	9.5%
2	7.0%	7.5%	8.5%
3	7.0%	5.5%	6.5%

We can use the information in these paths to create the hypothetical value of our security. Our computations proceed below.

---

[20]See L. F. Hayre, "Understanding Option-Adjusted Spreads and Their Use," *Journal of Portfolio Management,* Summer 1990.

Path 1 value: $\dfrac{\$80}{1.07} + \dfrac{\$80}{1.07 \times 1.09} + \dfrac{\$1,080}{1.07 \times 1.09 \times 1.095} = \$989.03$

Path 2 value: $\dfrac{\$80}{1.07} + \dfrac{\$80}{1.07 \times 1.075} + \dfrac{\$1,080}{1.07 \times 1.075 \times 1.085} = \$1,009.69$

Path 3 value: $\dfrac{\$1,080}{1.07} = \$1,022.80$

By averaging these path values together, we get our hypothetical value.

$$\dfrac{\$989.03 + \$1,009.69 + \$1,022.80}{3} = \$1,007.17$$

This would be the price if the market required no compensation for the uncertainty of repayment, and it is analogous to the values we obtained in Chapter 7.

If this security is trading in an efficient market for the price of $992.62, our hypothetical price is too high. To correct for this mispricing, we add a constant OAS to each of the interest rates and continue experimenting until our hypothetical price matches the actual market price of $992.62. Our experimentation in this case results in an OAS of 50 basis points.

Path 1 OAS value: $\dfrac{\$80}{1.075} + \dfrac{\$80}{1.075 \times 1.095} + \dfrac{\$1,080}{1.075 \times 1.095 \times 1.10} = \$976.46$

Path 2 OAS value: $\dfrac{\$80}{1.075} + \dfrac{\$80}{1.075 \times 1.08} + \dfrac{\$1,080}{1.075 \times 1.08 \times 1.09} = \$996.75$

Path 3 OAS value: $\dfrac{\$1,080}{1.075} = \$1,004.65$

Note that each of the discount rates above is adjusted upward by 50 b.p. By averaging these path values together, we find that our new OAS hypothetical value equals the market price.

$$\dfrac{\$976.46 + \$996.75 + \$1,004.65}{3} = \$992.62$$

To keep our example simple, we used only three interest rate paths. In practice, 500 or more paths are typically used.[21]

Many investments are marketed by revealing their OAS to potential investors. The use of this concept is quite common in the mortgage-backed securities market, for example. Exhibit 9.18 shows OAS ranges for a particular kind of

---

[21]The general formula for OAS determination is given below. Let s denote the interest rate paths, which are N in number. Let $CF(s,t)$ denote the cash flow for path s at time t, and let $r(s,t)$ denote the single-period interest rate for path s at time t. Then OAS is the number that sets the market price equal to the right-hand-side of the equation.

$$\text{Market Price} = \frac{1}{N} \sum_{s=1}^{N} \sum_{t=1}^{m} \frac{CF(s,t)}{\prod_{i=1}^{t}[1 + r(s,t) + \text{OAS}]}$$

Exhibit 9.18 FNMA Price List
(August 18, 1994)

Coupon Rate	Price Dollar	1/32s	Expected Coupon Weighted-Average	Expected Term (mo.)	Option-Adjusted Spread (b.p.)
			30-Year FNMA		
6.0	87	28	6.65	350	46
6.5	90	27	7.05	353	45
7.0	93	23	7.55	354	45
7.5	96	14	8.15	357	42
8.0	98	28	8.60	357	41
8.5	101	01	9.05	355	43
9.0	103	06	9.60	312	45
9.5	105	06	10.10	301	50
10.0	106	27	10.60	295	50
			15-Year FNMA		
6.0	92	11	6.55	172	39
6.5	94	20	7.05	174	37
7.0	96	27	7.65	177	33
7.5	98	30	8.10	177	33
8.0	100	24	8.55	177	37
8.5	102	13	9.10	132	58
9.0	104	01	9.60	121	58
9.5	105	07	10.10	115	57
			7-Year FNMA		
5.5	93	03	6.05	77	33
6.0	95	00	6.55	79	27
6.5	96	30	7.05	80	24
7.0	98	23	7.55	82	21
7.5	100	06	8.05	82	26
8.0	101	24	8.55	82	26
8.5	102	21	9.05	44	55

Source: *Mortgage Securities Research,* Goldman Sachs, August 19, 1994.

instrument in the mortgage-backed securities market. We report Federal National Mortgage Association "pass-through" bonds of various maturities, along with their current yield and option-adjusted spread. Notice both the general level of OAS for this instrument and how it varies across the sample. In general, OAS is a function both of coupon level and the average coupon (WAC) and average maturity (WAM) of the underlying mortgages,[22] as can be seen in this exhibit.

---

[22]WAC and WAM are acronyms in the mortgage market. See Chapter 13 for a further treatment of these terms and their precise meaning.

EXHIBIT 9.19   OAS under Different Volatility Assumptions

Security	Average Price ($)	Life (years)	Effective Duration	Assumed Volatility		
				8%	*12%*	*16%*
FNMA 8s	93.97	9.2	5.28	68	57	43
FNMA 9s	98.78	9.1	4.91	75	57	37
FNMA 10s	103.34	6.7	3.60	77	53	27
FNMA 11s	106.44	3.2	1.93	54	26	-2

Exhibit 9.19 looks at the FNMA instrument to analyze the effect of volatility on the estimated OAS. Notice that OAS declines as the volatility assumption increases. This is because the option to prepay a mortgage decreases in value when interest rates are insufficiently volatile to offer the prospect of substantially lower interest rates. In other words, the mortgage lender is less likely to have an attractively priced mortgage called away from him. The table includes a column for effective duration. This reports a duration calculation based on the simulation method we described in Chapter 8. Effective duration is given because the valuation technology takes into consideration the prepayment sensitivity to mortgage rates. This complexity associated with instruments having prepayment uncertainty will be discussed further in the next chapter.

Although OAS computations are helpful to investors considering the purchase of a security, they are subject to abuse and misinterpretation in practice. No two security analysts arrive at the same OAS, because their models of interest rates, or cash flow sensitivities to interest rates, differ one from another. Thus, it is best to treat OAS as indicative, not definitive.[23]

---

[23]See David F. Babbel and Stavros Zenios, "What's Wrong with Option-Adjusted Spreads?" *Financial Analysts Journal,* July/August 1992, pp. 65–69.

Summary

In this chapter, we have discussed four types of risks that affect the pricing and yields of financial instruments. Tax treatment probably has the most impact on prices and yields. Default risk, illiquidity, and payment timing risk usually have less impact, although extreme levels of default risk and illiquidity can have powerful effects on prices and yields.

Several tools are used to help analysts compare prices and yields of financial instruments of differing risks. Agency ratings, market-based measures of default, breakeven default rates, and zero- and par-spread curves are aimed at helping assess default risk. Bid-ask spreads and trading volume are used to assess liquidity risk. Tax adjustments are made to compare bonds with different tax treatments. Option-adjusted spreads are used to assess cash-flow-timing risk.

While these risks were considered independently, it is common in practice for a financial instrument to feature several of these risks, and they often act in concert with one another. For example, if federal taxes are lowered drastically, it may make it relatively more difficult for state and municipal governments to issue debt at attractive rates. If they are unable to issue new debt, their ability to repay existing debt may be impaired. The added default risk may decrease liquidity but reduce call risk. These reactions will also affect the interest rate risk discussed in an earlier chapter.

Key Concepts

Review Questions

1. You expect your employer to pay 20¢ on the dollar if it defaults on its only debt offering. The debt is a zero-coupon bond that promises to pay $1,000 in one year. The current market price of the debt is $914, while that of a similar Treasury bill is $921. What is the probability that your employer will default? What is the yield differential between the two bonds?

2. The typical muni offers a lower yield than a Treasury bond of similar maturity. How will this yield differential be affected by call risk, liquidity risk, and default risk?

3. Suppose that the yield on a Treasury portfolio is 6.25 percent. The yield on a similar risky portfolio is 125 b.p. higher. Both portfolios mature in five years and have the same tax treatment and liquidity risk. What is the breakeven default rate?

4. Suppose the example used in connection with option-adjusted spreads had a different call option. Suppose the bond was callable (at par and coupon) at 8 percent only after the end of the first year. What would be its value without the OAS, and what would be the implied

OAS to equate this answer to the price quoted in this chapter?

5. Suppose that you have an equally weighted portfolio of two bonds, one tax exempt and the other fully taxable. Both bonds have similar modified durations of 10 with respect to movements in their own yields. Suppose, further, that tax-exempt yields move in the same direction as taxable yields, but only 60 percent as much, given marginal tax rates of 40 percent. How would a portfolio duration of these two bonds be calculated?

6. Suppose that there are three possible outcomes for a corporate one-year zero: solvency, default with debt worth 40¢ on the dollar, and default where the debt is worthless. You know for a fact that the middle case has only a 15 percent chance of happening. The company's bond is selling for $74.56. A Treasury Zero of similar maturity is quoted at $88.76. What is the probability of default on the corporate debt if the expected return is the same as that on the Treasury bond?

7. A risky bond portfolio offers a 7.86 percent annual yield on a five-year investment. A

treasury portfolio with the same time horizon offers an annual yield of 6.52 percent. If the risky bonds are in default, they will pay their coupons and 25 percent of the principal. Assuming that the coupons are reinvested, what is the breakeven default rate?

8. Using the three interest rate paths given in this chapter, what is the hypothetical value of a bond paying a $75 annual coupon? Your broker quotes you a price of $996.50. Is this a possible price? Explain. What is the option-adjusted spread that will render this bond correctly priced by the model?

References

Altman, Edward I. "Measuring Corporate Bond Mortality and Performance." *Journal of Finance,* September 1989.

Altman, Edward I., and Scott Nammacher. *Investing in Junk Bonds.* New York: John Wiley, 1987.

Amihud, Yakov, and H. Mendelson. "Liquidity, Maturity and the Yields on U.S. Treasury Securities." *Journal of Finance,* September 1991.

Babbel, David F., and Stavros Zenios. "What's Wrong with Option-Adjusted Spreads?" *Financial Analysts Journal,* July/August 1992.

Bodie, Zvi; Alex Kane; and Alan Marcus. *Investments.* 3d ed. Burr Ridge, Ill.: Richard D. Irwin, 1995.

Boudoukh, Jacob, and Robert F. Whitelaw. "Liquidity as a Choice Variable: A Lesson from the Japanese Government Bond Market." *Review of Financial Studies* 6, no. 2 (1993).

Crabbe, Leland E., and Christopher M. Turner. "Does the Liquidity of a Debt Issue Increase with Its Size? Evidence from the Corporate Bond and Medium-Term Notes Markets." *Journal of Finance,* December 1995.

Fabozzi, Frank, and T. Dessa Fabozzi. *Bond Markets: Analysis and Strategies.* Englewood Cliffs, N.J.: Prentice Hall, 1989.

Fabozzi, Frank, and Gifford Fong. *Advanced Fixed Income Portfolio Management: The State of the Art.* Chicago: Probus, 1994.

Green, Richard C. "A Simple Model of the Taxable and Tax-Exempt Yield Curve." *Review of Financial Studies,* 1993.

Hayre, L. F. "Understanding Option-Adjusted Spreads and Their Use." *Journal of Portfolio Management,* Summer 1990.

Hickman, W. Braddock. *Corporate Bond Quality and Investor Experience.* Princeton, N.J.: National Bureau of Economic Research, 1958.

Homer, Sidney, and Martin L. Leibowitz. *Inside the Yield Book: New Tools for Bond Market Strategy.* Englewood Cliffs, N.J.: Prentice Hall, 1972.

Jarrow, Robert A., and Stuart M. Turnbull. "Pricing Derivatives on Financial Securities Subject to Credit Risk." *Journal of Finance,* March 1995.

Kadlec, Gregory B., and John J. McConnell. "The Effect of Market Segmentation and Illiquidity on Asset Prices: Evidence from Exchange Listings." *Journal of Finance,* June 1994.

Lee, Charles M. C.; Belinda Mucklow; and Mark J. Ready. "Spreads, Depths, and the Impact of Earnings Information: An Intraday Analysis." *Review of Financial Studies* 6, no. 2 (1993).

Litterman, Robert, and Thomas Iben. "Corporate Bond Valuation and the Term Structure of Credit Spreads." *Fixed Income Research.* Goldman Sachs, November 1988.

Longstaff, Francis A. "How Much Can Marketability Affect Security Values?" *Journal of Finance,* December 1995.

Longstaff, Francis A., and Eduardo S. Schwartz. "A Simple Approach to Valuing Risky Fixed and Floating Rate Debt." *Journal of Finance,* July 1995.

Moody's Investors Service. *Corporate Bond Defaults and Default Rates 1970–1995.* Moody's Special Report, February 1996.

Valuing Cash Flows in Foreign Currencies

This chapter broadens our view of financial markets to encompass the pricing of not only domestic instruments denominated in local currency but also foreign-currency-denominated instruments. To do so, however, requires knowledge of the foreign exchange market and the determinants of the exchange rate. Our treatment here is just an introduction. It begins with the need for foreign investment and foreign exchange, and it goes on to discuss the determinants of the price of foreign currency. The discussion ends with a review of other risks in foreign investment, including the differing nature of markets and institutions across the world.

Up to this point, most of our attention has been focused on prices, interest rates, and instruments in domestic markets. In this chapter, we broaden our focus to include the international arena. The analysis begins with a discussion of the need to look beyond your local market for financial investments, and the role foreign exchange plays in any transaction in foreign assets. It then introduces the reader to the new, different, and, at times, confusing terms in the market for foreign exchange. At the heart of this chapter is a treatment of the price of foreign exchange and how understanding the determinants of the price of a currency is critical to participation in the market for foreign-denominated assets.

Before we begin, however, it is important for us to point out that the treatment here is just an introduction to the subject. Volumes have been written on the role of foreign investments in asset management and the determinants of foreign exchange rates. This treatment quickly presents these topics in the context of understanding the values of cash flows from market instruments. Much more could and has been said elsewhere.[1]

Investing beyond Local Borders

In the U.S. market, we presume that financial assets can be purchased with dollars. In fact, most of us think that all money is green and that all of it has U.S. presidents on it! But to be a knowledgeable investor, one must look beyond all of this. We must realize that the world is a bigger place than Steinberg's cartoons imagine it to be.[2] In fact, the U.S. market, for all of its breadth and depth, is only one of many financial markets.

In these other markets, entrepreneurs, households, and large firms enter the market to obtain funds for investment, just as we do here. Likewise, individuals and institutions in those markets provide these funds, just as we do in our domestic market. However, the currency is different, assets may differ, and both institutions and markets conform to their local customs and needs. It is increasingly necessary to invest in and be knowledgeable about these markets. The business and financial world is becoming increasingly global, suggesting that avoidance of markets beyond our shores is a clear mistake. In fact, growth rates elsewhere around the globe are often higher than here in the United States. This suggests that the U.S. market is losing market share, even if it is not losing absolute size. Add to this the potential to diversify by adding foreign assets to your portfolio, and you can see why Americans have become increasingly interested in the global marketplace.

To participate in another market, however, takes know-how. Mistakes are costly in any financial market, and it is easy to make them when one crosses borders with different laws, customs, and market procedures on either side. Therefore, notwithstanding the attractiveness of global investing, care must be exercised to prevent a costly learning experience.

Here, you will begin this learning process in a somewhat less costly setting. We start by explaining the institutional structure and terminology of the market that links foreign currencies together—the foreign exchange market. Investors of

---

[1]See, for example, J. Orlin Grabbe, *International Financial Markets* (New York: Elsevier, 1990).

[2]For the reader unfamiliar with Steinberg's cartoons, they portray a particular locality, such as New York City, in exaggerated proportions relative to the rest of the world.

all types go to the foreign exchange market to obtain local currencies to invest in markets other than their own, and it is to this market that they return to convert these currencies to domestic-denominated money to be used for future consumption. Understanding how the foreign exchange market works is the first step on the road to global investing.

The second step on this road is to understand the determinants of the price one must pay for the foreign currency in this market. This is a long story because it is not an easy subject. However, to invest in another market requires that a foreigner (1) obtain local currency, (2) engage in a financial transaction, (3) receive payment, and, finally, (4) convert the proceeds to his or her local currency. As the first nine chapters of this book have indicated, understanding a domestic financial transaction is not trivial. Now we have an additional complexity to understand—namely, what determines the price of foreign currency today and what will happen to that price when one needs to convert the returns from foreign investment back into domestic currency. To grasp this, one needs to understand both the determinants of the current exchange rates between currencies and the factors that change these currency prices over time.

Foreign Exchange Markets

Investors wishing to participate in foreign markets may do so in one of two ways. They can purchase assets issued by foreign firms or governments that are denominated either in the investors' currency or in local currency. An example of the first case would be an American investor purchasing a **dollar-denominated** instrument issued by a foreign bank. In fact, many U.S. investors do purchase assets that are foreign-issued dollar-denominated debt, such as Eurodollars, Asia dollars, Eurobonds, and the like. These assets have returns that are equivalent to those discussed in the previous chapters. Of course, because the issuer is based in a foreign country, the uncertainty and possible payoff streams may differ, but the analysis already completed is unaffected by the distinction.

If the investor purchases a **foreign-denominated asset,** however, extra steps must be added to the transaction. The investor must first obtain the local currency by entering the market where currency is traded every day. Over $300 billion of currencies are traded each day in the **foreign exchange market,** making it among the largest markets in the world. The purpose of the foreign exchange market, like that of other markets, is to bring together buyers and sellers—in this case, buyers and sellers of currencies.

There are no centralized trading locations, such as an exchange or trading floor, for currencies. The currency markets are essentially over-the-counter markets with no set hours for trading. Market participants are "brought together" through an informal network using only wires, telephones, telexes, and satellites. There are no membership requirements or special rules to allow one to become a participant, although trading conforms to an unwritten code of rules among the larger, more active participants.

The participants in the market are usually large institutions. The employees of these firms enter the foreign exchange market either as brokers operating on behalf of their clients or as traders buying and selling currencies for their own accounts. In any case, the participants enter the market to buy one currency, using another in exchange. For example, a New York bank may buy Japanese yen, offering U.S. dollars in exchange, because it believes that the Japanese currency will go up in price relative to the U.S. currency. If the price does go up, the bank can sell the yen for dollars and make a profit, just as any investor or trader would if he or she had purchased a stock or bond. The distinction here, however, is that the investor has purchased a currency, not an interest-bearing financial asset. Therefore, when the bank purchases the Japanese currency, it invests it in local currency by buying a yen-denominated asset of some kind.

As noted above, foreign investment involves two steps, not just one. First, the local currency must be purchased in the so-called **spot market;** then, the local investment must be selected. The profitability of the investment depends upon both the performance of the investment selected in the foreign country *and* the future exchange rate between the two currencies. Therefore, foreign investment involves two risks rather than one—namely, currency and investment risk.

To limit this risk, investors can purchase or sell currencies in advance in the **forward market.** Here, investors can contract today to exchange currencies at a specified price and at a specified time in the future. This eliminates the risk of currency fluctuation from a foreign investment, but it also eliminates any potential gains from changes in the exchange rate. Accordingly, many investors and speculators prefer to invest **unhedged** in the currency—that is, without a fixed price of the currency in the future.

Of course, this is not always true. At least two types of participants in the foreign exchange market prefer **forward cover.** The first are investors who believe that the foreign currency is overpriced but the foreign financial investment is attractive. These investors would purchase a forward contract to sell the foreign currency in exchange for their local one. By so doing, these investors eliminate the currency risk while maintaining the investment risk associated with the firm, in the case of an equity investment, or interest rates, for a fixed-rate investment. The second class of participants are multinational firms. These companies frequently manufacture in one country and sell in another. For these firms, currency fluctuation adds a degree of uncertainty to their business that is clearly unwanted. They would tend to hedge their currency exposure and form an important client base for banks active in the foreign exchange market.

Determinants of the Exchange Rate

All of the players described above participate in the foreign exchange market. They buy and sell currencies, invest in foreign markets, or try to repatriate the funds earned from their normal overseas business activities. While all of this may be very nice and even informative, the real question here is how is the exchange

Box 10.1

The Recent Demise of the EMS

The European Monetary System (EMS) was created by the European Community in 1979. The EMS tied the various European currencies together in a system of semirigid exchange rates, based upon the presumption that the European Union would prove the fixed exchange rate sustainable. The exchange rate mechanism (ERM) tied 11 European currencies together such that exchange rates between these currencies would be allowed to fluctuate in bands 2.25 percent on each side of a central value (6 percent for the Spanish peseta and the Portuguese escudo). The Europeans hoped to stabilize the exchange rate between their currencies, with a goal of complete monetary union and a single European currency by the turn of the century. Unfortunately, the exchange markets were not accommodating to the EMS. Between the fall of 1992 and the summer of 1993, intense pressure on the relative exchange rates within the system ultimately caused its breakdown. The German currency, the deutsche mark, proved too strong to be contained within the allowable band, while the Italian lira and British pound showed consistent weakness that central banks could not contain. The result is informative, as it shows the limitations of central bank exchange rate regimes.

In the fall of 1992, the Italian lira was consistently hitting the lower bound of the EMS exchange rate mechanism. A crisis of confidence ensued, and the lira was forced to devalue relative to other countries. However, pressure remained on other countries, most notably England, where its currency, pound sterling, was viewed as overvalued relative to the deutsche mark. To stabilize the entire exchange rate system, pressure was then placed on Germany to reduce nominal interest rates during the summer of 1993, in the hope that real interest rates would also decline there and the mark would become less attractive. But the attempt was not successful. By August 2, 1993, the finance ministers and central bank chiefs of the European Community, recognizing the futility of a close EMS exchange union, agreed to let currencies fluctuate within a 30 percent band. In the words of Finance Minister Wim Kok of the Netherlands, "This is a face-saving way to prevent the system from collapsing." In the end, neither the system nor the face was saved. The president of the German Central Bank, Helmut Schlesinger, admitted to committing $35 billion dollars in support of weak currencies in the Bundesbank's futile attempt to maintain the narrow band.

rate determined between any two currencies in this market? And, equally important for the unhedged investor, what causes this exchange rate to change?

At some level, the answers are fairly straightforward. Exchange rates between currencies are determined in one of two ways. The first is by regulation. In the recent past, the exchange rate between currencies was regulated, and it still is in some countries. In this event, the central bank dictates an exchange rate at which local currency will be traded for all other foreign currencies, and it stands ready to buy or sell the local currency at that rate. These exchange rates change only when the central bank permits it, and this occurs only infrequently. However, history has shown us how difficult such **fixed-exchange-rate regimes** are to maintain. If the rate is incorrectly set (see Box 10.1), the system collapses, as investors and speculators anticipate a currency revaluation. For example, if the price of a currency is set too high, that is, if its true value in terms of other currencies is lower than the fixed exchange rate, then investors will sell the currency. This increases the selling pressure on an overpriced currency and eventually causes the central bank to lower the fixed price of the currency in what is called a **devaluation.** (See Box 10.2.) The reverse is also possible. In this case, a currency's value rises in what is referred to as an **appreciation** of a currency.

Increasingly, however, countries have preferred to allow their currency to **float,** changing price relative to other currencies based upon supply and demand for the currency rather than by regulatory fiat. In this case, the market and its participants dictate the price for a currency in much the same way that they dictate the price for any other financial asset or commodity. The value fluctuates as it becomes more or less attractive to potential buyers and sellers.

For a currency, which can be used to purchase any of the thousands of goods produced in an economy or any real or financial asset in the market, its value should be clearly related to its potential purchasing power in the home country. The relative value of any two currencies, therefore, should be closely related to their respective values in their home markets. Because currencies can be used to purchase both commodities and financial assets in each country, however, the application of the principle of relative purchasing power for exchange rate determination becomes a rather complicated notion.

Purchasing Power Parity Theory

The theory that describes the relationship between commodity prices and exchange rates is known as Purchasing Power Parity (PPP). It comes in two flavors: Absolute PPP and Relative PPP.

Absolute purchasing power parity holds that the equilibrium exchange rate is determined by the price of goods in the two countries. Specifically, the equilibrium exchange rate should be equal to the ratio of the prices of a representative market basket of domestic goods to the prices of an identical market basket of goods available in the foreign country. For the theory to be true, two conditions must hold: (1) the same goods must be included in each market basket, and (2) the goods must be included in the same proportions.

The theory was devised by Gustav Cassel, a Swedish economist, at the close of World War I. Trade had been interrupted during the war due to the treacherous conditions of shipping lanes, and therefore, exchange rates needed to be reestablished. Cassel attempted to derive a crude measure of equilibrium exchange rates by comparing prices of a market basket of goods in various currencies. The result was Absolute PPP. In equation form, the relationship is presented as follows:

$$\frac{\text{Price level }_{\text{domestic}}}{\text{Price level }_{\text{foreign}}} = e$$

where e is the exchange rate in terms of domestic currency per unit of foreign currency.

To illustrate this theory, consider the following basket of goods, priced in U.S. dollars and Japanese yen. Suppose it represents the typical consumption basket of a U.S. or Japanese citizen.

Commodity	Dollar Price	Yen Price
500 lbs. wheat	$ 150	¥ 22,000
30 lbs. rice	$ 10	¥ 2,200
200 gallons of unleaded regular gasoline	$ 220	¥ 26,000
1 videocassette recorder, remote control	$ 240	¥ 14,000
1 color television, remote control	$ 500	¥ 42,500
100 cans of soda	$ 32	¥ 5,100
20 double cheeseburgers	$ 38	¥ 9,200
TOTAL	$1,190	¥121,000

If these market baskets are truly representative, then the equilibrium exchange rate, in dollars per yen, should be:

$$\frac{\$1,190}{¥121,000} = 0.98347¢/¥ = e$$

Referring to the exchange rate in this way is termed a **direct quote**, because it values one Japanese yen in U.S. dollar terms—0.98347 cents per yen. This amounts to slightly less than 1¢ per yen. Alternatively, one could refer to the value of these currencies in another way; that is, the value of the dollar could be presented in terms of yen. This is referred to as an **indirect quote** from the U.S. perspective. Most countries use the direct quote method, but some, such as Great Britain, Australia, and the United States, use the indirect quote method of conveying exchange rates one to another. Translating our first result into an indirect quote (which we will denote with an uppercase E) is accomplished by taking the reciprocal of the direct quote, thus converting it into yen per dollar.[3]

$$\frac{¥121,000}{\$1,190} = ¥101.7/\$ = E$$

Note that Absolute PPP has produced an exchange rate but that not all commodities within the basket of goods are related across currencies at that same exchange rate. For example, it appears that wheat is overpriced and televisions are underpriced in Japan. Absolute PPP acknowledges that there are deviations when the price of any

---

[3]An analogy will make this concept simpler. For example, tomatoes will sell for 50¢ per pound or for two pounds for a dollar. Relating the price in terms of a pound of tomatoes would be analogous to a direct quote from the U.S. point of view, where the object being priced is a unit of foreign exchange. An indirect quote from the U.S. point of view takes the dollar as the object priced and relates the price in terms of how many units of foreign currency it takes to buy one unit of U.S. currency. This is analogous to how many pounds of tomatoes you can buy with one unit of U.S. currency—two pounds per dollar.

Box 10.2

Soros

September 1992 was a month international money managers won't easily forget. Especially George Soros, the legendary chairman of the Quantum group of funds. Soros and clients of his four Netherlands Antilles-domiciled pools cleared a cool $1.5 billion in just one month as a result of the upheaval in Europe's markets. Nor is that all the Soros crowd has made this year: Between the end of August and early October the new asset value of his flagship $3.3 billion (assets) Quantum Fund rose 31%, and it is up 51% year-to-date. As of mid-October his assets under management had swelled to $7 billion.

There were other big winners in the currency turmoil that toppled the pound sterling, the lira and other soft European currencies and humbled the central banks of Europe. The big winners include Bruce Kovner of Caxton Corp. and Paul Tudor Jones of Jones Investments. Kovner's funds made an estimated $300 million, increasing assets to about $1.6 billion; Jones's funds were up some $250 million, to $1.4 billion in assets.

The month of wild trading and sheer excitement that wrecked the European Exchange Rate Mechanism were also good times for leading U.S. banks with big foreign exchange operations, especially Citicorp, J. P. Morgan, Chemical Bank, Bankers Trust, Chase Manhattan, First Chicago and BankAmerica. Together, in the third quarter, they netted before taxes over $800 million more than what they normally earn in a quarter from trading currencies.

What did these people do to make so much money? They bet on the inevitable. They bet that the

Source: Thomas Jaffe and Dyan Machan, "Soros," *Forbes,* November 9, 1992. Reprinted by permission of *Forbes.* © Forbes, Inc., 1992.

pound and the other weaker European currencies were overpriced against the deutsche mark. They bet that the politicians and the central banks could not much longer maintain artificially high exchange rate in the interests of European unity.

Europe's Exchange Rate Mechanism was set up in 1979 by the then-members of the European Economic Community to keep the various European currencies relatively stable against one another. Relatively narrow fixed trading ranges were established within which the prices of 11 European currencies were supposed to fluctuate. But the system could work only if the various countries coordinated their economic policies. If one nation had, say, higher inflation than another, there would be great strain on the system. Differences in interest rates also would strain the system. When differences in interest rates and inflation rates among the 11 got out of line, the central banks had to intervene to buy and thus support the weakening currency against speculators and currency hedgers.

In former times, powerful central banks could usually frustrate speculators. They did so by simply buying massive amounts of the weaker currency and flooding the market with the stronger currency. But times are changing. While the central banks can mobilize tens of billions of dollars, trading in foreign currency markets now runs to a trillion dollars a day.

Andrew Weisman, director of currency fund management for French bank Credit du Nord, makes no apologies for the speculative operations mounted by his and other banks against the fixed rates. "The central banks brought September's debacle upon themselves," he asserts. Why does he say this? Because the exchange rates they were defending may have made political sense for the European leaders

---

commodity or handful of commodities is compared across currencies relative to the exchange rate, but on an aggregate basis, these deviations in price tend to cancel one another, resulting in a fairly reasonable equilibrium exchange rate.

If different exchange rates actually prevail, profit incentives are produced that should induce people to exploit them. For example, if things can be sold at

committed to the European Community but no longer made any economic sense.

Soros and the others who won big when the market overwhelmed the banks were mostly involved in one variation or another on a basic technique: Go short the weakest currencies. Going short a currency can be done in a number of ways. The simplest is simply to borrow money, say, Italian lire, and convert the borrowed money into, say, deutsche marks at the fixed rates. Then you wait for the lira to drop sharply against the DM, buy in the now cheaper lira to repay your debt and pocket a lot of extra deutsche marks.

In September the lira was trading at 765 lire to the mark. Four weeks later it took 980 lire to buy a single DM. A speculator who had performed this operation would have made a profit equal to 28% of the borrowed sum.

But his profit would have been much more than 28%. Speculators with substantial credit lines like Soros can borrow on a margin of 5% and get 20-to-1 leverage. That means you can borrow $1 billion for speculation by putting up just $50 million in cash. The result: Instead of having made 28% on your lira bet, you would have made 560%, or $280 million.

There are other ways, of course, to play the currency markets: through futures and options, for example. Soros actually evolved a complex play.

George Soros generally avoids the press, and in this moment of great triumph, he is as elusive as ever. But it is clear that he had concluded the European central banks were holding lousy hands in their game against the speculators and hedgers. That's why he was willing to bet the ranch.

Though Soros would not talk with *Forbes,* his spokesman did. He told us Soros has expected financial turmoil in Europe ever since the Berlin Wall collapsed in November 1989, leading to the reunification of Germany. These events, thought Soros, would doom the Exchange Rate Mechanism.

A Soros spokesman explains: "To have one [pan-European] currency and make it stick, you need one economy. But when one country was booming because it had essentially done a leveraged buyout of East Germany, while the others were in a recession, this made it inappropriate for the others to rely on Germany's monetary policy in trying to maintain their own currencies."

After German reunification, in Soros' view, it was only a matter of time before the European Exchange Rate Mechanism came unglued.

By this year it was clear to just about everyone that some European currencies—the British pound and Italian lira, for example—were fundamentally overvalued in relation to stronger ones such as the deutsche mark and French franc. As Britain and Italy struggled to make their currencies attractive, they were forced to maintain high interest rates to attract foreign investment dollars. But this crimped their ability to stimulate their sagging economies. While the British and Italians tried to deal with weak economies, Germany embarked on a policy of trying to restrain its own economy, overstimulated by the spending on eastern Germany.

There were plenty of players beside George Soros betting against the central banks and the ERM. Foreign exchange traders at money center banks and investment banks like Goldman, Sachs are constantly aware of what is happening in the international money markets. When large institutions, mutual funds and multinational corporations that do massive currency hedging to protect their profits started selling the weaker European currencies in September, the traders immediately picked up on the jump in volume they were handling for their customers. They could easily estimate just how great the selling pressure was and how much the central banks would have to spend to prop up those currencies. Then, the banks and

higher prices, adjusted for exchange rates, customs duties, and transportation costs in Japan as compared to the United States, profit seekers should be motivated to sell goods there. These actions will increase the supply of goods in Japan and reduce the supply in the United States until yen prices fall and dollar prices rise. In this case, the value of the yen must fall, resulting in more yen per dollar.

investment houses got into the game for their own accounts.

It was obvious, for instance, that the Bank of England wouldn't be able to support the pound successfully, so the banks started to use their own capital to heavily sell the currency short. Some of the more aggressive, like Citicorp and Bankers Trust, made roughly an extra $200 million apiece pretax from the trading turmoil in September. And it may have been even more. But the magnitude of these gains won't show up in the third quarter's results. When trading profits are that large, the banks often roll them over into succeeding quarters to minimize their tax bill.

We mentioned that Soros played a complex game. Here's how it went. Soros expected the following: the breakdown of the ERM and a substantial realignment of European currencies; a dramatic drop in European interest rates; a decline for European stock markets.

So, rather than simply shorting the weak currencies, he also placed simultaneous bets on interest rates and securities markets that would be affected by the currency realignments.

In carrying out this operation, Soros and his aides sold short sterling to the tune of about $7 billion, bought the mark to the tune of $6 billion and, to a lesser extent, bought the French franc. As a parallel play they bought as much as $500 million worth of British stocks even while they were shorting sterling, figuring that equities often rise after a currency devalues. Soros also went long German and French bonds, while shorting those countries' equities. Soros' reasoning on the French and German markets was that upward valuation was bad for equities but was good for bonds because it would lead to lower interest rates.

"When the Italians finally devalued the lira and the Germans lowered rates slightly," says the Soros spokesman, "it was almost like we'd been preparing for an exam for six months and now were finally taking our test."

After the lira was battered, Soros read that Helmut Schlesinger, president of the Bundesbank, had openly stated that Germany's central bank would not go to the wall for the pound. Soros has said that he saw this as a "clarion call for everyone to get out of sterling."

Because of his strong credit, Soros was able to maintain all these positions with just $1 billion in collateral. He was margined to the eyebrows, but he wasn't really gambling. "The profits that people like Soros recently made seem astronomical," says Gilbert de Botton, chief of London's $5-billion-plus (assets) Global Asset Management. "But do not rap them on the knuckles on one of the few occasions where they actually could make money. Even the pros have lost their shirts from time to time because of the absolute power of the central banks."

Soros knew this, but all his experience, all his instincts told him that this time he was betting with odds overwhelmingly in his favor.

Here's how his leveraged positions worked out: The pound dropped 10%, the mark and franc both rose roughly 7%, the London stock market gained 7%, German and French bonds were up about 3% apiece, and the German and French stock markets briefly rallied, but basically remained flat.

He has taken no pride in being referred to as the man who beat the central banks. One money manager who knows Soros well says: "George actually wants to be perceived as helping central bankers."

Was betting against them being helpful? In the sense that he was essentially betting on the inevitable, maybe yes.

The volatility in European currencies continues. Soros and other shrewd investors will no doubt continue trying to profit off the turbulence. But it will be a long time before a chance to make a killing like this year's appears again.

Until the exchange rate reaches a new equilibrium level, there will be an incentive for profit seekers to continue these actions. The profit opportunity is not a riskless one, however. Delays in shipping and in selling the commodity overseas could wipe out the profit. Similarly, a weakening of the yen prior to the sale of the commodities in Japan could also erode profits. Moreover, the imposition of a

EXHIBIT 10.1

Current currency quotes: direct and indirect

CURRENCY TRADING

Thursday, February 15, 1996.

EXCHANGE RATES

The New York foreign exchange selling rates below apply to trading among banks in amounts of $1 million and more, as quoted at 3 p.m. Eastern time by Dow Jones Telerate Inc. and other sources. Retail transactions provide fewer units of foreign currency per dollar.

Country	U.S. $ equiv. Thu	U.S. $ equiv. Wed	Currency per U.S. $ Thu	Currency per U.S. $ Wed
Argentina (Peso)	1.0004	1.0004	.9996	.9996
Australia (Dollar)	.7553	.7545	1.3240	1.3254
Austria (Schilling)	.09673	.09682	10.338	10.328
Bahrain (Dinar)	2.6532	2.6532	.3769	.3769
Belgium (Franc)	.03309	.03310	30.220	30.210
Brazil (Real)	1.0225	1.0225	.9780	.9780
Britain (Pound)	1.5375	1.5425	.6504	.6483
30-Day Forward	1.5363	1.5413	.6509	.6488
90-Day Forward	1.5341	1.5390	.6519	.6498
180-Day Forward	1.5307	1.5352	.6533	.6514
Canada (Dollar)	.7257	.7244	1.3780	1.3805
30-Day Forward	.7257	.7243	1.3781	1.3806
90-Day Forward	.7257	.7245	1.3780	1.3804
180-Day Forward	.7253	.7241	1.3787	1.3811
Chile (Peso)	.002435	.002438	410.75	410.25
China (Renminbi)	.1206	.1206	8.2928	8.2928
Colombia (Peso)	.0009779	.0009779	1022.55	1022.55
Czech. Rep. (Koruna) .	....	....	....	....
Commercial rate	.03702	.03702	27.015	27.016
Denmark (Krone)	.1759	.1759	5.6844	5.6835
Ecuador (Sucre)	....	....	....	....
Floating rate	.0003389	.0003389	2951.00	2951.00
Finland (Markka)	.2176	.2183	4.5959	4.5800
France (Franc)	.1978	.1981	5.0562	5.0475
30-Day Forward	.1979	.1983	5.0524	5.0433
90-Day Forward	.1981	.1985	5.0470	5.0379
180-Day Forward	.1983	.1987	5.0428	5.0324
Germany (Mark)	.6818	.6828	1.4668	1.4646
30-Day Forward	.6828	.6839	1.4647	1.4623
90-Day Forward	.6849	.6860	1.4600	1.4577
180-Day Forward	.6879	.6889	1.4538	1.4515
Greece (Drachma)	.004124	.004135	242.47	241.86
Hong Kong (Dollar)	.1293	.1293	7.7328	7.7321
Hungary (Forint)	.006913	.006915	144.65	144.61
India (Rupee)	.02737	.02738	36.540	36.520
Indonesia (Rupiah)	.0004363	.0004363	2292.00	2292.00
Ireland (Punt)	1.5820	1.5820	.6321	.6321
Israel (Shekel)	.3183	.3183	3.1412	3.1412
Italy (Lira)	.0006301	.0006303	1587.00	1586.50
Japan (Yen)	.009476	.009410	105.53	106.27
30-Day Forward	.009514	.009448	105.11	105.84
90-Day Forward	.009586	.009520	104.32	105.04
180-Day Forward	.009691	.009623	103.19	103.91
Jordan (Dinar)	1.4100	1.4100	.7092	.7092
Kuwait (Dinar)	3.3434	3.3422	.2991	.2992
Lebanon (Pound)	.0006293	.0006291	1589.00	1589.50
Malaysia (Ringgit)	.3932	.3933	2.5430	2.5427
Malta (Lira)	2.7701	2.7816	.3610	.3595
Mexico (Peso)	....	....	....	....
Floating rate	.1329	.1334	7.5250	7.4950
Netherland (Guilder) ..	.6088	.6099	1.6425	1.6397
New Zealand (Dollar) .	.6754	.6750	1.4806	1.4815
Norway (Krone)	.1557	.1557	6.4230	6.4220
Pakistan (Rupee)	.02915	.02915	34.300	34.300
Peru (new Sol)	.4237	.4237	2.3600	2.3600
Philippines (Peso)	.03828	.03823	26.120	26.160
Poland (Zloty)	.3922	.3922	2.5500	2.5500
Portugal (Escudo)	.006557	.006569	152.50	152.22
Russia (Ruble) (a)	.0002101	.0002103	4760.00	4756.00
Saudi Arabia (Riyal) ..	.2666	.2666	3.7504	3.7503
Singapore (Dollar)	.7079	.7074	1.4127	1.4137
Slovak Rep. (Koruna) .	.03322	.03322	30.098	30.100
South Africa (Rand) ...	.2735	.2743	3.6566	3.6452
South Korea (Won)	.001286	.001285	777.90	778.40
Spain (Peseta)	.008068	.008081	123.95	123.75
Sweden (Krona)	.1439	.1438	6.9492	6.9535
Switzerland (Franc) ...	.8352	.8369	1.1973	1.1949
30-Day Forward	.8377	.8395	1.1938	1.1912
90-Day Forward	.8427	.8444	1.1867	1.1842
180-Day Forward	.8492	.8510	1.1776	1.1751
Taiwan (Dollar)	.03642	.03642	27.460	27.460
Thailand (Baht)	.03964	.03964	25.230	25.230
Turkey (Lira)	.00001556	.00001562	64268.00	64035.00
United Arab (Dirham) .	.2724	.2724	3.6710	3.6710
Uruguay (New Peso) ..	....	....	....	....
Financial	.1379	.1379	7.2500	7.2500
Venezuela (Bolivar) ...	.003448	.003448	290.00	290.00
Brady Rate	.002353	.002370	425.00	422.00
SDR	1.4655	1.4624	.6823	.6838
ECU	1.2475	1.2495	....	....

Special Drawing Rights (SDR) are based on exchange rates for the U.S., German, British, French, and Japanese currencies. Source: International Monetary Fund.
European Currency Unit (ECU) is based on a basket of community currencies.
a-fixing. Moscow Interbank Currency Exchange

Key Currency Cross Rates   Late New York Trading Feb 15, 1996

	Dollar	Pound	SFranc	Guilder	Peso	Yen	Lira	D-Mark	FFranc	CdnDlr
Canada	1.3780	2.1187	1.1509	.83898	.18313	.01306	.00087	.93947	.27254	....
France	5.0562	7.7739	4.2230	3.0784	.67192	.04791	.00319	3.4471	....	3.6692
Germany	1.4668	2.2552	1.2251	.89303	.19492	.01390	.00092	....	.29010	1.0644
Italy	1587.0	2440.0	1325.5	966.21	210.9	15.038	....	1081.9	313.87	1151.7
Japan	105.53	162.25	88.14	64.25	14.024	....	.06650	71.946	20.871	76.581
Mexico	7.5250	11.57	6.2850	4.5814	....	.07131	.00474	5.1302	1.4883	5.4607
Netherlands ..	1.6425	2.5253	1.3718	....	.21827	.01556	.00103	1.1198	.32485	1.1919
Switzerland ...	1.1973	1.8408	....	.72895	.15911	.01135	.00075	.81627	.23680	.86886
U.K.	.65041	....	.54323	.39599	.08643	.00616	.00041	.44342	.12864	.47199
U.S.	....	1.5375	.83521	.60883	.13289	.00948	.00063	.68176	.19778	.72568

Source: Dow Jones Telerate Inc.

higher import duty or some other restriction on imports by Japan could obliterate any profits one would expect to make. Therefore, this is a profit opportunity accompanied by risk. Some of the risk can be transferred via contracts, such as a sales contract, forward exchange rate agreement, and so forth, but it is impossible to eliminate all of the risk from this profit opportunity.

Deviations from Absolute PPP can occur for several reasons. These include trade barriers, exchange controls, and variability of consumption across any two countries, to name just a few. Therefore, deviations from Absolute PPP can be expected to be larger for countries with a smaller relative foreign trade sector and less access to world markets. For instance, one would expect to find a closer conformance to Absolute PPP between the Netherlands and Denmark than between Germany and the United States because of the importance of trade to the first two countries relative to its importance to the latter two. This is true even though all of these countries feature fairly open economies. On the other hand, exchange controls or other barriers to international payments and the international movement of goods can lead to larger deviations from Absolute PPP. Thus, we would expect to find greater divergence between Russia and India than between Canada and Norway.

Another cause for deviation from Absolute PPP is the fact that the representative market basket of consumption goods varies both in proportion of goods and in identity of goods. For example, the Japanese market basket is likely to include less wheat and more rice than the American basket. Moreover, in some countries, fish is a more popular alternative to cheeseburgers, yet it is unlikely that it will convert many Americans away from the Big Mac. Thus, the "representative market basket of goods" is not the same across countries; therefore, the market mechanisms that act to close the pricing gaps are not operative to the same extent in all cases.

Relative purchasing power parity is a close cousin of Absolute PPP. The difference is that Relative PPP focuses not on price levels and exchange rates but on inflation rates and rates of change in exchange rates. The theory in its relative form states that even if price levels do not exactly correspond to Absolute PPP, the rate of change in the equilibrium exchange rate should be proportional to the difference in price level changes between the domestic and foreign countries. Relative PPP suggests that the expected rate of change in the exchange rate is proportional to the difference in inflation rates between domestic and foreign countries. In equation form, the relationship may be represented as follows:

$$\%\Delta e = \frac{1 + \pi_d}{1 + \pi_f} - 1$$

where π_d and π_f are the domestic and foreign inflation rates, respectively. To be concrete, suppose that domestic inflation is 20 percent and foreign inflation is 10 percent. In other words, domestic money is losing purchasing power at a faster rate than foreign currency. Therefore, we would expect that over time, it will cost more domestic money to buy a given amount of foreign currency. Substituting these values in the equation gives:

$$\%\Delta e = \frac{1 + 0.20}{1 + 0.10} - 1 = 9.091\%$$

Accordingly, we would expect the domestic currency to depreciate, relative to the foreign currency, at a 9.091 percent annual rate.[4]

---

[4]It is sometimes difficult to understand that if one country has 20 percent inflation and another has 10 percent, the first country's currency is losing value 9.091 percent faster than that of the

EXHIBIT 10.2

Relative purchasing power parity

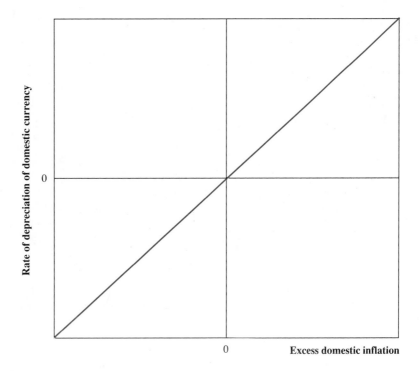

Relative PPP can hold true whether the absolute version of PPP holds true or not. For instance, due to a high tariff in a foreign country, the actual equilibrium exchange rate may be lower, in terms of domestic currency for a unit of foreign currency, than the natural (in the absence of tariffs) equilibrium rate. Nonetheless, if there is an inflation differential between the countries over time, the exchange rate can be expected to change at that same differential rate. This should be true even though the exchange rate at the outset was not at the natural equilibrium rate.

In Exhibit 10.2, we show the Relative PPP relationship between inflation differentials and rates of change in exchange rates. Again, Relative PPP applies retrospectively as well as prospectively—with realizations as well as with expectations.

In Exhibit 10.3, negative numbers on the horizontal axis indicate that domestic inflation is less than foreign inflation. Negative numbers on the vertical axis indicate that the domestic currency is appreciating rather than depreciating relative

---

second country. Intuition might lead us to think that 10 percent is the differential rate of inflation. To help understand the logic of the 9.091 percent number, consider the United States and Canada. Suppose that at the beginning of the year, the exchange rate is $1_{U.S.}$ to $1_{Canadian}$. Suppose further that in each country, it costs $100 for a basket of goods. At the end of the year, it costs $120_{U.S.}$ and $110_{Canadian}$ for the same basket of goods. While one number has grown by 20 percent and the other by 10 percent, the first number is only 9.091 percent higher than the second number $[(\$120_{U.S.} \div \$110_{Canadian}) - 1 = 9.091\%]$. Note that if we had expressed the rates of inflation in continuously compounded rates, we could have merely subtracted one from the other to get the continuously compounded rate of depreciation of the currency in the country with higher inflation.

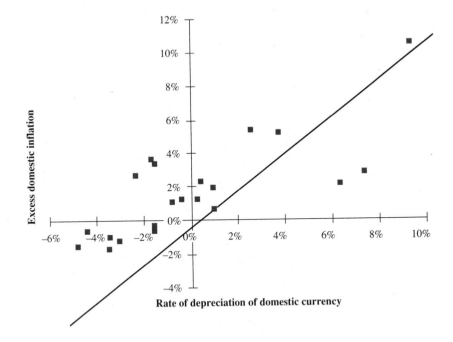

to the foreign currency. The relationship of exchange rate changes and inflation differentials is depicted with a simple 45-degree line. Countries whose experience may be plotted above the 45-degree line have their currencies depreciating more rapidly or, if in the upper portion of the lower left quadrant, appreciating less rapidly than would be indicated solely by examining inflation rate differentials. Similarly, countries plotted below the 45-degree line have currencies depreciating less or, if located in the lower portion of the lower left quadrant or in the lower right quadrant, appreciating more than inflation differentials explain.

Relative PPP tends to explain relatively more of exchange rate movements over long periods of time than over shorter periods. Moreover, when inflation differentials are based on inflation rates for traded goods, the relationships observed are closer to the 45-degree line. In Exhibit 10.3, we can see the actual rates of change in exchange rates relative to differential inflation rates. Note how several countries deviate from the equilibrium Relative PPP line by substantial amounts. Nonetheless, Relative PPP tends to explain at least the direction, if not the amount, of change in the exchange rate for most countries. Some of these deviations can be explained by structural factors, including changes in relative productivity gains in different economies; changes in tastes for goods, such as changes in the market basket of consumption; and so forth.

As mentioned above, the deviations from Relative PPP can be substantial over short periods of time, but over periods of many years, the deviations tend to diminish, as the overwhelming impact of differential inflation rates takes its toll. In Exhibit 10.4, we give evidence of this fact. While the numbers in Exhibit 10.3

EXHIBIT 10.4   Deviations from Relative Purchasing Power Parity:
Empirical Evidence from 22 Countries (1972–1992)

	<5%	*<10%*	*<25%*
1 year	37.7%	64.5%	95.7%
2 years	41.1	73.0	99.3
5 years	53.5	87.7	99.7
10 years	84.8	98.1	100.0

---

were averaged over 20 years, the numbers in Exhibit 10.4 are for periods of time ranging from 1 year to 10 years.

A Financial View of Purchasing Power Parity

Up to this point, the items purchased between the two countries were assumed to be commodities. We looked at the value of a representative basket of commodities in Absolute PPP and the percentage change in the price of the basket in Relative PPP. Some years ago, Irving Fisher considered an analogous problem for the value of financial assets across currencies.

In Chapter 4, we discussed Irving Fisher's theory of the relationship between expected inflation and nominal interest rates. His theory has been dubbed **Fisher Closed** by some economists because it deals with a "closed" domestic economy. Fisher also theorized about open economies and looked at interest rate differentials in an international context: this theory has been called **Fisher Open.**

Extrapolating from Fisher Closed, where nominal interest rates could be viewed as the sum of expected inflation and the real rate of interest (plus an interaction term), Fisher theorized that the differences in nominal interest rates on similar assets that are denominated in several currencies should equal the differences in expected inflation rates. Of course, Fisher was assuming that the real rate of interest was the same for all countries. Denoting domestic and foreign nominal interest rates as R_d and R_f, respectively, the formula may be expressed as follows:

$$\frac{1 + R_d}{1 + R_f} - 1 = \frac{1 + \pi_d}{1 + \pi_f} - 1$$

However, as we know from Relative Purchasing Power Parity, expected exchange rate movements are directly related to inflation differentials. Armed with this information, we may rewrite the above equation as:

$$\frac{1 + R_d}{1 + R_f} - 1 = E(\%\Delta e)$$

Fisher's rationale was simple. Investors will hold assets denominated in a currency only if the interest rates on those assets are sufficiently high to compensate

Exhibit 10.5

*Forward rate term
structures in the
United States
and Spain*

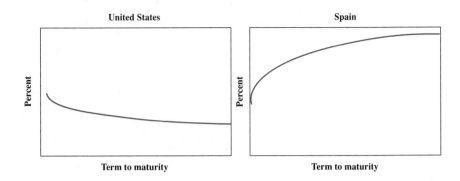

for any capital loss from the anticipated depreciation in the exchange rate. Likewise, they will hold assets featuring a relatively lower nominal yield only if they expect that the currency in which the asset is denominated will strengthen enough to offset that yield differential.

To give a concrete example of this theory, suppose that investors anticipate Mexican pesos to depreciate 10 percent per year relative to the U.S. dollar, perhaps because the Mexican price level is rising 10 percent faster than the American price level. If interest rates on peso-denominated bonds are less than 10 percent higher than those on similar dollar-denominated bonds, investors will sell peso bonds and buy dollar bonds. The price of the peso bonds will then decline, leading to an increase in their yields. Also, perhaps dollar-bond prices will increase in price somewhat, and yields will decline, due to increased demand, although most of the adjustment in interest rates occurs in the smaller country. These actions by investors will continue to cause the differential between Mexican and American interest rates to increase until it reaches 10 percent.

To Fisher, this relationship would have to hold for all maturities. Therefore, the theory has implications in the context of the term structure of interest discussion we had in Chapter 5 and the pricing of multiperiod bonds in Chapter 8. Consider two countries with term structures of interest, expressed in forward interest rates, as shown graphically in Exhibit 10.5. At the near term, U.S. interest rates are slightly higher than Spanish rates. Thus, the Spanish peseta can be expected to appreciate in the near term relative to the U.S. dollar. However, going out a few years into the future, the forward rates of interest in the U.S. are much lower than they are for Spain. Thus, the U.S. dollar can be expected to appreciate relative to the Spanish peseta after first undergoing a brief decline. Note that Fisher Open, in its original version, does not accommodate liquidity preferences or preferred habitats in the term structure. Rather, it most closely resembles the pure expectations theory discussed at some length in Chapter 5, as the differential in interest rates is precisely equal to the expected exchange rate devaluation. We depict the Fisher Open relationship in Exhibit 10.6.

While Fisher Open would certainly hold true in a world of certainty, in an uncertain world, there could be deviations. Risk premia may be demanded for

Exhibit 10.6

Fisher Open: The theoretical relationship

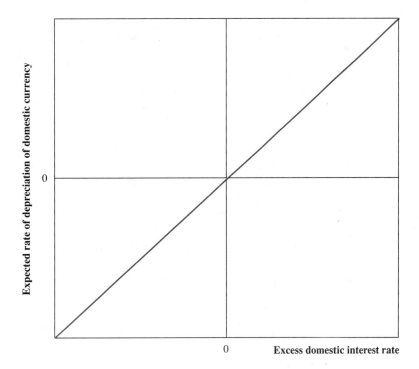

assets denominated in some currencies due to political risk, such as risk of expropriation or political instability; inflation risk associated with new political regimes; currency controls; or systematic financial risk, like correlation with broad market factors. Also, real rates of interest can diverge across countries due to impediments to the free flow of goods, labor, and capital. Thus, while deviations from Fisher Open may imply potential profits, those profits are fraught with risks. If the deviations from Fisher Open are random, then they would be expected to go away. If they are systematic and persistent, we must ask why investors have not exploited the profit opportunity. We may be looking at a free lunch, but more likely, we are about to be taken to the cleaners!

Interest Rate Parity Theorem

While investments across currencies, along the lines suggested above, are fraught with risk and potential loss, there are ways to substantially reduce the risks associated with foreign currency investment. Investors in the United States can invest in foreign-denominated bonds and cover their position by a forward currency contract to sell the foreign currency at the bond's maturity. If the bonds are issued by a strong and stable foreign government, and the other party to the forward contract is equally strong and default free, then the resultant return will be risk free to the

U.S. investor.[5] However, investors will choose this investment strategy if and only if the yield is competitive with any comparable domestic opportunities. On the other hand, if the yield is too attractive, all U.S. investors will move to the foreign market. In fact, the marketplace can only sustain both the domestic and the foreign markets if the forward exchange rate between the currencies exactly offsets the yield differential or interest rate spread in the two markets. This concept has been developed into a standard theorem in international financial markets known as the **Interest Rate Parity Theorem.**

The Interest Rate Parity Theorem (IRPT) relates exchange rates on forward contracts of specified maturities to the money market interest **agios,** or spreads, on similar assets denominated in different currencies. Before we discuss this theory, we should revisit a couple of definitions. A **forward exchange rate** is the price on a contract to exchange bank deposits denominated in different currencies at a specified future date. Common maturities are one month, three months, and six months. A **spot exchange contract** is a commitment to exchange deposits two business days after the date when the parties agree to the contract.

The theory holds that the ratio of forward and spot exchange rates will be proportional to the interest rate agio. It may be expressed mathematically as follows:

$$\frac{e_{\text{forward}}}{e_{\text{spot}}} = \frac{1 + R_d}{1 + R_f}$$

To illustrate this theorem by example, consider a situation in which the one-year foreign interest rate is 12 percent and the one-year domestic interest rate is 8 percent. Suppose the spot exchange rate between the two currencies is 10 per escudo. What is the current one-year forward exchange rate?

$$\frac{e_{\text{forward}}}{10\cent} = \frac{1 + .08}{1 + .12} \Rightarrow e_{\text{forward}} = 9.643\cent \text{ per escudo}$$

To show why this relationship must be so, it is helpful to consider what would happen if it were not so. Suppose that the one-year forward exchange rate on the escudo is 9.643¢ and the spot exchange rate is 10¢, as indicated above. Also, suppose that the domestic interest rate is 8 percent but the foreign interest rate is 14 percent, rather than the 12 percent shown in the previous example. What will happen? The foreign interest rate is too high relative to the spot and forward exchange rates and the domestic interest rate. Therefore, investors will be motivated to invest in escudo-denominated assets and earn the extra interest. Better yet, they can earn this extra amount without any exchange rate risk and without risking any of their own money! This is a free lunch if there ever was one.

Let us see how this can be accomplished. First, since we do not wish to risk any of our own money, we borrow money. A million dollars will do fine. Then,

---

[5]The point here is that repayment is not always certain in some parts of the world. Political and country risk lead some investors to question the willingness and ability of some sovereigns to repay their debt, even in local currency.

we convert the dollars to escudos at 10¢ per escudo to end up with 10 million escudos. At the same time, we contract in the forward market to buy enough dollars for escudos both to pay back all of our loan at a preset exchange rate of 9.643¢ per escudo and to repatriate our expected profit. After some simple calculations, it can be shown that this forward contract needs to be set at 11.4 million escudos, as will be seen shortly. Next, we take our 10 million escudos and invest them for a year at 14 percent interest. At the end of the year, we then have 11.4 million escudos (= 10 million × 1.14). We have already contracted in the forward market to sell 11.4 million escudos for $1,099,302 (= 11.4 million escudos × 9.643¢ per escudo), but we only need $1,080,000 (= $1 million × 1.08) to repay our borrowed dollar loan. Hence, we have $19,302 in profit, with no risk. And this is without using any of our own money, which we may not have had anyway. Since we made no investment, the rate of return on our investment is infinite. This is an attractive rate of return by anybody's standards, especially considering the lack of risk. Therefore, investors will take advantage of any such situation, thus driving the interest agio down or the forward exchange rate lower until the arbitrage situation is eliminated.

Unlike the Purchasing Power Parity theories and Fisher Open, we need not make any forecasts of exchange rates here to anticipate a profit. Every number in the equation is a number you can get simply from looking in your newspaper or calling a broker. You can contract for each element of the transaction immediately and without any uncertainty. Such a situation is too good to be true, or if true, it is too good to last. Hence, you must act quickly to exploit any such opportunity. If it does arise, other people like you will quickly drive away the opportunity.

Profit-seeking investors are not the only ones who hold this relationship in check. The forward exchange rates themselves are set by banks, who utilize this relationship to hedge forward contracts. Here is how it works. If you wish to buy, say, French francs at the forward exchange rate for delivery three months hence, your bank will borrow a commensurate amount of dollars today, convert them to francs at the spot exchange rate, and invest them in a three-month time deposit. The forward rate they will quote to you will be equal to the number of dollars they borrow plus the interest cost for three months on the dollar loan divided by the number of francs they will deliver to you. Most banks will quote virtually the same forward exchange rate because their costs of borrowing in the interbank market are similar and the interest rates they can earn on time deposits are also similar. However, any disparity in the opportunities faced by a bank can translate into a different forward rate, and occasionally, these differences can afford an investor who is swift afoot a (virtually) riskless profit opportunity.

Unbiased Forward Rate Theorem

With investors and banks constantly computing yield differentials across currencies, one would think that the exchange rates would adjust quickly. And they do. Deviations from interest rate parity quickly lead to exchange rate pressure and adjustment. Either the spot or the forward rate or both will adjust to maintain equilibrium. However, at that equilibrium, the spot and forward rates are not necessarily equal. For reasons analogous to the term structure of interest rates, spot and forward rates often diverge. If future spot exchange rates are expected to decline, this will be captured in the forward exchange rates, just as forward interests rates in the term structure are said to capture future short-term interest rates.

In fact, this was true in our previous example. Notice that the spot exchange rate for escudos was 10¢ per escudo, while the forward rate was computed to be 9.643¢ per escudo. The lower exchange rate associated with the forward exchange rate indicates that investors expected spot rates to move downward over the one-year term of the forward contract.

In the international financial markets, this relationship between spot and forward exchange rates is dubbed the **Unbiased Forward Rate Theorem.** The rationale for the theorem is that if forward rates are indeed biased, there exists an economic incentive to bet in favor of the bias, thereby generating potential profits if the bias persists. The potential profit is not without risk, however. If the investor covers his or her position with a forward rate contract, then he cannot make money if the exchange rate turns out to be different from that implied by the forward rate. Thus, the investor must assume an "open" position.

Again using the case above, the investor who thought that the value of the escudo would fall below 9.643¢ per escudo would not contract to reconvert his investment back into dollars. Rather, he would plan to do so when the one-year investment matured and the currency's value declined further than the amount embedded in the forward exchange rate. The investor would plan his bets and hope for the best if he or she sensed a deviation from the Unbiased Forward Rate Theorem.

This theorem is one of the most widely examined economic phenomena. Numerous studies have attempted to discern whether the forward exchange rate is a good, or at least unbiased, predictor of the future spot exchange rate. Some have found that the current spot exchange rate is a better predictor of the future than the forward rate, but others have found the forward exchange rate to be an unbiased predictor. In general, however, the results are not encouraging. The market may be willing to invest based on forward rates, but their forecasts tend to be rather inaccurate. The conclusion seems to depend on which currencies are considered, the time period under study, and the methodology employed.[6]

Implications for International Investment

The theories we have been discussing have important implications for investors interested in foreign investment. They indicate the causes of exchange rate movements, which in turn affect the dollar-denominated rate of return on nondollar investments. Understanding the causes of exchange rate movements leads to an appreciation of the

---

[6]A careful reader should have the sensation of déjà vú. This relationship is analogous to the pure expectations theory of the term structure of interest, which was discussed in Chapter 5.

EXHIBIT 10.7

*The Fisherian
framework*

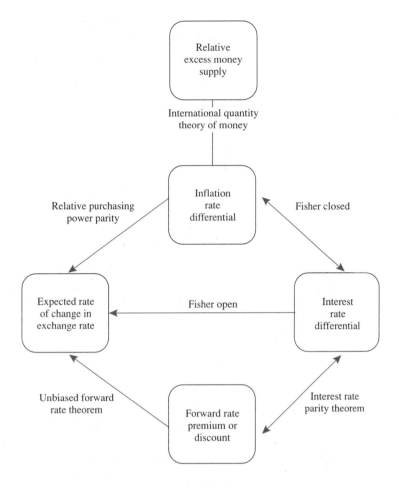

unique risks of foreign currency investing. To see this, let's put the theories' implications together to create a unified view of the causes of currency movements. Then, we will examine the implications for foreign-denominated asset risks.

Putting It All Together

The various theories we have discussed are known collectively as the **Fisherian framework.** The theories are linked together into a cohesive unit in several ways. Three theories—Relative Purchasing Power Parity, Fisher Open, and the Unbiased Forward Rate Theorem—give rise to predictions about the expected rate of change in the exchange rate. Relative Purchasing Power Parity and Fisher Open are linked together by Fisher Closed. Fisher Open and the Unbiased Forward Rate Theorem are linked together by the Interest Rate Parity Theorem. We link the theories diagramatically in Exhibit 10.7.

EXHIBIT 10.8

Quantity theory of money: empirical evidence

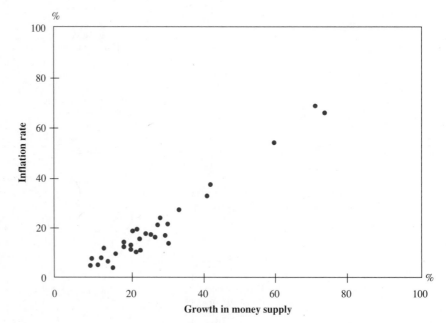

Source: Nigel Duck, "Some International Evidence of the Quantity Theory of Money," *Journal of Money, Credit and Banking,* February 1993.

Note that we have slipped in a theorem that has not yet been discussed in this chapter. The **International Quantity Theory of Money** holds that supply of money in excess of money demand will lead to a commensurate inflation rate. To the extent that different countries have excessive growth in money supply, this situation gives rise to differing inflation rates. Exhibit 10.8, drawn from a recent study of the subject,[7] illustrates the relationship between excess money growth and inflation. The chart covers 33 countries over a nearly 20-year period. The correlation between these two series is quite evident.

For individual countries, relative money growth results in differential inflation and, hence, expected changes in the relative price of any two currencies. The purpose of appending this theory to the diamond-shaped configuration of four theories is to add to your understanding of relative exchange rates and to show how additional theories can be incorporated into the Fisherian framework.

Other paradigms have been devised for linking exchange rates to interest and inflation rates. Some have far more sophistication than that included in this framework. However, in its simplicity, the Fisherian framework serves as a useful tool for identifying profit opportunities, both risky and riskless. This framework also links together a number of concepts in a unified manner. It argues that exchange

---

[7]See Nigel Duck, "Some International Evidence of the Quantity Theory of Money," *Journal of Money, Credit and Banking,* February 1993.

rate levels are determined by purchasing power in local tradable goods. The dynamic behavior of exchange rates is dependent upon inflation expectations across the two countries and real returns in the two economies. Those assets with higher return potential, net of inflation and the distortions of country political risk, taxes, and regulation, will offer investors an attractive return.

The Risks of Investing Abroad

At the outset of this discussion, the dual nature of the risks of investing in foreign currencies was noted. We indicated that investments in foreign-denominated instruments have all of the same risks as their domestic counterparts plus currency risk. The bulk of this chapter centered upon the determinants of the value of a foreign currency, as seen by domestic investors in the foreign financial markets.

The exchange risk associated with a foreign-denominated instrument, therefore, is a key additional element in foreign investment consideration. This risk flows from differential monetary policy and growth in real productivity, which result in differential inflation rates. The work of many academicians has clearly demonstrated the effects that such differences have on nominal rates and, by extension, on relative currency value changes. Some investors use their (assumed) knowledge of this relationship and of likely future policy discussions to speculate in the foreign currency market. It is just this bet on foreign economic policy that attracts some investors, making the forward market cover, even if possible, unattractive to most foreign participants. These individuals and institutions invest a substantial amount of time and effort in understanding future economic activity in foreign markets, and they use the exchange markets as a place to reap a return from their investments. Others would happily employ the forward markets to shed currency risk, and concentrate on the firm or project into which the local currency ultimately flows. However, while forward contracts can eliminate this risk for some types of investments, they are less helpful in eliminating the risk on investments whose rates of return are uncertain. In these cases, the quantity of needed forward cover is unknown, leaving the investor exposed to currency risk to the extent that the project's return differs from the amount of forward currency commitments.[8]

However, keep in mind that investing outside of your home market is not identical to investing at home, even after the exchange risk has been analyzed. The world is a big place with different customs, procedures, tax policies, and political risks. Before you enter a new market, you must recognize that "you're not in Kansas anymore."

As time progresses, there are more similarities than differences among the various national capital markets. However, there remains considerable latitude in

---

[8]A recently introduced class of securities, known as "quantity-adjusting forward and option contracts," is able to mitigate the exchange rate risk that arises from uncertain foreign asset returns. See, for example, David F. Babbel and Laurence Eisenberg, "Quantity Adjusting Options and Forward Contracts," *Journal of Financial Engineering,* June 1993.

the practices and conventions between some of the capital markets. In this section, we provide a sampling of these practices in order to convey a sense of the remaining disparities.

Transaction Costs.   The cost of transacting varies considerably across different markets. London is probably the least expensive European center for trading equities. Commissions average around 0.14 percent. When this is considered along with the excellent reputation, convenience, and expertise in trading securities that characterize the London market, it is not surprising that 95 percent of European stocks bought or sold outside their home markets are now traded in London. Similarly, Luxembourg is probably the cheapest place to issue and trade Eurobonds, so most of them are listed there. On the other hand, brokerage commissions and stamp duty for institutional investors on the Bombay Exchange in India range from 1.25 percent to 1.75 percent, approximately 10 times higher than the London market.

Settlement Delays.   Between the time a trade is made and actual settlement takes place, a number of days elapse. On the Hong Kong market, settlement takes place one or two days after the trade is consummated. In India, on the other hand, settlement is officially 14 days after the transaction date, although it is common to delay this for 28–31 days in practice. Most countries have settlement within a week after the transaction date.

Market Valuation.   There is a broad range in the price/earnings ratios of the various equity markets around the world. Part of the difference derives from disparities that exist in accounting and reporting methods. Other contributing factors include inflation differences, prospects for earnings growth, tax, regulatory structure, and general economic conditions within the country and within the markets in which its companies do business.

Taxation.   Most countries charge no taxes on capital gains, and many levy no taxes on dividends to foreign investors. Finland, for example, levies neither tax on foreign investors. Others levy taxes both on dividends and on capital gains. For example, India taxes dividends paid to foreign investors at 20 percent and capital gains at 10 percent. Denmark has a 30 percent withholding tax on dividends paid to foreigners but no capital gains tax. Moreover, through various bilateral tax treaties, the dividend tax may be reduced below 30 percent for investors from countries that are parties to such treaties. Turkey levies a withholding tax on interest paid on corporate debentures but not on government bonds or on dividends. Capital gains are exempt from tax for domestic companies but are subject to a 10.5 percent withholding tax on foreign securities.

Size of Market.   The largest equity markets are hosted by the United States, Japan, and the United Kingdom. In Europe, Germany, France, and Switzerland follow the United Kingdom in size. There were 626 companies listed on the

Zurich Exchange at the start of 1993. Australia had approximately 1,200 companies on its six exchanges in Sydney, Melbourne, Adelaide, Brisbane, Hobart, and Perth. Hong Kong had 390. Slovenia, on the other hand, had only 10 companies on its exchange. Botswana had 11 companies, and Ghana had 15.

Trading Hours. Some markets, such as Tokyo and Hong Kong, function virtually around the clock. Others operate on a much more limited scale. For example, during 1993, the Warsaw Exchange operated only on Mondays, Tuesdays, and Thursdays between 10:30 A.M. and 1:00 P.M.

Distribution. The degree of participation in the equity markets varies vastly by country, even among the developed nations. For example, almost 1 in 5 French own common stock, whereas only 1 in 25 Austrians own stock. In developing nations, the distribution of shares is often even more limited.

Foreign Ownership Limits. Again, in the area of limitations on the extent of foreign ownership, the practices among nations run the gamut of no restriction to virtually no allowance. In Sweden, for instance, restrictions on foreign ownership of Swedish shares were lifted at the beginning of 1993. Peru and Colombia place no restrictions on the purchase or transfer of shares on its exchange. Norway will lift its remaining restrictions in 1995.

India, on the other hand, has allowed foreigners limited access to its equity markets. Until February of 1992, the access was essentially nil. Since that time, India has opened its markets somewhat. Now, a license may be obtained to buy shares of Indian companies, provided that no more than 5 percent of outstanding shares are purchased by any single foreign investor. In the aggregate, foreign holdings of any Indian company may not exceed 24 percent. When that limit is reached, further purchases are suspended. Some countries issue a restricted kind of share to foreigners that allows participation in profits but no rights for voting or control.

Concentration. In some countries, such as the United States, market capitalization is spread among many companies. In others, relatively few companies account for much of the market capitalization and trading volume. For example, in the Netherlands, two stocks—Royal Dutch Shell and Unilever—account for approximately 48 percent of the market capitalization and much of the trading volume of the Amsterdam market. In Germany, 10 companies account for two-thirds of the market capitalization and trading volume. In Ireland, six companies are responsible for two-thirds of the market trading volume.

"A Shares" versus "B Shares." A number of countries allow companies to issue different classes of shares that carry different voting rights. For example, Swedish companies issue "A shares" and "B shares." Class A shares entitle holders to one vote per share, while class B shares carry one-tenth vote per share. Both shares pay the same dividend, but class A shares trade at a premium (and therefore lower dividend yield) due to the voting provision. Danish class B shares are similar.

Box 10.3

ADR Holders Feel Heat from Crisis in Mexico

Surprise!

You might have been buying stocks like Telefonos de Mexico on the New York Stock Exchange with dollars and receiving your dividends in dollars. But you were never protected from either the risk that the stock might tumble or that the Mexican currency might collapse.

Investors who have been active buyers of foreign stocks through the purchase of American depository receipts on U.S. exchanges are finding out the hard way that it's easy to buy them, but well nigh impossible to escape the risks—including the currency risk—foreign shares represent.

That's coming home with a vengeance in the case of Mexican ADRs, which had been popular vehicles for U.S. investors seeking to play what once was the darling of the emerging-markets crowd. With the peso losing 39% of its value since the crisis began on Dec. 20 through yesterday, four of the 10 worst-performing stocks on the New York Stock Exchange for the last quarter of 1994 were Mexican ADRs.

Double Whammy

ADRs are negotiable certificates or electronic entries that certify that the holder owns shares of a foreign company that are on deposit in the company's home market. Because they trade on U.S. exchanges and are priced in dollars they are a very convenient way for American investors to buy foreign shares. But their prices reflect not only the underlying value of the company in its home market, but also the relative value of the company's home-market currency against the dollar. In the worst case, both the stock price at home and the home currency could fall, as

they have in the case of Mexican stocks, dealing U.S. holders of ADRs a double whammy.

Foreign companies like ADRs because they can be used to gain additional exposure for their stocks and, less frequently, to actually raise new capital in the U.S. The booming ADR growth for the past few years—a record 7.2 billion ADR shares were traded in the U.S. in 1994—has given American investors access to stocks in countries as disparate as Germany and Belize.

The tremendous growth in ADRs has meant big business for the U.S. exchanges, depositary institutions (usually banks) and brokerage firms that deal in ADRs. At the end of 1994, there were 1,397 depository receipt programs in the U.S., according to Citicorp. Of the 254 new stocks listed on the Big Board in 1994, 52 were foreign companies, most of which used ADRs. The National Association of Securities Dealers has seven sales representatives scouring the globe to persuade foreign companies to list their shares in the U.S.

But Mexico's financial crisis, and the resulting losses to U.S. investors, is likely to slow the pace at which foreign companies come to U.S. markets, at least in the near term.

"We're cautious about Latin America in the short term," said Mark A. Bach, vice president and ADR global sales director at Citibank. "And the pace of activity from China has been slowing, and I don't see it increasing dramatically. But, in the long term, we still think the globalization of markets and the need for global capital raising won't go away."

Ownership of Chinese class A shares is restricted to Chinese companies and citizens. Class B shares are open to foreign investors. They are identical to class A shares in terms of equal earnings participation and voting rights, but they are denominated in U.S. dollars. Companies that issue class B shares are therefore given the opportunity to raise hard currency and may qualify for joint venture status, which carries the advantage of significantly lower tax rates.

These differences have had a severe damping effect upon foreign investment, at least traditionally. Knowing that customs, taxation, and regulation vary across countries, investors have been reluctant to send their funds beyond their national boundaries. Recognizing this, investment companies (such as mutual funds) have jumped into the breach, and the investment community has responded with financial innovation. The investment companies provide the investor the ability to purchase foreign companies through domestic investment vehicles. The investment community created the **American Depository Receipt** (ADR). ADRs are certificates or electronic entries that represent ownership of foreign securities. Through this vehicle, American investors can trade foreign securities in U.S. markets. Remember, however, that the currency risk of the investment remains with the investors; only the ease of the transaction has improved. (See Box 10.3.)

Summary

Up to this point in the book, we have centered our attention on the pricing of cash flows in instruments that are denominated in our home currency, presumably dollars. In this chapter, we consider the unique features of nondollar-denominated assets and introduce the notion of foreign investment. This is a big subject, and we have only skimmed the surface.

The present chapter chose to concentrate on two specific features of the world financial market. The first is the nature of the foreign exchange market—how it works, who works there, and what determines the price of one currency relative to another. While not simple, this story is understandable, and it will help you focus on currency values in the future. The key to this value rests upon a set of factors: the relative domestic purchasing power

of the currency; relative interest rates; and relative central bank policy, which determine inflation rates. Investments in foreign-currency-denominated instruments, therefore, involve risks that include not only standard financial risks but also currency risks associated with economic growth prospects and macroeconomic policy in both the home market and the market abroad.

Beyond these features, however, there are also institutional differences that affect value. Differences in transactions costs, taxation, liquidity, or ownership rights all have value implications. While the internationalization of investment markets is reducing these differential institutional features, some still remain and are quite important to keep in mind. Investors ignore them only at their own peril.

Key Concepts

Review Questions

1. Your broker gives you a direct quote of 0.98347¢/¥. In the coming year, inflation is expected to be 3.2 percent in Japan and 4.9 percent in the United States. What do you expect the exchange rate to be in one year?

2. You are reading a report that states that domestic currency is expected to appreciate 12.304 percent against foreign currency over a three-year period. Over this entire period, domestic inflation is expected to be 16.462 percent. What is the annual expected foreign inflation rate if the inflation rate is compounded annually?

3. The Fisher Closed theorem assumes that the real rate of interest is the same across all countries. Explain your reasons for agreeing or disagreeing with this assumption. How could the formula be adjusted if in fact there are differing real rates of interest?

4. If the dollar is expected to appreciate 5 percent against the British pound, and nominal interest rates are currently 7.5 percent (annually) in Britain, what is the current nominal interest rate in the United States?

5. The one-year domestic interest rate is 6.51 percent. The spot exchange rate is 157.5¢/£ and the expected one-year forward rate is 160.7¢/£. What is the nominal interest rate in Britain if the Interest Rate Parity Theorem holds? If the actual interest rate was below this, how would you take advantage of the situation (assuming no market impediments)?

References

Babbel, David F., and Laurence Eisenberg. "Quantity Adjusting Options and Forward Contracts." *Journal of Financial Engineering,* June 1993.

Bartov, Eli, and Gordon M. Bodnar. "Firm Valuation, Earnings Expectations, and the Exchange-Rate Exposure Effect." *Journal of Finance,* December 1994.

Bekaert, Geert, and Campbell R. Harvey. "Time-Varying World Market Integration." *Journal of Finance,* June 1995.

Bergstrand, Jeffrey H. "Selected Views of Exchange Rate Determination after a Decade of Floating." *New England Economic Review.* Federal Reserve Bank of Boston. May/June 1983.

Chrystal, K. Alec. "A Guide to Foreign Exchange Markets." *Review.* Federal Reserve Bank of St. Louis, March 1984.

Duck, Nigel W. "Some International Evidence of the Quantity Theory of Money." *Journal of Money, Credit and Banking,* February 1993.

Dumas, Bernard, and Bruno Solnik. "The World Price of Foreign Exchange Risk." *Journal of Finance,* June 1995.

Ederington, Louis H.; Jess B. Yawitz; and Brian E Roberts. "The Informational Content of Bond Ratings." *Journal of Financial Research,* Fall 1987.

Grabbe, J. Orlin. *International Financial Markets.* New York: Elsevier, 1990.

Humpage, Owen F. "Exchange-Market Intervention: The Channels of Influence." *Economic Review.* Federal Reserve Bank of Cleveland, Fall 1986.

Kubarych, Roger M. *Foreign Exchange Markets in the United States.* Rev. ed. Federal Reserve Bank of New York, 1983.

Moreno, Ramon. "The Eurodollar Market and U.S. Residents." *Economic Review.* Federal Reserve Bank of San Francisco, Summer 1987.

Officer, Lawrence H. "The Purchasing-Power-Parity Theory of Exchange Rates: A Review Article." *Staff Papers. International Monetary Fund,* March 1976.

Rose, Andrew K. "Explaining Forward Exchange Bias . . . Intraday." *Journal of Finance,* September 1995.

Sercu, Piet; Raman Uppal; and Cynthia Van Hulle. "The Exchange Rate in the Presence of Transactions Costs: Implications for Tests of Purchasing Power Parity." *Journal of Finance,* September 1995.

Williamson, John. *The International Monetary System, 1945–81.* New York: Harper and Row, 1982.

PART III

Instruments
in the Market

Understanding the Money Market

This chapter reviews the major assets traded in the short-term, highly liquid portion of the financial markets. This segment is known as the money market. For each instrument, a description of the market, borrowers and investors, and unique characteristics is presented. Next, a simple comparison of prices, yields, and liquidity is conducted.

As recently as 15 years ago, if you had asked the typical man or woman on the street about the money market, your inquiry would have been met with a blank stare. Nowadays, even the proverbial 80-year-old grandmother often knows about the money market, and chances are she has transferred money into and out of it

241

many times. Today, the typical man or woman on the street often does transactions that involve the money market, most often through the vehicle of money market mutual funds, Treasury bills, or negotiable certificates of deposit. Yet, in his or her mind, the money market is still likely to be shrouded in mystery and fraught with misconceptions.

In this chapter, we intend to remove as much mystery about the money market as is possible in one chapter. Entire volumes have been written on the subject,[1] so our brief treatment is bound to omit many details and skip over a number of money market instruments. Nonetheless, the treatment here will serve as an introduction to this important market, its many instruments, and its various features. You will undoubtedly have many dealings with this market in the future, if you have not already done so.

Overview of the Money Market

To finance their activities, governments, government agencies, financial institutions, and nonfinancial business enterprises need to obtain funds. As was explained in the first chapter of this book, this money is often obtained from the financial markets.[2] These groups can obtain these funds in any of a number of places within this broad marketplace. For example, they may offer participation or ownership shares (equities) for sale in the **equity market** (see Chapter 14), they may procure these funds through direct loans or through the issue of debt securities (bonds) in the **bond market**[3] (see Chapters 12 and 13), or they may acquire funds through the issue of debt instruments in the **money market.**

The money market has been described as a wholesale market for low-risk, highly liquid, short-term IOUs.[4] In truth, the money market is not just one market but a series of closely connected markets. This segment of the financial market brings together large economic units that have borrowing needs for short periods of time with those that have large sums to lend. These imbalances arise because the pattern of receipts of businesses, governments, and other economic units does not always coincide with their pattern of expenditures. At a given moment, one of these economic agents is likely to have a surplus or a deficit in cash. If the agent holds too much cash in the form of checking account balances, there is an opportunity cost in

---

[1]See Federal Reserve Bank of Richmond, *Instruments of the Money Market,* 7th ed. (Federal Reserve Bank of Richmond, 1991); and Marcia Stigum, *The Money Market,* 3d ed. (Burr Ridge, Ill.: Irwin Professional Publishing, 1990).

[2]Often the term "financial market" is used interchangeably with the term "capital market." If a distinction is made, the latter refers to that subset of the financial market that deals with stocks and bonds but omits the money market. See Charles Henning, William Pigott, and Robert Scott, *Financial Markets and the Economy,* 5th ed. (Englewood Cliffs, N.J.: Prentice Hall, 1988), p. 272.

[3]The bond market includes the corporate bond market, the Eurobond market, the long-term government securities market, the market for government agency securities, the municipal bond market, and the mortgage market.

[4]See Stigum, *op. cit.,* p. 1.

terms of the forgone interest it could have earned. If it holds too little, essential transactions may be delayed or opportunities lost. The money market serves as an efficient, low-cost mechanism to bring these short-term surpluses and deficits into balance.

The money market has both a **primary** and a **secondary market.** In the primary market, short-term funds are obtained quickly and easily at interest rates that vary according to the credit standing of the borrower, the nature of the borrowing instrument, the source of funds, and so forth. For most money market instruments, a secondary market also exists where claims are traded at interest rates that result from the interplay of supply and demand for those instruments.

However, the money market is unlike most other markets. Most markets, such as the supermarket, the flea market, commodities markets, and the stock market, operate from centralized, specific locations. This is not so with the U.S. money market. There are no physical location requirements to be a part of this market. All one needs is a desk, a telephone with multiple lines, and occasionally a license to do business.[5] Even at financial institutions with substantial operations in the money market, the location of money market operations is often referred to simply as the "money market desk."

There are, however, participants that have a dominating presence in this market. Many of them are located in New York City. This influential group consists of about 30 large commercial banks; four dozen government securities dealers, many of whom are foreign owned; and a handful of securities dealers who specialize in everything from certificates of deposit to bankers' acceptances. Also looming large on Broad and Wall Streets is the Federal Reserve Bank of New York. The Federal Reserve, the central bank of the United States, which is head-quartered in Washington, D.C., implements monetary policy through the intervention of its New York bank in this market.[6]

Instruments of the Money Market

Instruments that are traded in the money market have a number of characteristics in common. First, they are all debt obligations. Second, they have maturities ranging from one day to a full year, with most instruments having maturities of three months or less.[7] Third, these instruments typically exhibit a high degree of safety of

---

[5]Individual investors do not require a license, but market participants who trade these instruments, sell to the public, and/or issue such financial claims are regulated by either the Federal Reserve or the Securities and Exchange Commission. The issue of regulation is covered more fully in the following chapters on each type of institutional participant.

[6]Such money market intervention is accomplished through the Federal Open Market Operations Committee of the Federal Reserve. See Chapter 27 for a discussion of its function and operation.

[7]Certain securities with maturities exceeding one year are sometimes included under the money market rubric. This inclusion is usually based on other characteristics that these securities possess—such as short durations, liquidity, and trading practices—that render them close

principal. There are two reasons for this: (1) The short durations and minimal convexities of these instruments mean that they are subject to negligible interest rate risk, and (2) the debt instruments are issued by borrowers with generally high credit standing. Most debt obligations are from governments, federally sponsored agencies, central banks, large commercial banks, securities dealers, and prominent non-bank financial and nonfinancial business firms. Fourth, money market instruments have a high degree of liquidity. Most of the instruments of the money market have active secondary markets that allow them to be sold prior to maturity. Finally, these instruments are usually issued in high dollar amounts—units of $1 million or more.

While there are many classes of instruments in the money market, some with numerous variations, we will highlight eight of the most important ones. Three of these instruments represent claims to federal, state, and local government revenues: Treasury bills, federal agency discount notes, and municipal notes. Five—fed funds, negotiable certificates of deposit, commercial paper, bankers' acceptances, and repurchase agreements—are instruments of nongovernmental institutions, which include commercial banks, other financial institutions, and nonfinancial businesses and firms that have played an important role in the market recently. Our discussion of two other widely traded money market instruments, interest rate futures and options, will be deferred until Chapter 15, owing to the unique features of these instruments.

Treasury Bills

Treasury bills, or **T-bills,** as they are sometimes called, are debt obligations of the U.S. government. T-bills constitute approximately one-fourth of the total of all U.S. government marketable debt.[8] As of mid-1995, there were roughly three-quarters of a trillion dollars' worth of bills outstanding. As liabilities of the federal government, these obligations are generally considered to be free of default risk. In addition, they are traded in the most active of the secondary markets, which is characterized by low bid-ask spreads and extremely high liquidity.

T-bills have no coupon or stated interest, but they are issued at a discount from face value. The return earned is the difference between the discount issue price and the face value, which is paid by the Treasury at the bill's maturity. The size of the discount is determined in an auction, where the Federal Reserve Bank of New York, acting on behalf of the U.S. Treasury, auctions each new bill issue to dealers and other investors. The bills go to the bidders offering the highest price, thereby resulting in the lowest implied interest cost to the Treasury. As one might suspect, the amount of the discount will depend on the term of the bill and the prevailing market conditions.

---

substitutes for money market instruments that fit the narrower definition. Short durations of debt instruments exceeding a year in maturity are produced by featuring a variable interest rate linked to prevailing market rates.

[8]Other marketable debt obligations of the Treasury include notes and bonds. Certain Treasury debt instruments, such as savings bonds, special issues to U.S. government agencies and trust funds, and state and local series debt, are not marketable.

T-bills are issued with 91-day (3-month), 182-day (6-month), and 364-day (1-year) maturities. Because of the huge demand for funds to keep the U.S. government going and to refinance the outstanding debt, new three- and six-month bills are auctioned every week, and new one-year bills are auctioned every four weeks.[9] Since 1993, T-bills have been issued in denominations that are multiples of $1,000, with $10,000 being the minimum denomination. A round lot, which is the minimum amount major market participants desire to trade and is usually the amount with the lowest sales commission rates, is $5 million. Commission rates on round lots generally range from $12.50 to $25 per $1 million depending on the bill's maturity, with three-month bills commanding the lowest commission.

Interestingly, no certificate of indebtedness is issued when a T-bill is issued. There is no engraved piece of paper specifying the terms of the T-bill. Rather, the purchase is simply recorded in the book entry system on the computer at the Federal Reserve.

Because of the low risk and short maturity of these instruments, T-bills are attractive investments for many financial market participants. Individuals, corporations, state and local governments, and money market mutual funds have large holdings. To individual and commercial investors, T-bills have the added attraction of being exempt from state and local taxes. Foreign central banks also have large holdings in T-bills. These institutions hold government debt instruments for many of the same reasons as private domestic investors, such as the safe return they provide. From the U.S. government's perspective, T-bills have also become an important source of funds to finance the ever-growing U.S. debt outstanding. But foreign central banks also use these short-term instruments for another purpose. Foreign governments often accumulate cash to make debt service payments on their dollar-denominated foreign debt, and this cash is often placed in T-bills until debt payments are due. The Federal Reserve itself holds a large amount of Treasury bills and is an active participant in this market. The Fed usually holds well over $100 billion of bills and buys large quantities of bills from dealers in the secondary market when it wishes to inject money into the economy. The reasons the Fed does so, as well as the mechanics of such intervention, will be discussed at some length in Chapter 27.

Federal Agency Discount Notes

The U.S. government, like governments around the world, attempts to foster certain favored activities, such as housing, education, and farming. One way it can help these activities is by providing them with access to an inexpensive source of funds.

---

[9]Another kind of T-bill, known as a cash management bill, is issued at irregular intervals and has maturities ranging from a few days to as long as nine months. Maturities are usually scheduled shortly after one of the major mid-month federal tax receipt days in April, June, September, or December to facilitate repayment. Cash management bills are sold only in large blocks with minimum denominations of $1 million.

Because government debt is of such low default risk, it carries a low interest rate, and the resulting cost savings can be passed along to the favored activities.

The U.S. government could issue debt directly to support favored activities, but due to the negative impact such support would have on the recorded deficit, it rarely does. Rather, the government has established **federally sponsored agencies** that raise funds in the open market to support certain targeted activities. These organizations, which are either directly owned by the government or are federally sponsored, private agencies—sometimes referred to as **government-sponsored enterprises** (GSEs)—are set up in an effort to support particular sectors of the economy. Because of the separate status of these agencies, their debt was officially off the federal balance sheets for many years. Today, however, with the Balanced Budget and Emergency Deficit Control Act of 1985, all former off-budget entities are presented on the budget. While most of these debt obligations are not guaranteed by the U.S. government, many investors assume that the government will stand behind the debt if the agencies falter. They presume that if these agencies experience financial difficulty, the U.S. Treasury will come to their aid. In fact, in some cases, the U.S. Treasury is required to do so. Therefore, investors treat the debt as very low risk.

Such a proliferation of federally sponsored agency debt issues emerged over time that financial markets had difficulty keeping track of them all. Therefore, secondary market activity in these instruments dropped to low levels, resulting in illiquidity and higher interest costs. This led the federal government to consolidate and assume the fund-raising responsibilities for all federal agencies except six privately owned, federally sponsored credit agencies.[10] The federal agencies for which the government assumed responsibility are funded through the Federal Financing Bank using standard Treasury debt obligations. The other six agencies are financial intermediaries that issue their debt directly and then channel the proceeds of their debt issuance to lending institutions in the private sector. This is accomplished by lending to the private lending institutions directly or by purchasing their assets, thereby providing them with funds to make new loans.

Three of these agencies concentrate on raising funds for home mortgages: the Federal Home Loan Banks, the Federal Home Loan Mortgage Corporation (Freddie Mac), and the Federal National Mortgage Association (Fannie Mae). Another agency, the Student Loan Marketing Association (Sallie Mae), is charged with making funds for student loans more plentiful and affordable. The Farm Credit Banks, on the other hand, were established to provide low cost loans to agricultural producers. The sixth "agency," the World Bank, is not actually a *federally*

---

[10]One of these agencies, REFCO, or Resolution Finance Company, was established to help in the bailout in the Savings & Loan Association crisis. To date, REFCO has issued primarily 40-year debt and, unlike the other five federally sponsored agencies, has played no direct role in the money market. Therefore, we will not discuss REFCO in this chapter. Another debt issuer, the World Bank, is often lumped together with the federal agencies by market participants because it carries a similar, implicit government backing. We will treat the World Bank as the sixth federal agency in this chapter.

EXHIBIT 11.1

Federal agency discount notes outstanding

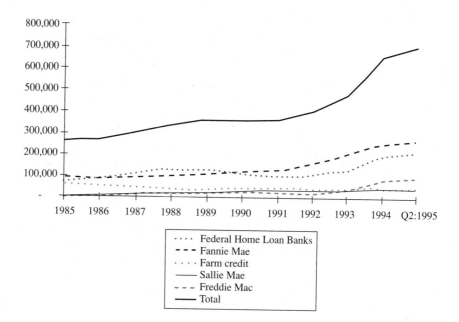

sponsored agency; rather, it is a bank sponsored by numerous countries around the world.[11] In addition to making loans to other private financial institutions, the World Bank often lends directly to private business firms and to foreign governments.

Each of these agencies has a need for long-term funds, which are raised by issuing interest-bearing bonds and notes. Moreover, they each have a need for short-term funds, which serve as "bridge financing" between major, long-term bond issues. These funds are often obtained by issuing **agency discount notes,** which resemble Treasury bills. Today, there are approximately $100 billion of these agency discount notes and over $700 billion of agency debt outstanding. (See Exhibit 11.1.)

Like T-bills, agency discount notes bear no interest but are offered at a discount from face value. Unlike T-bills, the amount of the discount is set by the agency. The agency will typically confer with dealers in the selling group prior to establishing a discount. Some agencies post discounts continually, but often at unattractive levels. If it desires to raise large amounts of money with a particular maturity, the agency will make the discount schedule relatively attractive.

Agency issues are smaller than Treasury issues and are traded less actively. In addition, most agency debt is held until maturity, contributing to the lessened liquidity. Bid-ask spreads are, therefore, wider than with T-bills of similar maturity. Round lots are $500,000. Thus, the round lot size of $5 million for T-bills would represent a large trade for agency debt. The discount notes are issued through dealers, who get five basis points for their service.

---

[11]Other development banks, such as the Asian Development Bank, issue similar securities.

Agency discount notes are priced so that their embedded yield is typically 10 to 30 basis points above the yields on T-bills of corresponding maturities. Part of this extra yield is due to the relative lack of liquidity of discount notes, and part is due to a small amount of nervousness among market participants about the lack of any explicit federal guarantee on much of the debt. Sometimes the credit spreads widen to more than 100 basis points when credit risk becomes of concern.

In addition to discount notes, the Farm Credit Banks offer interest-bearing securities that are a part of the money market with maturities of three, six, and nine months, while the Federal National Mortgage Association offers interest-bearing securities with six-month and one-year maturities. The Student Loan Marketing Association offers securities with six-month maturities once each month. Interest rates on these instruments are variable and are tied to six-month T-bill yields.

Major investors in agency discount notes (and their interest-bearing counterparts) are money market mutual funds and commercial banks. In addition, insurance companies, pension funds, thrifts, and even some individuals invest in these debt instruments. Notes issued by the Federal National Mortgage Association are fully taxable, as are those issued by the Federal Home Loan Mortgage Corporation. Notes issued by the Federal Home Loan Banks and the Farm Credit Banks are exempt from state and local taxes.

Short-Term Municipal Securities

State and local governments often have temporary needs for cash, such as in anticipation of the receipt of tax and other revenues or prior to the sale of bonds. To meet this need, they issue **short-term municipal securities.** These securities are issued in two forms: interest-bearing notes and discount notes. Of the two types, interest-bearing securities are more common. Interest-bearing securities often carry a variable interest payment that is tied to some other open market rate, such as Treasury yields. (For instance, the interest offered may equal T-bill yields less 100 basis points.) The extent of the rate movement, therefore, depends upon how the rate to which they are linked behaves over time.

The interest earnings, or the difference between·issue price and maturity value in the case of discount notes, are exempt from federal income taxes. Moreover, these earnings are often exempt from state and local taxes, provided that the investor is a resident of the state or city that issues the debt instrument.

The issuing bodies of short-term municipal debt include state, city, and county governments and the authorities, districts, and agencies established by state and local governments. Exhibit 11.2 lists the most common entities as well as the type of debt each employs. As is evident from this exhibit, two kinds of backing are available. First, the debt may have backing by the full faith and credit of the issuer. These issues are explicitly supported by the taxing power of the governmental body and are called **general obligation** (G.O.) securities. Alternatively, the issue may be backed by the revenues that are generated by the specific projects funded by the securities. These issues are called **revenue securities** and do not carry the

Exhibit 11.2   Issuers of Short-Term Municipal Securities and Types of Debt Issued

Issuer	*Types of Debt Generally Issued*
State government	G.O. and revenue
Local government:	G.O. and revenue
City	G.O. and revenue
County	G.O. and revenue
Authorities, districts, and agencies created by state and local governments:	
Public school	G.O. and revenue
Higher education	G.O. and revenue
Public power	Revenue
Water or sewer	Revenue
Transportation	Revenue
Health facilities	Revenue
Student loan	Revenue
Housing finance	Revenue
Pollution control	Revenue
Industrial development	Revenue
Waste management	Revenue

Note: G.O. denotes general obligation.

Source: *Instruments of the Money Market,* Federal Reserve Bank of Richmond, 1991.

backing of the full faith and credit of the issuer. Without this, revenue securities are perceived as significantly riskier than their G.O. counterparts.

Municipal securities usually have a minimum denomination of $5,000. Occasionally, to attract investors with more limited resources, the minimum denomination is dropped to $1,000. However, the transactions costs on such issues are higher to the issuer, and unless a very wide distribution of the debt is desired, this lower denomination is not offered.

Credit quality is an issue for municipal debt. Events such as the near bankruptcy of New York City and the default of Washington Public Power Supply System in 1983 have highlighted the need for careful evaluation of the credit quality of municipal issues. Accordingly, municipals often carry credit ratings provided by private credit rating agencies, with these credit ratings running the gamut from excellent to well below investment grade. To improve their credit ratings beyond what the municipality or revenue project could obtain, municipal issuers frequently offer some form of credit enhancement. The most common method of credit enhancement is to buy credit insurance from banks, corporations, and insurance companies. The debt issues are then rated according to the credit standing of the insuring entity.

Although municipals are subject to default risk, the yields they offer are often lower than those of Treasury obligations because of their tax exempt status.

EXHIBIT 11.3

*Holdings of short-term
tax-exempt securities*

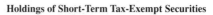

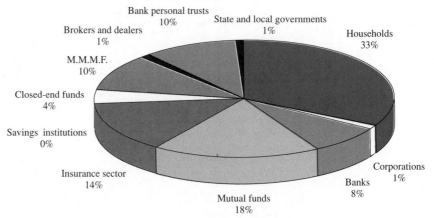

Holdings of Short-Term Tax-Exempt Securities

Bank personal trusts
10%

Brokers and dealers
1%

M.M.M.F.
10%

Closed-end funds
4%

Savings institutions
0%

Insurance sector
14%

State and local governments
1%

Households
33%

Corporations
1%

Banks
8%

Mutual funds
18%

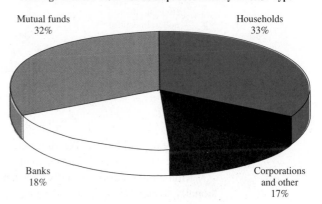

Holdings of Short-Term Tax-Exempt Securities by Investor Type

Mutual funds
32%

Households
33%

Banks
18%

Corporations
and other
17%

Source: Board of Governors of the Federal Reserve System, *Flow of Funds Accounts,* 1995.

Investors in municipal securities, therefore, are often individuals who find themselves in high federal tax brackets.[12] These individuals most often invest through tax-exempt money market funds, thereby diversifying the default risk among numerous municipalities. Bank trust departments also hold a sizable portion of outstanding municipal securities, usually on behalf of their clients. However, it is worth noting that financial and nonfinancial business corporations purchase nearly one-fourth of the securities issued. Federal and state taxes levied on corporations often combine to make these tax-exempt securities attractive to them as well.

Exhibit 11.3 summarizes the above discussion in a pie chart that illustrates the holders of short-term tax-exempt securities by sector. As is evident, the major

---

[12]See Chapter 9 for a discussion of the tax effect on security yields.

holders are households and mutual funds of various kinds, which hold these securities on behalf of retail individual clients generally. Accordingly, individual holdings *per se* grossly understate the true importance of individual investors in this tax-driven marketplace.

Fed Funds

Federal funds (fed funds) are the core of the overnight market for credit in the United States. They are the shortest-term liabilities of U.S.-chartered depository institutions: commercial banks, savings banks, savings and loan associations, and credit unions. About 80 percent of fed funds transactions are loans made between institutions from the close of one business day to the opening of the next, in the so-called overnight market. The remaining transactions, called **term fed funds,** may last for several days.

Transactions are executed by a transfer of funds from one institution's clearing account (checking account) at the Federal Reserve to the clearing account of another institution. These funds are, therefore, borrowed from one Fed account and transferred to another; hence, the name. There are two reasons that the fed funds market exists and is so active. First, there is an obvious need of institutions to manage their net cash position at the Federal Reserve. As will be discussed in a later chapter, balances at the Federal Reserve are required by regulation to be a certain fraction of some liabilities, but they pay no interest whatsoever. Therefore, depository institutions like to keep their excess balances in the non-interest-bearing reserve accounts as low as possible. Second, these same institutions have real financing needs. Just as governments and municipalities need transitory resources to finance their ongoing activities, institutions have similar needs. The first place they will seek these financial resources will be the fed funds market.

On any given day, due to the uncertain timing of cash inflows and outflows, a depository institution may have excess or insufficient reserves. Those with excess reserves may allocate them on the books of the Federal Reserve to institutions with shortfalls. In this way, they convert a surplus of nonearning reserves into earning assets. One additional attraction to depository institutions of borrowing from the fed funds market is that, unlike some other sources of funds that they have available, which require adding to reserves at the Fed, fed funds loans do not require any addition to reserves by the lending institution.

The needy institutions rent these reserves at the **federal funds rate.** The federal funds rate is competitively determined and is an important rate to which other money market rates are anchored. The rate also plays a key role in monetary policy, as the Fed can influence movement of the fed funds rate through the purchase and sale of government securities from its large portfolio. Competition is strong in this market, and usually, a single fed funds rate prevails. However, institutions with substandard creditworthiness may be charged a premium over the fed funds rate or excluded altogether. As in other markets, default risk matters here.

Lending institutions locate their needy counterparts through calls to their trading desk, through their banking relationships, or through specialized brokers who receive a fee for their services. These brokers maintain telephone contact with a large number of active participants in this market and can help put together buyers and sellers.

Like T-bills and the majority of agency discount notes, most fed funds are booked without a formal, written contract. This informality speeds the process and reduces transactions costs. Trust and experience are important elements in this kind of arrangement. Brokers can help a potential lender assess credit risk and gain access to potential new partners. At the same time, long-term relationships tend to develop between parties that trade frequently with one another. In fact, some fed funds transactions are continuing contracts. These are automatically renewed fed funds transactions at prevailing rates (or at some formula-generated number tied to prevailing rates) that continue unless terminated by the borrower or lender. The result is a longer-term instrument with open maturity.

As a general characterization, borrowers of fed funds are most often large money center banks whose loan demand from big corporate borrowers often exceeds deposits. Lenders of fed funds are typically smaller banks that collect more in deposits than they desire to lend locally or otherwise invest. While this market serves as an outlet for both types of institution, each must be concerned about its interest rate risk and, therefore, the effect that participation in this market will have on the institution. More will be said about this matter in Chapter 25.

Negotiable Certificates of Deposit

Earlier, we briefly discussed certificates of deposit issued by banks, which pay a stated interest rate over a fixed time period. **Negotiable certificates of deposit** (NCDs) are tradable (as is implied by the term "negotiable") time deposits. Like many other money market securities, NCDs are issued in denominations of $100,000 and higher. Most NCDs are in denominations over $1 million, with round lots in the secondary market in the $5–$10 million range. Maturities are from 7 days to 12 months, with most transactions in the 1- to 3-month area.

Most NCDs feature a fixed interest rate to maturity. However, some NCDs have variable interest rates, where the period of the instrument is divided into equal subperiods. Rates are reset at the beginning of each new subperiod, and interest is paid at the end of each subperiod. The reset rate is set at some fixed spread over a prevailing reference rate, usually the composite one-month secondary market CD rate or the one-month wholesale international rate, known as the **London Interbank Offer Rate** (LIBOR). The maturities of variable-rate NCDs typically range from 18 months to two years, which fall outside the usual definition of money market maturities. However, rate reset subperiods are every one to three months, so they are usually included in any listing of money market instruments.

There are four general classes of NCDs of differing rates, risk, and liquidity. **Domestic CDs** are issued by U.S. banks domestically. **Eurodollar CDs** are issued abroad by foreign and off-shore branches of U.S. banks. They are denominated in U.S. dollars, have maturities ranging from 1 to 12 months, and most have fixed interest rates. Historically, most of these CDs were issued in London, the center of the Eurodollar market; hence, their "Euro" name. **Yankee CDs** are NCDs issued in the U.S. by branches of foreign banks. Most of these are issued by the New York branches of well-known international banks. **Thrift CDs** are issued by large savings and loan associations. Many are issued in $100,000 denominations so that federal deposit insurance will apply. Sometimes, $100,000 thrift CDs of various institutions are packaged together into large-denomination CDs. The advantage is that each parcel is fully insured.

Unlike T-bills, most agency discount notes, and fed funds, NCDs actually are engraved certificates; hence, the use of the word "certificates" in their name. These certificates specify the amount on deposit, period until maturity, interest rate, and method of calculating interest rate. They are issued both in bearer and registered forms.

The credit risk of NCDs is rated by several rating agencies, including Standard & Poor's, Moody's, and several more specialized agencies. In the primary market, a bank will post its rates on NCDs for popular maturities: 1, 2, 3, 6, and 12 months. However, only some of these rates are likely to be competitive. These competitive rates apply to debt maturities to which the bank wishes to attract the most funds. Naturally, if an investor is bent on placing funds at a less desired maturity and at a noncompetitive interest rate, the bank is happy to oblige. In the secondary market, NCDs with remaining maturities of six months or less are most traded. Bid-ask spreads are typically around five basis points, and only the best banks have actively traded NCDs.

In addition to NCDs, the banking industry has recently turned to other types of instruments to finance its growth. Today, large banks use **deposit notes,** which are designed to resemble and trade like short-term corporate bonds. Deposit notes are somewhat longer than the NCD maturities, with original maturities of 18 months to five years, and they have a fixed rate of interest. Their original advantage to banks was that, as long as their maturities were 18 months or longer, they escaped non-interest-bearing reserve requirements. Now, however, no time deposits are subject to required reserves. Therefore, deposit notes are used solely as a mechanism for extending the maturity of the bank's liability structure. In addition, **bank notes,** a debt security similar to deposit notes, have appeared. Because they are not formally designated as deposit liabilities, bank notes can be issued without the required payment to the Federal Deposit Insurance Corporation (FDIC) for insurance. This assessment had been as high as 23 basis points only a couple of years ago, which is substantial in the competitive wholesale financial market.

Commercial Paper

Commercial paper is defined as short-term unsecured promissory notes. A growing number of financial and nonfinancial businesses have found this instrument to be a cheaper way to meet their needs for cash than traditional channels of NCDs, for depository institutions, or short-term loans, for nonfinancial business firms. As such, the commercial paper market has grown rapidly over the last decade.

Exhibit 11.4

*Investors in U.S.
commercial paper by
investor type (second
quarter 1995)*

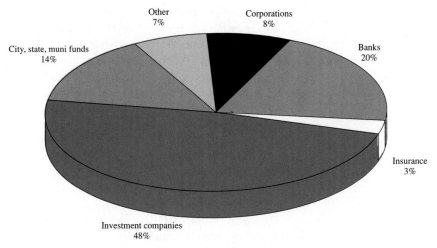

Other
7%

Corporations
8%

City, state, muni funds
14%

Banks
20%

Insurance
3%

Investment companies
48%

Source: Board of Governors of the Federal Reserve System, *Flow of Funds Accounts,* 1995.

Commercial paper is the second largest money market instrument, in terms of outstanding debt, behind T-bills, with the total value approaching $650 billion by mid-1995. Most commercial paper is rated by one or more of the credit rating agencies. Credit risk is perceived to be relatively low but present, and liquidity is also low. Accordingly, investors tend to hold to maturity. Consequently, yields on commercial paper exceed those on Treasury obligations of similar maturities.

Commercial paper is typically issued at a discount from face value, matures on a specific day, and is negotiable. Most maturities are in the 30- to 60-day range and often are repaid by the corporation through a succeeding issue. To guard against a sudden change in market conditions that would impair a borrower's ability to issue new paper and to comfort prospective lenders' concerns about credit quality, most issues are backed by standby lines of credit issued by banks.

Commercial paper is sold directly by the issuing institution or through dealers who purchase a block of commercial paper and then resell the debt to other investors. While dealer-placed paper had been the dominant type earlier in this century, large issuers' directly marketed paper now represents a majority of the market. In either case, the paper is usually issued in bearer form, although it can be issued in registered form. Minimum denominations are $100,000 to $250,000, and an average purchase is around $5 million.

Money market funds are the largest investors in commercial paper. Insurers, banks, thrifts, nonfinancial corporations, and state and local government bodies are also important investors in this instrument, as Exhibit 11.4 indicates. On the other hand, while historically, nonfinancial firms were the primary borrowers, today, financial companies account for approximately three-fourths of all issues, with most of the remainder being issued by nonfinancial firms. It is also worth

EXHIBIT 11.5

Commercial paper by Moody's rating category

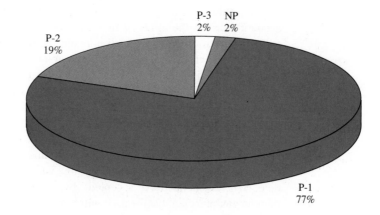

EXHIBIT 11.6

Rated U.S. commercial paper by sector

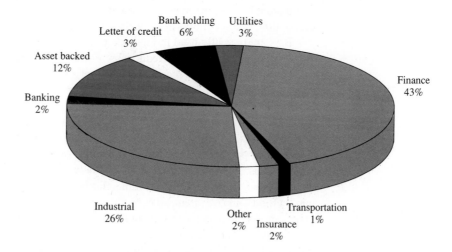

noting that the market is somewhat international, with about 10 percent of the dollar volume in the commercial paper market being raised by a foreign financial or nonfinancial firm or a foreign government.

The overwhelming majority of these firms are investment grade, but some activity still exists in the lower rating area (see Exhibit 11.5). Yields, of course, reflect this differential in credit risk and follow ratings quite closely. A summary of issuers' characteristics is presented in Exhibit 11.6.

Bankers' Acceptances

Many people write postdated checks in anticipation of an impending infusion of funds to their checking account. Sometimes, the inflow does not occur soon enough and the check bounces. Suppose you were to write a check and postdate it by a month. Suppose, further, that your bank stamped a guarantee on the check that it would be honored in full, 30 days hence, whether or not your checking account received the influx of funds. A creditor would be more likely to accept your postdated check if the bank making the guarantee merited its confidence. Moreover, the creditor could take your guaranteed check, endorse it, and use it to satisfy its own financial obligations to others. Naturally, since the recipient would need to wait for 30 days before obtaining cash in exchange for the check, anyone receiving the check, including the creditor, would regard its present value as less than the stated cash amount and discount it accordingly.

A **bankers' acceptance** (BA) has much in common with the check described above. It is little more than a time draft (read this as a postdated check) that orders the payment of a specified amount of money to the acceptance holder on a future date. BAs are stamped as "accepted" by the bank on which the draft is drawn, thereby guaranteeing that the draft will be properly executed and paid in full on its due date. In exchange for guaranteeing the time draft, the accepting bank is given international trade documents, temporary title to the goods that are related to the transaction, and a commission for its services.

BAs are typically used to facilitate trade between parties that do not wish to be exposed to each other's credit risks. For example, an importer may wish to delay payment for goods received until after it is able to resell the goods several months later. The importer could get a loan from its bank and pay the exporter immediately, but it is often cheaper to issue a BA. The exporter, or exporter's bank, is comfortable with the BA and will proceed with the transaction. In addition to financing foreign trade, BAs can also be used to finance the domestic shipment of goods; the domestic and foreign storage of grains, cotton, oil, and other staples; and the shipment of goods between foreign countries.

Investors in BAs include commercial banks, foreign central banks, money market funds, and nonfinancial corporations. They are sold at a discount from face value, are issued in bearer form, and are issued with maturities ranging from one to six months. There is an active secondary market for BAs. Yields are quoted on a discount basis and round lots are for $5 million in the broker's market. The yields are slightly lower than those on commercial paper because BAs are less risky due to the borrower's pledge to pay, the collateral of goods, and the guarantee of the accepting bank. Over the past 70 years, BA investors have not suffered any losses of principal.

Repurchase Agreements

In the previous section, we spoke of bankers' acceptances, which are IOUs guaranteed to the investor by the accepting bank and collateralized to the accepting bank by temporary title to the borrowers' goods. A **repurchase agreement** (REPO) is one step beyond such an IOU. A REPO is the purchase and repurchase of a given security by two parties at prices determined at the initial trade date. The security used may be a Treasury obligation, agency issue, mortgage-backed security, corporate debt issue, or money market instrument such as an NCD or BA, and the timing of the two transactions can be one day or several months apart. At the end of the period, the initial seller gets back the security and the purchaser gets back the funds provided, together with "interest."

This arrangement is referred to as a repurchase agreement due to the title transfer and/or possession of the security passing to the purchaser, who legally owns the security involved. However, unlike most holders of financial securities, the purchaser has little concern over what fluctuations may occur in the security's value because the initial seller enters into an agreement to repurchase it at a predetermined price at the end of the arrangement. The yield implied by the difference in the prices of purchase and repurchase is the **repo rate.**

The repo rate charged to the initial seller depends on the nature of the underlying security and the creditworthiness of the initial seller. A lower rate is charged if the security involved is free of default risk, highly liquid, and short in duration. A security of long duration could fluctuate substantially in value, exposing the purchaser to potential loss if the initial seller defaults on his obligation to repurchase it and leaves the purchaser stuck holding a security with depreciated value. To protect the purchaser against this eventuality, less than the full market value of the security is usually provided—from 0.1 percent to 5 percent less—depending on the term of the agreement and other characteristics of the security. Moreover, some repos that last for several weeks or months will have a "mark-to-market" provision whereby the initial seller is required to supply additional securities or repay a portion of the funds in the event that the underlying securities depreciate.

Many repos are overnight. Most are for less than three months and may involve a repo rate that resets daily or stays fixed over a longer period. Some repos extend as long as a year. Minimum denominations are $1 million, and a round lot is $25 million.

The major players in the repo market are banks, savings institutions, and nonbank securities dealers. Many of these firms need to finance their sizable inventories of securities. They seek investors such as banks, money market funds, and other nonfinancial firms who have funds to invest for short periods of time. Banks are not required to place funds in a non-interest-bearing reserve account for funds they place in the repo market, which enhances their attractiveness to banks. For the corporate treasurer, the repo rate clearly is an attractive alternative to the zero return received from idle balances in a checking account.

Summary of Money Market Instrument Characteristics

Exhibits 11.7 and 11.8 provide summary information with respect to the eight money market instruments we have discussed.

Exhibit 11.7 presents the borrowers and lenders in each of these markets, along with common denominations. Exhibit 11.8 offers risk profiles. As is evident here, the maturity of all of these instruments is quite short almost by definition. On the other hand, both the credit risk and liquidity differ substantially. Tax considerations come into play only with municipal debt, with others fully taxable for interest and discount yields.

EXHIBIT 11.7   **Money Market Instruments and Characteristics**

Money Market Instruments	Principal Borrowers	Principal Investors	Common Denominations
Commercial paper	Financial and nonfinancial corporations	Nonfinancial corporations, money market funds	$25,000 minimum
Treasury bills	Federal government	Individuals, nonfinancial and financial corporations, money market funds, foreign and domestic governments	$10,000 and higher
Fed funds	Banks	Depository institutions	Flexible
Municipal notes	State and local governments	Insurance companies, individuals	$5,000 for interest-bearing notes, $50,000–$100,000+ for discount notes
Negotiable certificates of deposit	Large banks and thrifts	Nonfinancial corporations, money market funds, individuals	$100,000 and higher
Repurchase agreements	Banks, securities dealers, other owners of government securities	Nonfinancial corporations and financial institutions	$10 million and higher
Bankers' acceptances	Financial and nonfinancial corporations	Nonfinancial and financial corporations, money market funds, governments	$100,000 minimum
Federal agency discount notes	Federally sponsored agencies	Individuals, money market funds, governments	$10,000, $25,000, $50,000, and higher, depending on the issuing agency

Finally, in Exhibit 11.9 on page 260, the outstanding volumes of the major money market instruments are presented for three subperiods spanning over 15 years. The exhibit reports outstanding balances in each of the instruments discussed above. In the case of NCDs, the Federal Reserve's series on large-denomination time deposits is used. In total, their value of approximately $2.6 trillion represents over one-third of nominal GDP for the economy of 1995. Clearly, these are large, deep, and efficient markets. However, their efficiency does not imply uniformity of yields. As indicated, the characteristics of each money market instrument are different, at least in degree. Accordingly, the yields of these instruments vary, as we illustrate in the next section.

Relationship among Interest Rates

In Exhibit 11.10 on page 261, we provide an indication of the yield spread across various money market instruments. The bar graph reports both the average rates for the individual markets and the variation in rates over a one-month period. The data

Eхнвт 11.8 Money Market Instrument Risk Characteristics

Money Market Instruments	Duration (Common Maturities)	Convexity	Credit Risk	Liquidity	Timing of Payments Risk	Taxability
Commercial paper	20–45 days	negligible	medium to very low, rated by credit agencies	limited secondary market	known	discount is fully taxable as interest income
Treasury bills	3, 6, and 12 months	low, positive	assumed to be none	very active secondary market	known	discount is fully taxable as interest income; exempt from state and local tax
Fed funds	1–7 days	none	very low	no secondary market	can be extended by borrower with agreement of lender, but at new rates	
Municipal notes	1–12 months	low, positive	rated by credit agencies	moderately active secondary market for large issuers	known	interest is exempt from federal income tax and state and local taxes of issuing locale; price appreciation is subject to tax
Negotiable certificates of deposit	1, 2, 3, and 6 months	low, positive	low to high; not guaranteed against default by FDIC	active secondary market	known	interest and price appreciation are subject to income tax
Repurchase agreements	1 day, 1 week, 3–6 months, flexible terms	none	low risk, collateralized by Treasury securities; collateral price risk	high liquidity but no secondary market	flexible	price differences taxed as interest income
Bankers' acceptances	1–9 months	negligible	very low; major banks are guarantors	active secondary market	known	
Federal agency discount notes	1–12 months	low, positive	assumed to be none	limited secondary market	known	discount is fully taxable as interest income; exempt from state and local tax

EXHIBIT 11.9

*U.S. money market
instruments
outstanding*

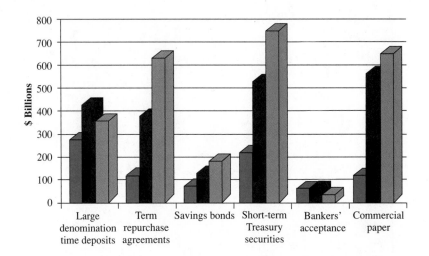

are for the month of July 1994. With the exception of the fed funds rate and the discount rate, all interest rates are for instruments with three-month maturities. As expected, for three-month maturities, Treasury yields are lower than bankers' acceptances and commercial paper. The absence of credit and liquidity risk makes these debts of the U.S. government highly desirable and, by implication, the lowest in yield. By contrast, commercial paper yields are 31 basis points higher on average, while bankers' acceptances yields are 22 basis points higher. NCDs, somewhat surprisingly, had a lower average yield than T-bills during the month, reflecting excess liquidity of banking institutions at the time. The fed funds rate varies greatly from period to period due to its role as a reflection of bank liquidity. Because fed funds are usually for shorter periods than three-month T-bills, their average yield was lower than that for T-bills, reflecting a steeply upward sloping term structure of interest at that time. In contrast, the discount rate, which is set by edict of the Federal Reserve Board, remained unchanged during the entire month.

Price Quotation and Yield Conventions

The pricing and yield conventions for money market instruments are often confusing and downright misleading. If the yields are computed, what you often get are numbers that are neither comparable nor helpful. This is because each market has different pricing conventions. To remedy this defect, the participants have adopted a practice to recast the money market yields, whether given in discount or outright terms or computed on a 360- or 365-day basis, into **bond-equivalent yields.** This is essentially a yield-to-maturity calculation using a semiannual yield convention. A more accurate measure, which doesn't resort to semiannual compounding, is the **effective annual interest rate,** which gives the true annualized rate of return over the period.

Exhibit 11.10

Yield ranges for money market instruments (July 1994)

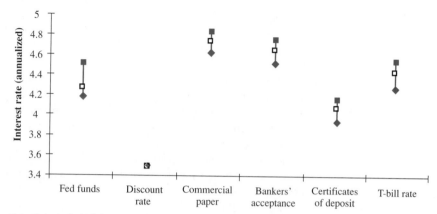

Note: ■ equals the high interest rate for July 1994, □ equals the average interest rate for July 1994, and ◆ equals the low intestest rate for July 1994.

To obtain effective annual interest rates, we begin by looking at the underlying cash flows of each instrument. For any instrument, we must consider two pieces of fundamental information: (1) what is paid for a money market security, and (2) what you get back in return. These two pieces of information can be related to each other by subtraction, resulting in the dollar return over a period, or by division, resulting in the total return over a period. Dollar returns will, of course, depend on the size of the investment, so their usefulness for comparative purposes is limited. Total return may be reported on a basis that reflects the length of the period, or it may be reported on an annualized basis, reflecting the compounding of returns over several periods. Because returns on an annualized basis are easily compared, we prefer to focus on them.

The market practice for some money market instruments, such as T-bills, bankers' acceptances, and commercial paper, is to quote prices on a **discount yield basis.** This means that you reduce the face value by the amount of the discount to get the price. This is analogous to the practice of a retail store that offers merchandise for sale at 10 percent (the discount) off list (face value) price. A shirt listed at $40 that is on sale at 10 percent off would sell for $36 [= $40 × (1 − .10)].

The key to calculating the prices of money market instruments quoted on a discount basis is to correctly compute their discounts. Here is where a knowledge of quoting conventions is important. Discounts are given on a simple "annualized" basis. Let us return to the shirt example to develop an analogy. Suppose that all shirts could be purchased for immediate or future possession on a "layaway plan." All shirts cost $40. However, a discount of 10 percent per year is offered on the price of the shirt for those who are willing to wait for delivery! Assume further that this 10 percent discount is available to all buyers, prorated by the portion of a year that you are willing to wait for delivery. For example, if you were willing to wait for only half a year, you would get a discount of 10 percent × ½ = 5%.

Now, for those of you who are attuned to haberdashery, this offer might not appear to be very attractive. After all, in a year's time, the shirt may be out of fashion or your girth may have changed. But money never goes out of fashion, and this is essentially how the money market for discount securities operates. In this market, a 10 percent discount for a 6-month, $100 T-bill means the instrument is selling at approximately $95.

There is only one additional element that has not been discussed: how many days there are in a year. The convention for most discount instruments is to use 360 days. This is done to avoid the occasional confusion that arises when a year changes from 365 to 366 days and to eliminate the need to remember which months have 28, 29, 30, and 31 days. Thus, the practice is to take the actual number of days until maturity and divide that total by 360 days to get the portion of a year by which the discount percentage is multiplied. Note that for some instruments, such as a 364-day T-bill, the portion of the year remaining can be greater than 100 percent.

Consider this example. A T-bill is quoted at a 7.55 percent discount, *d*, and has 157 days left to maturity, denoted below as *T*. What is its price per $100 face value? The general formula is:

$$\text{Price} = \text{Face value} \times [1 - (\tfrac{T}{360} \times d)]$$

Thus, for this example, the price is calculated as:

$$\text{Price} = \$96.7074 = \$100 \times [1 - (\tfrac{157}{360} \times .0755)]$$

Carrying out the calculation to four places beyond the decimal may seem to be overkill, but it is not. This is because the denominations and typical trade sizes of T-bills and other money market instruments are so large as to make the final digits important in terms of the money they signify. For instance, on a $10 million bankers' acceptance, the final two digits amount to $740.00.

We now know how to derive the first piece of useful information, the price. The next piece of useful information is to compute the value that we will receive when the investment matures—its redemption value. For a discount instrument, this calculation is trivial; it is simply the face value of the instrument.

Armed with these two useful pieces of information, we now can compute the **effective annual yield** (*EAY*). This calculation is based on the assumption that at the maturity of an investment, we could take the proceeds and invest in a like security with an identical return. In other words, the interest is compounded to an annualized rate of return. No fiction is involved here in terms of counting numbers of days in a year. In this case, we find 2.324841 (= 365 ÷ 157) compounding periods in a year. The calculation proceeds as follows:

$$\left(\frac{\text{Face value}}{\text{Price}}\right)^{\frac{365}{T}} - 1 = EAY$$

$$\left(\frac{\$100}{\$96.7074}\right)^{\frac{365}{157}} - 1 = 8.0946\%$$

Note that the effective annual yield differs substantially from the 7.55 percent discount rate.

The other main class of money market securities is comprised of interest-bearing instruments, such as fed funds, and certain nondiscount munis, agencies, and negotiable certificates of deposit. Fed funds and repos are not negotiable instruments, so the calculations for effective annual interest rates are simple. Consider fed funds or a repo quoted at 9.75 percent for overnight money. We will call this the **stated interest rate** (*SIR*). The first useful piece of information, from the investor's point of view, is what is paid for the investment. In both cases, it is simply the amount of the loan or, in the case of repos, the assumed agreed purchase price of the collateral securities. Since we are demonstrating our calculations on a per $100 basis, let us just assume that the amount is $100.

What is the redemption value? A day later, the investor will receive a day's worth of interest. The convention, again, is to use a 360-day year when computing interest due. Thus, the redemption value is:

$$\text{Redemption value} = \text{Loan amount} \times \left[1 + \left(\frac{T}{360} \times SIR \right) \right]$$

$$\$100 \times [1 + (\tfrac{1}{360} \times .0975)] = \$100.0270833$$

Do not overlook the redemption price digits far to the right. On a $100 million fed funds loan or repo, these numbers represent $27,083 of overnight interest earnings.

Next, let us utilize these two pieces of information to compute the effective annual interest rate. The calculation is as follows:

$$\left(\frac{\text{Redemption value}}{\text{Loan amount}} \right)^{\frac{365}{T}} - 1 = EAY$$

$$\left(\frac{\$100.0270833}{\$100} \right)^{\frac{365}{1}} - 1 = 10.389\%$$

The interpretation of the 10.389 percent effective annual yield is that it is the annual increase you would garner if you were able to reinvest your proceeds in a similar transaction each night throughout the entire year at a 9.75 percent rate of interest.

Negotiable certificates of deposit and other negotiable interest-bearing money market instruments are a bit more complex to tackle. This is due to the price-quoting convention that ignores accrued interest. By focusing again on the purchase price and redemption value, we can avoid any traps. Suppose you were to purchase a 180-day, 7.75 percent NCD, quoted at 7.40 percent, 23 days prior to maturity. Notice that the stated interest rate on the NCD of 7.75 percent differs from that of the quotation (7.40 percent) and that 157 days (= 180 − 23) have passed since the NCD was issued. The reasons that the stated rate differs from the quoted rate may be that the NCD is much shorter in remaining term than it was at issue and that market rates of interest have changed during the passage of 157 days since issue.

The task at hand is to determine the effective annual yield on such an investment. To derive this answer we proceed as follows. We must first compute the redemption value because, as will be shown, it is needed to compute the purchase price. The redemption value (*FV*) per $100 of principal amount (*P*) is given as follows:

$$\text{Principal} \times \left[1 + \left(\frac{\text{Days to maturity from issue}}{360} \times SIR \right) \right] = \text{Redemption value}$$

$$\$100 \times \left[1 + \left(\frac{180}{360} \times .0775 \right) \right] = \$103.875$$

The purchase price may be computed by discounting the redemption value by the market rate of interest for the remaining 23 days of this issue.[13]

$$\frac{\text{Redemption value}}{\left[1 + \left(\frac{T}{360} \times \text{Market rate of interest} \right) \right]} = \text{Purchase price}$$

$$\frac{\$103.875}{[1 + (\frac{23}{360} \times .0740)]} = \$103.386213$$

Now that we know the purchase price and the redemption value, we can obtain the effective annual interest rate to an investor.

$$\left(\frac{\text{Redemption value}}{\text{Purchase price}} \right)^{\frac{365}{T}} - 1 = EAY$$

$$\left(\frac{\$103.875}{\$103.386213} \right)^{\frac{365}{23}} - 1 = 7.77235\%$$

This is all the investor needs to know. Yet, at times, dealers will provide some extraneous yield information. In general, it is redundant and, at times, can prove to be misleading to the uninitiated investor. We prefer to focus on what you pay, what you get, and the annual effective rate of interest.

---

[13]To the seller of the NCD, this purchase price of $103.386213 is composed of two parts for tax purposes. One part is accrued interest, which is 157/360 × .0775 × $100 = $3.379861. The remainder of $100.006352 represents the sales price, which includes a very small capital gain above the initial issue price of $100.00. If a price is quoted by a dealer, it will be this sales price, and the investor is required to add accrued interest to get the total purchase price. When interest and short-term capital gains are taxed at equal rates, there is no economic substance to this calculation, yet it is required for tax reporting nonetheless.

Summary

In recent years, there has been a proliferation of money market instruments and a tremendous upsurge in the volume of issues. A few decades ago, much of what borrowers needed was obtained from their friendly local banker. Now, many borrowers bypass the banker and seek funds directly in the money market. This is particularly likely when the borrower is large and has known credit.

Today, individual consumers and small companies participate in the money market mostly on the investment side. However, there is much to learn in order to become a knowledgeable investor. Instruments differ, pricing conventions differ, and the investor often can make incorrect decisions.

This chapter reviews the main instruments of the money market. In each case, we outline the nature of the market, the reason for the instrument, and major market participants. An understanding of the idiosyncrasies of individual instruments is essential to an appreciation of the money market.

The last subject covered is that of pricing conventions. Here, too, pricing differs from instrument to instrument in a confusing manner. Quoted yields are often misleading because of differences in conventions that can substantially affect their meaning.

Therefore, we close the chapter with a return to basics. For each of these instruments, we can determine the effective annual interest rate associated with an investment in the instrument. Computing this true rate of return metric is frequently difficult but essential to comparing yields and deciding on relative value.

Looking ahead, we anticipate that as the information revolution continues to expand, even smaller investors and small borrowers will be able to access the money market through computer terminals. This will contribute to further expansion in the money market and will increase its importance as an investment vehicle for borrowers and lenders alike. As you enter this market, perhaps for the first time, know what you are buying and what your return will be!

Key Concepts

bankers' acceptances,   256
bond-equivalent yields,   260
commercial paper,   253
deposit notes versus bank notes
  versus NCDs,   253
discount yields,   261
domestic CDs,   252
effective annual interest rates,   260
Eurodollar CDs,   252
federal agency discount notes,   247
federally sponsored agencies,   246
fed funds,   251
general obligation versus revenue bonds,   248

government-sponsored enterprises,   246
instruments of the money market,   243
money versus bond versus equity markets,   242
negotiable certificates of deposit,   252
price quotations and yield conventions for
  money market instruments,   260–64
primary and secondary money markets,   243
relationship among interest rates,   258–60
repurchase agreements,   256
short-term municipal securities,   248–51
thrift CDs,   253
Treasury bills,   244
Yankee CDs,   253

Review Questions

1. If you are entering the money market for the first time by withdrawing from your savings account to invest in one of the instruments listed, what factors should you consider in selecting the instrument of choice? Compare these instruments with your simple savings account.

2. From the discussion in the text, it would seem that a commercial bank could raise funds using the commercial paper market,

the fed funds market, or the NCD market. How would you evaluate which avenue a banking institution should utilize to finance itself?

3. The U.S. government has recently embarked on a policy to shorten the maturity structure of its debt. It has argued that the cost of T-bills is usually below that of long-term Treasury bonds. Who are the likely buyers of this increased volume of T-bills? Given what you know about the term structure of interest, is this tactic likely to save the taxpayers money?

4. At a recent meeting of the Faculty Club, one of our learned colleagues from the humanities was heard making this statement: "The government should always raise its money by issuing Treasury bills. The discount rate on this portion of the money market is always lower than the yields quoted elsewhere." Please educate our dear friend.

5. Suppose that you are interested in a T-bill that matures in 212 days and is quoted at an 8.22

percent discount. What is the price per $1,000 face value? What is the annual effective interest rate?

6. Calculate the annual effective interest rate of an NCD using the following information. Its face value is $10 million, and it is subject to a variable interest rate with payments made quarterly and automatically reinvested. The relevant quarterly annualized interest rates are: 8.62 percent, 8.47 percent, 8.22 percent, and 8.21 percent. Assume you are the issuer.

7. What is the effective annual interest rate on a repurchase agreement that lasts one week and has a stated interest rate of 14 percent? Suppose that you could loan the same amount of money in the fed funds market at 13.92 percent compounded daily. If there is no risk, which is the better instrument?

8. Find the redemption value, purchase price, and effective annual interest rate of a 90-day, 6.31 percent NCD that matures in 47 days.

References

Federal Reserve Bank of New York. *Basic Information in Treasury Securities.* Federal Reserve Bank of New York, 1990.

Federal Reserve Bank of Richmond. *Instruments of the Money Market.* 6th ed. Federal Reserve Bank of Richmond, 1991.

Jensen, F., and P. Parkinson. "Recent Developments in the Bankers Acceptance Market." *Federal Reserve Bulletin,* January 1986.

Knez, Peter J.; Robert Litterman; and José Scheinkman. "Explorations into Factors Explaining Money Market Returns." *Journal of Finance,* December 1994.

Puglisi, D., and A. Vagnola. "An Examination of Federal Agency Debt Pricing Practices." *Journal of Financial Research,* Summer 1983.

Reinhart, Vincent. "An Analysis of Potential Treasury Auction Techniques." *Federal Reserve Bulletin,* June 1992.

Stigum, Marcia. *Money Market Calculations.* Burr Ridge, Ill.: Irwin Professional Publishing, 1981.

———. *The Repo and Reverse Markets.* Burr Ridge, Ill.: Irwin Professional Publishing, 1989.

———. *The Money Market.* 3d ed. Burr Ridge, Ill.: Irwin Professional Publishing, 1990.

This chapter reviews the major instruments in the government and corporate bond markets. For each, a description of the market, its borrowers and sellers, and its unique characteristics are presented. Special attention is given to the call feature and rating process. Finally, a simple comparison of prices, liquidity, and investor interest is offered.

Often, when a business or government entity is undertaking a project, such as building a factory or constructing a highway or school, the need for funds continues for many years. If money for these projects were to be obtained in the money market, a series of frequent borrowings would be required, with a new loan being incurred every few months to repay an existing loan. The problems with this approach are that more funds may be unobtainable at some point in the future, due to changes in market conditions or temporary deterioration of creditworthiness on the part of the borrower, or they may be obtainable but only at substantially higher interest rates. To guard against these potentially crippling possibilities, many

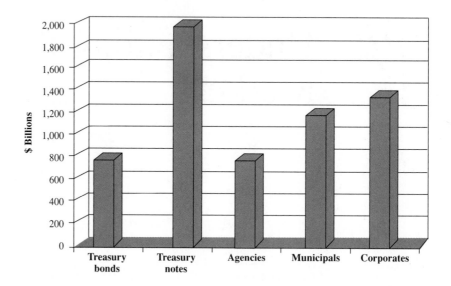

business and government entities seek to obtain funds with a longer payback period. These funds are obtained through long-term loans or in the bond market. As will be seen in a later chapter, banks and other lending institutions will make loans beyond one year, but they will rarely commit for over five years. Firms that seek funds for a longer term are usually forced into the bond market, where maturities can range well beyond five years. Recently, this market has become so competitive that it has also garnered a substantial fraction of the intermediate-term lending market at the expense of the depository institutions sector. Accordingly, it is an increasingly important market.

Overview of the Bond Market

The **bond market** is a market that brings together borrowers and suppliers of long-term funds through borrowing instruments known as bonds and notes. The initial maturities of these instruments are greater than 1 year, and they are sometimes 40 years or longer. Some bonds are even perpetual, promising to pay interest forever, though they never repay principal. The bond market is largely an institutional market; relatively few individuals invest directly in bonds. Major investors are insurance companies, pension funds, and mutual funds.

The bond market is composed of two sectors: government and corporate. The government sector can be further divided into the Treasury, federal agency, and municipal sectors. A glance at Exhibit 12.1 reveals the size of the U.S. bond market and the relative magnitude of each sector.[1]

---

[1]In this chapter, we treat only the U.S. bond market. The Eurobond market and Asian dollar markets are also huge in size, and they are growing in importance. These markets are described in

This market, because of its long maturity, is different from the money market in many respects. As a review of the operation of this market, two differences will be spotlighted here. First, only a fraction of the existing bonds mature in any one year, and correspondingly, only a fraction represent new issues. In contrast, the money market has, by definition, at least 100 percent turnover each year. Second, because maturity is so long, there is a large distinction between the primary and secondary bond markets; the mechanisms of each are complicated and quite distinct. Accordingly, in our review of each component of the bond market, separate emphasis will be given to each of these activities.

Instruments of the Bond Market

Treasury Debt

Treasury debt is often classified in three categories: bills, notes, and bonds. As was noted in Chapter 11, bills are non-interest-bearing, short-term (less than one-year maturity) discount securities that constitute an important part of the money market. In contrast, **notes** and **bonds** are interest-bearing securities with initial (on the date of issue) maturities of greater than one year. All three categories carry the full faith and credit of the U.S. government. The only material difference between notes and bonds is that notes have maturities at issue of 10 or fewer years, whereas bond maturities exceed 10 years at issue. Currently, the Treasury issues notes with initial maturities of 2, 3, 4, 5, 7, and 10 years, and it issues bonds with initial maturities of 30 years. In the past decade, the Treasury also issued bonds with maturities of 15 and 20 years, although it has discontinued that practice. The Clinton administration concentrated its debt issues at the short and long ends of the spectrum.

The primary market for government debt is a complicated affair. It works like this. Almost all negotiable Treasury debt is issued at auctions on a **yield basis.** Instead of bidding on the prices of the notes and bonds, investors submit sealed bids identifying the lowest yields to maturity that they are willing to accept. The bids are submitted through local Federal Reserve Banks and are opened at a prespecified time in the future. Each bid is exact to two decimal places, such as 9.64 percent, and also specifies the volume of Treasury debt desired to be acquired at that yield. Some bidders place orders as **noncompetitive bids,**[2] which means that they will pay a price equal to the average of the accepted bids. The Treasury is not a completely passive player. It sets a "stop-out" level above which it is unwilling to issue debt. At the appointed time, the various bids are compiled and

---

most international finance textbooks. Moreover, many developed countries have important bond markets that are increasingly of interest to U.S. investors. With the reduction of international barriers to the flow of funds, the separate bond markets are truly becoming pieces in a broader debt market.

[2]Noncompetitive bids are designed for small investors desiring very limited volumes of an issue, usually $1 million or less.

EXHIBIT 12.2   The Auction Process: Bidding Example

Bidders	Amounts ($ billion)	Bid (%)
Bidder A	$ 0.6	7.63%
Bidder B	$ 1.7	7.70
Bidder C	$ 1.2	7.71
Bidder A	$ 1.9	7.72
Bidder D	$ 3.0	7.75
Bidder A	$ 2.5	7.79
Bidder B	$ 3.5	7.83
Bidder E - - - - - - - - - - - - stop-out level - - - - - - -	$ 2.4 billion - - - - - -	-7.84%
Bidder F	$ 1.0	7.90
Bidder C	$ 4.0	7.92
Bidder C	$ 4.4	7.95
Noncompetitive bids	$ 5.3	—
Total	$30.9 billion	

the average level of the successful bids is calculated. The Treasury then sets a coupon on the debt issue to the nearest 1/8 of 1 percent, at a level that will make the average price charged to successful bidders equal to $100.00 (per $100 of face value) or less. Implicit prices are then computed that correspond with the levels of the accepted bids, and investors pay accordingly, with the noncompetitive bidders paying the average price.

To illustrate how this approach actually works, suppose that sealed bids on a two-year Treasury note are opened and the Treasury finds the bids contained in Exhibit 12.2, ranked downward from the most- to least-favorable bid. Notice that price (yield) and quantity are both listed and that several bidders have made multiple bids. Bidder A, for example, is willing to accept $0.6 billion at a 7.63 percent yield but will take an additional $1.9 billion if the yield increases to 7.72 percent.

At the outset of this process, suppose the Treasury announced that it wished to finance up to $20.0 billion through this two-year note issuance. Given the bid structure, the Treasury may decide that the bids are acceptable and then proceed to issue the even $20.0 billion. The Treasury then tallies the noncompetitive bids, which total $5.3 billion in our example.[3] This leaves $14.7 billion for the competitive bidders. Therefore, the highest seven bids will be accepted, and $0.3 billion of the $2.4 billion bid from bidder E will be accepted. However, each bidder receives the allocated quantity at the yield that he or she bid. Additionally, all of the noncompetitive bids are priced at the weighted average bid of those competitive bids that

---

[3]All noncompetitive bids are usually honored in full unless, as has happened a couple of times in the past, there are more noncompetitive bids than the total size of the offering. In those cases, bids for less than $100,000 were filled, and a pro rata share was distributed to the bidders desiring over $100,000.

EXHIBIT 12.3   Calculated Weighted Average Yield

Amount ($ billion)	Bid Yield (%)	Amount × Yield
0.6	7.63%	0.0458
1.7	7.70	0.1309
1.2	7.71	0.0925
1.9	7.72	0.1467
3.0	7.75	0.2325
2.5	7.79	0.1948
3.5	7.83	0.2741
0.3	7.84	0.0235
14.7	7.76%	→ Sum ÷ 14.7

were accepted, 7.76 percent. Exhibit 12.3 shows the calculation of the weighted average acceptable bid yield.

The Treasury will then set a coupon level within 1/8 of 1 percent of the average accepted yield, so that the average price charged to successful bidders will be equal to or slightly less than 100.0 percent of par value. In this case, 7.75 percent will be the coupon yield on the note, as it is just below the 7.76 percent weighted average accepted yield. This translates into a semiannual coupon of $3.875 per $100 of face value. Thus, the average buyer will receive the notes at a slight discount from par value.

The average price, per $100 of face value, is computed as follows:

$$\$99.9818 = \frac{\$3.875}{(1 + \frac{.0776}{2})^{1.0}} + \frac{\$3.875}{(1 + \frac{.0776}{2})^{2.0}} + \frac{\$3.875}{(1 + \frac{.0776}{2})^{3.0}} + \frac{\$103.875}{(1 + \frac{.0776}{2})^{4.0}}$$

This price will be charged to the noncompetitive bidders. Separate prices will be computed in a similar fashion for the competitive bidders, with the change reflected only in the discount rate.[4] Note that at this average price, the Treasury will collect slightly less than the $20 billion in face value that it will issue.

Treasury notes and bonds are issued on a regular schedule. The most currently issued notes and bonds within each maturity class, sometimes referred to as the **on-the-run** issues, are usually very liquid. This is because the initial purchasers of these securities are rarely the ultimate investors, with the exception of the

---

[4]The bidder's yield will be substituted for the weighted average yield to determine the price. This example is meant to be only illustrative of the process and is not exact. Day count conventions and other technical factors could alter the exact calculation. Certain features of this hypothetical auction have been exaggerated to promote exposition. For example, the auction illustrated would be termed a "very sloppy auction." Dealers measure sloppiness by the spread between the weighted average yield of accepted bids and the stop-out yield. Today, a typical auction on two-year notes may produce a spread of as little as two basis points. Our example features an eight basis points spread. Another distortion is that there are far greater numbers of bids than those shown. Moreover, the relative amount of noncompetitive bids is usually more along the lines of 10 percent or so.

noncompetitive-bid segment of the market. For the most part, initial purchasers are **primary dealers** in government securities. These firms subscribe to new issues through the bidding process fully anticipating the sale of their securities to other customers. Primary dealers form a highly liquid and very competitive market structure in which the government receives the highest possible prices for its debt and investors can quickly and easily gain access to the new issue.

In times past, the Treasury issued bonds with **call provisions,** which allowed it to retire certain bonds prior to maturity. This practice was abandoned during the last decade, as the call option began to inhibit innovation in the government bond market. Over the last 12 years, investment bankers have begun to separate the payments associated with government bonds, a process called **stripping.** In this way, the coupons and the principal from coupon-bearing bonds can be sold separately. A collection of coupons due at a certain date can be purchased as a simple zero-coupon bond by an investor with a certain time horizon. The practice of stripping has increased the market for government debt. When call provisions were in use, stripping was less popular, because the chance that some of the coupons could be called prior to maturity was somewhat disconcerting to the investment bankers issuing the zero-coupon bonds. Nowadays, with the elimination of new callable Treasury bonds, the Treasury itself strips coupons and principal from its bonds and sells them separately.

Marketable government debt is but a part of the total outstanding direct liabilities of the U.S. government. In addition to the instruments we have discussed, nonmarketable securities are also issued by the U.S. government and constitute part of the total Treasury debt. In recent years, the nonmarketable debt has accounted for close to one-third of all interest-bearing Treasury debt. Included in this category are savings bonds (designed primarily for individual investors), government account series bonds (sold by the Treasury directly to government agencies, trust funds, and other accounts), state and local government series bonds, and foreign series bonds, as well as a host of smaller issues. Exhibit 12.4 presents the division of total interest-bearing government debt securities as of the end of 1980 and as of the end of 1994. Over this 14-year period, the size has clearly risen, from $463.7 billion in 1980 to $2,719.9 billion in 1994, and the composition of U.S. debt has changed as well. Borrowings under one year have fallen from 47 percent of the interest-bearing debt down to 32 percent. At the same time, long-term debt rose to 12 percent from the 1980 total of 5 percent, and the 1- to 5-year and 5- to 10-year range increased as well. It seems as though the government has come to accept the notion that it is in this market to stay.

Agency Debt

A growing volume of securities is also being issued by **federal agencies.** Federal agencies are entities that are either owned and managed by the federal government or are federally sponsored, but privately owned. These securities are referred to generically as "agency debt." There are four different levels of federal

Exhibit 12.4

*Total outstanding
interest-bearing U.S.
government debt
(1980 and 1994)*

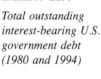

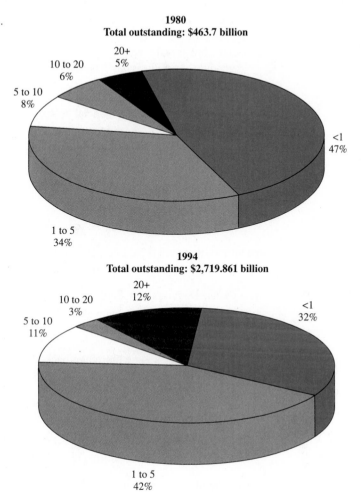

Source: *Economic Report of the President,* 1995.

backing for agency debt issues, each with a different value to the debt holder. In declining value order they are:

1. Securities with the backing of the full faith and credit of the U.S. government.
2. Securities with a guarantee by the U.S. Treasury.
3. Securities issued by agencies with borrowing privileges from the U.S. Treasury.
4. Securities issued by agencies with no *explicit* support but with some claim to government assistance.

In the case of no explicit support, it is generally presumed by investors that the federal government would step in to maintain the financial integrity of a federally sponsored, but private, agency.

Agencies currently issuing bonds to the public are:

- Farm Credit System
- Farm Credit System Financial Assistance Corporation
- Federal Home Loan Banks
- Federal National Mortgage Association
- Financing Corporation
- Maritime Administration
- Resolution Funding Corporation
- Student Loan Marketing Association

In addition, there are three international organizations, partially sponsored by the U.S. government, which also issue debt. They are:

- Asian Development Bank
- Inter-American Development Bank
- World Bank

Finally, four agencies issue mortgage-backed debt with both explicit and implicit government guarantees. They are:

- Federal Home Loan Mortgage Corporation
- Federal National Mortgage Association (also issues ordinary bonds)
- Government National Mortgage Association
- Federal Agricultural Mortgage Corporation

Other federal agencies (such as the Postal Service and the Tennessee Valley Authority) have issued debt in the past and continue to have debt outstanding. However, today, they seek financing through the **Federal Financing Bank,** which was established in 1973 to consolidate and reduce the government's cost of financing a variety of agency debt.

Because of the wide range of issuers and the uncertain claims they have on government support, it is difficult to generalize about agency debt. Even the way these agencies pay interest varies across the group. Interest payments may be made monthly, quarterly, semiannually, annually, or even less frequently. Some are in bearer form, others are registered in the name of the purchaser. Some are marketable; some are not. At times, even ownership is restricted to a particular class of investors. Interest may be subject to or exempt from federal, state, and local taxes. While most debt is denominated in U.S. dollars, some is denominated in foreign currency. Some have liquid secondary markets, while others do not.

In the face of all of this diversity, we can proffer four generalizations. First, the credit quality is perceived to be very high. Second, markets for agency securities are usually not as liquid as their Treasury counterparts. Third, yields are higher than marketable Treasury issues. Finally, the size of the market for agency securities is expanding continually.

Municipal Bonds

In Chapter 11, we spoke of municipal money market instruments. As indicated at that time, these short-term instruments are most often issued to tide over the state or local government between influxes of tax revenues, or in anticipation of a new bond issue. For the long-term capital needs of state and local governments, however, bond issues are generally of far more importance. It is this form of debt that state and local governments use to finance long-term investments, infrastructure costs, and capital improvements.

Municipal bonds have maturities up to 40 years, make semiannual interest payments, and are issued in $5,000 denominations. Their federal tax exempt status is the major attraction. Additionally, the interest payments of municipal bonds are excluded from local taxable income in the states of origin. Accordingly, individuals in high tax brackets, bank trust funds, mutual funds, and property/casualty insurers are major purchasers. Until a few years ago, most municipal bonds were bearer instruments, and they were the favored investments for those who wished to keep their wealth anonymous. However, the attractiveness of such investments to those that obtained their wealth through illicit and/or illegal means, such as drug traffickers, has led to a movement away from bearer bonds. Today, all new issues are registered to the purchasers so that their identity can be traced.

Typically, long-term municipal debt is sold as **serial bonds** rather than as **term bonds.** With serial bonds, a predetermined series of bonds matures each year until the maturity of the longest series. Term bonds, on the other hand, are repaid in full on a single maturity date. Serialization may help in marketing the bond because different investors prefer to purchase bonds with different maturities. Serialization allows the issuer to market selectively longer-term series to some investors, and shorter-term series to others. It may also increase the degree of comfort that investors have in the ability of the municipality to redeem the debt at maturity.

Municipal bonds have two other important characteristics. The first of these is their vulnerability to being called. Call provisions are common among municipal bond issues and must be considered when investment is made. They allow the issuer to retire the bonds beyond some specific call date but prior to maturity. The second feature is the nature of the credit risk inherent in the issue. In fact, given the large number of municipalities that issue debt, it should not be surprising that the quality of municipal bonds varies significantly. Recent crises, such as the near default of New York City and the Orange County problems that developed in 1995, have increased investor awareness of credit quality, as has the shift in financing methods employed by state and local governments. Fifty years ago, nearly all municipal debt was issued with the full faith and taxing power of the issuing governmental unit. It was **general obligation debt.** However, over the past half-century, this has dramatically changed. Today, **revenue bonds** are more common than general obligation bonds.[5] Revenue bonds rely solely on the income from the project or entity being funded by the issue for the payment of interest and principal, and accordingly, they are viewed as substantially riskier than their general obligation counterparts.

There are many potential explanations for this trend away from general obligation issues, but perhaps the most convincing is the attempt by municipalities to distance themselves from these liabilities. They may wish to do so for several reasons. For example, they may try to limit their liabilities in the event of an ill-conceived project. They may also wish to permit a greater use of user fees for proposed projects. But there are those that would argue that the goal is also to disguise the size of municipal activity itself. Revenue debt that has no claim on municipal assets can be held off the balance sheet and has no visible impact on the government's financial, to say nothing of political, future.

As municipal bonds are usually held by investors until maturity, there is not an active secondary market for most issues. Where one exists, the spreads tend to be wide, and trading sparse. This has led to the emergence of municipal bond funds and unit trusts to provide liquidity and serve as a substitute for a direct secondary market.

Corporate Bonds

The corporate bond market is where private firms obtain much of their long-term debt capital. Maturities on corporate bonds generally range from 10 to 30 years, and minimum denominations are $1,000 or more. (Maturities can extend up to 100 years or more! See Box 12.1.) Coupon rates range from zero (on zero-coupon bonds) to very high (on junk bonds), and they may be fixed or variable. Usually, interest rates are fixed, with coupons paid semiannually.

The major investors in corporate bonds are life insurance companies, state and local employee retirement funds, private pension funds, and foreigners. Institutions that purchase corporate bonds are seldom in need of liquidity, so more often than not, there is relatively little trading in these securities, and the secondary markets are therefore proportionately small.

Most corporate bonds contain **call provisions** that allow the issuer to retire the bonds beyond some specific call date but prior to maturity. Usually, there is a modest premium (e.g., one-half of a coupon) paid above par value by the corporation to the bond holders when exercising this call. Some bonds are **convertible** into common stock at a prespecified price. This is attractive to investors because investors can benefit from appreciating stock prices by converting into common

---

[5]An extreme example of this trend is the funding profile of the state of Kentucky. There, general obligation funding has proven so difficult that the state will have *no* general obligation debt outstanding by 1997.

shares, while being protected from depreciating stock prices by retaining the bond status. Because of this attractive feature, convertibles have lower promised coupon payments than ordinary bonds.

Corporate bonds come in five main varieties. Those backed by the full faith and credit of the corporation, but no specific collateral, are referred to as **debentures.** Debentures that have a secondary claim to the general assets and revenues of a firm are called **subordinated debentures.** In the event of a default, holders of such subordinated securities must wait until the claims of the senior debt obligations have been satisfied before they are eligible to receive the proceeds of asset liquidations. Bonds backed by mortgage collateral assets are referred to as **mortgage bonds;** bonds backed by rolling stock are termed **equipment obligations;** bonds backed by marketable securities are known as **collateral trust bonds.**

The nature of any bond is indicated by its **bond indenture.** The bond indenture is a legal document, often several hundred pages long, that accompanies a bond that spells out the rights and obligations of the issuer and the investor. In the bond indenture, the collateral is specified; protective covenants such as limits on executive salary, additional debt, and future dividends are listed; and payment dates are set forth. In addition, provisions are stipulated for default, call, and **sinking fund.** Many bonds have a sinking fund provision. This provision requires the corporation to retire a certain percentage, for example, 5 percent, drawn at random, of the par value of outstanding issues each year until maturity. Investors like sinking fund provisions because they reduce corporate indebtedness over time and lower default risk, as there will not be a huge sum of debt to refinance at maturity. The trustee, who monitors compliance with the indenture and initiates legal action in behalf of the bondholders, is also identified.

Determining Bond Value

There are two key features of corporate bonds that play a critical role in their value. Beyond the interest rate risk that affects nearly all debt, the price an investor is willing to pay for a corporate issue will be influenced by its callability and credit quality. While both of these features influence the value of other instruments, they are most important in the long-term corporate bond market. Accordingly, though these two features have been mentioned in general terms in Chapters 7 and 8, they warrant additional attention here.

Callability Provisions

As noted in the general discussion, most corporate bonds contain a call provision that allows the issuer to retire a bond at a prespecified price beyond some date that is prior to maturity. Obviously, the firm will exercise this option only if it is profitable to do so. Therefore, call provisions must have a negative effect on the value of the bond to the investor.

To see how a call provision affects the value and yield of a bond, let us return to the term structure of spot rates, forward rates, and the five sample interest rate paths

---

Box 12.1

The 100-Year Bond Is Coming Back, But Is It Good?

Like bell-bottom pants, 100-year bonds are coming back in style.

Taking advantage of some of the lowest long-term rates in a generation, **Columbia/HCA Healthcare** in Nashville, Tenn., issued $200 million of century debt Monday. More such issues are on the way, say Wall Street investment bankers and corporate consultants.

"I know of at least three companies that are thinking of doing it," says Fred Zuckerman, an independent consultant and former treasurer at International Business Machines, RJR Nabisco Holdings, and Chrysler.

Adds Rob Goldberg, head of capital markets for Merrill Lynch & Co., "I've had a lot of interest from companies in the structure."

But the reemergence of 100-year bonds isn't altogether positive for the bond market. The last time they blossomed in 1993 was just before interest rates rose sharply, heralding the bond market's worst year on record, 1994.

A bad bond market is even worse for holders of 100-year debt because its prices fluctuate more drastically than shorter maturities from 10 to 30 years customarily used by most corporations. For example, 100-year issues in 1993 by **Walt Disney, Coca-Cola,** and **ABN Amro** fell between 16% and 20% between their issue and their 1994 lows.

Columbia's 100-year issue is the first in two years and only the fourth since 1954, when the Chicago &

Eastern Illinois railroad issued bonds paying 5% annual interest until May 1, 2054.

David Anderson, treasurer of the fast-growing hospital company, says market conditions are some of the most favorable in his memory. "I mean, it's not a market you see every day," he says.

Why would investors buy the IOU of a company when chances are they won't live to see their principal returned?

One reason is that the buyers are institutions like mutual funds and pension funds—not individuals—which aren't making the investment with an eye to immediate repayment. Instead, they want the debt to help manage their portfolios' sensitivity to interest-rate changes.

A 100-year issue is one of the most interest-sensitive corporate bonds available, meaning buyers are likely purchasing it to make sure they get the most return for their money should interest rates fall further. Moreover, says Joseph Bellestrino, who oversees a $250 million portfolio of corporate bonds at Federated Investments in Pittsburgh, the additional interest payments are worth the risk.

"The market is inefficient on long paper like this," he says. While the Columbia bonds, which he bought Monday, are slightly more sensitive to interest-rate movements than 30-year corporate bonds, he believes he is being amply compensated by the 7.5%

---

that were introduced in Chapter 7. The paths are depicted in Exhibit 12.5 on page 280, and the numbers are provided in Exhibit 12.6 on page 281. Recall that these five paths are consistent with the spot and forward rates given in the term structure.

Now let us use this information to value two bonds, one noncallable and one callable, that are otherwise identical. Both bonds mature in five years and have a face value of $1,000. Both are assumed to be default free. In this example, we ignore default risk and isolate the problem of callability. Obviously, default renders the relationship more complex, because if a bond defaults prior to the call date, the call option is rendered valueless. Similarly, if a bond is called prior to maturity, its default risk beyond the call date is eliminated.

annual interest payments, now 1.25 percentage points more than the 30-year Treasury bond.

But most investors avoid 100-year bonds like the plague. "A lot of the railroad companies that issued 100-year bonds in the late 1800s didn't make it," says David Berry, head of credit research for Lincoln National Insurance in Fort Wayne, Ind.

Besides, he and others point out, even though investors get interest every year, by the time they get their principal back, inflation, even at its current low levels, would have eroded the principal's value to virtually nothing.

This financial nuance isn't lost on advisers like Mr. Zuckerman. He says it is so cheap for companies to issue debt like this now that "anyone who doesn't is dumb. I say to companies, 'Take the money and run,' even though I think rates are going lower."

The pact is a particular coup for Columbia. Although it is the largest for-profit hospital company in the country, it has only been around for eight years and unlike Coke, Disney, or ABN-Amro doesn't have a top credit rating. It is rated A3 by Moody's Investors Service and triple-B plus by Standard & Poor's. The others are rated double-A or higher.

Moreover, the company has been expanding quickly during the past two years with the rapid-fire acquisitions of Galen Health Care in September 1993, Hospital Corp. of America in February 1994, Medical Care America in September 1994, and Healthtrust in April of this year.

Mr. Goldberg of Merrill Lynch says more companies are likely to consider such bond issues because "100-year deals are attractive to senior management from a marketing perspective." Mr. Zuckerman explains: "Companies love it. It says to their constituents, 'These investors are willing to take my IOUs for 100 years. I must be the best credit in the world.'"

Source: Reprinted by permission of *The Wall Street Journal,* © 1995 Dow Jones & Company, Inc. All Rights Reserved Worldwide.

One-Hundred-Year Bonds Are Back

Issue	Date Issued	Amount (in millions)	Issue Price	High	Low	Current Price
Walt Disney	7/21/93	$300	$100.00	$104.59	$83.42	$103.17
Coca-Cola	7/22/93	150	100.00	109.51	83.22	106.50
ABN-Amro	10/13/93	150	99.18	96.68	79.69	95.25

Sources: BondNet; Morgan Stanley.

The callable bond may be called anytime after one year. Both bonds offer a 10 percent ($100) coupon, payable annually. The issuer of the callable bond has determined that it is in its economic interests to call the bond if the single-period rate of interest ever falls below 8 percent, and it has announced its intention to act accordingly.[6]

---

[6]Because this intention is a matter of public information, the market value of the bond will reflect it. In the absence of such public information, valuation methods utilize rational economic behavior principles to attempt to place a value on the callable bond. See, for example, Erol

Exhibit 12.5

*Simulating interest
rate paths*

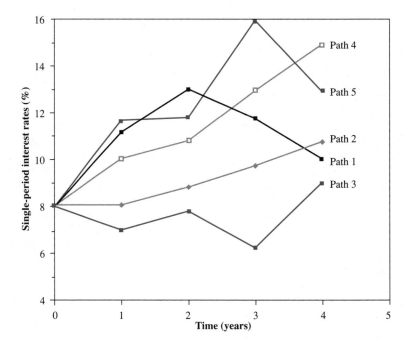

We can value the call-free bond in three ways: (1) use the spot rate term structure, (2) use the forward rates, or (3) use the interest rate paths. All three methods will generate the same final value. We will demonstrate the discounting by paths technique and confirm its validity by using the spot rate discounting method. Since we will be using only five interest rate paths, there will be five equally probable values produced by the paths technique. Thus, we will average these five values to get an implied market value.

First path:

$$\frac{\$100}{1.08} + \frac{\$100}{1.08 \times 1.11} + \frac{\$100}{1.08 \times 1.11 \times 1.13} + \frac{\$100}{1.08 \times 1.11 \times 1.13 \times 1.12} + \frac{\$1,100}{1.08 \times 1.11 \times 1.13 \times 1.12 \times 1.101} = \$974.25$$

Second path:

$$\frac{\$100}{1.08} + \frac{\$100}{1.08 \times 1.08} + \frac{\$100}{1.08 \times 1.08 \times 1.09} + \frac{\$100}{1.08 \times 1.08 \times 1.09 \times 1.10} + \frac{\$1,100}{1.08 \times 1.08 \times 1.09 \times 1.10 \times 1.11} = \$1,037.07$$

Third path:

$$\frac{\$100}{1.08} + \frac{\$100}{1.08 \times 1.07} + \frac{\$100}{1.08 \times 1.07 \times 1.08} + \frac{\$100}{1.08 \times 1.07 \times 1.08 \times 1.06} + \frac{\$1,100}{1.08 \times 1.07 \times 1.08 \times 1.06 \times 1.09} = \$1,097.67$$

Fourth path:

$$\frac{\$100}{1.08} + \frac{\$100}{1.08 \times 1.10} + \frac{\$100}{1.08 \times 1.10 \times 1.11} + \frac{\$100}{1.08 \times 1.10 \times 1.11 \times 1.13} + \frac{\$1,100}{1.08 \times 1.10 \times 1.11 \times 1.13 \times 1.15} = \$961.62$$

Hakanoglu and Emmanuel Roman, *Issues in Corporate Liability Management: The Refunding Decision* (New York: Goldman Sachs & Co., 1990).

EXHIBIT 12.6 Term Structure and Sample Interest Rate Paths

	One Year	Two Years	Three Years	Four Years	Five Years
Spot rates	8.0%	8.75%	9.33%	9.79%	10.13%
	1st Year	*2nd Year*	*3rd Year*	*4th Year*	*5th Year*
Forward rates	8.0%	9.51%	10.50%	11.18%	11.50%
Interest Rate Paths:	*1st-Year Single-Period Rate*	*2nd-Year Single-Period Rate*	*3rd-Year Single-Period Rate*	*4th-Year Single-Period Rate*	*5th-Year Single-Period Rate*
Path 1	8.0%	11.00%	13.00%	12.00%	10.10%
Path 2	8.0%	8.00%	9.00%	10.00%	11.00%
Path 3	8.0%	7.00%	8.00%	6.00%	9.00%
Path 4	8.0%	10.00%	11.00%	13.00%	15.00%
Path 5	8.0%	11.67%	11.79%	15.87%	13.00%

Fifth path:

$$\frac{\$100}{1.08} + \frac{\$100}{1.08 \times 1.1167} + \frac{\$100}{1.08 \times 1.1167 \times 1.1179} + \frac{\$100}{1.08 \times 1.1167 \times 1.1179 \times 1.1587} + \frac{\$1,100}{1.08 \times 1.1167 \times 1.1179 \times 1.1587 \times 1.13}$$

$$= \$936.82$$

The price is given by the average of the path prices:

$$\frac{\$974.25 + \$1,037.07 + \$1,097.67 + \$961.62 + \$936.82}{5} = \$1,001.49$$

We can use this information to compute the bond's yield to maturity. This is computed by setting the bond's price equal to its cash flows and solving for yield, as follows:[7]

$$\$1,001.49 = \frac{\$100}{(1 + YTM)} + \frac{\$100}{(1 + YTM)^2} + \frac{\$100}{(1 + YTM)^3} + \frac{\$100}{(1 + YTM)^4} + \frac{\$1,100}{(1 + YTM)^5}$$

This implies

$$YTM = 9.96\%$$

Since the cash flows of the noncallable bond are all fixed and certain, we could have used one of the simpler methods of discounting—spot rate term structure or forward rates of interest—to value this bond. Using the spot rates, we would obtain:

$$\$1,001.49 = \frac{\$100}{(1 + .08)} + \frac{\$100}{(1 + .0875)^2} + \frac{\$100}{(1 + .0933)^3} + \frac{\$100}{(1 + .0979)^4} + \frac{\$1,100}{(1 + .1013)^5}$$

---

[7]A standard iterative search technique is preprogrammed into most financial calculators for performing this calculation.

We used the path pricing method because it can also be used to value callable bonds.[8]

Next, let us determine the value of the callable bond. Note that only along Path 3 does the single-period rate trigger a call by reaching below the 8 percent threshold. It falls below this threshold at the beginning of the second period and again at the beginning of the fourth period. Because the bond can only be called once, we can safely ignore the latter occurrence. Thus, we compute a new Path 3 price to accompany the other four path prices. The principal will be repaid along with the first coupon payment at the end of the first period, when the drop in rates to 7 percent is observed. The third path price of the callable bond is:

$$\frac{\$1{,}100}{1.08} + \frac{\$0}{1.08 \times 1.07} + \frac{\$0}{1.08 \times 1.07 \times 1.08} + \frac{\$0}{1.08 \times 1.07 \times 1.08 \times 1.06} + \frac{\$0}{1.08 \times 1.07 \times 1.08 \times 1.06 \times 1.09}$$

$$= \$1{,}018.52$$

This path price is substantially below the $1,097.67 path 3 price of the noncallable bond because the call provision deprives the investor of a potentially large capital gain opportunity. By substituting this value for the path 3 price contained in the noncallable bond valuation and computing the new average of the path prices, we obtain the value of the callable bond.

$$\frac{\$974.25 + \$1{,}037.07 + \$1{,}018.52 + \$961.62 + \$936.82}{5} = \$985.66$$

The difference between the price of the callable bond and the $1,001.49 price of the noncallable bond is the value of the call provision. Therefore, in this case, the **call option value** is $15.83. We can use the computed value of the callable bond, along with its scheduled cash flows, to compute its yield to maturity (*ytm*) using an iterative search procedure.[9]

$$\$985.66 = \frac{100}{(1 + ytm)} + \frac{100}{(1 + ytm)^2} + \frac{100}{(1 + ytm)^3} + \frac{100}{(1 + ytm)^4} + \frac{1{,}100}{(1 + ytm)^5}$$

This implies

$$ytm = 10.38\%$$

Note that this yield is significantly higher than the 9.96 percent yield to maturity of the noncallable bond. Investors demand the extra yield (42 b.p.) to compensate them for the valuable option to call away the bond that they have granted to the bond issuer.

---

[8]Recall from earlier chapters that when using the path pricing method, the analyst uses many more than five paths to value the bond. Good pricing is sometimes achieved using as few as 500 paths, but better pricing is achieved using 10,000 paths. For pedagogical purposes, we have focused on five, well-chosen paths.

[9]For callable bonds, another number, referred to as yield-to-call, is sometimes computed. This yield gives the internal rate of return assuming the bond is called on the first call date. The computation is easy in this case because the bond is callable after one year. Thus, the yield-to-call is simply ($1,100 ÷ $985.66) − 1 = 11.60%.

In the above example, the value of the call option depended upon the level of interest rates at the time of issue, the interest rate level at which the issuer chose to call the bond, and the volatility of the interest rates in the future. If the level of interest rates throughout the simulation were lower, the likelihood of a call would increase, and more than one path would be shortened by a prepayment. Accordingly, the value of the call option issued to the firm would be greater, and the value of the callable bond would be relatively less in the face of a lower-interest environment.

Another way to view the importance of callability to the value of a bond is to look at the price-yield profiles of a noncallable bond and of a call option for different levels of interest rates. This is presented in Exhibit 12.7. A discussion of how these relationships are constructed will be deferred to Chapter 15. For the moment, you will have to trust us that the price-yield relationships are correctly sketched. Subtracting the value of the call option (shown at bottom) at each point along the price-yield profile from the commensurate value of a noncallable bond (shown at top), we get the value of a callable bond. As suspected, the value of the call option is highest when rates are low, and the likelihood of the firm to call the bond is high. At very high rates, calling loses value. But there is always some probability that rates will fall sufficiently for the call to be exercised. Therefore, the callable bond always has a lower value than its noncallable counterpart of equal coupon and maturity.

As indicated above, however, the value of a call depends on more than just the underlying bond yield. It also depends on the volatility of yields. The more volatile the yields, other things equal, the more valuable the call option is to the issuer because it is more likely that the issuer will be able to call the bond. Consequently, the market will require a higher coupon yield on a callable bond when interest rates are expected to be more volatile. The impact of volatility on the bond price is shown in Exhibit 12.8. The most volatile interest rates will give rise to the highest value of the call option and, hence, the lowest market price of the callable bond.

The call provision also has impact on the duration of the bond. By definition, the call provision has impact on the effective maturity, since the bond may be called away prior to maturity. Therefore, it will have an impact on the duration, or price sensitivity of the bond to changes in interest rates. What is interesting about this impact on duration, however, is that it will vary according to the volatility of interest rates.

Recall that the dollar duration of a bond is given by the slope of a tangency to the price-yield curve at a given yield, and that duration is given by the slope divided by the price. Note in Exhibit 12.8 on page 285 that as yields fall, the tangency lines (not shown) begin to slope more steeply, and later, less steeply. At the same time, prices rise rapidly at first, and then, less rapidly. This means that beyond some point, duration begins to fall, and fall quickly. The net effect of the changing slope and rising prices is shown in Exhibit 12.9 on page 286. Here, we show the duration of an 8% bond with a 10-year maturity that is callable after 5 years. There are two things of note in this chart. First, the

EXHIBIT 12.7

*The relation between
the values of a
noncallable bond, a
callable bond, and a
call provision*

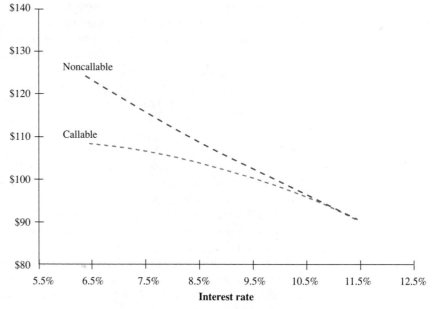

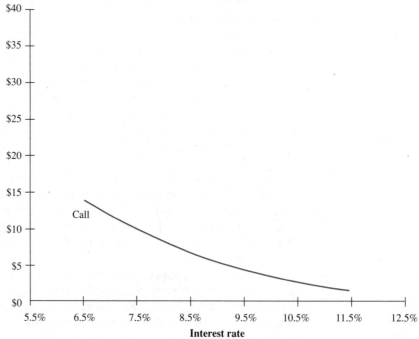

Exhibit 12.8

Relationship between bond price, option value, and interest rates

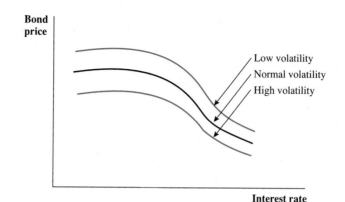

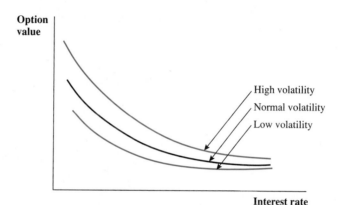

top and bottom lines show the durations of 10-year and 5-year noncallable bonds and demonstrate how these durations drift with market rates of interest. Since our callable bond is, in some sense, a hybrid of these two bonds, its duration should fall between those of these two "boundary" bonds. Second, where the duration of the callable bond lies within these boundaries depends on the current market rates of interest and on expected interest rate volatility. As interest rates rise, the duration is close to that of a 10-year bond; as interest rates fall, duration drifts downward and approaches that of a 5-year bond. The more volatile interest rates are, the more gradual the evolution of the bond's duration is from one extreme to another.

Default Risk and Bond Ratings

In Chapter 9, we discussed default risk and the attempts to capture this risk through the use of quality ratings assigned to bonds by various ratings agencies, such as Moody's and Standard & Poor's. We did not discuss at any length, however, the criteria used by these agencies to assign credit ratings. Given the

Exhibit 12.9

Duration sensitivity of a callable bond (8%; 10/s structure)

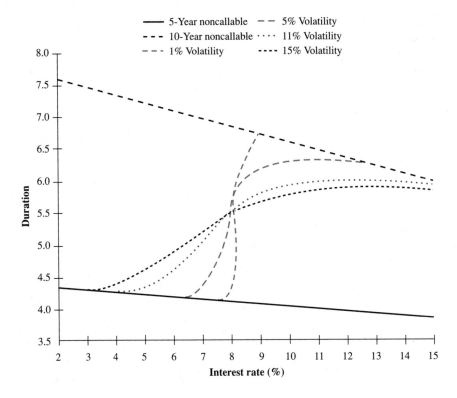

importance of such ratings on required yields in the bond market, it is appropriate to develop this issue more fully here. Because the treatment is somewhat different for corporate and municipal issuers, each will be discussed separately and in greater detail than before.

Corporate Bond Ratings.   Rating agencies collect and analyze accounting and other financial information that they feel may impinge on an issuer's future ability to repay its debt. Elaborate systems of financial ratio analysis, combined with economic analysis, are used to arrive at a rating that attempts to capture the probability of the issuer fulfilling the terms of the indenture and making all required payments in a timely fashion. While the weightings of various criteria associated with a corporate bond rating are fraught with an element of subjectivity, as emphasis will vary from firm to firm and from one analyst to another, these criteria have nonetheless contributed to a reasonably successful record of the agencies' abilities to distinguish risky bonds from those less likely to default.

The distribution of corporate bond ratings by Moody's for all outstanding rated issues as of December 31, 1995, is given in Exhibit 12.10. This exhibit shows the breakdown in terms of dollar values, while the bar chart in Exhibit 12.11 gives the

EXHIBIT 12.10   Distribution of Corporate Bond Ratings, December 1995
($ billions)

Ratings	Financials	Industrials	Utilities	All Corporates
Aaa	9.83	7.92	11.82	29.57
Aa1	2.92	9.06	4.25	16.23
Aa2	4.35	17.07	9.45	30.87
Aa3	52.11	32.4	13.85	98.36
A1	75.54	51.48	28.81	155.83
A2	70.38	59.01	31.1	160.49
A3	68.49	51.65	14.17	134.31
Baa1	21.96	28.53	20.3	70.79
Baa2	10.66	38.12	24.43	73.21
Baa3	6.63	63.75	15.95	86.33
Ba1	0.96	36.81	6.66	44.43
Ba2	2.1	27.81	3.87	33.78
Ba3	2.72	45.1	4.66	52.48
B1	1.23	44.74	1.91	47.88
B2	0.7	42.55	0.37	43.62
B3	0.42	41.94	0	42.36
Caa	0	19.64	0.32	19.96
Ca	0.7	5.32	0.69	6.71
C	2.45	0.86	0	3.31
Sum	334.15	623.76	192.61	1,150.52

Source: Moody's: *Special Report,* December 1995.

relative breakdown by category in percentage terms. As is apparent from the data, there is a surprising range of results. Total corporates vary considerably over the entire spectrum, with substantial volume in the low A range.

The financial ratios used to arrive at these ratings relate to coverage, profitability, leverage, and liquidity. **Coverage ratios** measure how many times the bond issuing company's annual income before taxes and interest on other debt could pay the annual interest and other charges associated with servicing the bond in question.

$$\text{Coverage ratio} = \frac{\text{Income before subtracting taxes and interest}}{\text{Total bond charges}}$$

For example, if total bond costs during a year are $10 million and the company earns $50 million before taxes and interest expenses, the coverage ratio would be 5.0. A ratio in excess of 1.0 means that a company has enough to make its bond payments, provided that its income does not fluctuate unduly over time. Many analysts like to see coverage ratios of 4.0 and higher for companies with stable earnings and ratios of 6.0 or higher for companies with cyclical earnings. Ratios of 2.0 to 3.0 are generally thought to be quite risky, although it would again depend on the nature of the debtor's business. The basic idea is that these ratios are thought to provide an indication of the issuer's ability to make bond payments.

EXHIBIT **12.11**

Distribution of corporate bond ratings, December 1995 (%)

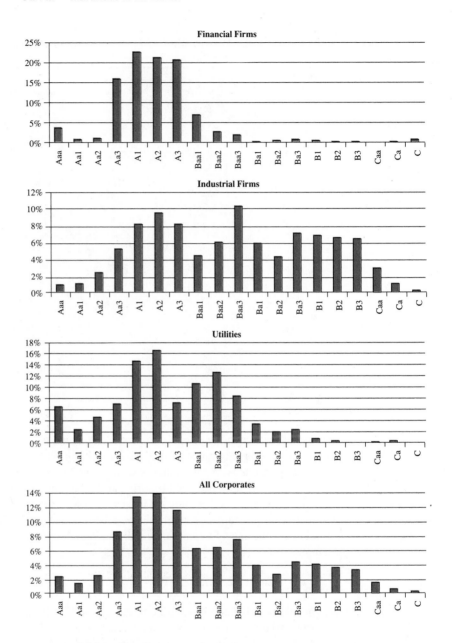

A low coverage ratio may result either from earnings that are too low or from debt that is too high. The source of a low ratio may be ascertained by examining other ratios. Low **profitability ratios,** relative to those of other competitors in the same business, suggest that low earnings are the problem, whereas relatively high **financial leverage ratios** indicate that a high debt level is the problem. Not only the levels but also the trends of coverage ratios are important. A rising coverage ratio may portend better times ahead, whereas a deteriorating coverage ratio may indicate troubled times ahead.

Profitability is an important measure of financial health. Better financial health makes debt less risky. Several measures of profitability are used, but one of the most important measures is the simple **rate of return on total assets.**

$$\text{Rate of return on total assets} = \frac{\text{Net income before taxes}}{\text{Total assets}}$$

Some analysts use sales in place of total assets to get a measure of the profit margin. What is considered to be a favorable rate of return will vary across industries and over time, but a relatively low rate of return for a given firm may indicate too many unproductive assets, low earnings, high costs, or other inefficiencies. Unless this situation is rectified, it could lead to lessened prospects of future financial strength.

Financial leverage ratios are measures of debt load. Leverage is a term used to denote the use of debt in funding a firm's operations, and several leverage ratios have been developed. One of the most popular is the total **debt-to-equity ratio.** Other measures attempt to distinguish between short-term debt, which may soon need to be refinanced, and long-term debt. Again, different types of businesses can support differing degrees of leverage.

Liquidity ratios are also important in assessing bond qualities. A problem arises when a firm has illiquid assets and liquid liabilities. In such a case, the firm will face short-term difficulties in converting assets to cash in order to liquidate debt, should the need arise. A firm may use little leverage, but unless it has enough liquid assets, it could still run into problems. The most commonly used liquidity measure is called the **current ratio.**

$$\text{Current ratio} = \frac{\text{Current assets}}{\text{Current liabilities}}$$

Here, current liabilities are liabilities due to be paid in one year or less. Current assets are assets, such as cash, marketable securities, accounts receivable, and inventory, that are expected to be converted into cash within one year or less. A current ratio of 2.0 or greater has proved to be comfortable for some types of business, but not for all. Analysts sometimes subtract inventory from the numerator because, in a cash crunch, it can be difficult to convert inventory to cash without suffering large losses. That modification results in a ratio known as the **quick ratio.**

Municipal Bond Ratings.   Financial ratios used in evaluating the quality of corporate bonds are often inappropriate for analyzing municipal bonds. Municipalities such as towns, cities, school and sewer districts, and toll road and bridge authorities often raise funds for construction projects by issuing municipal bonds. The issuing entities are not profit-making institutions but public institutions charged with performing certain public services. Accordingly, "municipal profitability ratios" are not applicable to their bond issue. Similarly, leverage ratios have little meaning because municipalities have few marketable assets and little "equity."

In the case of general obligation bonds, analysts look at two things. The first is the current financial condition of the municipality. Is it currently solvent? What is its debt burden? What is its long-term structural financial stability? Second, analysts examine the municipality's ability to raise additional income through new taxes, should they become necessary, or its capacity to service a bond through existing excess taxes. (Here, "excess" denotes taxes beyond the level needed to sustain the operating budget of the municipality.)

Several ratios are useful in assessing debt quality. **Debt per capita** considers the total municipal debt outstanding and divides it by the population. More than $300 per capita would be considered high for a small city, whereas $500 per capita might be acceptable in a larger city. Another ratio considers debt service as a percentage of the total municipal budget. Analysts look for something under 12 percent for high quality ratings. Some analysts consider the proportion of total debt that will mature in five or fewer years. Still others consider debt as a portion of total assessed value of taxable property. In this analysis, a ratio of under 8 to 10 percent is considered acceptable.

In addition to the ratios mentioned above, bond analysts consider sociological and demographic trends that might impinge on a city's ability to repay debt. Is the middle class vacating the city? Is there an expanding tax base? Is there a history of persistent deficit financing for normal operating expenses?

In the case of a revenue bond, only revenue earned from the specific project for which the bond was issued may be used to repay the bond. In this way, these types of issues are similar to corporate issues. An example would be a revenue bond issued to finance the construction of a toll bridge. Suppose the municipality intends to use toll revenues to repay the bond. If the toll revenues are insufficient, due to inadequate bridge usage, the bond will go into default. Taxes cannot be levied on local citizens to help repay the bond. Moreover, the collateral usually cannot be sold, as it is a public good. In the case of a general obligation bond, sales, property, and income taxes could be levied to help repay the bond. Not only any revenues generated by the project but also the full faith and credit of the municipal issuer stand behind the bond. Accordingly, investors must look quite closely at the underlying project and the viability of the issuing agency.

Coverage ratios are important in evaluating revenue bonds. Revenues are substituted for income in the numerator of the ratio, while the denominator remains total debt service charges. Analysts regard a coverage ratio of 1.5 to 2.0 as acceptable. The higher the ratio, the safer the bond issue.

Summary

Perhaps the best way to summarize the plethora of information given in this chapter about bond market instruments is in the form of a table. Exhibit 12.12 reports six characteristics of each of the instruments covered in this chapter. In terms of duration, these instruments are quite similar, with the important exception of callability features. The same can be said for convexity. Beyond this, differences increase. Credit risk varies from virtually none for U.S. Treasury debt to very high for high-yield

EXHIBIT 12.12   Bond Risk Characteristics

Bond Issuer	Duration	Convexity	Credit Risk	Liquidity	Timing of Payments Risk	Taxability
Treasury	Medium to very long, depending on maturity	Positive	None	Very high	Known	Exempt from state and local taxes in most jurisdictions
Agency	Medium to very long, depending on maturity	Positive to very negative, depending on interest rate, callability, and prepayments	Assumed to be none or very low	High to moderate	Known; some issues have modest call provisions, prepayment risk	Tax status varies according to issuer
Municipal	Medium to long, depending on maturity and callability	Positive to very negative, depending on interest rate and callability	Low to high, rated by credit agencies	Low for most issues	Most issues have call risk	Exempt from federal taxes, subject to risk if tax rates change
Corporate	Medium to long, depending on maturity and callability	Positive to very negative, depending on interest rate and callability	Low to high, rated by credit agencies	Moderate to low	Most issues have call risk	Taxable at all levels

bonds. Liquidity, likewise, varies dramatically, but not identically. From most to least liquid, Treasuries clearly top the list, while municipals, as a general class, are the least liquid because of their thin resale markets. Agencies and corporate debt fall somewhere in between, depending upon the size of issue, the reputation of issuer, and the bond indenture. On the timing of payment, bonds, as a class, exhibit little risk, once again with the exception of call provisions. Finally, taxability for bonds varies substantially, from complete tax exemption for municipal issues to full taxability for corporate bonds.

As with any financial asset, such summaries are only generalizations. Specific bonds, unique indentures, and special circumstances abound. If there is one rule that transcends all others in the financial market, it is that care must be taken to understand the exact nature of the instrument being considered. Failure to do so will make you wiser but certainly less wealthy.

Key Concepts

bond indentures,   277
call provisions and call option value,   272
convertible bonds,   276
corporate bond ratings,   286
coupon stripping,   272
coverage, profitability, and leverage
  ratios,   287–88
debenture, subordinated, mortgage, equipment,
  and collateral trust bonds,   277
debt per capita,   290
debt-to-equity ratio,   289
Federal Financing Bank,   274
general obligation versus revenue bonds,   276

liquidity, current, and quick ratios,   289
municipal bond ratings,   289
on-the-run,   271
primary dealers,   272
return on assets,   289
serial versus term bonds,   275
sinking fund,   277
Treasury, agency, municipal, and corporate
  bonds,   269–77
Treasury auctions and noncompetitive
  bids,   269–71
Treasury bills, notes, and bonds,   269

Review Questions

1. If there are only $3.0 billion in noncompetitive bids in Exhibit 12.2, what is the new weighted average yield and coupon?

2. The following bids were submitted at a Treasury auction:

Bidder	Amount ($ billion)	Bid (%)
A	$0.9 billion	6.77%
B	$1.2	6.81
C	$1.9	6.84
D	$2.4	6.86
C	$3.1	6.87
D	$3.2	6.88
E	$2.7	6.91
Noncompetitive	$4.4	—

After viewing these bids, the Treasury has decided to raise $11 billion from this auction.

a. What is the weighted average yield?

b. What is the coupon?

c. If these are two-year bonds, what is the price that each bidder will pay (per bid) per $100 of face value?

3. Which bidder ends up paying the most per $100 of face value? Which pays the least?

4. In the example using Exhibit 12.6, what is the value of a call option if the issuer does not call the bond until interest rates fall to 6.75 percent?

5. In Exhibit 12.6, if the price of the callable bond is $992.63, how much extra yield are investors demanding for the call option?

6. Today is July 25, 1995. Your bond dealer quotes the following:

    9.5   May 15,99   98.22+   98.25

What price will you receive for your $1,000 face value bond?

7. Exhibit 12.9 illustrated the fact that when interest rates are more volatile, the duration of a callable bond moves along a smoother pathway from the duration of a long-term bond to the duration of a shorter-term bond as yields decline than it follows when interest rates are not volatile. Why do you suspect this is the case?

References

Asquith, Paul. "Convertible Bonds Are Not Called Late." *Journal of Finance,* September 1995.

Benston, George, et al. *Perspectives on Safe and Sound Banking.* Cambridge, Mass.: MIT Press, 1986.

Bodie, Zvi; A. Kane; and A. Marcus. *Investments.* 3d ed. Burr Ridge, Ill.: Richard D. Irwin, 1996.

Fabozzi, Frank J. *Valuation of Fixed Income Securities.* Summit, N.J.: Frank J. Fabozzi Associates, 1994.

Fabozzi, Frank, and T. Dessa Fabozzi. *Bond Markets, Analysis and Strategies.* Englewood Cliffs, N.J.: Prentice Hall, 1989.

Fortune, Peter. "The Municipal Bond Market Part I: Policies, Taxes and Yields." *New England Economic Review.* Federal Reserve Bank of Boston, September 1991.

Hakanoglu, Erol, and Emmanuel Roman. *Issues in Corporate Liability Management: The Refunding Decision.* New York: Goldman Sachs, 1990.

Mitchell, K. "Interest Rate Uncertainty and Corporate Debt Maturity." *Journal of Economics and Business,* 1987.

Stigum, Marcia, and Frank J. Fabozzi. *The Dow Jones Guide to Bond and Money Market Investments.* Burr Ridge, Ill.: Irwin Professional Publishing, 1987.

Understanding the Mortgage Market

This chapter is devoted to the consideration of mortgage instruments. It begins with an analysis of the underlying financial instrument—the basic residential mortgage. This is followed by an explanation of the mechanisms by which mortgages are offered for sale in the secondary market. Next, an evaluation of the riskiness and relative prices associated with mortgage products is presented. The chapter concludes with a review of the major contributions to other areas made by the rapid development in the mortgage market.

The need to obtain a mortgage to finance home ownership has probably existed since shortly after early cave dwellers abandoned their caves to occupy single-family dwellings made of straw. One could imagine that as this trend took hold, straw became more expensive, and the need to finance it arose. Hence, the mortgage was born, or so the story goes.

Today for the average household, the purchase of a home is still its single largest financial transaction. The purchase of a home is costly to begin with, and it is even more costly to finance. For most of us, the house of our dreams comes complete with several bedrooms, a couple of baths, and a 30-year mortgage. Yet, in many respects, the average family in the United States is quite lucky. In the United States, mortgage loans to finance home purchases are readily available, and they are offered at terms that compare quite favorably with other financial claims. While politicians decry the rising cost of homeownership and we struggle to make ends meet each month, it is important to keep in mind the unique benefits flowing to households from the advancements and developments in the U.S. mortgage market. Today, the average home is purchased with little more than a 20 percent down payment. Through the miracles of finance, the rest is deferred and is converted into a long-term debt of the borrower. Accomplishing this feat is not easy, and it has only been achieved by years of increasing sophistication in what appears to be a very simple market. After all, it's only a mortgage!

Overview of the Mortgage Market

Since the 1930s, when the Federal Housing Administration (FHA) established it as a mortgage prototype, the 30-year fixed-payment mortgage has been the most prominent borrowing instrument in the residential mortgage market of the United States. Over the past 25 years, however, the diversity of mortgage instruments in the residential and commercial mortgage market has proliferated. There are adjustable-rate mortgages, graduated payment mortgages, and graduated equity mortgages, to name just a few.

At the heart of this market, however, the product and process of origination are fairly straightforward. For the average consumer, a **mortgage loan** is a multi-year loan obtained from a retail lender that uses the value of the real property as collateral. For those of us who were brought up in the 1950s and 1960s, these loans were obtained by visiting our local bank or savings and loan, filling out an application, and waiting. The financial institution would then investigate the creditworthiness of the borrower and have the house appraised to determine its value. Passing these hurdles, papers were drawn, and the loan was made. The institution provided the funds required and awaited the stream of monthly payments.

The papers, however, were, and still are, a key part of the transaction. They include a deed of trust or other document indicating that the lender has a security interest in the property. Borrowers give up some of their ownership rights as part of the deal.

How things have changed! Today, our mortgage loan is as likely to come from a bank of one sort or another as it is to come from a specialized firm established for the sole purpose of finding homeowners and making loans. These **mortgage bankers,** once a small part of the business, are now an essential element. Mortgage banks are often owned by financial firms such as banks or insurance companies, but they serve their market quite independently. In fact, we may not even go to their office, or any other office for that matter, to conduct transactions. Our real estate broker may facilitate the transaction through his or her office and steer us to a local partner for financing.

All of this has been made possible by a subtle but important change in the real estate market—the decoupling of loan origination and financing. This separation between origination and funding is an essential feature of the mortgage market revolution that has occurred over the past 25 years. It means that originators need not hold assets to maturity, and more to the point, they need not have the resources to do so. Originators create assets and sell them to others who view them in much the same way as any other fixed-income investment.

The result is a mortgage market that is mammoth in size. In fact, today, the largest market for private debt in the United States is the mortgage market. In terms of the value of debt outstanding, which totaled $4.5 trillion in 1995, the mortgage market eclipses the corporate bond market, and it is approximately equal in size to the value of Treasury debt or the stock market. Of this total, most are one- to four-family residential mortgages, although the commercial portion of the market totals reached nearly $0.75 trillion in 1995. (See Exhibit 13.1.) Growth has been substantial in all areas, but it is most noticeable in the residential category.

The expansion of the investor group can be seen with reference to Exhibit 13.2. Using 1995 data, this exhibit indicates that commercial banks and savings institutions hold only one-third of the outstanding mortgage totals. Adding life insurance companies, the institutions' total goes to $1.865 trillion of the $4.5 trillion market, or a little over 40 percent. The remainder of the outstanding mortgages are held primarily by the new entrants into the market, mortgage pools, and individual investors. Exhibit 13.3 on page 300 (that duplicates Exhibit 13.2 for your convenience) shows how these percentages have changed over the last decade. A comparison of the percentages held by the various investors in 1985 and 1995 shows the movement away from standard financial institutions and toward mortgage pools and trusts. Exhibit 13.3 indicates that the market share of mortgage pools has moved from 18 percent to 38 percent over the period, while the market share of standard financial institutions fell by the same 20 percent figure.

The securitization of mortgages, the innovative decoupling of principal and interest payments, and the alteration of payment timing characteristics via the creation of specialized mortgage-backed securities have transformed the market. In fact, the mortgage market has evolved more rapidly in terms of sophistication and complexity than any other market. Indeed, securities that are backed by mortgages are often considered to be the most complex of all traded securities. Even as we write this chapter, financial engineers are busy at work devising new ways to "slice and dice" the stream of payments associated with mortgage debt into new financial instruments. To understand the mortgage market, one must understand how all of this takes place.

Exhibit 13.1

Mortgage debt outstanding by type of property

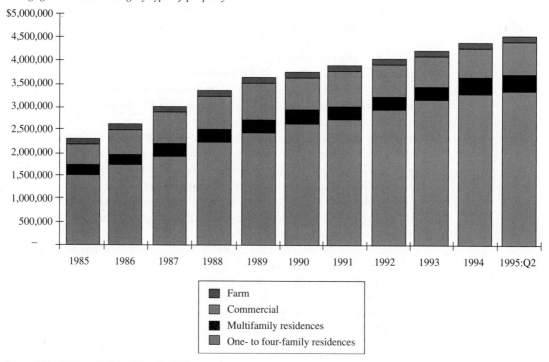

Source: *Federal Reserve Bulletin,* December 1995.

Before we venture to the frontiers of this rapidly evolving market, it is prudent to discuss and illustrate the key components of the traditional mortgage instrument. Then, we can proceed to analyze the operations of the secondary market for mortgages and the intricacies of the mortgage-backed securities market. This will allow us to explain how variations in the borrowing instrument, coupled with the repackaging of the cash flows, have transformed a stodgy market into the most dynamic of markets.

Mortgage Characteristics

As noted above, a mortgage loan is a loan secured by some form of deed of trust or other evidence that assigns real property. Most mortgages are secured by real estate, although some are secured by airplanes, trains, and financial assets. The real property can be claimed by the lender if the borrower does not make payments in accordance with the provisions stipulated in the loan agreement. Therefore, the credit risk inherent in any mortgage depends on both the creditworthiness of the borrower and the market value of the property securing the loan.

EXHIBIT 13.2   Totals by Type of Holder
(Second Quarter 1995)

	Total	*1 to 4 Family*	*Multifamily*	*Commercial*	*Farm*
Major financial institutions	1,865,144				
Commercial banks	1,052,881	648,815	40,519	339,983	23,564
Savings institutions	598,876	481,434	64,373	52,788	281
Life insurance companies	213,387	7,817	24,019	171,493	10,058
Finance companies					
Federal and related agencies	315,210				
GNMA	10	10	—	—	—
FmHA	41,917	13,217	11,512	5,949	11,239
FHA/VA	10,098	4,838	5,260		
Resolution Trust Corporation	6,455	2,870	1,940	1,645	—
FDIC	6,039	731	1,135	4,173	—
FNMA	178,462	162,674	15,788	—	—
Federal Land Banks	28,005	1,648	—	—	26,357
FHLMC	44,224	40,963	3,261	—	—
Mortgage pools or trusts	1,737,483				
GNMA	457,101	446,855	10,246	—	—
FHLMC	496,139	493,105	3,034	—	—
FNMA	543,669	533,091	10,578	—	—
FmHA	13	2	—	6	5
Private mortgage conduits	240,561	187,000	15,745	37,816	—
Individuals and others	609,264	406,770	93,218	96,413	12,863
Total holdings	4,527,101				

Source: *Federal Reserve Bulletin,* December 1995.

Mortgages also contain varying degrees of interest rate risk. Depending upon the nature of the contract, the interest rate may either be fixed for the full term of the mortgage or vary periodically. It may also contain limits on the movement of monthly payments or interest rate levels over the life of the loan. Though any variation may exist, the overwhelming percentage of mortgages can be characterized as either simple **fixed-rate mortgages** or **adjustable-rate mortgages.** Let's look at each in turn.

Fixed-Rate Mortgages

Most residential mortgages feature monthly payments that are fixed over a lengthy loan term. These payments consist of some principal and the interest due each month on the outstanding principal. Over time, the outstanding principal is paid off until the loan is amortized in full. The 30-year, fixed-rate, level-payment mortgage amortizes the principal in full over 30 years; another popular mortgage, the 15-year, fixed-rate, level-payment mortgage, amortizes the principal in full over 15 years, and so forth. In this respect, these level-payment, fixed-maturity,

EXHIBIT 13.3

Mortgage debt outstanding by type of holder (1985 and second quarter 1995)

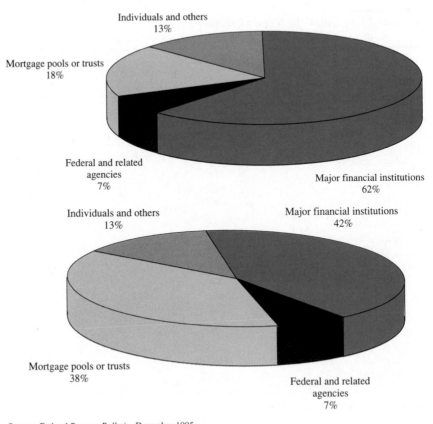

Individuals and others
13%

Mortgage pools or trusts
18%

Federal and related agencies
7%

Major financial institutions
62%

Individuals and others
13%

Major financial institutions
42%

Mortgage pools or trusts
38%

Federal and related agencies
7%

Source: *Federal Reserve Bulletin,* December 1995.

fixed-rate mortgages are similar to the annuities discussed in Chapter 6. We can therefore use the technology introduced there to value a mortgage, or to determine the monthly payment required for a given mortgage amount.

To determine the required monthly payment on a new mortgage, we can recast the annuity formula into mortgage terminology and solve for the payment. Recall that the value of an annuity is given by the formula

$$\text{Value}_{\text{annuity}} = \text{Payment} \; \frac{1 - \dfrac{1}{(1 + R)^N}}{R}$$

where R represents the interest rate per payment period and N is the number of payment periods in the annuity. In the case of a mortgage, the annuity value is redefined as the mortgage amount. The relevant payment becomes the monthly mortgage payment, R is the monthly interest rate (which, by convention, is equal to 1/12 of the stated interest rate), and N is the number of months until the mortgage is fully amortized. Therefore, we may rewrite the annuity equation in the following way for its mortgage counterpart:

EXHIBIT 13.3   Mortgage Debt Outstanding by Type of Holder
(1985 and Second Quarter 1995 $ Millions) *(concluded)*

	1985				
	Total	*1 to 4 Family*	*Multifamily*	*Commercial*	*Farm*
Major financial institutions	1,390,394				
Commercial banks	429,196	213,434	23,373	181,032	11,357
Savings institutions	760,499	554,301	89,739	115,771	688
Life insurance companies	171,797	12,381	19,894	127,670	11,852
Finance companies	28,902	28,902			
Federal and related agencies	166,928				
GNMA	1,473	539	934	—	—
FmHA	733	183	113	159	278
FHA/VA	4,920	2,254	2,666	—	—
FNMA	98,282	91,966	6,316	—	—
Federal Land Banks	47,498	2,798	—	—	44,700
FHLMC	14,022	11,881	2,141	—	—
Mortgage pools or trusts	415,042				
GNMA	212,145	207,198	4,947	—	—
FHLMC	100,387	99,515	872	—	—
FNMA	54,987	54,036	951	—	—
FmHA	47,523	22,186	6,675	8,190	10,472
Individuals and others	293,463	162,419	55,849	48,692	26,503
	Second Quarter 1995				
Major financial institutions	1,865,144				
Commercial banks	1,052,881	648,815	40,519	339,983	23,564
Savings institutions	598,876	481,434	64,373	52,788	281
Life insurance companies	213,387	7,817	24,019	171,493	10,058
Finance companies					
Federal and related agencies	315,210				
GNMA	10	10	—	—	—
FmHA	41,917	13,217	11,512	5,949	11,239
FHA/VA	10,098	4,838	5,260		
Resolution Trust Corporation	6,455	2,870	1,940	1,645	—
FDIC	6,039	731	1,135	4,173	—
FNMA	178,462	162,674	15,788	—	—
Federal Land Banks	28,005	1,648	—	—	26,357
FHLMC	44,224	40,963	3,261	—	—
Mortgage pools or trusts	1,737,483				
GNMA	457,101	446,855	10,246	—	—
FHLMC	496,139	493,105	3,034	—	—
FNMA	543,669	533,091	10,578	—	—
FmHA	13	2	—	6	5
Private mortgage conduits	240,561	187,000	15,745	37,816	—
Individuals and others	609,264	406,770	93,218	96,413	12,863

Source: *Federal Reserve Bulletin*, December 1995.

$$\text{Mortgage amount} = \text{Monthly payment} \ \frac{1 - \frac{1}{(1 + r)^N}}{r}$$

Now we can solve for the monthly payment by rearranging the formula.

$$\text{Monthly payment} = \text{Mortgage amount} \ \frac{r}{1 - \frac{1}{(1 + r)^N}}$$

Let us apply this formula to sample a few values. Consider a $100,000, 30-year, level-payment mortgage with a fixed annual stated interest rate of 12 percent. This translates into a 1 percent interest rate per month for 360 months. Solving for the monthly payment, we obtain

$$\$1,028.61 = \$100,000 \ \frac{.01}{1 - \frac{1}{(1 + .01)^{360}}}$$

Because $1,000.00 (= .01 × $100,000) of the first payment represents the interest due for that month, only the remaining $28.61 goes toward the repayment or **amortization** of principal. However, in the second month, the interest portion of the payment will be less because there is $28.61 less principal remaining to which to apply the interest. The interest portion of the payment will be $999.71 [= .01 × ($100,000 − $28.61)], and the remaining $28.90 of the payment (= $1,028.61 − $999.71) goes toward further reducing the principal. As can be seen, most of each of the early payments goes toward interest, not toward reducing principal. However, as the loan continues to be repaid—a process called **aging**—the principal is gradually reduced; thus, increasing amounts of the level payments go toward principal reduction. For example, at the end of 30 years, the last payment of $1,028.61 will consist of $10.18 interest and $1,018.43 to retire the remaining principal. The $10.18 interest represents 1 percent of the remaining principal.

The patterns of interest and principal payments for a 12 percent, 30-year mortgage are displayed in Exhibit 13.4. Note how remaining principal, depicted by the lower curve, declines with accelerating speed as time proceeds. Notice also that, at first, the level payment is mostly interest, but toward the end of the loan term, it is mostly principal.

The interest, principal, and amortization patterns are roughly similar for other mortgages, with the following differences. Mortgages of higher interest rates retire principal more slowly at first, whereas mortgages of lower interest rates tend to retire principal more quickly at first. This is shown in Exhibit 13.5 for two mortgages of identical size.

On the other hand, mortgages of shorter terms have a greater portion of each payment going toward principal; hence, amortization is more rapid. Unfortunately, this is accomplished through an increase in the monthly payment. In Exhibit 13.6, we have compared the monthly payments elicited by two popular

EXHIBIT 13.4

Distribution of mortgage cash flows (12% mortgage)

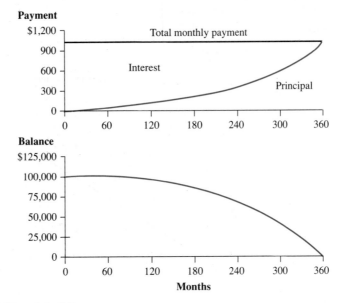

Source: Goldman, Sachs & Co.

EXHIBIT 13.5

Amortization principal payments (8% and 12% mortgages; $100,000 original balance)

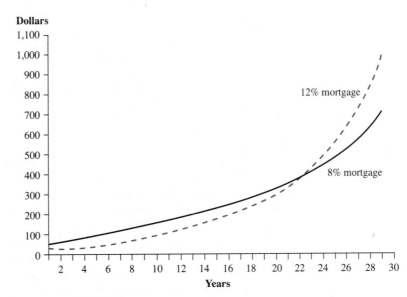

Source: Goldman, Sachs & Co.

fixed-rate, fixed-term mortgages—the standard 30-year mortgage and the 15-year mortgage—at stated annual interest rates ranging from 6 percent to 20 percent. The lowest curve of the exhibit gives the differences in monthly payments between the two mortgages. At low interest rates, the differences are rather pronounced, but at high rates, they are slight. Because amortization is more rapid in

Exhibit 13.6

Monthly mortgage payments: 15 versus 30 years

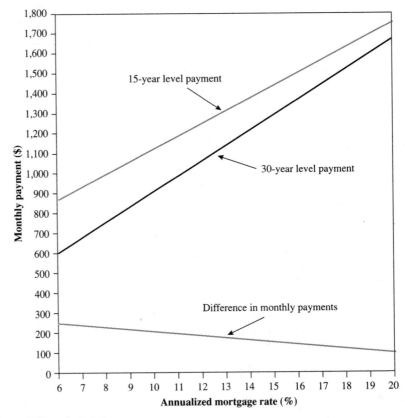

Source: Goldman, Sachs & Co.

shorter mortgages, total interest charges are lower. For example, the total interest paid over the life of a $100,000, 12 percent, 30-year mortgage loan is $270,299.60 [= (360 × $1,028.61) − $100,000], whereas for a 12 percent, 15-year loan, the total interest paid over its life is $116,030.60 [= (180 × $1200.17) − $100,000], less than half as much.[1] The differences in total interest are usually even more pronounced because 15-year mortgages are likely to feature lower interest rates than 30-year mortgages. In both of the cases above, at the 12 percent rate, interest payments over the lives of the loans exceed the original amount of the loan!

Most mortgages also charge **origination points.** Origination points are assessed to the borrower as an up-front fee for making the loan and for locking in a future interest rate prior to the execution of the loan. Today, most mortgage originators charge 1 to 3 points, where each point is 1 percent of the loan amount.

---

[1]The total interest calculations take the total of monthly payments that will be made over the 360-month life of the loan and subtract the total principal contributions, which must equal the initial amount of the loan. Anything left over must be interest.

EXHIBIT 13.7

*Theoretical default
risk on mortgages*

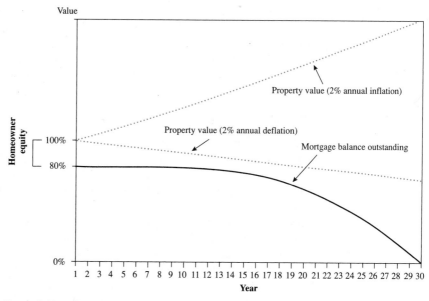

Source: Goldman, Sachs & Co.

Most mortgages may be prepaid at any time, at the option of the borrower. However, during the beginning years of the mortgage, there is occasionally a charge associated with liquidation of the loan. The amounts that the borrower may choose to prepay can vary from a few cents to the entire remaining loan balance, shown at each point in time by the lower curve of Exhibit 13.4. This will depend on the nature of the mortgage contract. Borrowers may desire to prepay their mortgage loans to reduce their overall debt loads, to refinance their homes at lower interest rates, or to sell their residence because of a need to relocate.

As indicated above, the credit quality of the mortgage is determined by both the creditworthiness of the borrower and the market value of the property itself. The lower the **loan-to-value ratio** (LTV), the more secure the loan—at least initially. However, of equal concern to the lender is the expected appreciation of the underlying asset supporting the loan. Exhibit 13.7 illustrates this point. This exhibit presents the degree of collateral protection afforded by an 80 percent LTV in two environments.[2] In one environment, shown by the upper curve, the property securing the loan appreciates 2 percent per year throughout the 30-year loan period. In the other environment, shown by the middle curve, the property depreciates by 2 percent per year throughout the loan period. The lowest curve gives the mortgage balance outstanding at each point in time. The difference between the property value curves and the mortgage balance outstanding gives the margin of

---

[2]An 80 percent LTV is standard in the new mortgage market, where a typical buyer must make a 20 percent down payment on the property being purchased. For example, on a house costing $100,000, a down payment of $20,000 would be required by the mortgage lender; thus, the mortgage amount of $80,000 would produce a loan-to-(house)-value ratio of 80 percent.

security to the lender. Note how this margin depends on both the loan-to-value ratio and the inflation assumption. In this example, the lender's risk is greatest in a deflationary environment and after 12 years. Other curves could be drawn portraying different mortgage rates and rates of appreciation in housing prices. In each case, one would arrive at a different theoretical default risk on the mortgage.

Adjustable-Rate Mortgages

An **adjustable-rate mortgage** (ARM) is a mortgage instrument that has its contractual interest rate tied to some interest rate index. The rate is periodically adjusted to reflect changes in the index. ARMs achieved popularity beginning in 1981, when regulators began to allow federally chartered thrift institutions, such as savings and loan associations, to offer them. They are attractive to lenders because they have low exposure to interest rate risk, as the mortgage rates on outstanding loans adjust periodically to conform to new market conditions. ARMs are attractive to borrowers, who can expect to pay less interest over the life of a loan than with a fixed-rate mortgage. By giving up the security of a long-term, fixed interest rate, the monthly payment need not incorporate an additional implicit charge to cover both the liquidity premium demanded for providing a fixed rate to the borrower and the homeowner's option to refinance the loan if rates decline.[3] But the lower expected rate is not without its cost. The variable-rate mortgage loan exposes the borrower to uncertain future interest rates and a variation in either monthly payments or loan term.

ARMs are designed to amortize the principal over time in a pattern much like fixed-rate mortgage instruments. Monthly payments are initially set according to the current interest rate, and they change when the interest rate varies. Generally, maturity remains constant. However, if interest rate levels change substantially, some maturity adjustment may be necessary. This will also be the case if there are restrictions on the amount that monthly payments can change over a given period. More will be said about this below.

There are numerous varieties of ARMs currently being offered. Each is distinguished from the others by variations in one or more of about a dozen contractual features. Some of the most important features are the interest rate index used, the margin above the chosen index, the frequency of rate and payment adjustments, the interest rate caps, and the monthly payment caps.

The Interest Rate Index.   Each ARM has its variable rate linked to one of several indexes. In the past, one of the most widely used indexes was the **cost of funds index** (COFI). This index, published by the Home Loan Bank of San

---

[3]Although the expected interest costs of ARMs are lower, the actual costs may be higher or lower, depending on what happens to interest rates over the term of the loan. See Lynn Bartholomew, Jonathan Berk, and Richard Roll, "Adjustable Rate Mortgages: An Introduction," *Mortgage Securities Research,* Goldman Sachs & Co., November 1986, as well as the discussion of liquidity premiums in Chapter 5.

Francisco, is constructed to reflect the actual cost of funds of thrift institutions operating in California, Arizona, and Nevada. Because of its accounting basis, the index does not adjust rapidly to current market rates of interest. For example, a thrift may have undertaken fixed-rate debt financing several years ago at a 14 percent rate of interest. This cost of funds is included in the index until maturity, even if similar borrowings are currently being undertaken at 8 percent. The COFI would still consider the cost of funds to be 14 percent on that particular portion of the thrift's debt. For this reason, among others, the COFI has fallen out of favor recently.

Today, the most popular indexes are the **constant maturity Treasury yield indexes** (CMTs). These indexes give the current yields on one-year or five-year Treasury securities. Of the two, the one-year CMT index is usually the more volatile. However, both indexes tend to move more rapidly than the COFI. Other interest rate indexes are sometimes used, but these three clearly dominate the ARM market.

The Margin. A margin is added to the applicable index to arrive at the mortgage rate used in computing monthly payments. The purpose of this margin is threefold. Set at origination, this margin adjusts for the borrower's risk of default, covers underwriting and administrative expenses, and provides for some anticipated profit. The usual margins vary from 150 b.p. to 275 b.p., with the majority of mortgages found in the upper half of the range. For example, the contract margin may be 250 b.p., implying that if the current index is at 7.0 percent, the mortgage rate over the ensuing period would be at 9.5 percent.

Adjustment Frequency. The frequency of adjustment stipulated in the mortgage document indicates the length of time that must elapse before a payment amount or applicable mortgage rate can be changed. The shorter the minimum time interval between allowable adjustments is, the more responsive the ARM cash flows are to current market conditions.[4]

Annual adjustments of both the mortgage rate and the dollar amount of the monthly payment are common provisions in ARMs, but other arrangements are often made. Some mortgages feature rates that adjust more frequently, such as monthly, while payments may adjust only annually. This can lead to negative amortization when rates are climbing. This results in a situation where a higher principal must be used in subsequent periods to compute the appropriate allocation of principal and interest. It is also likely to cause changes in the final maturity of the mortgage.

Rate Caps and Payment Caps. The vast majority of ARMs in the United States include **caps,** or limits, of some sort. The two most common caps are those that

---

[4]Even with frequent adjustment periods, the lender has the option not to increase the payments or applicable interest rate. While it may seem inconceivable that a lender may forgo such an opportunity, lenders occasionally do not raise the rates or payments to avoid precipitating unwanted mortgage prepayment behavior or defaults.

Exhibit 13.8

*The effect of rate caps
on mortgage rates*

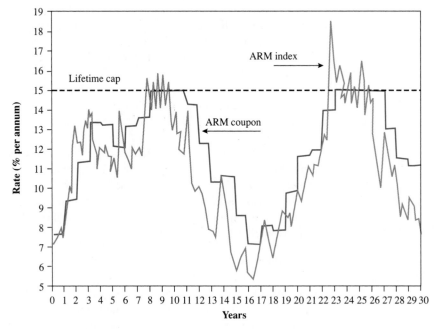

Source: Goldman, Sachs & Co.

limit the interest rate over the life of the mortgage to some spread above or below the initial rate, and those that limit the size of the adjustment between any two periods in either the mortgage rate or payment amount. For example, an ARM may have a 15 percent lifetime cap and a 2 percent annual adjustment limit. Thus, if the initial mortgage rate is 8 percent, the maximum rate chargeable would be 15 percent, and next period's rate could be no more than 10 percent, regardless of changes in the reference index rate. Caps sometimes work in both directions. In other words, they set both a ceiling and a floor between which adjustments must be constrained. An example of the existence of caps on the payments due on an ARM over a hypothetical series of interest rates is given in Exhibit 13.8. As shown in this exhibit, mortgage rates move more slowly when market rates jump substantially. However, if market rates remain at high (or low) levels, the mortgage interest rate catches up—that is, of course, as long as the market rate does not exceed the lifetime cap.

Prepayments on ARMs are undertaken for many of the same reasons that motivate prepayments on fixed-rate mortgages: debt load reduction or due to a move. However, unlike the refinancing-motivated prepayments on fixed-rate mortgages that occur when market rates decline, the prepayment behavior on ARMs is motivated somewhat differently. Since ARMs adjust to current market rates, borrowers of ARMs are often motivated to refinance at fixed rates of interest when they believe that variable rates of interest are about to rise. Moreover, they tend to prepay more rapidly just after their payments have been reset and when the payments are constrained to a low level by a periodic cap.

Other Mortgage Structures

In addition to fixed-rate, level-payment and variable-rate, variable-payment mortgages, there are several other variations. One is termed a **graduated-payment mortgage** (GPM). In this fixed-rate mortgage, the payments start off lower than would be the case in a level-pay, annuity-type mortgage. The payments increase over each of the first five or six years and then level off at an amount that is above that of an otherwise similar fixed-rate, level-pay program. Because the first few payments are less than the accrued interest, there is some negative amortization at the outset. This is added to the principal and retired in the later years of the mortgage life. Another type of mortgage, the **graduated-equity mortgage** (GEM), is similar to the GPM except that the initial payments are sufficient to cover the accrued interest. As payments rise over the first few years, an increasing amount goes toward the rapid retirement of principal.

Some mortgages have biweekly payments. The payments are often calibrated to retire principal more rapidly than with a monthly payment mortgage. Others have relatively low monthly payments, with a balloon payment due after a set number of years to retire principal.

Single-Family versus Multiple-Family versus Commercial Mortgages

Single-family mortgages are defined as mortgages that are provided for residences of one to four families. **Multiple-family mortgages** are secured by properties that house more than four families. Many multiple-family mortgages have scheduled terms of 15 years but payments based on a 30-year maturity. At the end of 15 years, a large loan-liquidating balloon payment is made to compensate the lenders for the lower monthly payments during the prior 180 months. Most of these loans cannot be prepaid during the first several years of the mortgage term, usually five years.

Commercial mortgages are secured by properties such as hotels, shopping centers, industrial complexes, and office buildings. Today, many commercial mortgages have prohibitions against making prepayments of principal and against refinancing. Little standardization of mortgage contracts exists for the commercial market.

The Secondary Market for Mortgages

Mortgages have been bought and sold by investors as single loans for a very long time. Financial institutions with deposits exceeding loan demand would purchase them from institutions in capital deficit areas. Many investors would not participate in this market, however, because of the extensive and specialized operational and underwriting capabilities that these investments required. The terms and provisions of mortgages diverged from one to another, and the creditworthiness of the borrower and quality of collateral varied widely. This made the mortgages difficult for investors to value confidently. Thus, the secondary market for mortgages was rather thin.

Several decades ago, in an effort to attract funds, issuers of mortgages began to package them in pools of several hundred individual mortgages.[5] They would then issue **pass-through securities,** which gave investors a pro rata share of the mortgage pool. Cash flows from the underlying mortgages were "passed through" to the investors via monthly payments of principal and interest. Mortgage-backed securities of this type usually have payments on a monthly basis, although some pay investors quarterly.

Although pass-throughs have existed for decades, they entered the market on a broad scale when three federal agencies began to provide credit guarantees and standards of uniformity for pass-throughs issued under their auspices. This enhanced the marketability of pass-throughs by making them easier to analyze and, therefore, more attractive to nontraditional mortgage investors. Additionally, the credit backing by a federal agency reduced investor concerns about payment collections.

Mortgage companies, commercial banks, savings and loans, and other mortgage originators pool mortgages to create pass-throughs. These originators may either issue the pass-throughs themselves or arrange to have the pass-throughs guaranteed by and issued through one of the federal agencies discussed in the previous two chapters.

The three federal agencies involved in the issuing of pass-through securities are the **Government National Mortgage Association** (GNMA, or Ginnie Mae), the **Federal Home Loan Mortgage Corporation** (FHLMC, or Freddie Mac), and the **Federal National Mortgage Association** (FNMA, or Fannie Mae). Pass-throughs not backed by any of the above agencies are known as private pass-throughs, or conventional mortgage-backed securities.

Each federal agency has its own standards for mortgages it deems acceptable for its mortgage-backed securities programs. The mortgage pools backing GNMA pass-throughs must contain mortgages that are insured either by the Veterans Administration (VA) or by the Federal Housing Administration (FHA). Ginnie Maes then impart a further layer of protection by providing a guarantee of the full faith and credit of the U.S. government for full and timely payments of principal and interest to the purchasers of the mortgage-backed security.

Freddie Mac pass-throughs are backed by pools of conventional single-family residential mortgages that usually are not VA or FHA insured. Nonetheless, timely interest payments and the ultimate payment (within one year) of principal are guaranteed by FHLMC, a private but federally sponsored credit agency.

Fannie Maes are similar to Freddie Macs, except that they carry a guarantee for full and timely payment of both interest and principal, similar to the guarantee of Ginnie Maes. However, the guarantee does not invoke the full faith and credit of the U.S. government. Like FHLMC, FNMA is a federally sponsored, private agency.

---

[5]For commercial mortgages, which often tend to be very large, the secondary market continues to be primarily a "whole loan" market. The loans are of sufficiently large size to make it worthwhile to analyze the credits in depth, and the loans are traded from one institution to another, either directly or through brokers.

Publicly sold conventional—privately issued—pass-throughs must be registered with the Securities and Exchange Commission (SEC). They are usually rated by credit rating agencies such as Standard & Poor's as AA quality or better. These high quality ratings are often acquired, in part, due to certain **credit enhancements** obtained by the issuer. The three main types of credit enhancements used for conventional pass-throughs are **mortgage pool insurance, letters of credit or guarantees,** and a **senior/subordinated structure.** Pool insurance is the most common form of credit enhancement. In the case of pool insurance or letters of credit, the institutions backing the credit must themselves have a credit rating at least as high as that which the mortgage originator desires for the pool. On the other hand, the senior/subordinated structure can be accomplished without the AA rating. With this method of issuing pass-through securities, the originator takes a subordinated position to other investors. In essence, the funds of the originator are placed at risk first so that others may view the investment as being of high quality.

Most conventional pass-throughs fail to meet the standards for purchase by FNMA or FHLMC. For instance, jumbo mortgages often constitute a large part of conventional pass-through pools. Jumbos are loans with outstanding balances greater than the congressionally established limits for purchase by federal credit agencies. While this limit changes periodically, at the end of 1994, it was $203,150. Alternatively, documentation may be nonstandard or incomplete. In any case, conventional pools generally include mortgages that are by some measure nonconforming.

Pooling Terminology

Numerous terms have been devised to describe aspects of the cash flows emanating from a pool of mortgages. Some of the concepts denoted by the terminology leave much to be desired with respect to their ability to convey information in its most precise and useful form for investment analysis. Nonetheless, it has become conventional to describe mortgages and prepayments with the following terminology.

Weighted Average Maturity (WAM)

Most mortgage pools have a range of final mortgage maturities. The differences between the shortest-term and longest-term mortgages in the pool may range from a few months to several years. WAM is calculated at the outset of a pool formation by taking the maturities of each mortgage in the pool and weighting them by their outstanding principal balances relative to that of the entire pool. This computation is illustrated in Exhibit 13.9 for a pool with four different maturities of different dollar values.

Weighted Average Remaining Term (WART)

After a pool begins to season, the WAM no longer accurately reflects the weighted average maturity. This is because all mortgages get shorter as time passes, with some shortening more than others due to different prepayment rates among mortgages of differing maturities. Therefore, one would like to have an accurate

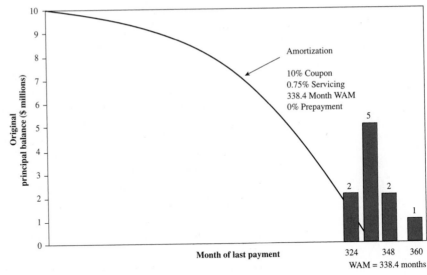

Exhibit 13.9

Weighted average maturity (WAM)

$$\text{WAM} = \sum_{i=1}^{n} w_i M_i$$
$$= (2/10)324 + (5/10)336 + (2/10)348 + (1/10)360$$
$$= 338.4$$

Source: Goldman, Sachs & Co.

measure of the remaining term of existing mortgage pools. However, no such standardized measure exists. Rather, the market convention is to ignore these pool-specific effects and compute something called the weighted average remaining term (WART). WART takes the initial WAM and subtracts the number of months of seasoning that have occurred.

Weighted Average Life (WAL)

The weighted average life (WAL) of a pool is computed by taking the scheduled times of principal payments, assuming no prepayments, and weighting them by their scheduled amounts of payment. As can be seen from Exhibit 13.10, WAL is shorter than WAM except for a pool of nonamortizing mortgages. Further, the exhibit shows the average life of the previously considered pool to be 242 months, or approximately 20 years. Assuming no prepayments, it will take this long for the investor to receive half of the face value of the mortgage pool.

Weighted Average Coupon (WAC)

Mortgages placed in a pool usually have different coupon rates.[6] Given this fact, a standard weighted average coupon (WAC) must be computed. The WAC is the average coupon paid by the household, and it should not be confused with investment yield. The amount passed through to investors is actually less than the

---

[6]An exception is the GNMA-1 in which all of the underlying mortgages have the same coupon.

EXHIBIT 13.10

Weighted average life (WAL)

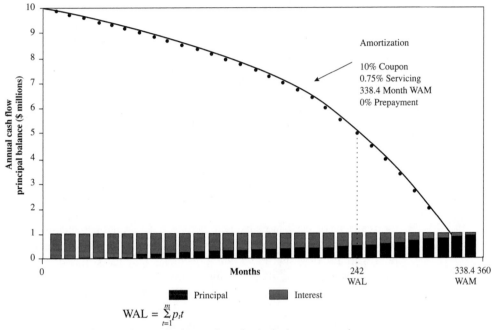

WAL $= \sum_{t=1}^{m} p_t t$

where p_t is the portion of principal amount at time t

Source: Goldman, Sachs & Co.

WAC because a servicing fee is first deducted. This fee includes the charge by the servicing institution for collecting the mortgage payments and managing the portfolio, as well as the guarantee fee for enhancements. These deductions are illustrated in Exhibit 13.11.

Other terminology is also used in this market, but the ones described here are the most common. Acronyms such as AOLS (average original loan size), WALA (weighted average loan age), and WARM (weighted average remaining maturity)—an improvement over the crude way WART is measured—are often used by analysts to describe the characteristics of a mortgage pool. These terms offer greater precision and more direct applicability to the modeling of cash flows from mortgage-backed securities but they are not as visible in the market.

Prepayment Terminology

Up to this point, we have centered the discussion of pool characteristics on stated mortgage terms, such as coupon, maturity, or principal schedule. However, as noted at the outset, prepayment is an option available to the borrower, who may prepay for any number of reasons. The borrower may wish to move, or reduce his or her debt burden, for example. In addition, if the borrower holds a fixed rate

Exhibit 13.11

Weighted average coupon (WAC)

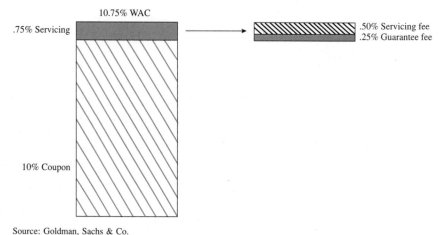

Source: Goldman, Sachs & Co.

mortgage, he or she is more likely to prepay in the event of an interest rate decline so as to refinance at a lower rate. This may not trigger a prepayment by a household with an ARM, but rapid rate movements may cause this borrower to refinance as well. As a result, prepayments are an important part of the dynamics of any pool. Consequently, one needs some better measure of the prepayment characteristics of a pool to determine its value and relative desirability.

A decade ago, many investors assumed that all mortgage pools had similar prepayment rates that resulted in a weighted average life of about 12 years. Today, mortgage-backed security analysts focus much more of their attention on mortgage prepayments in order to obtain a more accurate measure. This is because the interest rate risk—measured by duration and convexity—can vary drastically for different prepayment rates. This has led to the development of two alternative ways of picturing the pattern of prepayments. For each, the industry has employed a standardized index to capture the prepayment characteristics of a given mortgage pool.

Constant Prepayment Rate (CPR)

A simple, but imprecise, method of measuring prepayments is called the constant prepayment rate (CPR). This rate, expressed in annualized terms, gives the constant percentage of the remaining pool principal that is expected to prepay each month over its remaining life. For example, a monthly constant prepayment rate of 2 percent would imply an (annualized) CPR of 21.53 percent $[= 1 - (1 - .02)^{12}]$. Obviously, a pool of mortgages does not prepay at a constant rate throughout a year, much less over its entire life. However, the CPR is a useful convention for characterizing the assumed or current rates of prepayment on a given mortgage pool.

Public Securities Association Model (PSA)

Another method of characterizing prepayment speed is based on a model developed by the Public Securities Association (PSA). This method takes into account, in a simple and crude way, the seasoning effect that has been observed on prepayment rates. It assumes 0 percent prepayments for a new pool and then a linear progression of prepayments up to 6 percent by month 30. Beyond month 30, mortgages are assumed to continue to prepay at a 6 percent annual rate. Actual prepayment speeds are expressed as a fraction or multiple of PSA. For example, 200 percent PSA would translate to a 12 percent CPR for months beyond month 30.

Valuation of Mortgage-Backed Securities

Most mortgage-backed securities issued by federal agencies are treated as default-free securities. This is due to the interest and principal payment guarantees mentioned earlier. Nonetheless, they are fraught with interest rate risk complicated by prepayment risk.

Since cash flows are sensitive to interest rates, one of the interest-sensitive valuation methodologies discussed in Chapter 7 must be employed to value mortgage-backed securities. It happens that mortgage prepayments are sensitive not only to the level of interest rates but also to the paths taken to arrive at the interest rate level. That is because the mortgage prepayments at a particular interest rate level will depend, in part, on previous amounts of prepayments. Thus, we must use a valuation method that has a memory of how rates arrived at their present levels. Pure simulations and simulations through interest rate lattices like those discussed above are two commonly used methods that address this need.

Another complication is that mortgage prepayments are usually occasioned by declines in long-term interest rates, which are not necessarily accompanied by declines in short-term interest rates. This is because the long-term rates better reflect the refinancing rates on new mortgages, which motivate the prepayments. On the other hand, for reasons that were discussed in part in Chapter 7, sequences of short-term rates, not long-term rates, are appropriate for discounting interest-sensitive cash flows.[7] Thus, all modern mortgage valuation models simulate at least a two-factor model, with both short-term and long-term interest rates as factors. The simulations allow for some correlation in the movements of these rates but also preserve a degree of independence.[8]

Once the interest rate paths have been simulated, the mortgage cash flows—interest, scheduled principal amortization, and principal prepayments—can be

---

[7]The reasons for this are complex and highly technical. Because the cash flows emanating from mortgages are subject to behavior that is at least partly random, it is not altogether clear that riskless arbitrage is possible with mortgage-backed securities. For this reason, our valuation methodology may generate positive option-adjusted spreads to Treasuries, even in an efficient market.

[8]Some of the more refined mortgage-backed security valuation models also accommodate fluctuating basic volatilities of the interest rates. Because the value of mortgage-backed securities is affected by not only interest rates but also the volatility of interest rates (via its impact on the value of the prepayment option), a model that captures the random changes in volatility levels can more accurately value mortgage-backed securities. Other nondeterminate processes, such as prepayment speed, can also be modeled through simulation. This enhancement allows the same set of short-rate and long-rate paths (and perhaps even volatility paths) to give rise to several different levels of prepayment due to the somewhat random behavior of mortgagors.

EXHIBIT 13.12

*Annuity value and
mortgage value*

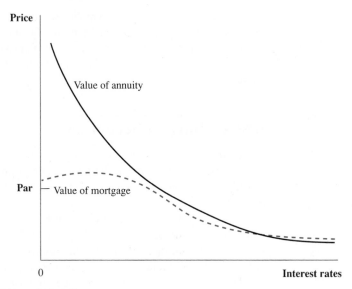

Source: Goldman, Sachs & Co.

linked to those long-term interest rate paths that would give rise to them. When the interest-sensitive cash flows are so mapped, they can be discounted by the short-rate sequences that are associated with the long-term rates driving the cash flows. Because this process is so complicated, it will not be developed here. However, one general characteristic of the results of this process can be illustrated.

By simulating interest rate paths with a variety of starting points, a curve can be drawn that relates mortgage-backed security value to market rates of interest. The result is a curve much like that shown in Exhibit 13.12, which is reminiscent of the interest sensitivity of callable bonds discussed in the previous chapter. In Exhibit 13.12, we have contrasted the value of a pool of mortgages to the value of an annuity with the same coupon rate and a maturity equal to the expected maturity of the mortgages. The differences between the levels of the curves are due to the prepayment behavior, which deprives the mortgage-backed security investor of large capital gains in the advent of declining interest rates. At moderate to low interest rates, convexity turns quite negative, while at high interest rates, it approaches the positive convexity of the annuity.

Recalling that effective duration is given by the negative of the slope of the value curve at a given point divided by the price at that same point, it is also apparent that effective duration goes from moderately positive to quite low, and even negative in the case depicted, as interest rates decline. Just as in the callable bond case, prepayment of the underlying debt substantially alters the price response as interest rates change. Indeed, the amount of effective duration drift is substantial and makes the ownership of mortgage-backed securities laden with risk.

Exhibit 13.13

Mortgage pass-through interest cash flow

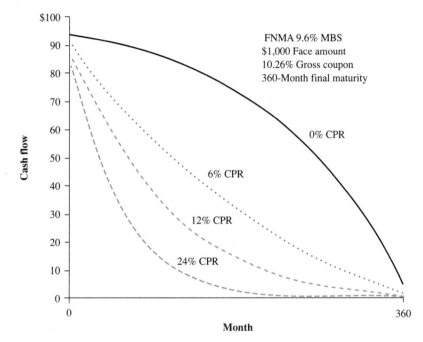

Source: Goldman, Sachs & Co.

Mortgage Strips

Not all mortgage-backed securities pass along the pool's cash flows to investors in strict, pro rata shares. Sometimes the total cash flow is allocated differentially among owners. **Strips** give disproportionately high shares of interest to some investors, while others receive a disproportionately large share of the principal repayments. Certain strips, called **IOs** (for "interest only"), pass along to the investors only the interest portion of each mortgage payment. Other strips, called **POs** (for "principal only"), return to investors only the scheduled amortization and prepayment portions of the mortgage payment.

Both of these strips are extremely sensitive to prepayment rates. For instance, investors in IOs will soon receive very little cash flow if mortgages are prepaid rapidly. On the other hand, they will receive interest payments long into the future if prepayments are low. This is shown in Exhibit 13.13, where cash flow is graphed against maturity for different CPR prepayment speeds. Note that total interest received over the life of the mortgage is given by the area under the curve representing the interest cash flow at various rates of prepayment. The effect of prepayment on total interest payments is presented more directly in Exhibit 13.14.

PO investors, by way of contrast, benefit from high prepayment rates. Unlike IO holders, who never know how much interest they will ultimately receive, PO holders will receive the entire principal in due course. Their only problem is that "due course" might be later rather than sooner. Obviously, since these investors

Exhibit 13.14

*Total lifetime
cash flow
(interest only)*

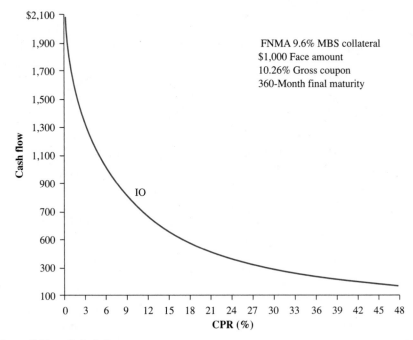

FNMA 9.6% MBS collateral
$1,000 Face amount
10.26% Gross coupon
360-Month final maturity

IO

Cash flow

CPR (%)

Source: Goldman, Sachs & Co.

will ultimately receive a fixed number of dollars, they would rather receive their money sooner than later. Because a PO may sell for deep discounts, say, 55¢ on the dollar, receiving the dollar soon can lead to very high rates of return on the investment. The pattern of principal cash flow, as a function of mortgage age and prepayment rate, is given in Exhibit 13.15. Note that total principal cash flow is equal to the area under a curve. In the case of POs, the areas under each curve are equal to each other, as the total principal ultimately received is unaffected by prepayment rates. However, the pattern of principal payments is dramatically different for different prepayment speeds. The PO analogue to Exhibit 13.14, however, would be a straight horizontal line intersecting the vertical axis at the face value of the mortgage.

In Exhibit 13.16, the values of an IO and a PO are shown together, along with their parent mortgage-backed security, across a wide range of interest rate scenarios. Note that at any interest rate, the heights of the IO and PO sum to that of the mortgage-backed security. If an investor purchases both an IO and a PO, he can reconstruct the identical cash flows from the entire pool of mortgages.[9]

---

[9]To exactly replicate the full mortgage payment stream, the IO purchased must be constructed from the same instrument as the PO. They must have the same "notional principal." This term is widely used to denote the reference amount on which the cash flows are based. The PO actually has a true principal, but the IO has only interest payments, which are based on a notional principal.

Exhibit 13.15

Mortgage pass-through principal cash flow

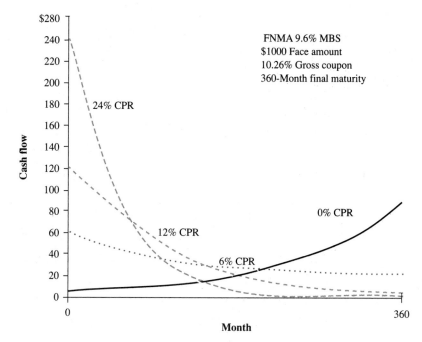

Source: Goldman, Sachs & Co.

By purchasing greater or lesser amounts of IOs per PO, an investor can synthesize mortgage-backed securities of varying coupons. This is shown in Exhibit 13.17. By purchasing 142.11 worth of IOs for every 100.00 (again, face value) of POs, an investor can synthesize a mortgage-backed security with a coupon rate of 13.5 percent from the decomposed 9.5 percent mortgage-backed security under consideration. However, because the underlying mortgage has a 9.5 percent coupon, the prepayment rate on the synthetic 13.5 percent mortgage will be that of a 9.5 percent mortgage, which will be much lower than that of a true 13.5 percent mortgage. The borrower will make his or her prepayment decision based on a comparison of the 9.5 percent mortgage rate with current refinancing rates; the borrower is totally unaffected by whatever coupon rate any particular investor may wish to synthesize with the cash flows stemming from the mortgage. In this way, the investor can create new securities that are not naturally occurring in the marketplace.

Indeed, this is a major attraction of mortgage-backed securities that decouple principal and interest payments. Investors can use these building blocks to construct whatever patterns of cash flows most closely meet their needs. Issuers, on the other hand, may be able to capture a slightly higher price by catering to the desires of investors in this way. For instance, in the aforementioned exhibit, the 9.5 percent mortgage-backed security sells for 98-03, whereas the synthetic 9.5 percent mortgage-backed security commands a price of 98-13, a full 10/32nds of a point higher.

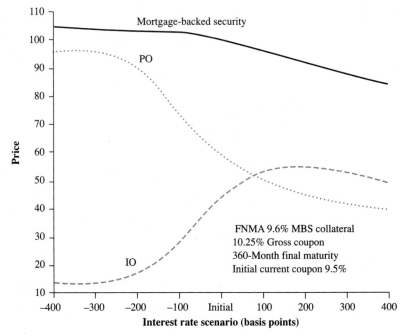

FNMA 9.6% MBS collateral
10.25% Gross coupon
360-Month final maturity
Initial current coupon 9.5%

Source: Goldman, Sachs & Co.

CMOs and REMICs

Collateralized mortgage obligations (CMOs) and **real estate mortgage investment conduits** (REMICs) are other types of variations on the theme of repackaging the cash flows of mortgage pools. Indeed, CMOs appeared on the scene several years prior to the first strips. REMICs are CMOs with special tax treatment of capital gains. There are no structural differences between these two types of instruments to the investor. Thus, in this section, we will refer to the broader CMO classification.

CMOs are debt obligations collateralized by a pool of mortgages or mortgage-backed securities. They are created by taking the cash flows on mortgage-backed securities and dividing them into groups that can be allocated on a prioritized basis. Then, new securities are issued whose payoffs are determined by the cash flows from the mortgage-backed securities that are allocated to their respective groups.

Perhaps the best way to characterize CMOs is to contrast them with IOs and POs, which we described in the preceding section. We can envision the cash flows emanating from a mortgage-backed security as a stream of payments composed of interest and principal extending over a number of time periods. IOs and POs take those chunks of cash flow illustrated in Exhibit 13.18 and divide them "horizontally/diagonally." The upper portion is called an IO, and the lower portion is called a PO. A CMO, on the other hand, would make the cut "vertically," where

**EXHIBIT 13.17   Creating a Synthetic Coupon Pass-Through Using FNMA
9.5 Percent Mortgage-Backed Security, IO, and PO**
(Combine IO and PO)

Synthetic Coupon (%)	IO per $100 PO	Price of Synthetic
1.5	15.79	62-00
2.5	26.32	66-18
3.5	36.84	71-04
4.5	47.37	75-21
5.5	57.89	80-07
6.5	68.42	84-24
7.5	78.95	89-10
8.5	89.47	93-28
9.5	100.00	98-13
10.5	110.53	102-31
11.5	121.05	107-16
12.5	131.58	112-02
13.5	142.11	116-19
14.5	152.63	121-05
15.5	163.16	125-22
16.5	173.68	130-08
17.5	184.21	134-26
18.5	194.74	139-11
19.5	205.26	143-29
20.5	215.79	148-14

Price Assumptions:

Mortgage-backed security:	98-03
PO:	55-06
IO:	43-07

Source: Goldman, Sachs & Co.

the principal portion of the payments would be divided into groups called **tranches.** The first tranche would receive all payments toward principal, whether scheduled or due to prepayments, until its allocation was full. In addition, it would receive interest payments on the outstanding principal allocated to that tranche. The second tranche would begin receiving principal payments only after the first tranche had been completely paid off. However, it would receive interest payments throughout the period on the amount of outstanding principal allocated to that tranche. This pattern would continue until the final tranche, dubbed the "Z" tranche. The "Z" tranche receives all remaining principal payments after every other tranche has been paid off. It receives no interest payments in the interim, but its principal accrues at the coupon interest rate until payments finally begin.

In the mid-1980s, most CMOs had four tranches, including the "Z" tranche. More recent CMOs feature as many as 30 separate tranches. CMOs were, in fact,

Exhibit 13.18

*Structures of CMOs
versus strips*

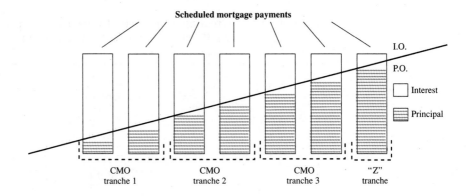

dominating the secondary mortgage market in the early 1990s. They have been popular for three reasons. First, they allow investors to have mortgage securities tailored to their maturity preferences. Commercial banks like the shortest-term maturities; thrifts, insurance companies, and commercial banks purchase the intermediate-term maturities; and insurance companies and pension funds purchase the longest-term maturities. Second, CMOs often have high book yields relative to debt instruments of similar quality. The high yields typically associated with mortgage-backed securities, due at least in part to the prepayment uncertainty, are also exhibited by CMOs that are manufactured from underlying mortgage-backed securities. Finally, CMOs typically have high credit ratings, usually AAA, owing to their backing by mortgage pools issued by GNMA, FHLMC, and FNMA.

CMOs are characterized by their coupon rate, average life (assuming prepayment and reinvestment rates as stated at issue), expected final maturity (using the same assumptions employed to get average life), and stated final maturity (assuming zero prepayments and very low reinvestment rates). If prepayments depart from the assumptions, the average life and expected final maturity of the tranches will change. Rising prepayments will shorten the average lives and expected final maturities, while declining prepayments will lengthen them. The values of later tranches are most affected by changes in the prepayment rates. CMOs pay on either a monthly, quarterly (the most common payment frequency), or semiannual basis.

In recent years, a variation on the CMO theme has been introduced with some success: floating-rate CMOs.[10] More will be said about these instruments in Chapter 16. The variations in CMO structures are so broad that it is difficult to make any more generalizations than those we have already made without introducing an

---

[10]Floating-rate CMOs are based on pools of fixed-rate mortgages. They create the floating-rate behavior by splitting the coupons into a floating-rate coupon and an inverse floating-rate coupon. (An inverse floating rate coupon goes down when market rates of interest rise and goes up when market rates decline. More will be said about inverse floaters in Chapter 16.) The sum of the floater and inverse floater never exceeds the fixed coupon rate.

incredible amount of detail.[11] Suffice it to say that this area of the secondary market for mortgages is developing rapidly, as investors are becoming increasingly sophisticated in their ability to analyze securities derived from mortgages. This broader investor interest expands the mortgage market, making money more readily available for the housing industry.

---

[11]A thorough treatment of this topic is available in Frank J. Fabozzi, Chuck Ramsey, and Frank R. Ramirez, *Collateralized Mortgage Obligations: Structures and Analysis,* 2d ed. (New Hope, Pa.: Frank J. Fabozzi Associates, 1994).

Summary

The market for mortgage securities has been transformed from a rather stodgy market to the most dynamic and innovative of markets. Much of the innovation was fostered by federal agency backing of pools of mortgages, which removed the credit risk from the mortgages. This allowed the market to innovate with the packaging of cash flows, and investors welcomed the opportunity to invest in instruments whose cash flows were better tailored to their needs, without the introduction of credit risk. Furthermore, federal regulations have been very receptive to the innovation taking place.

Two results of this effort are: (1) a mortgage market with rates charged to borrowers that are lower than they otherwise would be, and (2) a more "complete" market.[12] A third benefit of this innovation is that it has given employment opportunities to the select few that are willing to invest the time to master the concepts and mechanics of the instruments! Moreover, people who can understand this market are well situated to understand just about any other financial market. Finally, the innovations in the mortgage market have led to new financial valuation technologies, as traditional valuation methods were found to be inadequate for mortgage-backed securities. These valuation technologies have revolutionized our approaches to valuing other financial contracts as well.

---

[12]Recall from Chapter 1 that a complete market is a goal of financial economists because of the efficiency and opportunity that it would create. A complete market is characterized by a wide spectrum of assets—wide enough so that virtually any conceivable economic condition can either be bet upon or protected against by constructing a portfolio from existing liquid assets.

Key Concepts

aging and amortization,   302
COFI versus CMT adjustable-rate mortgages,   306–07
CMOs and REMICs,   320
CPR versus PSA,   314
credit enhancements,   311
fixed-rate versus adjustable-rate mortgages,   299
GNMA, FNMA, and FHLMC,   310
loan-to-value ratio,   305
mortgage bankers,   297

mortgage loan,   296
mortgage strips, IOs, POs, and tranches,   317, 321
origination points,   304
pass-through securities,   310
periodic versus lifetime caps,   307–08
secondary market for mortgages,   309–11
valuation of mortgage-backed securities,   315–16
WAM, WART, and WAC,   311–13

Review Questions

1. What is the monthly payment on a $125,000, 30-year mortgage that has a fixed annual interest rate of 9.5 percent? How much total interest will be paid?

2. If you were to make payments on the above mortgage on a biweekly basis, assuming the same interest rate and assuming that each payment is half as large as the monthly payment calculated in Question 1, how long would it take to pay down the mortgage? (Remember, there are 26 biweekly periods in a year.)

3. What is the constant prepayment rate (CPR) associated with a monthly constant prepayment rate of 1.75 percent? What is the monthly constant prepayment rate associated with a CPR of 17.5973 percent?

4. You have signed a mortgage with monthly payments of $1,697.25. The total amount financed was $170,000 at a fixed rate of 10.5 percent. What is the loan term?

5. Suppose that you are in the market for a $125,000 mortgage. You are given the choice of two monthly mortgages, one fixed and the other variable. The interest rate on the fixed-rate mortgage is 9.5 percent. The variable interest rate mortgage has a margin of 250 basis points and is based upon the five-year CMT index, which is currently at 6.25 percent. In your naiveté, you expect the relevant interest rate to stay at this level for five years and then increase to 6.75 percent for the remainder. If both mortgages are 30 years in length, which should you take?

6. Suppose that you are 10 years into a monthly, 30-year, fixed-rate mortgage. The interest rate on your mortgage is 11.25 percent. The remaining principal is $140,000. Currently, new fixed-rate mortgages are 11 percent. If the refinancing fee is $3,000, should you refinance? (Assume that there are no other fees and that you intend to reside at that same location for at least 10 more years.)

7. Consider a $100,000 30-year mortgage priced to yield 10 percent, assuming no prepayments and a flat yield curve. Suppose you were to sell the mortgage to two different investors, one with a short investment horizon and the other with a long-term investment horizon. The first piece consists of interest and principal payments on the mortgage for the first 10 years, while the second piece receives the remaining payments. How much is each piece worth? If interest rates were to increase immediately by 1 percent, how much would each piece be worth?

References

Archer, Wayne R., and David C. Ling. "The Effect of Alternative Interest Rate Processes on the Value of Mortgage-Backed Securities." *Journal of Housing Research,* 1995.

Asay, Michael R.; Leon Baudouin; Hal Hinkle; et al. *Mortgage Securities Research.* Goldman Sachs & Co., January 1988.

Asay, Michael R., and Timothy D. Sears. "Stripped Mortgage-Backed Securities: Basic Concepts and Pricing Theory." *Mortgage Securities Research.* Goldman Sachs & Co., January 1988.

Bartholomew, Lynn; Jonathan Berk; and Richard Roll. "Adjustable Rate Mortgages: An Introduction." *Mortgage Securities Research.* Goldman Sachs & Co., November 1986.

———. "Adjustable Rate Mortgages: Prepayment Behavior." *Mortgage Securities Research.* Goldman Sachs & Co., November 1986.

Belton, Terrence M. "Option Adjusted Spreads." *Secondary Mortgage Markets,* Winter 1988–89.

Brick, John R. "A Primer on Mortgage-Backed Securities." *Bankers Magazine,* January/February 1984.

Brown, Peter G., et al. *Introduction to Mortgage and Mortgage-Backed Securities.* New York: Salomon Brothers, September 1987.

Chen, Ren-Raw, and T. L. Tyler Yang. "The Relevance of Interest Rate Processes in Pricing Mortgage-Backed Securities." *Journal of Housing Research,* 1995.

Chinloy, Peter. "Public and Conventional Mortgages and Mortgage-Backed Securities." *Journal of Housing Research,* 1995.

Edens, Lynn M. "Understanding the Senior/Subordinated Structures in the Conventional Mortgage Pass-Through Market." *Mortgage Securities Research.* Goldman Sachs & Co., October 1989.

Fabozzi, Frank J. *Valuation of Fixed Income Securities.* New Hope, Pa.: Frank J. Fabozzi Associates, 1994.

Fabozzi, Frank J., ed. *The Handbook of Mortgage-Backed Securities.* 3d ed. Chicago: Probus, 1992.

Fabozzi, Frank J., and Franco Modigliani. *Mortgage and Mortgage-Backed Securities Markets.* Boston: Harvard Business School Press, 1992.

Fabozzi, Frank J.; Chuck Ramsey; and Frank R. Ramirez. *Collateralized Mortgage Obligations: Structures and Analysis.* 2d ed. Buckingham, Pa.: Frank J. Fabozzi Associates, 1994.

Green, Jerry, and John B. Shoven. "The Effects of Interest Rates on Mortgage Prepayments." *Journal of Money, Credit, and Banking,* February 1986.

Kau, James B., and Donald C. Keenan. "An Overview of the Option-Theoretic Pricing of Mortgages." *Journal of Housing Research,* 1995.

McConnell, John J., and Manoj Singh. "Rational Prepayments and the Valuation of Collateralized Mortgage Obligations." *Journal of Finance,* July 1994.

Sa-Aadu, Jarjisu, and Isaac F. Megbolugbe. "Heterogeneous Borrowers, Mortgage Selection, and Mortgage Pricing." *Journal of Housing Research,* 1995.

Shilling, James D. "Rates of Return on Mortgage-Backed Securities and Option-Theoretic Models of Mortgage Pricing." *Journal of Housing Research,* 1995.

Smith, S. D. "Analyzing Risk and Return for Mortgage-Backed Securities." *Economic Review.* Federal Reserve Bank of Atlanta, January/February 1991.

Understanding Equities

Financial resources necessary to run a nonfinancial firm come from both debt and equity holders. Short of default, debtholders typically receive a fixed, nominal return. On the other hand, equityholders explicitly receive a return that is tied to the earnings stream of the firm or the investment project being financed. This chapter evaluates the role equity plays in corporate finance. It analyzes the pricing of equities and the efficiency of the stock market in valuing the earnings stream associated with equity claims. It then reviews the changing role of debt and equity in corporate finance.

Financial resources necessary to run a nonfinancial firm come from both **debt** and **equity** sources. Up until this point in the book, we have concentrated on debt instruments. As noted several times before, short of default, holders of these debt instruments typically receive a fixed, nominal return. Equityholders, on the other hand, receive income that is much less certain, in both amount and timing, than debt holders.

In this chapter, we will discuss various aspects of equity securities. As in previous chapters, we will explain the nature of the instrument, its pricing, and its institutional characteristics. The discussion will be cursory, however, as separate books and courses are available to analyze equity investment in significantly more detail than is of concern to us here.

Equity as a Residual Claim

In all of this discussion about various financial instruments, we must not forget that real assets ultimately generate returns. Financial instruments, such as stocks and bonds, are simply claims on the return stream generated by the real assets. The purchase of any real asset is funded by capital raised through some combination of equity and debt, alternatively referred to as stocks and bonds.

For instance, consider the case of a cobbler in business for himself. His shoe repair firm is purchasing a machine that can be used to put soles on shoes for $100. The return on that machine, net of labor, material, and overhead costs, will depend on how many soles are resoled. We will assume in this illustration that the annual earnings from this machine follow a regular cyclical pattern, with $8 as the lowest return and $14 as the highest return over time. Now, if the machine is purchased entirely with equity, the net returns on the sole repair enterprise are entirely allocable to the equityholders who supplied all of the capital. Their stream of earnings is shown by the area under the curve in Exhibit 14.1.

Suppose, instead, that the $100 machine is financed with $50 debt, paying 10 percent per annum to the lenders, and $50 equity. To receive 10 percent returns on their $50 contribution, the debtholders will need to be paid $5 per annum, with the remainder (ranging from $3 to $9) going to equityholders. In Exhibit 14.2, the shaded area represents the portion of total earnings that will go to the lenders, with the remaining area under the wavelike curve going to equityholders.

Note that we have implicitly assumed that the same earnings stream is generated by the machine regardless of how the purchase of the machine is financed. Shoes wear out at a rate that is independent of how the machine is financed, and the replacement rate of the soles will be whatever it will be irrespective of the financing decision. Note also that the 10 percent rate paid on the debt is never enough to bankrupt the firm, as earnings are always more than sufficient to handle the debt service.

Finally, suppose that the machine is financed by 80 percent debt and 20 percent equity. Again, we are assuming, reasonably, that the earnings generated by the machine will continue to be unaffected by the financing decision. The cost of the debt continues to be 10 percent, or $8.00 per year (= .10 × $80). The debt remains riskless under our contrived assumption about the earnings pattern because interest payments never exceed annual earnings. Equityholders receive the

EXHIBIT 14.1

*Earnings stream
accruing from
real investment*

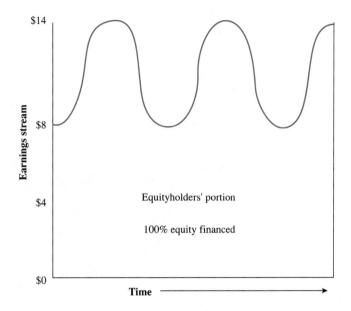

EXHIBIT 14.2

*Division of earnings
between debt- and
equityholders*

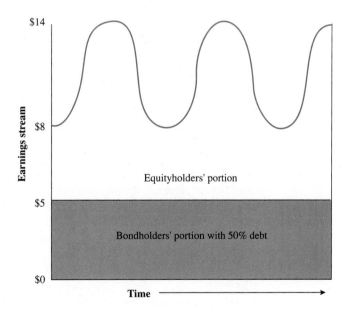

residual earnings, which range from $0.00 (= $8 − $8.00) to $6.00 (= $14 − $8.00). See Exhibit 14.3.

The return range to equityholders may not seem like very much, but remember that their investment is only $20. Therefore, the potential rate of return on their equity investment looks pretty attractive. The return may be as high as

Exhibit 14.3

*Division of earnings
for 80 percent
debt case*

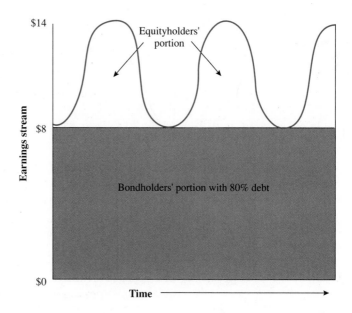

30 percent during those periods that the machine generates net (before interest) earnings of $14. In this case, $6.00 will be paid to the equityholders, which provides the 30 percent return on the $20 investment. Alternatively, at the low end of the earnings stream, the earnings are just sufficient to pay debtholders their required return. Equityholders receive nothing at all. This is the result of financial leverage—the use of both debt and equity to finance the operation of the firm. High leverage uses a larger percentage of debt and creates the possibility of higher rates of return for equityholders. This situation is illustrated in Exhibit 14.4.

It is instructive to note that the volatility of returns on assets (where returns range from 8 percent to 14 percent over time) is regular and constant regardless of how the firm is financed. The return on debt is always 10 percent. The returns on equity vary widely, depending on how much debt is employed in the financing of the firm. While the dollar earnings available to stockholders have a $6 range, the percentage return on equity varies widely, ranging from 8 percent to 14 percent for the all-equity-financed firm and from 0 percent to 30 percent for the mostly debt-financed firm. Of particular note is how the expected return on equity grows from 11 percent to 15 percent when heavy leverage is introduced.[1]

---

[1]Although we did not include the case of the firm financed by 100 percent debt, if we had, the value of the income stream would be discounted by a risk-adjusted interest rate of 11 percent rather than the riskless rate of 10 percent. Use of a risky discount rate is justified in light of the fact that the firm cannot guarantee payment every year of its expected earnings. This would equate the expected perpetual earnings per year of $11 to the value of the funding provided, $100 (= $11 ÷ 0.11).

EXHIBIT 14.4   Returns Distributed to Debt and Equity for Different Leverage Assumptions

Equity Investment (%)	Debt Investment ($)	Debt Returns ($)	Equity Returns ($)	Equity Returns (%)	Expected Return on Equity (%)
100%	$ 0	$0.00	$8–$14	8%–14%	11%
50	50	5.00	3–9	6–18	12
30	70	7.00	1–7	3–23	13
20	80	8.00	0–6	0–30	15

The preceding example was used as a device to explore the impact of financing choice on return patterns. Admittedly, there are several aspects of this example (aside from the fact that you cannot purchase a shoe repair machine for a mere $100) that are unrealistic. First, it is highly unlikely for the return pattern on a machine to have a perpetual, regular wavelike pattern with a floor at $8 per annum. A more likely pattern would exhibit some randomness, with a potential of lower or even negative earnings in some periods. Second, the machine is also prone to ultimate obsolescence and will need replacement at some point in time. For these reasons, as leverage is increased, the debtholders are likely to demand a higher rate of interest due to the fact that the firm's future solvency is in doubt. In these cases, the return to debt must include higher returns when the firm is successful, as the debtholder will not receive his contract returns when earnings fall below minimum debt payment requirements. At such time, our cobbler closes up shop, sells his machine, and works for someone else! While our example does not consider this important eventuality, the exhibits do demonstrate the residual nature of the equityholders' claim to the earnings on productive assets, and the varying returns available to equityholders. In essence, this example centers our attention on equity and its return rather than on the debt instruments that have occupied us up to this point.

Valuing Equity Claims

Given the nature of stock or equity returns, what is the value of these ownership claims? This, of course, is the next question. There are many approaches taken in valuing common stock. Indeed, as noted at the outset, there are investments and security analysis courses and industry-sponsored training seminars designed solely to consider stock-valuation techniques. Here, we will briefly discuss only the fundamental analysis approach, which is consistent with the approach we have taken in the valuation of fixed-income instruments.[2]

---

[2]For a detailed treatment of common stock valuation and a discussion of several competing approaches, see any one of a large number of textbooks on investments, including Robert

Fundamental analysis approaches the valuation of common stock by considering the cash flows, their timing, and their associated risks. So far, it sounds familiar. Therefore, let us use standard valuation techniques to determine the value of the cash flow received by the equityholder.

The cash flows considered are dividends and any other cash distributions a corporation may make to its shareholders.[3] The timing of these cash flows is typically quarterly, extending indefinitely into the future. The risks are that the cash flows may be less than expected, may be delayed, or may fluctuate in a manner that is otherwise undesirable.

Using standard present-value techniques, fundamental analysis would be based on the following general formula:

$$V_0 = \sum_{t=1}^{\infty} \frac{1}{N(t)} \sum_{s=1}^{N(t)} \frac{E(CF_{t,s})}{\prod_{i=1}^{t} (1 + r_{i,s} + \pi_{i,s})}$$

where:

> V_0 = the value of a common stock at time 0
>
> $E(CF_{t,s})$ = the cash flows (usually in the form of quarterly dividends) that are expected in the period t if state s occurs at that time
>
> $r_{i,s}$ = the "short rate," or single-period riskless interest rate, at time t if state s occurs at that time
>
> $\pi_{i,s}$ = the single-period risk premium that, when added to the short rate, gives the required rate of return on the security at time t in state s
>
> $N(t)$ = the total number of equally likely possible states during time period t

This formula is very similar to that used in previous chapters to value interest-sensitive cash flows. In words, it takes expected future cash flows, which are contingent on states of nature occurring at that time, discounts them by the interest rate and risk premia paths that are associated with those cash flows, averages the quotients across all states, and sums over all time periods. What a mouthful!

This formula is a bit much for most stock analysts. It calls for information that they are unlikely to have and for predictions that cannot be made with confidence. Put quite simply, this approach is overkill. Consequently, stock analysts make a number of simplifying assumptions.

One simplification is that dividends are usually assumed to be annual (as opposed to quarterly) cash flows. Thus, t denotes the number of periods in terms

---

Radcliffe, *Investment Concepts, Analysis, and Strategy,* 3rd ed. (Glenview, Ill.: Scott, Foresman and Company), 1990; and Jack Clark Francis, *Investments: Analysis and Management,* 5th ed. (New York: McGraw-Hill Book Company), 1991.

[3]We could have developed this analysis using the earnings of the firm rather than dividends. In this case, the cash flows are either paid to the owners or are reinvested in the firm in terms of retained earnings. Conceptually, these are similar approaches, but some have argued that they have different empirical implications. See Robert Shiller, "Do Stock Prices Move Too Much to Be Justified by Subsequent Changes in Dividends?" *American Economic Review,* June 1981.

Exhibit 14.5

Some assumed dividend growth patterns

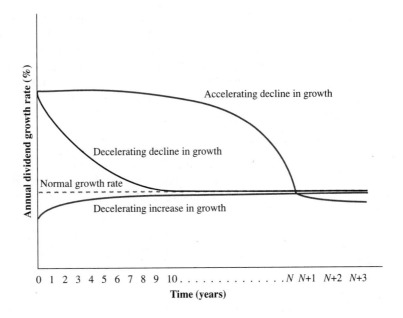

of years. Another simplification is that the potential cash flows across all future states during any given time period are simply averaged and lumped into a single number. As we saw in Chapter 7, this approach is attractive because it makes the analysis more tractable. However, it is also dangerous, because it does not take into account the interest sensitivity of cash flows in performing the valuation. The effect of this omission on estimated value can be quite large at times. In addition, many analysts do not attempt precise forecasts of future dividends, especially beyond the first five years; instead, they assume that dividends will follow a simple growth pattern. For instance, an analyst may assume a dividend growth path from among those portrayed in Exhibit 14.5. The kind of path selected would depend on the nature of the company and its past history. Note how all growth paths ultimately converge to a normal growth rate (or lower) after a number of years. If that were not the case, a single company would eventually grow to immense size and dominate much of the world economy! Alternatively, the analyst may use a single growth rate that represents some kind of average of the various growth rates over time, much like yield to maturity is an average (of sorts) of rates of interest.

The interest rates are typically simplified in two ways. First, in any one period, there is assumed to be only one possible interest rate, not a rate that varies across states of nature. This is tantamount to assuming that there is only one state in any given period. Second, analysts typically assume that a single interest rate will prevail across all time periods. As noted above, this also is a highly dubious assumption. But, when considered in light of the extremely uncertain cash flows, more than a single interest rate may be unwarranted precision.

Finally, instead of having a risk premium that varies across states and over time, a single risk premium is usually used. The risk premium can depend on one risk factor, for example, unexpected inflation; fluctuations in the stock market as a whole; or multiple risk factors; but it can be summarized by a single number.

After all of these simplifications are taken into account, the formula reduces to:

$$V_0 = \sum_{t=1}^{\infty} \frac{D_0 \prod_{n=1}^{t}(1 + g_n)}{(1 + k)^t}$$

where:

D_0 = the current annual dividend

g_n = the dividend growth rate during period n

k = the annual discount rate, or required rate of return on the particular security in question

This constant discount rate, k, is used in place of the fluctuating short rates plus their associated risk premiums in the general formula presented earlier.

Because the summation sign potentially goes to infinity for a corporation that may continue to exist indefinitely, this expression is often restated to capture the notion of an infinite series:

$$V_0 = \sum_{t=1}^{h} \frac{D_0 \prod_{n=1}^{t}(1 + g_n)}{(1 + k)^t} + \frac{\dfrac{D_{h+1}}{k - g}}{(1 + k)^h}$$

Here, beyond h years, dividend growth is assumed to be normal and smooth at g percent per year. The first expression values the first h dividends, growing at various rates, and the second expression values the remaining dividends, growing forever at the assumed constant rate. If dividend growth is assumed to be constant from the outset, the entire formula simplifies to:

$$V_0 = \frac{D_0(1 + g)}{k - g}$$

To be concrete about this formula, let us assume the following situation. A stock is currently paying a dividend of $10 per share, and this dividend is assumed to grow at a constant rate in the future of 5 percent per year. If the required rate of return on this stock is 12 percent, the value per share is:

$$V_0 = \frac{\$10(1 + .05)}{.12 - .05} = \$150$$

Riskiness of Equity Claims

Any number of things can change the value of equity claims. In the example above, returns may not grow at the assumed rate, interest rates may change, or dividend patterns may vary. All of these factors add risk to holding equity. This has led many to concentrate on ways both to measure and effectively reduce the riskiness of equity investment.

There are numerous ways of assessing the riskiness of equity, each of which has some validity. If only a single security is held by an investor, the risk can probably be captured by the potential variability in the present value of its stream of cash flow. This can be measured in various ways, as has been done in previous chapters. In general, the risk of a single security can be quite high.

However, if a portfolio of securities is held, the price fluctuations of individual securities tend to offset each other to some extent. This is known as the **diversification effect.** Thus, in a portfolio context, the riskiness of an individual security can be viewed as its contribution to the riskiness of the entire portfolio, net of the diversification effect.

While many measures of common stock risk have been developed, two are commonly used. The first is the **standard deviation of returns** of an individual security. This measures the variability of returns over a given period and is used as a measure of risk. It looks at the returns of an individual equity investment over time, computing its mean and variance. The square root of the investment's variance is the standard deviation of returns. For the computation of returns, the investor uses both dividends and price changes over each period. The rationale is that earnings will be partially paid in dividends this period and partially reinvested into further firm growth and future dividend payouts. Therefore, the correct return figure to measure both short-term returns and volatility of returns is the total rate of return, which includes not only current dividend payouts but also value changes in the underlying equity itself. However, this risk measure considers a security only in isolation.

Another measure of common stock risk is the **beta** of an individual security. The beta measures the tendency of a security's return to fluctuate relative to fluctuations in the stock market as a whole. Most often, beta is measured by regressing the total rates of return on individual securities against the total rates of return on the Standard & Poor's Index of 500 large stocks, or some other stock market index. The regression equation that determines a stock's beta takes the following form:

$$r_{it} = \alpha + \beta r_{Mt} + e_t$$

where:

> r_{it} = the rate of return for a particular stock over a period of time
> r_{Mt} = the rate of return for the chosen market index
> e_t = the error term in the regression

Such regressions use historical data and can be measured over any time interval. The regression would determine alpha and beta in the above equation.

The beta value indicates the relative movement of a particular stock with the overall stock market index considered. For example, a beta of 2.0 would mean that when the stock market rises x percent, the stock has a tendency to rise by twice as much, or $2 \times x$ percent. However, the stock may rise by more or less than that amount, depending on the specific circumstances facing the firm on a given day. This is the reason for e_t in the above equation. Because the specific circumstances do not affect all firms at once, they are therefore diversifiable. In other words, their effects tend to get canceled out in a portfolio of many diverse securities.

Notice that the beta measure is a two-sided concept. Thus, if the broad stock market index falls by y percent, the individual security with a beta of 2.0 would also tend to fall by $2 \times y$ percent.

Most stocks have betas somewhere between 0 and +3. An average stock would have a beta of 1.0, meaning that, on average, it fluctuates in the same direction as the market and by approximately the same amount, because the market as a whole is comprised of the individual stocks. Beta tends to explain a modest portion of the returns on stock—typically one-third or less. The remainder is referred to as "unsystematic, diversifiable, or idiosyncratic risk."[4]

Another, less commonly used, risk measure for equity securities is **stock duration.** The duration of stock is interpreted the same as it is for any financial instrument. It gives the relative fluctuation in stock value for a change in response to a movement in interest rates. Stock duration is measured by regressing percentage changes in stock prices against movements in interest rates. People who have measured the duration of the stock market as a whole have found it to be around 2.1. However, individual stocks have widely disparate durations. They range from −20 or less to +50 and even more. Unlike the duration measure for debt instruments, which often explains 80 percent or more of their price fluctuations, the duration measure for common stocks tends to explain only a small amount of the fluctuation in prices. For some stocks, it may account for as much as 40 percent, but for most stocks, it explains 10 percent or less of stock price fluctuations. The main reason for this disparity in the explanatory power of duration is that stock returns, unlike promised returns on fixed- and floating-rate debt instruments, are not contractually fixed or specified as a precise function of some index.

Equity Market Efficiency

Because of the large dollar volume of trading in equities and the considerable interest in equity value shown by institutional and individual investors, there is substantial interest in how well the equity market functions. This is generally couched as the question of **equity market efficiency.**

Efficiency can be looked at from several angles. One way to view efficiency is the speed with which transactions can be executed. Another is the professionalism evidenced by the brokers and market makers in providing services. The bid-ask spread, liquidity, and information dissemination are also elements of efficiency. Virtually every imaginable dimension of stock market efficiency has been thoroughly researched. (See Boxes 14.1 and 14.2.)

---

[4]Interested students should refer to the textbooks listed in the first footnote for more details on such things as estimation of betas from market data and its use in efficient portfolio construction. Further development here would take us too far afield.

Box 14.1

Niels Bohr's Ideas about Stock Market Efficiency

The author of quantum theory was a Danish physicist named Niels Bohr. During the early part of the twentieth century, Bohr developed insights into atomic structure and radiation and became the father of quantum mechanics. Not content to ponder only atoms, Bohr turned his brilliant mind to the stock exchange. Below, we quote a section from a volume of collected essays written in his honor.

> He considered a simplified case, that of people who deal only in reliable stocks and shares so that they are not subject to fraud, and confined himself to the short-term effects of buying and selling in a fluctuating market. A person who buys and sells completely at random is then equally likely to win or lose, if one neglects taxes and brokers' fees. Now there are people connected with a company who have advance information about how well the company is doing, and they are able to win money by using this information to control their own buying and selling. The question arises, From whom do they win it?

> They cannot win, on the average, from people who buy and sell at random. They can make their gains only from people who acquire limited knowledge, by studying business reports that are made public, and act according to that knowledge. Such people find, for example, a company that looks good and whose shares appear to be cheap with respect to its good prospects. They then buy those shares. But they are doing just the wrong thing. They ought to ask themselves why the shares are being sold cheap when the prospects appear good. The answer to this question is probably that there are people with advance information who know that the prospects are not as good as they seem, and who are therefore selling and depressing the price. The conclusion reached by Bohr was thus: the person who acts in accordance with limited knowledge will on the average do worse than the person who buys and sells at random.

Source: Paul A. M. Dirac, "The Versatility of Niels Bohr," in *Niels Bohr: His Life and Work as Seen by His Friends and Colleagues,* ed. Stefan Rozental (New York: Interscience, 1964), p. 307.

However, economists have tended to focus much of their research on one notion of market efficiency—the view that a market is efficient if the prices of securities reflect all available information and rapidly change to reflect new information. Although there are many stock markets and stock exchanges, most of the research considers the New York Stock Exchange (NYSE), which is the largest of the exchanges. The preponderance of evidence indicates that the NYSE is reasonably efficient. New information that is relevant to the value of a stock listed on that exchange, or the market as a whole, is rapidly and completely reflected in market prices. Indeed, this finding is so pervasive in the finance literature that when evidence of an inefficiency is uncovered, it usually makes the news and is documented in the academic literature. These inefficiencies are detected so rarely that they are referred to as **anomalies** and are usually transitory in nature. An example is the "equity premium puzzle" discussed in Box 14.2. Another is the "January effect," which documents the historically unusually large security returns for the month of January vis-à-vis returns in other months.[5] If the anomalies persisted after having been discovered, people could continually exploit them and

---

[5]See Robert Haugen and Philippe Jorion, "The January Effect: Still There after All These Years," *Financial Analysts Journal,* January/February 1996; and references contained therein.

Box 14.2

The Equity Premium Puzzle

Over the past decade, a perplexing puzzle regarding equity returns has been set forth. Dubbed the **equity premium puzzle,** it has challenged economists, using traditional financial models of investor and market behavior, to account for the high rates of return on equities relative to returns on fixed-income instruments.

The equity premium puzzle was first examined by Mehra and Prescott in a 1985 article published in the *Journal of Monetary Economics.*[*] The authors pointed out that during the 90-year period from 1889–1978, the average real rate of return on stocks was 6.18 percent higher than that on Treasury bills (or their early equivalents).[†] Mehra and Prescott contended that such a high equity premium is inconsistent with widely accepted financial models of asset pricing. The implications are twofold: (1) Either the stock market returns are unjustifiably high, the bill returns are too low, or both; or (2) The commonly used asset pricing models are wrong, or at a minimum, the parameters we typically use in these models are wrong.

This equity premium is of more than academic interest. Historical equity returns are often used by practitioners to form expectations of future returns and to anchor the discount rate applied to expected returns for stock valuations. For example, if current nominal yields on Treasury bills are 6 percent, an equity premium of 6.18 percent or so[‡] is added to it to get the expected rate of return on equities over the ensuing period.

Several attempts have been made to probe the robustness of the underlying data. Jeremy Siegel has reexamined the historical record, but over a longer time period.[§] He found that the 1889–1978 period

may not have been truly representative of the levels of return that have prevailed in the past and that can be expected to prevail in the future. Siegel compiled annual rates of return on stocks and Treasury bills (or their early equivalents) from 1802–1990. This period is almost 100 years longer than that upon which Mehra and Prescott based their conclusions. He found the equity premium to amount to only 1.90 percent over the 1802–1888 period and to 4.62 percent over the entire 1802–1990 span. The primary reason for this reduction in the observed equity premium is the higher real return on bills during the periods outside the period considered by Mehra and Prescott. While

---

[*]See Rajnish Mehra and Edward Prescott, "The Equity Premium: A Puzzle," *Journal of Monetary Economics,* March 1985.

[†]During that period, the annual real rate of return on equities was 6.98 percent, whereas it was only 0.80 percent on T-bills.

[‡]Actually, a premium higher than this would be added. This is because the equity premium needs to be restated in nominal terms. To convert the 6.18 percent into a nominal equity premium, we would have to know what average inflation rate prevailed over the historical period used for the measurement. If inflation averaged 5 percent, we would multiply the 6.18 percent by $(1 + .05)$ to get a 6.49 percent nominal equity premium for that period. In practice, this is not normally necessary. Returns are usually initially given in nominal terms, and real returns are then computed from the nominal returns and realized inflation rates.

[§]See Jeremy Siegel, "Stock and Bond Returns Since 1802: Will Equity Continue to Dominate?" *Journal of Monetary Economics,* 1992.

---

become exceedingly rich. But the exploitation of an inefficiency itself acts to restore equilibrium to stock prices, thereby removing the opportunity to exploit it.

The research on stock market efficiency is so voluminous that it could fill a small library.[6] This is undoubtedly due to the large number of people who would

---

[6]Some of the major studies include Eugene Fama, "Efficient Capital Markets: A Review of Theory and Empirical Work," *Journal of Finance,* June 1970; Eugene Fama, "Efficient Capital

this equity premium remains higher than is justified, the disparity is much lower.

A second approach taken is to examine the reliability of the historical average return spread as an indicator of the expected future equity premium. Using more advanced statistical techniques designed to uncover the basic return distribution, Cecchetti, Lam, and Mark found that an expected spread anywhere from 2.35 percent to 9.71 percent was consistent with the historical return distribution.[||] The lower end of this range is much closer to a theory-based equity premium than the historically observed average.

Several other approaches have been taken to reconcile the observed average equity premium with the predicted premium. Considered individually, they are incapable of accounting for the entire premium, but taken collectively, they may account for it. Rietz argued that if investors expected that large, sudden drops in consumption would be accompanied by a precipitous decline in stock dividends, as was experienced during the Great Depression from 1929 to 1933, investors would demand large equity premiums in order to entice them to invest in stocks. The reason for this premium is that equities serve as a poor vehicle to protect consumers against declines in consumption during hard economic times, because during these times, dividends and equity prices also typically decline.[#]

One tack taken is to recognize that, as we pointed out earlier, equities are leveraged claims on asset returns.[**] Because leverage tends to increase the riskiness of stock, an increased equity premium would be demanded by investors. However, when historically observed degrees of leverage are considered, there is insufficient risk to fully explain the historical equity premium.

Another line of research has been to generalize the asset pricing models so that they accommodate a more realistic formulation of economic circumstances and consumer behavior. The standard asset pricing models assume that all investors are identical in terms of wealth and attitude toward risk. The generalized models allow for differences in investor circumstances and attitudes toward risk, and they allow for the degree of risk aversion to vary with wealth or to depend on the consumption patterns of previous periods.

In sum, while we cannot say which explanation, if any, is closest to the truth, we can say that a reexamination of the statistical evidence, together with refinements in the asset pricing models, go a long way toward offering solutions to the equity premium puzzle.[††]

[||]Their data period extended from 1892 through 1988. This spread range represents the 95 percent confidence interval for the expected equity premium. See S. Cecchetti, P. Lam, and N. Mark, "The Equity Premium and the Risk-Free Rate: Matching the Moments," working paper, Department of Economics, Ohio State University, June 1991.

[#]See Thomas A. Rietz, "The Equity Risk Premium: A Solution," *Journal of Monetary Economics,* July 1988, and Rajnish Mehra and Edward C. Prescott, "The Equity Risk Premium: A Solution?" *Journal of Monetary Economics,* July 1988.

[**]See also Shmuel Kandel and Robert F. Stambaugh, "Expectations and Volatility of Consumption and Asset Returns," *Review of Financial Studies,* 1990.

[††]Some of the arguments are quite technical and beyond the scope of this text. However, for a useful summary article, see Andrew B. Abel, "The Equity Premium Puzzle," *Business Review,* Federal Reserve Bank of Philadelphia, September/October 1991.

---

like to make a sure profit and to the considerable academic interest in this theory. Virtually all of this research is subject to the caveat that an empirical test of stock market efficiency is really a joint test of the viability of a particular model of stock

---

Markets II," *Journal of Finance,* December 1991; Richard Roll, "R²," *Journal of Finance,* July 1988; and Eugene Fama and Kenneth French, "The Cross-Section of Expected Stock Returns," *Journal of Finance,* June 1992.

pricing (or equity returns) and the degree to which the market conforms to the model's predicted behavior. Thus, if the data reject the efficiency hypothesis, we really cannot ascertain whether it is because the model is inadequate or the market is inefficient. So many different models have been tried, however, that we may place some confidence in the efficiency of the market. While the degree of efficiency remains an open question, the informational efficiency of stock markets has been pretty well documented as an empirical reality.

Other aspects of market efficiency, therefore, have received more attention recently. These center on issues such as bid-ask spreads and liquidity measures. Under the title of market microstructure, there is increased interest in how markets function and how various aspects of the trading system affect prices, liquidity, and information value. While too new to report and summarize here, this area of micromarket investigation seems both fruitful and exciting to participants in this new research agenda.

Stock Ratings

Today, a number of companies provide investors with ratings of common stocks. These ratings are somewhat problematic, however, because stocks lack many of the characteristics of money market instruments and bonds that make them amenable to analysis. By definition, income from stocks is not secure. Stock prices are volatile even when interest rates are stable, and stock dividends are not fixed but subject to managerial discretion. Nonetheless, stock rating is a booming business in the investment community.

Ratings are available from individuals, firms, newsletters, and the standard rating agencies. Each has its own methodology, from the highly quantitative, objective formulaic approach to the more subjective, judgmental approach. The formulaic, quantitative approaches can be illustrated by a review of the procedures employed by the two major rating firms: Standard & Poor's Corporation and Value Line Investment Survey. While the procedures used by these two firms are somewhat unique, a review of their approaches to stock rating will give the reader some feel for the general methodology.

Standard & Poor's bases its ratings on a formula that is described in depth in its *Stock Guide*. The quality is assessed on the basis of only two factors—**earnings per share** (EPS) and **dividends per share.**

Earnings stability is a focus of the S&P analysis. They examine earnings over the previous eight years. For each year in which EPS are as great or greater than those for the preceding year, a basic score is given. If a decline in EPS takes place, the score is reduced. The eight scores are averaged, and the average becomes the basic earnings stability index.

Growth in earnings is also important. The growth index is computed by taking the average earnings over the most recent three years and comparing it to the average earnings over three base years (e.g., 1946–1949). The square root of the percentage by which earnings increased from the base period to the most recent period is then taken to create the growth index. This index is then multiplied by the stability index to get an index of their combined behavior. This combined index is compared to the general economy to see whether the company is doing better than, worse than, or as well as the economy as a whole.

The S&P ratings also consider dividends. The stability of dividends is checked over a 20-year period, with most recent years receiving greater weights in the index. A dividend growth factor is then created in a manner similar to that for earnings growth, and the dividend stability index and growth factor are multiplied together to get an overall measure of dividend strength.

Finally, the earnings and dividend indices are combined into a single numerical rating. The ratings of all stocks are divided into seven groups, ranging from highest to lowest.

A+	Excellent	B+	Average		
A	Good	B	Below average	C	Lowest
A−	Above average	B−	Low		

The astute reader will notice an element of "grade inflation" not dissimilar from that encountered in academia these days, where B+ is average and C is the lowest.

Because stock price is not considered, these stock ratings are not indicative of whether a particular stock is overpriced or underpriced, nor are they a prognosis of future expectations. Rather, they are simply measures of earnings and dividend performance in the past. Thus, they are no substitute for fundamental analysis.

Value Line Investment Survey, on the other hand, grades stocks from the point of view of an investor. Their ratings, based on an elaborate quantitative analysis that includes some subjective elements, indicate the relative performance of a given stock in comparison to other stocks in the same industry and to the market as a whole. (See Exhibit 14.6.) Some studies have shown that Value Line has a good track record in selecting securities that will outperform the market. Two questions remain. Will securities on Value Line's recommended list continue to exhibit such superior returns? Does the average investor receive the stock recommendations soon enough to be able to benefit from them?

The first question can be asked of any investment firm that makes recommendations. People in the firm change, systems of analysis change, and even if the people and systems do not change, the techniques and insights that were responsible for good forecasts in the past may no longer work in the future, as other analysts adopt similar methodologies. It's the old problem of the person in a movie theater who seeks to gain an unobstructed view of the screen by standing. If everyone in the theater adopts this behavior, the person is no longer at an advantage.

The second question is also important. If people know that Value Line has a good track record, when the recommendations come out, people will quickly bid up the price of the recommended shares. This very behavior helps to ensure the predicted price appreciation. Unless you are first or second in line, it is unlikely that you will be able to secure much benefit from following the recommendations.

EXHIBIT 14.6

Value Line report on Apple Computer

| APPLE COMPUTER OTC-AAPL | RECENT PRICE | 53 | P/E RATIO | 15.2 | (Trailing: 14.2 / Median: 18.0) | RELATIVE P/E RATIO | 1.03 | DIV'D YLD | 0.9% | VALUE LINE | 1082 |

| | High: | 18.0 | 17.3 | 17.4 | 31.6 | 17.2 | 15.6 | 21.9 | 59.8 | 47.8 | 50.4 | 47.8 | 73.3 | Target Price Range 1994 | 1995 | 1996 |
| TIMELINESS 3 Average (Relative Price Perform-ance Next 12 Mos.) | Low: | 11.0 | 6.8 | 5.4 | 8.6 | 10.9 | 7.1 | 10.9 | 20.1 | 35.5 | 32.5 | 24.3 | 40.3 | | | |

SAFETY 3 Average (Scale: 1 Highest to 5 Lowest)

BETA 1.25 (1.00 = Market)

1994-96 PROJECTIONS

	Price	Gain	Ann'l Total Return
High	95	(+80%)	16%
Low	65	(+25%)	7%

Insider Decisions

	D	J	F	M	A	M	J	J	A
to Buy	0	0	0	0	0	0	0	0	0
Options	0	1	0	0	0	3	0	2	0
to Sell	0	1	6	5	2	0	3	0	2

Institutional Decisions

	1Q'91	2Q'91	3Q'91
to Buy	125	156	147
to Sell	137	154	164
Hld's(000)	77237	86756	77566

| Percent shares traded | 30.0 20.0 10.0 |

Options: ASE

Shaded areas indicate recessions

9.0 x "Cash Flow" p sh

2-for-1 split

Relative Price Strength

1975	1976	1977	1978	1979	1980	1981	1982	1983	1984	1985	1986	1987	1988	1989	1990	1991	1992	©VALUE LINE PUB., INC.	94-96	
--	--	.02	.11	.55	1.21	3.03	5.10	8.30	12.51	15.51	15.18	21.10	33.16	41.85	48.18	52.80	61.55	Sales per sh A	89.75	
--	--	--	.01	.06	.14	.43	.68	.84	.80	.83	1.64	2.28	3.89	4.20	5.87	5.30	6.00	"Cash Flow" per sh	9.55	
--	--	--	.06	--	--	.35	.53	.64	.49	.50	1.20	1.65	3.08	3.16	3.77	3.74	4.15	Earnings per sh B	6.75	
--	--	--	--	--	--	--	--	--	--	--	--	.12	.32	.40	.45	.48	.55	Div'ds Dec'd per sh C	.75	
--	--	--	.01	.05	--	--	.23	.44	.33	.44	.53	.68	1.17	1.89	1.94	1.90	2.55	Cap'l Spending per sh	2.55	
--	--	.02	.11	.27	.27	1.60	2.25	3.19	3.84	4.45	5.54	6.63	8.17	11.77	12.54	14.00	15.95	Book Value per sh	25.15	
--	--	33.28	74.75	86.61	96.79	110.62	114.25	118.40	121.07	123.70	125.26	126.09	122.77	126.27	115.36	119.50	117.00	Common Shs Outst'g D	117.00	
--	--	--	--	--	--	24.3	16.1	30.6	26.7	22.1	11.6	20.3	13.6	12.9	10.5	12.9		Avg Ann'l P/E Ratio	12.0	
--	--	--	--	--	--	2.95	1.77	2.59	2.49	1.79	.79	1.36	1.13	.98	.77	.87		Relative P/E Ratio	1.00	
--	--	--	--	--	--	--	--	--	--	--	--	.4%	.8%	1.0%	1.1%	1.0%		Avg Ann'l Div'd Yield	.9%	

CAPITAL STRUCTURE as of 6/28/91

Total Debt $156.3 mill.

LT Debt None

Pension Liability No pension plan.

Pfd Stock None

Common Stock 117,959,416 shs. (100% of Cap'l) as of 8/2/91

334.8	583.1	982.8	1515.9	1918.3	1901.9	2661.1	4071.4	5284.0	5558.4	6308.9	7200	Sales ($mill)	10500	
22.3%	20.4%	15.5%	8.5%	9.9%	17.1%	16.5%	17.1%	14.4%	16.5%	7.5%	13.0%	Operating Margin	14.5%	
8.6	16.6	22.4	38.0	41.8	51.1	70.5	77.6	124.8	202.7	185	210	Depreciation ($mill) E	330	
39.4	61.3	76.7	59.2	61.2	154.0	217.5	400.3	406.0	474.9	448.7	490	Net Profit ($mill)	790	
48.5%	47.5%	47.5%	45.8%	49.0%	50.3%	47.0%	39.0%	39.0%	39.0%	38.0%	38.0%	Income Tax Rate	38.0%	
11.8%	10.5%	7.8%	3.9%	3.2%	8.1%	8.2%	9.8%	7.7%	8.5%	7.1%	6.8%	Net Profit Margin	7.5%	
156.8	231.3	340.2	432.4	526.7	712.4	828.7	955.9	1399.2	1376.2	1646.6	1660	Working Cap'l ($mill)	2500	
1.9	2.1	1.3	--	--	--	--	--	--	--	Nil	Nil	Long-Term Debt ($mill)	Nil	
177.4	257.1	377.9	464.6	550.5	694.1	835.5	1003.4	1485.8	1446.8	1766.7	1865	Net Worth ($mill)	2945	
22.2%	23.8%	20.3%	12.7%	11.1%	22.2%	26.0%	39.9%	27.3%	32.8%	25.4%	26.5%	% Earned Total Cap'l	27.0%	
22.2%	23.8%	20.3%	12.7%	11.1%	22.2%	26.0%	39.9%	27.3%	32.8%	25.4%	26.5%	% Earned Net Worth	27.0%	
22.2%	23.8%	20.3%	12.7%	11.1%	22.2%	24.2%	35.9%	23.9%	29.1%	22.0%	22.0%	% Retained to Comm Eq	24.0%	
--	--	--	--	--	--	7%	10%	12%	11%	13%	13%	% All Div'ds to Net Prof	11%	

CURRENT POSITION (($MILL))

	1989	1990	6/28/91
Cash Assets	809.0	997.1	889.7
Receivables	792.7	761.9	767.1
Inventory (FIFO)	475.4	355.5	733.3
Other	217.3	288.8	438.2
Current Assets	2294.4	2403.3	2828.3
Accts Payable	334.2	340.6	361.7
Debt Due	56.8	122.6	156.3
Other	504.2	563.9	768.8
Current Liab.	895.2	1027.1	1286.8

ANNUAL RATES

of change (per sh)	Past 10 Yrs.	Past 5 Yrs.	Est'd '88-'90 to '94-'96
Sales	NMF	27.5%	14.0%
"Cash Flow"	NMF	41.5%	12.5%
Earnings	NMF	44.0%	12.5%
Dividends	--	--	11.5%
Book Value	NMF	23.0%	12.5%

QUARTERLY SALES ($ mill.) A

Fiscal Year Ends	Dec.Per	Mar.Per	Jun.Per	Sep.Per	Full Fiscal Year
1988	1042	867	993	1169	4071
1989	1405	1247	1248	1384	5284
1990	1493	1346	1365	1354	5558
1991	1675	1598	1529	1507	6309
1992	1850	1750	1750	1850	7200

EARNINGS PER SHARE A B

Fiscal Year Ends	Dec.Per	Mar.Per	Jun.Per	Sep.Per	Full Fiscal Year
1988	.92	.61	.71	.84	3.08
1989	1.10	.44	.74	.88	3.16
1990	.96	1.04	.96	.81	3.77
1991	1.28	1.07	.72	.67	3.74
1992	1.10	1.00	1.05	1.00	4.15

QUARTERLY DIVIDENDS PAID C

Cal-endar	Mar.31	Jun.30	Sep.30	Dec.31	Full Year
1987	--	.06	.06	.08	.20
1988	.08	.08	.08	.10	.34
1989	.10	.10	.10	.11	.41
1990	.11	.11	.11	.12	.45
1991	.12	.12	.12		

BUSINESS: Apple Computer, Inc. is a major manufacturer of microprocessor-based personal computer systems. Micro-computers offered: Apple IIc, Apple IIGS, Apple IIe, and the Macintosh Family. Apple III discontinued in 1984, and the Lisa (Macintosh XL) in the summer of 1985. Apple also sells peripheral devices, operating systems and software. Manufacturing facilities are located in California, Ireland, and Singapore. Foreign sales: 41.7% of revenues. Research and Development: 8.6% of revenues. '90 depreciation rate: 24.0%. Has 14,530 employees, 32,750 stock-holders. Insiders own 9% of stock. Chief Executive Officer: John Sculley. Inc.: CA. Address: 10260 Bandley Drive, Cupertino, CA 95014. Telephone: 408-996-1010.

Apple ended fiscal 1991 on a sour note. (The year ended September 27th). The computer maker's decision to push lower-cost, less-profitable products in-creased unit sales dramatically, but took a toll on the bottom line since the company wasn't able to cut expenses fast enough to compensate for lower gross margins. Too, the stronger dollar trimmed profits as rev-enue from non-U.S. sources was translated back into dollars, helping to depress September-period share net below the year-ago level.

New products and cost-cutting efforts point to better results in fiscal '92, though. In October, Apple introduced two high-end Macintoshes, a more powerful version of its Classic Mac, and three long awaited entries in the fast-growing notebook field. Aid for Apple's hard-pressed margins will emerge as the year unfolds, thanks to a major restructuring effort that was initiated in fiscal '91. The company took a $224 million pre-tax charge (excluded from our earnings pres-entation) in the June period to cover the cost of reducing its 15,600 person work-force by about 10%, to consolidate facilities, and to move manufacturing to lower-cost regions. Most of these efforts won't pay off in a major way until the sec-ond half of the year; but, in all, we think share net will top $4.00 in fiscal '92.

Apple appears poised to post good an-nual share-earnings gains during the 3 to 5 years ahead. We expect to see a continued flow of products that should keep the company competitive in the per-sonal computing field, and the Macintosh user interface still has an ease-of-use edge over IBM-compatible competitors. Too, a pact to cooperate with IBM may well prove to be a boon. At the least, the tie should ease Apple's entree into the corporate world, since the first outgrowth of the deal will be tools to integrate Macintoshes into the IBM environment. However, the major impact of the deal won't be felt until the mid-Nineties, when a new operating sys-tem that will bridge the Apple, IBM, and UNIX worlds and new Macintoshes, utiliz-ing powerful new processors, are sched-uled to emerge from the alliance. Until then, these neutrally ranked, volatile shares will be average performers.

George A. Niemond   November 1, 1991

(A) Fiscal year ends last Friday in September. (B) Primary earnings. Excludes nonrecurring gains: '84, 8¢; '89, 37¢; loss: '91, $1.16. Next earnings report due mid-Jan.

(C) Next dividend meeting about Jan. 31. Next ex-date about Nov. 15. Approximate dividend payment dates: March 15, June 15, Sept. 15, Dec. 15.

(D) In millions, adjusted for stock split. (E) Depreciation on accelerated basis.

Company's Financial Strength	A++
Stock's Price Stability	30
Price Growth Persistence	60
Earnings Predictability	60

Source: Reprinted with permission, Value Line Investment Survey, New York, NY.

The results show the inevitable truth. While ratings schemes may be of value and may provide some information, they are not a panacea. Investment requires hard-core analysis, or random equity investment will result in random returns. In fact, unless you are willing to invest time as well as money you are likely to be last, rather than first, into a good investment idea. This has led many away from the market and many more into the open arms of professional money managers. These institutions provide investment management, diversification, and efficiencies of execution that many investors cannot obtain on their own. It is for this reason, among others, that their numbers and dollars under management have grown so rapidly over the last decade. (See Box 14.3.) More will be said about these firms, their products, and their financial management in the next section of this book.

Types of Equity Ownership

Thus far, we have discussed equity as if it were a single financial asset type. We have assumed that it was interchangeable with the words stock, ownership, and equityholder. In reality, there are at least two main types of equity ownership prevalent in the market: **common stock** and **preferred stock.** While others exist and these themselves are sometimes broken into classes, understanding these two generic types goes a long way toward understanding the equity market's institutional detail.

Common Stock

"Common stock is the first security of a corporation to be issued and, in the event of bankruptcy, the last to be retired. It represents an ownership share in the firm; it has the lowest-priority claim on earnings and assets of all securities issued."[7] Purchasers of common stock have the power to vote for a board of directors and to vote on major issues that may be presented before the shareholders. The more shares an investor has, the more votes he or she controls. An investor in common stock receives certificates of ownership similar to that in Exhibit 14.7. The certificate states the number of shares and a **par value** per share, if any. The par value often bears little relationship to market prices. For example, the par value of the Belmac Corporation is 2, whereas the stock was trading for approximately $5 per share in early 1991 and $22 a few months later. (Unfortunately, the holder of the **stock certificate** shown in Exhibit 14.7 sold her shares for $5 early in 1991, on the advice of a broker!)

Some stocks pay dividends, but not all. Companies in the early growth stages typically pay low or no dividends; rather, they retain as much earnings as possible to finance rapid growth. As companies become more established, they may pay a

---

[7]See Jack Clark Francis, *Investments: Analysis and Management,* 5th ed. (New York: McGraw Hill, 1991), p. 50.

Box 14.3

The Record of Index Funds versus Actively Managed Funds

Given the difficulty that professional investment managers have in selecting securities that will consistently outperform market averages, hordes of investors have been flocking in recent years toward investing in equities through "index funds." These are funds whose investment strategy is designed solely to match some broad-based index of securities returns. A popular index fund, offered by a number of mutual fund groups, is the Standard & Poor's 500 fund, or a close relative thereof. The following is an excerpt from the annual report of a company offering such a fund.

The chart below shows the percentage of general equity mutual funds outpaced by the Standard & Poor's 500 Index in each of the past 25 years . . .

Overall, the message is this: the Index rarely outperformed fewer than 30% of the equity funds and often outperforms more than 70%. To put a finer point on it, this summary presents the differences:

Percentage of Stock Funds Outpaced by the Standard & Poor's 500 Index	Number of Years
Less than 30%	2
30% to 49%	8
50% to 70%	5
More than 70%	10

Percent of General Equity Funds Outperformed by S&P 500 Index

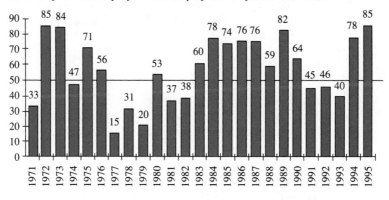

high percentage of profits as dividends. The amount of dividends paid is at the discretion of the board of directors but may be constrained by certain **covenants** that are designed to protect other claimants' interests.

Preferred Stock

Preferred stock, like common stock, is a form of equity ownership. As such, the holders of preferred shares receive dividends, not interest. If the corporation fails to pay dividends, the owners of preferred shares have little, if any, legal recourse. Moreover, preferred shareholders are not considered creditors in the event of bankruptcy.

In short, the secret of long-term performance success is: (1) not being very bad very often; (2) accepting the fact that most years will be in the average range; and (3) frequently being very good. Clearly, 1995 was an outstanding example of this final factor.

Both the chart and the summary table illustrate the inherent strength of the indexing concept. Nonetheless, I would emphasize, especially after the superlative 1995 return of the Standard & Poor's 500 Index relative to most equity funds, that there will be future years when sub-average returns *will* (not "may") occur. When such years occur, please don't be concerned. Indexing is not designed to be a year-to-year phenomenon, but a rational and productive long-range strategy.

Lest there be any mystery about the "secret" of indexing, the basis of its success is straightforward. It assumes that: (1) all investors (including professional managers as a group) will provide the same aggregate *gross* return as the stock market as a whole (say, +10% per year); and (2) that the *net* returns actually received by investors will equal their gross returns less any sales charges, advisory fees, other operating expenses, and portfolio turnover costs. That's really all there is to it.

Since the annual expense ratio for the average equity fund is 1.3% and its average transaction cost is "guesstimated" at 0.7%, such a fund would incur total annual costs of 2.0%. In a +10% market, then, its net return would be +8%. A Standard & Poor's 500 Index Fund pays no advisory fees, incurs only minimal operating expenses, and incurs very small transaction costs (because its portfolio is not actively managed, and is altered only as the stocks in the Index change).

The record of our 500 Portfolio in recent years suggests that these total costs can be held to about 0.2% (90% below those of the average fund), providing a net return to shareholders of 9.8% in a +10% market. One additional factor in our performance advantage results from our minimal cash reserves position, as compared to roughly 8% of assets invested in cash reserves for the typical stock fund. In a strong bull market, such as this past year, any cash holdings erode returns.

As the old saw goes "the proof of the pudding is in the eating." Over the past decade, the 500 Portfolio of Vanguard Index Trust has outpaced the average general equity fund by 2.0% per year, remarkably close, to say the least, to the 1.8% theoretical advantage described above. (Even this example materially *overstates* the record of the average equity fund, since it ignores fund sales charges where applicable, and Federal capital gains taxes, which, because of the higher turnover in an actively managed stock fund, are usually substantial.)

Source: The Vanguard Group. Reprinted by permission.

Preferred stock features a fixed-rate dividend or, in some cases, a floating-rate dividend, over an infinite life. Accordingly, preferred shareholders do not share in the profitability of a firm beyond the stated dividend rate. If a firm fails to make a scheduled dividend payment, the preferred shareholders usually are protected by **cumulative provisions,** which ensure that when the payment of dividends is resumed, they will receive current and omitted dividends before common shareholders receive any dividend.

It is rather curious that this class of equity shares would be called "preferred" since holders of preferred shares do not usually participate in the sizable upside earnings potential of the corporate issuer. However, they are superior in two areas:

EXHIBIT 14.7

Stock certificate

1. Although they have no *right* to receive dividends, if a corporation does allocate earnings to declared dividends, preferred shareholders must receive dividends at the stated rate before any dividends are paid to common shareholders.

2. In the event of forced liquidation, preferred shareholders have a claim on remaining assets up to the stated par value that has priority over that accorded to common shareholders.

Most preferred stock carries a par value. This par value is significant in three respects. Unlike the par value of common stock, which amounts to little more than an accounting entry, the par value of a preferred offering is equal or close to the initial amount received by the corporate issuer. Second, the dividend rate is linked to a par value. For example, a 13 percent preferred stock with a par value of $100 would pay a $3.25 quarterly dividend. Third, the par value represents the amount of the preferred shareholders' claim to funds in excess of those necessary to satisfy creditors.

EXHIBIT 14.8   Comparison of Preferred Shares to Common Stocks and Bonds

	Common	*Preferred*	*Bonds*
Cannot force firm into bankruptcy for failure to pay dividends	X	X	
Provides dividends	X	X	
Permanent source of financing, with no maturity date	X	X*	†
Dividends are partially tax-exempt to corporate investors‡	X	X	
Have a par value	X	X	X
No participation in firm profits beyond stated dividend or contractual interest		X	X
No voting rights		X§	X
May be convertible		X	X
May have a sinking fund		X	X
May have a call feature at par or a slight premium above par value		X	X
Cumulative dividend provision		X	
Provides interest			X
Payments by issuer are tax-deductible expense			X

*In rare cases, a preferred stock has a maturity date.

†Debt has a stated maturity with two exceptions: perpetual annuities (consol bonds) and perpetual floaters, a floating-rate debt instrument issued by some international banks.

‡The Tax Reform Act of 1986 left 80 percent of dividends tax-exempt to corporate holders.

§Some convertible preferred issues allow for voting rights if dividends are skipped.

Preferred stock has no maturity, but it often has a **sinking fund provision,** similar to that of many debenture issues, where shares are retired at par or at a slight premium above par. Other issues come with call features. Some are convertible into a prespecified number of common shares. As with convertible bonds, the convertibility feature increases in value as the common share price appreciates. Convertible preferred shares usually carry no voting rights unless the corporation fails to pay dividends.

In Exhibit 14.8, we have summarized the characteristics of preferred shares and contrasted them to common shares and bonds. It is evident in glancing at Exhibit 14.8 that preferred stock is, in many ways, a hybrid security with characteristics of both common stock and bonds. We would expect, therefore, that the market behavior of preferred share prices and their rates of return would be couched between the market behaviors of common stock and bonds. Our expectation is supported by the weight of empirical evidence.

In an early study by Bildersee,[8] evidence was presented that for high-quality preferred issues, preferred stock returns behave much like government bond

---

[8]See John S. Bildersee, "Risk and Return on Preferred Stocks," Ph.D. dissertation, University of Chicago, 1971.

EXHIBIT 14.9 **Preferred Stock Index Return Regressions with Bond and Common Stock Index Returns**

Preferred Stock Index	Bond Index			Common Stock Index		
	α	β	R^2	α	β	R^2
High grade	−.013	1.692	.393	−.139	.051	.017
Medium grade	.021	.842	.123	−.113	.190	.294
Speculative grade	.128	.231	.008	−.257	.228	.368

returns, yet for low-quality issues, these returns behave more like common stock returns. This finding is summarized in Exhibit 14.9. The exhibit presents results from regression analysis, where monthly holding-period rates of returns on preferred stock, the dependent variable, are compared to those of common stock and bonds over a 10-year period.[9]

The sample of preferred stocks was divided into three groups, depending on the Moody's quality rating. Three preferred stock indices were then formed—one for high-grade, one for medium-grade, and another for speculative-grade issues. Each of these indices was regressed against the returns on an index of government bonds and then against the returns on an equally weighted NYSE common stock index. The correlation coefficients are virtually mirror images of each other. High-grade preferred stock returns were 39.3 percent "explained" (in terms of R-square) by returns on government bonds but only 1.7 percent explained by returns on the common stock index. On the other hand, speculative-grade preferred stock returns were less than 1 percent explained by government bond returns, yet they were 36.8 percent explained by common stock returns. Medium-grade preferred stock returns were related to both bond returns and stock returns.

This same table can be used to extract rough estimates of the relative durations and betas of preferred stocks. Naturally, both estimates depend on the grade of preferred stocks under consideration. The beta estimates on the bond index return regressions provide measures of relative duration. High-grade preferred stocks exhibit durations roughly 1.7 times higher than the average bond in the government bond index. Medium-grade preferred stocks have durations slightly lower than those in the bond index, and speculative-grade preferred issues have durations less than one-fourth as long as the bonds. It is obvious from the low R-squares that these duration measures do not explain most of the returns on preferred stocks. However, we can surmise that interest rate changes impact

---

[9]The monthly holding-period rates of return include dividend and/or interest payments as well as any price appreciation or depreciation during the month. In the regressions, excess monthly returns were used for each variable. Excess returns are the monthly-holding-period rates of return after first subtracting the Treasury bill monthly yields for each period. They are termed "excess returns" because they are in excess of those available on riskless Treasury bills.

high-grade preferred issues much more than they impact speculative-grade issues, as the durations of the latter are only one-sixth the level of the former and the coefficients of determination are much lower on the speculative-grade issues.

The relative fluctuations of preferred stock returns with changes in common stock returns are given by the beta estimates on the stock index return regressions. All preferred issues in this data sample exhibit low betas, but the speculative-grade preferreds have much higher betas than the high-grade issues. While a typical common stock would exhibit a beta of around 1.00, the speculative-grade preferreds exhibit an average beta of around .23. The lower the grade of the preferred index, the more like common stock it behaves.

Blurred Distinctions between Debt and Equity

Thus far, we have discussed debt instruments (Chapters 11, 12, and 13) and two types of equity instruments—common and preferred stock. We noted that preferred stock shared several of the attributes of debt instruments as well as some of the attributes of common stock. The shared attributes were found both in legal/contractual parallels and in similar market price and returns behavior. While preferred stock is legally classified as a form of equity, due primarily to the nonbinding obligation of the issuer to pay dividends, its classification is less clear from a financial market point of view.

There are more than one hundred other types of securities issued by corporations whose characteristics and market behavior tend to blur the traditional distinctions between debt and equity.[10] Many of these were introduced during the past 15 years. Some were designed specifically to elicit favorable tax or regulatory treatment; others were designed to reallocate risk among the financiers of a firm.[11]

This proliferation of securities is making it difficult for regulatory/legal and tax authorities to keep pace. In some cases, we cannot be certain whether a particular security will be treated by the authorities as debt or equity. The market price behavior may also reflect this uncertainty, because regulatory and tax treatment may impact the economics (i.e., cash flows, risk) of the security.

Whatever tax and regulatory distinctions have traditionally developed between these two types of financial assets, it is worth pointing out that each is a bit like the other type of instrument. With the proliferation of variations of each type, the distinction has become even more ambiguous from both the investor's and the

---

[10]John Finnerty discusses 68 new types of securities and examines primary factors responsible for their introduction. See "Financial Engineering in Corporate Finance: An Overview," *Financial Management* 17, 1988.

[11]Optimal capital structure (that is, the proportion of debt versus equity in funding a firm) and security design are topics treated at length in the field of corporate finance. An excellent overview of these topics is given in Franklin Allen, "The Changing Nature of Debt and Equity: A Financial Perspective," in *Are Distinctions between Debt and Equity Disappearing?* Conference Series no. 33, Federal Reserve Bank of Boston, October 1989.

Exhibit 14.10

Earnings streams and funding claims

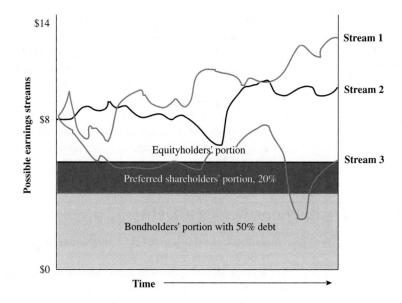

firm's point of view. This may be seen from both a financial perspective and a legal one.

A Financial Perspective

A strict financial perspective holds that "every corporate debt security is part equity if there is any chance at all of default; it is equivalent to a weighted average of a default-risk-free debt and a pure equity claim on the firm's assets. The more debt the firm issues, holding assets, earnings, and future opportunities constant, the greater the equity content. Thus, 'How much should the firm borrow?' is the same as asking how much implicit equity lenders should be induced to hold. When [one] asks, 'Are the distinctions between equity and debt disappearing?' finance theory answers, 'Of course. Riskier debt is more like equity.'"[12]

To see why this is the case, let us examine Exhibit 14.10. This exhibit is similar to Exhibit 14.4, except for two modifications. First, rather than a single, regular path of earnings over time, we have introduced three, more random paths representing possible earnings streams. Obviously, many other paths are possible. The drawing here is merely meant to be indicative of the randomness that a business firm may encounter in its earnings. Second, we have divided the equity category into both common and preferred stock to recognize the firm's option to use both in corporate finances.

---

[12]See Stewart C. Myers, "Still Searching for Optimal Capital Structure," in *Are Distinctions between Debt and Equity Disappearing?* Conference Series no. 33, Federal Reserve Bank of Boston, October 1989.

Exhibit 14.11

Dividing up the firm's cash flow: financial engineering

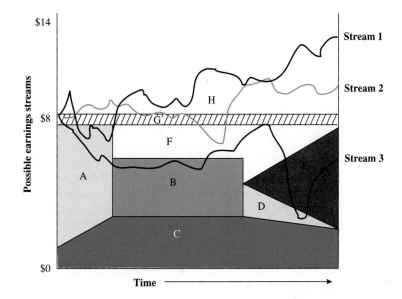

Several features of this exhibit are noteworthy. Income streams 1 and 2 are similar to the case portrayed in the earlier example. Debtholders, and in this case, preferred stockholders as well, are paid, and the residual earnings go to the common stockholders. However, unlike our previous example, income stream 3 is inadequate during several of the time periods to allow for full payment of preferred shareholder dividends. In addition, earnings are inadequate to make interest payments on debt during certain of the latter periods.[13] Thus, if the earnings of the firm followed the path traced by stream 3, in the cases of preferred stock and bonds, the earnings to investors may depend on the earnings on the firm's assets, thereby imparting an equity-like element to the instruments. In can also be shown that even when a firm approaches insolvency, as well as when it actually becomes insolvent, the bonds behave increasingly like equity securities.

However, this is only part of the story. As mentioned earlier, there are literally more than a hundred "hybrid" securities that occupy the spaces between pure equities and straight bonds. **Financial engineers** have created these by dividing up the asset returns in creative ways. In Exhibit 14.11, we have shown some hypothetical, rather arbitrary ways of dividing the cash flows. They can be divided vertically (time priority), horizontally (earnings priority), and diagonally. Security A looks somewhat like a first tranche of a mortgage-backed security. Security C is a type of default-free bond, at least when considered against the three illustrative

---

[13]We are assuming here, as we have assumed implicitly in prior diagrams, that all earnings are distributed each year to the claimants. If enough of the earnings are retained by the corporation, rather than paying out all excess earnings as dividends, there may be sufficient cash to pay preferred dividends during those deficit periods and to service debt in the latter periods.

earnings streams. However, the interest payments are not constant over the life of the bond. Security E would be difficult to value because the expected cash flows do not occur until far into the future. Security D is similar to Security E, but it is more secure because it has a priority to firm earnings and its cash flows are weighted a bit more toward the earlier years. Securities G and H are preferred and common stock, respectively. Note that given the income streams shown, all of these securities, except C, are subject to the possibility of default or payment delays. Thus, they all have both upside and downside potential, similar to an equity.

There are numerous other varieties of securities possible and currently available. They have bizarre names at times, reflecting the complex nature of their payoff commitments. Here are just a couple. ARPSs are **adjustable-rate preferred stocks.** PIK Preferreds are **pay-in-kind preferred stocks** that pay early dividends in the form of additional preferred shares. We could go on and on, but this chapter is just about done, so you will have to use your imagination. Perhaps you, too, will be a financial engineer!

A Legal Perspective

"Historically, the law has distinguished sharply between debt and equity, and between the duties a corporation owes to its stockholders and those it owes to holders of its debt securities and its other creditors. Over the past several years, changes in the business world, particularly the increase in leveraged buyouts and the use of nontraditional forms of securities, have put a strain on the traditional legal analysis."[14]

For the solvent corporation, the duties of management to shareholders is **fiduciary** in nature. That is, management is given very broad and general mandates to operate the business of the corporation responsibly and with appropriate regard to the interests of the stockholders. Management can exercise considerable discretion in following a course of action that it deems to be in the best interests of shareholders, a course that balances short-term with long-term interests.[15]

For a solvent corporation, the duties of management to creditors are primarily contractual in nature. They are specific and narrow in scope, and they are spelled out in detail in the **indenture agreement** (the list of terms) under which the credit is extended. Specific remedies are also set forth in the indenture to redress any breaches of its contractual provisions. Restrictions on the payment of dividends to shareholders and the repurchase of stock must also be adhered to strictly. Other

---

[14]Charles P. Normandin, "The Changing Nature of Debt and Equity: A Legal Perspective," in *Are Distinctions between Debt and Equity Disappearing?* Conference Series no. 33, Federal Reserve Bank of Boston, October 1989, p. 49.

[15]*Paramount Communications Inc. v. Time Inc.,* Civ. Action Nos. 10866, 10670, 10935 (consolidated) (Del. Ch. July 14, 1989)(1989 Del. Ch. LEXIS 77). "The corporation law does not operate on the theory that directors, in exercising their powers to manage the firm, are obligated to follow the wishes of a majority of shareholders. In fact, directors not shareholders are charged with the duty to manage the firm" (p. 34).

than these indenture conditions, management is not thought to have any fiduciary responsibilities toward creditors of going concerns.

When a corporation becomes insolvent, management owes fiduciary duties to creditors as well as to stockholders. The law requires that decisions must be made with due regard for the interests of all concerned. A problem may arise, however, because management's prior loyalties to the interests of shareholders may be difficult to redirect. Moreover, a corporation's directors continue to be elected by shareholders. If it becomes apparent that management is not properly executing its fiduciary duties to creditors, they may seek to have a court-appointed trustee designated in place of management.

Even if management seeks to exercise its fiduciary duties in a balanced way toward all creditors and shareholders during a period of insolvency, difficulties may arise. This is because it is difficult to determine the rights and relative standing of the various classes of creditors and shareholders. Even if these could be determined, how the rights and relative standing should be reflected in any plan of reorganization is subject to debate. This is particularly troublesome because a reorganization plan must be accepted by each impaired class of claimants. A vote is conducted, and for the plan to be accepted, a two-thirds majority in each class must vote in favor of the plan. A dissatisfied group may cause the plan to be scuttled (although the court may overrule it) and result in the firm's liquidation. Because the going concern value is usually far higher than the liquidation value, a liquidation would generally result in less total value to be distributed, so other claimants may be forced to make concessions to the dissatisfied group to keep the reorganization plan alive.

Many of the securities recently created share both the upside and downside risks of equities to a greater extent than do traditional debt instruments. The intricacies of the rights, priorities, and entitlements of some of the new financial securities have only begun to be examined by the courts. Debt created to fund corporate acquisitions is in the most precarious of positions. A bankruptcy court may be inclined to treat acquisition debt as a capital contribution, particularly in leveraged buyouts, basing their judgment on the notion that debt levels exceeded certain prudent norms. Even if this controversial view is accepted, the next area to resolve is how management will reallocate voting rights in the reorganization of such an insolvent company. Can debtholders be described as equity for distribution purposes and as debt for decision-making purposes? The answer is yes! Suffice it to say that these legal decisions and the subsequent legal debate are ongoing.

Summary

This chapter has introduced the concept of equity. As all other corporate securities, equity is a type of claim on corporate assets and their returns. We briefly demonstrated the process of equity valua-tion and the risk factors involved. As this is such a large area of academic and practitioner investiga-tion, this presentation has been only cursory in nature. Nonetheless, the techniques of valuation that have been applied to other financial assets are of considerable value here as well.

We then illustrated the distinction between the two most prevalent forms of equity: preferred and common. Several other instruments that have some

equity features were also discussed. Finally, we broached the subject of the blurring distinction between debt and equity. While we have reached the end of the chapter, we have only touched upon the beginnings of this vast field of inquiry.

Key Concepts

Review Questions

1. A firm that you are valuing will have a total life span of three years. During any one year, any of three possible states can occur. The associated probabilities are 60 percent, 30 percent, and 10 percent, respectively. Assume that the interest rate is constant at 6 percent in all states and at all times. The risk premium for each state in every period is 1 percent, 2 percent, and 3 percent, respectively. The cash flows begin at $10, $7, and $2 for each respective state in year one. Thereafter, each flow increases by 20 percent annually. If there are no expenses, what is the value of the firm?

2. Using the simplifying valuation assumptions, value a firm with the following information: the initial annual dividend is $3; the growth rate begins at 18 percent and declines 2 percent per year until 10 percent is reached, after which point it is constant; and the annual discount rate is 12 percent.

3. If the cash flows in the general formula for stock valuation are constant (zero growth),

what restrictions would have to be put on the other parameters in order for the formula to simplify to the constant dividend growth formula?

4. A company starts out with an initial annual dividend of $15. The next year's dividend will grow an additional 15 percent. The growth rate will decline by 10 percent annually (i.e., the next year's growth rate is 15% × 0.9 = 13.5%) for five years; thereafter it will remain constant. Using the simplifying assumptions and an annual discount rate of 9.5 percent, what is the value of the firm?

5. Occasionally, you see a company whose preferred stock is selling at a lower current interest rate than its bonds. Since preferred stock payments are subordinated to those of bonds, how could this be?

6. Professor Merton Miller of the University of Chicago received the Nobel prize in economics in 1992, in part based upon his work on corporate valuation. Central to this work is a

concept known as the Modigliani-Miller theorem, which indicates that under certain conditions, firm value is independent of the firm's debt-to-equity ratio. Discuss the relevance of this theorem to the cobbler example illustrated in Exhibit 14.4.

7. The same Professor Miller from Question 6 also analyzed the effect of taxation on corporate capital structure. How does the existence of the double taxation of equity (on firm earnings and on dividend payments, which are not deductible from earnings for tax purposes) affect the value of the firm that uses debt financing?

References

Abel, Andrew B. "The Equity Premium Puzzle." *Business Review.* Federal Reserve Bank of Philadelphia, September/October 1991.

Allen, H. F. "The Changing Nature of Debt and Equity: A Financial Perspective." In *Are Distinctions Between Debt and Equity Disappearing?* Conference Series no. 33, Federal Reserve Bank of Boston, October 1989.

Bildersee, John S. "Risk and Return on Preferred Stocks." Ph.D. dissertation, University of Chicago, 1971.

Brown, Stephen J.; William N. Goetzmann; and Stephen A. Ross. "Survival." *Journal of Finance,* July 1995.

Cutler, David M.; James M. Poterba; and Lawrence H. Summers. "What Moves Stock Prices?" *Journal of Portfolio Management,* Spring 1989.

Fama, Eugene F. "Efficient Capital Markets: A Review of Theory and Empirical Work." *Journal of Finance,* June 1970.

———. "Efficient Capital Markets: II." *Journal of Finance,* December 1991.

Fama, Eugene F., and Kenneth R. French. "The Cross-Section of Expected Stock Returns." *Journal of Finance,* June 1992.

Finnerty, John. "Financial Engineering in Corporate Finance: An Overview." *Financial Management,* 1988.

Francis, Jack Clark. *Investments: Analysis and Management.* 5th ed. New York: McGraw Hill, 1991.

French, Kenneth R.; William Schwert; and Robert Stambaugh. "Expected Stock Returns and Volatility." *Journal of Financial Economics,* September 1987.

Haugen, Robert A., and Philippe Jorion. "The January Effect: Still There after All These Years." *Financial Analysts Journal,* January/February 1996.

Kandel, Schmuel, and Robert Stambaugh. "Expectations and Volatility of Consumption and Asset Returns." *Review of Financial Studies,* 1990.

Kim, Wi Saeng; Jae Won Lee; and Jack Clark Francis. "Investment Performance of Common Stocks in Relation to Insider Ownership." *Financial Review,* February 1988.

Lintner, John. "The Valuation of Risk Assets and Selection of Risky Investments in Stock Portfolios and Capital Budgets." *Review of Economics and Statistics,* February 1965.

Lorie, James H., and Mary T. Hamilton. *The Stock Market: Theories and Evidence.* Homewood, Ill.: Dow Jones-Irwin, 1973.

Markowitz, Harry. "Portfolio Selection." *Journal of Finance,* March 1952.

Mehra, R., and E. Prescott. "The Equity Premium: A Puzzle." *Journal of Monetary Economics,* March 1985.

Mossin, Jan. "Equilibrium in a Capital Asset Market." *Econometrica,* October 1966.

Myers, Stewart C. "Still Searching for Optimal Capital Structure." In *Are Distinctions between Debt and Equity Disappearing?* Conference Series no. 33, Federal Reserve Bank of Boston, October 1989.

Normandin, C. P. "The Changing Nature of Debt and Equity: A Legal Perspective." In *Are Distinctions Between Debt and Equity Disappearing?* Conference Series no. 33, Federal Reserve Bank of Boston, October 1989.

Rietz, T. A. "The Equity Risk Premium: A Solution." *Journal of Monetary Economics,* July 1988.

Roll, Richard. "R². " *Journal of Finance,* July 1988.

Roll, Richard, and Stephen A. Ross. "On the Cross-Sectional Relation between Expected Returns and Betas." *Journal of Finance,* March 1994.

Shiller, Robert. "Do Stock Prices Move Too Much to Be Justified by Subsequent Dividends?" *American Economic Review,* June 1981.

Sharpe, William F. "Capital Asset Prices: A Theory of Market Equilibrium under Conditions of Risk." *Journal of Finance,* September 1964.

Siegel, Jeremy J. "Stock and Bond Returns Since 1802: Will Equity Continue to Dominate?" *Journal of Monetary Economics,* 1992.

Talman, Ellis W. "Financial Asset Pricing Theory: A Review of Recent Developments." *Economic Review.* Federal Reserve Bank of Atlanta, November/December 1989.

Chapter 15

Understanding Futures and Options

The last decade has seen a growth in markets in which futures and options are actively traded. These instruments have proved to be an important part of the financial menu for both hedging and risk-taking activity. This chapter reviews futures and options contracts, their use by institutions, and the factors that determine their value. It also provides an overview of the technicalities that frequently cause volatility in the marketplace—delivery dates and contract expiration times.

The financial assets discussed in the previous four chapters are all available for immediate delivery. Buyers enter the market for various money market instruments, bonds, mortgage debt, or equity with the understanding that a purchase will result in an immediate transaction. With the exception of a few days of settlement time to complete the transaction, necessitated by mail delays, international date lines, and administrative details, purchase of one of these assets results in ownership transfer at the time of trade. Over the last two decades, a second kind of market for financial claims has become increasingly important and diverse. In these markets, investors enter into financial contracts that involve implications for future real or financial market activity.

The first of these markets is the **futures market,** wherein future financial claims are actively traded. Here, investors may purchase financial assets that represent claims to real assets, such as gasoline, pork bellies, or corn, as well as other financial assets, such as Treasury bills or bonds, that will be delivered at some future date. The purchase of a futures contract involves a firm commitment to purchase something else at some future delivery date. The details of this market are rather complicated, and the mechanisms of trade are exacting, but as shall be explained, the futures market has greatly expanded investor opportunities to assume or transfer risk.

The second of these markets is the **options market,** wherein investors purchase the right to buy or sell an asset sometime in the future at a prespecified price. The contract to buy is referred to as a **call;** the contract to sell is referred to as a **put.** In either case, the options market provides investors with the ability to transact for real or financial assets, but it does not require them to exercise that option. This ability has also greatly enhanced investor opportunities, whether they are interested in speculation or in hedging the risk inherent in their underlying business activity.

No review of the financial markets would be complete without a discussion of the futures and options markets. These markets are complements for each other, and they are especially valuable for investors who wish to alter the risk associated with their activities. Whereas stock, bonds, mortgages, and money market instruments all involve the exchange of property rights, futures and options allow one to shift the risk associated with these property rights. Complete understanding of the financial markets is not possible without an appreciation of this new, burgeoning set of markets. As an introduction to these complex markets, we present an analogy; we then proceed to a more detailed discussion of the uses of futures and options and of the methods used to determine their values.

Games of Chance versus Futures and Options

Suppose you were offered the chance to play in either of two games of chance. In game A, we toss a coin into the air 10 times. Each time it lands on heads, we owe you $100. Each time it lands on tails, you owe us $100. The coin is balanced, and we flip the coin randomly. At the end of the game, the score is tallied and accounts are settled. You could win or lose as much as $1,000. Most likely, your winnings or losses will be less than those extreme results. In fact, on average, you will break even.

In game B, the rules are similar except that each time the coin lands on heads, you earn $100, whereas each time it lands on tails, you owe nothing. At the end of the game, your earnings could be as high as $1,000, but in no case will they be less than zero. In essence, heads you win, but tails you don't lose!

If there were an "entrance fee" for playing each game, which game would command the higher fee? If you are like most people, other things equal, game B would be your choice. Indeed, many people would be willing to pay only a very low entrance fee, or none at all, to play game A. Remember, you have an equal chance of both winning and losing money. Indeed, some risk-averse people might even require that they be paid in order to agree to play the game!

These simple games have two important distinguishing elements that make them useful analogues of futures and options. First, purchasers of futures receive two sides—an upside and a downside—to their potential profits (as in game A), whereas options purchasers receive only the upside potential (as in game B). Second, because of the absence of protection against losses, futures contracts are cheaper than options; indeed, they are often virtually costless (as was the entrance fee for game A).

Let us now add a few more elements to this game analogy. These additions will provide us with a better understanding of the contracts we will be describing shortly. Suppose, in our games, that we continue tossing the coin for many days. In game A (the futures analogue), we toss the coin many times each business day and continue to do so for three months. However, in no case can the net number of heads or tails in any single day exceed 10. If a net result of 10 is reached before the end of the day, the coin tossing ceases for that day. Rather than waiting until the end of the three-month period to tally the score and settling accounts, we tally the tosses each day and make payments to you or receive payments due from you on a daily basis. If you are unable to settle accounts on a given day, you are "bounced" and your participation in the game is abruptly halted.

In game B (the options analogue), we conduct a random number of tosses each business day for three months. There is no daily limit to the net number of heads or tails. However, the score is only tallied at the end of the three-month period. The account is settled at that time by tallying the total number of heads and tails. If the number of heads exceeds the number of tails, you win an amount based upon this difference. If the number of tails exceeds the number of heads, you neither receive nor owe anything. In this case, you pay nothing more than the entrance fee you were charged at the outset. Therefore, you receive an amount ranging anywhere from nothing to a very large sum of money at the end of the period.

By introducing these additional elements to our games, we have more closely approximated other important features of futures and options contracts. First, the time element of our two games is now more similar to that of futures and options, which may extend over several months. This time dimension has an impact on the value of the game to a potential participant. In the case of game B, there are two effects. The greater number of coin tosses over many days has the potential at least of generating very large positive payoffs to the players. This should increase the amount of money that a player would be willing to pay to participate in the game. On the other hand, since the payoffs, whether large or small, occur only after the passage of several months, the present value of the payoffs will be reduced below that which would prevail if all of the coin tosses were to be completed within a single day. At the same time, the entrance fee could have been invested and earned interest. These two effects of time influence the value of options contracts.

With game A, the effects of time are similar. While a longer period allows for a greater number of coin tosses, and a commensurate increase in potential gains or losses from playing the game, it also means that the present value of any gains or losses will be less. The same can be said about the effects of time on the value of futures contracts.

A second element to our games that has its analogue in traded futures and options contracts is the number of tosses. With futures, prices may increase or decrease, but only within a limited daily range. In game A, the upper and lower limits are implied by the ceiling on the net heads or tails that may result each day. In game B, an indefinitely large number of tosses is possible on any given day. With options, the size of price increases or decreases within a single day is not limited.

The scoring procedure of our games also has its counterpart in futures and options. In game A, the score is tallied daily and accounts settled on a daily basis. This is similar to the practice with futures. If the purchaser of a futures contract refuses or is unable to make settlement on a given day, the futures contract is closed out and the purchaser can no longer participate in the market. On the other hand, with options, accounts are settled only at the end, and an options purchaser is not at risk of being "bounced" from the marketplace.

One final element will be added to our games: an unbalanced coin. Suppose now that heads and tails are not equally likely. If all participants are aware of the bias of the coin, the entrance fee will reflect the coin's unusual nature. For example, if the imbalance is in your favor and both you and your counterparty know the degree of bias, you will be charged a compensative, higher entrance fee. You would willingly pay this premium given the favorable circumstances.

Futures and options prices often incorporate a premium similar to that which would occur in a game with an unbalanced coin. Market participants are often aware of and agreed about the tendency of certain prices to drift over time in a particular direction and at a particular speed. These tendencies are taken into account in the pricing of futures and options.

It should be noted that both in game A and game B, there are two players: a buyer (who pays the entrance fee) and a seller (who collects the entrance fee). While our example has consistently taken the viewpoint of the buyer, the seller is equally important and must absorb the risks of a random coin toss. In game A, it is the seller who must pay potentially large sums of money if the coin lands on heads a disproportionate number of times. However, the seller gains if the coin usually lands on tails. In game B, the seller again loses potentially large sums of money if heads predominates, but he gains nothing, apart from the entrance fee, if tails dominates the outcome. Obviously, the seller can only be induced to play game B if the nonrefundable entrance fee he receives is substantial. The analogy again carries through to sellers of futures and options. Their payoffs are opposite of those garnered by buyers of these instruments.

The Use of Futures and Options

By using the example of a game of chance, we unfortunately may have given the impression through analogy that futures and options are little more than risky gambles. This is not correct. Gambles are used to create new risks. Futures and options, on the other hand, are designed to transfer existing commercial risks among the parties to such contracts.

Nonetheless, the potential for risk taking in these markets cannot be denied. Investors who wish to **speculate** on the future course of interest rates, gasoline prices, or stock values can enter these markets for potential gain. Given the nature of the markets, a risk-taking participant can gain or lose vast sums of money through the leverage and risk inherent in positions taken here.

On the other hand, many other participants in the options and futures markets use these instruments to reduce their exposure to risk. Consider a farmer who will be harvesting thousands of bushels of wheat. He does not know at what price he will be able to sell the wheat when it is finally harvested. The farmer does know, however, that if the ultimate price is below his cost of producing the wheat, say $2.40 per bushel, he will lose money. Suppose the farmer sees that the futures price for the harvest month is currently set at $2.80. He could lock in a profit of $0.40 per bushel by entering into a futures contract to sell wheat at $2.80 per bushel.

A home builder may also be able to reduce risk by locking in interest rates. He may build homes efficiently, but if mortgage rates increase dramatically, he may be unable to sell the homes without discounting their prices. With higher interest rates and concomitant higher monthly payments, potential home owners may not be able to qualify for a loan at his original asking price. The builder could **hedge** against this risk by purchasing a futures contract involving a mortgage instrument. If mortgage rates increased, he would be able to purchase mortgage instruments at a discount in the marketplace and turn around and sell them at the contract price, making a profit equal to the difference in prices. This profit would allow him to sell the homes at a discount without an economic disadvantage.

Options have similar hedging uses but allow the purchaser even more flexibility. For example, the wheat farmer could purchase a put option that would allow him to sell the wheat at $2.80 per bushel if he wanted to do so. However, if the price of wheat at the time of harvest is actually above that figure, he would let the option expire unexercised and reap the higher rewards from the spot market. On the other hand, if the price of wheat at the time of harvest is lower than $2.80, he could exercise his right to sell wheat at $2.80 and lock in the profit of 40¢ per bushel. His profit, however, would be reduced by the amount he spent for the option.

The builder could also hedge his risk using an option rather than a futures contract. If interest rates fell sharply, the demand for home ownership would increase and home prices would rise. The builder could then sell his homes at a profit and, because he purchased an option rather than a futures contract, not exercise the mortgage option. While his profit from the home sale would be reduced by the cost of the option, it could be higher than it would have been if a futures contract had been purchased. On the other hand, if higher mortgage rates materialized because of inflation fears or an increase in real interest rates, the option could be exercised to recoup the losses from the slower home sales or discounted home prices.

Consider next an investor with a large portfolio of stock. Assume she is attracted to stock because of its upside potential, but she worries that the market might turn against her. She could protect her position by purchasing a put option on each of the stocks in her portfolio or by purchasing a put on the entire portfolio or something similar to it, such as the S&P 500 index. This would enable her to retain many of the benefits of a rising market, while avoiding the problems of a declining market.

In each of these examples, the principle to keep in mind is that futures and options can be used as hedges to offset a risky position. In the case of the farmer, it was an uncertain sales price for his produce; for the builder, it was an uncertain future mortgage rate; in the case of the stock investor, it was an uncertain future value of her portfolio.

As is the case in most of the financial markets, these instruments can be used for either speculation or hedging, depending upon the objectives of the investor. The examples above also indicate the complex nature of these transactions and the need to fully understand the potential effects of various investment alternatives. To aid in that understanding, the details of the contracts will be given in the following section.

Forward and Futures Contracts

When two parties agree to exchange a real or financial asset on a prearranged date in the future for a prespecified price, the agreement is known as a **forward contract.** Forward contracts are private agreements between two parties and are not negotiable instruments. The terms of the contracts are highly customized to the specific needs of the parties to the contract. The forward market operates through informal communication networks, and major participants include large financial institutions.

As an example, consider a forward foreign exchange contract. Suppose that a corporation owes a Swiss company 1 million Swiss francs, payable in three months, and seeks a forward rate agreement from its bank in order to avoid any exposure to a fluctuating exchange rate. This agreement by its bank is to sell 1 million Swiss francs (SF) to a corporate customer in three months at a fixed exchange rate of 1.24865 SF per U.S. dollar. Upon the passage of three months, the corporation must supply the bank with $800,865 million (= SF 1 million ÷ 1.24865 SF/$), and in return, it will receive 1 million Swiss francs.

A **futures contract** is similar to this forward contract. However, there are some important differences. The contract is a negotiable instrument, it trades on organized exchanges called futures markets, and it carries standardized terms, amounts, and maturity dates. While this standardization removes the flexibility characteristic of informal forward contracting, it does result in liquidity that forward contracts lack. Because these contracts trade in a centralized market, buyers and sellers can trade through brokers without personally searching for trading partners. Another important difference is that, unlike forward contracts, buyers or sellers of futures contracts who incur losses are subject to settlement procedures, wherein they must pay the **counterparty** each day an amount equal to their daily losses. Finally, futures contracts enjoy the benefit of having a clearing corporation that stands between the parties to the contracts to guarantee their performance of the contractual provisions.

Futures price quotations are given in several financial newspapers. *The Wall Street Journal* carries information on many of the futures contracts that are popular among U.S. investors. Exhibit 15.1 shows how futures are grouped into four broad categories: agricultural, foreign currencies, metals and petroleum, and financial

Exhibit 15.1   Registered Futures Contracts on Futures Exchanges Covered in *The Wall Street Journal*
(as of October 17, 1994)

Contract	Exchange	Contract Size	
AGRICULTURAL			
Grains and Oilseeds			
Barley	WPG	20	metric tons
Canola	WPG	20	metric tons
Corn	CBT	5,000	bu.
Corn	MCE	1,000	bu.
Flaxseed	WPG	20	metric tons
Oats	CBT	5,000	bu.
Oats	MCE	1,000	bu.
Soybeans	CBT	5,000	bu.
Soybeans	MCE	1,000	bu.
Soybean meal	CBT	100	tons
Soybean meal	MCE	20	tons
Soybean oil	CBT	60,000	lbs.
Wheat	CBT	5,000	bu.
Wheat	KCBT	5,000	bu.
Wheat	MCE	1,000	bu.
Wheat	MPLS	5,000	bu.
Wheat	WPG	20	metric tons
White wheat	MPLS	5,000	bu.
Livestock and Meat			
Feeder cattle	CME	50,000	lbs.
Hogs	CME	40,000	lbs.
Hogs	MCE	20,000	lbs.
Live cattle	CME	40,000	lbs.
Live cattle	MCE	20,000	lbs.
Pork bellies	CME	40,000	lbs.
Food and Fiber			
Cocoa	CSCE	10	metric tons
Coffee	CSCE	37,500	lbs.
Cotton	CTN	50,000	lbs.
Domestic sugar	CSCE	112,000	lbs.
Orange juice	CTN	15,000	lbs.
Rough rice	CRCE	2,000	cwt.
World sugar	CSCE	112,000	lbs.
Wood			
Lumber	CME	160,000	board ft.
FOREIGN CURRENCIES			
Australian dollar	CME	100,000	$A
British pound	CME	62,500	£
British pound	MCE	12,500	£

EXHIBIT 15.1 *(continued)*

Contract	Exchange	Contract Size	
Canadian dollar	CME	100,000	C$
Deutschemark	CME	125,000	DM
Deutschemark	MCE	62,500	DM
Deutschemark forward	CME	250,000	DM
Deutschemark—Fr. franc crossrate	FINEX	500,000	DM
Deutschemark—Jap. yen crossrate	FINEX	125,000	DM
Deutschemark rolling spot	CME	250,000	$
French franc	CME	500,000	FFr
Japanese yen	CME	12,500,000	¥
Japanese yen	MCE	6,250,000	¥
Sterling—mark crossrate	FINEX	125,000	£
Swiss franc	CME	125,000	SF
U.S. Dollar Index	FINEX	$500	x Index
METALS AND ENERGY			
Brent crude	IPE	1,000	net bbls.
Copper	CMX	25,000	lbs.
Crude oil	NYMEX	1,000	bbls.
Diammonium phosphate	CBT	100	ton
Gold—1 kilo	CBT	32.15	troy ozs.
Gold	CMX	100	troy ozs.
Gold—NY	MCE	33.2	fine troy ozs.
Heating oil—no. 2	NYMEX	42,000	gals.
Gas oil	IPE	100	metric tons
Gasoline—unleaded regular	NYMEX	42,000	gals.
Natural gas	NYMEX	10,000	MMBtu
Palladium	NYMEX	100	troy ozs.
Platinum	NYMEX	50	troy ozs.
Platinum	MCE	25	troy ozs.
Propane	NYMEX	42,000	gals.
Silver	CBT	1,000	troy ozs.
Silver	CBT	5,000	troy ozs.
Silver	CMX	5,000	troy ozs.
Silver	MCE	1,000	troy ozs.
FINANCIAL FUTURES			
Stock Indices			
All Ordinary Share Price Index	STE	A$25	x Index
CAC-40 Stock Index	MATIF	FFr 200	x Index
EuroTop 100 Index	CMX	$100	x Index
FT-SE 100 Index	LIFFE	25£	x Index
GSCI	CME	$250	x Index
KR-CRB Index	NYFE	$500	x Index
Major Market Index	CBT	$500	x Index
Mini Value Line Index	KCBT	$100	x Index

Exhibit 15.1 *(continued)*

Contract	Exchange	Contract Size	
New York Stock Exchange Index	NYFE	$500	x Index
Nikkei 255	CME	$5	x Index
Russell 2000 Index	CME	$500	x Index
S&P 500 Index	CME	$500	x Index
S&P Midcap 400	CME	$500	x Index
Toronto 35 Index	TFE	$500	x Index
Value Line Index	KCBT	$500	x Index
Interest Rates			
Canadian bankers' acceptance	ME	1,000,000	C$
Canadian gov't bonds	CBT	100,000	C$
10-year Canadian gov't bonds	ME	100,000	C$
3-year Commonwealth T-bonds	SFE	100,000	A$
Eurodollar	CME	1,000,000	$
Eurodollar	MCE	500,000	$
3-month Eurolira	LIFFE	1,000,000	Itl
Euromark	LIFFE	1,000,000	DM
Euromark	CME	1,000,000	DM
Euroswiss	LIFFE	1,000,000	SF
10-year French gov't bonds	MATIF	500,000	FFr
German government bond	LIFFE	250,000	marks
Italian gov't bond	LIFFE	200,000,000	Itl
LIBOR—1 mo.	IMM	$3,000,000	
Long Gilt	LIFFE	50,000	£
Sterling	LIFFE	500,000	£
Treasury bills	CME	$1,000,000	
30-Day interest rate	CBT	$5,000,000	
10-year T-notes	MCE	$50,000	
Treasury bonds	CBT	$100,000	
Treasury bonds	MCE	$50,000	
Treasury notes—2-yr.	CBT	$200,000	
Treasury notes—5-yr.	CBT	$100,000	

Exchange symbols:

Chicago Board of Trade (CBT)	London Int'l Financial Futures Exchange (LIFFE)
Chicago Mercantile Exchange (CME)	Marche A Terme International De France (MATIF)
Chicago Rice and Cotton Exchange (CRCE)	MidAmerica Commodity Exchange (MCE)
Coffee, Sugar and Cocoa Exchange (CCSE)	Minneapolis Grain Exchange (MPLS)
Commodity Exchange (CMX)	New York Cotton Exchange (CTN)
Financial Instruments Exchange (FINEX)	New York Futures Exchange (NYFE)
International Monetary Market (IMM)	New York Mercantile Exchange (NYMEX)
International Petroleum Exchange (IPE)	Sydney Futures Exchange (SFE)
Kansas City Board of Trade (KCBT)	Toronto Futures Exchange (TFE)
London Futures and Options Exchange (FOX)	Winnipeg Commodity Exchange (WPG)

futures. In recent years, the financial futures (and within that grouping, interest rate futures) have been the most popular. The exhibit also shows on which futures exchanges the contracts are traded, as well as the standardized contract size and unit of measure.

In Exhibit 15.2, we have reproduced a portion of a page from a *Wall Street Journal* dated Monday, October 17, 1994, that contains price quotations for the previous business day. Along the top of each column are various headings: the day's **opening price,** its high and low price for the day, its **settlement price** for the day, and the change in settlement price from the previous day's settlement price. These prices are established by a committee of clearinghouse officials that meet each day; the price is usually an average of prices that have prevailed over the last few trades of the day. Also reported are the lifetime high and low prices, which represent the extreme trading prices observed since the inception of the contract. Finally, the total number of contracts outstanding at the end of the day is reported as **open interest.** Because each contract outstanding has a buyer and a seller, open interest is calculated by taking both positions and counting them as one contract.

Let us examine a particular contract—unleaded gasoline—in more detail. The contract names, **trading locations,** and **contract sizes** are shown in boldface type across the beginning row for each contract type. The unleaded gasoline contract is traded on the New York Mercantile Exchange (NYM), and the contract calls for delivery of 42,000 gallons of unleaded regular gasoline. Contracts are available for settlement during each of the ensuing nine months. This is in contrast to the more limited choices for many agricultural commodities (e.g., wheat, barley, and oats), which are grouped around the normal harvest months. **Settlement dates** within a given month are established for each commodity differently, but the most common ones are the third Friday of the month and the business day prior to the last business day of the month.

The fifth column shows the settlement prices stipulated at the end of each trading day. Note that these settlement prices are not the same as the price of the final trade, which is typically reported as the "closing price" in other markets; rather, settlement prices are established by the committee of clearinghouse officials previously mentioned. Most of the settlement prices are around 55¢ per gallon. They tend to get higher as vacation season approaches in the late spring and then drop again as the autumn approaches. This contrasts with the heating oil contract (shown directly above the gasoline contract), which shows the highest prices in December, January, and February, when demand is highest. At the same time that wholesale gasoline prices on this futures market were hovering around 55¢ per gallon, unleaded gasoline was selling at the retail pump for close to double that price.[1] Most,

---

[1] Perhaps if you purchased gasoline in increments of 42,000 gallon lots, you would also get a price break. To store 42,000 gallons of gasoline would fill the basement of the average three-bedroom home approximately 6 feet high. While this may save you some expenses on gasoline, the increase in your homeowners insurance rates would probably more than offset your savings on the gasoline. Moreover, it would take you (if you drive an average amount and achieve 18 miles per gallon efficiency) approximately 63 years to consume that much gasoline!

Exhibit 15.2

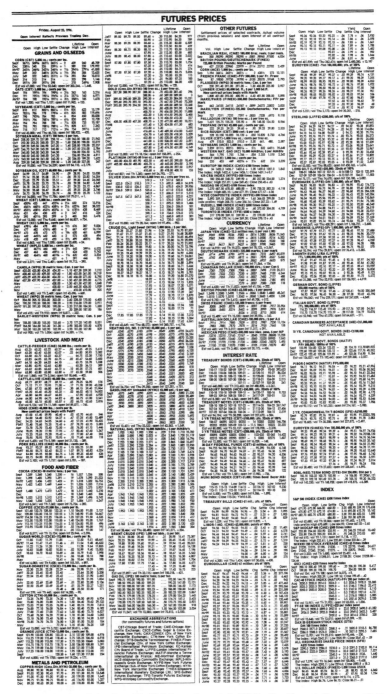

but not all, of the settlement prices fall between the high and low prices for the day. For an inactive contract, the settlement price may be outside these bounds because it is established as an average of several recent trading prices, and the trading prices may have been taken from other days. This happens to be the case for the March gasoline contracts. All of the settlement prices have declined by approximately 1¢ per gallon since the previously set settlement prices, as evidenced by the negative signs preceding the "change" figures. A 1¢ drop per gallon translates into a reduction in the value of a 42,000 gallon futures contract of $420.

The open interest numbers shown in the last column portray a general declining pattern as the period of the contract lengthens. More trading is usually done in the shorter-term contracts. Indeed, a typical pattern is for open interest also to decline in the month of expiration, as almost all futures traders (approximately 98 percent of them) prefer not to take delivery of the commodity but to "close out" or cancel their position by taking an offsetting futures contract. This sort of pattern is more evident where futures contracts settle in the current month (November 1994 in this case). See, for example, the cattle and hog futures.

Finally, at the bottom of each contract grouping, there are estimates of the **volume of trading** that occurred during that day and during the day preceding it. These volume numbers can be compared with the total open interest for all contracts in that commodity grouping. The open interest figure is followed by a number that gives the change in total open interest over the previous day. In the case of gasoline futures, there were 73,598 open interest, which represented a net increase of 2,253 from the previous trading day's level of open interest. This increase occurred in spite of the fact that there was an estimated volume of 26,048 gasoline contracts that day. Apparently, most of the contracts traded were existing contracts, which would not affect open interest; also, there were more new contracts opened out than old ones closed that day, resulting in the net increase in open interest.

Let's examine briefly a contract from the financial futures category. Consider the March 1995 Treasury bond contract listed on the Chicago Board of Trade (CBT). The settlement price is quoted as 98–22. That means that the contract settled that day for 98 and 22/32nds of par. The decimal equivalent of this value is 98.6875 percent of par. With a par value of $100,000 per contract, the cash price would be $98,687.50. The column to the right of this settlement price shows that the contract gained +8, or 8/32 from the previous day. That translates to $250 per contract (= 8/32 × .01 × $100,000). The minimum price fluctuation allowed is 1/32 of one full percentage point of face value, or $31.25. The normal maximum daily price swings allowed are three full points, or $3,000 per contract, although this limit can expand during periods of high volatility.

For a Treasury bond futures contract, a wide variety of bonds can be delivered to satisfy the contract at any given time. However, the bonds must have at least 15 years remaining until maturity or until their first permissible call date. Obviously, sellers of these contracts would be inclined to deliver the cheapest qualifying bond to satisfy their obligations. Therefore, to eliminate the incentive to deliver just one type of bond, which could cause a supply shortage and distort prices (as everyone on the short side of the contract would have the incentive to acquire and deliver the same bond, pushing its price upward), the CBT provides conversion factors that make it attractive to deliver several bonds in fulfillment of the contract.

There are numerous arcane regulations involving financial futures that will not be discussed here.[2] We will just caution the reader that "the devil is in the details," and a lot of money can be lost by the trader who does not pay careful attention to these details.

Valuation of Forward and Futures Contracts

Apart from a nominal fee paid to execute the transaction for a futures contract, forward and futures contracts are nearly costless. The forward and futures settlement prices are set so that no current cash outlay is required, except (in some cases) for a deposit to ensure performance of the contractual obligations. Accordingly, when we speak of valuation of forward and futures contracts, we are actually referring to the value of the cash or commodity flows embedded in the forward or futures contract.

Let us return to our example of the three-month Swiss franc forward rate of 1.24865 SF per U.S. dollar. How did the bank decide upon the forward rate at which to offer the Swiss franc to its corporate client? Most banks do not simply select a forward rate that reflects their expectations and then bet on it by offering it to their customers. Banks are far too risk averse to engage in such speculative behavior. Instead, they figure out what it would cost them to obtain these Swiss francs in the market today, through a set of transactions (described in Chapter 10) that deliver this amount of currency in three months. In essence, the bank will compute the implied market cost to **synthesize** a forward rate using today's current, or "spot," exchange rate along with the interest rates for both currencies in question. In finance, an instrument can be "synthesized" if it is possible to create identical net cash flows at stipulated points in time using alternative financial instruments. This approach is used throughout the markets for futures, options, and other derivatives that are developed in Chapter 16, and it is therefore essential to developing an understanding of the value of all forms of complex financial instruments.

In our forward exchange rate example, the facts at the time of the forward agreement were as follows:

Spot exchange rate: 1.26101 SF/$.

Three-month borrowing rate, in U.S. dollars: 8 percent simple interest, or 2 percent for 3 months.

Three-month investing rate, in Swiss francs: 4 percent simple interest, or 1 percent for 3 months.

---

[2]Two excellent sources of greater detail on these contracts are Chance, Don, *An Introduction to Options and Futures* (Philadelphia: Dryden Press, 1990); and Kolb, Robert, *Understanding Futures Markets,* 3rd ed. (Miami, Fla.: Kolb Publishing Company, 1991).

That is sufficient information for the bank to synthesize a forward rate of 1.24865 SF/$.

To synthesize a forward exchange rate, the bank would replicate the cash flow characteristics of a forward contract by using available spot market instruments. Because a foreign currency forward contract involves no immediate cash flow but only a deferred transfer of one currency for another, the bank will undertake transactions that involve no immediate net cash flow. The process involves two steps. Here is how they would do it.

Step 1: Determine the appropriate forward exchange rate, F.

This is computed by taking the spot exchange rate, S, and multiplying it by the ratio of the sums of 1 plus the interest rates of the respective countries:

$$F = S\ \frac{1 + r_{SF}}{1 + r_{US\$}}$$

$$1.24865 = 1.26101 \times \frac{1 + .01}{1 + .02}$$

Step 2: Synthesize the forward rate for the desired amount of Swiss francs by borrowing dollars today, converting them into Swiss francs today, and investing them for three months at the appropriate Swiss franc interest rate.

Through this process, the bank will have secured an appropriate amount of deliverable Swiss francs, and it can use the money collected from the corporate client to repay the dollar loan. Because the amount borrowed today will equal the amount invested today, there will be no immediate net cash flow to the bank.

To perform Step 2, the bank would work backwards. First, it would take the 1 million Swiss francs due to be delivered in three months and determine their present value in Swiss francs by discounting the amount due by the investment rate applicable for Swiss francs. In this case, there would be 1 percent earnings over the three-month period. Thus, the present value (*PV*) is:

$$PV = \frac{\text{SF } 1,000,000}{1 + .01} = \text{SF } 990,099$$

This amount of Swiss francs is equivalent to $785,163 (= SF 990,099 ÷ 1.26101 SF/$) at the applicable exchange rate. Next, the bank would borrow dollars in the amount of $785,163 for three months at 8 percent per annum simple interest. These borrowed funds would be converted immediately into 990,099 Swiss francs and invested at 4 percent per annum simple interest, until they are needed three months later. At that time, the invested sum would have accumulated principal and interest to total 1 million Swiss francs, precisely the amount desired by the corporate client. The three-month loan of $785,163 incurred by the bank would be repaid, with interest, at the end of the loan period. The amount due would be $800,866 (= $785,163 × 1.02), which is within a dollar of what the bank will be receiving from the corporate client. The discrepancy is due to rounding error and, customarily, would be resolved in the bank's favor.

The importance of these borrowing, exchange conversion, and investing transactions on the part of the bank lies in the fact that the bank knows exactly what the market price should be for the forward contract. If it conducts these transactions, it will not be exposed to any risk of fluctuation in the exchange rates. Through its actions, the bank has effectively synthesized a forward rate that will eliminate its risk. Similarly, by undertaking a forward transaction, the corporate client has eliminated its exposure to a fluctuation in exchange rates because it has locked in a current cost for the future delivery of the 1 million Swiss francs that it will need for the liquidation of an account.

You may be asking under your breath, "If it is so easy to synthesize a forward exchange rate, why doesn't the corporate client do so itself instead of going through the bank intermediary?" The answer is that, in fact, many corporate clients do synthesize forward exchange rates. Others prefer to work through banks because they may lack the bank's easy access to international markets, and their borrowing rate may be more expensive than that available to the bank.

One thing should be apparent in this example of producing a forward exchange rate. At no time was there any explicit consideration as to what the future spot exchange rate would ultimately be. Expectations did not enter the transaction in any direct way. Moreover, if other banks were offering and buying at a forward rate that was greater than the one derived through our synthetic approach, a profit opportunity would emerge. A bank could synthesize a forward rate at which it could purchase Swiss francs and then turn around and sell them at the higher forward rate to the other banks, making a nice profit in return for its astuteness.

This procedure is used throughout the forward and futures markets not only for foreign exchange but also for domestic financial transactions and commodity commitments. To illustrate its use in a domestic financial market context, Box 15.1 shows how forward rates of interest can be "locked in" through a pair of spot market bond transactions. Again, there is no immediate net cash flow. However, unlike the synthetic forward exchange rate transactions, this pair of transactions does create net cash flows—one positive and the other negative—on two different dates, a year apart, in the future.

In markets other than those for foreign exchange, the futures market plays a more vital role than the forward market. How are futures settlement prices determined? The answer must be that the same approach used for forward prices can also be used to derive appropriate futures prices. This is because if futures prices are set at a level that diverges too far from what traders or other economic entities could manufacture or synthesize on their own, there will be an arbitrage opportunity that will be difficult to resist. As people take advantage of the arbitrage opportunity, their actions will drive the synthetic and quoted futures settlement prices toward each other.

So how does one go about manufacturing or synthesizing a future settlement price for a commodity? Take the case of gold. Suppose that you are in possession of 100 ounces of pure gold, which you would like to sell as quickly as possible. If you were to sell it today, you could get, say, $400 per ounce, or $40,000. A buyer comes along and wishes to buy your gold in three months. What price would you

Box 15.1

Locking in Forward Rates of Interest

Imagine that you are in a situation where you will receive $1,000,000 one year from today, after your wealthy uncle's will passes through the probate period. You will not need the money until two years from now, when your twin daughters will enter an expensive West Coast university known more for its parties than its academics. Therefore, you would like to invest the money during the year prior to their departure for the university. There is no direct "forward market" for interest rates. You have two choices. You can wait and invest the money in a year at whatever interest rate happens to be offered at that time, or you can secure a forward savings rate by taking some actions in the current bond market that will "synthesize" a forward transaction.

You search the financial pages of the newspaper and find a pair of bonds that may be helpful. (You prefer to deal in coupon-bearing bonds because your experience is that zero-coupon bonds usually have a slight markup in price relative to coupon-bearing bonds.) The shorter-maturity bond of the pair matures in one year and pays an annual coupon of $100; it is currently selling at its par value of $1,000. The longer-maturity bond of the pair matures in two years and pays an annual coupon of $110; it may be purchased currently for $984.89.

This information is sufficient for us to figure out the term structure of spot rates of interest for the first two years, as well as the first and second year forward rates. To determine the one-year spot rate of interest, S_1 (and thereby the first-year forward rate, F_1), we simply set the sales price of the one-year bond equal to its future cash flows and solve for the discount rate:

$$\text{Price}_{1\text{-year bond}} = \frac{\text{Future cash flow}}{1 + S_1}$$

$$\$1,000 = \frac{\$1,000 + \$100}{1 + S_1}$$

$$\therefore S_1 = 10.0\% \text{ and } F_1 = 10.0\%$$

Now we can apply our findings about the 1-year spot and forward rates of interest to derive the implied 2-year spot rate and 2nd-year forward rate. We proceed as before, but since we already have derived the applicable 1-year spot rate, we need solve only for the discount rate applicable to the second year cash flow of the 2-year bond:

$$\text{Price}_{2\text{-year bond}} = \frac{\text{First year cash flow}}{1 + S_1}$$

$$+ \frac{\text{Second year cash flow}}{(1 + S_2)^2}$$

$$\$984.89 = \frac{\$110}{1 + .10} + \frac{\$1,000 + \$110}{(1 + S_2)^2}$$

Applying a bit of algebra, we proceed as follows:

$$\$984.89 - \$100 = \frac{\$1,110}{(1 + S_2)^2}$$

$$\therefore S_2 = \sqrt{\frac{\$1,110}{\$884.89}} - 1 = 12.0\%$$

$$\text{and } F_2 = \frac{(1 + S_2)^2}{1 + S_1} - 1 = \frac{1.12^2}{1.10} - 1 = 14.036\%$$

charge him? You will need to store and insure your gold for three more months. For 100 ounces of gold, storage for three months may run $5 and insurance will cost $10. Also, you will be forgoing three months of interest on the $40,000 that you could earn if you were to sell the gold today in the spot market. If simple interest is 8 percent per annum, you could earn 2 percent, or $800, over the three-month period on the $40,000 you could get by selling your gold in the spot market. If you were to agree to the forward sale of your gold, you would demand at least $40,815 (= $40,000 + $800 + $5 + $10), enough to compensate you for forgone interest,

Having completed the preliminaries, you must next decide whether the 2nd-year forward rate is sufficiently attractive that you would like to "lock it in" as your savings rate of interest for the year following the receipt of the $1,000,000 inheritance, or if you would rather take your chances and invest at whatever the prevailing interest rate happens to be a year from now. Suppose that you prefer to lock in the 14.036% 2nd-year forward rate. However, you have insufficient money today to buy any bonds. How could you accomplish this?

The answer involves the notion of **short selling** the 1-year bond and purchasing the 2-year bond with the proceeds from the short sale. This allows you to lock in a forward interest rate without spending any of your own money! Here is how the procedure works. First, to raise money today, you must short sell a bond.[a] If you short sell the 1-year bond, you will receive $1,000 (its sales price). You can use the proceeds to purchase the 2-year bond, which costs $984.89. Your financial situation across time now appears as follows:

	Period		
	0	*1*	*2*
Short sale of one-year bond	+$1,000.00	−$1,100	—
Purchase of two-year bond	−$ 984.89	+$110	+$1,110

Your net financial position at each point in time can be ascertained by summing the figures in the columns.

	Period		
	0	*1*	*2*
Net financial position	+$ 15.11	−$ 990	+$1,110

The problem with this net financial position profile is that it does not fit your needs (as we expressed them). Remember, the goal was to create a forward transaction synthetically, which involves no net cash flow today, either positive or negative.

If fractional shares of bonds were purchasable,[b] the necessary transaction would be straightforward.

---

[a] A short sale of a bond means selling a bond that you do not own. How is that possible? In modern financial markets, such an action is routine. You simply call your broker and tell her that you wish to sell a bond—in this case, the 1-year bond. "Do you own such a bond?" your broker may inquire. "Not really," is your response. "No problem. I'll borrow someone else's bond and sell it for you. You'll have to pay to me the cash flows that would have accrued to its owner so that I can make timely payments to him as if he still had possession of the bond," replies your broker. In practice, there may be further collateral arrangements to secure the short sale, but the essence of a short sale is as described above.

[b] Never mind for the moment that this cannot be done. The high volume traders can do this in sufficient volume to accomplish it without buying fractional shares of bonds.

---

storage, and insurance costs. If the buyer offers substantially more than that amount, you and others will have a strong preference toward selling the gold in the futures market rather than in the spot market. As this additional supply of futures sellers begins to emerge, coupled with the reduction in the number of people willing to sell in the spot market due to the more favorable prices in the futures market, the futures spread between the spot price and settlement price will be driven toward that which reflects the interest costs and the costs of storage and insurance.

What about a commodity, such as corn? Corn also has a storage cost, which will also include the forgone interest that could be captured by selling it in the spot

You would be able to purchase 1.015342 2-year bonds (= $1,000 ÷ $984.89) with the $1,000 proceeds from your short sale. Now, to compute your net financial position across time periods, you would simply multiply the second row figures from the two transactions by 1.015342. This would give you:

	Period		
	0	*1*	*2*
Short sale of one-year bond	+$1,000	−$1,100.00	—
Purchase 1.015342 two-year bonds	−$1,000	+$ 111.69	+$1,127.03
Net financial position	$ 0	−$ 988.31	+$1,127.03

One last problem remains. The size of transactions contemplated above does not provide an outlet to invest very much of the $1,000,000 you are scheduled to inherit. The transactions produce a savings outlet for only $988.31 of your funds one year hence, whereas you would like them to accommodate all of your inheritance. That means you will have to do the transactions in higher volume. How high? Simply divide the $1,000,000 inflow at Time 1 by the scheduled $988.31 outflow. The resulting quotient of 1,011.83 means that your transaction size must be 1,011.83 times higher than that shown above. Multiplying all three rows by this number gives:

	Period		
	0	*1*	*2*
Short sale of 1,011.8282 one-year bonds	+$1,011,828	−$1,113,011	—
Purchase 1.015342 × 1,011.8282 two-year bonds	−$1,011,828	+$ 113,009	+$1,140,360
Net financial position	$ 0	−$1,000,002	+$1,140,360

Now it is plain that if you undertake the preceding volume of transactions, you will need to supply $1,000,002 a year from now (which is just $2 in excess of what you are scheduled to inherit), but will receive $1,140,360 two years hence for your effort. That represents a 14.036% future rate of return, which is exactly the forward rate that you synthetically secured by your efforts. Sorry about the extra $2 that you will have to produce in one year. It represents a rounding error! Had you inherited more money, you would have been situated to perform the operations in such volume as to generate no fractional bond purchases, and no appreciable rounding error.

market. These costs will be reflected in the futures price of corn. There is an important difference, however. In the case of corn, there are periodic harvests that saturate the market with temporary excess supply. Thus, in months of harvest, the futures settlement prices may be lower than those that would be available through the storage process. How about gasoline? We noted that the futures price was not always above the spot price in some months. It is often cheaper to leave gasoline in the ground in the form of crude oil than to pump it to the surface and refine it. The forgone interest is lower because the investment is lower (e.g., no tanks are needed, no expenditure on electricity to run the pumps, no insurance against explosion, etc.). Nonetheless, there are patterns in oil and gasoline futures prices that are difficult to account for using the storage and forgone interest costs, or **cost-of-carry,** approach.[3] However, most commodity futures prices can be easily explained. Price divergences are most often the result of unusual circumstances, such as potential supply crises or political instability in areas of high production.

What about a financial futures contract? Here, there is no confusion generated by harvest uncertainty or alternative ways to store a commodity. The only cost of any substance is forgone interest. Accordingly, our approach works quite well. As an example, imagine that there is a financial futures contract that will secure an outlet for you to invest a sum of money at the end of one year at a prespecified interest rate. What we have shown in Box 15.1 is how an individual or business could "lock in" the forward rate of interest implicit in the term structure by purchasing a longer-term bond and short selling a shorter-term bond in appropriate proportions. Since the interest owed on the short-selling transaction is the cost of undertaking these transactions, it must be netted against the interest earned on the longer-term bond to derive the forward interest rate. The point is that if someone could synthetically create a viable forward interest rate by taking these simple actions, the market's futures rate could not be far from it; otherwise, there would be arbitrage opportunities that would be too good to resist.

Several theories have been put forth in the economic literature regarding the equilibrium forward or futures price. They go under such names as contango, normal backwardation, unbiased expectations, cost-of-carry, and so forth. We have not explained these theories of equilibrium forward and futures settlement prices, nor will we defend one against another. This is a subject of sufficient detail and complexity as to occupy a separate textbook and college course. Suffice it to say that some of these theories work well in certain markets or during some time periods, while others work well in other markets or during other time periods. None does a very good job of explaining observed settlement prices across all goods and services markets during any one time period. We can also say that the forces of eliminating arbitrage are so great that futures settlement prices cannot remain for long outside of certain bounds, which are dictated by the costs of performing the arbitrage.

Option Contracts

Let's now turn our attention to option contracts. Like futures contracts, an option is an agreement between two parties to exchange a real or financial asset at a later date for an agreed price. There are two classes of options. The first option may be exercised at the end of the predetermined period, while the second may be

---

[3]In all of these examples, we have ignored the impact of the "mark-to-market" daily settlement procedures. It has been shown elsewhere that this provision has only a marginal impact on the value of a futures contract, and so we have ignored it here. See Don Chance, *An Introduction to Options and Futures* (Philadelphia: Dryden Press, 1990) for a full treatment.

exercised at any time before the option expires. The former is referred to as a **European option,** while the latter, exhibiting more flexibility, is dubbed an **American option.** The price at which the option may be exercised is its **exercise price,** or more colloquially, the **strike price.** The clear distinction between these instruments and those previously discussed is inherent in their names: The bearer has an option, but not the requirement, to engage in the contracted transaction. For this right, the purchaser pays a fee, referred to as the **option premium,** that is the counterpart of the price of entry in our coin toss analogy.

While there are many types of options written, the bulk of the currently traded ones are of two types. **Call options** are contracts that give the bearer the right to purchase a given asset at the prespecified strike price. On the other hand, **put options** are contracts that give the bearer the right to sell an asset at a given strike price. The asset covered by the transaction is likely to be another financial asset such as a particular stock, various fixed-income instruments, or some index, such as the S&P 500. Moreover, traded options also involve commodities of various sorts and foreign currencies.

Standardized options are listed and traded on several exchanges in the United States, with the most active being the Chicago Board of Options Exchange (CBOE), the American Exchange (AMEX), the Pacific Coast Exchange (PSE), and the Philadelphia Exchange (PHLX). These options may be short term, a few months or less, or long term, one to five years. Exhibit 15.3 shows an example of the latter from the March 6, 1996, edition of *The Wall Street Journal*. The options reported here are long-term stock options (long-term equity anticipation securities, or LEAPS) from the five major exchanges. Although there are only a handful of LEAPS, the volume of transactions, on a contract-by-contract basis, is large relative to that of many short-term options. The expiration data for short-term and long-term options are given in monthly form only, as all exchange-traded options expire on the Saturday following the third Friday of each month.

Not all options are traded on exchanges, and both private and negotiated markets still exist. Yet, for the same reasons that futures markets tend to dominate forward markets, the emergence of listed options has led to the preponderance of transactions being conducted with listed options. The emergence of the Options Clearing Corporation, which functions as the issuer of all options on the four exchanges, has resulted in greater financial integrity and liquidity, which is appreciated by both sides of the option transaction.

Futures versus Options Revisited: Rights and Obligations

At the beginning of this chapter, we contrasted futures with options using the vehicle of two games of chance. Another way these instruments may be contrasted is in terms of the legal rights and obligations incumbent on the parties to futures and options transactions. At the most general level, it can be said that options decouple the rights from the obligations, whereas futures leave them fused together. To be concrete, the purchasers of options have rights (choices) but no obligations, while the sellers (writers) of options have obligations but no rights. The latter have no

Exhibit 15.3

LEAPS—Long-Term Options

LEAPS — LONG TERM OPTIONS

Option/Strike		Exp.	Call Vol.	Call Last	Put Vol.	Put Last
3Com	45	Jan 97	16	9 1/4	...	...
ABarck	17 1/2	Jan 97	1	11 3/8	20	7/8
25 1/4	25	Jan 96	53	4 3/4	...	...
25 1/4	30	Jan 96	13	2 3/4	...	...
25 1/4	30	Jan 97	20	4 3/4	...	...
AMD	15	Jan 96	20	9 5/8	...	...
22 3/4	20	Jan 96	20	6 3/4	2	2
22 3/4	25	Jan 96	137	4 1/4	10	5
22 3/4	30	Jan 96	222	3 1/4	...	...
AMR	50	Jan 96	...	...	20	5
ASA	45	Jan 97	...	...	300	4 1/2
49 5/8	55	Jan 96	...	...	90	8 1/2
AT&T	45	Jan 96	...	...	30	1 1/8
53 7/8	55	Jan 96	32	5 3/8	5	4 1/4
53 7/8	60	Jan 96	47	3 1/2	...	...
AbtLab	35	Jan 96	13	2 1/2	...	...
Alza	20	Jan 96	60	3 7/8	...	...
19 1/8	20	Jan 97	86	5 3/8	...	...
AmExpr	20	Jan 97	150	12 1/4	...	...
Amgen	60	Jan 96	101	6 1/2	...	...
AppleC	20	Jan 96	26	22 1/2	1110	5/16
41 1/8	30	Jan 96	20	14 1/4	...	...
41 1/8	40	Jan 96	19	8 1/4	35	5 1/8
41 1/8	60	Jan 96	30	2	...	...
AtlRch	100	Jan 96	16	8 5/8	...	...
BakrHu	15	Jan 96	100	5 5/8	...	...
BellAtl	50	Jan 97	...	...	28	4 1/4
BkBost	25	Jan 96	...	...	14	2
27 7/8	30	Jan 96	19	3	...	...
Boeing	40	Jan 96	30	7 7/8	25	1 7/8
44 5/8	50	Jan 96	18	2 5/8	...	...
BorInt	15	Jan 97	19	3	...	...
BrMySq	50	Jan 96	12	9 3/4	...	...
57 3/4	60	Jan 96	64	4	5	5
57 3/4	70	Jan 96	12	1 1/16	...	...
ChmBnk	30	Jan 96	...	...	20	1
Chrysl	30	Jan 96	17	18 1/2	...	...
46 7/8	40	Jan 97	35	12 7/8	8	4
46 7/8	50	Jan 97	40	8 1/2	...	...
46 7/8	60	Jan 97	212	4 5/8	...	...
Cisco	15	Jan 96	25	14 5/8	...	...
27 5/8	25	Jan 97	20	10 5/8	10	4 3/4
27 5/8	30	Jan 96	35	5 7/8	...	...
27 5/8	30	Jan 97	35	8 5/8	1	7 1/4
27 5/8	35	Jan 96	14	4 1/4	...	...
Citicp	30	Jan 96	22	14 1/2	...	...
CocaCl	30	Jan 97	50	22 5/8	...	...
50 5/8	40	Jan 96	10	12 3/4	45	3/4
50 5/8	50	Jan 97	13	8 3/4	10	3 7/8
Compaq	30	Jan 97	10	13	52	4 3/8
35 5/8	45	Jan 97	14	7	...	...
DellCptr	50	Jan 96	40	4 3/4	...	...
Digital	25	Jan 96	28	8	5	2 7/8
28 5/8	30	Jan 96	63	5 7/8	...	...
28 5/8	40	Jan 96	32	3 1/8	...	...
Disney	30	Jan 96	15	11 3/4	10	7/8
38 3/4	50	Jan 96	17	1 7/8	...	...
DuPont	60	Jan 96	15	5 3/4	...	...
Exxon	50	Jan 96	202	11 1/8	13	1 1/4
FordM	37 1/2	Jan 96	15	1 1/4	...	...
GaPac	65	Jan 96	17	18	...	...
77	85	Jan 96	14	7 5/8	...	...
Gap	35	Jan 97	50	8 1/2	...	...
GenEl	40	Jan 96	15	12 3/8	...	...
50 3/8	55	Jan 96	18	3 1/2	10	6 1/8
Glaxo	20	Jan 96	97	2 1/2	...	...
19 1/2	25	Jan 96	80	1 1/8	...	...
GnMotr	40	Jan 97	40	14 3/4	...	...
47 1/4	45	Jan 96	...	...	19	4 1/8
47 1/4	50	Jan 96	253	6 3/8	...	...
47 1/4	60	Jan 96	7	3	11	13 1/2
47 1/4	70	Jan 96	11	1 3/8	...	...
Homstk	25	Jan 96	23	2 7/16	...	...
IBM	40	Jan 96	...	...	36	3/16
73 1/8	50	Jan 97	1	28	36	1 1/4
73 1/8	60	Jan 96	47	17 3/8	251	2 1/16
73 1/8	60	Jan 97	25	21 1/2	...	...
73 1/8	70	Jan 96	54	11 1/2	2	5 1/2
73 1/8	70	Jan 97	8	15 1/4	17	6 5/8
73 1/8	80	Jan 96	268	6 3/8	2	10 5/8
73 1/8	80	Jan 97	155	11	13	11 7/8
IGame	30	Jan 96	50	1 3/8	...	...
IntGame	17 1/2	Jan 97	11	7	6	2 5/8
Intel	40	Jan 96	85	22 5/8	...	...
58 1/2	50	Jan 96	15	15 1/2	20	3 3/8
58 1/2	65	Jan 96	237	7 1/2	23	10 1/4
58 1/2	80	Jan 96	123	3 1/4	...	...
58 1/2	80	Jan 97	5000	6 3/4	...	...
JohnJn	45	Jan 96	...	...	20	1 3/8
52 3/8	50	Jan 96	62	7	40	2 3/4
52 3/8	55	Jan 96	43	4 1/4	...	...
52 3/8	55	Jan 97	20	6 5/8	...	...
K mart	15	Jan 96	18	3 1/8	...	...
16 3/8	20	Jan 96	18	1 1/4	...	...
MerLyn	25	Jan 96	250	11 1/4	...	...
34 3/8	40	Jan 96	...	...	20	7 3/8
34 3/8	40	Jan 97	14	5 1/8	...	...
Merck	25	Jan 96	753	12	...	...
36 1/4	30	Jan 96	235	7 7/8	8	1 1/16
36 1/4	35	Jan 96	14	4 3/4	4	2 7/16
36 1/4	40	Jan 96	107	2 5/8	...	...
Micsft	50	Jan 96	30	12 1/8	4	2 3/4
55 15/16	57 1/2	Jan 96	61	8 1/2	...	...
55 15/16	60	Jan 96	18	7 1/8	...	...
Monsan	70	Jan 96	20	12 3/4	...	...
Morgan	70	Jan 96	13	2 7/8	50	10 1/8
Motoria	50	Jan 97	...	...	20	5 1/8
53 7/8	60	Jan 96	1087	6 1/4	2	8 3/4
Novell	20	Jan 96	12	2 1/16	...	...
16	20	Jan 97	102	4	...	...
Oracle	35	Jan 96	250	15 1/2	...	...
PPG	42 1/2	Jan 96	20	2 7/16	...	...
PacT o	45	Jan 96	20	15 3/4	...	...
PepsiC	35	Jan 96	76	3 7/8	90	3
34 1/4	40	Jan 96	15	1 7/8	...	...
PhilMr	40	Jan 96	20	20 5/8	...	...
60 5/8	60	Jan 96	14	6 3/4	5	5 1/8
60 5/8	70	Jan 96	23	3 1/8	...	...
60 5/8	70	Jan 97	...	...	100	12 3/4
PlacrD	25	Jan 96	57	3 3/4	...	...
23 1/8	30	Jan 96	30	2 3/8	...	...
ProctG	65	Jan 96	13	4 3/4	...	...
RJR Nb	7 1/2	Jan 96	13	1	100	1 3/8
6 7/8	7 1/2	Jan 97	50	1 9/16	100	1 9/16
6 7/8	10	Jan 96	100	3/8	8	3 1/4
6 7/8	10	Jan 96	20	5/16	...	...
6 7/8	10	Jan 97	30	15/16	...	...
6 7/8	10	Jan 97	30	15/16	...	...
Salomn	50	Jan 96	40	1 7/8	...	...
SunMic	17 1/2	Jan 96	45	14 3/4	...	...
TelMex	40	Jan 96	320	25	1	15/16
63 1/2	45	Jan 97	...	...	12	2 5/8
63 1/2	55	Jan 96	240	14 1/2	2	4
63 1/2	55	Jan 96	...	...	80	4
63 1/2	65	Jan 96	342	9	10	8 1/4
US Surg	30	Jan 96	70	4 5/8	...	...
USXMar	15	Jan 96	15	3 3/4	...	...
UnCarb	17 1/2	Jan 96	20	15 3/4	...	...
Unisys	12 1/2	Jan 96	...	...	20	2 1/4
10 7/8	15	Jan 96	15	15/16	...	...
Upjohn	35	Jan 96	...	...	40	4 3/8
WMX Tc	20	Jan 96	15	9 7/8	...	...
29	30	Jan 97	...	...	100	3 3/4
29	35	Jan 96	12	1 5/8	...	...
29	35	Jan 97	100	3 1/2	...	...
WalMart	30	Jan 97	59	3	...	...
WalMrt	30	Jan 96	30	1 11/16	...	...
WstgEl	12 1/2	Jan 97	20	3 1/4	...	...
13	15	Jan 97	50	2 13/16	...	...
Xerox	110	Jan 97	21	19	...	...

VOLUME & OPEN INTEREST SUMMARIES

AMERICAN			
Call Vol:	8,640	Open Int:	368,559
Put Vol:	2,181	Open Int:	298,922
CHICAGO BOARD			
Call Vol:	5,836	Open Int:	578,404
Put Vol:	6,917	Open Int:	743,818
PACIFIC			
Call Vol:	929	Open Int:	59,831
Put Vol:	84	Open Int:	26,878
PHILADELPHIA			
Call Vol:	513	Open Int:	129,668
Put Vol:	185	Open Int:	66,513
NEW YORK			
Call Vol:		Open Int:	41,621
Put Vol:	89	Open Int:	18,408
TOTAL			
Call Vol:	15,918	Open Int:	1,178,083
Put Vol:	9,456	Open Int:	1,154,539

Source: Reprinted with permission from *The Wall Street Journal,* March 6, 1996. © 1996 by Dow Jones & Company. All Rights Reserved Worldwide.

ability to choose whether and when to buy or sell a particular good. Buyers and sellers of futures have both the right and the obligation to perform in certain ways. These rights and obligations are summarized in Exhibit 15.4.

Futures purchasers have the right to buy a good or security at a prespecified price when it is to their economic advantage. They are also obliged to buy a good or security at a prespecified price even when it is not to their economic advantage to do so. Futures writers are obliged to buy a good or security at a prespecified price when it is economically disadvantageous to do so. On the other hand, they also have the right to buy a good or security at a prespecified price when it is to their economic advantage.

Options purchasers, whether they buy calls or puts, are not obligated to do anything with their options. They may simply ignore them and let them expire. Rational options purchasers will exercise their rights to buy or sell a good or

Exhibit 15.4   **Futures versus Options: Rights and Obligations**

| Futures | | Options | | |
Writers	Buyers	Writers	Buyers	Type
Have the right and obligation to buy a specified amount of a good on an appointed future date at a prespecified price.	Have the right and obligation to sell a specified amount of a good on an appointed future date at a prespecified price.	Have the obligation, but not the right, to sell a specified amount of a good on or before an appointed future date at a prespecified price.	Have the right, but not the obligation, to buy a specified amount of a good on or before an appointed future date at a prespecified price.	Calls
		Have the obligation, but not the right, to buy a specified amount of a good on or before an appointed future date at a prespecified price.	Have the right, but not the obligation, to sell a specified amount of a good on or before an appointed future date at a prespecified price.	Puts

security at a prespecified price only when it is to their economic advantage to do so. Options writers, on the other hand, do not have the right to choose whether and when to buy or sell a good or security at a prespecified price. They must do so when the other party to the contract demands it. Buying or selling at the prespecified price may be to their economic advantage at some point in time, but they will not get a chance to take advantage of the situation unless the options purchasers require it of them. Naturally, rational options purchasers will never request that an action be taken in the interests of the options sellers. The sellers received their money up front in the form of an option premium, and they are not about to get any more.

This clear distinction between futures and options can be seen graphically by examining the payoff patterns for both types of securities given any range of price movement of the underlying asset. As seen in Exhibit 15.5, the payoff patterns of a futures contract with a settlement price of K would vary linearly with the price of the asset at settlement. Notice also that the payoffs at various prices, denoted as S_T, associated with the purchaser, are the mirror image of the implications of price movements for the seller of the contract. Both the purchaser and the seller are directly affected by price movement in either direction.

On the other hand, the payoff patterns for options market participants are not at all the same. Exhibit 15.6 illustrates the payoffs to both sides of a call option and a put option. As is apparent, these payoff lines are kinked at the exercise price for both participants in both markets. As indicated above, options yield either upside or downside gains, but not both simultaneously.

Valuation of Options Contracts

Close to a dozen option pricing models have been developed for valuing options on equities, foreign currencies, commodities, and options on futures. Another dozen or so have been developed for valuing options on debt instruments like

EXHIBIT 15.5

Futures payoff patterns

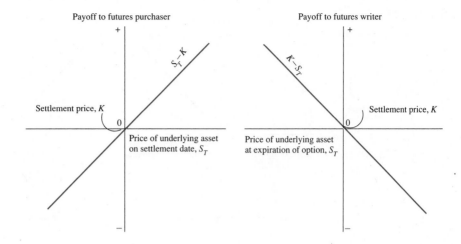

Payoff to futures purchaser

Payoff to futures writer

Settlement price, K

Price of underlying asset on settlement date, S_T

Settlement price, K

Price of underlying asset at expiration of option, S_T

Treasury bonds, T-bills, corporate bonds, mortgages, swaps, and others. All of these option models vary as to the assumptions they make regarding the price behavior of the underlying asset and about the economic environment (e.g., Are interest rates fixed or stochastic? Are markets complete? Is there continuous trading?). Most of these are presented through a set of equations that share at least one characteristic—they can be extremely intimidating to a novice.[4] This area is, in short, one of the most complicated in the financial market.

However, stripped of their continuous-time mathematics and statistical probability notation, the approach taken to pricing options is really quite simple and intuitively appealing. In this section, we shall describe two simple models. The first of these is based on the discounted values of cash flows. We shall then describe another

---

[4]For example, one of the earliest, and as it turns out, simplest, of the option pricing models was derived by Fischer Black and Myron Scholes. It is given below for a European call option.

$$C = S \cdot N(d_1) - Ke^{-rT} N(d_2)$$

where

$$d_1 = \frac{\ln(S/K) + (r + \sigma^2/2)T}{\sigma\sqrt{T}}$$

$$d_2 = d_1 - \sigma\sqrt{T}$$

and where

C = current call option value
S = current stock price
$N(d)$ = the probability that a random draw from a standard normal distribution will be less than d
K = exercise price
r = risk-free continuously compounded interest rate with maturity at expiration date
T = time to maturity of option in years
σ = standard deviation of the annualized continuously compounded rate of return on the stock

EXHIBIT 15.6

Option payoff patterns

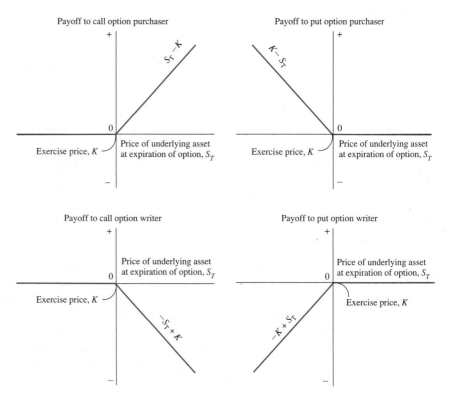

approach to pricing options that relies on replicating option cash flows using other instruments. As before, we combine cash flows to replicate those of the option we are trying to value. Then, by adding up the prices of the constituent parts of our "synthetic option," we can determine the value of a true option. This approach is similar to that taken earlier in valuing a bond as the sum of the values of the zero-coupon bond components implicit in the bond "package." If the values differ, arbitrageurs could take actions to drive the prices toward equilibrium with one another. Finally, we will discuss the nature of continuous-time models by way of an analogy.

We will first present the simplest model, which is implicit in many of the more complex models in one form or another.[5] This model involves taking each of the possible option payoffs, discounting them back to the present, and weighing these present values by the probabilities that they will ultimately materialize. If

_____

[5]This model gives correct pricing and is equivalent to some of the more complex models under the conditions of complete markets and risk-neutral market participants. In general, it should be viewed as a rough, first approximation to the value that would be derived through the more elaborate models. Several of the more elaborate models are discussed in John Cox and Mark Rubinstein, *Options Markets* (Englewood Cliffs, N.J.: Prentice Hall, 1985) and other resources cited in the reference section.

interest rates are assumed to be constant over time, this is exactly equivalent to taking the expected future option payoff and discounting it back to the present.

Consider a call option with a strike price of K on an underlying stock that pays no dividends. The option expires in one year, and the one-year interest rate is 10 percent. Suppose that S_T, the possible prices at the end of the year for the stock, range from $10 to $22. These possible prices are depicted, along with their probabilities, in Exhibit 15.7. If the exercise price, K, is $16, which in this example also happens to be the mean of the price distribution, the option will have a payoff of either zero or ($S_T - \$16$), whichever winds up being higher. Obviously, the payoff will be positive only if the final stock price exceeds $16. If the stock price ends up at $16 or less, there will be no payoff. These payoffs are also shown in the exhibit.

To value this option, we simply take the possible payoffs, ranging from $0 to $6 in increments of $1, discount them using an interest rate of 10 percent, and weigh the discounted values by their probabilities. This process is shown in the spreadsheet replicated in Exhibit 15.8. The value of the option is $0.6636. Because the interest rate is assumed to be constant, this is tantamount to taking the expected option payoff, which is $0.73, and discounting it by a 10 percent interest rate. Remember the distributive law of multiplication.

Now, taking the same option, let us assume that the probabilities of the final possible prices are distributed as in Exhibit 15.9. The mean of the price distribution again is $16, but the expected option payoff has risen to $1.68. Why has this increase occurred? The payoffs still range from $0 to $6, with increments of $1. However, the probabilities attached to the higher and lower payoff numbers have increased. The lower payoffs have no effect on the option's value because it will not be exercised at any price below $16. This means that only the higher payoffs will figure into the pricing of the option. In this case, the option is worth $1.5273, which is about 2.3 times higher than the option value that was based on the prior probability distribution. The spreadsheet analysis used to arrive at this figure is found in Exhibit 15.10.

This comparison illustrates an important point. When prices become more volatile,[6] call option values increase. The volatility is attractive to option purchasers because they get the benefit from the higher, and/or more probable, favorable outcomes while avoiding the losses associated with the lower outcomes.

Using the device of this example, we can also explore the influence on option value of changing the exercise price. If the exercise price were increased to $18, the option payoffs would range only from $0 to $4. In this case, the expected payoff would decline and the value of the option would be less. How much less would depend on which of the probability distributions we assumed for end-of-year stock prices. Assuming the less volatile distribution, the value

---

[6] Note that in our example, the range of final stock prices was the same; only the probabilities attached to the final prices were altered. Nonetheless, the variance and standard deviation measures of price volatility have increased from 3.7000 and 1.9235, respectively, to 14.56 and 3.8158, respectively. The same effect of increased volatility could have been shown if we had increased the range of outcomes while keeping the mean outcome constant.

Exhibit 15.7

*Option payoffs and
payoff probabilities*

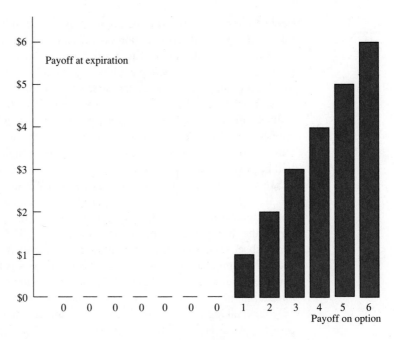

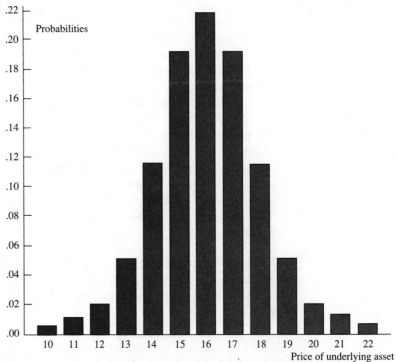

EXHIBIT 15.8   **Valuing a Call Option Using a Given Price Distribution**

Probability	Cumulative Probability	Underlying Price	Squared Deviation × Probability	Payoff	PV of Payoff	Probability × PV of Payoff	Probability × Payoff
0.0050	0.0050	10.0000	0.1800	0.0000	0.0000	0.0000	0.0000
0.0100	0.0150	11.0000	0.2500	0.0000	0.0000	0.0000	0.0000
0.0200	0.0350	12.0000	0.3200	0.0000	0.0000	0.0000	0.0000
0.0500	0.0850	13.0000	0.4500	0.0000	0.0000	0.0000	0.0000
0.1150	0.2000	14.0000	0.4600	0.0000	0.0000	0.0000	0.0000
0.1900	0.3900	15.0000	0.1900	0.0000	0.0000	0.0000	0.0000
0.2200	0.6100	16.0000	0.0000	0.0000	0.0000	0.0000	0.0000
0.1900	0.8000	17.0000	0.1900	1.0000	0.9091	0.1727	0.1900
0.1150	0.9150	18.0000	0.4600	2.0000	1.8182	0.2091	0.2300
0.0500	0.9650	19.0000	0.4500	3.0000	2.7273	0.1364	0.1500
0.0200	0.9850	20.0000	0.3200	4.0000	3.6364	0.0727	0.0800
0.0100	0.9950	21.0000	0.2500	5.0000	4.5455	0.0455	0.0500
0.0050	1.0000	22.0000	0.1800	6.0000	5.4545	0.0273	0.0300
Sum of Probabilities							Expected
			Variance =			Price =	Value =
1.0000			3.7000			0.6636	0.7300
			Standard Deviation =				
			1.9235				

would be $0.1273; under the more volatile distribution, the option would be worth $0.7273. We leave it as an exercise for the reader to verify these numbers. The reason for this decline in value is obvious. There are fewer future states in which the option would have a positive payoff. Prior to the change in exercise price, there were six states (S_T: $17, $18, $19, $20, $21, $22) in which there was a positive payoff to the option holder. After the increase in exercise price to $18, there were only four states (S_T: $19, $20, $21, $22) in which there was a positive payoff.

The effect on option value of increasing the time before expiration is also noteworthy. Today, the stock price is a single value. We have assumed that one year from now it could range from $10 to $22. If that wide of a range could unfold during a single year, imagine how wide the range would get after an even longer period of time. Because the upside potential would be higher, while the downside would continue to provide a zero return, it is likely that increasing the time to expiration would foster an increase in option value. This is not always the case, however. Remember that we will be discounting the (potentially higher) option payoffs by a larger number, reflecting the longer time period. Moreover, there may be other factors (e.g., an adverse price drift tendency, reversion toward the mean price, dividend payouts, etc.) that could offset the positive effect of increased time to expiration. Nonetheless, it is likely

Exhibit 15.9

*Option payoffs and
payoff probabilities*

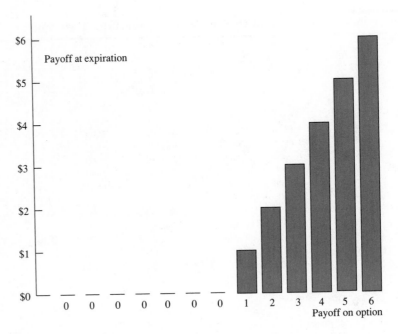

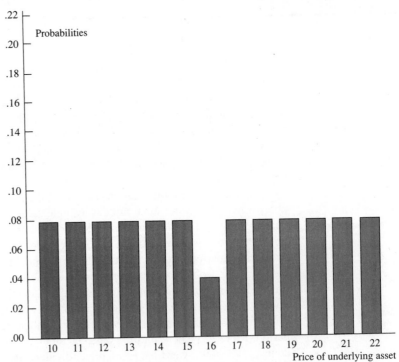

EXHIBIT 15.10   Valuing a Call Option Using a Given Price Distribution

Probability	Cumulative Probability	Underlying Price	Squared Deviation × Probability	Payoff	PV of Payoff	Probability × PV of Payoff	Probability × Payoff
0.0800	0.0800	10.0000	2.8800	0.0000	0.0000	0.0000	0.0000
0.0800	0.1600	11.0000	2.0000	0.0000	0.0000	0.0000	0.0000
0.0800	0.2400	12.0000	1.2800	0.0000	0.0000	0.0000	0.0000
0.0800	0.3200	13.0000	0.7200	0.0000	0.0000	0.0000	0.0000
0.0800	0.4000	14.0000	0.3200	0.0000	0.0000	0.0000	0.0000
0.0800	0.4800	15.0000	0.0800	0.0000	0.0000	0.0000	0.0000
0.0400	0.5200	16.0000	0.0000	0.0000	0.0000	0.0000	0.0000
0.0800	0.6000	17.0000	0.0800	1.0000	0.9091	0.0727	0.0800
0.0800	0.6800	18.0000	0.3200	2.0000	1.8182	0.1455	0.1600
0.0800	0.7600	19.0000	0.7200	3.0000	2.7273	0.2182	0.2400
0.0800	0.8400	20.0000	1.2800	4.0000	3.6364	0.2909	0.3200
0.0800	0.9200	21.0000	2.0000	5.0000	4.5455	0.3636	0.4000
0.0800	1.0000	22.0000	2.8800	6.0000	5.4545	0.4364	0.4800

Sum of Probabilities

1.0000

Variance =
14.5600
Standard Deviation =
3.8158

Price =
1.5273

Expected Value =
1.6800

that an increase in the time to expiration will be accompanied by an increase in call option value.[7]

Now how would our model change if the option payoffs were related to interest rates? We have already discussed the basics of valuing interest-sensitive cash flows. The option pricing models use the same valuation principles. Rather than give an elaborate example at this point, suffice it to say that the payoffs would be discounted by the interest rate paths that could give rise to those payoffs.[8] Again, the resulting present values would be averaged to obtain an appropriate value. One difference between this model and the preceding one is important. We cannot simply discount the expected option payoff by the riskless rate of interest to obtain

---

[7]Our simple option pricing model has abstracted from some elements, such as price drift, that make it difficult to derive the effect of increased interest rates on option value. Because an increased discount rate will reduce the present values of the option payoffs, other things equal, we might think that the effect of increased interest rates would be to reduce option values. However, this is not generally correct. The tendency of the price of the underlying asset (stock in this case) to drift may be positively related to the interest rate. For a full treatment of the interest rate effect, see Don Chance, *An Introduction to Options and Futures* (Philadelphia: Dryden Press, 1990); and Cox and Rubinstein, *Options Markets* (Englewood Cliffs, N.J.: Prentice Hall, 1985).

[8]Like the former example, this one also assumes risk neutrality. Otherwise, we must adjust the discount rates or path probabilities to take into account the market price of interest rate risk. For a detailed explanation of how to implement this adjustment in practice, see David Babbel and Craig Merrill, *Valuation of Interest-Sensitive Financial Instruments* (New Hope, Pa.: Frank Fabozzi Associates, 1996).

an equivalent option value. In this case, the average of the present values differs from the present value of the average. Thus, we cannot use the short-cut method.

Another approach to pricing options is based on arbitrage theory. Here, we attempt to replicate the payoff pattern of options exactly by using other instruments. Recall that this is analogous to the approach used before in valuing futures contracts. For an example of its application in the options market, consider a call option on 1,000 shares of stock. Assume that the exercise price on the call option is $100 and time to expiration is one year. At the end of the year, suppose that the stock price can be either $120 or $80. We will not bother giving you the probabilities of each outcome, as this information is not needed when using this approach. On the day of expiration at the end of the year, the option on a single share of stock will be worth either $20 (= $120 − $100) or zero (when the stock value falls to $80, which is below the exercise price of $100). These payoffs are shown in the table below.

S_T	Payoff on Option for One Share	Total Option Contract Payoff (1,000 Shares)
$120	$120 − $100 = $20	$20 × 1,000 = $20,000
$80	$0	$0

We will value the option by finding out how much we would spend out of our own pockets to replicate its payoffs by a leveraged stock purchase. We do not need to know the current price of the stock or the interest rate to construct the replica, although we will have to know them later in order to determine the exact cost of replicating the option contract.

To construct the replica, we will borrow x dollars to help in purchasing n shares of stock, with the remainder coming from our own pocket. What we want to do is to make sure that if the stock falls to its low value of $80, we can pay back the borrowed money without any additional out-of-pocket expense—which corresponds to our not exercising the option if the price falls. If the stock falls, we will get $80n from the sale of n shares of stock at $80 each; we must pay back a loan of x plus interest, so we have the first equation that must be satisfied:

$$\$80n - \$x(1 + r) = 0$$

We also want to get the same payoff from our leveraged stock purchase as we would from the option if the stock goes up to $120 per share. The option would yield a profit of $20 on each share of stock covered under the contract (the actual price of $120 per share less the exercise price of $100 per share), or $20,000 in all. Hence, a leveraged stock purchase to replicate the option must satisfy a second equation:

$$\$120n - \$x(1 + r) = \$20,000$$

Solve simultaneously to find $n = 500$ and $x = \$40,000 \div (1 + r)$. In words, replication of an option contract for 1,000 shares of stock with an exercise price of

$100 per share and with the array of final stock prices as given would require purchasing 500 shares of the stock directly, partially financed by a loan of $40,000 ÷ (1 + r), with the remainder coming out of our own pocket.

To determine how much it costs to replicate the cash flows of the option via the leveraged stock purchase, we now need to know what the current stock price is and what interest rate will be charged on the loan. Suppose that the borrowing rate is 9.59 percent percent per annum and the current stock price is $90. The purchase of 500 shares of stock will then cost $45,000 (= $90 × 500), and the loan to help fund our stock acquisition will be for $36,500 [= $40,000 ÷ (1 + .0959)]. The remainder of $8,500 (= $45,000 − $36,500) comes from our own pocket. Since the option contract covers 1,000 shares, the value of the option per share must be $8.50. If it were to cost any more than this, we could replicate the option more cheaply via a leveraged stock purchase. Arbitrageurs would exploit this difference in values, synthetically replicating the option payoffs and simultaneously selling short the actual option contracts, to reap a profit equal to the difference in their values. This activity would continue until option prices reached their appropriate level.

Contrariwise, if options were selling below their appropriate level, they could be used, together with savings deposits, to replicate the payoffs on shares of common stock more cheaply than if the stock itself were to be purchased. To see this, let us use the same numbers as before but refocus on the behavior of the stock.

If we were to hold 500 shares of stock, our investment would be worth either $40,000 (at $80 per share) or $60,000 (at $120 per share) at the end of the year. An option to purchase 1,000 shares at $100 each, together with an interest-bearing deposit of $36,500, will replicate the values of the common stock under each scenario. When the stock price is $120, the option payoff will be $20,000 and the deposit will have grown to $40,000, for a total of $60,000, exactly the value of the 500 shares of stock. When the stock price is $80, the option payoff will be $0, but the deposit will still have grown to $40,000, for a total of $40,000, again exactly the value of the 500 shares of stock. Thus, if the stock values can be replicated more cheaply through the purchase of stock options together with interest-bearing deposits, arbitrageurs will do so and will sell short the stock, reaping profits of the difference. Again, this activity would continue until the option and share prices reached their appropriate relation to each other.

In replicating the payoffs of the option and of the stock, this example called for a ratio of stock to options of 500 to 1,000, or 1:2. To replicate the option payoffs, we invested in stock and borrowed money. To replicate the stock payoffs, we invested in options and placed money in an interest-bearing deposit. The ratio of stock to options is not always 1:2; in general, the ratio will depend on the configuration of final possible stock prices. Similarly, the amount of the loan will depend on interest rates. We leave it to the reader to verify these claims through numerical experimentation with the same equation structures as used in the previous discussion.

This simple example may appear a bit contrived to you, but in practice, an elaboration of this approach is widely used and works quite well. Adjustments are often made to reflect cash distributions, such as dividends, that are scheduled to occur prior to the option expiration. Also, it is customary to value these options using many periods with numerous final price outcomes rather than just two final prices. In these cases, the ratio of stock-to-options that is necessary to replicate the option payoffs changes dynamically over time as stock prices unfold. Further adjustments are made to accommodate the possibility of exercising an option prior to expiration. Notwithstanding these complications, we have shown how an option can be priced through the principle of replication of cash flows.

All of the option pricing models considered thus far have assumed discrete price jumps at discrete points in time. Many option pricing models are based on continuous-trading arguments. These models assume a stochastic process for prices of the underlying asset and, for options whose payoffs are interest sensitive, a stochastic process for interest rates. These models may resemble some of the paths that were depicted in our discussion of interest rate processes (Chapter 7). One of these models assumes the diffusion process described in Chapter 7. To illustrate this, we will adapt the analogy employed in Chapter 7 for the present context.

Imagine that we are standing in your classroom with a bottle of perfume. We take a dropper and splash a bit of perfume onto the lectern. The perfume molecules get excited by this disturbance and begin to diffuse into the air in all directions. A given perfume molecule will head in one direction until it collides with an air molecule, which causes it to change directions. Some perfume molecules will go farther than others before colliding with air molecules.

After the passage of some time, those sitting on the rows closest to the lectern may catch the scent. Later, people on more distant rows may catch the scent. This dispersion of perfume molecules is a type of diffusion process, which would be akin to the random motion of stock prices. The row location would be akin to an exercise price, where the rows (exercise prices) set closer to the location of the splash on the lectern (current stock price) are most likely to get a whiff of the perfume first. If you placed a high time value on smelling the perfume, you would pay more for the front row seats! Similarly, a call option with a low exercise price would be worth more.

We could alter the movement of air in the room in two ways. We could open the doors at the front and rear of the classroom and create a slow drift of air to impact the diffusion process. Many option pricing models incorporate such price drifts as a part of the stochastic process. Alternatively, a sudden jolt to the building, such as that produced by an earthquake, by altering the placement of the air and your desk, could alter the speed with which you begin to smell the perfume, provided that you remain in the room through the disturbance. Some option pricing models incorporate such shocks, or "jumps" in prices, as a part of their stochastic process.

Regardless of the complexity that is incorporated into an option pricing model, whether in discrete or continuous time, the principles of option pricing remain the same. We look at potential cash flows, discount them, and weight them. The discount factors and weightings change from one model to another. If the arbitrage approach is taken, we attempt to replicate the cash flows using instruments whose prices are well known.

Summary

Understanding the financial markets of the late 20th century requires an awareness and knowledge of the futures and options markets. These instruments have become a major part of the marketplace, yet they are complicated instruments and tricky to value. In this chapter, we have given you a flavor of these markets.

At the outset, we offered an analogy that provided considerable insight and intuition into the nature of these financial contracts. Next, we offered explanations of the workings of the markets in which they are traded, as well as their potential use to both speculative investors and hedgers.

This was followed by a discussion on the pricing of these instruments. Here, we relied on our previous approach to valuing these assets using the discounted cash flow methodology developed in Chapter 7. We also introduced the notion of valuation through the use of replication of cash flows. This approach was fruitfully employed in the valuation of both futures and options, and it will prove useful in the next chapter as well.

Key Concepts

American and European options,   376
counterparty,   362
exercise or strike price,   376
forward and futures contracts,   362
futures market,   358
opening price, settlement price, and open
  interest,   366
option premium,   376

options market,   358
put and call options,   358
short selling and cost of carry,   375
speculation versus hedging,   361
synthesizing a security,   369
trading location, contract size, and settlement
  date,   366

Review Questions

1. A U.S. company will need ¥100 million in three months. The current spot exchange rate is 98.2¥/$. The relative interest rates are 7 percent in the United States and 5 percent in Japan. Describe the process that a bank would undertake in order to fulfill this contract.

2. A British firm will need $200 million in six months. The spot rate is 1.585 $/£. The current interest rate is 8 percent in Britain and 7 percent in the United States. What transactions will the bank undertake in the execution of a forward contract to meet this need?

3. While on a turbulent flight to France, you note that the person sitting adjacent to you is perusing the foreign exchange rate table in the European *Wall Street Journal*. The person notices your interest and comments that it appears that the franc will appreciate against the

dollar during the coming year. Politely explain to her the fallacy behind this reasoning.

4. You are expecting to win $2 million from the slot machines in Monaco in one year's time. You wish to invest your earnings upon receipt in one year for an additional year, but you wish to lock in your deposit rate now. Currently, a two-year bond with a 9 percent annual coupon is selling for $972.34, while the 8 percent, one-year bond is priced at $990.80. How would you lock in today your one-year return over the second period? What is the relevant one-year forward rate?

5. If the strike price associated with Exhibit 15.8 is $15 and the applicable interest rate is 9 percent, calculate the price of a one-year call option.

6. Change the extreme probabilities in Exhibit 15.10 to 0.07 and the central probability to 0.16. If all other parameters remain the same, what is the value of the call option?

7. If an American option and a European option are alike in all other attributes, describe how their values are related.

References

Babbel, David F., and Craig Merrill. *Valuation of Interest-Sensitive Financial Instruments.* New Hope, Pa.: Frank Fabozzi Associates, 1996.

Billingsley, R. S., and Don M. Chance. "The Pricing and Performance of Stock Index Futures Spreads." *Journal of Futures Markets,* 1988.

Black, Fischer. "The Pricing of Commodity Contracts." *Journal of Financial Economics,* 1976.

Black, Fischer, and Myron Scholes. "The Pricing of Options and Corporate Liabilities." *Journal of Political Economy,* May/June 1973.

Brennan, Michael J., and Eduardo S. Schwartz. "Arbitrage in Stock Index Futures." *Journal of Business,* 1990.

Chance, Don M. *An Introduction to Options and Futures.* Philadelphia: Dryden Press, 1990.

Chang, Eric C. "Returns to Speculators and the Theory of Normal Backwardation." *Journal of Finance,* 1985.

Chicago Board of Trade. *Financial Instrument Markets: An Advanced Study of Cash-Futures Relationships.* Chicago: Board of Trade of the City of Chicago, 1986.

Cornell, Brad, and Kenneth R. French. "The Pricing of Stock Index Futures." *Journal of Futures Markets,* 1983.

Cox, John C.; Jonathan Ingersoll, Jr.; and Stephen A. Ross. "The Relation Between Forward Prices and Futures Prices." *Journal of Financial Economics,* 1981.

Cox, John C., and Mark Rubinstein. *Options Markets.* Englewood Cliffs, N.J.: Prentice Hall, 1985.

Figlewski, Stephen. *Hedging with Financial Futures, for Institutional Investors.* Cambridge, Mass.: Ballinger, 1986.

Kolb, Robert W. *Understanding Futures Markets.* 3rd ed. Miami, Fla.: Kolb Publishing Company, 1991.

MacKinlay, Craig, and Krishna Ramaswamy. "Index Futures Arbitrage and the Behavior of Stock Index Futures Prices." *Review of Financial Studies,* 1988.

Modest, David M., and S. Sundaresan. "The Relationship between Spot and Futures Prices in Stock Index Futures Markets: Some Preliminary Evidence." *Journal of Futures Markets,*1983.

Ramaswamy, Krishna, and S. Sundaresan. "The Valuation of Options on Futures Contracts." *Journal of Finance,* 1985.

Stoll, Hans, and Richard Whaley. "Futures and Options on Stock Indexes: Economic Purpose, Arbitrage and Market Structure." *Review of Futures Markets,* 1988.

Understanding Floating-Rate Securities and Derivative Securities

There has been a revolution in the financial markets associated with the unbundling of basic characteristics of financial instruments. This has been followed recently by the repackaging of certain financial flows into alternative instruments. In the debt market, cash flows are decomposed and parceled out to separate buyers. Alternatively, pools of assets are collected to stabilize return and reduce risks. This chapter reviews these innovations in the financial markets, analyzes a series of derivative instruments, and looks at the pricing of their underlying cash flows. Our discussion ends with an analysis of the use of these instruments.

This is our final chapter concerned exclusively with instruments of the financial markets. There are more financial instruments than there are pages in this book, yet most are variations on a few major themes. In this chapter, we shall cover the remaining "themes" but leave largely untouched a discussion of the numerous "variations." Indeed, the variations are proliferating at a speed so rapid that any treatment of them is bound to be quickly outdated and incomplete. Nonetheless, a solid understanding of the fundamental security types discussed in this and previous chapters places the reader in a strong position to quickly understand most of the variations that he or she will encounter in the marketplace.

We begin our discussion with variable rate securities and then proceed to derivative instruments, such as inverse floaters, swaps, swaptions, warrants, caps, and floors. Although space limitations preclude a thorough discussion of the valuation of each of these security types, we do focus on one of these securities—interest rate caps—to demonstrate how our previously presented methodologies for valuation and duration analysis can be applied.

Variable-Coupon Securities

Variable-coupon securities is the generic name given to a class of securities that features interest payments, or coupons, that change at specified reset intervals according to a predetermined formula. On scheduled reset dates, the coupon rates are adjusted to prevailing market rates. When the coupons are changed, the security is said to be **repriced.** The effect of this repricing is to avoid large price swings in the security as the general level of interest rates fluctuates over time. The more frequent the reset dates and the less constrained the adjustments are to move with current interest rate levels, the closer to par value the security will trade. Therefore, as a general rule, variable-coupon securities tend to exhibit less price volatility than their fixed-rate counterparts. As is the case with all debt securities, however, credit quality change will also cause price movement here.

Although they had long been in existence in the Eurobond market, variable-coupon securities were introduced into the U.S. economy during the mid-1970s, when interest rate volatility began to increase. They have been popular ever since, and they are especially sought after by investors during periods of highly volatile or rising interest rates.

Types of Variable-Coupon Securities

There are several kinds of financial instruments that fit in the class of variable-coupon securities. They include **floating-rate notes** (FRNs), **variable-coupon bonds, perpetual floaters, variable-coupon renewable notes** (VCRs), **variable annuities,** and **adjustable-rate mortgages** (ARMs), among others. These various securities share at least two things in common: Their periodic payments vary and are linked to an interest rate index of some sort. Such indices include the London Interbank Borrowing or Offer Rate (LIBBR and LIBOR, respectively), the three-month T-bill rate, a long-term government bond rate index, or some sort of composite of short, long, and intermediate bond yields.[1] They differ from one another in sometimes subtle, and other times substantive, ways. For instance, floating-rate notes, variable-coupon bonds, and perpetual floaters differ in little more than maturity. Floating-rate notes are intermediate-term notes; variable-coupon bonds are longer-term bonds, and perpetual floaters never mature. On the other hand, the differences can be more substantial. For example, VCRs are FRNs with renewal options attached and interest bonuses to the purchasers who agree to renew. These differences can result in substantially different market values for each of these instruments and attract different buyers.

Some of these instruments include variability not only in interest payments but also principal payments during their life. This latter category includes variable annuities as well as various forms of adjustable-rate mortgage products. Variable annuities differ from the other securities in that their payments are set higher than the interest rate—high enough to amortize the principal over the expected life of the annuity. The maturity of variable annuities may depend on the longevity of the purchaser's life, or it may be for a fixed term. ARMs are backed by real property. Like variable annuities, the payments include a portion to amortize the principal over a fixed term. They also typically carry an option that allows the borrower to prepay the outstanding indebtedness. Often, these instruments contain a provision that limits the extent of interest and/or payment adjustment in any given period and throughout the life of the mortgage. Therefore, the adjustment does not always reflect the full extent of movement in general interest rates, and there can even be negative amortization, where the principal amount of the loan grows over time.

Valuation of Variable-Coupon Securities

It is tempting to view variable-coupon securities as equivalent to a sequence of single-period borrowings where the rate is reset to reflect the prevailing cost of credit during each period. However, this is not the case. Remember that rates adjust periodically *only* to capture movement in a general interest rate index. If a corporation were to borrow new money each period, the rate charged would reflect not only movement in the level of interest rates but also any changes over time in general credit market conditions and changes in the creditworthiness of the borrower. During some periods, it may not even be feasible to acquire funds due to the deterioration in credit. Thus, the spread above the benchmark rate of these instruments must incorporate a premium to compensate the investor for changing credit risk that a single-period loan would not have.

At issue, these variable-rate products typically sell for par value or very close to it. After issue, however, the price often deviates from par. Laurie Goodman has

---

[1]Even U.S. savings bonds are variable-rate bonds linked to an index of the better of short- and intermediate-term Treasury yields, whichever is higher, but they do not feature periodic coupons; all interest is accrued and paid out at maturity.

developed a simple approach to valuing floating-rate notes, or "floaters," after issue.[2] In her model, the price (P) of this instrument at any time after issue can be viewed as the sum of two positions:

1. The value, V, of a par floater offering the given spread over the benchmark rate.
2. An implicit interest subsidy to the borrower, or bonus to the lender, related to the change in credit quality since issue. The subsidy or bonus is equal to the discounted present value of the difference between the credit spread at issuance and the current credit spread. Denote this value the credit annuity, A.

Then, at any moment in time, the price of our hypothetical floater may be written as

$$P = V + A$$

If the borrower's credit quality has improved since issue, A is positive; if it has deteriorated, A is negative.

Goodman gives the following example of this approach. The 10-year Bank of New England FRN issued on July 15, 1986, was initially priced at 1/8 (12.5 b.p.) over three-month LIBOR. Two years later, on July 15, 1988, the required spread for this borrower was 42.5 b.p. over LIBOR because of the credit condition of the bank. Thus, due to deterioration in the bank's credit condition, the coupon, even though variable, would be yielding the investor 30 b.p. per year *less* than he or she should be receiving. This will cause the FRN to be selling at a discount, even after a rate reset. The size of the discount is exactly the present value of 30 b.p. per year per $100 par, discounted at the appropriate rate. Using the discount rate of 9.75 percent relevant to 1988, the value of this annuity is 1.64.[3] Therefore, the value of the floating-rate note becomes:

$$P = V + A$$

$$= 100 - 1.64$$

$$= 98.36$$

In fact, the selling price of the issue on that date was 98.375.

This example of the Bank of New England is useful for another reason. As you may remember from media coverage, our friends in New England were not exactly prospering during that period. Credit risk continued to increase, but once purchased, the FRN could not recognize this deterioration in its coupon reset policy. In this, like other debt instruments, credit risk remained with the lender,

---

[2] See Laurie Goodman, "Pricing Floating Rate Notes: A Simple Approach," *Financial Strategies Group*. Goldman Sachs & Co., July 1988. Our definitions and example closely follow those presented by Goodman.

[3] Goodman's justification for the 9.75 percent rate was based on the discount rate of a comparable maturity, comparable default risk, but fixed-rate bond.

even though the interest rate risk was shed by virtue of the FRN instrument's repricing provision.

Perpetual Floaters

In Chapter 6, we discussed perpetuities (consols)—fixed-coupon bonds that pay interest forever but never return principal. Variable-rate securities also have their perpetual analogues, called **perpetual floaters** (PFs). These instruments make interest payments that fluctuate with a constant spread above an interest rate index such as LIBOR but never return any principal.

During the 1980s, a number of large international banks issued perpetual floaters as a way of raising capital. Because principal is never repaid, bank regulators considered the funds raised from the sale of PFs as qualifying capital for regulatory purposes. This regulatory accounting concession was made even though PFs are, in fact, debt. Holders have no privileges of ownership such as dividends or profit sharing and voting rights. Moreover, tax authorities treat the periodic payments as deductible interest payments, similar to the treatment they accord any other debt. Therein lies the dual advantage of this product to banks: They can boost their regulatory capital while at the same time reducing their taxes.

Fixed-rate consol bonds would be a poor substitute, from the point of view of a bank, because of their very long durations. Banks typically have had limited access to the long-term debt market, partially because of the nature of their business and their assets. Both tend toward the short end of the maturity spectrum.

While perpetual floaters have long lives (indeed, supposedly infinite lives), their durations are quite short—typically only a few months. Their short durations stem from the fact that the interest payments are frequently reset to conform to current interest rates. Thus, there is little or no interest rate risk.

This is not to say that perpetual floaters are without price risk. While a change in market interest rates, in and of itself, should not have much impact on the prices of PFs, a credit quality change can have a devastating impact on prices. This risk is called **basis risk.** A basis change occurs when the credit quality of the company issuing the PF undergoes a change. If credit quality deteriorates, the market will demand a higher spread above the reference interest rate. However, since PFs feature a constant spread above the floating reference rate, the price will have to fall to accommodate the basis change. During the late 1980s and early 1990s, many PFs were trading at only 20 to 60 per dollar of principal because of credit quality erosion among large commercial banks.

In reality, very few commercial enterprises continue operation for more than a century or two. However, these same firms are making promises that stretch into eternity.[4] The skepticism, therefore, with which the market treats PFs is perhaps

---

[4]Preferred and common stock also are securities with supposedly infinite lives, but they don't carry promises about making certain payments. Consol bonds have infinite lives and do make promises, but they are *extremely* rare.

warranted. The price effects of a deterioration in credit quality would probably be even larger were it not for the fact that the present value of payments 60 or more years into the future is trivial. There is a secondary market for trading these instruments, but the market is characterized by low liquidity and large bid-ask spreads.

Inverse Floaters and Super Floaters

An **inverse floater** is a type of **derivative security** because its payoff stream is manufactured from other securities. Unlike floating-rate notes, which offer higher payoffs under rising interest rates, an inverse floater offers higher payoffs under falling interest rates, and diminishing payoffs as interest rates rise. Inverse floaters are "manufactured" out of a fixed-income instrument whose payments are divided into two parts and sold separately. A floating-rate instrument is sold to one group of investors, while an inverse floater is sold to the other group. The entity offering this arrangement hopes to make a profit for this service.

Here is how it works. Consider an eight-year corporate bond offering 10 percent fixed annual interest payments. The face value of the bond is $1,000, and therefore, the annual interest payments are $100. Suppose that the prevailing risk-free short-term rate of interest is 8 percent. Further, let's assume that the going rate on this corporate floater requires that its yield exceed the short-term rate by 100 b.p. Thus, initial payments on floating-rate securities are 9 percent interest. The financial engineer can decompose this fixed-rate bond into two parts. The first is a floating-rate security yielding 9 percent to the investor. The second is a security, called an inverse floater, that provides the residual yield from the fixed-rate issue, reduced by the engineer's fee.

In Exhibit 16.1 we have shown the hypothetical evolution of the short-term interest rate over time, along with the payments due to holders of floating-rate securities and inverse floaters. The floating-rate security holders are always paid the [(short rate + 100 b.p.) × par value], while the inverse floater holder receives a payment worth {[18% − (short rate + 100 b.p.)] × par value}. The par value of the fixed-rate bond is $1,000, and each investor is buying a security worth only half that amount; accordingly, the par values of the floater and inverse floater are $500 each. Because both the floater and inverse floater are paying the "going rate," they will be initially priced at their par values.

There are several things noteworthy about this example. First, the last two columns always sum to $90, which is the total cash outflow per period that needs to be paid to the holders of the floater and inverse floater. However, the second column, which designates the total cash inflow per period from the purchase of the fixed-rate bond, is always $100. The way we have set up the example, it looks like a pure arbitrage! Someone could offer a package of floaters and inverse floaters and, using a high-grade bond to secure the payments, earn a guaranteed profit.

Yet, there are two items that militate against this prospect. Note that if the floating rate ever exceeds 18 percent, the inverse floater holder is paid nothing.

EXHIBIT 16.1   Manufacturing Floaters and Inverse Floaters from an 8 Percent Fixed-Rate Bond

Year	Fixed Payment ($1,000 par)	Short Rate (SR)	Floating Rate (FR) (= SR + 1%)	Floating Payment (= FR × $500)	Inverse Floater Payment [= (18% − FR) × $500]
1	$100	8%	9%	$45	$45
2	100	6	7	35	55
3	100	9	10	50	40
4	100	13	14	70	20
5	100	10	11	55	35
6	100	7	8	40	50
7	100	3	4	20	70
8	100	8	9	45	45

Since the inverse floater investor can never receive less than $0 and is not obligated to pay if the floating rate exceeds 18 percent, the payments due the holder of the floater continue to increase and must be paid from the residual interest. If the floating rate ever exceeds 20 percent, the payment owed to the holder of the floater will exceed the $100 inflow from the fixed-rate bond, leaving the engineer vulnerable to cash outflows. To protect against that eventuality, the issuer of the floater/inverse floater package may wish to purchase an interest rate cap (see the section on interest rate caps and floors at the end of this chapter), thereby expending some of the profits he had hoped to reap. Alternatively, he could absorb the risk, in which case it is no longer a true arbitrage. By definition, arbitrage is achieved when you are able to generate a future cash inflow with no current outflow or a current inflow with no future net outflow. If interest rates soar during the eight-year period, the issuer could be placed at substantial risk. The second item that militates against this prospect is that a real floater issue is likely to be priced at a much smaller margin. Our example is excessively optimistic about the spread that is obtainable from splitting a fixed-income security into a package of floaters and inverse floaters. It did, however, get your attention! If the spread were really that large, arbitrageurs would enter into the fray and drive it away through their actions.

During the early 1990s, when interest rates plummeted, inverse floaters were very popular. A number of designs were offered to cater to the desires of investors. For example, some were levered so that for every percentage point that floating rates dropped below some threshold, the investor would receive an additional 2 to 3 percent interest payment. On the other hand, if interest rates rose above that threshold level, interest payments would decline 2 to 3 percent for each percentage point rise. There were also **super floaters,** which would offer the opposite side of the equation: For each percentage point increase in interest rates above some threshold, the investor would receive an additional 2 to 3 percent coupon. But for each percentage point decline in interest rates, the coupon would fall by 2 to 3 percent. Indeed, the varieties on this theme continue to expand beyond the limits of this paragraph!

Inflation-Linked Bonds

A close relative to the floating-rate notes and variable-coupon bonds is the inflation-linked bond, sometimes referred to simply as an indexed bond, or purchasing power bond. An **inflation-linked bond** has a variable coupon whose size is indexed to the purchasing power of money, rather than to prevailing interest rates. The purpose of this type of bond is to protect investors against the erosion of their investment occasioned by inflation. In contrast to a typical variable-coupon bond, whose coupons reflect changes both in real interest rates and *expected* inflation, as manifested in the nominal interest rate to which they are linked, the inflation-linked bond is indexed only to the *realized* inflation. The real rate offered is fixed at the outset.

The implications of this distinction are important. A change in either expected inflation or real interest, or both, will be captured by the adjustment to the variable-coupon bond. Thus, apart from changing credit conditions, a variable-coupon bond will tend to trade near par on the repricing dates. However, with the inflation-linked bond, only changes in the purchasing power of money are reflected in the variable coupon. A change in the real rate of interest will not be compensated in the payout pattern of the bond. Hence, the price of an indexed bond will be sensitive to changes in real rates.

There are two main types of inflation-linked bonds available. Both protect the investor against changes in the inflation rate, but they do so in different ways. Type #1 Bonds offer a coupon that is the sum of a fixed real rate and the inflation rate realized during the period.[5] Type #1 Bonds return the original principal at the maturity date without any adjustment. Type #2 Bonds offer a fixed real coupon rate based on a floating principal; the principal floats with the purchasing power price index. Thus, the Type #2 Bond's coupon is variable only to the extent that the principal on which it is based changes. Type #2 Bonds return the principal at the maturity date, adjusted to compensate for value erosion caused by inflation. We illustrate two hypothetical five-year bonds, linked to the consumer price index (CPI), in Exhibit 16.2. Notice how the Type #1 Bond has substantial variation in the periodic coupon payment, ranging from $52.00 to a high of $109.00. At maturity, however, it repays only the initial principal of $1,000.00. On the other hand, the Type #2 Bond has little variation in coupon payments but returns the

---

[5]Note that to be fully "inflation neutral," Type #1 Bonds should offer a coupon slightly higher than that indicated here. Using the Fisher equation discussed in Chapter 4, the full adjustment would require the coupon to be the sum of the real rate, the inflation rate, and the product of the real rate and the inflation rate:

$$R = r + \pi + r\pi$$

where R is the nominal coupon rate, r is the real rate, and π is the inflation rate. For example, if realized inflation during a period were 8 percent and the real coupon rate were 3 percent, Type #1 Bonds would pay a coupon of 11 percent (= 3% + 8%), whereas a fully adjusting coupon would pay 11.24 percent [= 3% + 8% + (3% × 8%)].

EXHIBIT 16.2   Inflation-Linked Bonds

(3 percent real annual coupon; $1,000 principal; issued August 30, 1997)

Year	Consumer Price Index	Inflation Rate (%)	Type #1 Coupon	Type #2 Coupon
1997	100.0			
1998	105.4	5.40%	$ 84.00	$ 31.62
1999	113.6	7.78	107.80	34.08
2000	118.0	3.87	68.70	35.40
2001	120.6	2.20	52.00	36.18
2002	130.2	7.96	109.60	39.06
Return of principal, August 30, 2002.			$1,000.00	$1,302.00

inflation premium in the principal repayment at maturity. It returns fully 30 percent more than either the Type #1 Bond or the initial bond principal.

There are many variations on the inflation-indexed bond presently available. Some indexed bonds are linked to the CPI, whereas others are linked to the GDP Deflator or some other price index. Guaranteed minimum nominal coupons may be a part of the bond covenant. There may be a provision to set the coupon rates "out of phase," so that each period's coupon adjusts to the prior period's inflation rate. This provision is usually for the convenience of the issuer, who needs to accumulate sufficient funds to pay the coupon and prefers to know in advance how much will be required at the end of a coupon period.

Type #1 Bonds have been issued in the United States, England, and elsewhere, but Type #2 Bonds are more popular in many countries fraught with higher inflation, such as Israel and Brazil. The durations of Type #1 Bonds are shorter than those of Type #2 Bonds because more of the cash flow is received sooner under the Type #1 structure.[6] The U.S. market for inflation-linked bonds is still very small, but in other countries, these bonds may be a dominant part of the capital market. In spite of the fact that many are issued by sovereign countries, most indexed bonds exhibit credit risk to some degree. The 1980s and 1990s have shown investors that even national government debt can contain credit risk.[7] When credit risk is present, the required real rate of interest can change over time, even though the real rate on riskless bonds has not changed. Any change in the required real rate of interest due to changing credit quality can produce large changes in the market price of the indexed bond, particularly bonds of Type #2.

---

[6]For a detailed analysis of the pricing and duration measurement of inflation-linked bonds, see David F. Babbel, "Real Immunization with Index-Linked Bonds," *Financial Analysts Journal,* November/December 1984, pp. 49–54.

[7]The world capital market has come a long way from the days when the then president of Citicorp, Walter Wriston, was quoted as saying, "Companies go bankrupt, not countries."

Swaps

A **swap** is a contract between two counterparties in which each agrees to pay the other's stream of payments on their debt issue over a period of time. Notice that the contract is to exchange the cash flow associated with two different debt issues, not to exchange the principal itself. The principal amounts involved in such transactions are generally equal and are referred to as the **notional principal** of the transaction. There are four broad types of swaps: interest rate swaps, currency swaps, commodity swaps, and mortgage swaps. Each of these types has several variations. The most common swaps today are interest rate swaps and currency swaps, which we will now discuss in turn.

Interest Rate Swaps

Interest rate swaps are arrangements in which parties "swap" interest payments on their debt issues. The interest payment streams are of differing character on the underlying notional principal amount. There is no exchange of principal. However, it is possible to construct a swap where notional principal is allowed to increase or decrease over the contract's life. The two main types of interest rate swaps are coupon swaps and basis swaps. In a **coupon swap,** one counterparty pays the other the fixed-coupon rate, and the other, in return, pays the coupon rate on a floating-rate instrument.

For example, one counterparty may agree to make semiannual, fixed-rate payments of 10 percent (per annum) for eight years on a notional principal of $100 million. Thus, he would pay $5 million every six months for 16 payments. In return, he would receive an agreement from the other counterparty to make payments based on LIBOR over an equal span of time. If LIBOR is currently quoted at 8 percent, he would be due $4 million [= (8% for six months) × $100 million] at the end of the first six-month period, resulting in a net outflow of $1 million during the first period. In subsequent periods, the net flow between the two parties could be higher or lower, depending on the LIBOR level prevailing during each period.[8] Basis point spreads off of the floating-rate index can be added or subtracted to adjust for differences in the relative credit standing of the parties to the agreement and are subject to negotiation.

In a **basis swap,** the counterparties exchange payments based upon floating-rate indices, but each coupon is determined by a different reference rate. For example, one counterparty may agree to pay interest payments based on LIBOR plus 100 b.p. in return for interest payments based on the T-bill yield plus 200 b.p. If LIBOR is initially 100 b.p. higher than T-bill yields, no net cash flow will take place during the first period. However, because the interest rate spread between

---

[8]This is considered a "fair swap" if the 10 percent fixed rate, over eight years, corresponds to a combination of forward three-month LIBOR rates implied in the swap yield curve over the same period.

LIBOR and T-bills narrows and widens over time, net cash payments will flow to one or the other counterparty in subsequent periods.

Swaps are useful ways of tailoring the interest rate risk characteristics of investments toward that which is desired. It is, in essence, a mechanism to reduce interest rate risk. You may be asking under your breath, "If the investor needs funding that exhibits a particular interest rate risk exposure, why doesn't he simply borrow in that market directly?" There are three reasons. First, the investor might issue debt in a particular market because he thinks it is underpriced but then be unable to find such an attractive price with the desired interest rate risk exposure. A swap lets him benefit from his acquisition of the underpriced resources without suffering from the unwanted effects of an adverse movement in interest rates.

Second, the investor's desired interest rate risk exposure may change over time. It is very costly to liquidate a position in bonds and issue a new one each time the desired risk characteristics change. However, it is quite inexpensive to alter this exposure through a swap.

Finally, and most importantly, it may be that one of the parties is better positioned to acquire one type of funding than another. For example, conventional wisdom has it that issuers of debt with high credit standing find it cheaper to issue fixed-rate debt, while borrowers with lower credit standing often find it cheaper to borrow at floating rates. Moreover, borrowers in some countries in Europe have more liquid markets in floating-rate securities, whereas borrowers in other markets, such as the United States and Japan, may find it easier to borrow at fixed rates. The type of debt that is cheapest or easiest to issue for a borrower may not necessarily have the borrower's desired payment pattern. A swap may alter the characteristics of the liability to conform more to that which is desired by the borrower. In this way, the borrower can benefit from his comparative advantage to borrow in one market, while avoiding the adverse consequences of having liabilities ill-suited to his business needs.

Currency Swaps

While interest rate swaps are a relatively recent introduction to the financial markets, currency swaps have been around for much longer. As we noted in Chapter 10, there are two bases on which currencies are traded in the foreign exchange market: spot and forward. A spot transaction involves the exchange of currencies two business days later, whereas a forward transaction involves the exchange of currencies further into the future, often several months or even years.

A **currency swap** is a pair of simultaneous spot and forward transactions in which the forward transaction offsets or unwinds the spot transaction.[9] For example, a holder of Swiss francs may wish to trade them for dollars in the spot market

---

[9] See Marcia Stigum, *The Money Market*, 3rd ed. (Burr Ridge, IL: Irwin Professional Publishing, 1990), pp. 272–275; and Eileen Baecher, "Swaps and the Derivative Markets," *Fixed Income Research*. Goldman Sachs & Co., January 1991.

and simultaneously enter into a forward contract to return the dollars for francs six months hence. This would be called a swap. The effect of the swap is to reduce the foreign exchange risk associated with acquiring and, later, selling dollars. During the period of the swap, the recipient of dollars can earn fixed or variable dollar rates of interest, while the recipient of Swiss francs can earn fixed or variable rates on that currency.

Swaptions

In recent years, yet another variation of the swap has been devised: the swaption. A **swaption** is the name that is applied to that class of financial instruments that combines options with interest rate or currency swaps.

The buyer of the swaption has the right, but not the obligation, to enter into a new swap or to cancel or extend participation in an existing swap on a future date. In both structures, the rates at which the options to enter into a new swap or to terminate or extend an existing swap are established at prespecified levels. The other terms of the swap are also specified at the outset. In the case of interest rate swaptions, rights to a stream of fixed-rate payments are traded for a stream of floating-rate payments. The trading language is similar to that for any other option, though to avoid possible confusion, the fixed-rate payments are regarded as the underlying commodity. Hence a **call swaption** gives the holder the right to receive the fixed rate and pay floating, whereas a **put swaption** gives the holder the right to receive floating and pay fixed. If interest rates increase, the put will be more valuable because the holder will benefit by receiving the higher floating-interest rates. On the other hand, if rates fall, the call swaption is more valuable.

Bond Warrants

A close relative to the swaption is a warrant on a particular bond. While swaptions are recent introductions to the capital market, warrants have been around for over 100 years. **Bond warrants** give the purchaser the right, but not the obligation, to purchase or sell the bond of a particular issuer at a specific price at some future date. Unlike most optionlike instruments, which expire in less than a year, the term to expiration of a warrant is generally several years long. In addition, the underlying bond also usually has a long term to maturity, typically 10 years or more.

Although swaptions and warrants have a number of elements in common, there are two important features of warrants that distinguish them from swaptions. First, the value of a warrant is sensitive to the new issue rate of a particular bond issuer, whereas a swaption is sensitive to the general level of corporate rates (e.g., LIBOR). Second, to exercise a warrant, the holder must actually purchase the underlying bond, whereas exercising a swaption does not entail the transfer of any underlying principal; only the difference between the fixed rate and the floating rate is exchanged. These two differences foster a much greater liquidity in the swaption market compared to that in the warrant market.

Interest Rate Caps and Floors

Caps are private contracts between two parties in which one party protects another against interest rate movements above a prespecified level. The investor pays a fee for the cap; in return, the cap's originator gives him monetary compensation whenever interest rates, as reflected in some specified interest rate index, rise above the cap, or **strike level.** A strike level is analogous to exercise price, or strike price, discussed in the previous chapter, except that it is an interest rate rather than a security price. In some sense, caps can be viewed as a type of "interest rate insurance policy"—protection against the effects of rising interest rates. An investment banker often acts as broker for the transaction. However, as in all over-the-counter transactions, the credit risk of each party is an important element of the agreement.

The compensation paid to the investor buying the cap depends primarily on three factors: (1) the degree to which the interest index exceeds the cap level, (2) the length of time of this positive spread, and (3) the size of the contract. It is easiest to explain the interplay of these three forces through an example. Consider a cap trading with the following features:

Underlying index: three-month LIBOR

Term of cap: five years

Rate determination: quarterly

Cap level (strike level): 10.00 percent

Underlying (notional) amount: $100 million

Price: $1.65 million

This cap agreement specifies a quarterly determination date. If, for example, the London Interbank Offered Rate (LIBOR) is quoted at 12 percent on the determination date, the investor will receive $511,111 at the end of that quarter. The payoff is computed as follows:

$$\left(\begin{matrix} \text{Reference} \\ \text{rate} \end{matrix} - \begin{matrix} \text{Cap} \\ \text{level} \end{matrix} \right) \times \frac{\text{Days in period}}{360} \times \begin{matrix} \text{Underlying} \\ \text{amount} \end{matrix} = \begin{matrix} \text{Periodic} \\ \text{payoff} \end{matrix}$$

$$= (12.00\% - 10.00\%) \times \frac{92}{360} \times \$100,000,000 = \$511,111$$

If, on the determination date, LIBOR is less than the cap rate, no payment will be received by the investor for that quarter. The amount paid to the investor for each ensuing quarter would be determined in exactly the same manner as described above, up through and including the final determination date for the chosen maturity of the contract. The higher the interest index is above the cap

Exhibit 16.3

Three-month LIBOR from 1986 through 1994

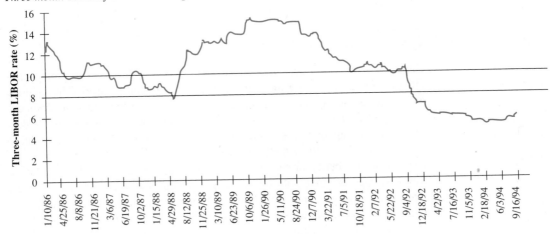

level, the larger the payment will be. The longer this spread remains positive, the longer the cap investor will receive periodic payments. The longer the cap maturity, the more periodic payments to the investor are possible. The lower the cap level is set, the more likely it is for the investor to receive payoffs.

Today, caps are available with a variety of features. The underlying index selected may be the one-month, three-month, and six-month rates based on LIBOR, the commercial paper rate, T-bill discount rates or yields, the prime rate, the municipal bond yield, and others. The determination date, the date on which the interest spread over the cap rate is calculated, may be anywhere from daily to annually over the term of the cap. Most common determination date intervals are monthly and quarterly. The term of the contract may be from three months to 12 years or more. Common terms are for three, five, and seven years.

To see how this hypothetical cap would behave over time, Exhibit 16.3 shows average monthly levels for three-month LIBOR from October 1986 through October 1994. The two horizontal lines represent 8 percent and 10 percent cap levels for two hypothetical 10-year caps purchased in October 1986. Exhibit 16.4 shows the actual payouts for a $100 million notional amount of such caps. As before, payouts are assumed to occur on a quarterly basis but in arrears.[10] As you can see from the graph, substantial payouts at the assumed cap levels occurred during the period from 1988 to 1991. Although, as would be expected, the 8 percent cap pays out more frequently and in greater amounts than the 10 percent cap, the 8 percent

---

[10]Caps are available in two types: (1) those that make periodic payments based on the then current interest rate spreads, and (2) those that make periodic payments based on the interest rate spreads prevailing at the previous reset date. The latter caps are "in arrears." The cap valued in Box 16.1 is not in arrears.

Exhibit 16.4

Hypothetical cap payouts from 1986–1994

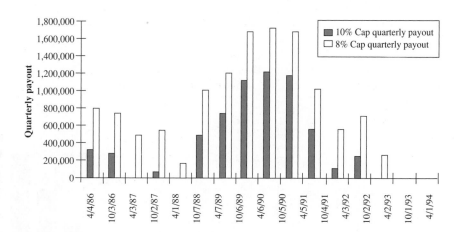

cap's price would have been larger because of the lower cap level. The determination of the cap's price will be discussed next.

Valuation of Interest Rate Caps

In Chapter 6, we showed how a coupon-bearing default-free bond can be valued as the sum of prices of zero-coupon bonds that can be assembled to replicate its cash flows. Interest rate caps can also be viewed in this fashion; they represent a package of single-payment caps whose maturity dates range from the earliest cap payment to the last cap payment. For example, a five-year cap that has semiannual reset dates can be represented as a series of 10 European-style[11] interest rate options, each expiring at a successively later date. The first option would expire in six months, the next in one year, and so forth. The values of the options with longer times until expiration will be higher than those expiring sooner, because the longer time period gives a greater chance for a substantial increase of market rates of interest above the strike level. This was noted in a similar context in our general discussion on options in Chapter 15. In Exhibit 16.5, the values of each of the implicit interest rate options are given by the black portions of the bars; the shaded portions represent the cumulative values of all interest rate options contained in caps with maturities ranging from six months to seven years. For instance, the five-year, 10 percent cap has an illustrated value of close to 1.6 percent of the notional principal of the cap,[12] whereas a single interest rate option expiring in five years would have a value of only 0.25 percent of the notional principal.

---

[11]Remember that a European-style option may be exercised only at expiration. An American-style option may be exercised any time prior to expiration.

[12]This illustration is based on an 8 percent flat spot rate curve and assumes 22 percent volatility of short rates. The value bars reflect the common practice of having the payment at the end of the period keyed to the interest rate spread at the beginning of the period. Thus, the interest rate option expiring at the end of the first six months is worthless, as the market rate of interest is below the cap rate at the outset.

Exhibit 16.5

Cap value equals sum of one-period caps (8 percent flat spot curve; 10 percent strike level)

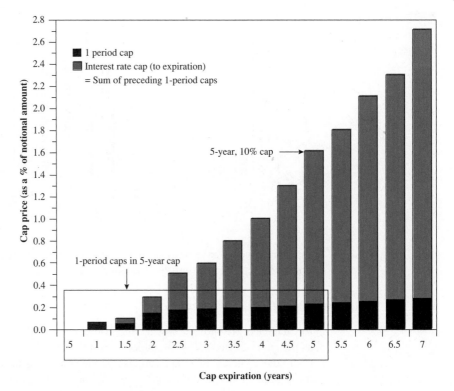

A second important point from Exhibit 16.5 is that the value of a cap should decline as it approaches maturity, assuming no changes in interest rates and volatility. Not only does the time value of each cap decline but, over time, there are also fewer and fewer interest rate options remaining. This also means that, all else equal, longer-term caps are worth more than shorter-term caps.

Although caps can be valued as a combination of interest rate options having successively longer expiration dates, in practice they are usually valued more directly using an interest rate lattice approach.[13] In Box 16.1 we provide an example of the mechanics of cap valuation using the lattice technique.

Price Sensitivity of Caps to Interest Rates

In Exhibit 16.6, we have drawn price profiles of interest rate caps featuring a 10 percent strike level with terms of three, five, and seven years. The exhibit illustrates cap prices as a function of market rates of interest. It is evident that cap prices increase with interest rates in a nonlinear fashion and that caps with longer terms to expiration are more valuable than those with shorter terms.

---

[13]The simulation approach can also be used but is not necessary since payoff amounts in any given period do not depend on the path that interest rates took to arrive at their level on the determination dates.

Exhibit 16.6

Price sensitivity by term of cap (price versus interest rates)

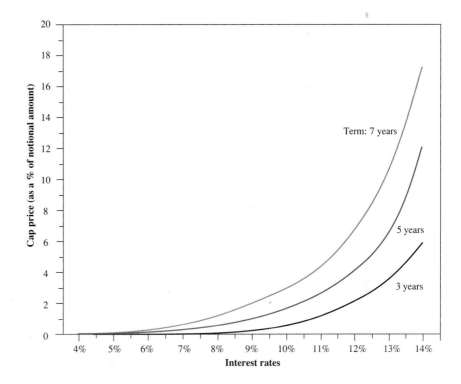

Cap price (as a % of notional amount)

Term: 7 years

5 years

3 years

Interest rates

Exhibit 16.7 shows the price profiles of five-year caps with varying strike levels of 8 percent, 10 percent, and 12 percent. Again, the exhibit illustrates cap prices as a function of market rates of interest. As in the previous exhibit, the price profiles are upward sloping and convex with increasing interest rates. Caps with lower strike levels command higher prices across all interest rates.

The price profiles give us the information necessary to compute duration and convexity measures. To compute the modified duration of a cap, we proceed as we have in previous chapters. The (negative of the) slope of the price profile is divided by the cap price at the current market rate of interest. Note that all cap price profiles slope upward. This is the opposite of the bond price profiles. Thus, while bonds have positive durations, caps have negative durations. In other words, bond prices decline when interest rates increase, whereas cap prices rise with increasing interest rates. If we were to perform the calculations, we would find that interest rate caps are highly convex instruments with very large negative durations. Indeed, it is not uncommon to find a cap with a negative duration of from 20 to 120 "years," whereas the duration of a coupon-bearing bond rarely exceeds 12 years.[14] Exhibit 16.8 provides

---

[14]The use of the "year" unit of measure for duration is curious in the context of interest rate caps. For a three-month cap to have a negative duration of 100 years does not have intuitive appeal, whereas with a bond, where duration is often computed as a present-value-weighted average of the

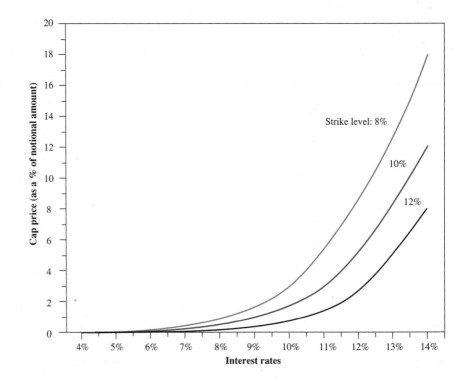

some sample cap values and durations under specified conditions. The positive convexity of interest rate caps means that caps will rise by increasing amounts at successively higher levels of interest. This positive convexity is a characteristic of most options that are held long.

Impact of Expected Short-Rate Volatility

Exhibit 16.9 portrays theoretical prices for caps of various terms and interest rate volatilities. Each line represents prices for various terms at each level of volatility. The main conclusions are that: (1) All else equal, greater expected volatility is correlated with higher cap values; and (2) as a cap ages, changes in volatility, as well as changes in interest rates, may have a greater impact on value than aging alone. For example, a five-year cap currently valued at 0.8 percent assuming 16 percent volatility (point A in Exhibit 16.9) should theoretically be worth .65 percent in six months (point B), but it could be worth 1.0 percent (point C) if volatility increases to 20 percent.

---

payment dates, the "year" label makes some sense. In the case of caps, durations are better interpreted as measures of relative price sensitivity. For example, a cap with a negative duration of 120 would increase in value approximately 120 percent for a 100 b.p. rise in interest rates, while a bond with a duration of 12 would decrease in value approximately 12 percent for a 100 b.p. rise in interest rates.

EXHIBIT 16.8   Cap Durations and Prices versus Market Interest Rates
(maturity of cap = 5 years; volatility* = 0.0775; quarterly payments)

Market Rate	Duration of 7% Cap	Price (%)	Duration of 8% Cap	Price (%)	Duration of 9% Cap	Price (%)
0.04	−90.8	0.99%	−106.1	0.46%	−122.3	0.21%
0.05	−69.9	2.16	−81.8	1.12	−94.2	0.55
0.06	−54.9	4.00	−64.8	2.29	−75.0	1.23
0.07	−42.8	6.55	−51.9	4.08	−60.7	2.40
0.08	−33.1	9.61	−41.7	6.52	−49.3	4.14
0.09	−25.6	12.91	−32.6	9.44	−39.7	6.48
0.10	−20.2	16.23	−25.4	12.61	−31.5	9.29
0.11	−16.3	19.47	−20.1	15.83	−25.0	12.34
0.12	−13.5	22.58	−16.3	18.98	−20.0	15.45

*The cap prices and durations are based on the Cox-Ingersoll-Ross (CIR) term structure model. A CIR volatility of 0.0775 and an annual speed of mean reversion of 0.4 were assumed. This translates roughly into standard volatility measures by dividing by the square root of the interest rate. For example, at an interest rate of 8 percent, a CIR volatility of .0775 translates into a standard volatility of .274 (= .0775 ÷ $\sqrt{.08}$). Modified durations were calculated in the usual way, by jiggling the interest rate lattice by 50 b.p. in each direction and dividing the difference in resulting prices by the initial price.

EXHIBIT 16.9

Price versus expiration and volatility
(8 percent flat spot curve; 10 percent strike level)

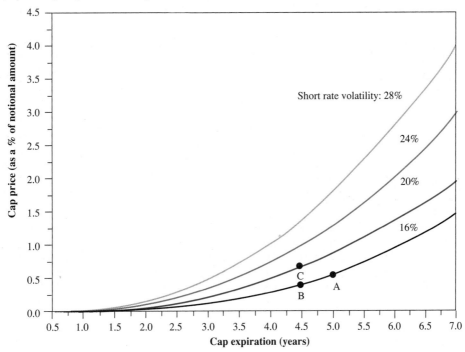

Box 16.1

Cap Valuation Using the Lattice Technique

In this example, we will value a three-year cap with a 9 percent strike level that has annual determination dates coinciding with the annual payment dates. Our cap has its payments keyed to the one-year T-bill rate, which is initially at 8 percent. Ensuing movements in this rate are described by a simple multiplicative process, where the volatility consistent with the current term structure of interest is 20 percent. The notional principal of the cap is $100,000. What is the cap worth?

To solve that question, we must first set up the interest rate lattice as follows:

Interest rate tree

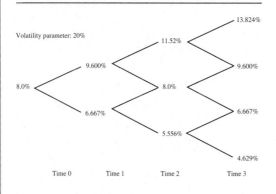

| Time 0 | Time 1 | Time 2 | Time 3 |

Time 3, the single-year rate may be 13.824 percent, 9.6 percent, 6.667 percent, or 4.630 percent.

Having set up our interest rate lattice properly, in a manner consistent with the observed term structure of interest rates (see Box 7.1 for an example of the term structure consistent with this 8.0 percent initial rate and 20 percent multiplicative volatility), we are ready to determine the payoff matrix. The payoff on a cap is given as follows:

$$\text{Maximum of } \{\$0, [(\text{Market rate} - 9.0\%) \times \$100,000]\}$$

Applying this formula to our interest rate lattice, we can compute the following payoffs:

Cash flow tree

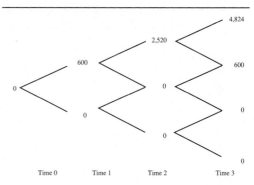

| Time 0 | Time 1 | Time 2 | Time 3 |

At Time 0, the single-year rate is 8 percent. At Time 1, the rate is either 9.6 percent (= 8% × 1.2) or 6.667 percent (= 8% ÷ 1.2). We will assume in our model that movements up or down in future short rates occur with equal probability. At Time 2, the rate may evolve to 11.52 percent (= 9.6% × 1.2), 8.0 percent (= 9.6% ÷ 1.2), 8.0 percent (= 6.667% × 1.2), or 5.556 percent (= 6.667% ÷ 1.2). Proceeding in a similar fashion, at

To verify one of the numbers, the $600 payoff was obtained by subtracting the strike rate of 9 percent from the 9.6 percent future single-period interest rate and multiplying this difference by the $100,000 notional principal. Since this product is higher than zero, it is the payoff at the end of year 1 if interest rates indeed climb to 9.6 percent by that time. On the other hand, if rates decline to 6.667 percent, the payoff is $0. The other payoffs are computed in a like manner.

Having computed the possible payoffs, we must now discount them by the interest rate paths that could give rise to these payoffs. The $600 payoff must be discounted by the interest rate prevailing at the beginning of the period, 8 percent. The quotient, $555.56, gives us the present value of the payment, provided that interest rates are sure to go up to 9.6 percent. Because, under our assumption, there is a 50 percent chance that interest rates will go down to 6.667 percent, with a accompanying payoff of $0, these two numbers must be averaged together to get the present value of the first year's possible payments. The result is $277.78.

At the end of the second year, there is one chance in four that the payoff will be $2,520 and three chances in four that it will be zero. (Remember, there are four interest rate paths at this point.) Interest rates could go up and up, or up then down, or down then up, or down and down. We discount the $2,520 by the first- and second-period interest rates that could give rise to it, 8 percent and 9.6 percent. The quotient of $2,128.95 is then multiplied by the one-fourth probability that it is received, giving $532.24. This is the present value of the second year's possible payments.

Finally, we take the potential payoffs at the end of three years and discount them to present values using the appropriate interest rates. The highest payment can only be received if interest rates increase for three successive years. There is only a one-eighth chance of that happening, according to the construction of our lattice. The present value of that payment is then:

$$\tfrac{1}{8} \ [\$4,824 \div (1.08)(1.096)(1.1152)] = \$456.80$$

Now there are three possible ways of getting a payoff of $600 at the end of the third year. Interest rates could go up twice and then down; down and then up twice; or up, down, and up. Each of these three paths

is equally probable and has a one-eighth chance of occurring. Thus, we must include all these possibilities in computing the cap price. We proceed as follows:

$$\tfrac{1}{8} \ [\$600 \div (1.08)(1.096)(1.1152)] = \$56.82$$

$$\tfrac{1}{8} \ [\$600 \div (1.08)(1.096)(1.0800)] = \$58.67$$

$$\tfrac{1}{8} \ [\$600 \div (1.08)(1.0667)(1.080)] = \$60.28$$

Having computed the present value of each potential cash flow and multiplied it by its probability of occurring, we can simply sum these products to get the value of the cap. The sum is:

$$\$1,442.59 = \$60.28 + \$58.67 + \$56.82 + \$456.80 + \$532.24 + \$277.78$$

Thus, the cap would be worth 1.44 percent of the notional principal of $100,000.

It should be noted in passing that under the same interest rate assumptions, $277.78 is the value of a one-year interest rate option, $532.24 is the value of a two-year interest rate option, and the sum of the other four numbers, $632.57, is the value of a three-year interest rate option, all with a strike level of 9 percent and a contractual underlying amount of $100,000. As was the case in Exhibit 16.5, the longer until expiration, the greater the value of each interest rate option. In setting up the interest rate lattice, it is also obvious that a higher volatility assumption generates higher potential payoffs and, hence, a higher cap value.

In practice, Wall Street analysts and investors use procedures very similar to those that we have employed in this simple example. However, they typically use monthly interest rate intervals instead of annual, and they may employ a more complex process to describe the movements and probabilities of interest rates than that used here. Moreover, there are algorithms that greatly simplify and speed the computational process. Nonetheless, what we have shown contains the gist of what goes on in the calculations.

EXHIBIT 16.10

History of three-month LIBOR volatility
(14-week rolling average)

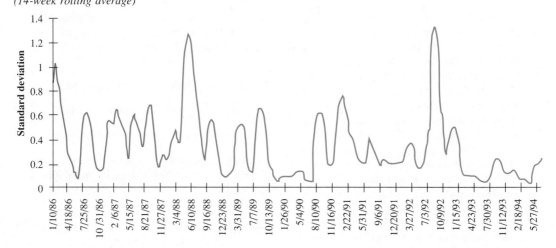

Exhibit 16.10 shows historical volatility levels from 1982 to 1988. It depicts a 14-week rolling standard deviation of three-month LIBOR. In general, volatilities between 15 percent and 30 percent (on a relative basis—i.e., $\sigma \div r$) are not unusual for three-month LIBOR, although short periods with much higher volatilities have occurred.

Relationship to Interest Rate Swaps and Floors

Interest rate floors are like caps in that they are also interest rate "insurance contracts." Unlike caps, however, floors provide protection against falling interest rates. Hence, a floor on three-month LIBOR with a 10 percent strike level entitles the owner to payments from the seller whenever three-month LIBOR falls below 10 percent on determination dates. Such payments would be based on the notional amount and the difference between three-month LIBOR and the 10 percent strike level.

You can synthesize an interest rate floor with a 10 percent strike level by entering into a swap (pay floating, received fixed) and purchasing a cap. The swap agreement must provide for the floating payer to receive 10 percent fixed payments in exchange for floating three-month LIBOR. The cap must make payments to the holder whenever three-month LIBOR is above 10 percent. Combining the two positions, the net payout is always zero for rates above 10 percent because the cap payment received plus the fixed receipt will exactly equal the floating payment due of three-month LIBOR. For rates below 10 percent, the cap does not make payments and the net cash received equals the difference between the 10 percent fixed rate received and the floating index paid. This payout pattern, across all levels of interest rates, is the same as that of an interest rate floor.

The general relationships[15] between swaps, caps, and floors are:

$$\text{Floor} = \text{Cap} + \text{Swap (pay floating, receive fixed)}$$

$$\text{Cap} = \text{Floor} + \text{Swap (receive floating, pay fixed)}$$

Thus, floors can either be purchased outright or created synthetically with a swap and a cap. Another implication is that the valuation of floors is related to the cost of setting up appropriate interest rate swaps and the price of an appropriate cap.

We will not take the space here to depict the behavior of interest rate floor prices vis-à-vis interest rate levels, volatility, and so forth, as the behavior is derived from the properties of caps and swaps. Suffice it to say that, other things being equal, a floor increases in value as interest rates decline, as volatility increases, as term lengthens, and as strike levels rise. Floors exhibit positive convexity and positive durations, often many times higher than those of long-term bonds.

---

[15]These relationships hold most precisely for like term and strike levels and a flat yield curve.

Summary

This chapter reviews several financial instruments that have become important parts of the portfolio of many individuals and firms. However, these instruments tend to be overlooked when one quickly lists the major assets traded in our financial markets.

The instruments considered here include variable-rate instruments of various types, derivative securities, and complex contracts that have developed in response to the needs of investors to hedge or protect their asset portfolios. The first group of instruments includes the ever-increasing number of variable-rate securities that have become a major part of portfolio management. The second group includes assets such as inverse floaters and the like that have achieved recent but substantial popularity. The last group includes swaps, caps, and floors. Although most investors neither see them nor understand them, these contracts have grown in importance in the market.

The pricing or valuation of these instruments is not hard, but it is complicated. Our standard techniques of using discounted cash flow across interest rate paths and constructing synthetic counterparts prove to be more than adequate. It is just difficult at times to see through the rhetoric to understand the underlying cash flows that must be valued. In the end, the financial engineers prove up to the task of applying known techniques to these instruments.

We have now completed our discussion of many of the important instruments of the financial market. There are very few traded instruments that are not somehow related to the ones discussed in the past six chapters. In Part 4 of this text, we turn our attention to the markets in which these instruments are traded and the institutions that play a central role in these markets. We will explore the structure of the markets, the nature of the financial institutions operating there, and the manner in which they use these instruments to address their risks as financial intermediaries.

Key Concepts

bond warrants,   402
call and put swaptions,   402
derivative securities,   396
floating-rate notes, variable-coupon bonds, and
  renewable notes,   392
inflation-linked bonds,   398
interest rate, basis, and currency swaps,
  400–01

interest rate caps and floors,   403–13
inverse and super floaters,   396, 397
notional principal,   400
perpetual floaters,   395
repricing and basis risk,   392, 395
variable-rate annuities and adjustable-rate
  mortgages,   392

Review Questions

1. After three years, a 10-year FRN originally
   issued at par has a discount of 50 b.p. per
   year per $100 par. Using the discount rate of
   8 percent, what is the value of the FRN
   according to Goodman's model?

2. "Perpetual floaters have infinitely long lives;
   therefore, they have infinitely long durations."
   Discuss.

3. Complete the following table of inflation-
   linked bonds:

(5% real annual coupon; $1,000 principal; issue May 15, 1990)

Year	CPI	Inflation Rate	Type #1 Coupon	Type #2 Coupon
1990	100.0	_____	_____	_____
1991	103.7	_____	_____	_____
1992	110.4	_____	_____	_____
1993	118.2	_____	_____	_____
1994	127.1	_____	_____	_____

4. What factors should be considered when deciding whether to buy a Type #1 or Type #2
   inflation-linked bond? Can present value
   analysis be used to compare their relative
   merits?

5. Using the interest rate lattice in Box 16.1,
   what would be the value of a three-year
   interest rate cap with a cap rate of
   9.6 percent?

6. Using the interest rate lattice in Box 16.1,
   what would be the value of a three-year
   interest rate floor with a floor rate of
   6 percent?

7. Using the multiplicative interest rate process
   described in Box 16.1, what would be the
   value of a three-year, 9 percent interest rate
   cap using only 10 percent volatility?

References

Abken, Peter A. "Beyond Plain Vanilla: A Taxonomy of
   Swaps." *Economic Review.* Federal Reserve Bank
   of Atlanta, March/April 1991.

Babbel, David F. "Real Immunization with Index-
   Linked Bonds." *Financial Analysts Journal,* No-
   vember/December 1984.

Baecher, Eileen. "Swaps and the Derivative Markets." *Fixed Income Research*. New York: Goldman Sachs & Co., January 1991.

Black, Fischer, and Myron Scholes. "The Pricing of Options and Corporate Liabilities." *Journal of Political Economy,* May 1973.

Cox, John C.; Stephen A. Ross; and Mark Rubinstein. "Option Pricing: A Simplified Approach." *Journal of Financial Economics,* September 1979.

Goodman, Laurie S. "Pricing Floating Rate Notes: A Simple Approach." *Financial Strategies Group.* New York: Goldman Sachs & Co., July 1988.

Hopper, Gregory P. "A Primer on Currency Derivatives." *Business Review.* Federal Reserve Bank of Philadelphia, May/June 1995.

Jarrow, R., and G. Oldfield. "Forward Contracts and Futures Contracts." *Journal of Financial Economics,* December 1981.

Kuprianov, A. "Money Market Futures." *Economic Review.* Federal Reserve Bank of Richmond, November 1992.

Merton, Robert C. "Theory of Rational Option Pricing." *Bell Journal of Economics and Management Science,* Spring 1973.

Siegel, D.R., and D.F. Siegel. *Futures Markets.* Chicago: Dryden Press, 1990.

Smith, C.W.; C.W. Smithson; and L.M. Wakeman. "The Market for Interest Rate Swaps." *Financial Management,* 1988.

Stapleton, R. C., and M. Subrahamanyam. "Interest Rate Caps and Floors." In *Financial Options: From Theory to Practice,* edited by S. Figlewski. Burr Ridge, Ill.: Irwin Professional Publishing, 1991.

Stigum, Marcia. *The Money Market.* 3rd ed. Burr Ridge, Ill.: Irwin Professional Publishing, 1990.

Markets and Institutions

Institutional Structure of Financial Markets

The common feature of financial markets and institutions is their ability to provide fundamental services to investors and borrowers. This chapter reviews the role performed by markets and institutions and introduces the institutional framework associated with them. The chapter focuses on three activities that are central: the creation of new securities, the exchange of existing securities, and the facilitation of trade.

This chapter marks the beginning of Part 4. In this part of the text, we turn our attention to the two types of financial markets and the institutions that perform various functions within those markets. This change of focus is the next step in a logical progression. In Part 1, we discussed cash flows. In Part 2, we developed

419

the determinants and valuation of cash flows, and in Part 3, we examined the packaging of cash flows into various financial instruments. This section begins with an overview chapter on the functions performed within financial markets. As you can well imagine by now, these functions also center around cash flows—how to promote the efficient flow of cash from those who have excess cash to those who need it for investment and consumption. Subsequent chapters in Part 4 will treat the market structure and major institutional players in the market. Our final chapters in the section will examine how financial institutions that participate in these markets manage the risks inherent in the markets. We will also review recent trends toward change and restructuring in these markets.

Functions Performed in Financial Markets

Financial markets are complex things. They involve thousands of institutions, millions of participants, and billions of transactions each day. These markets transcend geography and time zones, with traders operating from remote corners of the world and interacting at virtually any hour from any place. The globalization of the activity has even brought into question the role of national governments and their capacity to oversee the activity in this sphere. Increasingly global and functioning around the clock, these financial markets are constantly moving and constantly changing. At their core, financial markets perform only a small number of functions for the economies that depend upon them. However, these functions are central to any economy, and without them, investment could not take place, savings would lie dormant, and transactions would grind to a halt. Accordingly, it is critical that the role of financial markets in the economy and the functions they perform be clearly understood.

The three functions on which we concentrate here center upon the markets' role in transferring funds from surplus economic units in the economy to deficit economic units. As such, it is an expansion of the discussion of this activity that was presented in Chapter 2. In Chapter 2, we noted that these markets are central to an economy's need to ensure the smooth, orderly, and efficient flow of resources from one economic agent to another. To facilitate the flow of funds from those with excess cash to those in need of it, the financial markets provide the economy with three key services. First, they facilitate the creation and distribution of instruments of ownership and debt instruments. Second, they promote the development of mechanisms for converting these instruments back into cash and for increasing their liquidity. Third, they foster the development of institutions that ensure the integrity and promote efficient execution of security trades. These functions often are referred to as: (1) **underwriting services,** (2) **secondary market,** and (3) **trading and clearing facilities.** Each of these functions will be examined in turn in the remainder of this chapter. In subsequent chapters, a more in-depth treatment will be given to the structure of markets and institutions that perform these functions.

Creating New Securities

One of the most important functions performed in financial markets is the creation of new securities. While the resale of securities is critical, the first order of business in the market is to facilitate the exchange of resources between demander and supplier. Accordingly, this is the first activity that is reviewed here. To investors, the securities that are created represent ownership interests in the profit of a firm, in the case of equities, and claims to the assets and/or revenue stream of a firm, in the case of debt instruments. In any case, there are three main channels by which new securities are created and distributed to those with excess funds. These are: (1) private placement, (2) securities underwriting, and (3) and intermediary creation and purchase of new securities. In Chapter 18 we will take an in-depth look at the creation of new securities in the **primary market,** so we give only a brief outline on the topic below.

Private Placement

In a **private placement,** an "enabling institution," traditionally an investment bank, raises funds for a private or public entity seeking these funds. The institution arranges for one or more large institutional, or wholesale, investors to purchase all the new securities issued by the organization seeking the funds. The enabling institution receives a commission or fee as compensation for this service.

Because the securities are purchased by only a few large buyers, there is no need for the issue to be designed to appeal to a diverse market of potential investors. Rather, the terms of the issue may be highly customized and tailored to the joint desires of the investing firms and the issuing entity. In addition, since this process bypasses many of the "middlemen" and does not require Securities and Exchange Commission (SEC) registration, a private placement is often quicker and less expensive than a public offering of securities.

Underwriting of a Public Offering

A second way to channel funds from a provider to a user is through a **securities underwriting** of a new public offering. Here, the enabling institution, traditionally an investment bank or, in the case of a large offering a syndicate of investment banks, buys the new securities issued by the entity in need of funds. The price at which these securities are bought and the fees charged for services rendered to facilitate the transaction are arrived at either through a negotiation process or through a competitive bidding process. The enabling institution then distributes the securities to the broader investing community in a public offering. In most cases, the underwriting firm or firms commit to buy all of the securities offered by the issuing firm. In this way, the issuer is assured of a certain total amount of funds once the price per share is set. The underwriters are generally able to resell the securities at a higher price than that which they paid for them, and they will make a profit along with the fees paid for performing the underwriting service. However, these firms absorb the risk that they may be able to resell their securities only at a lower price, thereby incurring a loss. Sometimes, this loss can be substantial. (See Box 17.1.)

Another way to underwrite securities is on a **best efforts** basis. Here, the enabling institution does not buy the securities from the issuer at any guaranteed price. Rather, it agrees to use its facilities and goodwill to distribute as many of the total number of the securities as possible at the best price that can be obtained in the market. The enabling institution then conveys these funds, less sales commissions and fees, to the issuing entity. Often, the issuing entity will put a floor on the price of the security below which it will refuse to sell. The enabling institution then sells as many as it can above that price and returns the remaining securities to the issuer. Alternatively, if an insufficient number can be sold to the public, the issuer may withdraw the issue altogether. This procedure to raise funds is most commonly used by small firms and in some **initial public offerings** of new firms. Whether the sales price is guaranteed or not, the sale of new securities to the public is termed a **primary offering.**

An Intermediary Purchase of New Securities

Another way the market transfers funds to entities in need of additional resources is through an intermediary's purchase of new securities. This method differs from a private placement or a public offering of securities in that the enabling institution, a financial intermediary, actually purchases and retains the securities for its own account, at least for a time. In a way, all loans created and held by financial intermediaries, be they consumer or commercial loans, are of this type. However, the creation, funding, and servicing of standard loans by intermediaries really involves a more traditional lending relationship. Here, we concentrate on the part of the debt market that provides resources to large-scale financings through the issuance of securities to the debtholder.[1] This activity is somewhere in between standard commercial bank direct lending and investment bank underwriting. It is often referred to as **merchant banking,** and it involves considerable risk to the enabling institution's own capital, with the expectation of higher ultimate returns.

A situation where this method might be used is one in which the entity needing funds is somehow (and perhaps temporarily) not in a good position to seek funding through the regular distribution channels. The merchant bank may feel close enough to the situation to be willing to absorb the risk but uncomfortable in marketing the securities more widely until some business steps have been taken to make the securities more attractive to the general public.

---

[1]The more traditional forms of lending will be reviewed in Chapter 20.

Box 17.1

The British Petroleum Fiasco

In a typical underwriting, the investment bank will set the guaranteed price only a day or two prior to the public offering. The custom in Britain is to give a guarantee for a period of two weeks or longer. When the British Petroleum Company (BP), owned primarily by the government of the United Kingdom, decided to privatize a large part of its ownership, it contracted with some of the leading Wall Street investment banks, such as Goldman Sachs, Salomon Brothers, and Morgan Stanley, as well as Canada's Wood Grundy, to underwrite its securities offering. The idea was attractive at the time. The U.K. government would sell off 31.5 percent of BP and was issuing £1.5 billion of new shares as well. This share offer, valued at $7.2 billion, would be the largest ever.

The deal looked like a winner. With less than two weeks to go before the issue, 6.25 million people registered for the new share offering. A guaranteed price of $5.49 was set for the 2.19 billion share offering late in October of 1987. Unfortunately, this was just prior to the greatest single-day price decline in the stock market's history! On Monday, October 19, 1987, the Dow Jones fell 212 points. In London, the Financial Times Index fell an equally startling 249.6 points.

Tuesday was little better in the U.K., with another 12 percent decline, measured as 250.7 points on the FTSE index. In all, the U.K. market fell 22 percent in two days. The results were disastrous. The underwriting syndicate had to pay the British government the guaranteed price even though the value of the securities had declined substantially. By the time they were actually delivered to the syndicate of Wall Street banks, open market prices of the new securities had fallen far below the price guaranteed to the U.K. government. In that underwriting, Wood Grundy of Canada reportedly lost as much as $54 million, and Goldman, Salomon, and Morgan did not fare much better. In total, it has been estimated that the entire group lost an incredible $1.5 billion.

While the typical underwriting is priced to absorb some of the risk of fluctuating markets between the guarantee date and the sales date, the BP case had extra risk due to the long underwriting guarantee period. Moreover, there was no inkling that such a large market decline would occur. This is of small solace for the partners of the investment firms involved or for their colleagues pricing new issues in the increasingly complex and volatile markets of today.

Secondary Market Structure

Once securities are created, however, investors do not necessarily wish to hold them until maturity or, in the case of equities, forever. Accordingly, a second crucial function of the financial markets is the creation of a market for the exchange of preexisting securities. Newly issued securities are created and distributed in the primary market; previously issued securities are bought and sold in the **secondary market.** There are different ways for these securities to change hands; that is, several secondary market structures exist for the trading of existing securities. These include: (1) organized exchanges, (2) phone networks, and (3) shadow markets. The important functions of the secondary markets are to promote liquidity for the owners of existing securities and to provide a mechanism for valuing shares and claims on income streams. We shall devote all of

Chapter 18 to a discussion of the secondary market, so here we provide only a brief outline of the various ways in which exchange occurs.

Exchange Trading Structures

Organized exchanges exist for the trading of many securities. At an **organized exchange,** buyers and sellers of securities, or the agents and brokers of buyers and sellers, meet together in a central location to conduct trades. Examples of organized exchanges in corporate stocks and a limited number of bonds are the New York Stock Exchange and the American Stock Exchange; for commodity contracts, there is the Chicago Board of Trade. There are also exchanges that specialize in futures, options, and foreign currency instruments.

Two features distinguish an exchange from other secondary market structures. First, an exchange has a distinct physical location. Second, most exchanges have dealers, called **specialists,** who carry an inventory in certain securities and who stand ready to add to or subtract from that inventory.

The most important function of an exchange is to provide a continuous market, although some exchanges have had less than continuous trading.[2] A continuous market affords a person or institution the opportunity to buy or sell a security immediately at a price near or identical to that of the previous trading price. For this reason, exchange prices of a security are often used as reference points when a new security is being issued. Exchanges are also helpful in that the liquidity they provide to existing securities makes it easier to issue new securities, as investors have confidence that they can liquidate their investment if future contingencies arise that would induce them to do so.

Telephone Networks

Another secondary market structure is often referred to as the **over-the-counter** (OTC) market. This market gets its name from the fact that, originally, securities dealers typically sold securities over the counters at their offices. Today, however, the OTC is little more than a network of telephones linking dealers with one another and directly with customers. Their counters frequently are cluttered with computer screens and automated quote machines. If an investor wishes to acquire a particular security, he or she can contact directly a number of dealers who carry an inventory in the desired security and procure shares from the dealer who quotes the most favorable price. In contrast, on a securities exchange, if a particular security is desired, an investor usually transacts with the specialist for that security on the exchange.

This market originally emerged as a natural response to the growth in the number of securities available in the market. Only a few securities issues were sizable enough to warrant listing on the national or regional exchanges. Then, the OTC market began to compete directly for trades in listed securities as well. The

---

[2]The Paris Bourse, for example, did not have continuous trading as recently as two decades ago.

latter was made possible by exchange regulations that forced all members of an exchange to execute their trades of securities that were listed on an exchange through the exchange at a high fixed commission rate. Large traders could not achieve economies of scale under these conditions, so broker-dealers who were not members of an exchange began to make a market and trade securities at lower commissions. After the fixed commission schedules were abandoned in May 1975, this market continued to provide a valuable alternative for the trading of exchange-listed and nonlisted stocks, and especially for bonds. Today, almost any share or bond available on one of the exchanges may also be acquired over the counter. The prices quoted in the OTC market must therefore be competitive with those on an organized exchange.

Bond markets have historically been the most important component of the OTC market, but stock markets are gaining in importance. Virtually all government bonds—federal, state, and municipal—are traded OTC. Many bonds are bought in the primary market and held to maturity, so that they never enter into the secondary market. Stocks, however, have no maturity, and eventually, they will trade on a secondary market.

Shadow Markets

Besides organized exchanges and the over-the-counter markets, there are **shadow markets,** also known to some as the **third market.** These markets operate in a parallel fashion to exchanges and the OTC markets, but they are characterized by institutional investors and major dealers who often transact in very large blocks of securities. If such large blocks were to be traded on an exchange or through normal OTC channels, a severe distortion in price could result due to disruptions in supply and demand. In the shadow markets, the trades among large institutional investors can be conducted discretely and in high volumes without exerting any appreciable impact on exchange and OTC prices. Another characteristic of this part of the financial markets is that the buyers and sellers are often linked directly to one another, and as a result, more price negotiations can occur.

Players in the shadow markets use this vehicle for their trades because it often results in lower transactions costs than the more traditional trading arenas. This cost saving arises for two reasons. First, because the transactions involve high volumes between sophisticated wholesale investors, the per share cost of the trade is small. Second, many of the services provided to investors in the other markets, such as research, advice, and so forth, are not needed by the players in the shadow markets. By conducting their transactions through this market, they can avoid the associated costs of unwanted services and low-volume customers.

Clearing and Trading Facilities

The third key function performed by the financial markets is the clearing function. This function includes a number of services that are provided either as a package or as a set of individual services. It includes the process of clearing, settlement of accounts, and, frequently, custodial services for the securities purchased. Together, these services are essential to an efficient market. Trades must be certain, and the integrity of a transaction is central to providing immediacy and marketability in this and any other market. Yet, this is one feature of a financial market that is often overlooked. This is because it is too often taken for granted. However, a well-functioning financial market provides both the efficiency and the integrity of the trades that take place within it. There are numerous market mechanisms that ensure the integrity of the trading process and foster efficient trades. Below, we discuss a few of the more prominent mechanisms aimed at achieving these results.

Explaining the Clearing Problem

When a broker executes a trade on your behalf, a commitment is made for the specified number of securities to be delivered to you three business days later in return for an amount of cash to be surrendered by you at that same time. The three-day delivery is standard in securities markets, but not universal. Certain securities, such as Treasury bills, notes, and bonds, have a next-day delivery protocol. Foreign exchange has a two-day delivery protocol. Furthermore, special arrangements can be made to have the settlement date on a date different than that established in customary practice.

Typically, you do not present a suitcase of currency to the seller at that time; instead, you offer some other negotiable instrument, such as a certified check from a financial institution, to your broker. The check must be cleared and funds must be transferred from your account, just as your broker must transfer funds to the account of the seller of the security you wish to buy. This is the process of **settlement.**

Since the broker does not generally sell you shares out of his or her own inventory, the shares purchased need to be obtained from a seller. The seller may be in Moscow, Idaho, while you may be in Gainesville, Florida. If you entrust all of this to an agent, the agent will need to verify that the transaction is handled properly. The process of obtaining the shares from a previous owner in exchange for the predetermined monetary value is known as the **clearing process.** Market structures, known as clearinghouses, have been put in place to deal with clearing transactions and to rectify any problems that may arise in the process.

Once purchased, the securities may be sent directly to you, or they may be issued in your name and delivered to you from the transfer agent responsible for the shares purchased. Alternatively, you may leave the securities in the hands of your broker or bank for safekeeping. The latter is far more frequent and is referred to as **custodial** services. Custodial services are offered to investors to facilitate trading and sale, as well as to maintain the physical safety of the shares. It should be obvious that there are inefficiencies involved in the clearing process. To begin with, the physical transfer of security certificates and cash is clearly a cumbersome process. Suppose that on a given day, your brokerage firm sold 600 shares of IBM for one individual and 1,000 shares for another and then bought 1,500 shares of IBM for you from the fellow from Moscow, Idaho. Suppose further that all of these transactions occurred with the same dealer. On the settlement day, your brokerage firm would be receiving your 1,500 shares and delivering 1,600 shares sold by other clients. The net transaction in IBM for your brokerage firm on that day would be only a 100 share delivery. It would be more efficient for **netting** to occur and for the brokerage firm to be responsible only for the delivery of 100 shares. The brokerage firm and the dealer could accomplish this netting between themselves through a special arrangement. Then, the firm would have to figure out which of its customers should receive the shares sold and which should receive their monetary value. But if the trades all involved different dealers and brokerage firms, the ability to net the three transactions would be lost. Your trade would be cleared with your friend from Idaho, and the other two would proceed in a similar manner.

To facilitate this netting process, members of a **clearinghouse,** such as security brokerage firms, investment banks, and others, send records of their transactions each day to the clearinghouse. Then, after verification of all trades for consistency, the clearinghouse nets all transactions, and each member receives a list of the net amounts of all securities to be delivered and received, as well as the net amount of money to be paid or received. Thus, rather than settling many times with all the other firms that are parties to its transactions, each member of the clearinghouse settles only once each day.

However, what happens if one side of any one transaction fails to perform its contracted part? For example, what happens if your friend fails to deliver the shares you purchased? Occasionally, a failure by one of the parties to a transaction does occur. If, on the settlement day, the seller fails to make timely delivery of the securities purchased, delivers the wrong securities, or in some other way fails to make delivery in proper form, the trade becomes a **fail.** If this happens, the buyer of the securities is considered to be the owner of the securities as of the day of settlement. However, the buyer's broker is not required to make cash payment for the securities until they are actually delivered. This amounts to a free loan to the buyer's broker of an amount equivalent to the settlement price of the securities because the broker's client has paid for the securities, and the broker can deposit that money in the overnight market and receive interest daily until proper delivery of the securities is made.

Counterparty Risk

As indicated in the preceding paragraph, parties to a securities trade do not always fulfill their obligations. We call this **counterparty risk.** It is present whenever there are two sides to a trade. This risk includes both the unwillingness of the other side of any trade to fulfill its side of the bargain and its financial inability to do so. For example, suppose the value of IBM shares rises before delivery. The seller may wish to renege. Alternatively, suppose the seller defaulted on another financial commitment between the time of the trade and settlement. Other creditors may try to prevent the settlement, and this, too, can lead to a fail in the system. Were they not somehow reduced, these problems would negatively affect investors' willingness to conduct business and trade securities freely. The volume of trading would be diminished and the efficient allocation of securities would be hampered by this impediment to conducting business. However, there are mechanisms in place designed to mitigate this risk.

Two levels of protection are available to the investor. First, many trades are conducted through a brokerage firm, which in turn transacts on an organized exchange. If one party or another fails to live up to its responsibilities, the other party is not placed at risk, as the brokerage firm or the clearinghouse of the relevant exchange will make up the difference. In the futures market, the clearinghouse actually becomes a counterparty to each side of every trade. Thus, it is the only party that can be damaged if any party fails to fulfill its contractual responsibilities. This arrangement is particularly important for futures because they involve transactions that are constantly being marked to market, and a long time delay may be sufficient to allow a greater change in a counterparty's ability to fulfill those responsibilities. Second, if the brokerage firm itself is unable to make good on a promise, the **Securities Investor Protection Corporation** (SIPC) will indemnify the investor for any financial losses incurred. This organization was established in 1970 to insure customer accounts up to $500,000, and it is financed by insurance premiums levied on member firms.

We should also note that the use of netting by clearinghouses greatly reduces the amount of risk faced by trading firms because only the net amount of securities or cash is at risk, rather than the full amount of each trade. Still, the astute investor must recognize that not all commitments are fulfilled and that remedies must be in place to ensure both the integrity of the market and one's own financial safety.

Institutional Structures to Assure Good Trades

Along with clearinghouses and trading facilities, there are other mechanisms that have been developed to ensure good trades and promote a willingness to trade. While these do not ensure the integrity of an executed trade, they increase the availability of information on value and therefore assure traders that prices are fair and reasonable.

Foremost among these information tools is the widespread availability and use of electronic services that provide price quotes on a wide variety of securities. In days past, nonprofessional investors were at a substantial disadvantage in their investment decisions because there was no independent and timely way to confirm the value of their holdings or the competitiveness of a price quote, short of the burdensome process of soliciting quotes from a number of independent brokers. In today's market, an investor can get indicative quotes and actual bid and offer prices and volume quotes instantly. This increases the information available to investors and narrows the scope of potential manipulation by unethical market participants who might otherwise be tempted to exploit other participants in a misguided attempt to extract some extra profit from a transaction.

One such service is **NASDAQ** (National Association of Securities Dealers Automated Quotations), or Nasdaq (no longer an acronym), which aggregates bid and offer quotes from different dealers for particular issues and presents them to an investor. A qualified investor can then execute a trade by computer without the aid of a broker. There are other services, such as Reuters, Quotron, Telerate, and the like, that provide price quotes and relevant information on the full gamut of securities. Still other services provide data and analytic capability. Bloomberg is an example of a service that comes complete with analytical tools and historical data helpful to investors in security selection, portfolio management, and performance measurement. However, execution is not available directly through these machines.

Over the last 20 years, the Securities and Exchange Commission has also entered the fray. Fostered by regulation in 1975, the SEC developed the **Consolidated Quotation System,** which reports trades on the major national and regional exchanges and on Nasdaq. Two years later, the SEC developed the **Intermarket Trading System,** which links regional and national exchanges to provide brokers with quotes from a number of markets simultaneously. Together, these innovations allow brokers and market makers better access to markets and facilitate the execution of efficient trades.

Beyond electronics, other institutional structures have been developed to enhance the efficiency of trading. One such institutional structure is the **arbitration board,** which was established to reduce the costs of disputes between investors and their brokers. Through this board, disputes are supposed to be handled quickly and without expensive litigation. The reviews here, however, have been mixed. Some consumer advocates contend that the structure favors securities firms at the expense of the investing public. Nonetheless, some brokerage firms make it a requirement of clients to agree to such adjudication of possible future disputes as a condition to providing brokerage services.

In the end, of course, the investor may also turn to the courts or to regulatory bodies with jurisdictional oversight for recourse. Here, the SEC and other oversight bodies have clear jurisdiction to administer existing securities laws and legislation on required disclosure, insider information use, and stock manipulation activity. However, there are no guarantees in the market, and risks will remain. It is in the securities market that the phrase *caveat emptor* is perhaps best applied.

Summary

In this chapter, we have discussed the basic functions provided by a financial market. These functions may be reduced to three key activities provided by these markets—namely, the creation, trading, and clearing of financial assets. Virtually all the benefits of these markets to the real economy spring from the enhancement of one of these three functions, which are key to any market system.

The issues raised here in broad overview fashion will be discussed in some length in the chapters that follow. Some of the more important mechanisms to promote the creation and efficient trading of securities will be discussed in Chapters 18 and 19, respectively. In the latter, it will be shown that from time to time, new mechanisms are introduced to improve the trading process. The trend has been toward the provision and wider dissemination of information to investors and toward the encouragement of technologies that will allow investors to transact their business more directly and rapidly. To remain viable, structures and mechanisms that have served us well in the past will have to adopt new technologies in the delivery of information.

Many of the advances are best suited for knowledgeable investors who require little guidance, research, or other intensive services. For the rest of us, our broker will still be our main access to the market, and this is probably fine. We suspect that even with the information explosion that is transforming much of the business, there will always be firms or entities within a firm that will continue to service investors who need more attention and advice. But service comes at a price. The avid investor would do better to become a more knowledgeable investor by devoting some of his or her time to developing a better understanding of the workings of the markets.

Key Concepts

arbitration board,   429
best efforts contracts,   422
clearing and trading facilities,   420
clearinghouse,   427
clearing, settlement, and custodial services,   426
counterparty risk,   427
CQS and ITS,   429
initial public offering,   422
merchant banking,   422
NASDAQ and Nasdaq,   428

organized exchanges versus over-the-counter
  market,   424
primary offering,   422
primary versus secondary market,   420
private placement,   421
shadow or third market,   425
SIPC,   428
specialists,   424
underwriting,   420

Review Questions

1. Why should a firm worry about the liquidity of its equity?
2. Briefly discuss the three main functions that financial markets perform. List them in order of importance and explain your reasoning.
3. What is the distinguishing characteristic between an intermediary purchase and other methods of security creation?
4. When your local bank gives you a loan, in what sense is it creating a security? Suppose the bank packaged your loan with other similar loans and sold the group into the market as a loan-backed pass-through security. Would

it be easier for the bank to sell your loan to the market in this form than to sell your loan individually?
5. What are the two main functions performed by a secondary market?
6. Contrast private placements with shadow markets.
7. Both corporations and individuals depend upon the proper flow of information. Why is this the case? What is the role of information and why is it important to both sides of the market?

References

Altman, Edward I. *Handbook of Financial Markets and Institutions*. 6th ed. New York: John Wiley, 1987.

Bloch, Ernest. *Inside Investment Banking*. Homewood, Ill.: Dow Jones-Irwin, 1986.

Eccles, Robert G., and Dwight B. Crane. *Doing Deals: Investment Banks at Work*. Boston: Harvard University Press, 1988.

Fabozzi, Frank J., and Franco Modigliani. *Capital Markets: Institutions and Instruments*. Englewood Cliffs, N.J.: Prentice Hall, 1992.

Francis, Jack. *Investments*. 5th ed. New York: McGraw-Hill, 1990.

Kaufman, George. *Money Markets and Institutions*. 4th ed. Englewood Cliffs, N.J.: Prentice Hall, 1989.

Kaufman, George, and Larry R Mote. "Is Banking a Declining Industry? A Historical Perspective." *Economic Perspectives,* Federal Reserve Bank of Chicago, May/June 1994.

Logue, Dennis E. *The WG&L Handbook of Financial Markets*. Cincinnati, Ohio: Warren, Gorham and Lamont, 1995.

Securities Industry Association. *The U.S. Securities Markets: How They Work, Their Role in the National Economy*. New York: Securities Industry Association, 1980.

Primary Market Structure

Chapter Outline

This chapter reviews in greater depth the means by which borrowers obtain funds. The central role of underwriting via public or private offerings is reviewed in detail. Included in this coverage is a discussion of pricing, distribution procedure, and the transaction costs associated with the issuance of financial instruments. In addition, a review of the regulation of such activity is presented.

As we pointed out in previous chapters, financial markets include the capital market, for long-term securities, and the money market, for short-term securities. Each of these markets involves both a market for new issues, the primary market, and a market for trading in existing securities, the secondary market. The primary market is the focus of this chapter. Examples of primary market transactions include the private funding of a debt issue by a life insurance company for the construction of a new shopping mall, the issuance of Treasury bills by the U.S.

Treasury, a new municipal bond issue by the city of Philadelphia, and a new common stock issue by Ford Motor Company. In each of these transactions, the issuers receive an infusion of cash in exchange for ownership of a financial claim, either a debt or equity instrument, that did not previously exist.

Investment Banking Activity

The key financial institution in the primary market is the **investment bank,** or **underwriter.** Other financial institutions, such as certain large commercial banks and insurers, also engage in the underwriting function in various ways and have been increasingly active recently in this area. However, the primary market has traditionally been the lone province of the investment bank. Because "underwriter" is a broader term, inclusive of any institution performing the underwriting function, we will use it in this chapter to encompass all of those institutions that assist in the creation of financial instruments in the primary market. Those interested in a broader view of the activities of investment banks will have to wait until Chapter 20, where the industry's activities will be discussed in further detail. For present purposes, our interest is only on the function investment banks perform as an underwriter of securities in the money and capital markets.

The underwriter has the central role of obtaining funds for private and public economic entities via private placements or public offerings of securities. As a financial intermediary, the underwriter obtains funds from other investors and channels them into the enterprises that have retained its services and commissioned it to do so. The vehicle for transfer of funds is in the form of a security. The legal documentation accompanying a security, generally referred to as an **indenture,** spells out the terms of the fund transfer in detail and specifies the rights and duties incumbent on all parties to the exchange of securities for funds.

New Issues in the United States

Over the last two decades, as evidenced in Exhibit 18.1, the public offering of new securities issues has been fairly erratic. The data show that new security issues have not been steady in volume or in choice between debt and equity. Two trends are evident, however. Most noticeable is the increased volume in these markets and the fact that the relative importance of debt has substantially increased over the last two decades. Equity represented over 20 percent of new issues in 1986 but has fallen to an average of 12 percent for the last two years of available data.

These data are a bit incomplete, however, as they exclude private placements in both debt and equities. A recent study[1] sheds some light on this matter by reporting

---

[1]Board of Governors of the Federal Reserve System, "Recent Developments in the Market for Privately Placed Debt," *Federal Reserve Bulletin,* February 1993.

Exhibit 18.1

Public issues of debt versus public issues of corporate bonds ($ billions)

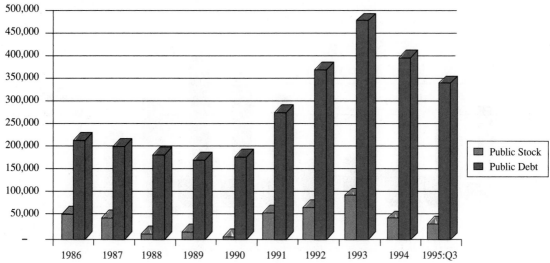

Source: Board of Governors of the Federal Reserve System, *Federal Reserve Bulletin,* December 1995.

private placement totals in both the debt and equity markets. Exhibits 18.2 and 18.3 report these totals through 1993, the time period of the study. Notice that private issues of equity vary considerably from year to year and reach their greatest relative importance during 1989 and 1990. On the debt side, private placements again add both significant volume and exhibit substantial volatility. These totals peaked at over $110 billion in 1989 and 1993 and fell to a low of $66 billion as recently as 1992. Likewise, there has not been a steady trend in the choice of private versus public distribution of securities, as evidenced in Exhibit 18.2. As can be seen, public issues of both stocks and bonds exceed 50 percent of the market over the eight years reported. Further, except for 1988–1990, the private placements of equity never exceed 20 percent.

Obviously, given these drastically changing patterns of activity, institutions that restrict their activities to underwriting securities and specialize only in the areas of either underwriting public securities or making private placements must go through some choppy economic times. This is part of the reason that many underwriting firms have branched into other financial services. We will discuss this further in Chapters 20 and 24.

While we have touched on private placements and public securities offerings in earlier chapters, we shall provide additional information in the sections that follow on the nature of the underwriting process and on the costs incurred in this process. We begin with private placements and then demonstrate the issuance process for public offerings, providing reasons for the use of each process.

Exhibit 18.2

Public versus private placement of new corporate stock issues ($ billions)

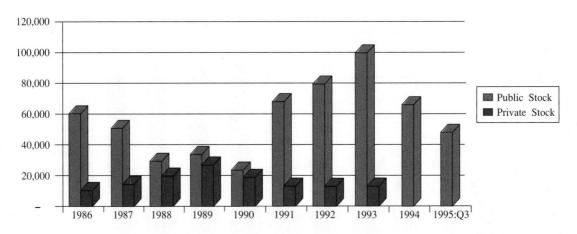

Source: Board of Governors of the Federal Reserve System, *Federal Reserve Bulletin,* December 1995.

Private Placements

A **privately placed security** is a security that is sold to fewer than 25 buyers. Because of its limited distribution, the issue need not be registered with the SEC, nor is the sale regulated by this governmental agency in any substantial way. As indicated in the exhibits above, most privately placed securities are bonds. The private nature of the transactions permits individual tailoring of bond maturity and covenants to conform to purchaser preference. Privately placed stock issues are generally new issues of young or nascent firms. As such, they are often placed with venture capital firms that devote their time and resources to funding and overseeing new firms. With these firms, control is often greater and monitoring of the new enterprise is easier. (See Box 18.1.) While it is true that most developing businesses are financed privately through the use of venture capital pools and private placements, it is also true that many of the largest companies obtain large sums of financing via private placements. They are, however, the exception rather than the rule in the equity placement market.

The recent review of the private placement debt market by the Federal Reserve illustrates these points. Exhibit 18.4 from that report shows the relative size of private and public debt issues. As is apparent, the preponderance of offerings is in the $10 million to $100 million range for the private market, with a median value for their 1989 sample of $34 million. This compares to the $100 to $250 million range and $150 median for public issues. Firms in this market, however, are not necessarily risky, even in a relative sense. Small issues and relatively smaller firms do not necessarily equate to credit risk. This is illustrated in Exhibit 18.5, where the credit ratings of private placements held by life insurance

EXHIBIT 18.3

Public versus private placement of new corporate bonds ($ billions)

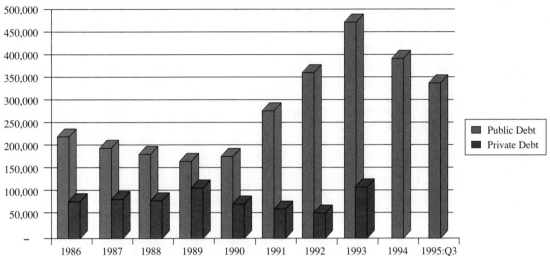

Source: Board of Governors of the Federal Reserve System, *Federal Reserve Bulletin,* December 1995.

companies in 1991 are recorded. As a major lender in the private placement market, the portfolio of life insurance companies may be viewed as being indicative of the market as a whole. Notice that the preponderance of issues carry an "A" or higher credit rating, with nearly 80 percent in the investment grade categories.

Maturity in the private placement market is somewhat shorter than in the overall bond market. Exhibit 18.6 illustrates this point using the private placement of new issues, again by life insurance lenders. As can be seen, the 3- to 10-year range accounts for more than two-thirds of the new volume over the sample period from January 1990 to July 1992.

While a small company typically has no recourse other than to obtain private financing, a large company may seek a private placement because of the disadvantages associated with the SEC registration process for public securities. By avoiding the SEC registration process, the firm may be able to obtain funding more rapidly. It also can avoid expensive underwriting services and the costly preparation of registration materials.

For firms seeking to privately place an issue, an underwriter is retained to advise on the pricing and terms of the issue and to locate an investor or group of investors. For finding investors, the underwriter is paid a comparatively modest finder's fee (1/4 percent to 1 1/2 percent). This fee, however, is primarily for services rendered in the placement, as the underwriter does not actually need to purchase the securities and absorb the risk of underwriting; it merely facilitates the placement by using its established contacts and knowledge of the institutional

<hr />

Box 18.1

Venture Capital: A Primary Market for Start-up Firms*

On the way to the limelight of an initial public offering of securities, a firm will often obtain financing through various other means. This process generally occurs in several stages, as depicted in Exhibit 18.A. As can be seen, venture capital is needed to finance a start-up firm prior to an **initial public offering** (IPO). Such venture capital funds are typically obtained through venture capital partnerships and, in some cases, through publicly traded venture capital funds. In any case, there is generally a long process between the first dollar raised and a public offering of shares in the open market.

EXHIBIT 18.A

Venture capital financing

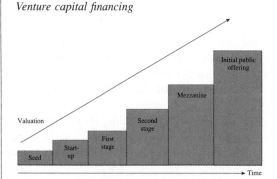

A start-up company's entrepreneurs usually provide **seed financing** to ascertain the feasibility of their concept. This financing often comes out of their own pockets. Next, **start-up financing** is sought to finance the product development and some preliminary forays into marketing.

When all of its initial capital is exhausted and a prototype of the product has been developed and appears to be marketable, the firm is ready to begin manufacturing and selling. At this stage, further financial support is normally required. **First- and second-stage financing,** often obtained through venture capital pools, fund the growth and provide the working capital needed to finance inventories, production processes, shipping, and accounts receivable at this stage. Financing provided during this period is often acquired at two or three different times in increasing amounts. The final stage prior to an IPO is often termed **mezzanine financing.** This stage can require substantial amounts of capital and often requires funding by large outside firms in addition to the funds provided by the venture capitalists.

When the firm has established itself with a viable product and market, this process ultimately culminates in an IPO. Often, however, an IPO will be undertaken prior to the establishment of a solid track record or evidence of a substantial market demand for the proposed product or service, provided that the capital needs are sufficiently high. In any case, for many of the providers of venture capital, this is the point at which they finally receive the reward for their patience. The payoff to the firm's financiers at this stage can be substantial. Indeed, were there not potentially large rewards, there would be very little venture capital provided, because the risks involved in financing a start-up company are often tremendous.

Not all of these stages are necessary for each firm, but they are meant to illustrate the normal stages of financing as the value of a firm grows. Gone are the days of simple financing and bootstrap capitalism. Business is just too capital intensive for the entrepreneurs of yesteryear.

<hr />

*This chart and explanation were adapted from Ernest Bloch, *Inside Investment Banking* (Burr Ridge, Ill.: Irwin Professional Publishing, 1986), Chapter 6.

Exhibit 18.4

Distribution of issue sizes (1989)

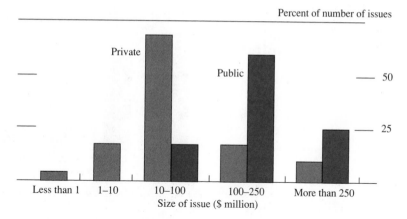

Source: Federal Reserve Board and IDD Information Services, *Federal Reserve Bulletin,* February 1993.

market. The private placement market has an additional advantage to the issuer in that the security covenants can be tailored to fit its specific needs, and those of its creditors, once the two sides of the deal are identified.

However, with all of these advantages, there comes one major disadvantage. The securities have very limited marketability. As a result, investors will typically require greater yields on these securities. This may offset the advantages. Therefore, firms in the private placement market must constantly weigh the advantages of this form of transaction against the yield differential that private issues require. At some point, the public offering becomes more cost effective.

Over the past decade, however, the private placement market has been providing funds at yields very close to those of similar publicly traded issues. This is perhaps because of the existence of the open market alternative. Unfortunately, the necessary documentation accompanying a typical private placement has increased dramatically as well, making it approach the detail, tedium, and cost of SEC registration. One reason for this increase in the documentation is the evolution of the market. Participants have for some time tried to expand the acceptability of the private placement market as well as the list of investors and issuers on both sides of the market. To do so, however, requires that the market's relative illiquidity be addressed.

To substantially increase acceptability, participants were required to create a liquid secondary market. Here, as elsewhere, the primary issuers needed to enhance the secondary market in order to develop the primary one. This cause was advanced in 1990 with the passage of Rule 144A by the SEC. Rule 144A permits greater, indeed unrestricted, trading in private placements by sophisticated institutions designated as qualified institutional buyers. As a result, both domestic and foreign participants have increased their activity in this market. Thus, the traditional distinctions between public and private placements have become blurry.

Exhibit 18.5

*Distribution of private
placement credit
ratings (1991)*

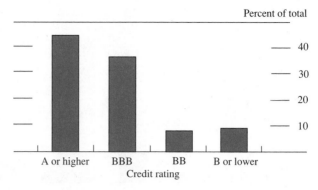

Source: From the Valuation of Securities CD-ROM. Used by permission of the National Association of Insurance Commissioners.

Public Issues

If a new security is sold to more than 25 buyers, it then becomes a **public security issue.** As such, the security must be registered with the SEC. However, if the registered security is subsequently sold to fewer than 25 investors, it still remains a public security issue. Thus, an issuer intending to place its security with fewer than 25 investors may decide whether to do so as a public or private security issue.

The purpose of an SEC registration is to assure the public that all relevant information is disclosed accurately. The information is quite voluminous and includes items ranging from the purpose of the issue to the remuneration levels of any officers receiving over $25,000 annually. To facilitate in the preparation of these documents and in the ultimate stock or bond offering, the interested firm contracts with both legal counsel and investment advisors. Legal counsel has become part of the reality of the security issuance process and the world of SEC regulation. Laws covering new issues and the SEC's control of the market are quite complex. We will review these statutes below. Some of these laws date back to the post-Depression reworking of U.S. financial rules and regulations, and all are sufficiently exacting to make legal assistance critical in the process. The presence of investment advisors is essential as well, for the realities of the stock and bond markets of Wall Street are often alien to Main Street, U.S.A. These firms will advise the issuer, price the offering, and ultimately place it in the hands of investors. The issuer can either contract separately for these services or arrange for one investment firm to handle all of them under one engagement agreement. In any case, advisors see this first step as an entree to the underwriting contract.

Although there is a statutory 20-day waiting period between filing all of the necessary paperwork and the actual issuance of new securities for an SEC registration, the period can be delayed for many months before approval is granted by the SEC. Because of the inconvenience that the document preparation process and

Exhibit 18.6

Distribution of average lives of private placements

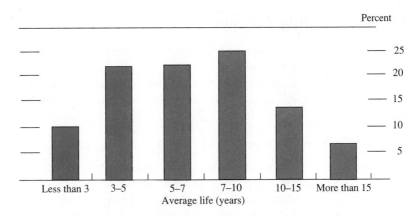

Source: American Council of Life Insurance, "Survey of Private Placement Commitments," *Investment Bulletin,* (several issues), Washington, D.C. Reprinted by permission.

waiting period sometimes cause, firms requiring substantial funding or just continual increases in financial resources may find it in their interest to seek a **shelf registration** from the SEC far in advance of the actual issue of a security. With this type of registration, a firm may issue securities on an ongoing basis or in several waves, thus allowing the firm to issue securities when funds are most needed or when market conditions are viewed as favorable. The firm with an active shelf issue has up to one year to sell its securities before the shelf registration must be renewed.[2]

Because the SEC registration process is burdensome, several public security issuers have sought and obtained permission to skip the registration process altogether. These include issuers of U.S. government obligations, state and municipal bonds, issues sold only within the boundaries of a single state, and obligations of commercial banks and savings and loan associations.[3]

Before an individual is allowed to purchase a new public security, he or she must be given a **prospectus.** This document duplicates in large measure the information contained in the SEC registration documents. Only some technical details are omitted from the prospectus.

The SEC is concerned that relevant information about the issuer be fully and accurately disclosed to prospective investors. However, registration by the SEC should not be construed as expressing an opinion about the riskiness of the security or as an endorsement of its merits as an investment. The SEC requires only that disclosure is adequate and accurate.

---

[2]The "shelf registration regulation" (Rule 415) appears to have led to greater investment banking industry concentration. See Marcia Cornett, Wallace Davidson, and Nanda Rangan, "Deregulation in Investment Banking: Industry Concentration Following Rule 415," *Journal of Banking and Finance,* March 1996.

[3]The exemption granted to commercial banks does not extend to their parent company, the bank holding company. See Chapter 21 for a discussion of the distinction.

The Underwriting Process

The process of underwriting a security includes three distinct elements: the valuation of the new instrument, the distribution of the securities, and the allocation of associated underwriting costs. Each step is critically important to understanding this rather cumbersome process. Therefore, we will review each element in turn.

Valuation of a New Instrument

When considering a new issue, the first question that must be addressed is its value. It is easiest to determine the value of an asset by finding a similar asset that already exists in the market and using the price of that asset as a reference point for value. How is this comparison done with security issues?

In many markets in the United States, there are distinct mechanisms through which new and old assets are traded simultaneously. Accordingly, comparisons of relative prices are straightforward. For instance, new car dealers and car lots for "previously owned vehicles" exist side by side in every town. One need only shop the two showrooms to obtain the different offering prices on the two vehicles. In the stock market, unlike the auto market, the prices of new and previously owned shares of a given company are exactly the same. Securities do not wear out like cars. The rights and income streams from new and previously owned shares to their respective owners are indistinguishable from one another. Thus, a company cannot expect to issue new shares to acquire additional capital at a price that will be any cheaper than that of its existing shares.[4] Therefore, one can easily determine the value of a new issue of shares of a firm if it already has existing equity shares trading in the market.

In the bond market, however, one cannot always make this claim. This is because there are usually substantive differences between newly issued bonds and seasoned ones. Four come immediately to mind. First, the liquidity of the newly issued bonds, often referred to as **on-the-run** current-coupon issues, is somewhat better than that of seasoned issues. Liquidity is an attractive attribute that is associated with a higher price and, hence, a lower yield, all else equal. For instance, as mentioned in Chapter 9, newly issued Treasury bonds, referred to as **current-coupon bonds,** usually yield a bit less than their seasoned counterparts.[5] But all else is rarely equal. New bonds may have different coupon rates and different remaining maturities than seasoned ones. Finally, new bonds may also have a different priority of claim to the issuer's assets or revenue streams, in the

---

[4]Indeed, due to underwriting and flotation costs, it is typically more expensive for a company or other economic entity to acquire new capital than to grow it over time simply by retaining more earnings. This will become explicit as we consider the costs in underwriting in an ensuing subsection of this chapter.

[5]The same phenomenon has been observed with corporate bond issues. See Robert C. Radcliffe, *Investment Concepts, Analysis, and Strategy,* 3rd ed. (Glenview, Ill.: Scott, Foresman/ Little, Brown Higher Education, 1990), p. 73.

case of a corporate issue. Thus, one would expect their yields to differ from those of seasoned bonds due to collateral, tax effects, and differences in the term structure of interest rates. Occasionally, an issuer, usually the U.S. Treasury, will "reopen" a seasoned issue and reissue additional bonds identical in every respect to existing bonds. In that case, we would expect all bonds to command the same prices and yields.

Often, however, a particular issuer has no previous equity or debt issues that are publicly traded upon which the prices of new issues can be based. In these cases, the underwriter will base its commitment price on **comparables.** This approach involves searching for securities of comparable risks and terms that are publicly traded. If there are no comparable economic entities, there may be a group of entities, or components of existing entities, that can be viewed as comparable to the issuer. For instance, a particular issuer may be a firm with operating units in several different areas, such as manufacturing and retail distribution of men's clothing. The underwriter can then attempt to locate separate firms in each industry that have operating and market characteristics similar to the firm looking to obtain financing. By pricing the pieces of the package and adding them together, a price for the entire firm is attained.

A second approach to valuation is also used. As a check to determine the reasonableness of any estimate or if comparables are not available, the underwriter will obtain the valuation of the underlying cash flows of the issue using the approaches we have already seen in previous chapters. A fundamental valuation analysis of the type described in Chapters 12 through 14 is performed to arrive at the fair market value of the cash flow, or offering price. If this procedure is carefully performed, the estimates derived should be an accurate predictor of the market's value of the new issue.

Valuations of the underwriter are not performed in the abstract. The underwriter knows that if he places too high a coupon rate on a bond issue, or too low a price on an equity issue, the issuer may withdraw its offering. On the other hand, as the coupon rate of the issue is lowered, or the issue price is raised, fewer underwriters will be willing to participate in the underwriting because of the difficulty they will have in selling the new securities. Thus, the underwriter must set the coupon rate or issue price just high enough to induce investors to buy all of the issue that the issuer wishes to sell. The underwriting syndicate can help in the valuation process by "premarketing" the issue to ascertain investor interest in the issue and to determine probable prices at which it can be sold.

The underwriter has some flexibility in this process if he or she is working for the firm under a **negotiated underwriting** agreement. In this case, the services performed and prices charged are negotiated between the firm and the investment banker. A fairly close relationship develops between the two organizations.

In a **competitive bidding,** as opposed to a negotiated underwriting, the issuer specifies the terms of both the offering and the services to be provided and prepares the registration statement. Then, the issuer puts the issue up for bid to competing underwriters, typically in a sealed-bid auction. The highest bidder wins the issue and may begin to sell the issue immediately. In a competitive bidding situation, premarketing cannot be done due to the uncertainty that a particular underwriting syndicate will win the bidding. Public utility companies and municipalities are among the frequent users of the competitive bidding system; indeed, many are required by law to utilize this system. Interestingly, there is little evidence that any appreciable advantage is gained by the process of competitive bidding.

Obviously, the market price of the security will be influenced by the terms of the offering. For example, in the case of debt instruments, the maturity of the instrument, its call provisions, and its sinking fund schedule all affect the required yield. In addition, covenants to limit additional debt issues; to restrict dividend payouts, which could jeopardize the creditors; and to specify minimum working capital maintenance will all impinge on the value of a bond. In each of these cases, there will be less of a cash cushion available to ensure full and timely coupon payments, and these provisions have a concomitant effect on price. This has already been demonstrated in previous chapters.

Distribution of the New Instrument

The typical distribution of securities in a public offering is accomplished by a **managing underwriter,** an **underwriting syndicate,** and a **selling group.** This structure is illustrated in Exhibit 18.7. In a negotiated firm commitment, the managing underwriter forms an underwriting syndicate and a selling group. This takes place about six weeks prior to the offering date. Each of the selling group's members is offered some tentative allotment of securities to be sold to the general public. It is often to the issuer's advantage to have its securities distributed widely, as this will help ensure a healthy secondary market for its securities; hence, a broad selling group is desirable.

Members of the underwriting syndicate place their own capital at risk by agreeing to purchase for their own inventory any securities that cannot be sold quickly to outside investors. On the other hand, members of the selling group agree only to use their best efforts to sell the securities. Any portion of their allotment that cannot be sold is simply returned to the syndicate. In most cases, underwriters are also members of the selling group, but the selling group usually includes nonsyndicate members as well.

A day prior to the offering, final terms such as coupon and price are decided and allotments to the underwriters are finalized. This information is placed on a **final prospectus,** which is given to the SEC for its approval.

On the first day of the public offering, each member of the selling group begins to sell its allotment. The shares or bonds are offered to the public at a specified premium above the price guaranteed by the syndicate to the issuer. The amount of the premium is set by the syndicate, and each member of the selling group is supposed to quote the same price to public investors. Occasionally, price concessions are granted by someone in the selling group to a valued customer, but such behavior is not appreciated by other members of the selling group and, if discovered, can lead to exclusion from future selling groups.

EXHIBIT 18.7

The underwriting structure

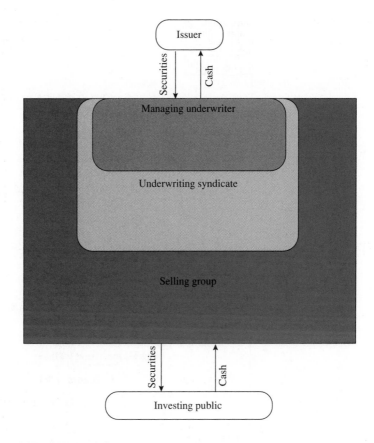

The historical record of a transaction is kept in several ways. Reporting to the SEC is the official form. In addition, the selling syndicate will often publish a **tombstone** in the financial press on or shortly after the issuance. This announcement is a form of public notification of the new issue and a method of marketing for the syndicate members. The advertisement reports the issuing firm, the offering price, and the members of both the underwriting syndicate and selling group. Exhibit 18.8 duplicates one such tombstone from the October 3, 1994, *Wall Street Journal*. As is evident, all of the above information is contained in this advertisement, along with the required disclaimer at the top of the page.

Costs in Underwriting

If the issue is sold out completely, the gross underwriting spread—the difference between guaranteed price to issuer and agreed-upon retail price—is divided among the participants. Each participant is paid for his part in the transaction: managing underwriters for preparing the issue, the underwriting syndicate members for risking their capital, and the members of the selling group as a commission for their

EXHIBIT 18.8

A recent tombstone

This announcement constitutes neither an offer to sell nor a solicitation of an offer to buy these securities. The offering is made only by the Prospectus, copies of which may be obtained in any State from such of the undersigned and others as may lawfully offer these securities in such State.

October 3, 1994

4,000,000 Shares

Commercial Net Lease Realty, Inc.

Common Stock

Price $12½ per Share

Smith Barney Inc.

Legg Mason Wood Walker
Incorporated

J. C. Bradford & Co.

Raymond James & Associates, Inc.

Bear, Stearns & Co. Inc.	Alex. Brown & Sons Incorporated	Dean Witter Reynolds Inc.
Dillon, Read & Co. Inc.	Donaldson, Lufkin & Jenrette Securities Corporation	A.G. Edwards & Sons, Inc.
Goldman, Sachs & Co.	Lazard Frères & Co.	Lehman Brothers
Merrill Lynch & Co.	Montgomery Securities	Oppenheimer & Co., Inc.
PaineWebber Incorporated	Prudential Securities Incorporated	Robertson, Stephens & Company
Salomon Brothers Inc	Wertheim Schroder & Co. Incorporated	William Blair & Company
Dain Bosworth Incorporated	Kemper Securities, Inc.	Piper Jaffray Inc.
The Robinson-Humphrey Company, Inc.		Wheat First Butcher Singer
Advest, Inc.	Robert W. Baird & Co. Incorporated	The Chicago Corporation
Crowell, Weedon & Co.	Dominick & Dominick Incorporated	First Albany Corporation
First of Michigan Corporation	Interstate/Johnson Lane Corporation	Janney Montgomery Scott Inc.
Ladenburg, Thalmann & Co. Inc.	Mabon Securities Corp.	McDonald & Company Securities, Inc.
Neuberger & Berman	Principal Financial Securities, Inc.	Rauscher Pierce Refsnes, Inc.
Stifel, Nicolaus & Company Incorporated	Sutro & Co. Incorporated	Tucker Anthony Incorporated
Brean Murray, Foster Securities Inc.	Allen C. Ewing & Co.	Fahnestock & Co. Inc.
Ferris, Baker Watts Incorporated	C. L. King & Associates, Inc.	Luther, Smith & Small Inc.
Mesirow Financial, Inc.	Pennsylvania Merchant Group Ltd	Ragen MacKenzie Incorporated
The Seidler Companies Incorporated	Wm Smith Securities Incorporated	Van Kasper & Company

sales efforts. Given that both effort and risk differ according to role, rewards are distributed accordingly. In the case of Commercial Net Lease Realty, Inc., shown in Exhibit 18.8, the managing underwriter, Smith Barney Inc., secures the most substantial fee from the issue, followed closely by other members of the syndicate that also put their own money at risk—Legg Mason Wood Walker, J. C. Bradford & Co., and Raymond James & Associates, Inc. The sellers, those firms at the bottom of the tombstone, receive rewards limited to their commission.

The size of the underwriting spread ranges from 4 percent or less to as high as 15 percent of the dollar value of the debt offering, depending on its size. For equity offerings, the underwriting spread tends to be even higher. A managing underwriter may receive around 0.5 percent for its services. The syndicate members may receive around 1.5 percent for risking their capital. The selling group may receive around 2.0 percent for its sales. Because the managing underwriter is often a member of the syndicate as well as the selling group, it can receive as much as 4 percent on its sales (= 0.5% + 1.5% + 2%). The syndicate members receive anywhere from 1.5 percent to 3.5 percent, as they are also typically a part of the selling group. After all accounts are settled, a typical allotment of total fees is 20 percent to the managing underwriter, including compensation for participating in the underwriting syndicate and sales group; 25 percent to the underwriting syndicate, including participation in the sales group; and the remaining 55 percent to the selling group, distributed in proportion to completed sales. Often, the managing underwriter and syndicate members receive an even greater share of total proceeds than those indicated above.

If the issue is fully subscribed, each of the participants exits with substantial fees. If, however, the issue does not sell out, the underwriters take back the remaining securities. They may retain the syndicate and try again to sell the securities at the initial public offering price. Alternatively, the underwriters may separate to pursue different strategies to place the unsold securities. It is at this point that the underwriters can lose a substantial amount of money, which is why they are compensated for putting their capital at risk.

The shares or bonds that are placed with investors either gain or lose value after issue. As a general characterization, gaining value is more likely, particularly for initial public offerings like those discussed in Box 18.1. For new firms, shares tend to rise in price, at least initially, and this tendency has led many to invest in these new ventures, with new ideas, products, or entrepreneurs. (See Box 18.2.) But like everywhere else in the financial markets, risk is part of the process. Even in the IPO market, there are winners and there are losers.

Regulation of Underwriting Activity

The laws, rules, and regulations covering underwriting activity are voluminous. Accordingly, any coverage would be deficient and omit large and important aspects of the regulation of underwriting activity. Here, we shall only make reference to the three most relevant acts upon which most regulation is based. Interested readers are referred to securities law for any level of detail.

Box 18.2

USSB Gets $224 Million in Initial Public Offering

United States Satellite Broadcasting's initial public offering Thursday may not have had the sizzle of last summer's IPO by Netscape Communications Corp., but USSB founder Stanley S. Hubbard can't complain. The market has valued his company at $3.1 billion, and his family controls more than 50 percent of the common stock. Besides that, USSB raised $224.1 million in the offering—$80 million more than Netscape, the California software company, got in its initial public offering.

USSB shares closed at $34.75 on the NASDAQ national market, up 28 percent from its issue price. The St. Paul company offered 8.3 million shares of common stock, compared with the 5.25 million shares of Netscape originally offered at $28. Netscape's stock doubled in price in first-day trading.

D. Forbes Tuttle of The IPO Value Monitor research firm in New York estimated that the USSB deal would certainly be among the largest in 1996. "Mature industrial companies re-entering the market will always be the largest deals," Tuttle said, "but for new emerging companies, as this was, that's a pretty fabulous valuation."

Like Netscape at the time of its offering, USSB has yet to turn a profit. In fact, it lost $74 million on revenue of $42.3 million for the year ended June 30. Investors, however, are betting on the promise of the satellite TV industry, which has grown from zero to upward of $1 billion in revenue within two years.

Recent announcements that AT&T Corp. would invest $137 million in USSB's partner, DirecTV, and the market entry of other large companies, such as MCI Communications and News Corp., have sparked more interest in the industry and in USSB, which sells satellite programming.

Anticipating increased demand for the 8.3 million shares of common stock, USSB's investment bankers—CS First Boston, Goldman, Sachs & Co., Invemed Associates Inc. and Schroder Wertheim & Co.—repriced shares to $27 on Thursday from an earlier projected price range of $21 to $24.

Like most IPOs, initial trading in USSB shares was made in large blocks by large institutions, and most of the volume occurred in the first hour. The first trade was made at $35, and shares dipped as low as $33 within an hour.

Brian Belski, technical analyst at Dain Bosworth Inc. in Minneapolis, cautioned about reading too much into one day's results. Even so, he said the stock turned in "a strong performance, in that it regained ground and did it in the face of a pretty flat market."

The past few months have been strong for IPOs nationally, and USSB's appeal was enhanced because it supplies a mass-market product, Tuttle said.

USSB provides subscription TV programming to U.S. households that buy an 18-inch satellite dish. Among USSB's 25 premium channels are multichannel HBO, Comedy Central, and Lifetime.

DirecTV, a unit of Hughes Electronics, which itself is owned by General Motors, entered into an agreement with USSB in which it manufactured, launched, and operates the satellite. DirecTV offers 150 channels, primarily of sports programming.

Source: Terry Fiedler, "USSB Gets $224 Million in Initial Public Offering," *Star Tribune,* February 2, 1996, Metro Edition.

The **Securities Act of 1933** is the bedrock of the new issue market. This act and its subsequent interpretations form the core of the underwriting legal structure. As its centerpiece, the Securities Act of 1933 has only one mandate: It requires the disclosure of all information that is material and relevant to the public issue of a security. Any misrepresentation or fraud is subject to severe penalties.

As such, this act is one of the major pieces of securities regulation relevant to underwriting procedures and legal process.

The **Securities Exchange Act of 1934** extends the Securities Act to apply to secondary markets, and it requires national exchanges, brokers, and dealers to be registered. Both the Securities Act and the Securities Exchange Act are administered by the Securities and Exchange Commission, the five-person body that is the major regulatory and oversight authority in the securities markets.

The **Banking Act of 1933** is also an important part of the legal structure. Sections 16, 20, 21, and 32 of this act, often collectively referred to as Glass-Steagall after their historical proponents, separated the underwriting activity from commercial banking activity by law. Thus, commercial banks traditionally have been precluded from underwriting corporate equity and debt issues. They have been permitted to underwrite general obligation government debt, however, by explicit rights granted elsewhere in the 1933 act itself. Therefore, underwriting syndicates for public debt often include broker-dealers as well as commercial banks. This regulation has been eroding as of late, with the increased presence of banks in underwriting activity. These institutions have been permitted to underwrite pass-through securities and commercial paper since 1987. In addition, a series of recent rulings has permitted them to engage in some standard debt and equity underwriting through an affiliate. The Banking Act of 1933 also distinguishes between U.S. underwriting activity and that which occurs in other countries, where commercial banks are often permitted much more latitude in securities underwriting. More will be said of this issue in our discussion of investment banks in both Chapters 21 and 24.

Offshore Funding: Euromarkets and Asian Markets

In addition to raising funds domestically, firms can obtain funds from the international market. This is a wholesale location where only the largest borrowers and institutional lenders tend to participate. Instruments of choice tend to be debt instruments of both long (bond) and short (money market) maturity.

The **Eurobond market** is the generic name given to the overseas bond markets, located mostly in Europe. The **Asian Dollar** market is the name sometimes used for the money market and bond market centered in Asia, but at times, these markets are also counted within the Euromarket classification. In any case, both areas are attractive alternatives to raising funds in the United States. The main attractions are: (1) lessened restrictions on the issuance of debt instruments and (2) a more favorable tax treatment to investors. Accordingly, both markets have attracted substantial underwriting activity. Over the past decade, the Eurobond Market has often outstripped the U.S. market in terms of the dollar value of new bonds issued. (See Box 18.3.)

The Eurobond market is centered in Luxembourg and London, where listing requirements are minimal, whereas the Asian Dollar market is centered in Singapore and Hong Kong. Other important centers for these markets include Paris,

---

Box 18.3

Euromarkets: Their Uses and Worth

"Euromarkets" and "eurocurrencies" refer to financial transactions denominated in currencies other than that of the country in which they take place. Thus a eurodollar loan or bank deposit is one denominated in dollars but made outside the US.

The prefix "euro" derives from the fact that such transactions, which are sometimes also described as "offshore" transactions, originated in Europe, with London as the main eurocurrency banking centre. Today, however, nearly half of so-called eurocurrency transactions take place outside Europe, through regional centres such as Hong Kong, Singapore and some Caribbean countries and, to a lesser extent, in New York and Tokyo. The US dollar is the main eurocurrency, followed by the yen and deutschemark, reflecting their roles in international trade and finance.

Limited banking transactions in US dollars and sterling, the then dominant world currencies, were made in Germany during the hyperinflation that followed the first world war. The modern, worldwide, network of eurocurrency transactions developed in the 1960s, following the relaxation of exchange controls carried out by western European countries in 1958. Nearly 80 percent of international banking transactions are made in eurocurrencies; and, in addition, active markets have developed in eurocurrency security issues, especially in eurobonds and, to a lesser extent, in euro-commercial paper and equities.

The Advantages of Eurocurrency Transactions

The growth of euromarkets began mainly as a way of avoiding various restrictions and costs in domestic banking and securities markets. These included interest rate ceilings, restrictions on foreign investment imposed in the US and the prohibition, in 1957, on the

use of sterling bank loans to finance trade between countries outside the UK.

Today only the imposition by central banks in some countries of noninterest-bearing reserve requirements on domestic bank deposits remains as a major domestic regulation favouring eurocurrency banking transactions. Even so, euromarkets have continued to grow as a result of other advantages they possess.

These include: the convenience to a customer of transacting in a foreign currency with a local bank instead of one overseas; the ability to follow daylight hours across countries; the assembly of very large bank loans through syndication (95 percent of syndicated international bank loans are in eurocurrencies); low taxes in some centres; and the ability to separate currency from political risk (the former Soviet Union preferred to hold its dollar deposits outside the US during the 1950s and 1960s).

Other Factors in the Growth of Eurocurrencies

Special factors influence the pace of growth in eurocurrency banking transactions from time to time. The sharp rise in oil prices in 1973 and again in 1979–80 led oil-exporting countries to have large balance of payments surpluses, which they invested to a great extent in dollar bank deposits, held partly outside the US. But this phase of expansion was brought to an end by the Mexican debt moratorium of 1982.

The eurocurrency transactions of individual banks are to a considerable extent portfolio adjustments made in response to perceived currency and interest rate risks. Interbank transactions play a larger part in these adjustments than they do in domestic banking, so that the volume of "gross" eurocurrency transactions is perhaps three times that of "net" transactions with non-bank customers.

The extent to which non-banks choose to hold deposits as eurocurrency rather than as domestic currency deposits depends on a comparison of relative returns and costs in the two types of markets. High reserve requirements, for example, force banks to offer lower interest rates on domestic as opposed to eurocurrency deposits. The reduction in reserve requirements in several countries in recent years is one reason why the proportion of eurocurrency deposits in international banking markets has fallen from 90 percent to just under 80 percent over the past decade.

Eurobonds

About half of international borrowing is now in the form of bond issues, and about 80 percent is in the form of eurobonds. (Euro-commercial paper programmes and, even more, medium-term euronote programmes have also grown substantially, the latter exceeding Dollars 200bn in 1994.)

Originally the term "eurobond" was reserved for bonds denominated in a currency other than that of the location of issue, but nowadays it is also used to apply to issues by a foreign lender in the currency of the country where it is issued, as long as distribution is largely to international investors made through a syndicate of investment houses. Eurobonds are always unsecured and are mainly fixed-interest bonds. About four-fifths of eurobond issues are said to be swapped into another currency in some years.

Like that of eurocurrency banking the initial development of eurobond markets was a reaction to restrictions on, and the transaction costs of, foreign bond issues in the currency of domestic markets. As eurobonds are unregistered 'bearer' bonds, from which withholding tax is not usually deducted, they also offer tax benefits. But the disadvantages of domestic currency bonds have become relatively unimportant for one reason or another.

Despite this, and despite improvements in domestic bond markets, the share of eurobond issues in international borrowing has continued to grow, from 20 percent in 1980 to over 40 percent in 1993, at the expense of syndicated bank loans.

Eurobonds now account for three-quarters of the total stock of international bonds. This growth has been helped by the standardisation of issue arrangements such as the form of the issue document and interest payment and clearing arrangements, which has kept issue costs down. The eurobond issue market is a flexible and competitive one, free from the high transaction costs typical of cartelised markets such as France, Germany and Switzerland and of highly regulated markets such as those of New York and Tokyo.

Eurobonds are usually listed on the London or Luxembourg stock exchange. London is thought to have three-quarters of trading in the secondary market, which is usually an over-the-counter market, in which banks act as dealers. Small issues may have relatively low liquidity, but bid-offer spreads on high-quality bonds have fallen as improvements in the market have been made.

The Benefits of Euromarkets to Business

The development of euromarkets has widened the access companies have to loan markets and has brought down borrowing costs relative to the underlying level of interest rates. Even relatively small companies can tap eurocurrency markets through their banks; and companies can borrow in whatever market is most advantageous to them and swap proceeds into the currency they need to spend.

Competition from euromarkets has helped to break up cartelised domestic markets and has played a large part in the liberalisation of domestic markets, to the benefit of borrowers. By facilitating international financing and helping to reduce real interest rate differences between countries, euromarkets have played a part in creating a world capital market, to the benefit of world economic growth.

Source: Harold Rose, "Euromarkets: Their Uses and Worth," *The Financial Times Limited*, November 24, 1995. Reprinted with permission of Harold B. Rose. London Business School.

Frankfurt, Zurich, Dublin, Bahrain, Sydney, Wellington, Tokyo, and Taipei. These markets are characterized by innovative features on the debt instruments, such as index linkage to commodity prices, floating rates, currency options, and so forth. One of the characteristics of the market is that primarily better-known companies have access to funding there, while upstart companies have little chance of gaining much interest due to the difficulty of assessing credit risk and market information.

The existence of these alternative capital markets acts somewhat as a constraint to the costs that the SEC or any other domestic regulator can impose on would-be issuers of securities. If the regulations become too onerous, companies with some market standing can simply go elsewhere to access funding. This would be harmful to the profitability of the U.S. financial industry, so the SEC has been forced to keep the costs of compliance that it imposes on others in mind when it designs and administers its regulations.

We could go on at some length about these markets, but this would lead us too far afield. Suffice it to say that underwriting occurs in each of these financial centers in a fashion that is analogous to the approach used here. However, there are differences—in disclosure, process, and access, to name just a few. Yet, in a global market, issuers and investors are increasingly aware of these alternative markets and their investment potential.

Choosing among New Instrument Forms

Part 3 of this textbook delved into a number of securities issued by private and public entities. There were many alternatives. If an economic entity desires funding, how is it supposed to decide which form of security to offer? If it is a government, the choices are narrowed, because a government typically does not issue common or preferred equities; it will issue only debt instruments. For a private corporation, the variety of possible securities is even larger.

The choice of a new instrument form depends on the objective of the funding, the economic environment, and the economic constraints of the issuer. For example, a corporation may already be so indebted that an additional debt issue will jeopardize its solvency; in such a case, an equity issue, common or preferred, would be the security of choice. If interest rates are particularly low, a corporation with good equity capital may choose to issue a debt instrument with fixed interest rates in order to take advantage of the low rates. If interest rates are perceived to be temporarily high, the same corporation may desire to obtain funding through a variable interest rate instrument.

In any case, the issuer will usually consult with an expert underwriter for advice on the form and timing of a securities issue. The nature of the assets and revenue streams of the issuer will factor importantly into a decision about the preferred form of security to issue. Occasionally, a particular form of security falls out of favor in the market, and the underwriter will advise the issuer about the kinds of instruments that appear to offer the least expensive form of financing at any given time. With the ever-expanding menu of possible security forms, the solicitation and acquisition of expert advice have become more important in recent years.

Summary

The primary market is of primary importance. It is the market that funnels funds directly to the end-users. Nonetheless, the secondary market tends to get the most press because of its visibility and glamour. However, it is important to remember that many countries are able to survive without any well-organized, efficient secondary market. However, few can operate without a primary market that provides needed capital to the industrial sector.

Within the primary market, there are numerous security types that can facilitate the transfer of funds from providers to users, such as common and preferred stock, bonds, notes, mortgage loans, and money market instruments. There are several modes for obtaining funds, including a negotiated public offering, best efforts public offering, competitive bid public offering, and private placement.

The institutions that participate in this market have changed over time and will continue to change in the future. Rules that regulate the primary market have clear goals, but these rules have also changed over time, and they are currently undergoing significant revision in the United States. While this is happening, the security types that are used in the transfer of funds from provider to user have proliferated, and new ways of conveying funds are bound to be developed.

Yet, amidst all of this change, the role of the primary market has remained fundamentally the same. That goal is to transfer funds from savers to investors—from economic entities with a surplus to those with a deficit. The primary market provides the fuel for the operation of the economic machine.

Key Concepts

Banking Act of 1933,   449
comparables,   443
indenture,   434
initial public offering,   438
investment bank,   434
managing underwriter, underwriting syndicate,
  and selling group,   444
negotiated versus competitive bidding
  underwriting,   443
on-the-run and current-coupon bonds,   442
public security issue,   440

privately placed security,   436
prospectus and final prospectus,   441
Securities Act of 1933,   448
Securities Exchange Act of 1934,   449
seed, start-up, first-stage, second-stage, and
  mezzanine financing,   438
shelf registration,   441
tombstone,   445
Eurobond and Asian Dollar markets,   449
underwriter,   434

Review Questions

1. How would you go about valuing a conglomerate company?
2. The three primary acts dealing with regulation of underwriting activity could be described as answering the questions: Who,

   What, and How? Why is this an apt description?
3. While at a frat "tea party," you overhear the following statement: "Look at the exorbitant profits that the investment banking industry is

reaping. They don't produce anything, so what good are they?" How would you reply to this sudden outburst?

4. In what ways has the growth in alternative capital markets served as a check on the proliferation of government regulation?

5. Discuss the trade-off connected with the number of members included in a selling group.

6. As commercial banks have entered the underwriting business, some members of their community have contended that they are stealing resources and market share from the basic lending business. Present the arguments both for and against this assertion.

7. In several local communities, there has been a movement toward legally mandating a competitive bid process for issuing municipal debt. Discuss the pros and cons of such legislation.

References

Admati, Anat R., and Paul Pfleiderer. "Robust Financial Contracting and the Role of Venture Capitalists." *Journal of Finance,* June 1994.

Affleck-Graves, John; Shantaram P. Hegde; and Robert E. Miller. "Trading Mechanisms and the Components of the Bid-Ask Spread." *Journal of Finance,* September 1994.

Bhagat, S. "The Effects of Management's Choice between Negotiated and Competitive Equity Offerings on Shareholder Wealth." *Journal of Finance and Quantitative Analysis,* 1986.

Bhagat, S.; M.W. Man; and G.R. Thompson. "The Rule 415 Experiment: Equity Markets." *Journal of Finance,* December 1985.

Bloch, Ernest. *Inside Investment Banking.* Burr Ridge, Ill.: Irwin Professional Publishing, 1986.

Board of Governors of the Federal Reserve System. "Recent Developments in the Market for Privately Placed Debt." *Federal Reserve Bulletin,* February 1993.

Chu, J.F. "The Private Placement Market Comes of Age." *The Bankers Magazine,* September 1989.

Cornett, Marcia Millon; Wallace N. Davidson III; and Nanda Rangan. "Deregulation in Investment Banking: Industry Concentration Following Rule 415." *Journal of Banking and Finance,* March 1996.

Francis, Jack Clark. *Investments.* 5th ed. New York: McGraw-Hill, 1990.

George, Thomas J.; Gautam Kaul; and M. Nimalendran. "Trading Volume and Transaction Costs in Specialist Markets." *Journal of Finance,* September 1994.

Hansen, R. "Evaluating the Costs of a New Equity Issue." *Midland Corporate Finance Journal,* Spring 1986.

Lerner, Josh. "Venture Capitalists and the Oversight of Private Firms." *Journal of Finance,* March 1995.

Logue, Dennis, and Robert Jarrow. "Negotiation vs. Competitive Bidding in the Sales of Securities by Public Utilities." *Financial Management,* 1978.

Loughran, Rim, and Jay R. Ritter. "The New Issues Puzzle." *Journal of Finance,* March 1995.

Mikkelson, W. H., and M. M. Partch. "The Valuation Effects of Securities Offerings and the Issuance Process." *Journal of Financial Economics,* 1986.

Radcliffe, Robert C. *Investment Concepts, Analysis and Strategy.* 3rd ed. Glenview, Ill.: Scott Foresman/Little Brown, 1990.

Ritter, Jay R. "The Cost of Going Public." *Journal of Financial Economics,* 1987.

———. "The Long-Run Performance of Initial Public Offerings." *Journal of Finance,* March 1991.

Ross, Stephen; Randolph Westerfield; and Jeffrey Jaffe. *Corporate Finance.* 3rd ed. Burr Ridge, Ill.: Richard D. Irwin, 1996.

Secondary Market Structure

Markets for existing securities can be organized in many ways. The world has seen negotiated trades, exchanges, and intermediaries serve as mechanisms for trading existing securities. This chapter reviews the services provided in the secondary market and the various ways the market has been organized. Considerable attention is devoted to the exchange structure, the mechanism of trade, and its relative importance. In addition, U.S. regulation of the secondary market is briefly reviewed.

The broad and deep secondary market is an essential ingredient for an efficient capital market system. Without it, anyone who purchased a security would have to hold it until maturity, if the security featured a maturity, or until death, if the security were a perpetual issue such as preferred stock, common stock, or consols. In such a case, buying a security would be a sobering decision, knowing full well that it is likely to stay with you longer than most of us keep our jobs! If secondary markets exist but are as inefficient as they are in many countries and in the markets for some security categories, it may be possible to unload a purchased security prior to maturity, but only at a significant loss. We could liken this situation to working with a partner. It takes more time and money to undo the relationship than to begin it, sometimes much more time than the time spent building the business that you wish to dissolve. On the other hand, to continue the analogy, an efficient secondary market is much like being a consultant. When the engagement turns sour, you pack your bags and move to the next client.

Secondary markets are available for most publicly issued securities. Indeed, as we noted in the previous chapter, some investment banks even make a market for private placements, although the volume of this kind of business is usually quite light and trading is sporadic. This secondary market can be important, nonetheless, in that it provides a mechanism for an institutional investor to divest of an unwanted investment, albeit sometimes only at a steep discount.

There are, however, many ways in which a secondary market can be organized. All of these markets accomplish the same end—connecting buyers and sellers—but they do so in different ways. In this chapter, we review these alternative structures and the mechanisms of trading in each.

Secondary Market Structures

If you wished to sell your used car, there are several ways you could go about it. You could canvass your friends and neighbors, tack a note on a bulletin board, place an ad in a newspaper or two, or use some other approach that would put you in touch directly with an interested party. There may be a person in the next county willing to pay a higher price for your vehicle, but you might never be aware of this fact. It may be just too costly to advertise that broadly or to search to find that individual.

Or you could use an alternative method of selling your car. You could employ the services of an acquaintance, in the capacity of a broker, who has wide contacts with dealers and other auto buffs and an ability to market your vehicle to a number of potentially interested parties. The acquaintance/broker is more likely to find the interested party across town quickly and obtain the better price, but it may cost you a commission to employ his services.

On the other hand, you might prefer to go directly to a preowned car dealer who buys and sells preowned cars for her own inventory and profits from the spread between her buying and selling price. The spread would also need to compensate her for the cost of carrying the inventory and for any other operating costs that she incurs. However, you may find this method of sale both more convenient and cost effective, considering the time and cost involved in selling the vehicle yourself. However, even in this case, you may have to visit several dealers in order to secure the most favorable offer.

Finally, you could offer to sell your car at an auction. If the auctioneer is able to attract a large crowd, you could take comfort that the price you receive will be close to the highest price that the car would command in the market. Of course, the services of the auctioneer are not free, as it is expensive for him to operate that kind of enterprise on a scale likely to attract the volume of participants necessary to make the auction a viable opportunity that is attractive to you as a seller.

Each of these four approaches to selling your vehicle are available to any car seller. Generally, however, the broker and auction approaches are more commonly used in the commercial and wholesale sides of the business, while direct search and dealer sales are most common for the type of transaction described above.

Similarly, if you wish to trade a "used security," you can do so in the used security market, or secondary market, in a number of ways. In fact, there are four types of market structures in the secondary securities market that parallel our examples above quite closely. They are **direct search markets, brokered markets, dealer markets,** and **auction markets.** Each type of market is characterized by the approach used to find a suitable trading partner. Let us now consider each of them in turn.

Direct Search Markets

In a direct search market, the buyer or seller of a given security must search out the other side of the trade directly. In this case, the full cost, in terms of time and expense, of locating a suitable trading partner is borne by the individuals wishing to make the trade. They may seek a trading partner relying on word-of-mouth communication, advertising, or some other informal mechanism. Unfortunately, given the unique characteristics of any individual security that its owner is attempting to sell, these costs can be substantial. You not only must find a person interested in trading the particular security you have in mind, but you must also find an individual who is willing to pay a price for your security that meets your expectations. If you wish to buy a security, you have a similarly difficult situation finding the individual willing to offer it to you at an acceptable price. Despite these difficulties, however, the direct search approach is common for securities with only local or regional interest. For example, if you have a small local bank in town, their shares are often traded only by word of mouth. The same can be said for many of the small firms in the economy. These issues trade infrequently and generally have no third party, such as a broker or a dealer, interested in facilitating the trade. As you can guess, however, these transactions are not the mainstay of the secondary market. Rather, the direct search market is relegated to handling thinly traded securities.

Brokered Markets

If the trading volume or interest in a security becomes sufficiently high, however, the situation changes. In this case, the services of brokers may be available. As long as these services can be used to locate a trading partner who is willing to transact at a price at least as favorable as that which you were able to find through direct search, and as long as the services are less costly than the cost of a direct search, there will be a demand for the broker's services.

Such brokerage services will be supplied whenever it makes economic sense for the broker to offer them. In general, this means that there is a prerequisite level of investor interest in the security, as manifested by trading volume. This satisfied, the broker can justify the time and effort associated with providing his services to parties interested in the particular security. Otherwise, he would have to charge too high a price for his services and the investor would be better off finding trading partners via the direct search approach.

There are two reasons that trading volume affects the broker's decision to become active; in both, economies of scale can be achieved in connection with facilitating transactions in a particular security. First, there are high fixed costs in acquiring the communication technologies and trading infrastructure that allow the broker to keep in touch effectively with a large number of investors, dealers, and other brokers interested in the security. The broker must maintain a current knowledge of investor interests via continuous contacts with a number of the investors. Second, the cost can be high for obtaining investment analysis and other information needed to maintain the broker's knowledge of the value of the security that he wishes to trade.

After incurring the large fixed setup costs, the broker may incur close to zero marginal costs to share the information with clients. He therefore has an incentive to charge a commission that is lower than the cost of direct search but high enough to eventually cover the large setup costs. In this way, investors will have an incentive to utilize his brokerage services.

Examples of brokered markets are the retail market for individual investors in municipal bonds, the placement of "term federal funds" for periods longer than one day between financial institutions, and the market for some negotiated certificates of deposit. In each of these cases, brokers are retained to search out compatible trading partners when the need arises to trade in these securities. Brokers do not, however, buy the security in question themselves. The trading is sufficiently thin that the cost to dealers of providing continuous liquidity and immediate execution of trades is deemed too expensive to be justified. As this implies, there is a level of trading activity above which a dealer market may emerge.

Dealer Markets

Although brokers may command several advantages over the direct search markets, they do have a disadvantage in that they cannot guarantee the prompt execution of investor orders. While they are searching for alternative potential trading partners for a client, the market prices may move adversely or the seller may just become impatient because of his or her critical need for cash. Thus, the investor dependent on brokerage services is faced with both price risk and potential delays stemming from the uncertainty surrounding the amount of time it will take to locate a suitable trading partner and execute the transaction.

If trading is sufficiently active in the security, dealers may arise who will take advantage of the situation by maintaining an inventory in the security. This will allow them to buy and sell the issue at any time for their own inventory. Dealers would quote bid and offer prices and stand ready to execute orders at these quoted prices. This is attractive to investors, who then know that they can immediately buy or sell a given amount of their securities at the quoted prices.

In such a situation, a dealer offers two quotes for a particular security, one at which he is willing to buy the security, a **bid,** and one at which he is willing to sell the same security, an **offer** or ask. For example, a dealer in a nonexchange listed stock may offer a quote of, say, 8 1/4–1/2, indicating his willingness to purchase this security at $8.25 per share and sell it at $8.50. In such a situation, the dealer is compensated for his services by selling securities at offer prices higher than those that they bid to pay for the securities. (See Box 19.1.) The prices quoted may vary from one dealer to another because they may have different inventory positions, different investment objectives, or because their views differ on the value of the securities being traded. Thus, it behooves the investor to contact more than one dealer in order to secure a favorable price.

Examples of dealer markets are the market for U.S. Treasury issues, the market for most corporate bonds, and the OTC market for common and preferred stock. Each of these dealer markets has distinctive features. The Treasury market is characterized by relatively few different issues (200 or thereabouts), each of which is huge (several billion dollars). This has attracted dozens of active dealers who trade with each other, with financial institutions, and with the investor public at relatively small bid-offer spreads. Transaction sizes are often very large (in the millions of dollars range) in the interdealer portion of the market (dealers trading directly with other dealers), but range from several thousand dollars to tens of millions of dollars in the dealer-public portion of the market.

The corporate bond market, by way of contrast, is comprised of thousands of issues, each of which is typically less than $250 million. Although this size is relatively small and the issues are heterogeneous, the nature of fixed-income instruments—instruments with fixed coupon payments for a specified number of years—means that they can often be viewed as close substitutes for one another. Thus, the most successful bond dealers make markets in a full range of bond issues and are willing to buy almost any bond for their inventory. However, because this market is characterized by large, infrequent trades, corporate bond dealers need to have a strong capital base in order to absorb the risk of carrying an inventory over relatively long periods of time. Thus, this market is dominated by a few large investment banking firms, such as Goldman Sachs, First Boston, and Salomon Brothers.

Finally, there are tens of thousands of stock issues that trade over the counter. OTC stocks are generally not close substitutes for each other, and they do not

Box 19.1

Dealer Services and the Bid-Ask Spread

Traditional wisdom refers to the bid-ask spread as the "jobber's turn," suggesting that it provides compensation to the dealer for the provision of services. Demsetz[†] (1968) formalized this rationale for the spread, defining the particular service provided as "predictable immediacy" and offering a simple model to describe the spread.

Market buy and sell curves with and without the provision of immediacy

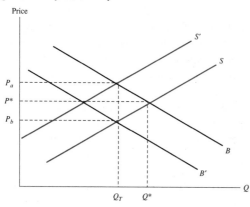

Consider a continuous market with aggregate supply (sell) and demand (buy) schedules, S and B, for a

security (see figure at left). In an idealized world, investors would come together simultaneously, and the market would clear at price P^* and quantity Q^*. In this marketplace, however, such coordination of trading is impossible. By assumption, the market is continuous, and there is no mechanism (e.g., a limit order book) for holding orders over time. Thus, S and B do not represent standard static supply and demand schedules, but rather time rates of supply and demand. At any given instant, there may be no orders on either side.

Instead, we introduce a monopolistic market-maker who allows the trading to occur by standing in as a counterparty to all trades. In the process, he provides a service to investors that Demsetz labels "predictable immediacy." The market-maker knows the aggregate supply and demand propensities. The supply and demand curves that he presents to the public, S' and B', however, are both shifted leftward. Investor purchases clear for price P_a, at the intersection of the market demand schedule, B, with the market-maker's supply schedule, S'. Similarly, investor sales clear at the intersection of S and B', for price P_b. The differences: $P_a - P^*$ and $P^* - P_b$ are liquidity premia. In the figure, the quantities, Q_T, purchased and sold by the market-maker happen to be equal, so that no market-maker inventory is accumulated. His profit thus equals $Q_T(P_a - P_b)$; this is the "jobber's turn."

[†]See Harold Demsetz, "The Cost of Transacting," *Quarterly Journal of Economics*, February 1968.

Source: Mark D. Flood, "Microstructure Theory and the Foreign Exchange Market," *Review,* Federal Reserve Bank of St. Louis, November 1991.

often trade in large blocks. Therefore, there are many dealers in OTC stocks who tend to specialize in a narrow range of issues. Every dealer, however, performs a similar function. They buy and sell securities for their own account and serve as a source of trading activity for the range of securities in which they choose to trade. As in the case of bond markets, dealers in OTC stocks face considerable risks. Accordingly, large relative capital positions are maintained, and these firms are overseen by the regulators of the OTC market-makers.

Auction Markets

Beyond the dealer markets, one enters the auction market arena, where trade is generally more frequent. There are reasons that this market structure emerges. Dealer markets provide the advantages of rapid execution of a trade and of lower search costs than brokered or direct search markets. However, they do carry two disadvantages. You can never be sure that a more favorable price could not have been attained by contacting other dealers. Furthermore, you will always face the expense of a dealer's bid-offer spread.

By contrast, an auction market offers a centralized market where trades are carried out in a single location at publicly announced prices. In such a situation, all traders, whether they be dealers or other investors, have access to the trading opportunity. An auction market avoids both of the disadvantages enumerated above. The prices attained represent the most favorable prices available from the participants in the auction market, and they do not carry with them a bid-offer spread. Moreover, auction markets allow investors to execute their transactions immediately when they are willing to accept the auction price.

For an auction market to be successful, however, a high dollar volume of trading in a security is not enough. What is required is a large number of transactions. For example, three issues could exhibit a similar average total dollar trading volume of $10 million per week but a vastly different number of transactions. For example, security A might typically involve 2,000 trades per week of $5,000 per transaction. With such high and nearly continuous volume, this security would be suitable for continuous auction markets such as those featured on a stock exchange. Security B might typically involve trades in an average amount of $500,000 about 20 times per week, or four times per day. This type of security might be more suitable for a dealer market, and a dealer's spread would compensate for the price risk of holding a security in inventory between the infrequent trades. Security C may trade in $20 million bunches, with only one trade, on average, occurring every two weeks. While this also translates into an average weekly volume of $10 million, the trades are so infrequent that it is unlikely a dealer would be willing to bear the price risk. Such a security is more likely to be traded in the brokered or direct search markets.

Where auction markets emerge, they require frequent presentations of purchase and sale orders within a single market. Strict priority is given to highest bid and lowest offer in the execution of trades. In Chapter 13, we described the operation of auction markets in the primary market for newly issued Treasury securities. This is the type of priority rule that must be both established and understood by market participants in order for an auction market to exist. However, the clearest example of an auction market structure is the trading of broadly held securities in both the computer-linked OTC market and large organized exchanges. In fact, these are the images conjured up in people's minds when one makes reference to the stock market or one of the major exchanges. They immediately think of the Nasdaq automated quotation system and the trading of listed securities on an organized exchange, such as the national or regional stock exchanges or option and futures exchanges. Let's look more closely at how these markets work.

The Mechanics of Trading

The Ordering Process

Trading stock on an exchange is a bit like to going to a fast food restaurant. It entails entering an order and then waiting to be served. How long you wait to be served depends, in part, on what you order and, in part, on the number of other patrons already waiting in the queue. But entering an order is not as simple as it may sound, because the menu in the secondary market for securities is rather lengthy. Indeed, there are at least 768 kinds of orders in common use today. Most people will use only a few of these order types, but there is a baffling array of possibilities.

To decide on the exact nature of your stock order among the many choices, it is useful to go through the following set of questions.

1. *What security do you wish to trade?* While we won't offer you much help here, there are many places to look for help, advice, and simple information. Entering an order is serious business, and investors ought to do so only after they have researched the matter thoroughly. Some good sources are *The Wall Street Journal, Financial Times, Investors Daily,* and *Barron's,* in the newspaper category; *CNBC, Nightly Business News,* or *Wall Street Week* on your tube; and references such as *Value Line* or research reports from *Standard & Poor's* and *Moody's.* Annual reports help as well.

2. *Do you wish to buy it or sell it?* If you decide to sell the security you selected, do you wish to conduct a **long sale**? In a long sale you are selling a security that you already own; owning a security is often referred to as being "long" the security. Or do you wish to **short sell** the security? In this case, you will borrow somebody else's security and sell it with a promise to restore the borrowed security at a later date. Selling a security that you do not own is called "shorting" the security.[1]

3. *What is the size of your order? How many shares do you wish to trade?* Exchanges divide order quantities into **round lots** and **odd lots.** The brokerage commission structure generally favors trading in round lots; that is, the cost of transactions on a per share basis usually runs lower on a round lot. The size of a round lot varies across exchanges and also depends on the trading activity in a particular security. For example, a round lot on the New York Stock Exchange is 100 shares or some integer multiple thereof, but for some inactive shares, a round lot is only 10 shares.[2] Thus, depending on the trading activity in the security, odd

---

[1]Exchange rules usually dictate that short sale orders can be executed only after the price of a security has risen, a so-called uptick. So, your order may not be achieved in all cases.

[2]According to the *New York Stock Exchange Fact Book* of 1994, the average trade size in that year was 1,495 shares, with more than 30 percent of trades in excess of 25,000 shares.

lots would be for 1–99 shares or 1–9 shares. On other exchanges, a round lot may be 25 or 50 shares.[3]

4. *What is the price at which you wish to conduct the trade?* Here your choice is whether to buy or sell **at the market** or to place a **limit order.** With a market order, you will buy or sell your stock at whatever the most favorable prevailing market price happens to be at the time your order reaches the auction location. When placing a limit order, you decide in advance to place a limit on the range of prices at which you would be willing to trade. For example, suppose Goodyear common stock is currently selling for $58 per share. You may place a limit order to buy 100 shares of Goodyear at $56 per share. The trade will be executed at the limit price, or better if possible. In the case of your Goodyear order, it will be filled if and when the market price reaches the limit price of $56. Alternatively, you could place a limit order to sell Goodyear whenever the share price reaches as high as $60. In placing a limit order, there is a risk that the trade will not be consummated in the near future, and perhaps not at all, if the market price of the security does not cross the limit threshold.

5. *Do you wish to impose any time limits within which you wish to conduct the trade?* You can place a limit order that expires in a day, a week, or even a month in the event that the trade is not able to be consummated within that period. You can also place a **good-until-canceled** (GTC) order, in which case the order will remain effective indefinitely unless it is canceled at some point in time.

6. *Do you wish to impose any other conditions on the execution of a trade?* For example, you may wish to place a stop order. A **stop-loss order** is a sell order that becomes a market order when the stock sells at or below the stop price. A **stop-buy order** becomes a market order whenever the prevailing market price reaches or exceeds the stop price. In a sense, a stop order is the opposite of a limit order. While in a limit sell order, the limit price is placed above the current market price, in a stop-loss order, the stop price is placed below the current market price. A limit sell order is designed to help you achieve a certain amount of profit, whereas a stop-loss order is designed to help you avoid a loss that exceeds a prespecified level. A limit buy order and a stop order to buy a security have an analogous relationship. There are dozens of types of orders that we will not mention here, each of which is designed to accomplish a particular goal of the trader.[4] Suffice it to say that the menu of alternatives is a full one.

---

[3]Some market observers, called "technical analysts," closely track the trading statistics of "odd-lot traders." Such traders are presumed to possess less financial acumen than the wealthy investors, who typically trade in round lots. Thus, the technical analysts holding to this persuasion watch what the odd-lot traders are doing and then do the opposite for their own accounts on the presumption that the odd lotters are bound to be wrong. The paradox with this sort of investment philosophy is that these technical analysts, who purport to have financial acumen, are letting their judgment and behavior be determined solely by those whom they judge to be less cunning, rather than letting their investment decisions reflect any independent judgment or analysis.

[4]A useful discussion of various types of orders and their execution is found in Richard J. Teweles and Edward S. Bradley, *The Stock Market,* 4th ed. (New York: John Wiley & Sons, 1982), chapters 7 and 8.

Executing a Trade

Most individual investors place a security trading order through a broker, although some work directly with dealers. Priority for order execution depends on the time and price at which the order was placed. Market price orders are executed on a "first come, first served" basis.

Orders placed on an exchange are transacted in a **free double auction.** In a free double auction, bids to purchase stock are arranged from highest to lowest, and offers to sell stock are arranged from lowest to highest offer price. Then, and only then, do transactions occur. This procedure achieves the highest price for the seller and the lowest price available for the buyer, given the collection of orders available at any time.[5] It also maximizes the number of trades possible from any set of orders. When these transactions are completed, the order book may still contain limit orders that cannot be satisfied at the current price, so stock is purchased from the seller offering the lowest price. At any moment in time, the difference between the prices of standing limit orders is known as the bid-offer (or bid-ask) spread. The bid-offer spread is analogous to the dealer spread referred to earlier.

If the bid-offer spread gets too large, a member of the exchange charged with assuring an efficient market in a particular security may take the opposite side of the transaction and purchase (or sell) the security for (or from) his or her own inventory. This individual is referred to as a specialist, and his role will be discussed at length in the next section of this chapter. As a result of the specialists' actions, securities trading on organized exchanges tend to have rather narrow spreads. In a 1990 study reported in the 1992 *New York Stock Exchange Fact Book,* 84.5 percent of the securities quoted on the NYSE exhibited a bid-offer spread per share of 1/4 point ($0.25) or less. Moreover, market depth was generally good. The average trade of 3,000 shares produced no price change or a small price change (1/8 point) 84.4 percent of the time. **Price continuity,** or the variation in price from one trade to the next, was also good. The same study reported that 95.8 percent of all transactions occurred with no change or with only a 1/8-point variation.

The sale is completed by a transfer of ownership to the buyer at the time payment is made for the security. In fact, the transaction really involves transferring the stock from the seller's broker to the buyer's broker. For most securities, this **settlement** occurs between two and three business days after the trade date. For certain securities, such as U.S. Treasury bonds, notes, and bills, settlement for round lots occurs on the first business day following the date of trade, and settlement for odd lots takes place three business days after the trade date. While these practices represent the majority of all trades, other settlement days are possible. For example, **cash contracts** call for settlement on the same day as the trade.

---

[5]Recently, there has been a considerable amount of research centering around the rules of trading. The field is known as market microstructure. See the references at the end of this chapter to investigate the issue further.

The Role of Specialists

It is often maintained that organized exchanges function so efficiently due to the activity of **specialists.** Specialists are members of an exchange who are selected by the exchange to specialize in buying and selling one or a few specific issues of listed stock. Specialists are expected to stabilize stock price movements by buying or selling these securities from their own account against the prevailing market trend in security prices. For instance, they may purchase a stock at a higher price than anyone else is willing to pay at the time or sell a stock at a lower price than anyone else is willing to accept. Over 83 percent of specialist transactions were directed toward this type of stabilization.

A specialist may engage in transactions either as a broker or a dealer. When acting in a broker capacity, the specialist will execute orders for other brokers in exchange for a commission. When acting as a dealer, the specialist will act for his own account and absorb the risks associated with his profit-seeking activities. While much of this activity is aimed at market stabilization, the specialist's hope is that he will profit by reversing the "stabilizing" transactions when the market turns around. Only about one in four members of the exchange are specialists. They interact with other members of the exchange but do not transact business with the public directly.

The specialist is motivated to take "contrarian" trades for two reasons. First, it is a requirement of the exchange and of federal regulation. A specialist must maintain a continuous market with close bid and offer prices, and he must minimize the effect of a temporary imbalance between public supply and demand in the securities for which he makes a market. Second, the total compensation earned by a specialist depends on maintaining investors and speculators interested in trading his stock. Investors and speculators prefer to trade in a good market with narrow spreads and continuous prices. Therefore, it is in the self-interest of a specialist to promote as close and continuous a market in his stock as possible.

A specialist has information that is not shared with other members of the exchange or the public at large. This is because the specialist maintains a **specialist book** that contains information regarding the relative strength of supply and demand for the particular securities in which he specializes. The book lists all of the limit and stop order prices and the desired trading volumes associated with each order. To prevent abuse of this special information, the specialist is prohibited from buying for his own account when he has an unexecuted market order to buy, and he is prohibited from selling for his own account when he has a market order to sell. Similarly, he is forbidden from buying for his own account at a price below that at which he has a limit order to buy. Further, the specialist cannot sell for his own account at a price at or above that for which a limit sell order has already been placed. If he were permitted to do otherwise, he would, in effect, be competing against his own customers and acting improperly as their agent.

As noted above, trades can be executed outside an exchange in a manner similar to the process described above. If investors enter a computer-linked trading environment, they obtain all the benefits of an auction market, except there is no specialist

EXHIBIT 19.1

1994 dollar volume of equity trading in major world markets ($ billions)

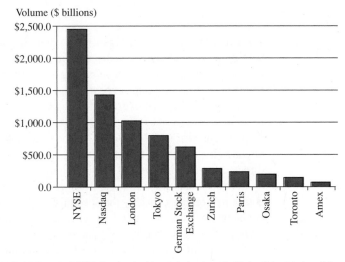

Volume ($ billions)

Source: *NASDAQ Fact Book 1995*, Reprinted with permission from the National Association of Securities Dealers, Inc.

involved or overseeing the transactions. Rather, an order is entered through a broker, who in turn seeks to execute the trade through a dealer in the desired securities. While business conducted on an organized exchange must be transacted through specialists, each of whom has a monopolistic position over the securities business in which he or she specializes, there may be many dealers who indicate that they **make a market** in a given security listed on the computer screen. To make a market implies that the dealer has an interest in the security and will generally buy and/or sell the security in question. In fact, most dealers will offer a two-sided quote for the security, offering firm prices at which they will either buy or sell. In any case, an interested party will, in all likelihood, receive a bid or offer from the dealer who is contacted. However, without a specialist, one dealer may quote a price less favorable than another dealer, so it behooves the broker to shop around.

The Organized Exchanges

There are many examples of organized exchanges in both the United States and the rest of the world. Internationally, the most visible exchange by far is the New York Stock Exchange (NYSE). As illustrated in Exhibit 19.1, the NYSE volume of equity trading surpasses the total equity trading volume in all of Europe. Nonetheless, markets in London, Tokyo, Frankfurt, Zurich, and Paris are also enormous. Note also that within the United States, the NYSE is followed by Nasdaq and, much further behind, the American Stock Exchange (AMEX). However, this ranking is somewhat misleading. Because Nasdaq allows transactions in exchange-listed securities, some of the Nasdaq volume reported in Exhibit 19.1 relates to securities whose primary listing is on other exchanges.

EXHIBIT 19.2   U.S. Equity Markets Share and Dollar Volumes, 1994

	Share Volume		Dollar Volume	
	(millions)	*(percent)*	*($ millions)*	*(percent)*
Nasdaq	74,353	44.51%	$1,449,301	32.80%
Nasdaq market-maker trading in exchange-listed securities	6,891	4.13	230,364	5.21
AMEX	4,523	2.71	58,511	1.33
Regionals (BSE, CSE, MSE, PSE, Phlx)	7,859	4.70	225,806	5.11
NYSE	73,420	43.95	2,454,242	55.55
Totals	**167,046**	**100.00%**	**$4,418,224**	**100.00%**

Source: *NASDAQ Fact Book 1995*, Reprinted with permission from the National Association of Securities Dealers, Inc.

This point is illustrated in Exhibit 19.2. In this table, the relative distribution of equity market volume in the United States, both in terms of shares and dollar volumes, is reported, and the Nasdaq volume is divided between Nasdaq securities and exchange-listed Nasdaq volume. Notice also the growing relative importance of regional exchanges in this exhibit. The combined volume of the five major regional exchanges is considerably larger than AMEX, and it approaches Nasdaq trading of listed securities. Nonetheless, the American Stock Exchange accounted for 4.523 trillion shares in 1994, representing $58.51 billion. To be sure, the NYSE, AMEX, and the regional exchanges are clearly important parts of the secondary market. Below, we shall review some of the history and structure of these exchanges to give you a sense of their size and relative importance. We begin with the largest.

The New York Stock Exchange

The **New York Stock Exchange** (NYSE) has its roots in history. It began operations on May 17, 1792, when 24 stockbrokers and merchants signed a document known as the "Buttonwood Agreement," which contained the initial rules for membership and participation in the exchange. The NYSE has grown into a corporate association of 1,366 members. These members are said to "own a seat" on the exchange. This seat on the exchange allows members to trade on the floor of the exchange, a physical location in lower Manhattan, New York City. Some of the members perform the role of brokers, while others are the specialists referred to earlier.

The NYSE is perceived to be the leading securities exchange in the world, listing stocks with equity valued at over $4.4 trillion. As seen in Exhibit 19.3, this market valuation comes from 3,060 equity issues that are issued by 2,570 different companies. In addition to equity, the NYSE is involved in the trading of bonds, futures, and options. The bottom of Exhibit 19.3 offers some data on NYSE-listed bonds. Notice that while the value of these issues has risen from

Exhibit 19.3   Market Value of Securities Listed on the NYSE

Stocks

End-of-Year	Number of Companies	Number of Issues	Shares Outstanding (millions)	Market Value ($ billions)
1984	1,543	2,319	49,092	$1,586
1985	1,541	2,298	52,427	1,950
1986	1,575	2,257	59,620	2,199
1987	1,647	2,244	71,802	2,216
1988	1,681	2,234	76,175	2,457
1989	1,720	2,246	82,972	3,029
1990	1,774	2,284	90,732	2,819
1991	1,885	2,426	99,622	3,712
1992	2,088	2,658	115,839	4,035
1993	2,361	2,904	131,053	4,540
1994	2,570	3,060	142,281	4,448

Bonds

End-of-Year	Number of Issuers	Number of Issues	Par (Face) Value ($ billions)	Market Value ($ billions)
1984	1,024	3,751	$1,084	$1,022
1985	1,010	3,856	1,327	1,339
1986	951	3,611	1,380	1,458
1987	885	3,346	1,651	1,621
1988	846	3,106	1,610	1,561
1989	794	2,961	1,435	1,412
1990	743	2,912	1,689	1,610
1991	705	2,727	2,219	2,227
1992	636	2,354	2,009	2,044
1993	574	2,103	2,342	2,528
1994	583	2,141	2,526	2,367

Source: *New York Stock Exchange Fact Book,* 1994.

1984, in part due to the declining rate of interest during the interim, the number of issues has declined by nearly one-third. This is in face of a growing volume of bonds outstanding, as was indicated in Chapter 13, which suggests a declining market share.

Futures are offered through a wholly owned subsidiary, the New York Futures Exchange, but volume has been fairly low. Options, too, are traded, but again, they account for a small fraction of exchange activity. In truth, the NYSE is primarily a stock exchange, trading only the equity shares of their listed companies in any appreciable volume.

However, for a firm to achieve listing on the NYSE is not easy. Only the largest and most widely held firms need apply. The leading firms that are listed on the exchange are household names. (See Box 19.2.)

Box 19.2

Leading Stocks on NYSE by Share Volume

The 25 most active stocks during 1994, ranked by reported share volume on the NYSE, are listed below. Share volume is based on round-lot trades. In paren-theses, adjacent to each company name, we have pro-vided the 1993 ranking.

Company Name	1994 Reported Share Volume
1. Telefonos de Mexico (TMX) (4)	937,012,100
2. General Motors (GM) (6)	574,748,500
3. RJR Nabisco Holdings (RN) (5)	565,884,700
4. Merck & Co., Inc. (MRK) (2)	521,695,900
5. Wal-Mart Stores (WMT) (3)	496,447,300
6. International Business Machines (IBM) (7)	492,335,600
7. Ford Motor (F) (14)	480,090,600
8. Philip Morris (MO) (1)	479,286,300
9. Chrysler Corporation (C) (8)	443,742,600
10. Hanson PLC (31)	439,791,300
11. AT&T Corp. (T) (10)	434,747,100
12. COMPAQ Computer (CPQ) (37)	428,344,700
13. General Electric (GE) (40)	390,148,500
14. Motorola, Inc. (MOT) (27)	380,790,800
15. Citicorp (CCI) (9)	380,495,200
16. American Express (AXP) (13)	342,415,175
17. PepsiCo, Inc. (PEP) (16)	337,068,800
18. Coca-Cola Company (KO) (19)	329,141,200
19. Micron Technology Inc. (MU)	323,999,200
20. Kmart Corp. (KM) (22)	283,442,000
21. Glaxo Holdings (GLX) (11)	279,631,200
22. EMC Corporation (EMC)	278,614,400
23. WMX Technologies Inc. (WMX) (24)	270,159,500
24. American Barrick (ABX) (30)	258,453,900
25. Disney (Walt) Company (DIS) (17)	257,092,300

Source: *New York Stock Exchange Fact Book,* 1994.

Current rules state that a firm must meet five minimum requirements to be listed on the NYSE. First, it must demonstrate earning power of $6.5 million before taxes over the previous three years. In addition, certain rules regarding the breakdown of these earnings over those three years also apply. Second, the firm must have net tangible assets of at least $18 million. Third, the market value for publicly held shares must be greater than $18 million. Fourth, a total of at least

Exhibit 19.4

Distribution of NYSE share volume and trades by trade size, 1994

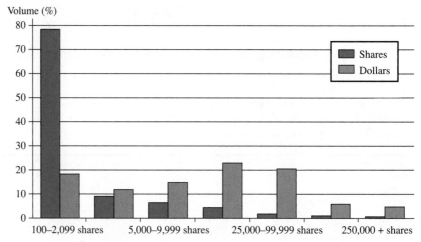

Source: *New York Stock Exchange Fact Book*, 1994.

1.1 million shares must be outstanding. And fifth, there must be at least 2,000 holders of more than 100 shares of stock.

Trades on the NYSE vary substantially in size. While the average transaction size was 1,495 in 1994, nearly 80 percent of all transactions were between 100 and 2,099 shares. Of the total volume of trades, less than one-fourth of 1 percent of trades exceeded 100,000 shares. Less than 0.03 percent of the transactions exceeded 250,000 shares. In dollar volume terms, however, the data are substantially different. More than half of the dollar volume of all transactions arose from trades exceeding 10,000 shares. Both of these breakdowns are reported in Exhibit 19.4, covering the year 1994.

One of the stated goals of the NYSE is to maintain a fair and orderly market so as to maintain the interest of both small and large participants in engaging in NYSE transactions. To this end, all market participants are under continuous surveillance during the trading day. The NYSE regularly reviews the performance of specialists to ensure that they are fulfilling their role in achieving this goal. Further, the NYSE has instituted what it refers to as **circuit breakers.** The goal of these circuit breakers is to stop huge swings in stock value. For example, if the Dow Jones Industrial Average declines or increases by 50 points or more, some computer trading activity can be subject to restriction. Then, if the Dow moves by 250 points from the previous day's close, trading is halted for an hour or more in order to stop momentum. Also, there is a program called **sidecar** that diverts all computer program trades for a few minutes if the S&P 500 futures contract declines by more than 12 points from the previous day's close. Without going into the details of program trading, this slowdown of such trades is designed to allow the market to respond to large order inflows without worrying about computer trades.

Opinions differ on whether these rules are effective or even desirable. Proponents note that these procedures slowed trading 30 times in 1994 and can be viewed as aiding the stability of the market. Opponents argue convincingly that suspending trading does not solve the underlying problem; rather, it only defers it to another day. Given the recent increase in volatility, there is renewed interest in reevaluating the limitations placed on trading activity. (See Box 19.3.) As you might suspect, this debate is part of the larger debate about the role of regulation on markets, and it will not be solved here. Suffice it to say that some like the procedures, while many do not.

The American Stock Exchange

The American Stock Exchange (AMEX) is very similar to the NYSE. Membership entitles a firm to participate in the exchange. While not as large as the NYSE in terms of listed equity value, the AMEX does an impressive volume of trade. For example, in 1994, over 4.5 billion shares of stock were traded on the AMEX. Exhibit 19.5 on page 474, which is similar to Exhibit 19.3, reports the number of firms with primary listing on the American Stock Exchange. Here, unlike the NYSE, the number of issues has not risen appreciably over the last decade and is down from the high of 1,100 in 1988 to its present total of 981. The major listings on the AMEX, while large firms, do not have the same degree of visibility as their NYSE counterparts. (See Box 19.4 on page 475.)

As in the case of other exchanges, the AMEX also trades bonds and options of various kinds, along with common and preferred stock. The value of bonds is in the second panel of Exhibit 19.5, while the options trading is reported in Exhibit 19.6 on page 476.

The mechanics of exchange on the AMEX are quite similar to those described for the NYSE. As on the NYSE, specialists are obligated to maintain a fair and orderly market. They play the role of exchange facilitators to bring together buyers and sellers, and they also act as dealers when necessary to maintain an orderly market.

The AMEX's bond program began in 1975 with the introduction of trading odd-lot quantities of bonds on the exchange. Now, T-bills, long-term Treasury bonds, agency issues, and corporate bonds are listed on the exchange.

Also in 1975, the AMEX began listing options on stocks. At first, options on only six securities were listed. The program was expanded in 1983 to allow listing of options on broad market and industry-based stock indices. In 1985, the AMEX began the trading of options on OTC securities. By the end of 1994, the AMEX was trading more than 48 million contracts on more than 440 individual stocks. Further, long-term options on 50 common stocks, five broad-based index options, and seven industry-based options were trading.

As the above facts illustrate, an exchange can facilitate the trading of securities. Exchanges allow a wider variety of securities to emerge in order to meet the needs of both borrowers and lenders.

The Regional Exchanges

There are several regional exchanges including the Pacific, Philadelphia, and Cincinnati exchanges. However, some would contend that these regional exchanges do not meet the criteria for auction exchanges as discussed in the

---

Box 19.3

Are Constraints of Trade a Thing of the Past?

The New York Stock Exchange rule that almost shut down the Big Board during last Friday's frenetic trading could be in for a change soon.

Responding to concerns about last Friday's near-halt in trading on a relatively minor sell-off, the Securities and Exchange Commision and the New York Stock Exchange are reconsidering the "circuit breakers" that the Big Board instituted following the October 1987 stock market crash. The most controversial of those rules is one that calls for stock trading to stop for an hour whenever the Dow Jones Industrial Average falls 250 points in a day. Beyond that, a 400-point drop would cause a two-hour stoppage.

Calls for Change

The Dow Jones industrials came within an eyelash of tripping over that curb shortly after 3 p.m. Friday when it sank 217 points below Thursday's close. That scare prompted some market professionals to call for change. Among others, officials of the National Association of Securities Dealers, which operates the Nasdaq Stock Market, have asked the SEC to consider changing the rules. Nasdaq and the American Stock Exchange have agreed to stop trading whenever the Big Board trading halts are triggered.

The Big Board instituted the trading-halt rules in October 1988, in the wake of the stock market crash a year earlier, to prevent a free-fall. Back then, a 250-point drop in the Dow represented a 12% decline. Since then, the Dow has climbed more than 3400 points, reducing 250 points to a drop of less than 4.5%.

Most market analysts consider last Friday's sell-off a healthy and minor correction in a market that has marched steadily higher for a year. Some were hoping for an even bigger correction. But few, if any, believe there was any need for a forced halt to trading. NASD officials have said they would prefer tying the trading halts to percentage changes, instead of using absolute numbers that will have be changed repeatedly if the stock market continues rising.

Regulators and exchange officials seem inclined to agree that it's time for some changes. Richard R. Lindsey, director of the SEC's division of market regulation, said the agency is "trying to build consensus" on what those changes will be.

"There's some value in circuit breakers when you have very rapid movements on heavy volume," Mr. Lindsey said. "The question is, where should the levels be?"

In meetings at trading firms in New York yesterday, Mr. Lindsey said, he heard differing views. He

---

previous sections of this chapter. Their volume appears to some to be too small and isolated to bring together the broad spectrum of investors and borrowers necessary for a well-functioning market. Yet these exchanges have done well as of late, and their market share has been rising. Nonetheless, an investor in Philadelphia, for example, would like to be sure that the price being bid on XYZ stock is as good as the price that can be obtained on the NYSE or AMEX. In order to bring together the largest number of investors and borrowers as possible, and also to assure that intermarket prices are consistent, the **Intermarket Trading System (ITS)** has been put in place. The ITS links nine markets: the New York, American, Boston, Chicago, Cincinnati, Pacific, and Philadelphia Stock Exchanges; the Chicago Board Options Exchange; and the NASD. This system enables brokers representing public customers, as well as specialists and market makers trading

summarized one camp as the "if it ain't broke, don't fix it" crowd. But, he added, the SEC isn't waiting for the 250-point rule to be triggered before changing it.

Talks Among Exchanges

Big Board officials, previously opposed to changes in the post-crash trading curbs, are beginning to budge. A Big Board spokesman said the exchange has renewed talks with officials of other exchanges about how to modify the 250-point and 400-point rules. However, he said, the Big Board remains "steadfastly committed" to the collars that limit certain computer-aided index-arbitrage trades whenever the Dow rises or falls 50 points in one session. Those collars kicked in yesterday for the 31st time this year, the most in any year.

This is the second round of talks about changing the circuit breakers in less than a year. An intraday drop of 134 points, or 2.9%, on July 19 led to discussions between officials of the SEC and Big Board last summer. But no changes resulted from those talks.

At the rate the Dow has been rising, some changes appear inevitable. During the past few weeks, the stock market has become increasingly volatile, with intraday swings of as much as 100 points becoming less worrisome. At current prices a 12% move—the size represented in 1988 by that 250 points—would be about 675 points.

"There probably still are mixed views about circuit breakers and whether they should be widenend,"

Mr. Lindsey said. "There are a number of people that say they should be widened. We'll talk with the firms and the exchanges to see if some kind of consensus can be reached. The fact that we got close to triggering them on Friday means it's surely time for a dialogue about that. The SEC's general view is that we like the markets trading whenever the markets can be trading."

Limits on Exchange

A summary of the trading curbs put in place by the New York Stock Exchange after the crash of October 1987:

- **50-POINT COLLAR:** When the Dow Jones Industrial Average is up or down 50 points from the previous day's close, limits are placed on program-aided index arbitrage trades. Stays in effect until the DJIA is within 25 points of previous close or the session ends.

- **100-POINT SIDECAR:** When the S&P 500 futures contract is down 12 points—the rough equivalent of 100 points on the DJIA—program trading is halted.

- **250-POINT CIRCUIT BREAKER:** When the DJIA falls 250 points, trading is halted for an hour.

- **400-POINT CIRCUIT BREAKER:** When the DJIA falls 400 points, trading is halted for two hours.

Source: Reprinted by permission of *The Wall Street Journal,* © 1996 Dow Jones & Co., Inc. All Rights Reserved Worldwide.

for their own accounts, to interact with their counterparts in other markets whenever the nationwide Composite Quotation System shows a better price in another market. In 1994, volume on the ITS was 2.8 billion shares.

Regulation of the Secondary Market

Secondary markets around the world are generally regulated by security laws and governmental oversight agencies. Many reasons are offered for this regulation, from an interest in well-functioning efficient markets to the attainment of social goals that range from equal access to some notion of the fair pricing of services. Most economists and financial experts give little credence to the second set of

EXHIBIT 19.5   Market Value of Securities Listed on the AMEX*

Stocks

End of Year	Number of Issues	Shares Outstanding (millions)	Market Value** ($ billions)
1983	948	5,357	81
1984	930	5,517	70
1985	940	6,340	87
1986	954	7,451	96
1987	1,073	8,253	99
1988	1,100	8,730	111
1989	1,058	8,817	131
1990	1,063	9,768	102
1991	1,055	10,814	125
1992	943	10,178	109
1993	1,005	10,612	135
1994	981	10,925	114

Bonds

End of Year	Number of Issues	Par* (Face) Value ($ billions)	Market Value ($ billions)
1983	262	8,765	7.4
1984	290	12,671	9.7
1985	347	22,853	17.7
1986	341	24,118	19.9
1987	324	25,462	19.1
1988	309	25,557	21.0
1989	279	27,279	21.4
1990	260	27,195	29.5
1991	236	25,415	18.9
1992	183	23,290	16.9
1993	125	15,341	12.4
1994	103	13,679	8.7

*Includes securities with unlisted trading privileges.
**For companies that trade ADRs, only the value of ADRs outstanding (not the underlying shares outstanding) is included in this total.
Source: *AMEX Fact Book*, 1995.

arguments; they believe that regulation should have as a goal an efficient secondary market where participants can obtain accurate information and where representatives are professionals who behave in an ethical manner.

With this as an objective, regulation seeks to prevent actions that violate these tenets. These abuses include: **fraud,** deliberate deception and misrepresentation; illegal **insider trading,** where trades by insiders are motivated by nonpublic information; **unauthorized trading,** trading a client's account without prior consent; **illegal solicitation,** such as selling a security without first giving the

Box 19.4

Leading Stocks on AMEX by Share Volume

The 10 most active stocks during 1994, ranked by reported share volume on the AMEX, are listed below. Share volume is based on round-lot trades.

Company Name	*1994 Reported Share Volume (millions)*
1. XCL Ltd.	236.7
2. Cheyenne Software, Inc.	173.2
3. Echo Bay Mines Ltd.	166.5
4. Viacom Inc. (Class B)	164.6
5. Royal Oak Mines Inc.	115.7
6. IVAX Corporation	107.6
7. Energy Service Company, Inc.	93.0
8. Amdahl Corporation	80.4
9. Hasbro, Inc.	69.2
10. InterDigital Communications Corporation	61.4

Source: *AMEX Fact Book,* 1995.

investor a prospectus that details the relevant information; and **churning,** trading a customer's account excessively to generate commission income. The above list is not exhaustive but merely indicative of the fact that such abuses are indeed possible in these complex markets.

In the United States, abuses were presumed to be so rampant during the early part of this century that Congress completely revamped the securities regulations in the aftermath of the Great Depression. In fact, the current form of financial regulation in the United States, covering both financial institutions and financial markets, dates back to the 1930s. Specifically, trading in the secondary market is now governed primarily by two acts that were enacted at that time, the Securities Act and the Securities Exchange Act. The Securities Act of 1933 requires full disclosure of all information relevant to a new securities issue. It requires federal registration of large corporate securities issues, and it mandates audited financial statements. In addition, the 1933 act prosecutes acts of alleged fraud and deception that violate this law.

The Securities Exchange Act, passed in 1934, established the Securities Exchange Commission (SEC). The SEC was empowered to implement the provisions of the 1933 act and also undertake some supplementary oversight responsibilities,

Exhibit 19.6   Historical AMEX Options Trading
Number of Contracts Traded (thousands)

Year	Calls	Puts	Total
1983	28,069	10,899	38,968
1984	28,731	11,373	40,104
1985	35,186	13,414	48,600
1986	48,875	16,568	65,443
1987	52,952	17,997	70,949
1988	34,225	10,776	45,001
1989	37,448	12,408	49,856
1990	26,958	13,930	40,888
1991	25,422	13,383	38,805
1992	27,922	14,393	42,315
1993	32,151	15,735	47,886
1994	32,621	15,858	48,479

Note: The AMEX was trading 440 individual stock options (including 136 options on OTC securities) by the end of 1994.

Source: *AMEX Fact Book,* 1995.

including the regulation of commission rates on organized securities exchanges and the stipulation of initial margin requirements for securities purchases that are financed, in part, by borrowing. Taken together with the 1933 act, this regulatory structure has proved to be a model for the world. Counterparts of this legislation and the SEC itself exist throughout the world financial community.

However, the U.S. financial regulation structure continues to evolve. The Maloney Act of 1938 expanded the purview of the SEC's oversight to include the over-the-counter markets for securities. The next year, the Trust Indenture Act of 1939 was passed, mandating that each bond issue be governed by an indenture contract, which contains policies and procedures that involve both the issuer and the bond investors. The Trust Indenture Act also required the appointment of a third party to act as trustee and enforce the provisions stipulated in the indenture. In addition, this act required that any new information relevant to the financial health of the issuer be provided to the trustee on an ongoing basis.

Later, in 1964, the Securities Act was amended to require a more extensive and frequent disclosure of financial data for publicly traded securities, including those in the over-the-counter market. This was followed in 1975 by other Securities Act Amendments, which directed the SEC to nullify exchange rules that were deemed anticompetitive, such as uniform brokerage commission schedules. These amendments also required the SEC to develop a national market system and permitted investor orders to be executed without the participation of an exchange specialist.

Two other acts are worthy of mention here as well. In 1970, the Securities Investor Protection Corporation Act established the SIPC so that clients of bankrupt brokerage firms could be indemnified. Under this system, all registered brokers and dealer firms pay approximately 1 percent of their gross income into a fund that is used to pay investors who have been harmed by the failure of a brokerage firm. Later, in 1974, the Commodities Futures Trading Commission was established to replace the Commodities Exchange Authority, providing a higher degree of regulatory oversight of the trading of futures contracts.

At the same time, in an effort to ensure that markets perform efficiently and participants are treated fairly, the industry itself has been active in various forms of self-regulation. The exchanges promote norms and standards and attempt to enforce them on member firms. Likewise, the Securities Industry Association promulgates codes of ethics and high standards of conduct. In the end, a market that is seen as fair and efficient is as important to members of the industry as it is to any governmental body.

All of these activities, procedures, rules, and regulations are designed ultimately to promote the integrity of the financial markets in the United States and to increase the confidence of investors who must engage in both primary and secondary market transactions. While some of these regulatory tools are burdensome, they nonetheless have resulted in a market of both stability and integrity that plays a central role in world finance.

Summary

In this chapter, we have discussed the secondary market, its structure, the mechanics of trading, and its regulation. We found that there are various kinds of secondary markets for securities, all of which coexist. There are direct search markets, ones that rely on brokers, some that use dealers, and still others that are set up as organized exchanges. Which structure is most appropriate depends on the breadth and depth of the market for a particular security and, most importantly, on its trading patterns.

We then turned to the mechanics of trading securities in the secondary market. Here, much of our commentary was directed toward trading on organized security exchanges. However, the processes for trading in alternative market structures are quite similar, particularly in the dealer market, where market-makers function in a manner similar to that of the specialist on an exchange.

Finally, we turned to the regulation of secondary markets. Much of the regulation was directed toward reducing the abuses that were believed to be rampant in the less-regulated securities markets prior to the Great Depression. Whether the past really was as rife with abuse as some have suggested is arguable. In fact, recent investigators have shown that the securities markets were not nearly as problematic as history suggests. Nonetheless, the characterization at the time led to the regulatory structure currently in place in the United States. These regulations have fostered the development of a secondary market in the United States that is unparalleled in the world today and have contributed to the viability of the primary market as well.

However, we must end on a cautionary note. The benefits of these regulations come with costs. The burdens of regulation, which include the direct expense of satisfying regulatory mandates and the constraints on what can and cannot be done, are substantial. The challenge is to weigh these costs against the benefits that accrue from the regulatory structure. Many in the industry would argue that the current form of regulation is too restrictive and expensive, while others might disagree. Here, as elsewhere, the role of government should be carefully scrutinized and limited to only those areas where there is a clear need that outweighs the cost.

Key Concepts

at-the-market versus limit orders, 463
auction markets, 461
bid-offer spread, 459
brokered markets, 458
cash contracts, 464
circuit breakers and sidecar, 470
dealer markets, 458
direct search markets, 457
fraud, insider, and illegal solicitation, 474
free double auction, 464
good-until-canceled and stop orders, 463

Intermarket Trading System, 472
long versus short sale, 462
making a market, 466
New York, American, and regional
  exchanges, 467–73
price continuity, 464
round versus odd lots, 462
settlement, 464
specialist, 465
specialist's book, 465
unauthorized trading and churning, 474–75

Review Questions

1. What is the primary difference between brokers and dealers?
2. What is the relationship between trading volume and the four secondary market structures?
3. Describe and contrast limit, market, and stop-loss orders.
4. A specialist profits from his or her role as broker and dealer. Briefly discuss how this is accomplished.
5. Explain the role of information in the abuses cited as the motivation for laws and government oversight of the secondary market.

References

American Stock Exchange. *American Stock Exchange Fact Book.* New York: American Stock Exchange, 1995.

Benston, George. *The Separation of Commercial and Investment Banking: The Glass Steagall Act Revisited and Reconsidered.* New York: Oxford University Press, 1990.

Demsetz, Harold. "The Cost of Transacting." *Quarterly Journal of Economics,* February 1968.

Glosten, Lawrence R. "Is the Electronic Open Limit Order Book Inevitable?" *Journal of Finance,* September 1994.

Flood, Mark D. "Microstructure Theory and the Foreign Exchange Market." *Review.* Federal Reserve Bank of St. Louis, November 1991.

Hamilton, James. "Off Brand Trading of NYSE-Listed Stocks: The Effects of Deregulation and the National Market System." *Journal of Finance,* December 1987.

Hasbrouck, Joel. "Measuring the Information Content of Stock Trades." *Journal of Finance,* March 1991.

Kadlec, Gregory B., and John J. McConnell. "The Effect of Market Segmentation and Illiquidity on Asset Prices: Evidence from Exchange Listings." *Journal of Finance,* June 1994.

Kidwell, David S.; Richard L Peterson; and David W. Blackwell. *Financial Institutions, Markets and Money.* 5th ed. Fort Worth: Dryden Press, 1993.

Mayer, Martin. *Markets.* New York: W.W. Norton and Co., 1988.

New York Stock Exchange. *New York Stock Exchange Fact Book.* New York: New York Stock Exchange, 1995.

Schwartz, R.A. *Equity Markets: Structure, Trading and Performance.* New York: Harper and Row, 1988.

Teweles, Richard J., and Edward S. Bradley. *The Stock Market.* 4th ed. New York: John Wiley & Sons, 1982.

| CHAPTER | The Investment Banking |
| 20 | Industry |

Chapter Outline

A Brief Historical Perspective
The Investment Banking Function
   Advising Function
   Administration Function
   Underwriting Function
   Distribution Function
Investment Banking Structure
   Boutique versus Full-Service Banks
   Investment Management Activity
   Mergers, Acquisitions, and Other Activities
   Full Service: Good or Bad?
   The Major Players
   The Cyclical Nature of Profits
Regulation of Investment Banking
   Major Regulatory Legislation
   Role of the SEC
   Role of the NASD
   Roles of the Federal Reserve and SIPC

This chapter looks at the investment banking industry in the United States from a historical, functional, and industry perspective. It begins by reviewing the recent history of this industry. Next, it examines investment banking's main lines of business—underwriting, investment management, and advisory services. Following this is an examination of the ongoing restructuring of the industry. The chapter concludes with a short review of the regulations under which U.S. firms provide investment banking and other financial services.

It would probably seem curious to you to enter a retail shoe store and find, upon entering, a sign that said "Shoe Department." It would seem more sensible to encounter such a sign in a large department store. Yet this is precisely the curiosity that awaits the visitor to a large investment bank. You will find not only an **investment banking** department but also perhaps a dozen or more other departments. Some of their names are arbitrage, asset management, capital markets, commodities, equities, fixed income, mortgages, foreign exchange, futures, insurance and pensions, merchant banking, and mergers and acquisitions. Together, these departments are just as important to the financial fortunes of a modern full-service investment bank as its investment banking department. Today, there are several investment banks that are analogous to this department store concept of financial services.

This chapter reviews the key activities of the investment banking industry, starting with the most obvious, the activity of the investment banking department. For some firms in the industry, this is their only activity. These are referred to as boutique firms, analogous to the single-department retail stores, which, in this case, specialize in investment banking services. These boutique firms may further narrow their market by focusing on a particular segment, such as high-technology firms, utilities, or municipalities.

Other firms, however, may do much more. These firms, the department stores' counterparts, engage in a broader array of activities in the capital market. They offer products and services across a wide range, where opportunities present themselves. In fact, these investment banks are rapid to respond to market niches, and they are equally quick to retrench when the market changes. As such, these firms are dynamic forces within the capital market, expanding and contracting with the ebb and flow of the markets they serve. Their reason for doing so will be made clear as we proceed.

We will begin our review of the activities of these firms by revisiting their role in their primary market—investment banking services. This area was discussed in depth in Chapter 18. To distinguish it from the other activities of these firms, we will refer to it as the **investment banking function** performed within an investment bank. This function involves the creation and subsequent purchase of newly issued securities, such as bonds and stocks, from business concerns and governments seeking resources from the financial market. Once purchased, the securities are then resold by the investment banking department to individual or institutional investors in smaller quantities. Below, we sketch briefly the development of investment banking in the United States. The scope of this activity is changing rapidly even as we write, so our sketch is only meant to be suggestive of the operations of these major financial firms in the U.S. market.

A Brief Historical Perspective

Before the Great Depression of the 1930s, it was common for securities underwriting and distribution, the two major parts of investment banking services, to be performed by many different types of financial institutions, including commercial banks, trust companies, insurance companies, private banks, and stand-alone investment banking institutions. These institutions all saw this activity as a logical extension of the services they offered to their corporate or municipal customers. Frequently, they would provide this service along with shorter-term loans. When funding needs became sufficiently large to require seeking capital through bond and stock offerings, these institutions would be there to provide needed assistance and expertise. They would facilitate these firms' fund-raising efforts by underwriting and distributing their securities.

The Great Depression, the stock market crash, and the widespread failures of commercial banks led to increased scrutiny of financial markets and all of the institutions operating within them. It was found, or at least alleged, that a number of commercial banks had underwritten new securities for their client firms, some of which were nearly bankrupt. The monies received from these securities sales were then allegedly used to repay the bank debt, often to the very same institution that had underwritten the securities offering. The net effect of this activity was that the commercial banks were made whole, while shifting their risks to investors. What made those accusations especially troublesome was that the underwriters had failed to inform investors in the securities of the precarious financial condition of the corporate issuers. Whether these practices were as widespread as alleged or were merely a part of the hysteria of the time is unclear. Recent authors have contended that the abuses were far less prevalent than suggested.[1] In any case, the result was a perception that remedial action was necessary to address the fact or the appearance of impropriety.

There was an obvious **conflict of interest** for a commercial bank with a loan in jeopardy. Two things could have been done to rectify the situation, either of which probably would have sufficed. Either the federal government could have prohibited commercial banks from pursuing investment banking activities, or it could have made laws requiring full disclosure of information relating to the corporate client seeking funding through a securities offering.

In fact, with the passage of the Banking Act of 1933, the federal government did both. In Sections 16, 20, 21, and 32 of the act, more commonly known as the Glass-Steagall Act (sponsored by Senator Carter Glass of Virginia and Representative Henry Steagall of Alabama), commercial banks were prohibited from engaging in corporate securities offerings. This act has been referred to in Chapters 18 and 19, as it is still viewed as a key piece of legislation defining allowable activities of commercial banking institutions.

At the same time, the Securities Act of 1933, which required full disclosure of information and contained antifraud provisions, was passed by an activist Congress. This act also provided remedies for investors against salespersons who disseminated false and misleading information about securities. Then, with the passage of the Securities Exchange Act of 1934, the Securities and

---

[1]For a full analysis of this issue and the historical record, see George Benston, *The Separation of Commercial and Investment Banking: The Glass Steagall Act Revisited and Reconsidered* (New York: Oxford University Press, 1990).

Exchange Commission (SEC) was established and a policing mechanism was put in place.

Considering the financial information disclosure requirements contained in the Securities Act, many now view the provisions of Glass-Steagall, which prohibited commercial banks from engaging in investment banking activities, as being unnecessary. Nonetheless, the separation of commercial banking activities from investment banking activities is likely to continue to at least some degree for a while longer. Attempts by recent administrations to repeal this prohibition have failed. At this writing, interstate banking has arrived in the United States, but security limitations on commercial banks are still in place. However, we can probably expect further efforts to remove some of the remaining barriers between investment banking and commercial banking. Recent research on the Glass-Steagall Act finds no evidence that conflicts of interest induced commercial banks to fool the public into investing in securities in an attempt to rid their balance sheets of underperforming loans. Instead, the public appears to have rationally accounted for the possibility of conflicts of interest, and this appears to have constrained the banks to underwrite high-quality securities. If further research corroborates these findings, much of the justification for Glass-Steagall will be eroded.[2]

This continued limitation of access to the market is due in no small part to entrenched interests that now exist. Financial institutions who provide investment banking services have had their domains protected from outside competition for 60 years or longer. While other financial institutions have successfully broadened their areas of operation to include at least some access to this activity, existing firms have argued against what they see as encroachment from other types of institutions into areas that have been their preferred and protected domain. Yet, as will be made clear in the following chapters, the debate goes on. Institutions wishing to enter lines of business within the capital market have developed a capability to achieve this end even while prohibitions continue to exist. In the end, as we will argue in Chapter 24, there are more similarities than differences among the various financial institutions. Therefore, when one talks of investment banking as an activity, it is best to define it as a function rather than as a "stand-alone" industry.

The Investment Banking Function

With the backdrop of this historical perspective, we turn our attention to an examination of investment banking from a functional point of view. As this activity is central to the industry and is the set of expertise that will be used in other product lines, it follows that a careful description of this activity is key to understanding the industry.

---

[2]See R. S. Kroszner and R. G. Rajan, "Is the Glass-Steagall Act Justified? A Study of the U.S. Experience with Universal Banking before 1933," *American Economic Review,* September 1994.

Individual firms may also engage in other activities such as merger and acquisition advising, investment management, securities sales and trading, and so forth. Each of these will be explained later. However, a bank's ability to offer these services will depend upon its underwriting reputation and capability, as well as whether it operates as a specialized or boutique firm or chooses to operate in other areas of the market. Ultimately, the firm's reach will depend upon the extent to which it sees itself as a full-service provider of financial services.

The investment banking function performed by a typical firm includes the following activities: **advising, administration, underwriting,** and **distribution.** These services are performed as part of the basic investment banking business and are central to any firm. Let's examine each of these activities in turn.

Advising Function

In advising a corporate or governmental client, an investment bank will first assist its customer in making an assessment of its funding needs. Then, the investment bank will acquaint the client with the respective costs and benefits of various alternatives for raising funds. They will provide advice regarding current market conditions and the timing of any one option that may emerge as most advantageous. The process should lead to the investment bank suggesting a funding mechanism and structure that it feels will best fit the client's needs. It may, at this point, also recommend a team of institutions that could assemble the package that would address the funding needs.

Administrative Function

Once a financing strategy has been adopted, the investment bank can perform a vital administrative function. This service involves a myriad of details associated with a new issue, such as recordkeeping, title transfer, and tax and regulatory filing on behalf of the issuing firm. Because financial covenants and regulatory structures of the securities business are routine considerations for the investment bank but obscure issues for the general business community, the investment bank can provide valuable administrative services. It aids its client in traversing waters that, to the client, are uncharted. While fees for this service are only a small fraction of the offering value, the amount is not trivial in absolute dollar terms. While these fees may seem high, they are typically far cheaper than the disaster that could result if the client attempts to traverse the regulatory morass and financial marketplace on its own.

Among the administrative functions that an investment bank can render is assistance in the completion of the legal documents necessary for SEC filing, including the creation of a prospectus associated with any new issue. Indeed, the investment bank shares responsibility with the issuer for ensuring that everything is done in compliance with relevant securities laws. Here, as elsewhere in the financial market, intimate knowledge of both law and procedures is critical. The client expects its underwriter to know the ins and outs of the administrative procedures associated with any offer. As noted in Chapter 18, these procedures differ across offerings. For example, not all securities must have a registration statement and prospectus approved by the SEC. The investment bank is required to know that federal, state, and municipal issues, as well as some companies that are sponsored or regulated by governmental agencies, are exempted from the registration requirements. Additionally, certain small issues and private placements are generally exempted from SEC registration. This is all part and parcel of the knowledge of law and process that clients expect their investment bank to employ in providing this administrative function.

Underwriting Function

The underwriting function is provided by an investment bank when it agrees to bring an issue to market on behalf of its client. When an investment bank guarantees a fixed price to the security issuer in exchange for its securities, it is said to have "underwritten" the security offering. The underwriter is at risk if it sets the guarantee too high because it may be unable to resell the securities at a price sufficient to cover the guarantee. However, if it sets too low a guarantee, it may lose the underwriting business to a competitor. Thus, proper valuation of a security is extremely important to an underwriter.

One way for the investment bank to reduce the underwriting risk is to delay, as long as possible, the price-fixing date. This allows the syndicate time to test the market for the new shares and line up purchasers at the proposed price. However, the client may not be happy with such a delay. Nonetheless most underwriters will try to wait and set the **guaranteed price** at the end of the registration period, which could be as little as a day or two before the actual **security flotation** takes place. By choosing a pricing date close to the flotation date, the underwriter has more up-to-date information on which to base a guarantee price, and it has some knowledge of the demand for the issue. Also, there is less intervening time for new developments to drastically alter the price.[3] Unfortunately for the client, this leaves the issuing firm in limbo, unable to determine the exact value of its new issue.

While overpricing an issue can be disastrous to profitability, underpricing a security can also have bad consequences for the underwriter, even if it wins the bid to serve as the underwriter. A reputation for underpricing a security, as evidenced by a repeated pattern of securities' prices climbing rapidly after the commencement of the offerings, can lead prospective corporate issuers to seek alternative investment banking firms.[4] Obviously, it is in the corporation's interest

---

[3]Recall the underwriting of British Petroleum stock in November of 1987, mentioned in Chapter 18. The underwriters set the guarantee price about 15 days in advance of the flotation date. Due to the stock market crash in the interim, the underwriters lost in excess of $1 billion.

[4]See R. Carter and S. Manaster, "Initial Public Offerings and Underwriter Reputation," *Journal of Finance,* September 1990; and R. Beatty and J. Ritter, "Investment Banking, Reputation and the Underpricing of Initial Public Offerings," *Journal of Financial Economics,* 1986.

to obtain as much cash from its securities offerings as possible while still maintaining the goodwill of its investors.

The investment bank makes its profit by selling the new securities at a price higher than the net price that is guaranteed to the issuing firm. It is widely considered that a successful pricing and offering results in a rapid sale of securities, within a day or two after the offering begins, and involves a modest appreciation of the securities' prices in the weeks immediately following the offering. This modest appreciation pleases the investors in the company and fosters goodwill.

Many securities are not brought to the market in this manner. These securities are not formally purchased by the investment banker; instead they are merely distributed through either a **best-efforts-basis public offering** or through a private placement to a select group of investors. In these cases, the investment bank does not incur the risks of an underwriter, and it is compensated through fees for bringing buyer and seller together. This fee is lower than that associated with a price guarantee, at least on a risk-adjusted basis. For some firms, only a best-efforts underwriting is possible because of the high risk or limited market recognition of the institution seeking financing. For others, private placement is a cleaner alternative and one that is easily accomplished by an investment banker with good contacts.[5]

Distribution Function

The distribution function involves the placement of newly issued securities into the hands of investors. This is an essential part of the underwriting process, and it distinguishes some investment bankers from other members of the financial community who do not have the ability to access large pools of funds for their clients. The distribution function represents the essential value of the underwriting function to the corporate client, as it places the firm's securities into the hands of final investors.

A good investment bank is able to quickly reduce its risk through the way it structures its distribution network for the new issue. As noted in Chapter 18, there are two groups that the underwriter depends upon to accomplish this risk reduction during the crucial, albeit short, period of price vulnerability. First, through the formation of an **underwriting syndicate,** the lead underwriter is able to share in the price risk of the issue. Each member of the syndicate absorbs a share of the risk that the ultimate selling price will be inadequate to cover its portion of the costs of the guarantee. Syndicate members are also expected to bear the risk associated with the **price stabilization function.** It is common for underwriters to

---

[5]Those interested in the mechanics of these offering options are referred to Chapter 18. For studies on the choice between an underwritten offering and a best-efforts offering, see S. Bhagat, "The Effect of Management's Choice between Negotiated and Competitive Equity Offerings on Shareholder Wealth," *Journal of Financial and Quantitative Analysis,* 1986; and D. Logue and R. Jarrow, "Negotiation vs. Competitive Bidding in the Sales of Securities by Public Utilities," *Financial Management,* 1978.

agree to stabilize the price of a newly issued security for up to a month or more beyond the issue date. If the market price begins to sink below some predetermined level, the underwriters will step in and buy shares. This serves to stabilize prices, or at least ensure that they stay above some threshold level deemed acceptable. The risk arises if, after the period of stabilization, the underwriters carry a large inventory of securities that cannot be sold at prices sufficient to recover their costs.

The second group established by the underwriter to reduce risk is the **selling group.** The underwriter is able to sell the issue more widely and rapidly through such an arrangement than if it were to undertake all sales alone. While other firms of the group are not liable for their inability to sell the issue, a firm's inclusion in the group is predicated on the presumption that it has the ability to enhance the distribution network and that it also has a financial incentive to do so. While an underwriting syndicate can include anywhere from four to a hundred or more members, a sales group usually includes not only the syndicate members but also additional brokerage houses.

Investment Banking Structure

Boutique versus Full-Service Banks

As noted above, underwriting and distribution are just two of the many activities that can be offered by today's investment banking firms. But for most of these firms, these activities constitute their only line of business. In fact, most investment banks are of the boutique variety in that they engage in only a small portion of the securities industry's activities. These firms limit themselves not only to underwriting exclusively but also usually to a small subset of the market that they believe they know well. For example, there are four boutique firms that specialize in underwriting securities only for magazine publishers; several specialize in raising funds for small computer companies; and a handful focus on assisting broadcasting firms. This procedure leads to a keen underwriting knowledge and, perhaps, to specialized distribution capability as well. Unfortunately, it also limits diversification and increases the market risk associated with specialized firms.

Therefore, a sizable number of investment banking firms are of the department-store variety and seek to be full-service financial institutions. These institutions use the expertise of their firm to engage in activities beyond the simple, or perhaps not so simple, investment banking business. In each case, the organization uses its inherent capabilities to broaden its product line and to both deepen and broaden its customer relationships.

The rationale here should be clear. These and other diversified investment banking firms have developed capabilities in each of the four primary areas—advising, administration, underwriting, and distribution—as prerequisites for their investment banking activity. They then use these same capabilities to extend their activities and profit potential beyond their traditional underwriting activity. This has led to a substantial increase in the size of such firms, as full-service investment banks will have separate departments in the areas of **investment management, mergers and acquisitions,** and **securities sales and trading,** to name just the most prominent areas.

In each case, the firm's natural advantage is its knowledge of and activity in the underwriting business. They are able to leverage this into other areas of the securities market. For example, these firms have a keen awareness of market value, which is a crucial ingredient in both investment management and the mergers and acquisitions business. Likewise, their active trading in new issues makes them well suited for both long-term investment management and the short-term trading activity that is part and parcel of sales and trading. In fact, their activity in the markets in all of the above areas and their awareness of the availability of investment funds makes them an obvious player in securities sales and trading. As full-service banks proceed down each of these roads, these product areas have developed into profitable, separable lines of business. Other companies willingly employ these firms' services because these firms are cost effective and because they have developed a close relationship with their customers over the years.

Investment Management Activity

In recent years, one area of growth has been the investment management business. The reasons for entering this area are twofold. First, as was pointed out above, investment banks have strength in analyzing securities and the firms that issue them. Investment management serves as an excellent avenue for investment banks to leverage their expertise into another profitable activity. Second, investment banks noticed that in recent years, as profit margins and commissions on traditional investment banking services and the brokerage business have reflected increased competition, there was much money to be made on Wall Street in the investment management business.

However, some investment banks entered the investment management business only after considerable debate and delay. It was feared by their management that by entering into this business, investment banks would be alienating their traditional constituencies for securities' sales and distribution. Much of what investment banking firms distributed was marketed to investment management and other financial institutions. Thus, in a real sense, entry by investment banks into the investment management business would require that they compete directly with their own clients. These clients might harbor suspicions that the investment banks were able to gain an unfair competitive advantage, keeping for their own investment management subsidiaries some of the best securities issues or transferring them at lower commissions, even if the law precluded such approaches. These clients might therefore conduct their business elsewhere.

But where? After enough investment banks went into the business, even the reluctant ones finally entered the market as well. After all, if virtually all of their competitors were in the business, a decision to avoid the area would force existing clients who required access to this service to deal with another investment bank. More importantly, even if there were a few holdout investment banking firms who refused to enter a business in direct competition with their clients, many of the major investment banks who were in the investment management business had products and services that were sufficiently attractive and important to the marketplace that client reservations about dealing with them were overcome. Therefore, most full-service firms entered the market whether they wanted to or not.

To lessen the suspicion about self-dealing, investment banks erected **Chinese walls** between the securities underwriting and sales operations and the investment management business. It is common for an investment management business to have a policy that all securities purchased or sold must be done through an outside broker-dealer. For example, Goldman Sachs Asset Management would buy and sell its securities from Merrill Lynch or Salomon Brothers, but not from Goldman Sachs brokers. This policy has alleviated some, but not all, of the concern about self-dealing. However, it has reduced one of the advantages that investment banks would naturally have over their competitors. Even so, clients of investment banks' investment management services apparently believe that these firms have the advantage of being closest to the securities markets and will use their information and know-how to achieve superior investment performance.

Investment banks engage in investment management in a number of different ways. For example, they may provide individual investment management services, known as private banking services, for wealthy clients. Alternatively, they may offer such services to firms as well as individual investors by pooling funds into a partnership for joint investment. Such an investment pool may be designed to meet a specific investment strategy or style; performance would then be measured and evaluated against an index reflecting that particular portfolio management style.

Investment banks may also be asked to manage funds so as to achieve returns that mimic a liability facing the client, such as funding cost or actuarial return assumptions. In such a case, an index is created to mirror the liability cost structure of the client. The objective is for the assets to return more than the liabilities cost. Because the liabilities of many financial institutions are not readily traded in public markets, the financial characteristics of the liabilities are mathematically modeled, and a set of liquid securities is selected to mirror the behavior of the liabilities over time. The customized index is then based on the returns of these securities.[6]

Some investment banks have also chosen to go directly to the general investor public through the introduction of mutual funds. Aimed at either the institutional market or the retail customer, these investment companies are used as a way of raising funds for the investment management group to invest on behalf of their

---

[6] See Babbel, Stricker, and Vanderhoof, "Measuring Investment Performance in an Asset/Liability Context." *Managing Asset-Liability Portfolios,* Association for Investment Management and Research, 1992.

customers. More will be said about these trends in Chapter 23, where the details of mutual funds are discussed at some length.

Finally, it is common for investment banks to be consulted regarding investment strategies and opportunities, even if someone else is engaged to actually manage an investment program. Sometimes, this advice is rendered gratis, in anticipation of a greater volume of transactions directed toward the investment bank by a grateful client. At other times, it is rendered on a fee-for-service basis.

In all of these cases, the firm provides investment management expertise to the investor-client in exchange for a fee or other considerations. Given the expansion of this portion of the business, all large firms have entered the area and competition has become fierce at all levels.

Mergers, Acquisitions, and Other Activities

In addition to investment management, investment banking firms have been active in advising their clients in many different financial areas. For example, an investment bank may be contacted to advise a client in the area of mergers and acquisitions. It may help a client locate a suitable merger partner or an acquisition target. It may be retained to perform a valuation of the target and to arrange desired financing. Or it may be asked to help devise and implement a strategy to acquire a targeted firm, including the raising of sufficient funds to consummate the acquisition. As corporate restructuring continues in the United States, such activity has become commonplace (so common, in fact, that some firms are learning to "do it yourself"; see Box 20.1). On the other hand, an investment bank may be enlisted to help a potential target of acquisition fend off any unwanted suitors by devising defense mechanisms. However, in each case, these services are contracted separately and may be viewed as a separate customer service relationship.

In recent years, investment banking advisory services have expanded far beyond traditional bounds. Today, an investment bank may be sought for advice on insurance product design, pension plan design, hedging, foreign currency positions, real estate, and many more areas. Their services are sought both here and abroad. Indeed, the U.S. investment banking industry is seen as a dominant force worldwide. (See Box 20.2.) The talented and informed personnel of an investment bank can often provide a valuable "market perspective" on corporate plans.

Full Service: Good or Bad?

As was noted at the outset of this review, the quest to be a diversified provider of financial services is fraught with problems. For example, offering asset management services may be viewed to be in conflict with the business interest of asset management clients who purchase securities from the equity and fixed-income departments. A client could perceive such an investment bank as a competitor who has an unfair advantage when it comes to buying and selling securities. Another example of a potential conflict is when an investment bank has been underwriting securities of two firms, and one firm wishes to engage the services of the investment bank's

---

Box 20.1

More Companies Shun Investment Bankers, Do Their Own Deals

When investment bankers at Merrill Lynch & Co. heard in August that Illinois Tool Works Inc. was readying a bid for Elco Industries Inc., they pounced. Brit Bartter, a Merrill banker, quickly called Illinois Tool Chairman John Nichols to pitch his services.

Mr. Nichols' curt reply: No thanks.

"Maybe in 38 years of doing this, I have picked up a thing or two," Mr. Nichols says now. Mr. Bartter declines to comment.

Even as mergers and acquisitions sizzle, investment bankers are often being left out in the cold. After a decade of M&A experience, more and more companies are shunning Wall Street and are negotiating and completing mergers with little, if any, help from bankers.

Walt Disney Co.'s $19 billion acquisition of Capital Cities/ABC Inc. last summer was the most-celebrated deal crafted with scant help from bankers. But in recent years, a slew of companies, such as Computer Associates International Inc., Norwest Corp., RJR Nabisco Holdings Corp. and PepsiCo Inc., have relied mostly on in-house finance teams in making acquisitions.

Strategic Moves

Fueling the trend is a spate of strategic mergers in which corporate chieftains, seeking to acquire businesses they know well, sit down and hammer out deals face-to-face. Nearly 80% of last year's $344.7 billion of M&A activity constituted acquisitions by U.S. corporations, up from 42% of the $279.7 billion in 1988, says Morgan Stanley & Co., which studied deals of $100 million or more. And while U.S. financial buyers, mostly buyout firms, accounted for 34% of M&A activity in 1988, they were behind just 6.3% of last year's acquisitions. Unlike acquisitions by financial buyers, those by corporations usually are strategically driven.

Two of the biggest transactions in U.S. history reflect the change. The 1988 leveraged buyout of RJR Nabisco produced $203 million in merger fees for six Wall Street investment banks and Kohlberg Kravis Roberts & Co., but, by contrast, the Disney/Cap Cities deal, the second-biggest takeover behind RJR, cost investors less than $6 million in banking fees. All Disney needed from bankers was a simple fairness opinion, a review of the proposed merger to determine its fairness to stockholders.

"The more people you have in a deal, the more you have to pay," notes Sanjay Kumer, president of Computer Associates, which estimates it has saved $64 million in the past eight years by negotiating its own acquisitions. He adds that he won't negotiate with bankers, and, unlike many corporate chieftains, he wouldn't call on a banker even if contemplating a hostile takeover. "I don't want to ever live with somebody else's deal," he explains.

---

mergers and acquisitions department to orchestrate a hostile takeover of the second firm. A third example is the case in which an arbitrage department charged with trading the firm's own, or so-called proprietary, account gets wind of some merger or corporate finance transactions being worked on in another of the firm's departments that could impact the prices of shares in the proprietary trading account.

To address these potential conflicts, investment banks have attempted to carefully segment their activities in different parts of the firm. These divisions,

The Traditional Approach

At one time, bankers, with their vast network of contacts, would bring an acquisition idea to a corporate client. If the client liked the prospect, the banker would negotiate the entire deal, handling everything from pitching the proposal to drawing up the fairness opinion. Today, with more in-house corporate-finance teams, bankers are relegated to mundane tasks such as setting prices, structuring purchases or simply blessing deals with bare-bones fairness opinions.

Such jobs are far less profitable than advisory work. Lazard Freres & Co. earned $13 million advising Pet Inc. on its $2.6 billion sale to Grand Metropolitan PLC last year. But when Raytheon Co. negotiated to purchase E-Systems Inc. for $2.3 billion, Morgan Stanley and CS First Boston Inc., representing E-Systems, split $4 million in fees for fairness opinions.

The pressure to hold down fees is intense. Last year, according to Securities Data Co., securities firms booked $990 million in M&A fees for 5,887 mergers, acquisitions and leveraged buyouts valued at $388.2 billion. For the year ended Sept. 30, 1989, by contrast, they earned far more—$1.3 billion—on far fewer deals—3,880 totaling $264.1 billion.

The fee pressure was apparent in Chemical Banking Corp.'s two big mergers. When Chemical merged with Manufacturers Hanover Corp. for $2 billion five years ago, Morgan Stanley and Goldman, Sachs & Co. pocketed $8 million in fees, 0.4% of the value of the deal. But when Chemical unveiled a $10 billion merger with Chase Manhattan last year, the fees going to three Wall Street firms totaled a mere $11 million, only 0.1% of the market value. Chemical declines to comment.

Investment bankers say competition is forcing them to do more than just plain-vanilla work. . . .

Basic Business Fading

"The bread-and-butter business is getting scarcer and scarcer," says Michael Madden, former investment-banking chief at PaineWebber Inc.

Certainly, investment bankers are still used in most M&A transactions, especially for maneuvers such as tender offers, and their work continues to produce fat profits for Wall Street. And not all do-it-yourself deals fly; indeed, Illinois Tool lost out on Elco after Textron Inc. topped its bid.

Moreover, bankers can play a crucial role by greasing the wheels. When Lockheed Martin Corp. and Loral Corp. began discussing a merger, Bear, Stearns & Co. got the ball rolling by setting up meetings with top executives. The upshot: Lockheed bought most of Loral for $9.1 billion.

Nevertheless, the bankers' role has changed as corporations have grown savvier. "A lot of companies are thinking about acquisitions as a line of business, and they have developed their own expertise," says Richard Barrett, Salomon Brothers Inc.'s former investment-banking chief and now head of the financial-institutions group at UBS Securities Inc.

Source: Reprinted by permission of *The Wall Street Journal,* © 1996 Dow Jones & Company, Inc. All Rights Reserved Worldwide.

the so-called Chinese walls referred to earlier that are erected between certain departments, are set up as policies to prevent abuses. Nonetheless, some corporate clients prefer to operate through specialized boutique firms to reduce the potential for problems arising from inherent conflicts that characterize the full-service investment bank. However, it should be remembered that even an unaffiliated firm has a powerful incentive to trade private information for a price. Thus, the top investment banking firms can only occupy their positions with a

---

Box 20.2

Top Dogs
U.S. Financial Firms Seize Dominant Role in the World Markets

Heard all about the globalization of finance?

Forget it.

What's really happening is the *Americanization* of finance. Some evidence:

• Worldwide, seven of the top 10 merger advisers are American, and two others are partly American-owned.

• The top four global underwriters of stock offerings in the past three years have been American firms.

• Goldman, Sachs & Co., the 1995 leader in global stock offerings, won the job of co-coordinator in the privatization of Deutsche Telekom AG—the world's largest such deal—and the lead role in the biggest-ever equity offerings in Denmark, Spain, Sweden, Mexico and Singapore.

• Hoechst AG, the German chemical giant, turned to J.P. Morgan & Co. to guide its $7.1 billion takeover of Marion Merrell Dow, the biggest trans-Atlantic acquisition last year.

• When Credito Italiano SpA made a successful hostile bid for Italy's Credito Romagnolo SpA last year, J.P. Morgan advised the former, and Goldman Sachs and Morgan Stanley Group Inc. the latter.

• In August, Merrill Lynch & Co. became the first non-Swiss institution to lead-manage a Swiss-franc corporate bond issue for a Swiss company, cement giant Holderbank Financiere Glaris SA.

Sophisticated Operators

With muscles and skills developed in the frantic competition of the world's biggest financial market, U.S. investment and commercial banks emerged last year as the international juggernauts. They are adept at arranging huge loans, underwriting stock offerings and putting together multinational mergers. They employ the most sophisticated technology while capitalizing on the status of English as the financial world's lingua franca.

To compete, American firms push "innovation after innovation," says Lowell Bryant, head of the bank-consulting practice at McKinsey & Co. in New York. "Whether you're talking about derivatives, structured credits or any kind of innovative cross-border finance, the players that first discovered how to do these things are U.S. players."

In other countries, by contrast, finance "has been an insider's game consisting of very close relationships" between banks and their corporate clients, he says. "In the U.S. market, those days have been gone since the 1970s."

Growing Appeal

The upshot: The U.S. market's appeal keeps growing. "In the U.S.," says Joseph MacHale, J.P. Morgan's head of credit, "you can do financing for almost any quality of credit, as opposed to international markets, which demand that borrowers be rated double-A or triple-A."

The U.S. regulatory environment is unusually conducive to innovation: many countries' regulators are biased against capital markets. In America, innovation is held in check only by specific legal prohibitions. But in France, many financial innovations are considered illegal unless specifically sanctioned. Asset-backed securities, dreamed up by Americans, could be introduced in France, Spain and Italy only after legislation permitted their use.

Walter Gubert, J.P. Morgan's chief for Europe, the Mideast and Africa, adds that the Securities and Exchange Commission's strict enforcement and its strong emphasis on investor protection "push market participants toward quality and rigor."

Cultural Advantages

Culture plays a big role, too.

Americans' frontier spirit, appetite for risk, can-do attitudes and rags-to-riches dreams explain U.S. success in global finance. Noting Americans' immigrant roots and entrepreneurial tradition, Frederic C. Rich, a Sullivan & Cromwell partner in New York, says, "Social mobility is one of our great strengths."

The way money has supplanted class as the arbiter of status in America is cited by Benjamin Appen, a vice president at D.E. Shaw & Co., a New York investment bank. "You don't read about Brooke Astor anymore; you read about Donald Trump and George Soros," he says. "Money is a pure playing field; it's a forum for competition where brains are what anybody brings to the table. For those reasons, it has attracted the best and the brightest who previously didn't enter finance because it was considered crass or vulgar."

Foreigners aren't taking all this lying down. European banks such as Deutsche Bank, Swiss Bank Corp., Union Bank of Switzerland, ING Group NV of the Netherlands and National Westminster Bank of Britain have made big acquisitions or invested large sums to build top-flight investment-banking operations. And although Japan's big banks and securities firms have been humbled by a lame economy, bad loans and the Daiwa Bank scandal, no one thinks they will slink off the financial stage.

But foreign banks won't find it easy to regain market share. Bankers wonder how long European banks will continue to benefit from low payments on deposits and passive shareholders. Others note the difficulty of trying to expand through acquisitions, especially those that meld differing national cultures. And Japan's consensus management and practice of rotating executives into different jobs every few years clearly slow innovation and hamper their ability to react quickly to change.

Tad Rybczynski, a visiting professor at City University in London, predicts that the Europeans and Japanese will need five to 10 years before they can challenge the Americans. He says Europe's big universal banks—banks in both commercial and investment banking—"must build new organizational structures and acquire skills and introduce new cultures distinct from old-fashioned commercial banks to compete with the Americans." He adds:

"Americans have experience derived from the breadth and width of their capital markets. They are people with an extraordinary knowledge of underwriting, financial markets and, above all, capital markets. And they have been able to use this knowledge in a very innovative way, which has enabled them to change investment banking from the old-fashioned raising of funds for industry and commerce into the aggressive restructuring of industry."

By exporting those skills to other countries, U.S. securities firms, Mr. Rybczynski says, "have built powerful units with very strong capital bases and appropriate organizational structures designed to compete globally. . . . The rest of the world is merely catching up."

Some U.S. Troubles

Not all major U.S. financial firms will survive the battle to become truly global, of course. Kidder, Peabody & Co. and Drexel Burnham Lambert Inc. have already fallen by the wayside. Lehman Brothers Holdings Inc. crops up in constant takeover rumors, and Salomon Brothers Inc. remains troubled since its 1991 bond-trading scandal. Some bankers say U.S.

investment banks, in particular, suffer from a boom-bust mentality and volatile earnings that could force even the best of them into the arms of cash-rich European banks.

Bankers Trust New York Corp. is enmeshed in management changes and lawsuits involving its sale of derivative products. "Two years ago, it was rated up with J.P. Morgan as the finest bank in the country," says Richard Watkins, chief executive of Latinvest Securities Ltd. in London. And noting that Chase Manhattan Bank and Chemical Banking Corp. (which has already absorbed Manufacturers Hanover Trust Co.) will soon be merged, he says that only a few years ago "all three regarded themselves as world-class organizations with an outstanding future."

Ironically, much of the U.S. firms' success abroad stems from the Glass-Steagall Act, which separated commercial and investment banking. Overturning that 1934 law has long been sought by U.S. banks, but, meanwhile, the legislation prevented U.S. investment banks from subsidizing their activities with large retail banking bases, as Europe's big banks do. It "forced U.S. institutions to work harder than their counterparts in other countries to make money," says William Lewis, a McKinsey partner in Washington.

The domestic competition has been intensifying for two decades. In 1975, fixed commissions on securities transactions were abolished. In the early 1980s, the U.S. introduced "shelf-registrations," which allow companies to register securties with the SEC and market them at an opportune time. And recently, the Glass-Steagall Act's erosion allows commercial banks to encroach on investment banks' turf.

Competition in Banking

Meanwhile, U.S. commercial banks faced more competition because of the creation of money-market checking accounts in the late 1970s and the subsequent deregulation of interest rates on bank deposits.

U.S. investment and commercial banks alike have to deal with the growth of financial-service giants such as General Electric Credit Corp. and the emergence of big fund-management companies.

The force of that competition is indicated by the costs that firms incur and the fees that they can charge clients. Before Morgan Stanley backed away from merging with S.G. Warburg Group PLC last year, it found that the British firm's cost of processing a trade was about 80% higher than its own. And in the U.S., a typical brokerage customer would pay an average commission of about six cents a share on a $50,000 trade; in Japan, the cost would run 30 cents a share, McKinsey estimates.

Unlike Germans and Japanese, American firms "had to innovate to earn higher profits," Mr. Lewis says. Or even to survive. The result has been a flood of new ideas, ranging from better methods of calculating risk to creation of sophisticated securities and derivatives that stretch far beyond the old plain-vanilla loans.

"As it exists today, international finance is trading in secondary markets and applying technology to that trading," says Till Guldimann, executive vice president at Infinity Financial Technology Inc., a Mountain View, Calif., provider of financial-software systems. "Americans are very good at technology, and the faster the cycle of markets, the better the Americans are. They like quick change, experimentation and diversity."

An Innovative Plan

When Continental AG wanted to increase its employees' stake in the company to 5% from 0.5%, the big German tire maker first had to overcome Germans' traditional fear of stocks. Working with Dresdner Bank, which handled the administrative, legal and tax issues, J.P. Morgan three months ago came up with a plan: Continental workers can buy shares by putting up 20% of the cost, borrow the remaining 80% at no interest and collect all dividends. Using options paid for by Continental, the workers also are protected against any drop in share prices for two years but get the full amount of any increases. "Morgan had a product other German banks didn't have," says Gregor Schoess, Continental's group treasurer.

In contrast to top U.S. firms, European and Japanese rivals have tended, until recently, to stick with familiar ideas and products. Despite big capital bases, few European banks have been willing, for example, to take the risks required to make major inroads into the U.S. market. They are risk-averse even on their home turf.

In October, for example, Abbey National PLC, a British bank, issued £300 million ($464 million) of bonds convertible into preferred stock. In a maneuver European banks would shun, Merrill Lynch purchased the entire offering and sold it to clients. Similar transactions in the U.K. are handled on a "best-efforts" basis—the bank tries to sell the issue but won't risk its own capital. In a similar example of a U.S. firm's willingness to put its capital at risk, Goldman Sachs bought 80% of Diamond Cable Communications PLC, a British cable-TV company, and raised $75 million in equity and $400 million in debt. In October, Goldman registered to take Diamond public in the U.S.

"Europeans get into too much thought, too much planning, too much strategy," Mr. Watkins of Latinvest says. "Therefore, we build up teams selling too many old-fashioned products."

To the Rescue

U.S. firms sometimes step in where foreigners have stumbled. Three years ago, Japan's Nomura Securities Co. acted as global coordinator of a $1 billion stock offering by Ireland's GPA Group PLC, the aircraft-leasing giant. Launched amid an airline-industry slump, the deal flopped; GPA had to scramble to renegotiate loan extensions with its banks. Six months ago, Morgan Stanley devised a long-term solution to GPA's cash problems: a complex $4 billion restructuring that would convert bank debt into marketable securities, using 230 GPA planes as collateral.

U.S. banks' coups extend to ordinary commercial banking. This fall, J.P. Morgan teamed up with Deutsche Bank to lead-manage a four-billion-mark ($2.75 billion) loan for Volkswagen AG. Days later, it muscled aside the German bank to arrange on its own a $2 billion syndicated loan for Germany's Siemens AG.

Initially, some Europeans rebelled at the "barbarity" of spartan American business mores, which included power breakfasts and banned alcohol at lunch. When a U.S. securities executive suggested a breakfast meeting with a French colleague, the Frenchman replied, "Why don't you come a half-hour early, and we can shower together."

But such attitudes may be changing. When O'Connor & Associates, a Chicago options-trading firm, first linked up with Swiss Bank Corp. in the early 1990s, says Leslie Grant, an executive director at WBC Warburg, "if you looked in at 7 a.m. or 7 p.m., it tended to be people in front of the O'Connor [trading] machines who were at work. Now everybody works as hard."

Even so, Daan Potger, a Dutch student at the London School of Economics and Political Science, complains, "Americans work too hard; they work six, seven days a week." He tells of beeper-wearing American bankers "who go out to dinner with their wives, and when the beeper goes off, they go back to their offices."

Source: Michael R. Sesit, "Top Dogs: U.S. Financial Firms Seize Dominant Role in the World Markets," *The Wall Street Journal*, January 5, 1996. Reprinted by permission of *The Wall Street Journal*, © Dow Jones & Company, Inc. All Rights Reserved Worldwide.

EXHIBIT 20.1   **The Ten Largest Investment Banks, Year-End 1994**
($ billions)

	Equity	*Assets*
Merrill Lynch	$5.8	$163.7
Goldman, Sachs & Co.	4.8	95.3
Salomon, Inc.	4.5	172.7
Morgan Stanley	4.5	116.0
Lehman Brothers	3.4	109.0
Bear, Stearns & Co.	2.3	66.8
Smith Barney	2.2	44.4
CS-First Boston	1.8	109.8
PaineWebber	1.6	38.2
Donaldson, Lufkin & Jenrette	1.0	33.1

Source: *Institutional Investor,* April 1995.

reputation for trust that they have built up over the years, a reputation they guard jealously.

The Major Players

The largest national, full-line firms in the United States include Merrill Lynch, Goldman Sachs, Salomon Brothers, Bear Stearns, Morgan Stanley, and CS-First Boston. Of these firms, Merrill Lynch is most active on the retail side, while the others concentrate more on the corporate side and are highly active in trading securities. In addition to these full-line firms, there are specialized investment bank subsidiaries of commercial bank holding companies, such as J.P. Morgan and Bankers Trust; specialized discount brokers who offer transactions services without investment advice, such as Charles Schwab; and regional securities firms that concentrate their efforts on serving clients in their particular region.

The cadre of investment banks that underwrite the bulk of corporate America's securities firms are collectively known as the "bulge bracket." This is because of their enormous capital and assets, relative to the rest of their competitors. In Exhibit 20.1, we identify the 10 largest investment banking firms by capital and assets. All of the investment banks ranked in the top 10 are full-service banks.

These firms can also be ranked by volume of activity rather than balance sheet equity and assets. For example, Exhibit 20.2 reports the relative ranking of the major investment firms for both 1994 and 1995 according to the volume of U.S. debt and equities underwritten. Exhibit 20.3 provides similar rankings for non-U.S. securities. Some of these names are already familiar from Exhibit 20.1, but there are also new names, and the ordering changes. Most notable is the presence of several foreign investment banks in Exhibit 20.3. Finally, to round out

Exhibit 20.2   Top Underwriters of U.S. Debt and Equity

| Manager | Full-Year 1995 | | Full-Year 1994 | | |
	Amount ($ billions)	Market Share (%)	Amount ($ billions)	Rank	Market Share (%)
Merrill Lynch	$122.3	17.9%	$116.1	1	16.5%
Lehman Brothers	70.3	9.9	78.3	2	11.1
Goldman, Sachs & Co.	68.5	9.7	64.9	4	9.2
Morgan Stanley	68.5	9.7	58.7	5	8.3
Salomon Brothers	68.1	9.6	56.7	7	8.0
CS-First Boston	64.6	9.1	72.2	3	10.2
J.P. Morgan	40.2	5.7	26.3	9	3.7
Bear, Stearns & Co.	25.4	3.6	34.7	8	4.9
Donaldson, Lufkin & Jenrette	22.2	3.1	23.6	10	3.3
Smith Barney	20.7	2.9	13.8	12	2.0
Top 10	570.8	81.2	545.3		77.2
Industry Total	$709.3	100.00%	$705.7		100.0%

Source: Reprinted with permission of *The Wall Street Journal,* © 1996 Dow Jones & Company, Inc. All Rights Reserved Worldwide.

Exhibit 20.3   Top Underwriters of Non-U.S. Securities

Manager	Amount ($ billions)	1995 Market Share (%)	1994 Market Share (%)
SBC Warburg	$ 19.3	6.4%	6.0%
Merrill Lynch	17.7	5.9	5.6
Deutsche Bank	15.6	5.2	3.8
ABN Amro	14.1	4.7	2.8
Goldman, Sachs & Co.	13.7	4.6	6.1
Morgan Stanley	13.5	4.5	4.5
J.P. Morgan	13.4	4.5	4.2
CS-First Boston	13.3	4.4	5.7
Lehman Brothers	12.5	4.2	3.0
Banque Paribas	12.5	4.2	3.4
Top 10	145.6	48.6	45.1
Industry Total	$299.8	100.0%	100.0%

Source: Reprinted with permission of *The Wall Street Journal,* © 1996 Dow Jones & Company, Inc. All Rights Reserved Worldwide.

the picture, Exhibit 20.4 offers these rankings for the mortgage-backed debt market, Exhibit 20.5 shows rankings for the municipal market, and Exhibit 20.6 offers a product listing for the same two-year period.

However, the ranking of firms need not be based only upon total balance sheets or volume of underwriting. As the cliché goes, bigger may not be better.

EXHIBIT 20.4   Top Underwriters of Mortgage-Backed Debt

Manager	Amount ($ billions)	1995 Market Share (%)
Bear, Stearns	$ 7.3	15.5%
Lehman Brothers	6.4	13.6
Paine Webber	5.0	10.6
CS First Boston	4.9	10.4
Donaldson Lufkin	4.4	9.4
Morgan Stanley	3.8	8.1
Merrill Lynch	3.3	7.0
NationsBank	3.2	6.8
Salomon Bros.	2.5	5.3
Prudential Securities	1.4	2.9
Top 10	42.2	89.6
Industry Total	$47.0	100.0%

Source: Reprinted with permission of *The Wall Street Journal,* © 1996 Dow Jones & Company, Inc. All Rights Reserved Worldwide.

EXHIBIT 20.5   Top Municipal Underwriters

Manager	Amount ($ billions)	1995 Market Share (%)	No. of Issues
Goldman, Sachs & Co.	$ 19.8	12.8%	307
Merrill Lynch	17.0	11.0	350
Smith Barney	13.0	8.4	413
PaineWebber	12.7	8.2	283
Lehman Brothers	9.8	6.3	137
J.P. Morgan	7.3	4.7	89
Morgan Stanley	7.0	4.5	89
Prudential Securities	6.5	4.2	228
Bear, Stearns & Co.	6.2	4.0	92
A. G. Edwards	2.3	1.5	183
Top 10	101.6	65.6	2,171
Industry Total	$154.9	100.0%	9,818

Source: Reprinted with permission of *The Wall Street Journal,* © 1996 Dow Jones & Company, Inc. All Rights Reserved Worldwide.

With this in mind, several publications, including *Euromoney, Institutional Investor,* and *Financial World,* periodically rank the investment banks operating around the world based on extensive surveys of investment banking corporate clients and peer institutions. A portion of the 1995 *Euromoney* survey, which reports borrower responses for both the U.S. domestic market and overall capital

Exhibit 20.6   Who's No. 1 in Each Market?

Manager	Full-Year 1995		Full-Year 1994	
	Amount ($ billion)	Top-Ranked Manager	Amount ($ billions)	Top-Ranked Manager
U.S. domestic	$709.3	Merrill Lynch	$705.7	Merrill Lynch
Straight debt	442.5	Merrill Lynch	361.8	Merrill Lynch
Convertible debt	5.4	Morgan Stanley	4.7	Goldman, Sachs & Co.
Junk bonds	24.8	Donaldson, Lufkin & Jenrette	27.4	Merrill Lynch
Investment grade debt	238.6	Merrill Lynch	196.7	Merrill Lynch
Mortgage debt	47.0	Bear, Stearns & Co.	178.2	PaineWebber
Asset-backed debt	107.1	Merrill Lynch	75.4	Merrill Lynch
Collateralized securities*	154.1	Merrill Lynch	253.6	PaineWebber
Preferred stock	16.3	Goldman, Sachs & Co.	15.5	Goldman, Sachs & Co.
Common stock	81.7	Goldman, Sachs & Co.	60.3	Merrill Lynch
IPOs	30.1	Goldman, Sachs & Co.	28.3	Goldman, Sachs & Co.
Closed-end funds	0.2	Smith Barney	5.5	Merrill Lynch
International debt	280.1	SBC Warburg	322.4	SBC Warburg
International equity	19.7	Merrill Lynch	22	Goldman, Sachs & Co.
U.S. issuers	725.6	Merrill Lynch	709.6	Merrill Lynch
Municipal new issuers	154.9	Goldman, Sachs & Co.	161.9	Merrill Lynch

Source: Reprinted with permission of *The Wall Street Journal,* © 1996 Dow Jones & Company, Inc. All Rights Reserved Worldwide.

raising capability, is given in Exhibit 20.7.[7] In that survey, the top five firms in the United States are also ranked in the top 10 worldwide. However, rankings differ. As noted in Box 20.2, U.S. firms are major players on the world stage, but they are clearly not the only ones in the game! Rankings were also given for numerous subcategories, but those are not reported here. Underwriting was broken down into nine subcategories, and firms were ranked separately in each. These subcategories included equities, Eurobonds, medium-term notes, syndicated loans, private placements, Euro commercial paper, asset-backed securities, and foreign bonds.

Peer reviews and rankings are also offered. Here, interest centers on firm capability as a trading house, as a syndicate member or leader, and in the advisory area. Trading was comprised of various subcategories, including a number of derivatives, foreign currencies, government bonds, equities, Eurobonds, medium-term notes, and Euro commercial paper. The same set of firms find their way into each of the rankings, although in different positions for different products. In the syndicate list, the same is true.

Where such ratings are conducted for the advisory category, it also includes a number of subcategories, including merger and acquisitions, short-term economic

---

[7]This table is based on *Euromoney* magazine's investment banking poll of polls from September 1995. Because it is getting increasingly difficult to distinguish between investment banks, commercial banks, and the universal banks of Europe, all institutions included in the broadest definition of investment banking have been included.

EXHIBIT 20.7   Borrower Ranking of Quality, 1995

U.S. Domestic Markets

Which bank is best at raising capital in U.S. public domestic markets?

Rank 1995	1994	Bank	Score
1	2	Merrill Lynch	92
2	1	Goldman, Sachs & Co.	56
3	3	Morgan Stanley	48
4	4	Lehman Brothers	42
5	—	J. P. Morgan	30

Overall Capital Raising

Overall, which bank has served you best in raising capital through the international markets?

Rank 1995	1994	Bank	Score
1	6	J. P. Morgan	76
2	2	Merrill Lynch	70
3	*	SBC Warburg	68
4	5	Morgan Stanley	66
5	1	Goldman, Sachs & Co.	48
6	4	CS-First Boston	42
7	—	HSBC Markets	38
8	8	Barclays de Zoete Wedd	30
9	3	Lehman Brothers	28
10	10	Deutsche Bank	26

*Swiss Bank Corporation ranked 9.
Source: *Euromoney,* September 1995.

research, long-term economic research, European government bond research, European equity research, Asian economic research, and industry specialists.

The *Institutional Investor* and *Financial World* surveys emphasize different areas of excellence (e.g., less European focus), and therefore these rankings of investment banks should not be considered the final word. Moreover, the rankings often change dramatically. For example, due to its role in the Treasury bond bidding scandal, Salomon fell from a top ranking in trading as recently as 1992 to a spot off of all the charts in 1995. Scandals can be costly. (See Box 20.3.)

The Cyclical Nature of Profits

Wall Street has long been characterized as a feast or famine business. There are many cycles that affect the business climate, including interest rates, exchange rates, commodity prices, equity prices, and so forth. Each of these cycles will produce massive amounts of potential business in a particular domain. Because the economy is cyclical, there can be an embarrassment of riches as numerous nonfinancial corporations often enter the market near the same time to make public stock offerings, retire debt early, engage in mergers and acquisitions, seek hedging assistance, invest in real estate or commodities, or whatever else the fashion of the month happens to be. On the other hand, if a firm is specialized, say, to make debt offerings for high-technology firms, and there is a dearth of such offerings, it can be famine for that firm and result in massive layoffs.

For this reason, many investment banks have sought to operate diversified firms with a maximum of flexibility. There may be feast in some departments of the firm and famine in others. However, the diversified firm as a whole is able to navigate the fickle waters of fortune and keep intact a cadre of experienced experts in each field, knowing that sooner or later it will be well positioned for the proper moment in a business cycle when highly profitable opportunities will arise. In the interim, slack resources can be reallocated within the investment bank to those areas where there is a temporary deficit. Because there are always some departments that are not performing well at any given moment in time, this diversified strategy does not produce the gluttonous feasts that characterize the specialized firm whose moment has arrived; however, it tends to produce a steadier profit stream and greater market power in the long run.

Another thing that investment banks do to help them survive the low points in their profitability cycles is to increase their capital. At the end of 1994, the industry as a whole had close to $150 billion in capital, supporting total assets of approximately $1.5 trillion. At the same time, there are fewer investment banking firms than prior to the stock market crash of October 19, 1987. The total number of firms operating in this specialty decreased by almost 25 percent over the ensuing five years, yet there remain close to 5,000. These firms include the so-called national full-line firms who service retail customers (acting primarily as broker-dealers) as well as corporate customers (including new issue underwriting and advisory services). Even with these efforts to reduce the cyclical nature of profits, the investment banking industry of today continues to manifest wide profitability swings. For example, during 1994, many of the largest full-line investment banks suffered reductions of as much as 70–80 percent from their 1993 record profit levels. By contrast, 1995 was a very good year!

Regulation of Investment Banking

The broad aims of the regulatory bodies that oversee the investment banking industry are to (1) promote competition and limit monopolistic practices; (2) foster the dissemination of accurate information to investors; (3) prevent agents with inside information from using that information to their own advantage and to the disadvantage of others; and (4) reduce the effects associated with insolvency. To achieve these aims, several regulatory bodies have been established and share jurisdiction over the investment banking industry. These include the Securities Exchange Commission (SEC), the National Association of Securities Dealers (NASD), the

---

Box 20.3

The Death of Drexel

In the end Drexel Burnham Lambert proved as much a creation of Mr. Michael Milken as were so many of the former junk-bond king's *nouveau riche* clients. The once high-flying Drexel is now bust, just over a year after it pleaded guilty to six felonies and paid $650m in fines, and only eight months after Mr. Milken resigned when he was served by the federal government with 98 indictments for criminal fraud.

The demise of this always-controversial investment bank, which made $1.1 billion in pre-tax profit in 1986, was shockingly swift even by the fickle standards of Wall Street. At the end of 1989 Drexel said it had $800m in equity. Yet on February 13th its holding company could not come up with $100m to pay off short-term loans falling due. This default, said Drexel in a terse (under) statement, "could result in other defaults."

Later that day Drexel's holding company filed for Chapter 11 bankruptcy protection against its creditors which, in the peculiar circumstances of the securities business, meant the firm (and its 5,300 employees) was no longer in business. With no one willing to extend any more credit, Drexel could not trade a single bond nor underwrite a security. It remained only for the regulators, such as the New York Federal Reserve, the Securities and Exchange Commission (SEC) and the New York Stock Exchange, to make sure that Drexel unwound its outstanding positions in as orderly a manner as possible.

Drexel's problems were partly short-term liquidity, partly basic questions of insolvency. The solvency issue stemmed from Drexel's overwhelming dependence on the $200 billion junk-bond market, the legacy of Mr Milken. Drexel lost money in both 1988 and 1989, raising questions about both the size and quality of its junk inventory (including private placements). Wall Street guesses put this at $2 billion (i.e., the stated value in Drexel's latest accounts) though it was probably higher.

The inventory probably also consisted of the worst sort of junk. After all, if Drexel could have sold the bonds it surely would have done so. The firm also increased its junk holdings last year when it took bad bonds back from clients in return for persuading them to buy billions of dollars of RJR Nabisco bonds underwritten by Drexel.

As the junk-bond market's collapse has fed on itself in recent months, with the latest plunge in prices triggered by Moody's downgrading on January 26th of $19.5 billion of RJR Nabisco debt, Drexel's losses when valued according to the market price must have looked increasingly ugly. These woes were compounded by a decision in December by Groupe Bruxelles Lambert, a Belgian holding company which owns 35% of Drexel, to turn down the investment bank's plea for more capital. As a result, creditors grew increasingly and understandably anxious. The message was that Drexel's main shareholder was prepared to wash its hands of the connection and write down its once lucrative investment to zero rather than risk deeper involvement.

The Belgians were terrified by the unquantifiable contingent liability posed by legal claims from companies and individuals that stemmed from Drexel's

---

national and regional securities exchanges, and the Federal Reserve Board. In addition, the Securities Investor Protection Corporation (SIPC) also plays an important part, albeit not as a regulator but as an insurer of balances on deposit.

Major Regulatory Legislation

Since the onset of the Great Depression, several major pieces of legislation have been enacted in an attempt to regulate the securities markets. Most important are the Securities Act of 1933 and the Securities and Exchange Act of 1934, which

admission to six felonies. This is also why no other institution has been willing to invest a cent in Drexel. Refuseniks included such rich high-profile Drexel clients as Mr. Ronald Perelman, a corporate raider turned chairman of Revlon, Mr. Henry Kravis, Wall Street's leveraged buy-out king, and Mr. Carl Icahn, a corporate raider turned TWA chairman.

Despite this string of bad news, Drexel's chief executive, Mr. Fred Joseph, has continued to talk up the firm's prospects in a way that might have been awkward if Drexel had not been privately-owned. As recently as February 5th Mr. Joseph told *The Wall Street Journal*: "I see daylight. The worst is behind us." It now transpires that Drexel had apparently borrowed up to $600m from its commodity-broking subsidiary in a last-ditch effort to keep rolling over its debts.

Drexel's finances were, in fact, even worse than the gloomiest gloomsters suspected. The final straw was when commercial banks' growing anxieties about their credit lines backing Drexel's commercial paper resulted in a full-scale liquidity crisis. On February 12th Drexel managed to pay off $30m in commercial paper falling due only by getting special consent from the SEC to remove excess capital from its broking subsidiary. That alerted regulators to the scale of the problems.

These became public knowledge also on February 12th when Drexel issued a statement saying it had "liquidity problems" and that it was seeking a big investor or merger partner. Since nobody on Wall Street believed that any sane person would invest in Drexel, this was seen as an admission that the firm's condition was terminal. Other Wall Street firms, which lacked much love for the upstart Drexel, imme-diately stopped trading with it. Squeezed out of the markets, Drexel had ran out of luck, credit and time.

From the sheer speed of Drexel's demise it is clear the firm made the wrong choice in January 1989 when it settled with the government by paying a fine of $650m and sacrificing Mr. Milken, agreeing to cooperate in the government's investigation of him and not to pay him his 1988 bonus of some $200m. That way, Drexel avoided a criminal indictment under the Racketeering Influenced Corrupt Organisations (RICO) act. But it was a controversial decision within the firm. That is why Mr. Joseph, Wall Street's master of double-talk, voted at a Drexel board meeting against the deal ditching Mr. Milken that he had himself negotiated with Mr. Rudolph Giuliani, then United States attorney for the southern district of Manhattan.

Mr. Joseph's fast footwork had one effect. It saved his job. Regulators could easily have demanded his departure for (at the very least) being asleep at the switch in New York while Mr. Milken was committing his alleged crimes in Drexel's Beverly Hills junk-bond headquarters. Mr. Joseph further helped himself by agreeing to bring in as Drexel's new chairman Mr. John Shad. He was a former chairman of the SEC and, previously, Mr. Joseph's mentor when both men were at another Wall Street firm, E.F. Hutton. Mr. Joseph also agreed to have a posse of Drexel lawyers second-guessing every business decision, which made it increasingly hard for the firm's investment bankers to do any at all. Junk-bond underwriting does not lend itself to rule by committee.

Drexel would have had a better chance if it had fought beside Mr. Milken. For it is not a coincidence that the junk-bond market has been collapsing almost since his departure. The junk market was first and

was passed to correct certain omissions and inadequacies discovered in the 1933 act. These two acts continue to govern securities markets even today. The major purpose of these acts was to require disclosure of information in primary distributions of securities. The Securities Exchange Commission was established to police the disclosure requirements.

Coinciding with the passage of the 1933 and 1934 acts was the passage of the Banking Act of 1933, which, among other things, separated commercial and investment banking and prohibited commercial banks from certain investment

foremost Mr. Milken's own private market. He it was who knitted it all together, raising money for a favoured group of clients, be they insurance companies, savings-and-loan associations or industrial holding-companies, in return for these same clients buying each other's bonds. With Mr. Milken's departure, the ability to raise money vanished as well as the knowledge of where the bonds were held. This dual expertise was the prime source of Drexel's underwriting and trading profits in the 1980s and Mr. Milken's gargantuan bonuses.

It is not then surprising that, like Drexel itself, Mr. Milken's favoured junk-bond-financed creations are themselves now having problems. Examples include First Executive, an insurance company based in Beverly Hills, which set aside $800m at year-end to cover losses on its $8 billion junk-bond portfolio; Centrust, a junk-bond-addicted thrift in Miami whose chairman, Mr. David Paul, was recently kicked out by federal regulators; and Integrated Resources, a property and financial-services company, which on February 13th also filed for Chapter 11 bankruptcy protection. Its creditors include Centrust ($39m), First Executive ($49m), and Drexel itself ($41m), a fine example of Milken knitting.

Drexel's collapse raises a wider issue: its effect on Wall Street and the rest of the economy. So far the verdict is perversely sanguine. The Dow Jones industrial average actually rose five points on February 13th, while junk-bond prices fell only slightly. There has been no panic partly because Drexel's troubles were well-known and thus discounted, and partly because the junk market is only a $200 billion cog in a $5 trillion economy.

Panic could yet come. First, it is unlikely that the junk market has hit bottom. There is the by-no-means small matter of selling off Drexel's own inventory. Other Wall Street firms may also be sitting on big losses on their own junk holdings. Drexel's collapse has also confirmed for now the end of takeover mania, risk arbitrage and merchant banking, the businesses of betting on, lending to and investing in takeovers. These were the most profitable areas on Wall Street during the late 1980s.

Insurance companies and mutual funds, which between them own 60% of all junk bonds, will also be hurt. Insurance companies' shares are already under pressure because of worries about junk, while traders are scared stiff of any mass redemptions by the public of mutual funds invested in junk bonds. So far this has not happened. If it does, and Drexel's collapse could yet trigger it, the junk market could really collapse; money managers have already dumped the best-quality issues in the rush to raise cash.

Salutary though it is to see excesses punished by the free market, the Drexel debacle also has troubling implications for the economy. For it is another sign that the interest-rate spread is widening between good and bad credits, and that lenders are increasingly willing to lend only to the most creditworthy borrowers. Junk bonds were not all evil. They created jobs and fuelled economic growth in the debt-happy 1980s. Conversely, the increasing rationing of credit now evident is contractionary in an economy where credit growth is already slowing sharply. Roll on credit revulsion? Roll on deflation?

Source: *The Economist*, February 17, 1990. © 1990 The Economist Newspaper Group, Inc. Reprinted with permission. Further reproduction prohibited.

banking activities. Later, in 1975, Congress passed the Securities Acts Amendments, one of which made fixed sales commissions illegal. Today, there is no fixed commission scale common to all firms operating as broker/dealers. The 1975 amendments also authorized the SEC to develop a national market system (NMS), which was intended to serve as an auction market for all securities that could feasibly be included. As of this writing, designs for such a system are still being studied and have not been fully implemented. In 1986, Congress passed the Government Securities Act, which requires the Treasury, in consultation with the SEC

EXHIBIT 20.8   Information Included in SEC Registration Statement

1. **General information**
   - Copy of issuer's articles of incorporation.
   - Information on issuer's products, history, and location.
   - Names and remuneration of any officers receiving more than $25,000/year.
   - Names and addresses of issuer's officers, directors, and underwriter.
   - Names and addresses of any investor owning more than 10 percent of any class of stock.
2. **Purpose for which the proceeds of the issue will be spent**
3. **Offering price**
   - To the general public.
   - To specific individuals or groups, if different from public offering price.
4. **Underwriting agreement**
   - Copy of the underwriting agreement.
   - Underwriting fees.
   - Fees provided to promoters and/or developers.
   - Net proceeds to issuer.
5. **Financial information**
   - Detailed balance sheet.
   - Detailed income statements for three preceding years.
   - Detailed statement of capitalization.
6. **Legal**
   - Copies of legal opinions on matters related to the issue.
   - Copies of any indentures affecting the new issue.
   - Details about any pending litigation.
   - Details of any unusual contracts (e.g., management profit sharing plans).

---

and the Fed, to promulgate rules regarding the activities of brokers and dealers in government securities. These rules are concerned with capital adequacy, custody and use of customer securities, financial reporting, record keeping, the treatment of customer deposits or credit balances, and the mechanics of repos and reverses.

In this section, we do not give a historical overview of how the regulatory bodies came into being, nor will we trace the evolution of securities markets laws. Rather, our focus is on the current regulatory environment. Suffice it to say that much of the legislation arose during the Great Depression in an effort to prevent the immense problems of that period from occurring in the future.

Role of the SEC

The SEC oversees the issuance of new securities and mandates specific disclosure rules for the issuers. A securities registration statement must be filed with the SEC, and a prospectus containing all relevant information pertaining to a new security must accompany its distribution to the public. (See Exhibit 20.8.) Prior to final approval by the SEC for selling the securities to the public, a prospectus must carry a statement on it, written on the front page in red ink, disclosing that the security has not yet been approved for sale. This kind of prospectus is known as a **red herring.**[8]

The SEC also has issued regulations regarding the disclosure, on a regular basis, of updated information regarding the companies that have publicly traded securities outstanding. These disclosure requirements include the annual filing of detailed balance sheets, income statements, and supporting documents in statements known as **Form 10K.** In addition, less detailed statements must be filed semiannually as **Form 9K.** When significant economic events occur that relate to an issuing company, **Form 8K** must be filed at the end of that month. For example, a major change in the valuation of assets, a change in control, or a finding of legal liability are the kinds of information that would require the filing of Form 8K.

The SEC also regulates all organized exchanges and participating brokerage firms and specifies capital requirements for broker/dealers. All government securities brokers and dealers are required to register with the SEC. While it provides the general guidelines and has broad enforcement powers, the SEC leaves the day-to-day regulatory duties as a responsibility of local regulatory or trade associations such as the NASD and the exchanges themselves.

Role of the NASD

The NASD is an acronym for the National Association of Securities Dealers, a trade and oversight body whose member firms are securities market participants. In the spirit of self-regulation, NASD issues mandates designed to prevent unfair and illegal security trading practices, to assure that trading takes place in an orderly fashion, and to deal with customer complaints. It regulates how securities purchased by clients of broker/dealers must be held in safekeeping for the customer in a denominated, segregated account in which the customer is afforded significant protection. NASD is also responsible for overseeing the annual auditing of broker/dealers' financial statements. The security exchanges carry out the same duties, but they restrict their activities to policing their respective exchanges.

Roles of the Federal Reserve and SIPC

The Federal Reserve Board also exerts its influence, but only indirectly through its power to determine margin requirements[9] for security purchases and its oversight of the U.S. government securities market. The SIPC, while having no regulatory

---

[8]To minimize the economic burden of complying with SEC registration requirements, exceptions are granted for issues that are for less than $1.5 million, securities that are privately placed, securities issued in exchange for outstanding stock in a merger, and debt securities with maturities of less than 270 days. Also, securities issued offshore and seasoned in overseas markets for 90 days may then be sold in the United States and are not required to have prospectuses.

[9]Many securities are purchased "on margin." This means that the securities were not paid for completely with cash, but were financed, in part, by loans from the brokerage firm. This allows the investor to obtain greater leverage in his investment and thereby control a greater number of securities. However, it also means that the investor faces greater risk from an increased exposure to a fluctuation in the prices of securities.

authority, nonetheless offers insurance on cash and securities left on deposit with a brokerage firm. The SIPC does, however, have the authority to liquidate a failing brokerage firm. Currently, the insurance limit is $500,000 per investor. All registered brokers must pay periodic premiums to the SIPC to cover the costs of insurance and of maintaining an insurance fund. In addition to its own resources, the SIPC has borrowing authority of up to $1 billion from the SEC and an additional $500 million from a group of banks. However, these borrowing options are expected to be used only to handle a temporary cash drain from unusually high claims experience.

Summary

Among all types of financial institutions, the investment banking firm stands out as perhaps the most innovative and adaptable of firms. A good investment bank will profit handsomely by being quick to exploit situations and market imbalances that may last only a short time. Even when there are few cycles in the bank's favor at any given time, the clever and innovative firm tends to use its time to develop new products and markets, leading to new business opportunities that will get it through the tough times until more of its departments become profitable.

The continuing evolution of the global financial marketplace is more in evidence year by year. To be successful in today's markets, an investment bank must have an ability to blend knowledge of significant local markets with an understanding of how those markets relate globally. This environment is vastly more complex than what had existed in past decades and is always evolving, vulnerable to events, and keenly competitive. In addition to the interpersonal skills that have characterized successful investment banks of the past, today sophisticated analytical, information technology, trading, and financing skills are needed to survive.

The strategic ideas and capabilities that foster success today are not necessarily those that will be the most appropriate tomorrow. To remain profitable, the investment bank must understand and adapt to change as a way of life. It must continue to look with a fresh eye for ways to improve services, refine its vision, and attract and retain individuals of high caliber. Yet with all of these challenges, and in a highly competitive and volatile world, the profit potential remains high for the best investment banks. Therefore, strong incentives exist to respond positively to the challenges, and we trust that investment banking will be of increasing importance to the economy over time as the challenges are met.

Key Concepts

advisory services,   485

administrative services,   485

asset management,   491

best efforts versus fixed-price offerings,   487

conflicts of interest and Chinese walls,   483, 490

distribution services,   487

investment banking versus investment banking
  function,   482

mergers and acquisitions,   489

price stabilization,   487

prospectus and red herring,   507

SEC forms 8K, 9K, and 10K,   508

securities sales and trading,   489

security flotation,   486

underwriting syndicate and selling group,   487–88

underwriting services,   486

Review Questions

1. Briefly outline the four functions that an investment bank performs. How are they interrelated? Does doing one function give the bank an advantage in performing all of the other functions associated with securities underwriting?

2. Why is it important for the corporation issuing a new security to have the underwriter correctly price the offering?

3. Scan through today's financial papers. Look for advertisements of initial public offerings and note the members of the underwriting syndicate versus the members of the selling group. Why is it that many of the same firm names appear on so many announcements? Why are the members of the selling syndicate often less well known than those of the underwriting syndicate?

4. Analyze the relative proportion of debt and equity issued over the last quarter of this year. How does it compare to the previous several years? Explain why it differs from the quarterly pace of offerings during the previous two years.

5. The focus of securities regulation is information disclosure. Some have argued that certain firms should be prohibited from issuing new securities because their activities are too risky. Contrast the view of appropriate regulation that is central to the establishment of the SEC with that of this lunatic fringe.

6. One of the rationales for entering into full-line investment banking services is to avoid the pitfalls of underwriting profit cyclicality. Which additional functional areas of a full-line investment bank are more likely to reduce this cyclicality?

References

Beatty, R., and Jay R. Ritter. "Investment Banking, Reputation and the Underpricing of Initial Public Offerings." *Journal of Financial Economics,* 1986.

Benston, George. *The Separation of Commercial and Investment Banking: The Glass-Steagall Act Revisited and Reconsidered.* New York: Oxford University Press, 1990.

Bhagat, S. "The Effects of Management's Choice between Negotiated and Competitive Equity Offerings on Shareholder Wealth." *Journal of Finance and Quantitative Analysis,* 1986.

Bloch, Ernest. *Inside Investment Banking.* Burr Ridge, Ill.: Business One Irwin, 1986.

Carter, R. and S. Manaster. "Initial Public Offerings and Underwriter Reputation." *Journal of Finance,* September 1990.

Chemmanur, Thomas J. and Paolo Fulghieri. "Investment Bank Reputation, Information Production, and Financial Intermediation." *Journal of Finance,* March 1994.

Eccles, Robert G. and Dwight B. Crane. *Doing Deals: Investment Banks at Work.* Boston: Harvard University Press, 1988.

Francis, Jack Clark. *Investments.* 5th ed. New York: McGraw-Hill, 1990.

Jaffe, Dwight M. *Money, Banking and Credit.* New York: Worth Publishers, 1989.

Kohn, Meir. *Financial Institutions and Markets.* New York: McGraw-Hill, 1994.

Kroszner, R. S., and R. G. Rajan. "Is the Glass-Steagall Act Justified? A Study of the U.S. Experience with Universal Banking before 1933." *American Economic Review,* September 1994.

Logue, Dennis, and Robert Jarrow. "Negotiation vs. Competitive Bidding in the Sales of Securities by Public Utilities." *Financial Management,* 1978.

Williamson, J. P. *The Investment Banking Handbook.* New York: J. Wiley & Co., 1988.

The Commercial Banking Industry

This chapter reviews the central role that banks play in both the financial and payment systems of the United States. The banks' balance sheets, profitability, and risk exposure are discussed in some detail, as is the regulatory structure under which they function. The history of commercial banking in the United States over the post-Depression era is also presented. The chapter concludes with an examination of the changing nature of commercial banking in the dynamic financial services industry.

Like many of his fellow graduating seniors, Joe had grown to like the small town in which his college was located, and he wanted to linger there awhile longer. The problem was that there were insufficient employment opportunities to make it economically viable for him to stay there. To earn a living in that town, Joe would have to be an entrepreneur.

Joe had been taught on the farm by his father that the big money was to be made not as a farmer but as a middleman. He learned in his economics class that a successful middleman is one who can parlay his location and knowledge of a market to his advantage.

Joe thought back to his days as an undergraduate and remembered the frustration that was common to many of his fellow students. There were no auto rental places in town, so students had to drive 25 miles to the nearest airport in order to rent one there. But with no convenient bus service, this begged the question: How does one get to the airport to rent the car in the first place? And another: After one has finished using it, how does one get from the airport back to campus? The only practical alternative was to persuade a friend with a car to twice make the 50-mile round-trip to the airport automobile rental agency.

This gave Joe an idea. He would merge his lifelong aspiration to be a middleman with the perceived need of students to be able to rent a car conveniently. Joe's car rental service would be different from others in one important respect. Instead of owning a fleet of vehicles, Collegiate Car Rental would rent them from the airport at their favorable weekly or monthly rental rates. Joe could then turn around and rent the cars at higher daily rates to students, thereby earning a profit. Joe's intimate knowledge of the community, which included access to information about the driving habits and creditworthiness of potential student customers, and his convenient location would give him a comparative advantage that would aid him in turning his venture into a profitable one.

In several ways, Joe's venture is similar to **commercial banking.** A commercial bank is a middleman of sorts, although we use the elegant name of a depository financial intermediary. It produces or manufactures nothing of its own, and unlike most middlemen, a commercial bank buys and sells very little. Instead, it has one commodity—money rather than cars—which it ''rents'' from one party and then ''rents out'' to others. The rent a commercial bank pays for money is in the form of interest, in the case of savings and time deposits, and in the form of the cost of providing convenient transfer and payment services, in the case of checking deposits. The rent it charges for use of the money is in the form of fees and interest on loans and investments. Like Joe's firm, a profitable commercial bank benefits from several important competitive advantages. These include an intimate knowledge of the community, familiarity regarding the creditworthiness of potential borrowers, and a convenient location. Unlike Joe's firm, a bank benefits

Exhibit 21.1   **Aggregate Commercial Bank Liabilities**
(December 1995)

	$ Billions	% of Total
Deposits		
Transaction accounts	$ 770.3	18.5%
Nontransaction accounts	1,878.5	45.1
Large time deposits	421.3	10.1
Other time deposits	1,457.1	35.0
Borrowings	673.7	16.2
Foreign offices	258.6	6.2
Other liabilities	222.0	5.3
Total liabilities	3,803.1	91.2
Total equity	364.8	8.8
Aggregate liabilities and capital	$3,633.1	100.0%

Source: *Federal Reserve Bulletin,* Table 1.26, March 1996.

in other areas as well. A bank has an insurance guarantee on its deposits, and therefore it has the ability to attract funds at a low cost.

In the sections that follow, we will examine in detail the financial intermediary known as a commercial bank. We will review its sources and uses of funds. Then, we will explore the business risks that face the commercial bank in its endeavor to earn a spread between the cost of funds and the returns from the use of funds. Finally, we will outline the regulatory framework established to assure that the commercial bank sector functions well and provides needed services to consumer and commercial clients.

Sources of Funds

Commercial banks obtain their funds from several sources. Perhaps the most visible sources are checking deposits and savings accounts of various forms. However, these institutions also raise funds from the issuance of various types of nondeposit securities. In addition, commercial banks issue equity capital of various forms both to sustain operations and to satisfy the regulators. The relative magnitude of each income source is indicated in Exhibit 21.1, which looks at all sources of funds for the commercial banking industry as a whole. Notice that this figure is $4.2 trillion (seasonally adjusted) as of December 1995. Of this total, transaction accounts constitute slightly less than 20 percent of the industry's funding. Nontransaction accounts, other than large time deposits, provide 35 percent, while nondeposit borrowing and large time deposits provide 16.2 percent and 10.1 percent, respectively. We will now discuss each of these income categories in turn.

Deposits at Commercial Banks

Banks attract funds through the administration of various depository accounts that, combined, represent the majority of their funding base. There are two main types of depository accounts: transaction accounts and nontransaction accounts.

Transaction Accounts.   The term **transaction accounts** refers to what were once widely known as checking accounts in the United States. In other places they are often referred to as sight deposits. Certain transaction accounts are primarily used by businesses and pay no interest. These are commonly called **demand deposits.** Other checkable deposits are held primarily by consumers and can pay interest. **Negotiable orders of withdrawal (NOW)** account is the term given to what is perhaps the most visible interest-bearing checking account. Some of these accounts require very little by way of balances to pay interest, while others offer more favorable interest rates but require a high minimum balance, for example, $2,500 dollars. In many cases, these deposit accounts charge transaction fees or monthly maintenance charges to cover these services, but in any case, they serve as the basic transaction account for both households and firms.

A recent innovation in these transaction accounts is the issuance of debit cards. **Debit cards** can be used to withdraw or deposit funds in checking and savings accounts via an **automated teller machine** (ATM). In addition, these plastic cards may also be used to make purchases, much in the same way as checks and cash, in what is referred to as a **point of sale** (POS) transaction. The purchaser simply presents the plastic card to the vendor and enters a password; the vendor then enters the dollar amount of the transaction. In this way, funds are transferred from the buyer's checking account to the vendor's account, without the need of paper checks and the accompanying processing costs.

The main purpose of holding balances in a transaction account is to facilitate monetary exchange, that is, to permit payments to be made in exchange for a purchase. The costs to the bank for the funds deposited is the rather substantial administrative and check processing costs and, for some of these checkable accounts, the interest cost associated with average balances.

Savings and Time Accounts.   Sometimes referred to as **nontransaction deposits** or **time deposits**, these accounts are a major source of bank funds. This category includes various types of deposits that earn interest but are generally not used to pay bills. These types of accounts include retail **savings accounts, money market accounts**, and various kinds of **certificates of deposit.**

The first of these accounts is the standard retail savings account, sometimes referred to as a **passbook savings account.** This account derives its name from the passbook that is used to track the deposits and withdrawals and is presented for each transaction. In any case, the passbook savings account is the most flexible of the savings vehicles. Deposits and withdrawals can be made at any time, as often as desired, and in any amount without invoking a penalty, unlike with time deposits and some money market accounts.

Money market accounts are the second form of savings account. These deposits may offer a somewhat higher yield to depositors, who are generally required to hold higher balances in the accounts. An outgrowth of the banks' attempt to compete directly with money market instruments and mutual funds for the consumers' investment dollars, the money market account's name reflects its aspiration. In fact, yields are often below open market rates and are frequently slow to change. In these kinds of accounts, the investor may have the ability to draw checks to pay bills. However, there is usually a low limit on the number of checks that can be written against each account in any given month—such as two drafts per month.

The rates of interest paid on savings accounts and money market deposits are typically somewhat lower than returns that can be obtained through direct capital market security purchases. Nonetheless, these accounts have remained competitive. Depositors willingly accept these lower rates due to the increased convenience of these accounts, which provide easy access at any time, and the existence of deposit insurance up to $100,000.

Certificates of deposit, while also covered by deposit insurance up to the same $100,000 limit, impose somewhat more restrictive conditions upon the investor. They are designed to be held until maturity and bear a fixed interest rate stated on a printed certificate. If redeemed prior to maturity, certificates of deposit may carry a substantial interest penalty, amounting to several months of lost interest. They are held for investment purposes, mostly by individuals, and carry maturities generally ranging from three months to five years. When issued in denominations of $100,000 or more, certificates of deposit are usually negotiable instruments. These are denoted "large time deposits" in Exhibit 21.1 and are held primarily by other banks and nonfinancial businesses.

Nondeposit Liabilities

In addition to depository accounts, banks issue a variety of debt obligations to attract funds. These securities, unlike the deposit liabilities discussed above, are not covered by federal deposit insurance, but they can be used to raise large amounts of cash quickly and to provide funds of a particular desired maturity. At times, it is cheaper to raise funds in this way than through deposit taking because these instruments escape levies for deposit insurance and come with no expectation of services to be provided by the bank. Some of these borrowing instruments have been discussed in prior chapters. For example, **federal funds** may be borrowed from other commercial banks, a discount loan may be obtained from the Fed, and a bank may borrow from financial and nonfinancial corporations via security repurchase agreements (REPOs) or floating rate notes. Banks also obtain funds by borrowing from their holding companies, which, in turn, issue their own debt. This issuance may be in the domestic capital market, as in the case of commercial paper issued by the bank's holding company. Alternatively, the bank may tap the Eurodollar market, where they can obtain U.S. dollar-denominated deposits from foreign investors and from foreign branches of U.S. banks. You will notice that 6.2 percent of the funding of the U.S. banking system is obtained through foreign offices, as shown in Exhibit 21.1. There are a plethora of places to borrow money if you are large, supported by government regulation, and willing to pay the right price!

Equity Capital

Beyond these debt instruments, the bank has its own **equity capital** supporting bank activity. A bank will attract equity capital through the issuance of both common and preferred stock. In addition, the banking industry has a large amount of retained earnings, which, over time, can increase the bank capital account. By the same token, losses over time can reduce the capital account. For instance, if a bank or bank examiner determines that a particular loan is unlikely to ever be repaid, the loan is removed as an asset on the bank's balance sheet and a corresponding reduction is made in the bank's loan loss allowance account. If this proves insufficient to cover the loss, funds are transferred from the bank's capital account. While equity constitutes a relatively small portion of the funds raised by a typical bank—generally between 4 and 8 percent of total capital—it is nonetheless a very important source of funds because it provides the cushion against losses and deleterious economic events. It is for this reason that regulators around the world have paid increasing attention to this area of bank balance sheets.[1]

The cost of this bank capital is equal to the dividend stream that investors expect. Remember, investors here are the same as investors in any other equity issue. They measure their return, as we have shown in Chapter 14, by looking at current dividends paid plus whatever capital gains they expect to receive. This expected total return must be sufficient to entice them to hold the equity.

In addition to straight common stock, the industry has been increasing its issuance of various hybrid financial obligations. These securities are referred to as hybrids because their behavior falls somewhere between debt and equity in terms of their claim on bank earnings, their seniority, or their maturity. The simplest of these securities is perpetual noncumulative, **variable-rate preferred stock.** These issues are clearly equity of the financial institution. However, because their return is tied to current market interest levels, as well as the bank's profitability for the period, they are similar to floating-rate debt instruments.

At the other extreme, the bank may issue **subordinated debt** with either a fixed or variable rate of return. This is an obligation that is independent of the bank's ability to pay. Indeed, if the bank cannot cover the interest on its debt, it may well be forced into bankruptcy or liquidation. The differentiating feature of this instrument from other nondeposit liabilities, however, is that its covenants

---

[1]The issue of bank capital is larger than the space we can devote to it here. For a discussion of the issue, see Anthony Santomero, "The Bank Capital Issue," in *Financial Regulations and Monetary Arrangements after 1992,* M. Fratianni, C. Wihlborg, T. Willett, editors (North Holland Press, 1991). In addition, see Box 21.2 (pp. 532–33) for a discussion of current regulation.

place its claim on assets below others—hence, the use of subordination in the title. Such debt generally has a maturity beyond seven years at issue. These two features, subordination and long maturity, have led regulators to define it as secondary capital and to allow banks to include it with common and preferred stock of various kinds in the definition of total capital for regulatory purposes.

In recent years, several of the large banks have been attracted to one particular type of hybrid security, **perpetual floaters.** A perpetual floater is actually a debt instrument that pays an interest rate that floats with a spread over some recognized short-term interest rate index, such as LIBOR. Because interest paid is deductible for tax purposes, it represents an attractive alternative to common and preferred equity. Although a perpetual floater is actually a debt instrument, the perpetual nature of it—whereby the principal is never repaid—has led some bank regulators around the world to treat it as equity capital rather than debt for capital adequacy regulation purposes, just as in the case of subordinated debt mentioned above.

The fact that perpetual floaters always pay current interest rates may lead one to suspect that the value would always trade near par, but this is not the case. The interest paid is tied to an index of short rates, but a deterioration in the credit quality of the particular bank issuer can render the interest rates paid woefully inadequate to compensate for the default risk. The latter has led to dramatic reductions in market value, to 40 percent of par value for some issues and even lower at times.

Uses of Funds

The commercial bank seeks to deploy all of the funds it raises in a manner that generates income above and beyond the expense incurred by the institution to obtain the funds. In this regard, the commercial bank is actually no different from any other profit-seeking firm. What distinguishes a bank is the manner in which it raises funds and the ways in which it deploys them. As we have just reviewed the first, let us now look at the second—uses of funds.

There are several categories of assets in which a commercial bank deploys its funds: cash and cash equivalents, deposits, investment securities, loans, and physical capital. The relative importance of each category for the industry as a whole as of the end of 1995 is demonstrated in Exhibit 21.2. As is evident, each of these broad categories has several elements.

Cash and Cash Equivalents

Banks cannot deploy all of their funds. Because there is always a demand for ongoing transactions that require cash, and because of regulatory concern over liquidity, banks maintain some of their resources in highly liquid form.[2] Accordingly, a bank maintains **vault cash** for day-to-day contingencies, and it also

---

[2]Some have argued that this is just a mechanism to gain implicit revenue, as requiring banks to hold non-interest-bearing reserves allows the Federal Reserve to finance the government debt more cheaply. At the end of each year, Federal Reserve profits revert to the Treasury.

EXHIBIT 21.2   **Aggregate Uses of Commercial Bank Funds**
(December 31, 1995)

	$ Billions	% of Total
Cash items	$ 221.2	5.3%
Securities		
U.S. government	708.7	17.0
Other	274.6	6.6
Loans		
Interbank	198.6	4.8
Commercial	710.8	17.1
Real estate	1,073.6	25.8
Individual	492.8	11.8
Other	233.3	5.6
Other assets	230.4	5.5
Total assets	$4,167.9	100.0%

Source: *Federal Reserve Bulletin,* Table 1.26, March 1996.

maintains deposits in a **clearing account** at the Fed. Both of these types of balances pay no interest. However, bank regulators require that a certain amount of funds be maintained both in vault cash and in the clearing account. This required amount is referred to as **required reserves.** The size of required reserves is based upon the structure of the bank's liabilities. Currently, reserves are required only against transaction accounts, but they have been traditionally assessed against various types of time and savings deposits as well. (See Exhibit 21.3.)

Beyond the required minimum level of reserves, a bank may wish to maintain **excess reserves** in order to have sufficient liquidity to conduct its daily business efficiently and to handle any unforeseen contingencies that may arise. However, because reserves are not earning assets, it is generally desirable, from a profitability perspective, to keep these balances as low as is practicable.

At any moment in time, a commercial bank is likely to be in possession of numerous checks and drafts issued by other banks and their customers. These are treated as **cash in the process of collection**, and they are usually considered to be liquid assets. Beyond this, most banks have deposits at other banks. A small bank will deposit some funds with a large one in return for help in executing its transactions. Large banks may have clearing balances with one another, particularly internationally. These deposits may be interest bearing, but they are intended to compensate the recipient bank for its correspondent banking services.

On the other hand, banks may be holding deposits for the earnings they offer. Like other investors, they see CDs of other institutions and Eurodollar CDs as viable investment vehicles that offer both return and a certain degree of liquidity in the secondary market. Additionally, these assets offer a maturity choice that may fit nicely into the bank's goals to limit the mismatch between the duration of assets and liabilities. More will be said on this point in Chapter 25.

EXHIBIT 21.3   **Reserve Requirements of Depository Institutions**

Type of Deposit	Percentage of Deposits	Effective Date
Net transaction accounts		
$0 million–$52 million	3%	12/19/1995
More than $52 million	10	12/19/1995
Nonpersonal time deposits	0	12/27/1990
Eurocurrency liabilities	0	12/27/1990

Required reserves must be held in the form of deposits with Federal Reserve Banks or vault cash. Nonmember institutions may maintain reserve balances with a Federal Reserve Bank indirectly, on a pass-through basis, with certain approved institutions. For previous reserve requirements, see earlier editions of the *Annual Report* or the *Federal Reserve Bulletin.* Under the Monetary Control Act of 1980, depository institutions include commercial banks, mutual savings banks, savings and loan associations, credit unions, agencies and branches of foreign banks, and Edge Act corporations.

Transaction accounts include all deposits against which the account holder is permitted to make withdrawals by negotiable or transferable instruments, payment orders of withdrawal, and telephone and preauthorized transfers for the purpose of making payments to third persons or others. However, money market deposit accounts (MMDAs) and similar accounts subject to the rules that permit no more than six preauthorized, automatic, or other transfers per month, of which no more than three may be checks, are savings deposits, not transaction accounts.

The Monetary Control Act of 1980 requires that the amount of transaction accounts against which the 3 percent reserve requirement applies be modified annually by 80 percent of the percentage change in transaction accounts held by all depository institutions, determined as of June 30 of each year. Effective Dec. 19, 1995, the amount was decreased from $54.0 million to $52.0 million.

Under the Garn–St Germain Depository Institutions Act of 1982, the Board adjusts the amount of reservable liabilities subject to a zero percent reserve requirement each year for the succeeding calendar year by 80 percent of the percentage increase in the total reservable liabilities of all depository institutions, measured on an annual basis as of June 30. No corresponding adjustment is made in the event of a decrease. Effective Dec. 19, 1995, the exemption was raised from $4.2 million to $4.3 million. The exemption applies only to accounts that would be subject to a 3 percent reserve requirement.

The reserve requirement was reduced from 12 percent to 10 percent on Apr. 2, 1992, for institutions that report weekly, and on Apr. 16, 1992, for institutions that report quarterly.

For institutions that report weekly, the reserve requirement on nonpersonal time deposits with an original maturity of less than 1½ years was reduced from 3 percent to 1½ percent for the maintenance period that began Dec. 13, 1990, and to zero for the maintenance period that began Dec. 27, 1990. The reserve requirement on nonpersonal time deposits with an original maturity of 1½ years or more has been zero since Oct. 6, 1983.

For institutions that report quarterly, the reserve requirement on nonpersonal time deposits with an original maturity of less than 1½ years was reduced from 3 percent to zero on Jan. 17, 1991.

The reserve requirement on Eurocurrency liabilities was reduced from 3 percent to zero in the same manner and on the same dates as was the reserve requirement on nonpersonal time deposits with an original maturity of less than 1½ years.

Source: *Federal Reserve Bulletin.*

Investment Securities

In light of our earlier observation that a bank raises funds in part by issuing securities, it may seem curious that a bank also invests in securities. The conundrum becomes more curious when one observes the kinds of securities predominately held in bank portfolios. These are issues of federal, agency, state, and municipal governments. How is a bank going to earn a profit on these securities unless it is able to issue its own securities at lower rates of interest than the government's securities? Rarely is a bank safer than a city or state government, and even more rare is the bank that is safer than the U.S. government, which can always resort to printing money to repay its debt. Thus, the bank should not be able to issue securities that pay a lower rate of interest than that paid by the government securities. Yet banks do hold these assets, and in substantial volume. Why?

Unfortunately, there is no one answer to this conundrum. Rather, there are six different but reasonably valid explanations for this phenomenon. First, a bank will often invest in securities of a different maturity than those it issues. For example, it may raise money in the fed funds market, which is typically an overnight market, and reinvest in securities with a longer maturity. If the term structure of interest is positively sloped, the bank may be able to earn more on its securities investments than it is paying for funds, even though its own creditworthiness is less than that of the governments that issue the securities in which it invests. This strategy is fraught with interest rate risk and is limited to some degree by regulatory authorities. In days of yore, before interest rates exhibited the kind of volatility of the 1980s and 1990s, this practice was more widespread. More will be said about the dubious nature of this strategy in Chapter 25.

Second, the purchase of governmental securities may induce the government to conduct other, more profitable business with the bank and to maintain profit-making accounts there. Thus, the government securities themselves may appear to be unprofitable, but considered as a package, the business becomes profitable.

Third, government securities are often quite liquid, and holding them can serve as a secondary source of reserves, if needed. Accordingly, some are held for this reason even if the bank has no other relationship to the governmental unit.

Fourth, some state and local securities offer attractive yields that can yield more to a bank than it costs to raise funds. This is due to one of two reasons: (1) Some municipalities have more credit risk than certain banks and can therefore carry higher yields than bank paper, or (2) the tax-exempt status of the issue offers an after-tax effective yield sufficiently high to warrant investment. The first of these reasons may make you run to your bank to withdraw your money, but the second is classic tax planning by the institution.

Fifth, government securities can serve as a convenient vehicle to invest funds temporarily until some more profitable lending opportunity comes along or can be negotiated. Here, the shorter maturity offers a temporary abode that yields low but not insignificant returns.

Finally, security purchases and sales can be used to quickly alter the duration of an asset portfolio to some desired level. Accordingly, it may be part of a proactive risk reduction strategy along the lines suggested earlier for CD purchases. As we have already noted, more will be said of this in Chapter 25.

In addition to government securities, commercial banks are also able to hold the securities of other financial institutions beyond those formally designated as deposits. Some of these, such as bankers' acceptances, are a key part of the investment portfolio for all of the same reasons outlined above. However, under current regulations, commercial banks are prohibited from holding nonfinancial corporate securities for their own investment account. They are, therefore, limited to the government and financial institution market for investment opportunities.

Loans

The major category of investments for many commercial banks has been loans. This makes economic sense. It is difficult for any institution to make profits consistently by issuing generic liabilities, such as deposits and other debt securities, and then turning around and investing the proceeds in other generic securities, such as commercial paper, notes, or government bonds. While the bank's position in its local market may permit it to raise its funds somewhat less expensively than open market borrowers, its total profit must not depend on this source alone. Considering the costs associated with raising and servicing deposits, an institution using this strategy is more likely to be losing money than to be making it, unless it has a large competitive advantage such as superior skill in selecting those securities that will outperform the market.

That is why many banks seek to parlay their natural advantage—having superior information about their clients—into a profitable enterprise. They do this by issuing mostly local liabilities, such as personal checking and savings accounts, and investing the money in individual or commercial loans made to their own customer base, about which they have detailed knowledge. In focusing on specialized liabilities and assets, both of which require a substantial amount of local information, a bank is able to earn larger spreads between their cost of funds and the return on their investments than a simple money manager who tries to make the best picks among assets at prices set in the open market. The advent of the information age, however, is reducing the bank's ability to keep this information advantage. With the availability of credit reports, nonbanks have recently invaded many of the previously bank-only markets such as credit cards and mortgage lending. This trend, discussed further in Chapter 24, has led banks themselves to look beyond their local market and simple products for profit. We will illustrate this in the next section of this chapter.

This trend notwithstanding, banks still depend upon lending for a substantial portion of their profit and activity. Many of the loans a bank makes to individuals and firms are secured by real estate. This area of banking is referred to as **mortgage** lending. From Exhibit 21.2, it should be noted that this component of lending accounts for more than 25 percent of the total assets of the banking industry. In addition, consumers borrow for durable goods, such as automobiles, and to finance current consumer spending. Some of this lending is secured; some is not. In the latter category is the burgeoning market for unsecured consumer debt, also known as **credit card receivables.** This is a natural service for banks to offer since they can take advantage of the information they already have about the creditworthiness and financial condition of their depositors. However, the product itself is fairly complicated.

When a consumer makes a purchase using a Visa or MasterCard issued by a bank, the bank makes immediate payment to the vendor, but at a discount of 1 to 6 percent. The funds with which the bank makes payment to the vendor come from the bank initially, as the consumer has done nothing but sign the slip. The bank then collects the full value of the funds from the consumer on his regular billing cycle due date, thereby profiting from the spread. Another profitable opportunity is presented to the bank if the consumer is unable to make full payment on the due date. In this case, a loan is automatically extended to him, at an amount not to exceed his prearranged credit limits and at a preset interest rate. Periodic payments are expected thereafter until the debt is settled. Most credit card issuers charge a steep interest rate on credit granted under these terms, and consumers sometimes take several years to pay off the credit card balances on their accounts. Therefore, they represent fairly attractive returns.

However, there are costs that must be subtracted from this wide margin. The difference between the full value charged to the consumer and the discounted amount paid to the vendor represents only the gross profit to the bank issuer. From this gross profit must be subtracted the costs of funds, the cost of bad consumer credit, and the administrative costs of processing the bills. These costs are quite substantial and reduce the profitability of this product line from excessive to only attractive, as will be shown below.

In addition to consumer lending activity, the commercial bank has a large and important **commercial and industrial loan** portfolio. Indeed, the industry's name rests upon the assumption that its primary role is to provide the funds needed for the commercial sector. Such business loans are often a large and important part of the bank's balance sheet. Here, however, the challenge is to find projects that are both worthy of investment and can pay an interest rate sufficient to cover the bank's transactions costs and cost of funds. Yields on these loans are generally lower than on consumer lending, yet commitments are large. Therefore, a smaller interest rate spread still leads to high dollar profit per customer, at least if the loan is repaid. With a small capital base, relative to total assets, the bank must be exceedingly conservative in its lending. Losses can quickly erode capital and cause failure.

Tangible Property

One final category of assets that a commercial bank typically holds is real property, such as buildings, furniture, equipment, computers, and the like. These are included in the "other assets" category of Exhibit 21.2. These assets are usually not very liquid and constitute a small part of a bank's asset portfolio. By accounting tradition, these assets are kept at original purchase price less depreciation, and they account for only a fairly small fraction of total assets. Your local bank may have a formidable edifice, but it doesn't use much of its resources on physical plant and equipment. However, for banks that own, rather than rent, choice property, this asset category can be rather important.

Activities beyond the Bank Balance Sheet

Thus far, we have discussed the activity of the commercial banking industry by reviewing the assets and liabilities on the bank's balance sheet. However, today, banks have outgrown their own balance sheets and the restricted set of activities in which they are allowed to engage. They have sought to move beyond their initial area of activity in two ways. First, most institutions have formed holding companies. A **bank holding company** is a corporate entity that owns the commercial bank and may also own a whole set of other firms that are engaged in various kinds of financial activities, including mortgage banking, consumer lending, and a whole host of other related businesses. These firms expand the reach of the bank, while frequently bearing the brand name of the so-called **lead bank** of the holding company.

The second way a banking institution may increase its activity is to engage in businesses and provide products and services that do not show up on its balance sheet directly. In the ever-changing financial markets, there are many opportunities to offer services or sell products that do not directly involve the bank's balance sheet. The reason bankers have increasingly looked for these activities can be summed up in one word: competition. There has been tremendous competition facing the modern bank, forcing the spreads between the cost of funds and the return on investments to narrow and causing its market share to decline even in those areas where it has traditionally concentrated. Exacerbating this situation is the increased economic volatility of recent decades and the accompanying uncertainty regarding the ability to maintain any given spread over time.

Hence, many commercial banks today derive a sizable portion of their revenues from both subsidiary and **off-balance-sheet** activities. Rather than retain assets and liabilities on the bank's balance sheet for long periods of time, these firms generate much of their income from subsidiary activities and from fees charged for various services performed beyond any part of the banking firm's balance sheet. In the first case, new business opportunities are pursued without the constraints and regulation that are part of the banking industry.[3] In the second case, much of the financial risk—interest rate risk, credit risk, liquidity risk, and foreign exchange risk—is passed through to the parties being serviced by the commercial bank.

We will not attempt to provide an exhaustive list of all of the areas of bank activity in which fees may be generated for services, but we will give a few examples below. Because this area of a bank's operations is rapidly expanding, any list must necessarily be incomplete by the time it is published in a textbook. Nonetheless, most of the important services can be grouped into the areas of traditional banking services, investment management, advisory services, brokerage services, and underwriting.

Banking Services through Subsidiaries

As noted above, bank holding companies, through their subsidiaries, have traditionally offered many services that are closely related to or are equivalent to banking products. In fact, by regulation, the activities of the bank holding

---

[3]However, bank holding company activity is regulated, albeit somewhat differently, by the Federal Reserve.

company and its subsidiaries are restricted to these areas. The Federal Reserve, which is responsible for the authorization of bank holding company activity, must find that the business conforms to these criteria. Nonetheless, the holding company structure has permitted geographic and product expansion by commercial banks into a wide range of financial activities, including mortgage banking, consumer lending, leasing, real estate appraisal, and credit insurance.

Investment Management Services

For many commercial banks, investment management is a major revenue producer. Although they are prohibited from making certain investments in corporate securities for their own accounts, banks manage billions of dollars worth of securities for wealthy individuals, corporate clients, and various kinds of retirement asset funds through their trust and investment departments or subsidiaries. They also manage assets for corporate and/or union pension funds; various types of mutual funds, including money market mutual funds; and other investment companies. In each case, commercial banks exploit their investment skills and knowledge of the securities markets. This has made trust and investment management a rapidly growing part of bank activity and a new, fierce competitor to other investment managers in the financial markets.

Advisory Services

Because of their expertise in financial markets and their relationships to depositors and borrowers, banks are also well situated to offer other advisory services. These advisory services include economic analysis, investment and financial advising, asset valuation services, and bankruptcy-workout counseling. While a commercial bank does not act as a real estate broker, it often provides real estate appraisal services for its clients. Its access to valuable databases and familiarity with regulatory and tax matters also enable the bank to provide bookkeeping and data processing services to both nonfinancial and financial corporate clients, as well as to individuals.

Brokerage Services

In recent years, several bank holding companies have begun to offer securities brokerage services, including discount brokerage. An early example was Bank of America's foray into discount stock brokerage through the acquisition of Charles Schwab and Company. Other banks have entered into the market as well. Although these services are officially offered through a separate subsidiary of the bank holding company, the services may be provided within the confines of the commercial bank offices, and the separation of a commercial banking subsidiary from a stock brokerage subsidiary is not particularly apparent to the bank customer. Banks also may be broker/dealers in gold, silver, and rare coins.

Another area in which banks act as brokers is insurance. Credit insurance, which is often used to insure repayment of loans, is offered directly by banks.

Other kinds of insurance may be offered through banks under certain restricted conditions, but the restrictions against bank activity in insurance have eroded in recent years. More will be said about this issue in Chapter 24.

Underwriting

Banks are prohibited from underwriting most corporate securities other than commercial paper, but this prohibition is eroding. Currently, all banking institutions are able to underwrite general obligation bonds and debentures of municipalities, states, federal agencies, and the U.S. government. Some banks are major players in these markets, where they may have an advantage over investment banks when it comes to underwriting state and local bond issues. The political ties and geographical proximity that commercial banks have to the issuer are not irrelevant considerations. At the same time, the size of these banks gives them stature in the federal agency and Treasury markets.

However, more recently, several institutions have also been able to directly compete in the market for both corporate debt and equity. Banks entered this market through a loophole in the Glass-Steagall Act. This portion of the Banking Act of 1933 prohibited commercial banks from directly engaging in or affiliating with institutions that were principally engaged in underwriting securities. Over time, however, the corporate parent of the commercial bank, the so-called bank holding company, has been allowed to establish a separate subsidiary to engage in securities market activity. These Section 20 subsidiaries, named after the section of the aforementioned law, have substantially increased the presence of the commercial banking industry in the underwriting area. Although a bank's underwriting of corporate debt and equities is limited to 10 percent of its securities unit's annual revenue, there is currently a strong push to get that limit relaxed to 25 percent of revenue, or even abolished altogether. This effort is pressing because, early in 1996, some banks have been bumping up against, and even exceeding, that limit. Banks are in these businesses to stay, and the competition with their friends in the investment banks is likely to heat up over time.

Profitability of Commercial Banking

With all of these products and activities, how well is the industry performing? An idea about the profitability of this industry can be gleaned from Exhibit 21.4, which presents the two most frequently cited measures of performance—**return on assets** and **return on equity**—over a 60-year horizon. These figures report the profit per dollar of either total assets or equity capital on the balance sheet.

The results are surprisingly volatile, and the return on assets are quite small. For all its efforts, the industry achieved a profit of less than 1 percent on assets over the past 60 years. Over the last decade, these numbers have been no better. While the returns of the industry over the past three years are impressive, they follow two periods of below-average profit. Also, volatility has substantially increased over the past decade.

EXHIBIT 21.4

Return on assets (ROA) and equity (ROE) (1934–1995)

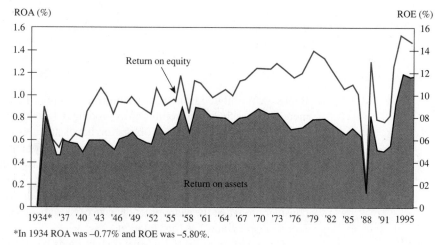

*In 1934 ROA was −0.77% and ROE was −5.80%.

Source: Federal Reserve System, Washington, D.C.

Reasons can be offered for this mediocre performance, and some explanation is in order. Exhibit 21.5 offers some insight, focusing on the past five years of U.S. banking experience. Panel A shows that the U.S. banking system had seen a substantial deterioration in the quality of its loan portfolio. Past due and problem loans, labeled here as noncurrent loans, plus repossessed real estate, were a substantial problem in the 1980s and into the 1990s. In 1991, the problem peaked at above 5 percent of total loans for the industry as a whole. This caused severe losses over the period for some institutions. In fact, in 1989, almost 12 percent of the commercial banks lost money. This number rose to 13 percent in 1990. The recovery in earnings during 1992 and 1993 was a direct result of an improving asset portfolio, as the cyclical decline of the last business cycle was overcome. As asset quality improved, profitability increased rather dramatically, as evidenced by the strong recovery of the return on assets since 1991.

The return on equity tells a similar story. The return on assets is leveraged up to obtain the return on equity. As profitability returned to the industry, the return on equity rose in concert with the return on assets. However, the return on equity increased less than the return on assets because of a large build-up of capital in the banking industry that occurred during the same period. This build-up was partially a result of increased emphasis on capital by the regulatory authorities and concerns about solvency by the industry itself.

Followers of the industry are far from convinced, however, that the recent surge in profitability is sustainable. The industry and all its members are under increasing pressure from the full range of financial institutions, making profitability more difficult to achieve. This has led many to forecast a decline in the banking industry in general, as commercial bank customers move to investment banks and the nondepository institutions described in Chapter 23. Others, however, have argued that the environmental change will force the industry to

Exhibit 21.5

Financial ratios for U.S. commercial banks

A. Noncurrent assets to total loans
Commercial banks

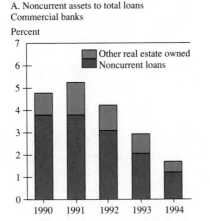

B. Percent of institutions losing money
Commercial banks

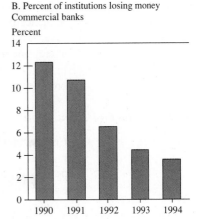

C. Return on average assets
Commercial banks

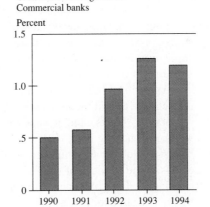

Source: Federal Reserve Bank of Kansas City, *Financial Industry Trends,* 1995.

change and respond to the new challenges. They point out that it is these same factors that explain the movement to broader product lines and off-balance-sheet activities. In fact, the move to fee-based services has led some institutions to report earnings in which more than 50 percent of their income comes from off-balance-sheet, fee-based services. Suffice it to say that such a transformation will be required if the banks of today are to be the banks of tomorrow.

Commercial Bank Regulation

Commercial banking in the United States is perhaps the most regulated business of all. The early history of its regulation is reminiscent of attempts to diminish the size of a balloon by squeezing it. In the case of a balloon, this is usually an exercise in futility, as the air quickly rushes to another area of the balloon and causes it to protrude there. Only if the grasp is sufficiently encompassing can an influence be exerted upon the ultimate size of the balloon. However, even in this case, extreme care must be exercised to prevent the balloon from bursting while attempting to constrain its shape. Similarly, the history of bank regulation is one in which regulators have attempted to fully encompass the industry without breaking it in the process. To see this, let us begin with the basics.

The Structure of Regulation

Commercial banks in the United States must have a charter to operate. The charter may be granted by either the federal or state government. The choice of a charter determines the degree of regulatory oversight by federal and state agencies. Federal supervision is generally more stringent, but state regulation stringency varies somewhat from state to state. Most banks have elected to be chartered by states; those choosing a federal charter are called **national banks.** National banks are generally larger than **state banks,** although some of the nation's largest banks, such as J. P. Morgan, operate under state charters.

Banks operating under state charters are supervised by a **state bank commissioner,** or **Superintendent of Banks.** Banks operating under a national charter are supervised by the **Comptroller of the Currency,** who is an official of the U.S. Department of the Treasury.

All national banks are members of the Federal Reserve System. A state bank may choose to join the Federal Reserve System. The Federal Reserve supervises its member banks, and it supervises bank holding companies, regardless of whether or not the bank itself is a member of the Fed. Member and nonmember banks are subject to a number of regulations of the Federal Reserve and have access to the services of the Federal Reserve System (FRS) lending and check-clearing facilities. All banks must maintain the statutory reserve requirements set by the Fed. In addition, as the central clearinghouse for checks and reserve balances, the Fed affects all banks through its policies and rules. (More will be said about this and the important role of the Federal Reserve in Chapter 27.)

Deposits in commercial banks are generally insured by the **Federal Deposit Insurance Corporation** (FDIC), which came into existence in 1933 by congressional charter. However, in the past, some deposits were insured by state insurance agencies. Now, all banks subscribe to the insurance of the FDIC by paying periodic premiums that are related to their total deposit base and level of risk. The FDIC examines its subscribers for safety and sound banking practices. Deposits are insured up to $100,000 in each account in the event of a bank default resulting in a situation where a bank is unable to repay its depositors.

Purposes of Commercial Bank Regulation

Regulation can be established for several purposes. Bank regulation was established primarily to maintain the stability of the banking system. This purpose leads bank regulators to consider two goals, namely, limiting the risk that banks incur, and promoting competition. The real fear of a regulator, however, is a crisis of confidence in the system that results in a full **banking panic.** Let's look into the regulator's nightmare.

Understanding a Banking Panic.   Commercial banks and other depository institutions are in an inherently unstable situation. To some extent, they have liquid liabilities and frozen, or at least illiquid, assets. Their assets are largely in loans that have fixed future dates for repayments; there is little banks can do to accelerate the payments in the event that immediate cash is required. Their liabilities, on the other hand, are largely checking and savings deposits, which, in large measure, can be converted to cash and withdrawn immediately. In this sense, they are liquid. These conditions provide the fuel necessary for a run on a bank and a full blown banking panic. All that is needed is a spark to ignite a run. The spark usually comes in the form of a rumor, which may be true or false, that some economic event has reduced the value of a bank's assets and has impaired its ability to meet its obligations to depositors.

This may lead to a **panic,** where a run at one bank precipitates runs at other, inherently healthy, banks. The contagion to other banks arises due to the incomplete information that bank depositors and equityholders have about the soundness of their banks. They know that banks may fail due to a deterioration in general economic conditions as well as due to problems that are peculiar to a particular bank. At any point in time, investors have only imperfect estimates as to whether the causes afflicting a particular failing bank will have more widespread impact. As a precautionary measure, they may seek to withdraw their funds from other banks. If enough investors do this, even the best-managed bank will suffer from liquidity problems, and a panic will ensue. The problem with a panic is not that the weak banks fail but that many of the ones operating on a perfectly sound basis will also fail. The disruption to the economy from such a phenomenon is greater than society is willing to accept.[4]

Methods of Commercial Bank Regulation

To reduce the likelihood of the problem illustrated above, bank regulators have been given a host of tools to ensure the stability of the banking system. In fact, many experts would argue that they have too many! But before we discuss this view, let's review these regulatory tools and their purposes. For expositional ease, these regulations may be broken into three distinct groups, each aimed at a different part of the problem: (1) procedures and institutional arrangements established to reduce the likelihood and severity of a banking panic; (2) regulations instituted to limit the risk that any one bank may take, with a goal of limiting the vulnerability of the system as a whole; and (3) procedures established to promote the health and competition within the sector. We now consider each in turn.

---

[4]Interested students may wish to investigate the U.S. history of bank runs by reading Ben Bernanke, "Nonmonetary Effects of the Financial Crisis in the Propagation of the Great Depression," *American Economic Review,* June 1983; or Milton Friedman and Anna Schwartz, *A Monetary History of the United States: 1867–1960* (Princeton, N.J.: Princeton University Press, 1963).

Box 21.1

Anatomy of a Bank Run

To illustrate how a bank run develops along the lines outlined in the text, consider the following situation. A bank has 100 depositors, each of whom has deposited $1,000. Thus, the bank has $100,000 in liabilities. Coupled with the bank's equity of 5 percent, the institution had total resources of $105,000. Prior to the precipitating event, let's assume that the bank holds all $105,000 in loans. Now, suppose that one of its borrowers announces that it cannot repay its loan. This causes the bank's assets to decline. The first to lose as a result of this turn of events are the equityholders. But their capital may be insufficient to absorb the loss. Suppose, for example, that the result is that assets are reduced in value to $95,000. This means that each depositor now has only 95¢ of assets backing each dollar deposited. In other words, the average depositor has lost $50 per $1,000 deposited, as shown in the exhibit below.

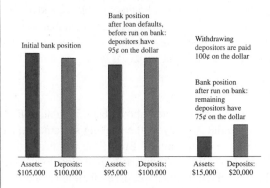

As you can imagine, the average depositor is not enamored with the prospect of losing money. How-

ever, she knows that until the bank is shut down by regulators, she can withdraw her funds at 100¢ on the dollar, provided that she gets toward the front of the line of depositors seeking to withdraw their funds. As other depositors come to the same realization, the line gets longer. The specter of a long line arouses worry among the less informed public, and soon, they, too, join the forming crowd.

The well-meaning but troubled bank continues to honor its deposit withdrawals as long as it can liquidate its assets and obtain the needed cash to pay off its depositors. Suppose that $15,000 of the remaining $95,000 in assets are in long-term, and therefore illiquid, loans and that the remainder is in cash, reserves, and money market instruments. The bank will be able to satisfy the withdrawal demands of the first 80 people in total. Each will receive 100¢ per dollar deposited. When their liquid assets are exhausted, the bank will have to stop honoring withdrawal demands. This will leave the bank with 20 customers and only $15,000 in asset value. Thus, each remaining customer will receive only 75¢ in present value on the dollar! Moreover, it is likely that there will be delay until the withdrawal demands can be met, because the bank cannot collect on its loans earlier than specified in the due dates.

Instead of each bank customer sharing equally in the bank's misfortune, it is only the slow afoot who will suffer. In this example, they will suffer to the tune of $250 each. The knowledge of this phenomenon exacerbates the tendency for people to run to the bank to secure a more favorable priority for withdrawal of funds—hence the term "run on the bank."

Prevention of Bank Runs.   The government acts to prevent runs in two ways. One is by having the Federal Reserve serve as a lender of last resort. As we stated before, a problem may arise due to insufficient liquid assets at a time when depositors in extraordinary numbers make a demand for cash. In such a situation, the Fed can loan cash to its member banks to satisfy withdrawal demands. This allows the commercial bank to remove from its balance sheet a liability with the highest level of liquidity—a demand or savings deposit—and replace it with a liability that may exhibit more patience—a loan from the Fed. The loan from the Fed can be repaid in a matter of days or weeks, whereas the depositor expects immediate liquidity.

A second, and perhaps a more important, way the government has reduced the risk of runs is by providing insurance on the safety of deposits. The insurance is provided by the FDIC, and even though the FDIC itself has insufficient reserves to handle a major crisis, it is generally assumed that the federal government will step in to bolster the FDIC if the need arises. Because depositors have confidence about the ultimate safety of their deposits, they are less likely to participate in a run on a troubled bank.

If the past is any guide, we can say that these measures have met with a good measure of success. There were significant banking panics in 1861, 1873, 1884, 1890, 1893, 1907, and 1933. With the exception of the banking panic of 1890, each of these panics was followed by economic disruption and a deep depression. For more than 60 years, however, the U.S. has not experienced a significant banking panic. Much banking legislation was passed during the years following the Great Depression, and undoubtedly, it has been a major factor in stopping widespread bank runs.

Limiting Bank Risk-Taking Activities.   Another major thrust of bank regulation is to limit the risks that banks take. There are three ways in which regulations exert control over the risk-taking activities of banks. First, the government imposes certain asset restrictions on the industry. For example, banks in the United States are restricted from investing in equity securities, real estate, and junk bonds. Moreover, they are constrained from lending to any one customer an amount that exceeds 15 percent of bank capital.

Second, regulators may place restrictions on the lines of business in which both the bank and its bank holding company (BHC) may be engaged. The thrust of the restriction is that BHCs must limit their activities to those that are deemed "closely related to banking." Earlier, we listed a number of such activities that have met the standards of a closely related activity, and it is apparent from the list that a substantial amount of latitude exists in what is deemed closely related to banking.

Third, regulators are able to stipulate a minimum capital requirement. This is an important mechanism to control risk since capital provides the cushion against adverse experience. In 1994, minimum equity capital was set at 8 percent of adjusted total assets. A bank is considered inadequately capitalized and is subject to closure unless it has at least a 4 percent capital ratio. (See Box 21.2.) In addition, regulators have the authority to set higher capital standards for individual banks that are deemed to have especially risky investment portfolios. If a bank is found to be in noncompliance, it can achieve the required capital ratio either by raising new capital or by decreasing its asset base.

While regulators attempt to limit the risk of banks, it is not their responsibility nor desire to limit the failure of poorly operated banks. Rather, regulators

Box 21.2

Risk-Based Capital Standards for Commercial Banks: Improved Capital-Adequacy Standards?

In August 1988, the Board of Governors of the Federal Reserve System agreed to adopt risk-based capital standards for U.S. commercial and savings banks and bank holding companies. The new standards, which substantially changed U.S. regulatory standards for assessing bank capital adequacy, replaced simple flat-rate standards with standards that explicitly incorporated risk. While well-run banks had their own "risk-based" systems for allocating capital, business plans had to be revised to incorporate the new regulatory standards. Interim minimum risk-based capital standards, which allowed for a transitional period, became effective at year-end 1990. The new standards became fully effective at year-end 1992.

The risk-based capital standards address credit risk in a limited fashion and make crude adjustments for country-transfer risk. This is accomplished by assigning assets to risk categories, based upon the type of collateral, guarantees, and the identity of the obligor. Off-balance-sheet commitments are first converted to credit-equivalent amounts, then assigned to risk categories on the same basis as bank assets. Capital requirements are set against the value of risk-weighted assets, which are computed as the sum of risk-weighted balance-sheet assets and off-balance-sheet commitments. Assets and credit-equivalent amounts of off-balance sheet commitments considered to possess little or no credit risk are given risk-weights of zero percent and thus require no capital backing. Riskier assets and off-balance-sheet commitments are assigned higher risk-weights of either 20, 50, or 100 percent. The risk-weights of various bank assets and off-balance-sheet commitments are given in [the accompanying table].

A bank's capital requirements are determined by total risk-weighted assets. After a phase-in period which ended at year-end 1992, banks must have at least 4 percent Tier 1 capital and 8 percent total risk-based capital, where both capital ratios are measured as a percent of risk-weighted assets. Tier 1 capital is composed of common equity capital, noncumulative preferred stock, and minority interests in consolidated subsidiaries, minus intangible assets other than purchased mortgage servicing rights and credit-card receivables. Total risk-based capital is composed of Tier 1 capital, plus Tier 2 capital, where the qualifying amount of Tier 2 capital cannot exceed the level of Tier 1 capital. Tier 2 capital is composed of cumulative perpetual and long-term and intermediate-term preferred stock, qualifying subordinated debt and mandatory convertible debt, and general loan- and lease-loss allowances in amounts up to 1.25 percent of risk-weighted assets. As with the former primary and secondary capital constraints, bank supervisors were given the ability to set higher minimum risk-based capital requirements for banks that were not considered well-run or in sound condition. Again, however, no formal guidelines were established on how these minimums would be adjusted with increased risks.

FDIC Risk-Weightings of Assets and Off-Balance-Sheet Commitments

	Balance-Sheet Items
Risk-Weight (%)	*Risk-Asset Variable*
0%	Cash and balances due from Federal Reserve Banks and other OECD central banks.
0	Direct claims on, and portions of claims unconditionally guaranteed by, the U.S. Government and its agencies or other OECD central governments.
0	Direct local currency claims on, or guaranteed by, non-OECD central governments.

Balance-Sheet Items

Risk-Weight (%)	*Risk-Asset Variable*
0	Gold bullion and Federal Reserve Bank stock.
20	Cash items in the process of collection.
20	All claims on U.S. depository institutions and other OECD depository institutions and short-term (remaining maturity one year or less) claims on non-OECD banks and non-OECD central banks.
20	Portions of loans and other claims conditionally guaranteed by the U.S. and other OECD countries' central governments.
20	Securities and other claims on U.S. Government-sponsored agencies (*i.e.,* not explicitly U.S.-backed).
20	Portions of loans and other claims collateralized by securities issued or guaranteed by the U.S. Government, or by U.S. Government agencies or Government-sponsored agencies or other OECD central governments.
20	Portions of loans and other claims collateralized by cash on deposit in the lending bank.
20	General obligations backed by the full faith and credit of U.S. state and local governments and political subdivisions of other OECD governments.
20	Claims on official multilateral lending institutions or development institutions.
20	Privately-issued mortgage-backed securities representing indirect ownership of a U.S. Government agency or U.S. Government-sponsored agency.
20	Investments in the shares of mutual funds whose portfolios contain assets qualifying for 0% or 20% risk-weight.
50	Loans fully secured by first mortgages on 1-to-4 family residential properties (if made in accordance with prudent lending practices).
50	Certain privately-issued mortgage-backed securities representing indirect ownership of a pool of residential mortgages which meet the criteria for the 50% risk-weight.
50	Revenue bonds and similar obligations, including loans and leases, that are obligations of U.S. and other OECD municipal governments.
50	Credit-equivalent amounts of interest-rate swaps and foreign-exchange rate contracts.
100	All remaining assets or portions of assets not falling into above categories.

Off-Balance-Sheet Items*

Credit Conversion Factor (%)	*Off-Balance-Sheet Variable*
100	Direct credit substitutes backing financial claims.
100	Participants in bankers' acceptances.
100	Forward agreements (excluding those involving foreign-exchange rate contracts).
100	Securities lent (where the lending bank faces some risk of loss).
50	Transaction-related contingencies.
50	Unused commitments with an original maturity exceeding one year.
20	Short-term, self-liquidating, trade-related contingencies.

*Note: Off-balance-sheet obligations are first converted to credit-equivalent amounts, then assigned to risk-weight classes based upon the identity of obligor or guarantor or collateral used.

Source: John P. O'Keefe, "Risk-Based Capital Standards for Commercial Banks: Improved Capital-Adequacy Standards?" *FDIC Banking Review*, Spring 1993.

attempt to limit the cost to the public coffers and the damage to individual consumers of poorly run banks. They achieve this by taking early action, before the financial woes of a bank get too large. In recent years, there have been increasing bank failures, yet a panic has not ensued.

Promoting Bank Competition.   Regulators frequently talk in terms that suggest that a key goal of the regulatory structure is to provide for a sufficient number of banking institutions in order to encourage and ensure competition. Judging from the structure of banking, it would appear that they have been successful. In the United States, there are more commercial banks per capita than in most other industrialized countries. However, whether this is due to proactive bank regulation or the result of the patchwork of historical state regulations is an open question. (See Box 21.3.) In fact, regulators have often worried aloud that fostering bank competition is at odds with other regulatory goals, such as promoting the solvency of banks.

When banks must compete with each other, the story goes, they are often enticed to proceed with as little capital as possible in order to secure attractive rates of return on equity. This obviously reduces the banks' safety cushion against adverse experience and makes them more susceptible to failure. The regulators therefore frequently find that it is a difficult balancing act to carry out one regulatory goal without contradicting the aims of another goal. Accordingly, the goal of competition has traditionally been viewed as secondary to preventing bank runs and limiting risk taking.

Is this view of competition as a secondary goal a problem? At first glance, it would seem that competition could be sacrificed for the stability that might result from limitations on risk taking. However, it is not that easy. It should be clear from other parts of this book that one cannot constrain, limit, or exclude competition in the financial sector. Attempts to do so usually lead to innovation around the regulation and a loss of market share by the constrained sector of the industry. As we noted above, this is what has happened to commercial banks in many different segments. Investment banks have brought many commercial bank customers to the capital markets. Products such as mortgages and credit cards, once the sole territory of banks, are increasingly being offered by many different types of institutions. On the liability side, the same erosion of market share is taking place.

In the end, therefore, the regulator really does have to worry about the competitive position of the banking sector and the competition within this sector. Failure to do so will lead to a decline in market share and a decline in the fortunes of the individual institutions in the industry being protected by regulation.

Although the United States does have by far the highest number of banks in the world, many are quite small. A disproportionate amount of assets are placed in relatively few banks. Most of the largest banks are what are referred to as **money center banks** because of their location at the center of the money markets. These few are followed by a set of institutions with large geographic franchises, often covering many states. This class is referred to as **super-regional banks.** The names and sizes of these institutions are reported in Exhibit 21.6. This exhibit reports the largest 25 banks at the close of 1995, and Exhibit 21.7 presents the list as it will

EXHIBIT 21.6 Largest 25 U.S. Bank Holding Companies
(December 1995)

Rank	*Bank Holding Company*	*Total Assets as of 12/31/95 ($ millions)*
1	Citicorp, New York	$256,853
2	BankAmerica Corp., San Francisco	232,446
3	NationsBank Corp., Charlotte, N.C.	187,298
4	J.P. Morgan & Co., Inc., New York	184,879
5	Chemical Banking Corp., New York	182,926
6	First Union Corp., Charlotte, N.C.	131,880
7	First Chicago NBD Corp., Chicago	122,002
8	Chase Manhattan Corp., New York	121,173
9	Bankers Trust Corp., New York	104,002
10	Banc One Corp., Columbus, Ohio	90,454
11	Fleet Financial Group, Inc., Providence, R.I.	84,432
12	PNC Bank Corp., Pittsburgh	73,404
13	Norwest Corp., Minneapolis	72,134
14	Keycorp, Cleveland	66,339
15	First Interstate Bancorp, Los Angeles	58,071
16	Bank of New York Co., Inc., New York	53,685
17	Wells Fargo & Co., San Francisco	50,316
18	Bank of Boston Corp., Boston	47,397
19	SunTrust Banks, Inc., Atlanta	46,471
20	Wachovia Corp., Winston-Salem, N.C.	44,981
21	Republic New York Corp., New York	43,882
22	Barnett Banks, Inc., Jacksonville, Fla.	41,554
23	Mellon Bank Corp., Pittsburgh	40,646
24	National City Corp., Cleveland	36,199
25	Comerica Inc., Detroit	35,470

Source: *The American Banker,* March 18, 1996.

appear after announced mergers are completed. It is evident that the top of the industry is increasing in size and market share, with both money center and super-regional banks causing a rather substantial consolidation in the industry's numbers.

Bank Regulation in the 20th Century: A Brief Historical Sketch

In early American financial history, paper money was issued by the federal government with mixed results.[5] This right was shared with chartered banking institutions, which printed their own separate currencies. However, with the **National Bank Act of 1864,** a uniform national currency was established and banks were

[5]Historians will recall the "greenback" period and the somewhat less disastrous U.S. Note experience.

Box 21.3

Are Big U.S. Banks Big Enough?

According to some observers, international banking is like sumo wrestling in at least one respect. An institution needs to be big enough to compete, and generally, bigger is better. The analogy is motivated by the prominence of Japanese and European banks among the world's largest banks. A decade ago, the U.S. had most of the largest banking organizations in the world by asset size, and only one Japanese bank and a few European banks ranked among the top 10. But today, the list of the 10 biggest banking organizations includes 6 Japanese banks, 2 European institutions, and only 2 American banks (see exhibit below). This apparent reversal of fortune has been used to support the argument that U.S. banks are not big enough to compete internationally.

Largest 25 World Banking Companies

Rank	Bank	Total Assets ($ millions)	Fiscal Date
1	Sumitomo Bank, Japan	$565,873	3/31/95
2	Mitsubishi Bank, Japan	547,642	3/31/95
3	HSBC Holdings, United Kingdom	316,942	12/31/94
4	BankAmerica, USA	215,475	12/31/94
5	Dai-ichi Kangyo Bank, Japan	576,555	3/31/95
6	Sanwa Bank, Japan	578,000	3/31/95
7	Sakura Bank, Japan	553,890	3/31/95
8	Fuji Bank, Japan	562,785	3/31/95
9	Credit Agricole, France	382,178	12/31/94
10	Citicorp, USA	250,489	12/31/94
11	Credit Lyonnais, France	327,911	12/31/94
12	National Westminster, United Kingdom	248,608	12/31/94
13	Deutsche Bank, Germany	369,148	12/31/94
14	ABN-AMRO Holding	291,630	12/31/94
15	Banque Nat'le De Paris, France	271,641	12/31/94
16	Union Bank of Switzerland, Switzerland	243,968	12/31/94
17	Industrial Bank of Japan, Japan	429,539	3/31/95
18	Barclays, United Kingdom	256,088	12/31/94
19	Indust. Comm'l Bank of China, China	337,761	12/31/93
20	Societe Generale, France	277,035	12/31/94
21	Swiss Bank Corp., Switzerland	161,113	12/31/94
22	NationsBank Corp., USA	169,604	12/31/94
23	Chemical Banking Corp., USA	171,423	12/31/94
24	Bank of Tokyo, Japan	268,806	3/31/95
25	Int'le Nederlanden Greop, Netherlands	206,749	12/31/94

Note: On March 31, 1996, Bank of Tokyo and Mitsubishi Bank merged to become Bank of Tokyo-Mitsubishi Ltd., the world's largest bank. On April 1, 1996, Chemical and Chase banks merged to become Chase Manhattan Corp., the largest U.S. bank.

Source: *Institutional Investor—International Edition,* August 1995, Vol. XX #8.

The Changing Banking Structure in the U.S.

The American banking system is less concentrated than the banking systems of many other countries. In part, this is due to the U.S.'s historical restriction on banks' geographic expansion. Over the past 15 years, however, these legal barriers to bank consolidation have been relaxed. The hard-fought battle ended in 1994. Then, interstate banking legislation was passed by Congress under the title of the Riegle-Neal Interstate Banking and Branching Efficiency Act of 1994. Under this legislation, banks in different states will be permitted to merge and form an interstate banking network across state lines by mid-1997 unless the individual states pass specific legislation prohibiting such interstate mergers. We have come a long way in 15 years.

While further consolidation in the U.S. banking system will occur as a result of this legislation, it is not likely that the U.S. banking system will become as concentrated as the ones in many other countries, both because of historical remnants of geographic limitations and because of the greater emphasis that the U.S. places on the anticompetitive effects of bank mergers. In fact, some are concerned that these regulations obstruct the economic forces that would naturally give rise to mega-banks in the U.S. In particular, they argue that restrictions on consolidation, particularly for large banks, sacrifice efficiency, which is detrimental not only to the U.S. banks' international competitiveness but also to their domestic customers.

Size and Efficiency

The empirical research on efficiency in banking raises doubts about how far the advantages of size go. Most studies on cost efficiency suggest that scale economies are exhausted well below the size of the larger U.S. banks. Moreover, recent studies find that unexploited scale economies account for a relatively small part of the overall variation in efficiency among banks. This means that, beyond a point, the efficiency gains owing to size may be small.

However, a look at which banks are active in international banking suggests that size does matter to some extent. Around the world, large banks are generally the only ones with any meaningful global presence. In the U.S., for example, only the largest banks ($50 billion or more in assets) are materially involved in international banking. It is interesting to note that most studies find that scale economies for U.S. banks are exhausted well before that point. This suggests that it is possible that scale economies in international banking continue beyond the point at which they are spent in other aspects of banking.

The advantages of size in international banking, however, do not necessarily increase indefinitely. In the U.S., many banks with over $50 billion in assets are involved to a significant extent in overseas business. Among these large banks, size does not seem to have much bearing on the degree of globalization. More specifically, among the large banks, the importance of foreign activities relative to domestic banking is not strongly related to the size of a bank. Moreover, the ability of some moderately large U.S. banks to have 50 percent or more of their activity related to international banking suggests that they can compete effectively. It is also important to note that a good deal of international banking involves off-balance-sheet items, such as options, swaps, and forward contracts. In this area, U.S. banks have been very strong competitors, which tends to belie the notion that U.S. banks are at a disadvantage owing to their size relative to larger foreign banks.

---

*This section contains excerpts from an essay by Fred Furlong that appeared in the August 7, 1992, Federal Reserve Bank of San Francisco *Weekly Letter.* This material is used by permission of the FRBSF and the author.

given the option of obtaining a federal banking charter. The Comptroller of the Currency issued charters, supervised these institutions, and controlled U.S. Note issues. This latter task was ultimately transferred to the U.S. Mint. Since that act, there have been flurries of legislation aimed at defining, limiting, and then expanding the role of banks. We will briefly review the main legislative initiatives in their order of occurrence below.

- The **Federal Reserve Act of 1913** created the Federal Reserve System. One of the main innovations of this act was to offer a facility called the discount window, where banks could borrow currency. At the time, nationally chartered banks were required to become members of the Federal Reserve System. They thereby obtained access to the check clearing facilities and discount window, but they were required to adhere to Federal Reserve System regulations.

- The **Edge Act of 1919** regulated the international activities of U.S. banks. It provided that U.S. international banks could operate subsidiaries in the United States and engage in interstate banking activities directed toward servicing the accounts of their customers involved in international commerce. The justification for this privilege, which was denied to many domestic banks, was that the U.S. international banks needed to compete effectively with foreign banks in the United States that had this ability.

- The **McFadden Act of 1927** dealt with the issues of branching and interstate banking. Some states permitted banks to operate with a number of branch offices, while others permitted just one office. At the same time, interstate banking was permitted by some states but not by others. Prior to the act, the Comptroller of the Currency had banned branching and interstate banking for national banks, which had placed national banks at a competitive disadvantage to state banks operating in states that permitted these practices. With the McFadden Act, national banks were allowed to branch within home states where state banks were permitted to branch. The 1935 amendments allowed these institutions to follow whatever opportunities for branching and interstate banking were available to state banks in their states of operation.

- The **Banking Act of 1933** had three major provisions. First, it established the FDIC and required all national banks to join. Second, it required commercial banks to cease their investment banking activities in the so-called Glass-Steagall portion of the legislation. Through Sections 16, 20, 21, and 32 of the legislation, banks were prohibited from underwriting corporate securities. Third, interest payments on demand deposits were prohibited, and the law provided for regulation of rates payable on savings and time deposits. All of these provisions were aimed at reducing the risks of bank panics and industry insolvency.

- The **Banking Act of 1935** affirmed the right of the Federal Reserve to regulate the rates of interest payable on time deposits of commercial banks and restructured the Federal Reserve into its present form, with a Board of Governors and chairman holding greater authority. It also extended the McFadden Act provisions to include statewide branching, where permitted, for state banks.

- The **Bank Holding Act of 1956** and its 1966 and 1970 amendments were directed toward bank holding companies that had managed to avoid regulations

EXHIBIT 21.7   **Pro Forma Ranking with Mergers in Progress**
(December 1995)

Rank	Bank Holding Company	Total Assets as of 12/31/95 ($ millions)
1	Chemical/Chase, New York	$304,099
2	Citicorp, New York	256,853
3	BankAmerica Corp., San Francisco	232,446
4	NationsBank Corp., Charlotte, N.C.	187,298
5	J.P. Morgan & Co., Inc., New York	184,879
6	First Union Corp., Charlotte, N.C. (3 deals pending)	134,257
7	First Chicago NBD Corp., Chicago	122,002
8	Fleet Financial/National Westminster Bancorp, Boston	114,048
9	Wells Fargo & Co./First Interstate, Los Angeles	108,387
10	Bankers Trust Corp., New York	104,002
11	Banc One Corp., Columbus, Ohio	90,454
12	Norwest Corp., Minneapolis (6 deals pending)	76,656
13	PNC Bank Corp., Pittsburgh	73,404
14	Keycorp, Cleveland	66,339
15	Bank of Boston Corp., Boston	47,397
16	Bank of New York Co., Inc., New York	53,685
17	National City Corp./Integra Financial Corp., Cleveland	50,545
18	Republic New York Corp./Brooklyn Bancorp, New York	48,021
19	SunTrust Banks, Inc., Atlanta	46,471
20	Corestates/Meridian Bancorp/United Counties, Philadelphia	45,990
21	Wachovia Corp., Winston-Salem, N.C.	44,981
22	Barnett Banks/First Fin'l Bancshares Polk City, Jacksonville	41,686
23	Boatmen's Bancshares/Fourth Financial Corp., St. Louis	41,046
24	Mellon Bank Corp., Pittsburgh	40,646
25	First Bank System/FirsTier Financial, Omaha	37,459

Source: *The American Banker,* February 5, 1996.

restricting branching and interstate banking by virtue of their status as holding companies. The practice had grown more widespread during the 1950s. This act and the amendments gave the Federal Reserve the authority to regulate the activities of bank holding companies. While bank holding companies were prohibited from pursuing interstate banking in states that did not expressly permit it through so-called "affirmative legislation," they were empowered to pursue their non-banking businesses on an interstate basis.

• The **Bank Merger Act of 1960** was enacted to set up an approval mechanism whereby the Justice Department could approve or disapprove of proposed bank mergers based on their compliance with antitrust laws. Its amendments in 1966 recast the focus to include benefits of mergers that were not strictly related to increased competition. For example, favorable consideration was accorded to a proposed merger if it would increase services or convenience to the public or strengthen a problem bank.

- The **Truth in Lending Act of 1968** was designed to require lenders to fully disclose the terms of the loans. Prior to this act, it was more difficult for the consumer to compare the costs of loans because there was no standard of comparison, such as effective annual interest rate, required to be computed and disclosed to the consumer.

- The **Fair Credit Billing Act of 1974** contained Federal Reserve Regulation Z, which prescribed how consumer credit card complaints are to be dealt with, and also contained regulations dealing with housing and mortgages.

- The **International Banking Act of 1978** regulated the activities of foreign banks on U.S. soil. It made foreign banks subject to many of the same rules as domestic banks.

- The **Depository Institutions Deregulation and Monetary Control Act of 1980** eliminated interest rate ceilings on savings deposits, allowed interest to be paid on transaction accounts, eliminated state usury ceilings on mortgage loans, and raised the insurance amount provided by the FDIC to $100,000 per account. At the same time, this act substantially increased allowable activities for savings and loans, presenting the banking industry with a greater competitive challenge from that sector than ever before.[6]

- The **Depository Institutions Act of 1982,** sometimes referred to as the Garn-St. Germain Act, raised the limit of capital that a bank could lend to a single client to 15 percent and authorized regulators to aid failing banks (and other financial institutions) by promoting their merger with healthier banks (and other financial institutions) on an interstate basis. This policy was extended to both state and nationally chartered financial institutions.

- The **Competitive Equality in Banking Act of 1987** was directed to avert a growing crisis of failing financial institutions. It authorized emergency interstate bank acquisitions and created "bridge banks," operated by the FDIC, to assume control of failed banks for up to two years before their stock must be sold. Prior to this act, failed banks were liquidated, depositors were paid off, or the bank (or at least acceptable assets and deposits) was sold to another healthier banking institution.

- The **Financial Institutions Reform, Recovery, and Enforcement Act of 1989** allowed commercial banks to purchase healthy savings and loans institutions, whereas prior to the act they could acquire only failing ones, and allowed savings and loans that meet banking standards to convert to commercial banks.

- The **Federal Deposit Insurance Corporation Improvement Act of 1991** addressed several issues around the deposit insurance fund. It authorized the FDIC to borrow up to $30 billion to increase the fund. It established a requirement for prompt corrective action to resolve troubled institutions, and instituted risk-based insurance fees for covered institutions.

- The **Interstate Banking and Branching Efficiency Act of 1994** permitted interstate branching at the holding company level and the acquisition of banks

---

[6]The savings and loan industry did not use the expanded powers wisely. See Chapter 22 for the full story, known as the "thrift crisis."

nationwide as of September 29, 1995. In addition, interstate branch networks and holding company mergers are permitted as of mid-1997 across all states that do not pass specific legislation prohibiting such interbank expansion.

Summary

The commercial banking industry is a central part of the financial sector, and it is the most visible of a series of financial intermediaries. In the most elementary terms, the commercial banking industry borrows funds from one part of the market to lend them out in another. However, its sources and uses of funds are much more complicated than this simple summary. Banks operate in many markets and deal with a plethora of instruments. Only some of these sources and uses of funds are presented on the bank's balance sheet, but all are part of highly competitive financial markets.

The competitive nature of these markets is, in fact, a central part of the story of commercial banking in America. The traditional markets of commercial banks have substitutes available; as a result, they have entered into previously nonbanking product areas. With all of this activity, however, the profit of the industry has been volatile and risk has been expanding. The former is documented here. The latter is obvious in the competitive nature of financial markets, the increasing presence of non-U.S. banking institutions, and the dramatic increase in innovation in the financial markets over the last decade.

These factors have not gone unnoticed. Regulation, which is a tradition in the industry, has been the focus of the debate over the banking structure of the United States. Industry advocates favor more flexibility and deregulation in order to more effectively compete in the market for financial services. Proponents of a greater role of government argue that the past has shown a need for further regulation to assure depositors and the rest of the economy that their banks are safe and sound. It is likely that this debate will continue through our lifetime and beyond.

Key Concepts

Review Questions

1. Briefly outline the components of the commercial bank's balance sheet. From which areas would you expect the bank to make most of its profit?

2. Consult your local newspaper to find the rates of interest being paid on passbook savings accounts, money market accounts, and certificates of deposit. Compare these rates with the capital market alternatives to determine the value people place on the convenience of their local institution.

3. Commercial banks have substantial holdings of fixed-income securities. What explanations for these holdings were offered in the chapter? Given each of these explanations, what type of fixed-income security would be most desirable?

4. Discuss the aims and methods used by the federal government to ensure the stability of the banking system. Explain the trade-off that is inherent in the regulatory mandate.

5. Commercial banks have traditionally been seen primarily as financial intermediaries. Explain this view and discuss the value added that these institutions bring to the capital market. Furthermore, how has the value of commercial banks changed over time?

6. The use of minimum capital requirements helps ensure bank stability. Are there any limits to the ability of the regulator to impose higher capital standards to achieve this end?

7. Society is concerned about nonfinancial firms and nonbank financial institutions in addition to commercial banks. Would it be advisable to use capital standards and risk limits on these firms as well?

References

Barth, J. R.; D. Brumbaugh; and R. Litan. *The Future of American Banking*. Armonk, N.Y.: M. E. Sharpe, 1992.

Berger, A. N.; A. K. Kashyap; and J. M. Scalese. "The Transformation of the U.S. Banking Industry: What a Long Strange Trip It's Been." *Brookings Papers on Economic Activity*, 1995.

Bernanke, Ben. "Nonmonetary Effects of the Financial Crisis in the Propagation of the Great Depression." *American Economic Review*, June 1983.

Board of Governors of the Federal Reserve System. "Recent Developments Affecting the Profitability and Practice of Commercial Banks." *Bulletin*, July 1995.

Boyd, J. H., and M. Gertler. "U.S. Commercial Banking: Trends, Cycles and Policy." *NBER Macro Annual*, 1993.

Clark, J. A. "Economies of Scale and Scope at Depository Financial Institutions: A Review of the Literature." *Economic Review*. Federal Reserve Bank of Kansas City, September/October 1988.

Craine, Roger. "Fairly Priced Deposit Insurance and Bank Charter Policy." *Journal of Finance*, December 1995.

Friedman, Milton, and Anna Schwartz. *A Monetary History of The United States: 1867–1960*. Princeton, N.J.: Princeton University Press, 1963.

Gorton, Gary, and Richard Rosen. "Corporate Control, Portfolio Choice, and the Decline of Banking." *Journal of Finance*, December 1995.

Humphrey, David B. "Cost Dispersion and the Measurement of Economies in Banking." *Economic Review*. Federal Reserve Bank of Richmond, May/June 1987.

Kaufman, George G., and Larry R. Mote. "Is Banking a Declining Industry? A Historical Perspective." *Economic Perspectives*. Federal Reserve Bank of Chicago, May/June 1994.

Klebaner, Benjamin. *Commercial Banking in the United States: A History*. Hinsdale, Ill.: Dryden Press, 1974.

Litan, Robert E. "Taking the Dangers Out of Banking Deregulation." *The Brookings Review,* Fall 1986.

Merton, R. C. "An Analytic Derivation of the Cost of Deposit Insurance and Loan Guarantees: An Application of Modern Option Pricing Theory." *Journal of Banking and Finance,* 1977.

Santomero, Anthony. "The Bank Capital Issue." *Financial Regulations and Monetary Arrangements after 1992,* M. Fratianni, C. Wihlborg, and T. Willett, editors. North Holland Press, 1991.

Spong, Kenneth. *Banking and Regulation: Its Purposes, Implementation and Effects.* Federal Reserve Bank of Kansas City, 1985.

Sprague, Irvine H. *Bailout: An Insider's Account of Bank Failures and Rescues.* New York: Basic Books, 1986.

Other Depository Institutions

This chapter reviews the history and evolution of the three major nonbank depository institutions: savings and loan associations, savings banks, and credit unions. It reviews their original charge and the evolution that has taken place toward the homogeneity of depository institutions. The thrift crisis and its implications for future regulatory change are discussed in some detail.

Lawyers call it "making a distinction without a difference." Others dismiss it as mere nomenclatorial sophistry. Regardless of the interpretation, the fact is that the

United States has a series of distinct financial intermediaries that are all depository institutions. These include the commercial banks discussed previously and other institutions such as savings and loan associations and savings banks, collectively known as thrifts, and credit unions. In the not-too-distant past, these institutions served different and separate parts of the consumer population; they were therefore viewed as distinct parts of the depository structure and were regulated separately from commercial banks and from each other. Today, because of all the changes each group has undergone, they are difficult to tell apart.

Currently, all depository institutions have far more in common than in contrast, and it is only at the margin that they can be distinguished one from another. Historically, however, they developed quite separately and for different purposes. And thanks to the fact that once government bureaucracies are created they tend to perpetuate themselves even after outliving any useful purpose, these depository institutions may ever remain separately categorized and regulated.

In this chapter, we will review the origins of each of these three types of depository institutions and discuss their original roles. Then, we will discuss how these institutions, in their attempts to compete with each other and with commercial banks and to adapt to a changing marketplace, have lost their distinctive character over time. Today, their importance in the marketplace is substantial, and they play a key role in channeling household savings into productive uses.

Savings and Loan Associations

The first of these institutions is **savings and loan associations** (S&Ls). These entities are consumer thrift institutions that have their roots in providing mortgage finance and still tend to specialize in mortgage lending today. In the United States, S&Ls are the largest providers of residential mortgage loans. Most of these funds are raised by issuing fixed time deposits and offering savings accounts to their consumer clientele.

Evolution of Savings and Loan Associations

Historically, banks and insurance companies did not lend to individuals for home construction. To fill this need, individuals aspiring to home ownership got together, formed groups, and pooled their money to lend it to members of the group for home construction. At first, only a small number of members could purchase homes with the available resources. However, as the loans were repaid over time, the funds were redeployed in new loans to other group members so that they could, in turn, finance the construction of their homes. The first S&L was established in Pennsylvania in 1831 under the name Oxford Provident Building Association.

S&Ls were originally organized as **mutuals,** dubbed "building and loan associations." This form of organization has no equity owner. Instead, the individuals providing the resources are the true owners of the institution. Profits are distributed to members in return for their funds. Remaining income beyond that which is distributed to owners is retained in reserves and in a capital surplus account for future use. Equity capital, as such, does not exist. Rather, to connote their ownership role, all depositors are said to have share balances rather than deposits. Those having such share balances have voting rights, where their board of directors is not self-perpetuating. Voting rights are proportionate to funds on deposit.

Over time, the demand for loans increased, and the associations responded to this increased demand by expanding beyond their original group members to attract other funds. They changed their name to "savings and loan association" as a part of this outreach for new members. Later, some were organized as private stock associations to facilitate the acquisition of equity capital. Today, most S&Ls continue to be mutuals, but stock associations are usually larger and hold the majority of industry capital and assets.

The industry as a whole has had a rather rough ride in its short history. Expansions have led to crisis and contraction. Boom has led to bust. This roller coaster ride was most evident in the 1920–1935 period, around the Great Depression, and the 1980s period, known recently as the **thrift crisis.** In these cases, rapid growth in industry assets was followed by a crisis of confidence precipitated by large losses.

In the earlier period, assets of the industry rose nearly 300 percent from 1922 to 1929, with the number of institutions reaching 12,000. But 1929 was not a good year! The U.S. Depression triggered massive losses throughout most of the financial sector, and the S&L industry was hit hard. Losses mounted as workers were unable to make mortgage payments. Foreclosure was epidemic, as was the crisis of confidence in the industry. The industry that emerged from the 1930s was far different from the one that had entered it. Assets contracted by more than one-third, and the number of institutions fell to 7,000.

Stability and growth were the watchwords for the 1940s and the 1950s. The industry recovered and prospered in the post–World War II period, with the demand for mortgages high and inflation low. The same could be said for the 1960s.

Then came the 1970s. This was a period when inflation rose and interest rates skyrocketed and became exceedingly volatile. It was not a good time to be in the business of making long-term fixed-rate loans financed by retail short-term deposits. The industry was reasonably protected from all this, at least at the beginning. Federal regulation, known as the Interest Rate Adjustment Act of 1966, restricted the interest rate that could be paid to depositors. This, coupled with rate ceilings on commercial banks under authority granted to the Federal Reserve under the Banking Act, insulated the interest spread between lending and borrowing rates for the two industries, primarily at the expense of retail depositors. However, faced with low interest rates at their local savings and loans, customers moved. Slowly at first, they moved out of S&L and bank deposits and into other types of assets that did not have these interest rate ceilings. This phenomenon became known as **disintermediation.** As we will note in the next chapter, this period was one of tremendous growth for the mutual fund industry, most notably money market mutual funds, which functioned as an alternative to savings deposits.

This withdrawal of deposits from the S&L industry caused additional problems. At the same time that their deposit base was declining, institutions with long-term assets found the values of their mortgage loans and other assets headed downward due to the higher interest rate environment. The problem was exacerbated when depositors withdrew their funds at full value, causing these institutions to suffer a loss as they attempted to liquidate the supporting assets. Regulators and industry leaders felt a need to correct this problem by loosening restrictions on both deposit interest rates and asset investment alternatives. While recognizing the need to lift the cap on interest rates paid to depositors, the industry argued successfully that regulatory relief should follow any price flexibility. The resultant legislation, the Depository Institutions Deregulation and Monetary Control Act passed in 1980, permitted S&Ls access to the demand deposit arena, with broad authorization of negotiable orders of withdrawal (**NOW**) accounts, which could be offered nationally to individuals and not-for-profit institutions. This type of account was an innovation of a Massachusetts institution back in 1972, and it had become a common interest-bearing substitute in New England over the ensuing period. At the same time, the deposit insurance limit for both banks and savings and loan associations was raised from $40,000 to $100,000 per customer. Moreover, institutions were allowed entry into the general consumer loan market. In 1982, all federally chartered S&Ls were permitted to offer money market deposit accounts, were granted greater access to the consumer market (up to 30 percent of assets), and gained new access to commercial lending for a portion of their asset portfolio. According to this legislation, denoted the Garn-St. Germain Depository Institutions Act, savings and loan associations could not continue to expand into consumer lending beyond 11 percent of their assets to commercial loans, 40 percent to commercial mortgage loans, and 3 percent into other commercial ventures.

But this period was too volatile for the industry to sustain reasonable financial performance. Its historical balance sheet problems, coupled with misadventures in the newly authorized lending and borrowing arenas outlined above, led to substantial operating losses. The industry as a whole began to experience substantial losses as the decade progressed. Losses led to bankruptcy, and regulators closed or forced the merger of many S&Ls. This, in turn, led members of the industry to act more aggressively to diversify their activity into real estate lending and development, consumer lending, and other financial products. With regulatory approval, the industry's assets rapidly increased, although their basic business and balance sheets continued to deteriorate. Expansion, unfortunately, was often ill-conceived and frequently led to even greater losses to institutions that badly needed both profits and capital. With neither, bankruptcy often resulted. Industry ranks continued to shrink. Over the ensuing two decades, the industry lost more than 50 percent of its members to failure, merger, and forced acquisition.

Today, there are close to 1,500 S&Ls, and they operate in every state in the United States. In terms of total assets, the size of the S&L industry has fallen substantially over the period of the crisis, and the number of S&Ls has also decreased sharply. Currently, there are fewer than 15 percent of the number of institutions that existed in 1925. However, in absolute terms of the amount of assets held on the industry's balance sheet, it is the second largest financial intermediary, surpassed only by commercial banks. In terms of assets, the average savings and loan association is approximately twice the asset size of the average commercial bank, although the largest S&Ls are much smaller than the largest commercial banks. For example, in 1995, World Savings was the largest S&L and held assets of $33 billion. By way of contrast, Citibank and Bank of America held $257 billion and $232 billion in assets, respectively.

Regulation

The regulation of S&Ls is not the responsibility of the Federal Reserve. However, a parallel structure was established in the 1930s to oversee these institutions. As with other regulations, this was precipitated by the crisis in the industry during the Great Depression. The **Federal Home Loan Bank System** (FHLBS) was established in 1932 to oversee S&Ls in a manner that is similar to the way in which the Federal Reserve System oversees banks. There were 12 district offices headed by the Federal Home Loan Bank Board (FHLBB). Members of the FHLBB were chosen and appointed by the president of the United States and served for fixed terms. In 1933, the FHLBB was further empowered to act as a chartering agency for federal S&Ls, and it governed them by setting minimum capital requirements, requiring regular financial reports, and conducting periodic examinations. The FHLBB was also responsible for approving mergers and setting branching rules for these federally chartered S&Ls. Finally, in 1934, the National Housing Act established the Federal Savings and Loan Insurance Corporation (FSLIC) to insure deposits in a manner equivalent to the commercial banks' FDIC.

All of this changed as a result of the trend toward deregulation in the 1980s and the ensuing crisis that followed. As noted above, the 1980 act raised deposit insurance coverage to $100,000. The 1982 legislation increased allowable asset categories, including adjustable-rate mortgages (ARMs), for the first time. It also permitted institutions to convert to federal savings banks, a category of institution created only two years earlier.

As a result of the collapse of the industry the regulatory structure also underwent change. In 1989, regulatory control of the industry was restructured in the **Financial Institutions Reform, Recovery and Enforcement Act** (FIRREA). First, the FSLIC was abolished. This became necessary because the losses it had sustained more than absorbed its financial resources. In short, it was bankrupt. Next, in light of the large number of failures in the industry, it was felt that a stronger regulatory authority was required. Therefore, the FHLBB was disbanded, and regulatory control of the industry was removed from the Federal Home Loan Bank System. Regulatory control was vested in the **Office of Thrift Supervision** (OTS), which was formally part of the U.S. Treasury Department. Deposit insurance was shifted to the **Savings Association Insurance Fund** (SAIF), which became part of the FDIC. Finally, the **Resolution Trust Corporation** (RTC) was established with the expressed purpose of facilitating the liquidation of bankrupt institutions that

Box 22.1

A House of Mortgages Comes Tumbling Down

In a town that was becoming a real estate graveyard, Michael R. Wise thought he had found the fountain of youth. Instead of cutting back, as did other Denver thrifts caught in the mid-1980s oil bust, his Silverado Banking Savings & Loan Assn. invested heavily in real estate development—often using stock, not cash, to fund deals.

Silverado's assets soared, as did its influence. Neil M. Bush, a Denver oilman and son of the Vice-President, joined the board. Wise was named president of the thrift industry's advisory council to the Federal Reserve Board and a director of the Federal Home Loan Bank in Topeka, Kan., which supervises regional thrifts. When the market turned, says a local consultant, "Wise planned to be on top."

Less than Zero

The problem was that the market turned straight down. That left Silverado saddled with millions of dollars in bad loans. In early August, Silverado announced a $198 million write-off, leaving it with negative net worth, and began looking for a buyer. The downfall raised questions about Silverado's ties to developers, especially MDC Holdings, a national homebuilder with $800 million in revenues. The Se-

curities & Exchange Commission is investigating MDC's dealings with Silverado and several other thrifts. And on Aug. 31, citing possible conflict of interest if his father were to become President, Neil Bush resigned from the board.

Developers linked to Silverado have seen their $53 million stake in the thrift erased. MDC alone was forced to write off $28 million. Among others hit is Bill L. Walters, one of Denver's largest builders. If Silverado is forced to dump its real estate on an already battered market, the carnage could spread.

To some industry experts, the sequence of highly leveraged land speculations looks like a classic case of high-risk self-dealing. "They were just trading paper for paper," says Nicholas L. Scheidt, president of Apex Realty Investments Inc. in Denver. "They created equity on the balance sheet but no real value."

Less-than-arm's-length transactions between thrifts and developers are often blamed for many of the U.S. thrift industry's woes. But Silverado and its partners vehemently deny wrongdoing. Wise defends the deals as a strategy for survival in a tough market, adding that other major corporations frequently finance deals with stock. "It's obvious we went too far," he says. "But we did nothing illegal or immoral."

resulted from the 1980s debacle. The loosening of portfolio restrictions, too, was reconsidered. Institutions were required to hold 70 percent of their assets in mortgage loans or securities, commercial real estate holdings were limited, and high-yield investments were relegated to a subsidiary. This was followed by the **Federal Deposit Insurance Corporation Improvement Act** of 1991, which further tightened regulatory control. This act mandated prompt corrective action for troubled institutions, and it centered increased scrutiny on the institution's capital position. Firms are divided into well-capitalized, adequately capitalized, undercapitalized, significantly undercapitalized, and critically undercapitalized groups, with increasingly onerous remedial measures demanded from institutions in lower tiers. Further, to limit regulatory forbearance, a big term for passivity, the 1991 act requires better accounting, less discretion by regulators, and risk-based insurance premiums. As

Silverado shed its traditional thrift image soon after Wise arrived nine years ago. By the mid-1980s, it had nearly stopped making home mortgage loans and plunged into land development. As other thrifts cut back on loans, Silverado could charge developers lofty fees: In 1986, when many thrifts were struggling, it made $15 million, a hefty 28% return on equity. Assets grew tenfold, to $2.4 billion, from 1982 to 1987.

Silverado bought distressed properties from developers, allowing them to book a profit. The thrift paid cash, but then the developers often plowed their gain back into Silverado stock. By issuing new stock, Silverado improved its capital position, at least on paper, allowing it to make more deals.

For example, in 1986, Silverado bought two troubled downtown office properties from Walters for $53 million, while helping him finance another property. Wise says that Walters put his $15 million in stated profits back into new Silverado common stock. A $15 million capital infusion then would have let Silverado make $500 million more in new investments. "It was cash for trash . . . a way for both sides to keep deferring the bad news," says Denver developer James M. Sullivan.

Round-Trips

MDC dealt heavily with the thrift. In 1986 it sold a Silverado joint venture 5,900 homesites for $38 million, booking a $14 million profit. Earlier land deals with Silverado and another thrift netted MDC $23.5 million on sales of $38 million. Some land took quick round-trips: In 1986, MDC sold housing land in California to Silverado for $13.3 million, then bought it back for $17.8 million. Silverado also bought $119 million in high-risk, cut-rate mortgages that MDC had originated; it paid mostly in new Silverado stock.

The spiral ended early this year. With bad loans piling up, Silverado's outside accountant demanded action, a former officer says. Today, Wise points out, only 45% of the portfolio is in commercial property, which often sells for half its 1982 value. But residential real estate might not be faring much better. As a result, some experts predict even bigger write-offs to come.

MDC, too, is reeling: It lost $20 million on operations alone in the second quarter. It slashed its national ambitions and is taking steps to save cash. With $967 million of debt, "it's a company in distress," says Barbara K. Allen, analyst with Prudential-Bache Securities Inc. Responds MDC President David D. Mandarich: "We've got a tough year ahead, but we've got enough liquidity to make it." It also has $6 million in Silverado preferred stock that it could convert into control. MDC says it won't. This time, Wise, whose personal Silverado stock was once worth more than $15 million, isn't finding eager takers for his paper.

Source: Reprinted from September 26, 1988 issue of *Business Week* by special permission, copyright © 1988 by The McGraw-Hill Companies, Inc.

this makes clear, an outgrowth of the debacle that resulted from the losses and failures was a complete revamping of the thrift regulatory structure.

Little remains of the original purpose of the FHLB System. The Federal Home Loan System and its regional banks remain, however. The revitalized organization has found a niche in the market by granting loans to its member institutions in order to finance their activity in the home mortgage market. These funds are obtained through long-term debt issues in the bond market. However, these loans have no guarantee, no governmental implicit guarantee, and no presumed Treasury access. These loans are long-term funding sources for member organizations, which include both S&Ls and commercial banks.[1]

---

[1]Other depository institutions can also elect to become members of their local FHLBB. These may do so for similar reasons, namely the access to long-term funding at favorable rates.

The Savings and Loan Industry Today

The S&L industry continues to function in spite of these regulatory changes—and perhaps because of them. With added supervision and control, the industry has progressed beyond its meltdown period, and new entrants have added to its numbers. In any case, to be a member of the industry in good standing requires that the institution hold a minimum of 70 percent of its assets in real estate mortgages and/or mortgage-backed securities.

S&Ls may enter by obtaining either a federal or a state charter. Federal charters are currently granted by the Federal Office of Thrift Supervision. Entry parallels commercial bank charter requirements, with minimum capital standards, proof of competency, and a viable business plan. If a state charter is selected, state authorities set chartering requirements. In this case, the branching laws are determined by the state, and they are usually more liberal than the branching laws for commercial banks.

Virtually all S&Ls have their deposits insured up to $100,000 by the SAIF fund, which is overseen by the FDIC. In prior years, this insurance function was handled either by the Federal Saving and Loan Insurance Corporation or by state insurance funds. Then came the deposit insurance crisis. For reasons outlined above, institutions began to fail. This led to losses at the FSLIC. The thrift crises of 1986 in Ohio and Maryland put pressure on the state system, as many S&Ls had their deposits insured by state agencies. However, with the inability of these states to satisfy depositor demands for withdrawal funds, people lost confidence in the viability of state insurance agencies. The result was that state systems were abandoned throughout the country, and covered institutions were moved into their national counterpart, the SAIF system, which dominates today.

Sources and Uses of Funds

Historically, most funds were raised by the S&L industry through savings accounts and to a lesser extent, certificates of deposit. This was followed by a period in the 1980s in which the S&L industry began offering a spate of new savings vehicles to the public. As noted previously, negotiable orders of withdrawal (NOW) accounts were allowed nationally beginning in 1980. These accounts provided depositors with a relatively modest rate of interest on their account balances and also allowed them to draft checklike instruments, called negotiable orders of withdrawal, for consumption and business expenditures. Later, in 1982, **money market deposit accounts** (MMDA) were introduced to compete directly with money market accounts offered by brokerage firms that offered checking privileges. These MMDA accounts offered competitive current rates of interest on account balances. Other funds were raised by offering Keogh and IRA plan retirement accounts to retail depositors.

These sources are supplemented by two others. As previously noted, the Federal Home Loan Bank System continues to perform a financing function for the industry. Currently, approximately $75 billion is provided by this source alone. In addition, many of the institutions have shifted their corporate form from a mutual to a stock company structure. This permits direct equity capital inflows, and has expanded the funding base over the last decade.

At the same time, institutions began to shift their focus from creating assets that they expected to hold to maturity to creating assets for resale to other investors. In short, the industry became a major factor in creating mortgages for the mortgage-backed securities market discussed in Chapter 13, and in the move to **securitization.** In securitization, the S&L issues debt securities backed by a given bundle of pooled assets, such as consumer installment loans. The intent of securitization of assets, like the mortgage-backed securities market, is to raise funds more cheaply than could be done if the S&L were to maintain the assets in its own portfolio. An additional benefit of such programs is that risk is transferred away from the institution to other market participants. At the same time, assets are removed from the S&L's balance sheet, thereby improving the capital-to-assets ratio and, concomitantly, regulatory compliance. In some cases, the S&L will engage just in **whole loan sales,** where individual large loans are sold to investors in the secondary market. All of these methods of financing lending activity supplement the capacity of S&Ls to make loans.

Today, the assets in the S&L's balance sheet include direct holdings of residential mortgages; mortgage-backed securities such as GNMAs, CMOs, IOs, and POs; and participation certificates (PCs) issued by the Federal Home Loan Mortgage Corporation.[2] Other areas of S&L investment include mobile home loans, home equity loans, education loans, real estate, business loans, and investments in service corporations that fund land development and housing rehabilitation projects. In addition, S&Ls may be able to invest in credit cards, consumer loans, commercial paper, mutual funds, municipal revenue bonds, and investment-grade corporate securities. However, each institution is mindful of its need to satisfy the criterion for 70 percent mortgage assets contained in the 1989 FIRREA legislation outlined earlier.

Savings Banks

Evolution of Savings Banks

Savings banks started in the United States well before the Civil War, somewhat predating their S&L counterparts. The first savings bank was the Philadelphia Savings Fund Society (PSFS), which was organized in 1816. The rationale behind these savings banks, however, was quite different. Established in urban settings, primarily in the Northeast, these institutions were focused on savings rather than on mortgage finance or on credit itself. In fact, in the early history of savings banks, few loans were made to depositors, and deposits were invested in government bonds and in time deposits in local commercial banks.

---

[2] See Chapter 13 for a full discussion of these instruments and recent developments in mortgage finance.

Savings banks, as originally envisioned, were quasi-charitable institutions that were established to foster savings and encourage wealth accumulation among the low-income, newly arrived, working class. Boards were sometimes self-perpetuating and were frequently populated by the social class of the city involved. Originally, these institutions were exclusively state chartered and began as mutuals. Accordingly, the industry itself is often (incorrectly) referred to today as the **Mutual Savings Bank** (MSB), part of the depository network.

In any case, these institutions did accomplish their goal, at least historically. Over time, their roots in the working class gave way to more general acceptance, and they grew rapidly over the next 100 years. Even the Depression did not affect adversely their growth and stability. While their S&L and commercial bank counterparts were undergoing a substantial crisis and were experiencing a reduction in numbers, savings banks experienced few failures and enjoyed an expansion in deposits over the 1920s and 1930s. The growth of this group of institutions has been relatively slow since World War II. This is primarily because savings banks exist in competitive marketplaces where both commercial banks and S&Ls have increasingly seen their savings deposit base as an attractive source of funds. The savings bank industry's response has been to shift its focus from being simply a savings institution to becoming a more general-purpose consumer bank.

This transformation was facilitated by legislation drafted to address savings and loan needs in the 1980s. Along with S&Ls, savings banks were given authority to offer a fuller range of deposit products in both the 1980 **Deposit Institutions Deregulation and Monetary Control Act** (DIDMCA) and the 1982 Garn-St. Germain **Depository Institutions Act.** In addition, the 1980 legislation permitted federally chartered savings bank institutions for the first time in U.S. history, *and* it also allowed mutuals to demutualize and convert to standard corporate structure. The national chartering capability greatly expanded the geographic area of the industry from its original set of 16 Northeastern states plus Washington. The conversion potential added interest and visibility as well. As a result of these new opportunities, coupled with permission granted in the 1982 act that allowed S&Ls to shift to federal savings bank charters, the industry has been substantially transformed in terms of both numbers and character over the last decade.

The Savings Bank Industry Today

Members of this industry traditionally have not been large in size. However, as savings banks evolve into more standard financial institutions, this is changing. The typical savings bank has a deposit size greater than either commercial banks or savings and loan associations, with average asset holdings in excess of $800 million. However, many money center commercial banks have greater deposits than their counterpart savings banks.

In the past few years, savings banks have gained in both number and size due to the conversion of savings and loan associations into savings banks, and the rapid expansion of the federal savings banks with home offices in California. In fact, 6 of the 10 largest institutions by asset size in 1995 were headquartered in this one state.

Nonetheless, most of the approximately 500 savings banks operating today are still found in the northeastern states. Massachusetts, New York, and Connecticut house a significant number of both institutions and deposits, with a large number of savings banks operating in Maine, New Hampshire, New Jersey, Pennsylvania, Rhode Island, Vermont, and Wisconsin. West of the Mississippi River, savings banks were previously permitted only in Washington and Alaska. Today, however, there are members of this industry in 31 states plus Puerto Rico.

Savings banks may be federally chartered by the Office of Thrift Supervision, or they may be state chartered by the various state banking departments. Institutions granted a federal charter are referred to as federal savings banks (FSB). The OTS is also the agency to which petitions for conversion from an S&L charter to an FSB franchise are submitted. State savings banks have been relatively less attractive recently, as evidenced by the emergence of federal savings banks in the list of the top 25 institutions in the industry. Nonetheless, state banking departments still play an important role in the oversight of savings banks. They are involved in the approval process of any new branches that may be sought, even by federally chartered institutions, and they supervise state institutions and coordinate these activities with the FDIC, the agency now responsible for all deposit insurance. In addition, mergers and acquisitions must be approved by the Office of Thrift Supervision, the FDIC, and state banking departments.

Sources and Uses of Funds

For mutual savings institutions, their reserves and/or surplus are the counterpart of equity capital for stock organizations. As is the case for the mutual portion of the S&L industry, these resource categories serve as the equity buffer for financial and regulatory purposes. For stock firms, capital is raised directly and serves its usual role as a source of funds for lending activity. Given the rocky history of S&L institutions, regulators demand that capital ratios of savings banks conform to regulatory standards for other depository institutions. Accordingly, capital has been increasing in the industry to reach these standards.

Nonetheless, for both mutuals and stock organizations, the principal source of funds is time deposits that carry a fixed rate of interest over a predetermined period of time. As is the case for their counterparts in the S&L industry, savings banks generate other funds by offering NOW accounts and MMDAs. Each of these types of accounts can be used for settling transactions via an instrument that behaves much like a commercial bank check. The advantage to the consumer of holding a savings bank account rather than a classic bank checking account is that the accounts bear interest, generally at a somewhat higher rate than even the bank counterpart of these consumer transaction accounts. Some savings banks even offer straight demand deposits, but the availability of this type of an account depends upon state statute and the conditions imposed by the state banking commissioner. Deposits are insured up to $100,000 by the Bank Insurance Fund within the FDIC.

Savings banks' principal use of funds is for mortgages—typically first mortgage loans, as is the case for the S&L industry. In addition they, too, have gone heavily into the creation and resale of mortgages for subsequent packaging by three federal agencies—FNMA, GNMA, and FHLMC. Beyond mortgage assets and some consumer loans, savings banks have a somewhat broader array of assets than savings and loan associations. Like other institutions, they invest in U.S. government and agency securities and state and municipal securities. However, savings banks are also allowed to invest in corporate bonds and even in corporate equities under the charters granted by some states. While such holdings are small in total, the flexibility offered to some state-chartered savings institutions is noteworthy.

The Thrift Crisis and Beyond

Savings and loans and savings banks are often referred to collectively as **thrifts.** These institutions are lumped together because of their joint history, which, as we have seen, is actually fairly distinct. But those not so well versed in the history of each segment see them as identical institutions that take savings deposits and make residential mortgages. The recent charter conversions of large S&Ls and the emergence of a national federal savings bank industry have lent credence to the notion that both of these types of institutions are best treated as one thrift industry. So, we will do the same from here forward, even though it does somewhat of a disservice to the relatively conservative mutual savings banks to include them along with the S&Ls under a single label. Nonetheless, a considerable amount has been written about the thrift industry and its recent performance, particularly regarding the so-called thrift crisis of the 1980s.

Understanding the Thrift Crisis

The thrift industry went through a series of crises during the 1980s and early 1990s that rocked the entire industry and left a huge debt for the taxpayers of America to satisfy. It all started in the late 1970s, when interest rates rose to extreme levels. Because both S&L and savings bank investments were primarily in long-term mortgages with long durations, the values of these investments declined precipitously with the increases in interest rates. Thus, the assets were worth far less than the nominal loan value reported on the balance sheet.

At the same time, deposit yields did not keep pace with general market interest rates. As a result of Regulation Q, thrifts had been offering predominantly low-yielding savings accounts up to that time. Even when these interest rate ceilings were lifted in 1980, these institutions had difficulty keeping pace with the interest rates offered by competing institutions and open-market instruments because their investment portfolios were locked into long-term, fixed-rate mortgages. The duration of the liabilities was, effectively, shorter than the duration of the assets—a sure recipe for disaster whenever interest rates rise. It did not take long for there to be a substantial erosion of capital, and soon, the buffer was depleted. As a result, depositors began to withdraw their funds *en masse* in search of safer and higher-yielding investments.

Regulators recognized this problem but seemed both unwilling and unable to assist the industry. You see, regulations were written using book-value accounting rules. Therefore, assets were listed according to purchase price, even if their subsequent market value changed. Liabilities, too, remained at their initial value. Therefore, while assets were yielding low returns, they still were carried at their purchase price on the banks' balance sheets, which recorded adequate but declining capital accounts. But in economic terms, where market values are used, the capital of many of the institutions was often completely gone. In fact, it was negative.

A perverse incentive faces the institution when it has little or no capital to lose. The incentive is to **bet the bank,** or in this case, bet the thrift. This is accomplished by making very risky investments. The risk can be in the form of illiquidity, credit quality, prepayment risk, or calls uncertainty, as well as our old standards of duration and convexity risk. The hope is that the risk will be rewarded by high returns. If it is not, there is nothing more for the institution to lose than what has already been lost. Moreover, a safe investment is unlikely to generate sufficient return to restore the capital position within any acceptable time horizon. Hence, the risky behavior is perceived as the rational choice for the management of an impaired institution.

This is exactly what happened to the industry. Remember that Congress passed legislation in 1980 and 1982 that permitted thrifts to raise funds by issuing instruments, such as NOWs, MMDAs, and other more competitive savings vehicles, to consumers in an effort to stem the disintermediation. It worked. Yet this provided new, costlier sources of funds to the industry at a time when their economic surplus had already eroded and was, in many cases, negative. Consumers and investors were not overly concerned about the riskiness of their savings because their accounts were sponsored by government-backed deposit insurance. To promote confidence among depositors, Congress even raised the amount of insurance coverage on deposits from $40,000 to $100,000 as part of the 1980 legislation. In effect, Congress had provided additional fodder to play the "bet the bank" game.

Many would argue, in fact, that the regulatory structure, by its inactivity and permissiveness, actually encouraged this behavior. **Regulatory forbearance,** a practice of bending the rules or delaying action by the regulator in the hope of financial recovery, became commonplace. Institutions with negative capital accounts could be found throughout the industry. In fact, they were only half jokingly referred to as "zombie thrifts." Regulators even invented a new form of "regulatory accounting" whereby phantom capital, called "net worth certificates," was recognized for regulatory purposes, thus allowing insolvent S&Ls to stay in business and keep "spinning the roulette wheel." Hundreds of institutions went "belly up" when their risky investments did not generate the necessary level of returns. The more they lost, the more these institutions would "double up" on their risky bets in an effort to recoup their losses. To increase the size of their bets, they sought to attract more funds by offering even more attractive rates of interest on deposits. This, of course, increased their cost of funds and made the bets even more precarious.

Finally, Congress put a stop to much of the risky behavior and began to clean up the mess. Insolvent institutions were shut down or merged with healthier institutions. Regulations were more rigorously enforced. In attempting to satisfy the

Exhibit 22.1

The industry continues to shrink in number of associations and assets

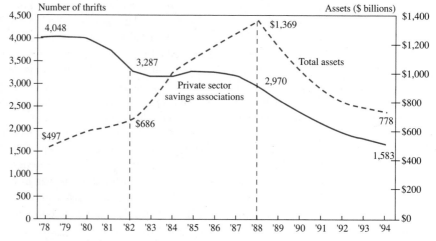

Source: Federal Reserve Bank of Kansas City—*1995 Annual Review.*

Exhibit 22.2   Nationwide Thrift Failures: 1989–1995

Year	Failures
1989	168
1990	355
1991	149
1992	62
1993	27
1994	64
1995	2

Note: Thrift failures include those that have undergone pass-through receivership and/or have been fully resolved.

Source: Failure data were obtained from the Resolution Trust Corporation.

demands of withdrawing depositors, the FSLIC quickly went bankrupt. This is what ultimately led to the passage of FIRREA in 1989. Responsibility for insuring S&L deposits was transferred to the FDIC, and the RTC was charged with closing bankrupt institutions and disposing of their assets. The results are evident in Exhibit 22.1, where a time series of savings associations' assets and number of institutions is reported for the 15 years of the crisis. The "go for broke" strategy led to a rapid expansion of assets even as firms were exiting the industry. Assets reached a pinnacle in 1988 at nearly $1.4 trillion, or three times their level only a decade earlier. Over the next six years, assets in the industry declined by over $600 billion, and the number of institutions fell by more than 45 percent. As Exhibit 22.2 illustrates, failures accounted for the largest percentage of this decline.

EXHIBIT 22.3   **Financial Assets and Liabilities of FDIC-Insured Savings Institutions**
(Year-end 1995; $ Millions)

Assets		Liabilities	
Loans and leases, net	$ 647,908	Deposits	$ 741,892
Securities	288,563	Other borrowed funds	182,514
Other real estate owned	3,157	Subordinated debt	2,581
Goodwill and other intangibles	6,864	All other liabilities	12,691
All other assets	79,249	Total equity capital	86,063
Total	$1,025,741	Total	$1,025,741

Source: Federal Deposit Insurance Corporation, *Quarterly Banking Profile,* Fourth Quarter 1995.

The Thrift Industry Today

Today, the industry is quite different than it was during the late 1980s. For the most part, institutions have returned to profitability and have adjusted to a smaller industry. FSBs have taken the place of many of the former S&Ls, and strict regulation of asset quality and equity capital have replaced regulatory accounting and forbearance, phrases used to connote regulatory tolerance. The RTC still has 49 institutions to dispose of by the first quarter of 1996, but this process is progressing nicely. The balance sheet for the entire thrift industry as of the end of 1995 is reported in Exhibit 22.3. These numbers include all FDIC-insured institutions, whether they are part of SAIF or BIF insurance funds, that is, whether they are savings and loans or state or federal savings banks. Notice that capital now represents over 8 percent of total assets for the entire industry, up substantially from the crisis years of 1985 through 1990. The 1995 income statement is presented in Exhibit 22.4 for these same institutions. Again, notice that net income has returned to a robust $7.6 billion for the year. As noted above, the largest of these institutions are small by commercial bank standards, but they are not trivial. See Exhibit 22.5 for a list of the largest institutions and their home office locations.

There is no question that the thrift crisis was indeed a mess. What is less clear is who was to blame. In Washington, D.C., many would contend that industry and its management were the villains, and the "go for broke" story above lends credence to this view. However, regulatory oversight was clearly inadequate. Many reasons have been offered to explain this fact. Some would contend that well-meaning regulators hoped that interest rates would decline and turn the industry around; however, they fail to ask if this was appropriate regulatory behavior. Others have argued that the regulators had become captives of the industry, unwilling to regulate and close institutions for fear of recognizing their failure to regulate. According to this theory, deregulation was used as a mechanism to allow the institutions further leeway to speculate. In short, the extent of the loss was a direct result of the captive regulator granting greater latitude to a troubled industry. In the end, legislative

EXHIBIT 22.4   Income and Expense of FDIC-Insured Savings Institutions
(Calendar Year 1995; $ millions)

Total interest and fee income	$70,994
Total interest expense	42,528
Net interest income	28,466
Provisions for loan and lease losses	2,110
Total noninterest income	7,119
Total noninterest expense	21,831
Gains (losses) on securities	464
Applicable income taxes	4,161
Extraordinary gains, net	(321)
Net income	**$ 7,627**

Note: A total of 2,029 FDIC-insured savings institutions were in existence during the calendar year of 1995.
Source: Federal Deposit Insurance Corporation, *Quarterly Banking Profile,* Fourth Quarter 1995.

EXHIBIT 22.5   Largest 25 Thrift Institutions in Assets
(Totals as of June 30, 1995; $ millions)

1. Home Savings of America, FSB, Irwindale, Cal.	$53,247
2. Great Western Bank, FSB, Chatsworth, Cal.	41,987
3. World Savings & Loan Assn., Oakland, Cal.	33,050
4. Dime Savings Bank of New York, FSB, New York, N.Y.	19,909
5. American Savings Bank, FA, Irvine, Cal.	19,369
6. Washington Mutual Bank, Seattle, Wash.	18,805
7. Glendale Federal Bank, FSB, Cal.	16,054
8. First Nationwide Bank, FSB, Dallas, Tex.	14,736
9. California Federal Bank, FSB, Los Angeles, Cal.	14,325
10. Citibank, FSB, San Francisco, Cal.	14,321
11. Standard Federal Bank, Troy, Mich.	12,947
12. Bank United of Texas, FSB, Houston, Tex.	11,345
13. Guaranty Federal Savings Bank, Dallas, Tex.	9,221
14. Roosevelt Bank, FSB, Chesterfield, Mo.	9,002
15. Coast Federal Bank, Los Angeles, Cal.	8,598
16. First Federal of Michigan, Detroit, Mich.	8,524
17. Household Bank, FSB, Newport Beach, Cal.	8,061
18. Sovereign Bank, FSB, Wyomissing, Pa.	7,321
19. LaSalle Talman Bank, FSB, Chicago, Ill.	7,170
20. First Federal Savings & Loan Assn., Rochester, N.Y.	6,867
21. First Bank, FSB, Fargo, N. Dak.	6,856
22. People's Bank, Bridgeport, Conn.	6,667
23. Greenpoint Bank, New York, N.Y.	6,665
24. Astoria Federal Savings & Loan Assn., Lake Success, N.Y.	6,423
25. Bank of America, FSB, Portland, Ore.	6,407

Source: *American Banker,* November 3, 1995.

action came too late, and necessary resources to address the problem were withheld until Congress had no choice. Estimates of the cost of this fiasco have been as high as $500 billion. We will be paying off that debt long after this book is no longer in print, so there seems to be plenty of blame to go around.

Credit Unions

Credit unions are cooperative nonprofit associations oriented toward consumer savings and credit needs. In contrast to the setbacks and slow growth of the S&Ls and savings banks in recent years, credit unions have been the fastest growing among the depository institutions. Still, they are the smallest in terms of total assets under management, with a little over $300 billion as of mid-1995.

Evolution of Credit Unions

Credit unions were established early in the 20th century to serve the needs of low-income individuals and families. Their role was to provide inexpensive credit to their members and serve as an outlet for their savings. Until the 1950s, credit union growth was modest; membership was under five million persons. At that time, aggressive institutions began offering new services and conducted advertising campaigns in a successful effort to broaden their appeal to middle-income individuals. Today, membership in the United States is in excess of 55 million—one person out of every five belongs—and it is over 85 million worldwide. There are now 36,000 credit unions spread among 80 countries. In the United States, there are over 20,000 institutions, a total that is down some-what from the heyday credit unions experienced in the late 1960s and early 1970s. However, even this number exceeds the total number of other depository institutions combined.

Not just anyone can join a credit union. From their inception in the United States, membership has been restricted to people having a **common bond,** around which the credit union is established. Usually, you have to either belong to a sponsoring organization or be a family member of someone who belongs to such an organization. Most often, the sponsoring organization is an employer. However, about one out of every six credit unions is organized around a nonprofit organization such as a labor union, a church, or a fraternal or social organization. Others are organized around a common area of residence or age; for example, a credit union might be established to serve retired persons. One credit union even organized around a family surname—Lee—and was fairly successful in the San Francisco Bay area, where many Chinese Americans share that surname.

Credit unions enjoy some advantages over other depository institutions. Often, they receive free office space and other facilities from the sponsor. Their officers and directors usually serve as unpaid volunteers. Since credit unions operate as not-for-profit institutions, they are also exempt from both federal and local taxation. Because of all of this, the low-cost structure of a credit union enables it to provide low-cost loans while offering attractive interest rates on deposits. As these institutions are mutuals, the payments made to shareholders are technically dividends. Earnings above anticipated dividends will generally be retained in reserves or capital surplus or, on occasion, will be paid to shareholders in the form of an extra dividend. Sometimes, the credit union will even grant borrowers a refund of interest charged on loans.

Credit unions are fairly democratic institutions. Members feel a real linkage with both the institution and the common bond that supports it. All officers and board members are elected by shareholders, with each member getting one vote regardless of the size of his or her account.

With all of these advantages comes a disadvantage. Credit union management has traditionally been viewed as far less experienced than that of competing depository institutions. This is due, in large measure, to the small, unprofessional, and volunteer nature of its staff, and has also led to less innovation and product expansion. Most credit unions offer only the basic deposit-type accounts and simple consumer credit. It has also led to some failures associated with the very nature of these institutions.

The typical credit union has only about $10 million in assets. This is far smaller than the average commercial bank, at about 1/20th the size, and still smaller than the average S&L, at about 1/35th the size, and the average savings bank, at about 1/70th the size. However, today credit unions are the third largest supplier of consumer installment debt, ranking behind only commercial banks and finance companies. They supply approximately 15 percent of all such debt in the United States.

Credit unions are overseen by a separate regulatory structure that was established along with the others during the Depression era. Federal chartering began in 1934, but it was not until 1970 that the National Credit Union Administration was established. The **National Credit Union Administration,** an independent U.S. government agency, issues federal charters and is responsible for conducting periodic examinations of the credit unions and regulating them. Deposits are insured up to $100,000 by the **National Credit Union Shares Insurance Fund** (NCUSIF), which is managed by the NCUA. A small number of state-chartered credit unions are insured and regulated by state agencies. However, state-chartered credit unions can qualify for the NCUSIF insurance if they desire to do so.

There have been some recent discussions about altering the regulation and structure of credit unions. Proposals have ranged from integrating the deposit insurance fund into the FDIC to eliminating the industry's tax-exempt status. However, members of credit unions are a loyal lot, and prior attempts to change the industry have failed.

Sources and Uses of Funds

Credit unions obtain their funds largely from their members. Their primary vehicle for raising funds is interest-bearing time deposits, called "shares." Since 1978, credit unions have been able to offer money market certificates that earn

EXHIBIT 22.6   **Financial Assets and Liabilities of Credit Unions**
(Second Quarter 1995; $ billions)

Assets		*Liabilities*	
Checkable deposits and currency	$ 7.5	Checkable deposits	$ 30.1
Time deposits	17.3	Small time & savings deposits	239.2
Fed. funds & security RPs	8.6	Large time deposits	7.9
U.S. government securities	63.5	Fed. Home Loan bank loans	0.3
Home mortgages	64.5	Miscellaneous liabilities	4.3
Consumer credit	126.4		
Open market paper	1.3		
Miscellaneous assets	17.4		
Total	**$306.4**	**Total**	**$281.8**

Source: Board of Governors of the Federal Reserve System, *Flow of Funds Accounts,* 1995.

current interest rates. They also offer "share drafts," which are similar to interest-bearing checking deposits, the industry's version of a NOW account. Share drafts were authorized by the Depository Institutions Deregulation and Monetary Control Act back in 1980 but had appeared somewhat before in states that permitted institutions to develop this product. Employer-sponsored credit unions often offer payroll savings plans that make it convenient for their employees to set aside a portion of their earnings for a savings account. This service gives the credit union industry a stable flow of funds into its share accounts.

Funds are used primarily for consumer loans. Most of these loans are short-term; as a result, there is less problem of disintermediation during times of changing interest rates. Credit unions can make unsecured loans to members for periods not exceeding 5 years, and secured loans for periods as long as 30 years. Historically, auto loans have been a major type of loan granted to members. However, with the intense competition of automobile finance companies such as GMAC and Ford Motor Credit, as well as banks and finance companies, credit unions have increased their activity in providing residential mortgages, credit cards, education loans, home improvement loans, and loans to the small businesses of members. Credit unions can invest in U.S. government and federal agency securities, and they have recently expanded their holdings of mortgage-backed agency debt. They can also place funds in deposits at federally insured commercial banks, savings and loan associations, savings banks, and other credit unions. These uses of funds provide needed liquidity to satisfy an upsurge in loan demand or share withdrawals. The industry's balance sheet for the second quarter of 1995 is presented in Exhibit 22.6.

In addition to these credit and share services, some credit unions offer other nonbanking services. Traditionally, share life insurance was a benefit of membership. However, institutions are now offering third-party life insurance, financial planning, and other products to their members.

Distinctions and Differences

As noted at the outset of this chapter, most of the differences between the various depository institutions are historical in nature and, today, have become blurred. At the margin, however, there remain some distinctions. For instance, some institutions invest more heavily in consumer loans, while others invest more heavily in mortgage loans, securities, or business loans.

There are many more distinctions than real differences, however. Credit unions offer "share drafts," savings banks and S&Ls offer NOW accounts, and commercial banks offer checking accounts, both interest bearing and noninterest bearing. All of these instruments are available on small 2 3/4-inch by 6-inch printed paper, all are accepted interchangeably for the satisfaction of debts and conducting of transactions, and all can bear interest.

Other distinctions are made between time deposits, certificates of deposit, and shares, but the consumer will see no real differences. Each type of institution offers its own brand of money market certificates, money market share accounts, or money market deposit accounts. Drafts may be written against these accounts to satisfy debts or conduct transactions in an identical manner. Each institution can manage IRAs, has insurance on deposits up to $100,000, and can make consumer and mortgage loans. Each can be either federally or state chartered. All of these institutions offer credit cards, traveler's checks, and other services.

It is not surprising that the real differences among these institutions are dwindling. There is intense competition among financial institutions. With the trend toward deregulation, these institutions have sought to gain or retain their market share by providing their clients/consumers/depositors/owners needed services. A focus in today's market is on convenience, and it would compromise an institution's competitiveness if it were not able to offer a reasonably full line of desired services. We see a continuing trend toward the evolution of a full-service financial institution. As will be discussed in the next chapter, competition is increasing from nontraditional areas such as mutual funds, insurance companies, and finance companies. Some of these institutions are offering interest-bearing checking-type accounts and a myriad of other services that eclipse those available at many standard depository institutions. It is often said that "only time will tell." In this case, it will tell that we are right!

Summary

The financial markets have many and varied institutions operating within them. A critical part of the sector is the depository institutions. For most, this is synonymous with the commercial banking industry. However, there are three other important depository-type institutions that provide needed financial services to both borrowers and lenders. Each has its own history, regulatory structure, and constituency, yet each is evolving toward a common form. The future will be one in which all four subsectors may remain, but only because of historical accident. All of these institutions service the depository market and lending market in much the same way.

Key Concepts

bet the bank, 557
common bond, 561
credit unions, 561
Deposit Institutions Deregulation and Monetary
  Control Act, 554
Federal Deposit Insurance Corporation
  Improvement Act, 550
Federal Home Loan Bank System, 549
Financial Institutions Reform, Recovery and
  Enforcement Act, 549
money market deposit accounts, 552
mutuals, 546

National Credit Union Administration, 562
NOW accounts, 548, 552
Office of Thrift Supervision, 549
regulatory forbearance, 557
Resolution Trust Corporation, 549
savings and loan associations, 546
Savings Association Insurance Fund, 549
savings banks, 553
securitization, 553
thrift crisis, 547
thrifts, 556
whole loan sales, 553

Review Questions

1. Since the 1970s, the S&L industry has contracted significantly. Is this contraction necessarily bad? Cite and explain some favorable effects of the contraction of the S&L industry.

2. Why is the likelihood of disintermediation less severe for credit unions than for savings banks and S&Ls? How have the recent changes in credit union portfolios altered this likelihood?

3. The thrift crisis was precipitated by rapidly rising interest rates. In response, the government undertook various measures in the effort to address the problem. Enumerate and discuss the wisdom of these actions. Be sure to consider both the short- and long-term effects of these regulatory changes.

4. Consult the financial section of your local paper and examine the different yields offered to depositors at local financial institutions. What is the range of the deviation

from the mean, and how can you explain these differences?

5. A recent presidential commission suggested the conglomeration of depository institutions with a single regulatory oversight body. Given what you have read in this chapter, evaluate the wisdom of such a proposal and discuss the pros and cons of its implementation.

6. The current deposit insurance structure has three funds and two insurers. Some have proposed pooling these different entities into a single depository insurer. Discuss the pros and cons of doing so in light of the recent history of each type of depository institution involved.

7. Who is to blame for the thrift crisis?

8. The incentive to "bet the bank" by undertaking risky investment practices can become overwhelming when capital and surplus are low. What can regulators do to prevent this behavior?

References

Barth, James R. *The Great Savings and Loan Debacle.* Washington, D.C.: American Enterprise Institute Press, 1991.

Barth, James R.; Philip F. Bartholomew; and Michael G. Bradley. "Determinants of Thrift Institution Resolution Costs." *Journal of Finance,* July 1990.

Benston, G., et al. *Perspectives on Safe and Sound Banking.* Cambridge, Mass.: MIT Press, 1986.

Credit Union National Association, *CUNA Yearbook.* Madison, Wis.: Credit Union National Association, 1995.

Davids, Lewis E. "Comparing Bank, Savings and Loan, and Credit Union Installment Loan Costs." *The Bankers Magazine,* July–August 1982.

Dunham, Constance R., and Gary G. Heaton. "The Growing Competitiveness of Credit Unions." *New England Economic Review,* Federal Reserve Bank of Boston, May/June 1985.

Dunham, Constance R., and Margaret Guerin-Calvert. "How Quickly Can Thrifts Move into Commercial Lending?" *New England Economic Review,* Federal Reserve Bank of Boston, November/December 1983.

Fraser, Donald R., and James W. Kolari. "The 1982 Depository Institutions Act and Security Returns in the Savings Industry." *Journal of Financial Research,* Winter 1990.

Goldstein, Steven; James McNulty; and James Verbrugge. "Scale Economies in the Savings and Loan Industry before Diversification." *Journal of Economics and Business,* August 1987.

Kane, Edward. "Principal-Agent Problems in S&L Salvage." *Journal of Finance,* July 1990.

———. "Dangers of Capital Forbearance: The Case of the FSLIC and Zombie S&Ls." *Contemporary Policy Issues,* January 1987.

Merton, Robert C. "An Analytic Derivation of the Cost of Deposit Insurance and Loan Guarantees: An Application of Modern Option Pricing Theory." *Journal of Banking and Finance,* 1977.

Pearce, Douglas K. "Recent Developments in the Credit Union Industry." *Economic Review,* Federal Reserve Bank of Kansas City, June 1984.

Santomero, Anthony M. "The Intermediation Process and the Future of the Thrifts." *Expanded Competitive Markets and the Thrift Industry,* Federal Home Loan Bank Board, San Francisco, 1988.

White, L. J. *The S and L Debacle.* New York: Oxford University Press, 1991.

Nonbank Financial Institutions

This chapter reviews the fastest growing segment of the financial institutions industry—nondepository organizations. It analyzes the growth in the insurance industry, examines pension funds and mutual funds as alternative savings vehicles, and looks at the growth in special-purpose finance companies. Current developments in interindustry competition are reviewed in light of the dynamics of the financial services industry.

Beyond the standard depository institutions covered in the previous two chapters, there are a large number of nondepository institutions in the financial sector. These entities run from the mundane to the esoteric. Some are well-known parts of our own financial planning, such as insurance companies or pension funds. Others, such as mutual funds, are evident only to some of us. And lastly, there are institutions that have very little visibility but many assets under their control. Special-purpose finance companies are a case in point. This chapter will review these institutions in some detail and outline their activities and their place within the capital market.

Nondepository financial institutions, while quite distinct, have one important attribute in common. They are all in a part of the financial market that is growing most rapidly. In fact, the emergence of these institutions over the past several decades can be viewed as the cause of changes that have occurred in the behavior of depository institutions and have resulted in the decline in their market share. The story of nonbank institutions is really a tale of change, innovation, and regulatory avoidance. It is, in short, a success story.

The Insurance Industry

The notion of "saving for a rainy day" is shared by many cultures. However, two problems arise with this notion. First, one never knows if he or she will ultimately experience the feared "rainy day" once, twice, thrice, or not at all. Second, if the rainy day does come, it may arrive at a time in one's life before sufficient savings have been accumulated to confront the event. **Insurance** is the savings vehicle that has been developed to provide for the rainy days in our lives, no matter when and how often they occur. It is a mechanism that can reduce financial uncertainty.

Everyone is a potential victim of numerous perils that could wreak financial havoc in his or her life. For example, fire could destroy a family's home, or death could take away a family's wage earner. To the individual family, the occurrence of either peril would have devastating financial consequences. Insurance cannot prevent the peril from occurring. Rather, insurance reduces the uncertainty of future financial losses that could result from the occurrence of various perils. An uncertain, future loss of potentially great magnitude can be avoided by incurring a small cost today. That small cost is the insurance **premium** paid by the policyholder to buy protection from the financial consequences of unfortunate events.

Financial uncertainty for the individual is reduced because risk is transferred to an insurance company. An insurer accepts this risk because various techniques, such as risk pooling and competent statistical/actuarial projections, allow the company to estimate accurately the total amount of loss under its policies. The insurer does not know when a given individual will die, have an automobile accident, get sick or injured, or have a house fire. Yet, through the law of large numbers, and with the help of actuaries, who are specialists in assessing risk, the insurance company can make an accurate estimate about the number of deaths, the incidence of disease or injury, and the number of accidents and fires that will occur during any given year to a large group of people. Thus, a price, which the industry refers to as a premium, can be charged to the insured population that is adequate to cover the expected losses of its members during any given period.

Along with risk bearing, insurance companies also engage in spread lending. This is a less obvious but equally important part of the overall business of insurance. Since premiums are paid in advance and any claims that arise from policies are not likely to be settled, or paid, until some time in the future, the issuance of an insurance contract creates a pool of funds available for investment. The "spread" is the difference between the returns achieved on the invested funds and the ultimate cost of the funds to the insurer. This spread is not known at the outset because it depends on the earnings realized from invested funds and on the underwriting profit or loss experienced on the underlying policies. Nonetheless, a reasonable estimate of the spread can be made based on the characteristics of the investments chosen and the statistical properties of the risks assumed under an insurance contract.

Structure and Financial Position of the Industry

Three major segments make up the insurance industry: **life/health insurance, property/casualty insurance,** and **reinsurance.** Each segment has its own set of issues, although some firms are active in all areas. Companies whose activities span more than one segment of the industry are referred to as **multiline insurers.** Below, we consider each part of the industry in turn.

The Life/Health Insurance Sector.   Life/health insurers offer products that are based upon life expectancy and health, including health insurance and death benefit life insurance and annuity products. The underlying risks absorbed by these companies involve **mortality risk,** which is the risk of bad health or injury and the uncertain time of death. These firms are organized in two ways, either as stock companies or as mutual companies. The primary distinction between the two forms of organization is found in the ownership of the entity. A stock company is owned by its stockholders, who have contributed the capital necessary to operate the company; a mutual company is owned by its policyholders, who have capitalized their company through the payment of excess insurance premiums. There are approximately 1,700 stock companies and 100 mutuals in the United States today.

At the end of 1995, assets of U.S. life insurers exceeded $2 trillion. Exhibit 23.1 shows, for December 31, 1994, the total assets, capital and surplus, premium income, and investment income of the life insurance industry, and it distributes these quantities between the mutual and stock sectors. Note that despite the disparity in number of companies, the two sectors are relatively comparable in terms of total assets. The stocks control close to 60 percent of the industry's assets, while the mutuals hold the remainder. It was not long ago that this situation was reversed, with mutuals dominating the industry.

The Property/Casualty Insurance Sector.   Property/casualty companies offer products that insure personal or real property, and reimburse damages occurring

EXHIBIT 23.1

1994 U.S. life insurance industry: stocks versus mutuals ($ billions)

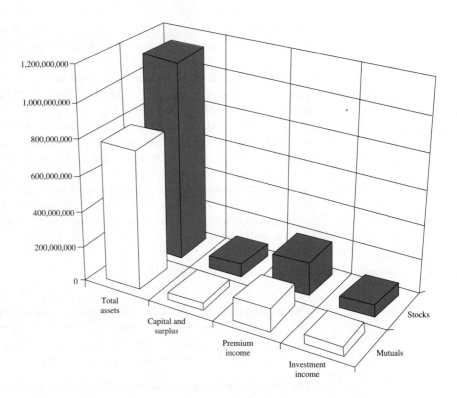

as a result of accident, fire, or malfeasance. The risks absorbed here revolve around the randomness of **event risk,** that is, the chance that something will go wrong. Firms in this part of the business are usually organized as either **stock** or **mutual** companies. However, property/casualty companies may also be organized as reciprocal exchanges or Lloyds-type associations. A **reciprocal exchange** is comprised of "subscribers" essentially insuring each other. The **Lloyds-type organizations** are associations of individuals who are personally liable for a specified portion of each policy issued. The much more common varieties, however, have standard organizational forms. Of the 1,187 property/casualty companies reported on in the 1995 edition of *Best's Aggregates and Averages,* 702 are stocks and 414 are mutuals, while 56 are reciprocals and 15 are Lloyds-type associations. The number of institutions offering property/casualty insurance, however, is larger than this total. According to the Insurance Information Institute, there were approximately 3,500 property/casualty companies in operation in the United States at the end of 1994.

Exhibit 23.2 uses year-end 1994 data to illustrate the total assets, capital and surplus, premiums earned, and investment income of the property/casualty industry. It also distributes these quantities across the mutual and stock sectors. Notice that in contrast to the life insurance industry, stock companies have an even more dominating position in the property/casualty industry.

EXHIBIT 23.2

*1994 U.S. property/
casualty insurance
industry: stocks versus
mutuals ($ billions)*

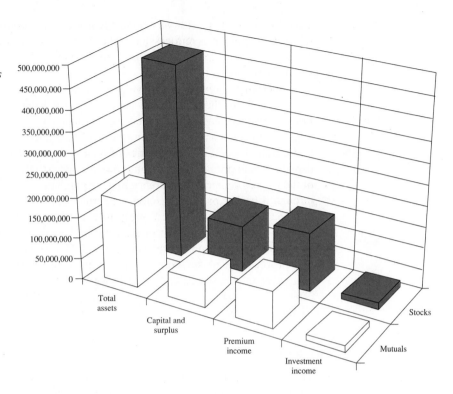

The Reinsurance Sector.   Reinsurance is a mechanism used by the insurance industry to spread the risks it assumes from policyholders. Through it, the industry's losses are absorbed and distributed among a group of companies so that no single company is overburdened with the financial responsibility of offering coverage to its policyholders. Catastrophes, unexpected liabilities, and a series of large losses that might be too great for an individual insurer to absorb can be handled through reinsurance. Without reinsurance, most insurers would be able to cover only the safest of ventures, leaving many risky but worthwhile ventures without coverage.

A reinsurance contract is an insurance policy issued by one company—the reinsurer—to another company, usually called the ceding company, primary carrier, or the direct underwriter. The ceding company is the insurer that underwrites the policy initially and then later, by purchasing reinsurance, shifts part or all of the liability for coverage to a reinsurer. This reinsurance provides reimbursement to the ceding insurer for claims payments covered by the reinsurance agreement. It does not alter the underlying reinsured policies or the obligations created by those policies. However, the reinsurance does provide protection to the ceding insurer against frequent or severe losses.

The quantity of insurance ceded to a reinsurer is called the cession. If more of the risk is shifted to the reinsurer than it desires, the reinsurer may in turn reinsure a portion of the risk with yet another reinsurer. This reinsurance purchased by reinsurers is known as retrocessions. The retrocession of risks often proceeds in a chainlike fashion, spreading exposure to risks throughout the international reinsurance community.

Much of the reinsurance coverage is available through German and Swiss reinsurers. Also, there are some large reinsurers located in the United States, France, Sweden, and Japan, while a few other key players in the reinsurance market are scattered about. Reinsurance can be obtained from professional domestic insurers, located in the countries of their respective clients; from reinsurance departments of primary carriers; and from foreign-based reinsurers located outside of the client's country. Reinsurance may be purchased directly from the reinsurer, through a broker or other insurance intermediary, or through an insurance exchange, such as the ones at Rotterdam and Chicago. The advantage of going through a broker is that some of the large brokerage firms will provide advisory services about the nature of the contract and the quality of the reinsurer and will help negotiate the most favorable price for the contract desired. However, they do charge for their services, and some brokers do not offer and are not capable of offering these services. Rather, the brokers act merely as an intermediary for a handful of companies with which they conduct virtually all of their business.[1]

Assets Held by Insurance Companies

The insurance industry occupies a dominant role in the capital markets. Perhaps no financial institutions own more corporate bonds than insurance companies. This dominance arises from their role as managers of pension funds, managers of mutual funds, and providers of insurance, which carries long-term obligations that make bonds a natural asset class for insurers. The insurance industry's annual appetite for new corporate bonds often exceeds the supply of new issues in the United States, so these companies supplement their bond purchases with mortgages, common and preferred stock, real estate, short-term and medium-term notes, government bonds, mortgage-backed securities, and foreign bonds. Exhibit 23.3 shows the year-end 1994 composition of insurers' asset portfolios for stock and mutual life/health organizations combined. It also contains comparable information for the property/casualty industry. If more detail could be shown that would permit an examination of the differences in asset allocation by ownership type, one clear distinction would surface. It is generally the case that stock companies own relatively more bonds and fewer mortgages and policy loans than their mutual counterparts. Otherwise, the mutuals and stocks invest rather similarly.

An examination of Exhibit 23.3 reveals that both life/health and property/casualty companies are heavily invested in fixed-income securities. However, one finds that there is a distinct difference in the roles of mortgages and equities. The

---

[1]An extensive treatment of reinsurance—the purposes, contracts, institutions, and investments—is available in McIsaac and Babbel, *The World Bank Primer on Reinsurance* (Washington, D.C.: World Bank Financial Sector Development Department, 1995).

Exhibit 23.3

1994 portfolio composition: U.S. life/ health versus U.S. property/casualty

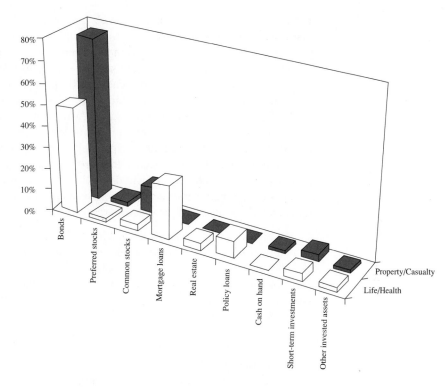

life/health companies are heavily invested in mortgages and light in equities, but the property/casualty companies hold few mortgages and are heavily invested in equities. More will be said about this below.

The Regulation of Insurance Companies

Insurance companies are regulated by the states. There has been little federal regulation ever since the passage of the **McCarran-Ferguson Act of 1945.** This federal statute relegated authority to the states to regulate virtually all insurance company activity. The mandate includes both firm solvency and product specification. Firm solvency issues are generally addressed by the state of domicile of the insurance firm, although some states, such as New York, require firms offering products within their borders to demonstrate a financial capability similar to those headquartered within the state. Indeed, in the case of New York, this practice of requiring compliance to New York insurance regulations regardless of where else a firm may conduct business, coupled with the size, experience, stature, and stringent regulations of the New York Department of Insurance, has led insurers to regard New York as the *de facto* national insurance regulatory authority.

Notwithstanding New York's special role in the regulation of insurance, it remains the case that there are over 50 insurance regulatory authorities with disparate rules and approaches. To promote a convergence of state insurance regulatory standards, state insurance commissioners formed the **National Association of Insurance Commissioners** more than a century ago in 1871. This organization provides various services to state commissioners and has recently developed the standardized examination system known as the **Insurance Regulatory Information System** (IRIS). Regulators examine the IRIS financial ratios for indications of insolvency risk. Also, the NAIC has proposed "Model Investment Laws" both for the life/health and the property/casualty industries, which states may choose to adopt, that regulate the composition of insurance investment portfolios.

State regulators have ultimate responsibility for stipulating which asset categories are authorized for inclusion in the portfolios of insurers. This, in turn, has a significant impact on the investment flexibility of members of the industry. While the laws regulating insurance company investments currently vary from state to state, they share at least four stated purposes:

1. Prevent management from making "speculative" or otherwise inappropriate investments that would endanger the solvency of the insurer and thus impair the rights of policyholders. To achieve this goal, state laws typically set standards on quality and diversification of the portfolio, both among classes of assets and on individual assets.

2. Stabilize the financial position of the insurer to prevent the insurer from being unduly vulnerable to dramatic shifts in the economy. Here, too, the goal is often used to restrict the set of allowable assets and to require evidence of diversification in the asset portfolio.

3. Restrict insurers from gaining control of an industry or company that is beyond the influence of the insurance regulatory authorities. Such constraints can be used to prevent an insurer from directly acquiring a large block of stock in another firm outside the insurance industry.

4. Achieve certain "social goals" as they are seen relevant to local regulatory authorities.

How these goals are converted into regulation is a different matter. From these lofty goals to line-by-line regulation, state authorities have established a fairly rigid set of constraints on the industry's asset selection.

Regulation of Life Insurers' Investments.   Historically, life insurers have dealt in long-term, fixed-rate contracts, with premiums and reserves that are based on conservative, fixed interest rates. While recent product trends, as we will review later, stress products that provide few guarantees, investment restrictions faced by life insurers still reflect the need to provide guarantees. Accordingly, life insurers are largely restricted to placing their cash flows in high-grade bonds and mortgage loans. Most states have specific rules on the amounts that can be placed in real estate, common stocks, and preferred stocks. For example, one state restricts common stock investments for life insurers to 10 percent of total assets or 100 percent of surplus, whichever is lower.

States have also adopted specific quality requirements for life insurer investments. For example, one state requires that the issuing company of a qualified bond must earn at least one and one-half times its fixed charges on all debt during the previous year. Investments in low-grade bonds must be accompanied by supplying extra reserves, up to 20 percent, to provide a cushion against adverse default or market price experience. More uniformity is anticipated as states begin to adopt the NAIC's Model Investment Law.[2]

A life insurer can establish "separate accounts," which are subject to less stringent restrictions. Through separate accounts, such as for pension assets or variable life insurance, a life insurer can compete for access to significant pools of assets without the normal investment restrictions placed on the "general account" of a life insurer. Recognizing a need to give life insurers a reasonable degree of investment flexibility, several states have adjusted their laws to permit life insurers to hold a small percentage of assets in "unregulated" investments. Moreover, most state regulators permit investments in options and futures to hedge the portfolios against interest rate and market risks.

Regulation of Property/Casualty Insurers' Investments.   Property/casualty insurers are subject to fewer investment restrictions than life insurers. However, an NAIC Model Investment Law that imposes more restrictions than before is currently under consideration by property/casualty insurers. Several states require that all domiciled property/casualty insurers invest assets equal to the required minimum capital surplus in government securities such as U.S. or state bonds, mortgage loans, and, in a few states, public utility bonds. Several other states are more demanding and require that the insurer use the foregoing investments to offset *all* required reserves, including all loss reserves and unearned premium reserves. A few other states expand the allowable investments for offsetting reserves to include bonds and/or preferred stock of corporations that meet minimum standards of solvency and earning power.

Beyond the requirements to offset either capital/surplus or reserves, property/casualty insurers have latitude to invest in common stock, real estate, and other risky investment classes with only a few limitations on the quality of these investments. Most states also permit investments in options and futures contracts if they serve a hedging purpose.

Regulation of Product.   Beyond firm solvency and investment restrictions, the state commissioners must also approve products for sale within their borders. This requirement has led to a massive bureaucratic headache for the industry, as it must receive authorization from all 50 states to offer a product nationally. To ease this burden, the NAIC has worked to develop common standards, and individual states will often accept another's approval. For example, approval within New York is frequently sufficient to obtain authorization in many other states.

However, product authorization may not be sufficient. For some highly visible products, such as automobile insurance or workers' compensation, the state

---

[2]See David F. Babbel, "A Perspective on Model Investment Laws," *Journal of the American CLU and ChFC,* September 1994.

commissioner may also have authority to control prices. Through their role as public advocates, some state commissioners have chosen to set price ceilings and even availability criteria for certain insurance products. Experience in New Jersey, Massachusetts, California, Washington, D.C., and elsewhere has shown that this approach often backfires, as insurers drop products that are made unprofitable by price ceilings, and sometimes even withdraw from states imposing such strictures. Product availability and consumer choice typically suffer, and in the long run, lessened competition among insurers may mean that prices do not decline at all.

Insurance Liabilities

Insurance companies raise funds primarily through the sale of insurance policies. Unlike other liabilities, which pay a stipulated interest rate or dividend, insurance liabilities are customized to direct indemnification payments to those customers or their beneficiaries who have experienced a covered event, such as an accident, fire, disability, disease, or death. Accordingly, any discussion of liabilities is really a discussion of insurance products themselves.

There are four principal groups of products sold by life/health insurance companies: life insurance, annuities and guaranteed investment contracts, disability insurance, and health insurance. Each of these product categories contains subproducts that are unique and respond in different ways to movements in both the underlying insurance risk and asset values in the market. For some of these subproducts, their overriding determinant is future movements in interest rates.

In today's complex and dynamic financial markets, each life insurance company is faced with the difficult task of designing and pricing insurance products that meet the needs both of target markets and selected distribution channels. Product development must also consider the need to match assets with liabilities for the company as a whole. Within this context, the following life insurance products are evaluated in more detail:

- Term insurance.
- Nonparticipating and participating whole life insurance.
- Universal life insurance.
- Variable life insurance.

Together, these products account for about 95 percent of the life insurance offerings of the industry. In terms of insurance in force, term and whole life account for the bulk of it, but universal life, variable life, and the very popular universal-variable life hybrid are also important products and account for most of the remainder of what the industry sells.

Term Life Insurance.   Term life insurance pays a death benefit if the insured dies within a specified period of time. If the insured survives this period, the contract expires and there are no future benefit rights. Most term insurance sold today is renewable and/or convertible. Renewable term insurance guarantees the insured the right to renew the policy each year, up to a maximum age, for example 60, without evidence of insurability, that is, good health. The renewal provision is an option granted to the policyowner. This option raises the premium slightly beyond that for a nonrenewable contract. However, it is seen by many as an attractive option. With annual renewable term insurance, the premium rate for each year of coverage is specified and guaranteed by the insurance company. Of course, the rate per $1,000 coverage goes up each year, as the insured ages and remaining life expectancy decreases. Given that term insurance liabilities typically are for a short duration, they do not create a need for the insurer to build reserves. Thus, they do not lead to significant accumulation of assets by the insurer.

Convertible term insurance gives the insured a right to convert a term insurance contract into a form of permanent insurance. When the policyowner has exercised the option to convert, the premiums increase to the level required for a new policy, which is generally a whole life or universal life policy. For many life insurers, term insurance is sold primarily as a first step toward the ultimate sale, through conversion, of a cash-value permanent policy. Thus, an insurer with a significant amount of term insurance policies may be positioned to acquire significant assets when a predictable portion of these contracts is converted each year.

Whole Life Insurance.   Whole life insurance comes in two varieties: nonparticipating and participating. Both kinds of policies call for periodic level premiums throughout the life of the insured. The life insurance company establishes a policy reserve that is designed to be an amount sufficient to meet the maturing obligation contained in the whole life insurance contract. Under the level annual premium plan of whole life insurance, premiums paid in the early years are more than sufficient to cover the cost of providing current policy benefits, because mortality rates are low. In the later years, as mortality rates increase with age, premiums are inadequate to cover the promises of the insurer. This gives rise to a need for a life insurance policy reserve, which is the amount required to make up the difference, at any time, between the net present value of prospective benefits and prospective premiums. Thus, the reserves in a whole life policy and the matching assets held by the insurer increase as the contract remains in force and approaches maturity. A whole life insurance policy with a face amount of $100,000 would generate policy reserves that would accumulate to the full face value of the policy by age 99 or 100. This is shown graphically in Exhibit 23.4.

The policies remain in effect for as long as the fixed premium is paid. Should the policyholder decide to discontinue payment, the contract could be surrendered for its cash surrender value. The insured can access these cash values prior to surrender by incurring a policy loan. This way, the insurance will remain in force, but any death benefit will be reduced by the amount of the loan outstanding until it is fully repaid. These cash values grow at an increasing rate as the policy reserves increase.

In **nonparticipating contracts,** issued primarily by stock life insurance companies, the level premium and annual cash surrender values are typically guaranteed

EXHIBIT 23.4

*Reserve buildup
pattern on whole
life insurance*

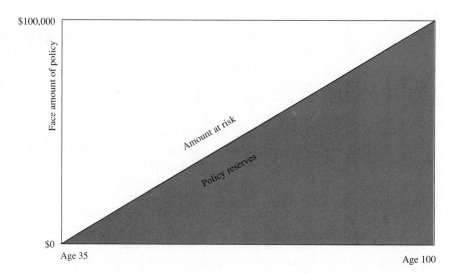

for every year of the contract. In **participating contracts,** issued primarily by mutual life insurers, policy dividends are earned at the end of each year. These dividends are adjusted depending on the mortality experience, overhead expense, and investment performance that the insurer achieved relative to its conservative assumptions for each of these items on which premiums were based. The lower the mortality experience, the lower the overhead expense, and the better the investment performance, relative to projections, the higher the dividend to policyholders.

Universal Life Insurance.   Universal life unbundles the component parts of a permanent (whole life) life insurance contract. We can view universal life insurance as a flexible-premium deposit fund. Each year, the policyowner pays a premium, the size of which is flexible within stipulated bounds. From this premium is subtracted an annual charge for mortality expenses and a charge to cover administrative/marketing costs. The remainder is placed into a fund that is credited with an interest rate that is reset annually. In addition, because it is permanent life insurance, the funds accruing interest in a universal life policy are tax deferred.

Universal life also allows the policyowner to exercise a "withdrawal" option that gives the insured access to cash values without forcing him to surrender the contract or take a policy loan. A withdrawal simply reduces the funds in the universal life account that accrue interest and reduces the death benefit by the amount of the withdrawal. However, from the companies' perspectives, the availability of a withdrawal option increases the sensitivity of the universal life policy liability to changes in interest rates and may affect the company's profitability.

There are several approaches insurers use to develop the interest rate credited on universal life insurance. Many insurers tie the interest rate to a market standard such as the one-year T-bill rate less some figure, such as 100 basis points. Others do not tie the credited rate to any financial index; rather, they set a rate based on competition or based on the yield on their asset portfolio. This portfolio yield is an average on all investments in the insurer's general account, unadjusted for current market conditions. Accordingly, crediting rates set by this method may appear favorable during periods of declining interest rates but unattractive during periods of rising rates.

Most insurers guarantee the interest rate quoted at the time of purchase for 6 to 12 months. After this period, the rate is adjusted to reflect the current rate quoted by the company on new universal life insurance policies. Some insurers provide two sets of interest rates: one rate for new contracts and another rate for continuing/renewal contracts. To compete successfully in the market for new clients, the new contract rate is often a slightly higher interest rate.

Variable Life Insurance.   Variable life insurance is similar to traditional permanent life insurance with one major difference: the cash value, or savings element, is not guaranteed. Variable life resembles a whole life contract with cash values invested in a balanced mutual fund. In fact, several major mutual fund companies provide investment products and services to insurers who wish to enter the variable life insurance market. The cash values in a variable policy increase or decrease with the yield on the separate fund in which the variable life insurance assets are invested. The cash values in a variable policy are marked to market. Today's variable life insurance policyowner typically can select from several investment choices and has the ability to switch, with some restrictions, between alternative investment funds. The provision of such investment flexibility has contributed to the growth of variable life insurance products.

Annuities and Employee Benefit Funds.   An annuity is a contract that promises the holder periodic payments for a specified length of time, which could refer to the holder's lifetime. To purchase a stream of future income, the investor transfers assets to the insurer, either in a single premium or through periodic premiums. During the accumulation period, all funds in the annuity accrue tax deferred. Then, an annuity systematically liquidates previously accumulated assets.

The benefit payments under an annuity may be either fixed or variable. In a fixed annuity, the insurer guarantees a specific periodic payment amount; in a variable annuity, the amount of benefit payments depends on the performance of the portfolio in which the assets are invested. At the end of the accumulation period, the investor can usually convert the accumulated investment from a variable to a fixed annuity, or vice versa.

The amount of the fixed annuity that can be purchased depends on the period of time over which it is to be received and the rate of return that the insurance company uses in pricing the annuity benefit. Under a variable annuity, the insurer guarantees to pay a fixed number of variable annuity units per period, as long as the annuitant lives. The value of the unit fluctuates with the value of the separate portfolio of securities. Annual benefits equal the number of units received multiplied by the current value of each unit. In selling a fixed annuity, the insurer

Box 23.1

If I Sue Myself, Will I Win?

The litigation frenzy continues unabated. In an ironic twist, however, the plaintiffs are, in essence, suing themselves in some recent cases. In a very real sense, this sort of litigation is like the situation in which you have $5 in each of your two front pockets, and you transfer $3 from your left to your right pocket. You still have a total of only $10. If someone persuades you, for a fee, to let them oversee the cash transfer between your pockets, you will wind up with even less than $10.

In late 1995 and early 1996, we have witnessed several dozen class-action lawsuits levied against life insurers over the alleged misrepresentation of so-called "vanishing premium" policies whose premiums did not vanish. Some of the most notable of these suits have been against large mutual life insurance companies. This is a type of lawsuit that we find most ironic. In such cases, the policyowners are truly suing themselves, and they may be placing themselves in a situation just as dubious as the individual who tries to get ahead by shuffling money between pockets.

The purpose of this commentary is neither to criticize nor to support the vanishing premium concept. Rather, it is to point out that in the case of mutual life insurance company policyholders, there is little point to the lawsuits. A typical firm has both debt holders and equity holders. It owes money to its creditors (bondholders), and it provides its owners (stockholders) with returns on their equity. Mutual life insurers are similar in this respect. They have

both debt holders and equity holders. However, they do not generally issue either bonds or stock. Rather they issue insurance policies, which act as a combination of both debt and equity instruments. The debtlike instrument is the guaranteed benefit of the insurance policy. The equitylike portion is in the form of dividends that either lower the premiums due on the policy or increase the benefits payable. Thus, policyowners are not only the firm's *customers* but also its *creditors* and its *owners*. When you buy a policy from a mutual insurance company, the product you are buying is its debt *and* its equity.

Dividends that are declared and paid each year on a participating insurance policy depend on four things: 1) actual versus projected operating costs; 2) actual versus projected mortality expenses; 3) actual versus projected investment income; and 4) the amount of insurer surplus that is generating additional earnings. (Surplus funds provide an extra cushion for contingencies such as an unexpected rise in benefits payable and for adverse changes in the value of securities.) If the insurer does better than expected, the policyowners will ultimately receive the benefit. After all, they own the company. Similarly, if the insurer does worse than expected, the policyowners will receive reduced benefits.

The so-called "vanishing premium" policies at issue in these lawsuits were sold primarily during the 1980s. These policies were really little more than traditional participating whole life policies with

assumes both an investment risk and an annuity/insurance risk. With a variable annuity, the insurer retains the annuity/insurance risk but transfers the interest/investment risk to the policyowner.

One type of annuity, the single premium deferred annuity (SPDA), has been a popular asset accumulation vehicle for individuals recently. As its name implies, the annuity is bought with a single premium. Cash accrues at a specified rate, which is reset periodically. At the end of the deferral period of the SPDA, the accrued funds are annuitized to provide periodic payments to the investor.

high *illustrated* dividends. These dividends were sufficiently high that, if maintained into the distant future, they would be more than sufficient to offset scheduled premiums beyond some point in time.* In essence, the policyowner would pay premiums for a number of years—say 7 to 15 years—and own a policy without needing to make further payments. Thus, the premiums "vanished." Of course all of this was contingent on the illustrated dividend schedule remaining in force throughout the life of the policy.

Now, what happens if the policyowners sue their own firm because they have received reduced

---

*The illustrated dividend schedules were usually based on dividend scales that were in effect at the time of illustration to policyholders. In other words, the scales were based on the dividends actually being paid to extant policyholders. They were not projections into the future but merely illustrations of what could happen if dividend scales remained unaltered for decades to come. Accompanying each dividend illustration was typically some statement to the effect that dividend scales were provided for informational purposes only, and that no warranty was implied about the size of future dividends. During the 1980s and early 1990s, these dividends appeared to be high relative to the market levels of interest rates, owing to the portfolio yield method of determining dividends. The portfolio yield is an accounting concept that averages coupon rates without regard to current prices. In a declining interest rate environment, these coupon rates on seasoned bonds are higher than current yields, giving rise to high illustrated dividends.

benefits—at least compared to what they may have been expecting? In an aggregate and very real sense, they will receive even lower benefits. They are suing nobody but themselves because there is no one else obligated to "make good" on the dividends. As illustrated above, the policyowner in a mutual insurance company has two pockets. One is for debt claims (the guaranteed insurance benefits), and the other is for equity claims (like dividends). A lawsuit does nothing more than transfer a dollar from the equity pocket to the debt pocket. There are no equity owners in a mutual insurance company other than its policyowners, and there is no outside third party insurance available to the mutual insurance company to pay the "winning" plaintiffs.

If the policyowners "win" their lawsuit against themselves, what has really happened is that they receive higher *promised* contractual values, in their roles as creditors, but lower nonguaranteed values, in the form of dividends and insurance values, in their role as owners of the firm. Moreover, the higher *promised* contractual values cannot in the aggregate yield higher total *expected* values of the policies because there is now less surplus backing the claims. The surplus has merely been transferred out of the policyowner's equity pocket and into his debt pocket. In effect, what these policyholders have done is akin to taking a high-grade bond and transforming it into a junk bond with higher promised yields but lower credit quality. Furthermore, there is now a shrinkage in the total amount of money in the pockets. The drain is the rather substantial fees of the attorneys.

Alternatively, the investor may surrender them and choose to receive the funds in a lump sum. These funds can then be exchanged for another SPDA. The tax on accruals within an SPDA is deferred until the contract is either annuitized or surrendered. The tax deferral is continued if the funds from a surrendered annuity are exchanged for another annuity. Most current SPDAs are sold with surrender charges known as "back-end loads." These charges start at 5 percent to 10 percent in the first year and typically reduce to zero by the seventh year. Interest on the SPDA is normally guaranteed for a 12-month period, with interest on future years changed to reflect market rates. Most SPDAs provide for a book-value surrender less any applicable surrender charges and any excise tax on surrenders prior to age 59 1/2. However, some insurers have sold SPDAs with mark-to-market adjustments.

Insurance companies are also heavily involved in the pension fund business. In fact, approximately one-third of pension plan assets are held by insurance companies, amounting to $1 trillion in 1995. The assets are managed for the pension plan sponsor and are credited with the interest rate earned on the insurer's general account. Some insurers use a portfolio rate, while others use a new money method for determining the credited rate.

One contract of particular interest is the guaranteed investment contract (GIC). These contracts promise a guaranteed rate of return over a specified period. A single-premium GIC with a lump sum maturity payment replicates the financial pattern of a zero-coupon bond. Yet, a GIC is considered an insurance contract, not a security. The GIC market is huge, with close to $200 billion of outstanding contracts.

Qualified retirement plans have historically been the most active buyers of GICs, which are used to lessen the volatility of plan portfolios and to reduce the reinvestment risk of fixed-income securities. GICs sold to pension plans are usually of the single-premium variety, whereas GICs sold to profit-sharing plans or 401(k) plans may allow recurring periodic deposits during a "window," usually ranging from 90 days to 1 year. Moreover, they may allow the option of switching from one kind of investment vehicle to another at points in time and receive the yield on the investment vehicle selected.

Disability Insurance.   Disability insurance provides a monthly income benefit in the event of a loss of income from a covered peril such as an accident and/or illness following a waiting period of 30, 60, or 90 days from the onset of disability. The cost of disability insurance reflects the insurer's expected expenses for insured claims, investment earnings, and administrative and marketing costs associated with issuing and maintaining the contracts.

Contracts are available that cover either a short period, one to two years, or a long period, up to age 65 or for life. A major product innovation that was introduced to the market a few years ago was "universal disability insurance." This product creates a new provision for disability insurance: cash values that can be accessed by the insured at the termination of the contract. Universal disability insurance has an investment component clearly attractive to an insured, and it has accordingly attracted considerable attention.

Health Insurance.   A huge fraction of our gross domestic product is spent for health care. Recently, it was estimated that upwards of one-seventh of our GDP is directed toward health care. Federal and state insurance programs, such as Medicare and Medicaid, cover a large portion of these expenses for the aged and poor. Other health care is provided by several types of organizations, including commercial insurers, Blue Cross and Blue Shield associations, preferred provider organizations (PPOs), health maintenance organizations (HMOs), and point-of-service (POS) plans. In addition, some employee benefit plans facilitate an individual by providing supplemental self-insurance through pretax payroll contributions.

With such a huge portion of the GDP directed to health care, it may be surprising that health insurers have relatively low assets at any given time. The reason for this is that reserves for health insurance payments are typically quite low, as premium inflows are used to pay for current expenses. It is common for a health insurer to have no more in assets than what would be required to cover costs over a two- to three-month period. Even the vast "trust funds" of Medicare are more illusory than real, as the funds amount to little more than book entries on a computer. In reality, the taxes collected for Medicare are transferred to other government agencies for use there in return for IOUs. This does little to build up the capital market, although it is great for the record-keeping industry.

Contrast this with life insurers and pension funds, who often build up reserve assets to cover periods stretching 30 years or more. Because of the short duration of the health insurance policy liabilities, assets that are acquired are kept in short duration instruments, typically in money market assets or short-term notes. Thus, health insurers have little importance to the capital markets.

Health care expenditures have been rising more rapidly than inflation over the past two decades, and costs are reaching the explosive stage. To cope with these increasing costs, many health care plans are being developed that differ from the traditional practices. But until health care changes from a "pay as you go" type of system to a funded system, it will have an unimportant direct role in the capital markets. However, health care does play an important indirect role, because the existence of Medicare and other forms of health insurance acts as an economic disincentive for consumers to "save for a rainy day" in their lives; thus, less money flows into the capital markets than would otherwise be the case.

Property/Casualty Insurance.   The two major property/casualty product groups—**personal lines** and **commercial lines**—provide coverage for different segments of the market, consumers and firms, respectively. They also have different implications for investment needs. The basic distinction is in the timing of the cash flows of premiums and claims.

Most personal property/casualty insurance is purchased in the form of multiperil comprehensive contracts, specifically the homeowner/renter contract and the family auto policy. This is the insurance with which we are most familiar, as it represents the bulk of consumer experience with the industry. Homeowner/rental policies provide coverage for fire, theft, and other hazards faced by individuals in their homes or apartments. Automobile insurance covers the daily hazards we face each day on the road. It is in these areas that product and price regulation have been most active, as they are issues that are closely related to consumer—or should we say voter—interest. As with any other product, however, the price is ultimately determined by actuarial risk, administrative cost, and investment returns.

From an investment perspective, it is important to recognize that the liabilities generated by most personal property/casualty insurance have durations that are relatively short. Durations for many forms of property/casualty insurance have been found to range from less than one year to four years, with most lines having a duration of less than two years.[3]

Property risks, by their nature, involve only a short time lapse between the insured event and the settlement of the claim. These losses occur quickly and are quickly settled. To the industry, these lines of insurance are often referred to as **short tailed.** Property coverage contracts, which are the most basic form of business insurance, seek to restore a business facility that has been damaged by some natural disaster such as a fire or windstorm or by an unnatural event such as a riot, civil commotion, or falling aircraft.

Another kind of coverage, called business interruption, may be a separate policy or an enhancement of a basic property policy. Business interruption coverage covers profits and certain expenses for things such as fixed costs that would continue during the period of shutdown and rebuilding following a covered loss. One specialized form of this coverage, called contingent business interruption, protects the firm in the event that a covered loss forces a customer or supplier on which the firm is dependent to close its doors.

Some industries are particularly sensitive to shutdown for any period of time. Newspapers, for example, often will print abbreviated editions following a loss rather than yield the field to competitors. These editions may be printed at considerable additional expense and can add significantly to the total loss the firm suffers. Firms in other highly competitive industries that do not have the capacity to make up for the loss of production facilities could find it necessary to purchase production from their competitors, in the form of subcontracts, at a much higher than normal cost. The insurance policy that covers this risk is called extra expense; it provides funds to protect against loss of market during rebuilding.

In some industries, such as food, clothing, and banking, crime is a major source of loss. Crime policies cover losses due to the dishonesty of employees, losses of money or securities by breaking and entering into the insured premises, or the robbery of an employee away from the insured location. Also covered are losses resulting from the acceptance of counterfeit currency or money orders and from depositors' forgery of the firm's debt.

Liability insurance covers claims filed for injury or property damage arising out of the alleged negligence of the insured. The obligation may be determined by a court decision or by a settlement reached by the parties in anticipation of such a decision. Losses are paid over many years because of the time it takes to litigate, or because the full extent of injury is not immediately apparent; hence these risks are often referred to as **long tailed.** One unique attribute of liability insurance is

---

[3]See David F. Babbel and David R. Klock, "Measuring the Interest Rate Sensitivity of Property/Casualty Insurer Liabilities," in *Insurance, Risk Management, and Public Policy: Essays in Honor of Robert I. Mehr,* edited by Sandra Gustavson and Scott Harrington (Boston: Kluwer Press, 1993).

that the policy is responsible for the defense of the insured against any covered claim or suit even if such a claim should prove to be groundless.

A contract provision that significantly changes the timing of insurance payout is whether the policy features the claims-made or occurrence trigger. Under occurrence-basis policies, an insurer is responsible for all events occurring in the policy period. On a claims-made basis, the policy in force when the claim is recognized and filed is responsible for the loss. The importance of this distinction can be seen in the case of lung disease, where the effects of asbestos may not be diagnosed until 20 years after the claimants' exposure.

Liability insurance policies come in various forms and cover a myriad of liabilities. There is insurance to cover any liability arising from the ownership, maintenance, or use of an automobile, truck, bus, or other motor vehicle. There is liability insurance for products that "go bump in the night," called product liability. There is liability insurance for "errors and omissions." This kind of insurance is designed to cover anyone professing to be an expert, such as a doctor, attorney, accountant, engineer, consultant, corporate officers/directors, and other professionals. It is the only form of liability insurance in which the insurer cannot settle a claim without the prior approval of the insured. This provision arises out of the simple fact that the only commodity a professional provides is his or her reputation, and an insurance settlement might be construed as an admission of less than professional ability. This kind of insurance coverage is always written using a claims-made coverage trigger.

General liability insurance is a broader kind of liability insurance that is designed to protect a firm from other kinds of liability, such as that arising from the ownership or occupancy of real estate, business operations, and so forth. Umbrella liability is another kind of insurance that is designed to fill any gaps in coverage that might exist between the various liability insurance policies and to increase the total amount of coverage provided beyond that contained in the other liability policies.

Another kind of long-tailed coverage is known as workers' compensation. This is a no-fault insurance for work-related accidents or illnesses. Injured employees need not prove negligence on the part of the employer; they need merely show that the injuries arose out of employment. Each state has its own workers' compensation law that establishes benefit levels. These benefits typically cover 100 percent of all medical expenses, two-thirds of lost wages for the duration of the disability, rehabilitation expense, if so indicated, and a survivor annuity benefit in the event that the employee is fatally injured.

Pension Funds

Approximately 60 percent of nonagricultural workers in the United States are covered by private pension plans. Government plans cover over half of the remaining nonagricultural workers. The rest are on their own, except for Social Security and any retirement programs they devise and fund for themselves. Much of the

EXHIBIT 23.5

Assets of private and public pension funds by type of fund, 1993

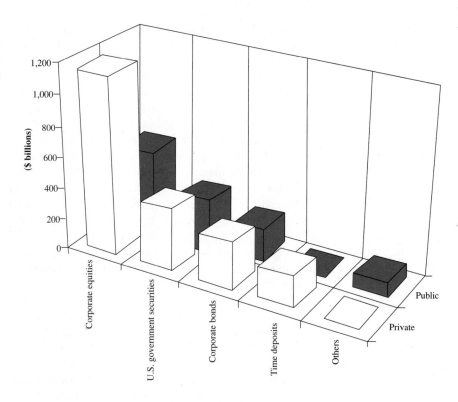

development and growth in private pension plans has been fostered by enabling federal regulation, particularly the **Employee Retirement Income Security Act of 1974** (ERISA). ERISA established minimum pension standards to protect the rights of participating employees, and subsequent legislation, such as the Tax Equity and Fiscal Responsibility Act of 1982, the Tax Reform Act of 1984, and the Tax Reform Act of 1986, has shaped the private pension system to an enormous degree.

The private pension system plays a more important role in the capital markets than the public system in the United States for one very important reason: It is funded. There are actual investments backing the promises of the pension plan sponsor. The federal system, on the other hand, which is the largest of the public systems, is not funded, although many state and local systems are. Yet another instance of what is good for the goose is not good for the gander! Private pension plans invest largely in stocks and bonds. Pension funds are long-term investors with limited need for liquidity. The mix between these asset categories for private plans usually ranges from 50 percent to 80 percent in stocks, with most of the remainder in bonds and government securities. State and local government plans tend to have a much higher proportion of their investments placed in corporate and foreign bonds and in U.S. government securities. (See Exhibit 23.5.)

There are two basic types of pension plans: defined-contribution plans and defined-benefit plans. In a **defined-contribution plan,** a contribution rate is fixed, but the retirement benefit is variable and will depend on the performance of the investments selected. Under today's regulations, the maximum amount of money that can be salted away into a defined-contribution plan is either 25 percent of compensation or $30,000, whichever is lower.

In a **defined-benefit plan,** the retirement benefit is stipulated, usually as a percentage of final average salary, but the contributions will vary according to the amount needed to fund the desired benefit. Today, the maximum amount of defined benefit is equal to either $100,000 or 100 percent of the average compensation a participant receives during his or her highest three earning years under the plan, whichever is lower. The $100,000 figure is adjusted annually to reflect inflation.

These two types of plans create very different investment problems for the plan sponsor. The defined-benefit plan creates a liability pattern that must be anticipated and funded. Sponsors of this kind of plan tend to long-term fixed-income instruments so that the defined liabilities can be met with a high degree of certainty. The defined-contribution plan, on the other hand, creates a liability only as large as the investments happen to be worth at any point in time. With this kind of plan, it is not necessary to direct investments toward fixed-income instruments. During the past 15 years, increasing numbers of plan sponsors have changed their pension plans to the defined-contribution design. Some people believe this suggests there will be a relatively lower demand for fixed-income instruments.

Defined-benefit plans are insured by the **Pension Benefit Guaranty Corporation** (PBGC) up to a maximum amount (around $2,000) per participant per month in the event that the plan sponsor and fund are unable to meet their obligations to retirees. The PBGC is a government agency headed by a board of directors comprised of the Secretaries of the Treasury, Labor, and Commerce. The Treasury Secretary also serves as chairperson of this board. Defined-benefit pension plans are charged an insurance premium to pay for this guarantee. In the event that the fund is unable to meet its obligations, it has borrowing authority from the U.S. Treasury.

If the pension fund complies with certain requirements of federal law and the Internal Revenue Service code, it is qualified to receive favorable tax treatment. Employers' contributions to such qualified plans are deductible from taxable income as an ordinary business expense, and these contributions are not considered taxable income to the employees. Likewise, any employee contribution is deductible for federal tax purposes. Moreover, any investment earnings are not taxed until the employee retires and receives the funds.

The value of assets in private pension funds exceeded $3.3 trillion in 1993, while state and local government retirement plans, railroad retirement programs, and federal civilian plans added another $1.1 trillion. Roughly one-third of private pension funds are managed by insurance companies. Private plans were 55 percent of the defined-benefit design, whereas 45 percent were of the defined-contribution design. The recent trend is toward more defined-contribution plans and fewer defined-benefit plans.

Investment Companies

Steel magnate and philanthropist Andrew Carnegie counseled, "To get really rich, place all your eggs in one basket, and then watch that basket!" However, most people who follow this advice do not get really rich, but they expose their fortunes unnecessarily to the vicissitudes of time. Placing our money in a diversified portfolio is a time-consuming hassle for most of us, and we often lack the expertise to do so. Therefore, many consumers have chosen to place their money in an investment company as a way to, in effect, place all of their eggs in one basket, yet have them redistributed to many separate baskets. It is not a recipe for vast riches, but it is a means of having some safety while receiving the attractive returns that characterize many of the securities in our capital markets.

Investment companies are divided into three distinct categories: (1) face-amount certificate companies, (2) unit investment trusts, and (3) management companies. In this section, we will review the salient features of each type.

Face-Amount Certificate Companies

A **face-amount certificate company** is engaged in the business of issuing face-amount certificates, which contain a promise of the company to pay a specific amount of money to the investor on a specified maturity date in the future. To receive this payment, the investor must make periodic installment payments to the company. If all the payments are made, the investor receives the face amount of the certificate. The face amount is the amount paid plus compound interest. The company itself, however, invests these funds in the interim. In essence, these firms are like the depository institutions in Chapters 21 and 22, with two important distinctions. First, they are not chartered institutions subject to the same regulatory structure that is relevant for the standard depository firms. Second, they do not offer deposit insurance, which is so important to valuing a bank's liabilities. For these reasons, the certificate company must offer higher returns to investors.

The Investment Company Institute does not track statistical information regarding face-amount certificate companies because of their size. Such companies generally account for an exceedingly small percentage of the total assets of all registered investment companies. Nonetheless, investors must be aware of their existence and should recognize both the rewards and risks associated with investing in these companies.

Unit Investment Trusts

A **unit investment trust** is an investment vehicle that (1) is organized under a nonvoting trust indenture or similar instrument, (2) does not have a board of directors, and (3) issues to the public redeemable interests in units of specified securities that the trust owns. Unlike a mutual fund, the composition of the portfolio is fixed for the life of the fund. Most unit trusts hold only fixed-income securities. The most common vehicles of this type are the unit investment trusts that invest in municipal bonds. In addition, some unit trusts are periodic payment plan companies established for the purchase of mutual fund shares.

A unit investment trust will be organized by a depositor who registers the trust, promotes the sale of its securities, and may thereafter provide bookkeeping and administrative services to the trust. Any person, company, or financial institution may act as an organizer, referred to as the depositor of the trust. The depositor operates under a trust agreement entered into with a bank or trust company that serves as trustee. All income and principal repayments are paid by the fund's trustee to the shareholders. The trusts expire as the securities mature. Neither the depositor nor the trustee has discretion as to investment decisions, which are predetermined by the trust instrument and fixed for the entire life of the trust.

Investment Management Companies

Investment companies are financial firms that purchase assets using only equity shares. **Investment management companies** comprise all investment companies that are neither face-amount certificate companies nor unit investment trusts. Depending upon the redeemability of their shares, investment management companies are classified as either **open-end** or **closed-end** investment companies. Although both are commonly referred to as **mutual funds,** it is incorrect to refer to a closed-end fund as a mutual fund; open-end investment companies and mutual funds are synonymous.

These investment management companies rely on a sponsor or promoter to be established. This person, company, or financial institution acts as a promoter in the expectation that, once established, the new company will use the promoter's services as an investment advisor to manage the funds obtained from new shareholder subscriptions. Upon creation, the shareholders of the newly formed firm elect a board of directors to oversee its operations and to select an **investment advisor, administrator,** and **custodian** of the purchased financial assets. These directors and various subcontractors are paid from the proceeds of the investments made on the shareholders' behalf.

Closed-end funds have a fixed number of shares authorized and issued.[4] In addition, they do not have any redeemable securities outstanding. After the initial offering, the shares of closed-end companies are sold either on a stock exchange or in the over-the-counter market. Consequently, the shares may be traded in the marketplace at a price greater or less than the value of the securities contained in the fund. During the past two decades, the shares of closed-end funds have typically traded at a discount relative to the values of the underlying securities. Exceptions to this rule, however, are not rare, and discounts tend to fluctuate considerably over time. Explanations for the often observed discounts have been unsatisfactory to date.

---

[4]Closed-end funds may occasionally expand this number through subsequent flotations, or rights offerings. However, the number of shares cannot be expanded or contracted without further underwriting activity and SEC filings.

Open-end management companies, the more frequent and visible type of mutual funds, continuously offer shares for sale to the public. In addition, they stand ready to redeem their shares at net asset value at any time when requested by an investor. The number of outstanding shares of an open-end company varies as new shares are sold and other shares are redeemed. By February of 1996, the open-end mutual fund complexes in the United States had over $3 trillion under management. Other countries had another $2.1 trillion under management, with France and Japan managing close to half a trillion dollars each and Luxembourg managing approximately $250 billion. In the United States, the size of this segment is almost 20 times larger than the closed-end investment fund segment.

As noted above, mutual funds contract out for three key services. The first of these, investment advisory services, is obtained from a registered investment advisor or, more commonly, an investment advisory firm. This contract is renewed annually. Mutual funds also generally contract out for clerical and administrative services, including recordkeeping and stockholder services. Again, this service is renewed annually by the board of directors. Finally, mutual funds are required to place and maintain their securities and similar investments in the custody of a custodian. Qualified custodians include banks with capitalization in excess of $500,000, national securities exchange member firms, and securities depositories of a national securities exchange or association. Management companies may maintain custody of their securities themselves provided they meet certain requirements. In each case, these services are provided for a fee that is based on assets under management and is reported quarterly to stockholders.

Regulations Applicable to Investment Companies

The Securities and Exchange Commission is the main oversight body responsible for the investment company industry. As public companies, investment companies fall directly into the SEC's jurisdiction. In addition, the flotation of new securities, which occurs only infrequently with closed-end funds but continuously with open-end funds, must satisfy all underwriting regulations set forth in the Securities Act of 1933 and the Securities and Exchange Act of 1934. If an underwriter engages in retail distribution of investment company securities, the underwriter-distributor must register as a broker/dealer with the SEC. Underwriters registered as broker/dealers must be members of the Security Investor Protection Corporation (SIPC), which provides for compulsory insurance for the protection of customers of insolvent broker/dealers. Excluded from membership are those broker/dealers whose business consists exclusively of (1) the distribution of shares of registered open-end investment companies or unit investment trusts, or (2) the business of rendering investment advisory services to one or more registered investment companies or insurance company separate accounts.

Underwriters for investment companies need also to join the National Association of Securities Dealers, Inc. (NASD) and to register their sales representatives with the NASD, because NASD rules exclude nonmembers from underwritings in which members participate. Members of the NASD qualify by passing examinations administered by that organization. An underwriter must also register under applicable state laws.

In addition, the **Investment Company Act of 1940** directly relates to the mutual fund industry and delegates regulatory authority to the SEC. In that role, the commission oversees the activity of the funds, the nature of contracts with service providers, and the oversight activity of the board of directors.

A mutual fund can elect to qualify under Subchapter M of the Internal Revenue Code. Under this provision, if the fund meets diversification requirements and distributes all realized capital gain and dividend income to the separate account in the form of dividends, it is then not taxed on this income. Its owners, of course, are subject to taxation on these earnings.

Size of Investment Company Business

The amount of money in unit investment trusts is well over $100 billion, with close to 90 percent of it placed in tax-free debt instruments. Most of the remaining funds reside in taxable bonds. Unit investment trusts are sponsored by giant investment firms such as Bear Stearns, John Nuveen, Kidder Peabody, Merrill Lynch, Paine Webber, Prudential-Bache, and Smith Barney. Closed-end investment companies are even more popular. Unlike a mutual fund, a closed-end investment company issues a limited number of shares that trade on a stock exchange or in the over-the-counter markets. The value of closed-end funds' shares is determined by market supply and demand. Some of the larger investment companies, such as MFS Intermediate Income Trust, Duff & Phelps Utilities Income, Nuveen Municipal Value Fund, and Templeton Global Income Fund, have asset values in excess of $1 billion. However, open-end mutual funds dominate the business in terms of size. Exhibit 23.6 gives the top 20 open-end mutual fund complexes in the United States. We refer to them as mutual fund complexes because many of these investment companies offer more than one mutual fund to the public. For example, Fidelity has more than 150 retail funds in its complex and manages over $250 billion in investments. Including its brokerage funds, trust funds, and other funds, it manages over half a trillion dollars.

Just about every financial magazine and newspaper publish mutual fund rankings from time to time, and *Barron's* is no exception. The criteria for ranking performance are most often along the lines of "What have you done for me lately?" Some of the rankings adjust realized rates of return for the risk of the fund, but most do not. In the case of *Barron's,* their performance index is based on the observation that many people, including large numbers who are planning for retirement through corporate plans, tend to stick to a single fund family. In *Barron's* listing of fund families, only those families that offer at least three equity funds, three taxable bond funds, one fund investing in both stocks and bonds, and a minimum of one fund each for international stocks and the money market are eligible for ranking. There are three things important to note about these fund rankings. First, a family that has performed well in stock (e.g., General Electric/GNA Capital, who achieved top ranking) or in taxable bonds (such as Piper Capital, who also achieved top ranking)

Exhibit 23.6   Top 20 Open-End Mutual Fund Complexes in the United States
(as of October 31, 1994)

Order	Complex Name (Mutual Fund Family)	Assets Value ($ millions)	Name of Parent Company
1	Fidelity	$278,562.4	Fidelity Investments (a privately owned company)
2	The Vanguard Group	137,472.9	The Vanguard Group of Investment Companies
3	Merrill Lynch Asset Management	125,405.7	Merrill Lynch, Pierce Fenner & Smith
4	Capital Research & Management	112,081.3	Capital Group Incorporated
5	Franklin/Templeton Group	90,248.6	Franklin Resources, Incorporated
6	Dreyfus Corporation	64,815.3	Mellon Bank
7	Putnam Funds	62,981.6	Marsh & McLennan Companies, Incorporated
8	Federated	62,443.1	Federated Investors
9	TIAA-CREF	61,941.4	Teachers Insurance and Annuity Association
10	Dean Witter	58,053.5	Sears, Roebuck and Company
11	Smith Barney	54,981.2	Primerica
12	Prudential Mutual Funds	52,090.6	Prudential Insurance Company of America
13	IDS Mutual Fund Group	47,022.2	I.D.S. Financial Corporation
14	T. Rowe Price	39,921.1	T. Rowe Price Associates, Incorporated
15	Kemper	39,414.5	Kemper Financial Services, Incorporated
16	Scudder	33,218.4	Scudder, Stevens & Clark, Incorporated
17	SEI	30,682.1	SEI Financial Services
18	Oppenheimer/Centennial	29,247.8	British & Commonwealth Holdings P.L.C.
19	Twentieth Century	26,462.1	Twentieth Century
20	Massachusetts Financial	25,356.5	Sun Life of Canada U.S.
	Total of 358 Complexes of Funds	$2,199,216.0	

Source: *1994 Data,* Investment Company Institute, Washington, DC.

during the past year may not rank very high in tax-exempt bonds (G.E. was ranked 24th) or international stocks (Piper was ranked 55th). Second, the rankings are very fickle over time. They are sometimes akin to the Philadelphia Phillies baseball team, which went from worst to first and back to worst during a three-year period in the mid-1990s. A particular management style that performed well during 1995, when interest rates were declining, may perform poorly in other economic scenarios. Moreover, a manager that does well may get promoted or retire, and someone else with a different investment style may be directing fund investments next year! However, not all is based on luck. A fund that has consistently low management fees has a good chance of doing well in the long-run rankings. Third, notice how only 6 of the top performing fund families (shown in Exhibit 23.7) ranked among the top 20 in size (shown in Exhibit 23.6). The largest of all fund complexes ranked 45th in the *Barron's* survey.

The variety of funds available to the public is staggering. For example, several mutual fund complexes, such as State Street Funds of Boston, offer specialized mutual funds that restrict their investments only to a single country. You can invest in Germany, England, Japan, or Australia, or in numerous other countries, through their funds. Indeed, you can invest in the fixed-income side, the small equity side, or

EXHIBIT 23.7   *Barron's* Top 20 Performing Mutual Fund Families

			Ranking by Category			
Rank	*Management Company Name*	*Stocks*	*International Stocks*	*Balanced Funds*	*Taxable Bonds*	*Tax-Exempt Bonds*
1	Vanguard Group	4	9	4	5	23
2	General Electric/GNA Capital	1	22	16	13	24
3	Piper Capital	20	55	12	1	3
4	Kemper Financial Services	36	5	32	7	9
5	Putnam Investment	2	35	7	28	31
6	Miller Anderson & Sherrerd	8	57	10	33	4
7	Fleet Financial Group	25	11	5	31	36
8	AIM Advisors	9	2	1	40	62
9	First Union Evergreen	39	43	14	11	10
10	Sunbank Capital	15	21	33	16	15
11	USAA Investment	37	40	34	2	7
12	Capital Research	32	7	15	34	30
13	Massachusetts Financial Services	3	27	22	32	37
14	Colonial Management Associates	51	23	18	24	22
15	New England Investment	5	53	43	6	16
16	Eaton Vance	21	41	3	54	17
17	T. Rowe Price Associates	12	18	38	26	26
18	Alliance Capital	23	50	35	29	2
19	Van Kampen/American Capital Investment	7	24	28	22	47
20	Goldman, Sachs & Co.	54	4	8	44	41

Source: *Barron's*, February 5, 1996. Reprinted by permission of *Barron's*, © 1996 by Dow Jones & Company. All Rights Reserved Worldwide.

the large company equities of each of these countries through one or another of such funds. Other fund families, such as Fidelity or Vanguard, offer sector mutual funds that specialize in only one industry. There are mutual funds that invest only in high-technology electronic companies, only in biotech firms, only in utilities, only in oil stocks, and so forth. There are corporate bond funds, municipal bond funds, Treasury bond funds, small capitalization firm stock funds, large capitalization stock funds, and virtually anything that you can conceive. In all, there were 5,357 different mutual funds in the United States at the end of 1994. Exhibit 23.8 reports the mix of these funds for 1989 and 1994 by investment objective. By having specialized funds, an investor can switch his or her money into and out of one or another of these funds in an effort to achieve higher investment performance. Investors following this strategy put their money in those areas that they feel will be currently most profitable and take it from areas that are not. If a given mutual fund complex offers many specialized funds, it is often possible to transfer funds from one to another of the funds without sizable transactions costs. Whether this will ultimately enhance the investor's yield depends upon his or her ability to predict sector or country returns. For those of us without this skill, the broader investment strategy of the more general mutual funds may still be preferred.

EXHIBIT 23.8

Number of mutual funds classified by investment objective

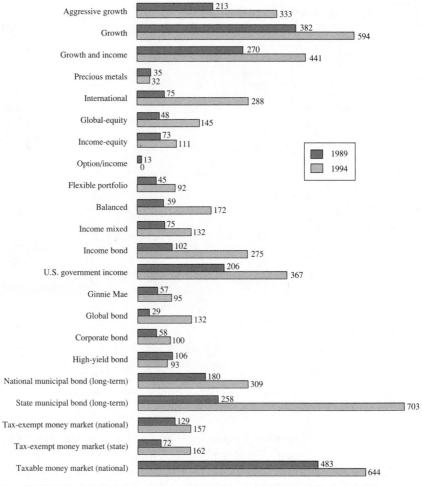

Note: In 1989, there were 13 funds in the Option/income category. As of January 1992, funds in this category were reclassified as Income-equity.

Source: *1995 Mutual Fund Fact Book,* Investment Company Institute, Washington, DC.

The decade of the 1980s saw a dramatic increase in investor interest in mutual funds, as shown in Exhibit 23.9. From 1980 to 1994, the number of accounts grew from about 12 million to more than 107 million, while assets rose from $135 billion to over $2 trillion, as seen in Exhibit 23.10.

Investment banks also participate in the investment management business and often offer a family of mutual funds. For example, on January 12, 1996, *The Wall Street Journal* listed Dean Witter as offering its investors a choice among 56 separate mutual funds. Goldman Sachs offered 19, J. P. Morgan, 9; Lazard, 11; Merrill Lynch, 152; Morgan Stanley, 30; Paine Webber, 68; Salomon, 9; Smith Barney, 79; Warburg, 17; and Lehman Brothers, 1. Of course, the numbers of

EXHIBIT 23.9

*Mutual fund
shareholder accounts
(millions)*

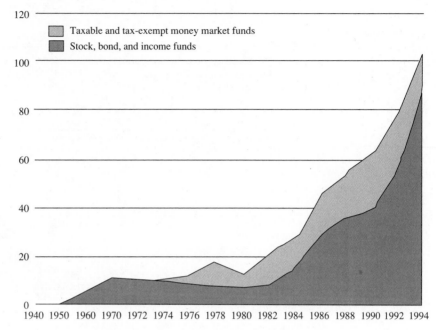

Source: *1995 Mutual Fund Fact Book,* Investment Company Institute, Washington, DC.

mutual funds managed is not a good indicator of market interest in these funds, because some of the funds are quite small in capitalization, and others are enormous. Participation in some of the funds is limited to institutional investors, while others allow participation from all classes of investors.

Below, we show a sample of a family of funds offered on January 12, 1996, by Morgan Stanley to its institutional clients.

NAV	Net Chg	Fund Name	Inv Obj	YTD %ret	4Wk %ret	Total Return						Max Init Chrg	Exp Ratio
						1Yr-R		3Yr-R		5Yr-R			
		Morg Stan Instl:											
20.18	+0.10	AsianEq	IL	+3.6	+5.9	+18.4	A	+23.7	A	NS		0.00	1.00
9.86	+0.03	Bal	MP	−1.2	−0.5	+21.0	D	+10.3	D	11.5	D	0.00	0.70
8.77	+0.04	EmMkDbt	WB	+2.1	+6.6	+55.3	A	NS		NS		0.00	1.49
13.75	+0.13	EmMkt	IL	+4.6	+6.9	+3.1	E	+14.5	C	NS		0.00	1.75
14.22	−0.04	EuroEqt	IL	+2.2	+3.9	+14.6	B	NS		NS		0.00	1.00
9.83	+0.08	Gold	SE	+15.0	+13.5	+34.5	B	NS		NS		0.00	1.25
10.63	+0.01	Hi Yld	HC	+1.6	+2.7	+25.2	A	NA		NS		0.00	0.75
9.39	−0.12	JpnEqty	IL	+1.3	+2.4	−0.6	E	NS		NS		0.00	1.00
20.64	+0.10	Muhlenkmp	MP	−3.0	−1.5	+27.8	A	+12.3	A	+19.9	A	0.00	1.57

Exhibit 23.10

Assets of mutual funds ($ billions)

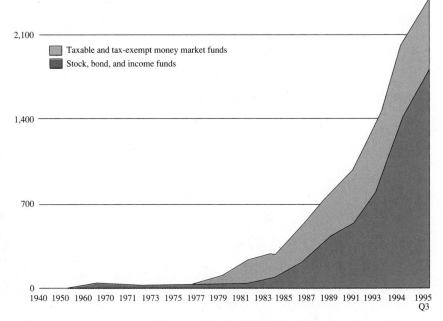

Taxable and tax-exempt money market funds

Stock, bond, and income funds

Source: *1995 Mutual Fund Fact Book,* Investment Company Institute, Washington, DC.

This excerpt from *The Wall Street Journal* highlights a number of different items of information. The first column shows the NAV, or net asset value of each share of the fund, expressed in dollars. More will be said about this in Chapter 23. The second column shows the gain or loss in the NAV, based on the prior day's NAV. The third column shows the fund name. In the first row below the header, in boldface type, is the fund family name. Subsequent rows show the name given to each fund. The abbreviations shown usually convey the basic content of the portfolio. For example, AsianEq denotes common stock, or equity securities from selected Asian countries. JpnEqty has common stock only from Japan. EuroEqt has common stock from the developed European countries. EmMkDbt and EmMkt denote debt and equity securities, respectively, from emerging market countries. Hi Yld denotes high-yield or "junk bond" investments. Occasionally, an abbreviation will not convey the basic content of the portfolio. For example, Muhlenkmp stands for Muhlenkamp, which is a fund named after the individual who devised the investment strategy.

The next column gives a two-letter symbol that denotes the general classification of mutual fund objectives. A legend is provided in *The Wall Street Journal* for 26 classifications defined by Lipper Analytical Services, Inc. Lipper also publishes average performance indices for funds in most of these classifications. In this excerpt, we encounter five of these objectives: IL denotes international (non-U.S.) stock; MP denotes some sort of multipurpose fund, such as

---

Box 23.2

In the '90s, as in the '60s, Money Pours In

Did you buy your $447 worth?

That is what the average person in the United States—man, woman and baby, rich and poor—invested last year in mutual funds that buy American stocks. At the end of the year, that average person owned such funds with a value of $4,074.

These two figures, each a record, illustrate both how widespread the fund mania has become, and how fast it is growing. A year earlier, the average American had domestic stock fund assets of just $2,704.

Some argue that not much is really happening here—that if you look at the overall picture Americans are really not doing that much more in the stock market. Sure, they are buying a lot of mutual funds, but they are buying fewer individual stocks, and a lot of those mutual fund purchases are really replacing pension fund assets.

Such arguments, however, should be allowed only to color the picture, not to erase it. A glance at the newsstand shows that publishers think there is much more interest in the market than there used to be. This is a boom brought on by rising stock prices and baby boomers' growing worries about how they will pay for retirement.

The late 1960s was the previous period of mutual fund mania, when young fund managers could start new funds, with investors showering huge sums on them. In 1968, the peak year of the last mutual fund mania, the average American put $10 into stock funds. That is equivalent to $45 in 1995 dollars, or about a tenth of the flow into domestic stock funds in 1995. The holdings of that average American, also adjusted for inflation, were about $1,000. It looks as if this mania is a lot bigger.

If it is fund mania that is helping to drive up prices now, the question becomes how it will end. The answer probably is that it will not be panicky fund investors who bring on a bear market; just the reverse.

The 1960s binge did not stop even when the performers of the formerly hot funds fell off sharply; it took a couple of years for that message to sink in sufficiently for withdrawals to begin affecting the industry. Withdrawals reflected poor performance, but they no doubt helped to perpetuate the slide of stock prices in the great 1973-74 bear market. And it was years before the public came back.

Source: Floyd Norris, "In the '90s, as in the '60s, Money Pours In," *The New York Times*, January 29, 1996.

a balanced, convertible fund; WB denotes short world multimarket and single-market and general world income foreign bonds, or emerging-markets debt; SE denotes sector stock funds (e.g., health/biotechnology, natural resources, environmental, utility, gold-oriented funds, etc.); and HC denotes high-yield, high-risk bonds.

The fifth column, labeled YTD %ret, gives the year-to-date total return, which is comprised of NAV change plus accumulated income for the period, in percent. This figure assumes reinvestment of all distributions. The sixth column gives the same information, but for the most recent four-week period. The next three columns give total rates of return over the previous year, three years, and five years, respectively. Percentages are annualized for periods exceeding one year. Each of the figures in these three columns is followed by a letter—A, B, C,

D, or E. These letters indicate the relative performance (using total rate of return as the ranking criterion) among funds with the same investment objectives for the time periods listed. Each letter represents a quintile of performance. For example, A is for the top 20 percent and E is for the bottom 20 percent.

The next to last column gives the maximum initial sales commission, or "load," in percent. The Morgan Stanley Institutional Funds carry no load in each case, but it is not uncommon to find loads for some funds ranging from 3 to 8 percent. The final column shows annual expenses as a percentage of assets under management. These expenses include administrative expenses and advisory fees paid to the investment manager. A typical range for these expenses is from 0.2 percent to 2 percent. However, it is not uncommon for a fund to incur additional expenses for research, computers, stock-quote systems, and even phone calls and newspaper subscriptions, which are paid in the form of "soft dollars." These payments are made in the form of extra-generous commissions paid to the broker. They typically do not show up in the last column as expenses but are reflected over time in a slightly lower rate of return earned on investments.

Money Market Funds

Up to this point, we have concentrated on mutual funds that have invested in various types of stocks and bonds. However, there are also mutual funds that only invest in short-term money market assets. These latter funds are a recent phenomenon in the marketplace, but have grown very rapidly since their inception about 25 years ago.

In 1972, the first money market funds were introduced to the United States. The purpose of these funds was to exploit government-imposed interest ceilings that stipulated the maximum interest rates payable on the deposits at commercial banks and savings banks. Money market funds had no such restrictions, nor did they impose a stiff penalty for early withdrawal of funds. They could, therefore, attract depositors from standard depository institutions. Today, banks and savings banks can compete against money market funds with NOWs, MMDAs, and other such accounts that were enabled by the Garn Bill in October, 1982. When money market funds were first introduced, however, banks and savings banks had no such competitive offerings. Accordingly, hundreds of billions of dollars flowed into money market mutual funds, and they remain there to this day.

Money market funds invest in high-quality, short-term money market instruments such as commercial paper, T-bills, repurchase agreements, bank CDs, bankers' acceptances, and short-term government agency debt. (See Exhibit 23.11.) Because the investment vehicles are short term and exhibit low risk of default, there are low fluctuations in the value of money market fund asset portfolios. Due to this fact, the SEC has permitted these funds to maintain a fixed price of $1 and fluctuate their daily yield based upon asset yield. However, to make this possible, the SEC severely restricts investments to short-term, top-quality securities. It also prohibits

EXHIBIT 23.11

Taxable money market fund asset composition, year-end 1994

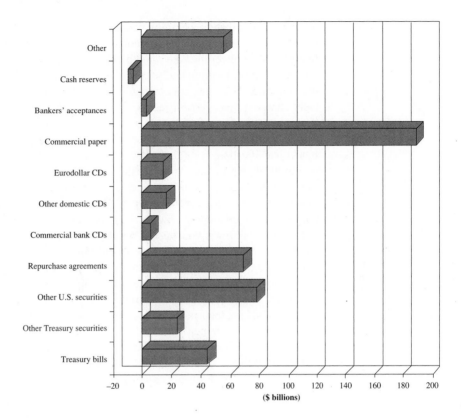

low-quality investments from constituting more than 5 percent of total invested assets, with a maximum of 1 percent directed toward a single issuer. Because of their short-term investment horizon, money market instruments also enjoy high liquidity. This is necessary, as money market mutual fund customers can write checks on their accounts to redeem shares, provided that such checks exceed some minimum amount, say $500. Thus, money market funds function, in key ways, like interest-bearing checking deposits.

Money market funds do not carry federal deposit insurance; accordingly, some funds buy private insurance. Still others invest only in government securities in an effort to attract investors worried about bank solvency. Most money market funds do not charge either entrance or exit fees. There are no commissions for opening an account, purchasing additional shares, or redeeming shares for cash.

Performance of Mutual Funds

One of the attractions of investing through mutual funds is that they are able to offer the investor a highly diversified portfolio, but without all of the paperwork, research, and transaction costs. Another of the attractions of investing through mutual funds is that they employ people who are experts at security selection and portfolio management. It is commonly believed that the individual investor is likely to make fewer mistakes, and perhaps even earn higher returns, by delegating the security selection and portfolio management tasks to the professionals of the investment management companies. For these services, these companies typically charge a management fee to cover investment selection, fund administration, and securities safekeeping.

The preponderance of evidence indicates that the first attraction of a mutual fund, diversification, is valid. However, the second attraction of a mutual fund, that of improved performance, is highly dubious. Most studies have shown that mutual funds, on average, perform no better over time than a random security selection method. It is true that over short periods of time, some funds do outperform a portfolio based on random security selection or on a broad-based stock index such as the S&P 500. But if you were to simply create several mutual funds, each based on random security selection, there would obviously be some that outperformed others during any given period of time.[5] The question is whether one can consistently outperform a stock index. The answer appears to be that only very few can.

There are **no-load** and **load funds** from which the investor can choose. The no-load funds get their money through management fees based on the amount of assets under management. The load funds charge a commission to get into the fund and also charge a management fee based on assets under management. Most studies have shown no systematically superior performance from those funds that charge a load over those of the no-load variety.

Finance Companies

Finance companies cater to the particular needs of the individual borrower and deliver a highly personalized credit service. Today, finance companies account for close to $700 billion in assets, which include consumer credit, loans to businesses, and mortgages. They obtain their funds largely through the sale of large-denomination debt securities, primarily commercial paper for the larger finance companies, and marketable and nonmarketable longer-term bonds and stock for the smaller ones. Additionally, finance companies have lines of credit at commercial banks that can be used to supplement their primary sources of funds in the event of a need. There are three basic types of finance companies: firms that specialize in consumer credit, firms that specialize in sales finance, and firms that specialize in small business firm lending. However, the larger finance companies may operate across two or more of these domains. The first two types have declined over the past

---

[5]A mutual fund complex could take advantage of this. It could institute several new mutual funds each year, granting a small amount of "seed money" to several aspiring managers. At the end of a period of two to five years, certain of these pilot funds are bound to have outperformed a broad-based stock index, and they could be touted to the public, who would willingly commit large amounts of funds to the manager. Therefore, investors should not rely solely on past returns to form their expectations of the future.

two decades, as they have lost market share to credit unions, commercial banks, and S&Ls. The last type has seen rather substantial growth over the same period. Some of the largest companies, such as General Electric, are increasingly effective competitors in numerous areas. This has led to a further blurring of the distinctions between finance firms and commercial firms.

Consumer Finance Companies

These companies make small and medium-sized installment loans to households for the purchase of automobiles, recreational vehicles, home appliances, mobile homes, vacations, and other such items, or for the refinancing and consolidation of a group of smaller consumer debt obligations. These companies often lend to people who are unable to obtain credit elsewhere, such as from a commercial bank or credit union. Consequently, consumer finance companies carry relatively high interest rates to compensate for an increased propensity of default, higher servicing costs, and higher loan origination costs. Many of the borrowers are from low-income, less-educated segments of the population, and therefore, consumer finance companies are regulated by the states and are restricted from making loans that exceed a specified size. These companies also may be regulated on the maximum interest rates that they can charge and on the measures they can take to collect loans that are past due.

Some consumer finance companies have obtained bank charters so as to offer time deposits that are insured by the FDIC. Again, we see the distinctions eroding between commercial banks and other financial intermediaries. There are approximately 1,700 consumer finance companies operating 10,000 offices throughout the United States. Some, such as Household Finance and Beneficial Finance, are large and operate hundreds of offices; most are much smaller.

Sales Finance Companies

These companies make loans to both consumers and businesses to finance the sale of items such as automobiles, pleasure boats, refrigerators, and other consumer durables. Many of the better known sales finance companies are **captives** of the dealer or manufacturer of the product sold. For example, General Motors, Ford Motor Co., Sears Roebuck, Montgomery Ward, Motorola, and General Electric all have sales finance companies. The loan contracts are standardized, and the dealer will complete the forms with the consumer in order to obtain cash from the sales finance company at the completion of the sale. These companies compete directly with commercial banks, credit unions, and credit cards, all of which offer alternative sources of financing for consumer purchases.

Business Finance Companies

Businesses that carry inventory and use equipment often need to finance these items. Business finance companies specialize in lending to this group, particularly to small and medium-size firms. They are particularly adept at tailoring their financing package to the particular needs of these businesses. One of the services they provide is known as **factoring,** a process by which they purchase the accounts receivable of a business at a discount. They pay cash to the business and then receive payment directly from the firm's customers. Other business finance companies specialize in the leasing of equipment. Some of the larger business finance companies offer lease financing for the purchase of capital equipment and "rolling stock" such as airplanes and railroad cars. They also may make short-term unsecured business loans.

Summary

Institutions in the financial markets come in many shapes and sizes. When one thinks of financial institutions, commercial banks and thrifts come immediately to mind. However, as has been demonstrated in this chapter, there are many more types of institutions, each of which provides valuable services to different parts of both the financial community and the real sector of our economy. Taken together, these institutions have grown rapidly in number and have transformed

the financial landscape. The insurance sector has broadened its product line and substantially increased the assets under its control. The investment companies have virtually revolutionized the market for investment and deposit-type services. Finance companies continue to innovate to provide customer service in this growing but competitive market. And the change these institutions have initiated continues unabated.

Key Concepts

consumer, business, and sales finance companies,   600
defined-contribution versus defined-benefit plans, 586–87
Employee Retirement Income Security Act of 1974,   586
face-amount certificate company,   588
factoring,   602
insurance,   568
Insurance Regulatory Information System,   574
investment advisor, administrator, and custodian,   589
Investment Company Act of 1940,   591
investment management company,   589
life/health insurance,   569
McCarran-Ferguson Act of 1945,   573
money market mutual funds,   598

mortality risk versus event risk,   569–70
multiline insurers,   569
National Association of Insurance Commissioners,   574
open-end versus closed-end funds,   589
participating versus nonparticipating contracts, 577–78
Pension Benefit Guaranty Corporation,   587
personal and commercial lines,   583
premium,   568
property/casualty insurance,   569, 583
reinsurance,   571
short-tailed versus long-tailed risks,   584
stock, mutual, reciprocal, and Lloyds-type insurers,   570
unit investment trust,   588

Review Questions

1. The regulation of insurers' assets is an attempt to protect the consumer. Can you think of any trade-offs that have resulted from this legislation?

2. Contrast the benefits and drawbacks of fixed and variable annuities.

3. We noted in this chapter the movement toward defined-contribution pension plans. Contrast the benefits of both defined-contribution and defined-benefit pension systems from the point of view of both the employer and the employee.

4. What do you think is the government's rationale for creating the PBGC for defined-benefit plans and not for defined-contribution plans?

5. Find examples of closed-end funds of various types. Calculate the premium or discount from net asset value. Is there any discernible pattern in these numbers?

6. Loads on mutual funds come in two varieties: an initial charge, or front-end load, and a redemption fee, or back-end load. Evaluate the load structures of several of the emerging market mutual funds and compare them for different investment time horizons.

7. The proportions of investments in taxable and tax-exempt money market funds versus stock funds and bond funds changed drastically from 1983 to 1993. In 1983, money market funds constituted 61.2 percent of all mutual fund investments, whereas in 1995, they constituted only 28.9 percent of mutual fund investments. Stock and bond mutual funds grew substantially during that same period. To what do you attribute this shift in popularity?

References

Abken, Peter A. "Corporate Pensions and Government Insurance: Deja Vu All over Again." *Economic Review.* Federal Reserve Bank of Atlanta, March/April 1992.

American Council of Life Insurance. *Life Insurance Fact Book.* Washington, D.C.: American Council of Life Insurance, annual publication.

American Council of Life Insurance. *Pension Facts.* Washington, D.C.: American Council of Life Insurance, annual publication.

Babbel, David F. "A Perspective on Model Investment Laws." *Journal of the American CLU and ChFC,* September 1994.

Babbel, David F., and David R. Klock. "Measuring the Interest Rate Sensitivity of Property/Casualty Insurer Liabilities." In *Insurance, Risk Management, and Public Policy: Essays in Honor of Robert I. Mehr,* edited by Sandra Gustavson and Scott Harrington. Boston: Kluwer Press, 1993.

Brown, Keith C.; W. V. Harlow; and Laura T. Starks. "Of Tournaments and Temptations: An Analysis of Managerial Incentives in the Mutual Fund Industry." *Journal of Finance,* March 1996.

Brown, Stephen J., and William N. Goetzmann. "Performance Persistence." *Journal of Finance,* June 1995.

Falkenstein, Eric G. "Preferences for Stock Characteristics as Revealed by Mutual Fund Portfolio Holdings." *Journal of Finance,* March 1996.

Investment Company Institute. *Mutual Fund Fact Book.* Washington, D.C.: Investment Company Institute, annual publication.

Investment Company Institute. *1994–1995 Directory of Mutual Funds.* Washington, D.C.: Investment Company Institute, 1995.

Harris, Maury. "Finance Companies as Business Lenders." *Quarterly Review.* Federal Reserve Bank of New York, Summer 1979.

Malkiel, Burton G. "Returns from Investing in Equity Mutual Funds 1971 to 1991." *Journal of Finance,* June 1995.

Mayers, David, and Clifford W. Smith. "Ownership Structure and Control: The Mutualization of Stock Life Insurance Companies." *Journal of Financial Economics,* May 1986.

McIsaac, Donald, and David F. Babbel. *The World Bank Primer on Reinsurance.* Washington, D.C.: World Bank Financial Sector Development Department, 1995.

CHAPTER 24

Change and Competition in Financial Structure

Chapter Outline

This chapter overviews the increasing overlap between the objectives of various financial institutions. It explains the motive forces behind this increase in competition and the trend toward a single market for financial services. It ends with an evaluation of the feasibility and advisability of the separation between finance and commerce.

The past two decades have ushered in a revolution in the nature of financial institutions. Although we have presented an analysis of institutions on a functional basis in Chapters 18 through 23, the traditional distinctions between commercial and investment banks, credit unions, savings and loan associations, savings banks, insurers, investment companies, pension funds, and mutual funds have blurred and, in some cases, disappeared altogether. It may very well be that some future edition of this textbook will altogether dispense with the traditional separate institutional analyses and focus entirely on the market functions described in Chapter 17.

This chapter will be devoted to explaining the revolution in the financial service industry. We do not have sufficient space in a single chapter to review, in depth, the evolution—indeed, revolution—that has taken place among all financial institutions. Instead, we will adopt the perspective of a single institution and follow it through the post-Depression era to the present. The perspective will be that of commercial banks. However, this choice of perspective could just as easily have been that of insurers, investment banks, savings and loan associations, or some other financial institution. The economic forces felt and the lessons learned by one were experienced and learned by all. Thus, our focus on the banking perspective is intended to be instructive but not exclusionary.[1]

The Evolution of the Banking System

We begin by recounting the evolution of the U.S. banking system over the recent past. This will serve as an opening perspective on why these institutions have changed and how they have come to view both the securities industry and the insurance industry as areas of potential penetration and growth.

The U.S. depository institution industry in general, and the commercial banks specifically, have gone through a period of transition from highly regulated firms to ones with fewer constraints on both their product and geographic markets. Let us review how this all occurred.

Product Market Expansion of Commercial Banks

The mid-20th-century commercial banking structure can be traced back to the Banking Act of 1933, especially those sections normally referred to as the **Glass-Steagall Act.** As discussed in Chapter 21, this legislation separated both commercial and investment banking and is the root of product-price regulation. In terms of the former, this act effectively established product market barriers to entry in the commercial and investment banking businesses by separating deposit-taking activity from securities and underwriting. It divided a once seamless industry by severely restricting the product lines that could be offered by commercial banks and by forbidding banking activity within their investment banking counterparts. After much debate, trust and investment activity, which some felt was subject to divestiture, was retained by the commercial banking sector.

In the subsequent decade, little was done to challenge this regulatory structure surrounding the banking industry, as the economy of the 1930s and the following war period did not lend itself to experimentation. If anything, this era was one of consolidation of regulatory control and restrictions. Then, in 1945, Congress passed the **McCarran-Ferguson Act.** This act exempted the insurance industry from antitrust prosecution and specifically permitted the free exchange of information between companies. It also granted, and effectively fully relegated to states, the authority to regulate insurance activities.

---

[1]Sources that can be consulted for a review of changes that affected the other institutions include Frederic Mishkin, *The Economics of Money, Banking and Financial Markets,* 2nd ed. (Glenview, Ill.: Scott, Foresman and Co., 1989); and Tim S. Campbell, *Money and Capital Markets* (Glenview, Ill.: Scott, Foresman and Co., 1988).

It was not until the late 1950s that banking firms tried to broaden their markets through product expansion. The process accelerated, but always within the severe regulatory restrictions on allowable bank activity. To ease these restrictions, banks made use of the **holding company form,** which led to substantive relief from regulation and increased flexibility of activity. With this structure, banks wishing to expand their activity could do so through the establishment of a holding company that owned the bank itself. Because this company was not a bank, it transcended the restrictions and regulations that were relevant to the wholly owned banking subsidiaries. It also permitted one firm to own several banking institutions, so-called **multibank holding companies.** The holding company form did not, however, solve the industry's problems in insurance. Because of the 1945 act, states had full discretion over who could sell insurance within their borders, and most states excluded banks from the list of institutions permitted to do so.

In 1956, the passage of the **Bank Holding Company Act** gave the Federal Reserve Board the authority to determine the permissible activities and products of these multibank holding companies, subject, of course, to existing legislation. To some, this was seen as the first step in an attempt by regulators to control the expansion of this form of financial firm. As a result of the legislation, the Federal Reserve could now determine allowable activity for both the bank, the bank holding company, and its subsidiaries. However, to avoid the restrictions imposed on multibank holding companies, many banks exploited a loophole in the law and maintained a one-bank holding company structure. This allowed continued expansion of bank activities without regard to national regulatory approval.

The 1970 amendment closed this last loophole by forcing one-bank holding companies to adhere to all of the provisions of the 1956 Bank Holding Company Act. This new law enabled the Federal Reserve Board to maintain closer control over the activities of commercial bank holding companies, which were in turn restricted to those product areas that were "consistent with or equivalent to" the business of banking. Yet, to some extent, the law sanctioned the use of a holding company structure to broaden bank activity into the other arenas. If a case could be made that an activity was closely related to the banking business, chances were good that it could be added to permissible holding company functions. In the securities area, allowable activities expanded into various forms of asset management and discount brokerage activity. In the basic banking business, consumer finance, mortgage banking, and factoring were all added to the list. But for insurance, the holding company structure offered little help. States' rights remained strong, and the McCarran-Ferguson Act was clear. The only exception was the explicit exemption contained in the National Banking Act of 1916 whereby insurance sales are permitted by banks in towns of fewer than 5,000 people.

Nonetheless, the trend toward expansion of securities activity continued with the movement toward the elimination of the boundary between commercial and investment banking. The product lines of these two parts of the financial services industry were becoming more intertwined. Investment banks expanded into a relatively large segment of the retail banking market with the introduction of money market mutual funds and cash management accounts. Likewise, commercial banks had expanded their activities in private placements, corporate finance, and commercial paper—areas that had been the traditional province of investment banks The main participants in this expansion were originally money center banks, but major regional firms had also garnered an appreciable market share in these areas.

By the mid-1980s, the U.S. industry was quite different than it had been only 50 years earlier. Banks had expanded through holding company structures to a substantially larger product area. This included a wider array of corporate banking services and a larger set of consumer retail products. The former group of products, operating either through a subsidiary of the bank or holding company, offered commercial clients advice, the *de facto* underwriting of commercial paper, and private placement, to mention just a few. The business unit, commonly referred to as a Capital Markets Division, looked increasingly like an investment banking subsidiary. At the consumer level, expanded liability products aimed at a broader segment of household savings flourished, as did trust and investment management services. On the credit side, open lines of credit, credit cards, and mortgages of various types all added to the bankers' options.

However, this did not end the industry's evolution. Banks continued to push the boundaries of Glass-Steagall in the move to become full-service institutions. This movement received a substantial boost from interpretations of the 1933 act that would allow the major banks to be engaged in limited security underwriting business through affiliates. On June 13, 1988, the Supreme Court let stand the Federal Reserve Board's approval for commercial bank affiliates to underwrite commercial paper, municipal revenue bonds, and securities backed by mortgages and consumer debt under the condition that a bank affiliate's underwriting is limited to a small percentage of the affiliate's gross revenue. The ruling was based on the interpretation of the Banking Act that prohibits bank affiliation with firms that are "principally engaged" in securities activities. The percentage limits on underwriting that would keep bank affiliates from being "principally engaged" in securities became the determining factor on permissible association.

Although this ruling made the new powers useful only to the largest banks, which could develop huge affiliates engaging in government securities trading or other nonbanking activities, it was only the beginning. Many banks subsequently established such subsidiaries, known as **Section 20 subs,** to engage in securities activity. And in the ruling's aftermath, the Federal Reserve has given specific permission for these entities to formally underwrite the full range of debt and equity, subject to the size constraint listed above and to strict regulatory oversight.

What was once a prohibition has been converted to a regulatory framework for permissible activity. To be sure, the system is cumbersome. Banks interested in engaging in securities activities must establish a separate legal entity and build firewalls around it in order to conduct business activities that their competitors can transact directly. However, once the structure is in place, the large banks are fully competitive with their investment banking counterparts, and they now frequently appear on "league lists" such as those reported in Chapter 20.

Each year, Congress promises to repeal the remaining features of the Glass-Steagall prohibitions, but each year it fails to do so. Even with two consecutive presidents (Bush and Clinton) recommending repeal, the statutes remain, but to a large extent, they exist in name only.

Expansion of Geographic Markets

The control of geographic expansion of commercial banks is traced to the 1927 **McFadden Act** in which the historical tradition of a state's right over the allowable expansion of commercial banks was reaffirmed. This was clearly the case for all state-chartered institutions. In addition, this act stated that national banks were allowed to branch within a state only where state-chartered institutions were granted this right. The 1935 amendment subsequently allowed these institutions to follow whatever opportunities for branching and interstate banking were available to state banks in the state of operation. The 1956 **Douglas Amendment** of the Bank Holding Company Act continued the deference to state policy on geographic expansion of both nationally and state-chartered institutions. Specifically, it indicated that out-of-state expansion could not occur unless the host state expressly permitted such entry. The 1960 **Bank Merger Act** continued the tradition of states' rights on this issue. Together, these three acts had effectively erected barriers to entry in interstate banking: (1) by prohibiting banks from operating branches outside their home state (McFadden Act); (2) by forbidding banks from purchasing banks outside their home state unless the laws of this acquired bank's state expressly permit such an acquisition (Douglas Amendment); and (3) by establishing guidelines for the approval of mergers between federally insured banks (Merger Act).

In the interim, large banks and bank holding companies wishing to expand their geographic presence were forced to do so through holding company nonbank subsidiaries that could provide a variety of services across state lines. These services were offered through facilities such as loan production offices (LPOs); domestic branches that were engaged in international activities, referred to as Edge Act offices; as well as a variety of bank holding company nonbank subsidiaries that ranged from leasing companies and real estate appraisal firms to investment management groups that provided trust services.

As this process of nonbank product expansion continued, the basic vehicle of financial product distribution began to change. Telecommunication and electronics began to replace brick and mortar as a delivery system of retail products. An example of the technology-driven changes in the delivery of retail products was the emergence of automated teller machines (ATMs), which expanded the potential service area beyond arbitrary branching restrictions. Yet branching remained the domain of state legislation and was largely restricted to intrastate limits.

State control was nearly complete; but it was eroding. Legislation passed in 1960 and 1966 permitted bank mergers that provided benefits to the community that outweighed the potential competitive aspects of a merger. The Bank Merger Act provided the Justice Department with a basis for developing compromise guidelines to be employed in evaluating bank merger proposals. In addition, the emergency provisions of the **Garn-St. Germain Depository Institutions Act** of

1982 provided that banks could cross state boundaries to acquire failing domestic institutions under certain circumstances. This was the first of a growing number of areas in which the previously sacred state boundary began to be crossed in the new wave of mergers. The once clear limitation of geographic expansion, made official in the Douglas Amendment to the McFadden Act, was undergoing significant erosion. This development added new dimensions and opportunities to the geographic expansion potential of the bank holding company.

The year 1975 was the beginning of formal state legislation that changed the course of interstate banking. Then, Maine enacted the first state law permitting general entry of out-of-state banking units. The result was a period of rapid acquisition of Maine's holding companies. Seeing the results of this experiment, additional states did not follow Maine's lead until seven years later. At that point, both New York and Massachusetts passed interstate banking laws. The latter, however, was considerably different from the former. While New York authorized out-of-state bank activity within its borders without reciprocity, Massachusetts established a regional banking statute that provided access on a limited basis according to the home state of the holding company.

Litigation followed quickly, with the future of regional pacts subject to considerable debate. On June 10, 1985, the Supreme Court of the United States delivered its opinion on the **Northeast Bancorp case** with an 8–0 court ruling upholding regional banking. As of the beginning of 1992, less than a handful of states had not enacted legislation that would allow some kind of interstate activity for banks. For those that had, the results of opening up their borders were immediate, with substantial cross-boundary acquisitions and regionalization in some cases. This led the Treasury to propose the complete elimination of state restrictions. Their proposal, more radical than the action of the recent past, would have allowed both bank acquisition and bank branch expansion across state lines. In the end, however, it was defeated, and by the end of the Bush administration, interstate banking seemed destined to remain a patchwork of regional compacts.

However, politics are often difficult to predict. In 1994, legislation was passed under the title of the Riegle-Neal **Interstate Banking and Branching Efficiency Act.** The legislation puts an end to state authority to prohibit interstate bank holding company acquisitions as of September 29, 1995. Then, as of June 1, 1997, banking institutions will be permitted to establish interstate branch networks unless the state explicitly prohibits such actions. This provision is sometimes referred to as an "opt-out" clause, in that interstate banking will take place unless the state legislature takes definite steps to prevent it. It would appear that interstate banking has finally come to the United States.

The Reasons for Product Line Expansion

As is evident from the above review, much has been changing in the commercial banking scene. The old lines dividing commercial from investment banking are quickly eroding. State boundaries have also fallen to regional banking trends and the quick evolution to interstate banking. This is a fairly idiosyncratic experience brought about by the historical structure and regulation of commercial banking in the United States. However, the forces that led to the decline in the regulation of both product and geography are important to understand. Appreciating them is a prerequisite to understanding the institutional evolution reported.

The motivating forces behind the evolution of the commercial banking system center around two fundamental issues. First, the product line offered to the industry's natural constituents, firms, and households cannot be arbitrarily segmented across industry lines. Attempts by bank regulators to do so were inherently inefficient and opened the way for economic forces consistent with an expansion in the product line offered by various financial entities. Second, technology ultimately made geography less meaningful as a constraint on the delivery system of financial services. This led to an inevitable trend to expand product markets and to substitute technology, telecommunications, or mail service for physical space. In most cases, this has resulted in increased competition and a reduction in the number of competitors in the industry as a whole.

In terms of the first of these forces, it should have been apparent as early as 1933 that the arbitrary division of products offered to the corporate sector was doomed to fail. In any case, as the previous sections recount, banks sought to expand their product menu to satisfy customer needs. This was done first by an expansion into investment banking areas with longer duration, such as private placements and venture capital pools. It was followed by a realization that a substantial portion of investment banking activity was essentially a substitute for the lending function even at the short end of the maturity spectrum. Commercial paper facilitation and Euromarket syndication are clear cases of loan alternatives into which commercial banks have sought entrance.

It should be pointed out that commercial banks were not the predators in this expanding product-line process. Indeed, it could be argued that our investment banking community, subject to much less explicit regulation, was the first to see the opportunity to expand its product franchise into commercial banking products. Their success led to a further decline in the already small position of commercial banks in the American financial system. Junk bonds, commercial paper, and venture capital pools were the product alternatives used by investment banking firms to enter the traditional bank market of major industrial corporate lending. And these were successful. Their position was further advanced by the process of securitization, in which a substantial portion of the standard bank portfolio could be initiated and sold without the need of a depository source.

The result of this confrontation between the two divided parts of the banking industry was the virtual elimination of the division proposed in the Glass-Steagall Act. Major participants are now defined not along industry lines but by their chosen strategy of market concentration. In commercial lending, Goldman Sachs, Bankers Trust, and Morgan Guaranty are more alike than are regional and money center commercial banks, for example.

At the consumer level, the same process was at work. Increasingly, household portfolio choice was viewed as being hampered by arbitrary restrictions along industry activity lines. The simple savings account gave way to a complex array of portfolio options, only a few of which were previously viewed as allowable activities for commercial banks. Institutions that refused to innovate found themselves losing household market shares to a securities industry that adapted well to the consumer's desire for participation in a wider array of debt instruments and access to the equity market. Mutual funds, money market funds, and tax-deferred and tax-exempt instruments all developed as an alternative to the previous rather staid and increasingly obsolete bank savings vehicles. In order to follow their customers' needs for greater savings vehicle flexibility, banks had little choice but to evolve.

At the same time, technology was changing the face of the industry and its delivery system. Corporate banking shifted from a simple single-bank relationship and passive corporate finance to unbundled product marketing. Rollover financing directly from the market substituted for bank seasonal borrowing, as lenders were linked more easily with the corporate treasurer's office. Cash management moved from manual systems to on-line, real-time cash controls.

On the consumer side, the telephone became a substitute for location in retail deposit gathering. Computer home banking, debit cards, wire transfer, and the mailbox slowly replaced the teller line. In a search for higher yields, portfolios shifted from one bank to another, or from banks to their counterparts in the mutual funds industry or the brokered deposit market. Today, as we look at the prospects of internet banking and point-of-sale transactions with "smart cards" or prepaid cards, it is hard to believe that geography was once taken so seriously.

Credit instruments have also evolved. Spearheaded by some aggressive banking firms looking for market share and a different distribution network, the credit card industry has also pushed product innovation. In each case, the institution offering the new product saw it as an opportunity to harness new technology and to substitute electronics for geographic presence.

This, in turn, led to increased concentration of certain product lines, as well as emphasis on off-site operation centers to achieve low-cost production. As location became less central, the need for efficient production increased. In many cases, the lowest-cost producer was not the banking firm or even part of the banking industry. Accordingly, here, too, market share was lost to aggressive yet efficient competitors from outside the narrow commercial banking sector. Once again, the evolution meant a decline in bank influence and market share.

The internationalization of markets and greater competition from abroad are also contributing to the quickening pace of change among financial institutions. Many countries outside of the United States do not impose the same constraints on the operating latitude of their financial institutions. A single institution will often offer commercial and investment banking services, as well as a spate of insurance products, mutual funds, and the like. As a result, U.S. institutions are often at a disadvantage when competing with such firms, and their managers are not afraid to point it out. They have often complained that it is difficult to compete on an equal footing with these institutions given the inability of U.S.-based banks to operate easily in this full range of activities.

In all, the above story tells an interesting tale. Banks had been put into a narrow box as a result of the Great Depression. Glass-Steagall, the Bank Holding Company Act, and states' rights had restricted their ability to evolve. Banks circumvented these restrictions over time through regulatory avoidance and financial innovation. One well-known critic of the regulatory environment, Professor Edward Kane of Boston College, refers to this as the **regulatory dialectic.** Regulation leads to a response by the regulated. This response, in turn, causes regulation to change, thus starting the whole process over again. The story outlined above of product expansion into securities activity fits this model quite nicely. Through the development of the bank holding company and the evolution of products, banks have increasingly moved into the securities industry. Bank regulators responded by changing regulation, which merely caused another reaction. In the geographic expansion, too, the regulatory dialectic seems to be an accurate characterization of the interaction between regulators (at times state legislatures) and the regulated.

While our comments have been directed primarily toward commercial bank movement into investment banking, other financial institutions experienced similar pressures and responded in a similar manner. In fact, each of the depository financial institutions has been broadening its products and markets in response to these competitive pressures. Savings and loan associations, as well as credit unions, have joined the trend toward broadening their roles. Many have chosen to become full financial service firms for individuals, and they are expanding their services to the commercial sector as well. In an effort to avoid severe constraints on their investment activities, many of these institutions are converting to commercial or savings banks, as was noted in Chapter 22.

At the same time, insurance firms have been converting themselves into general financial service firms. Beginning as a relatively small part of the financial market, insurance companies have changed their role and broadened their menu of services into deposit- and investment-type products. Resources that had been maintained previously in bank balance sheets have shifted not only to securities firms but also to their insurance counterparts. Using its financial expertise and name recognition, the insurance industry has garnered an increasing share of the financial pie. It has done so through product expansion into investment products and direct acquisition of securities and investment banking firms. Without the prohibitions of legislation and regulation, insurance companies have bought and have been bought by securities firms over the last 20 years.

However, direct market interaction between insurance and banking has thus far been limited by regulation. With the inevitable convergence of their product lines, one would suspect that this division will not be sustained. Insurance firms would like to market standard insurance products such as annuities, universal life, and credit facilities that can easily compete with the depository and lending products that are the core of the banking franchise. For their part, the banking industry sees the insurance industry as a direct competitor and a potentially interesting arena into which to expand.

Banking and Insurance: What Is Next?

The general consensus is that there will be more interaction between banks and insurance firms in the future. Each industry is expanding into the other's area, as noted above. Indeed, in Europe, the two subsectors are substantially intertwined. The insurance industry is aware of this and of the interest that commercial banks have in their industry. Yet they don't quite appreciate the forces driving this interest. The consensus in the insurance industry is that banks wish to engage in the distribution activity of insurance. According to this line of reasoning, the goal of banks is to increase fee income in order to enhance their return on capital and leverage their existing retail distribution system.[2] It is presumed that banks are most interested in competing with the insurance agency function to gain the commissions usually accruing to sales agents. Most often, it is argued that banks have little interest or comparative advantage in underwriting and that they prefer life insurance products to property and casualty insurance products. (See Box 24.1.)

While correct, this perspective on the banking industry's interest in insurance is less than complete. It misses a fundamental part of the banking industry's history and motivation: Banks want and need added products. This is true for two reasons. First, the basic position of banks in the financial industry is contracting. Banks' efforts to broaden the product lines for their customers are an attempt to stem this decline. Second, banks are interested in more than just sales commissions. The distribution business that displaces a free-standing, expensive independent agent and broker system is just the banking industry's first foray into insurance products. The goal is to cross-sell corporate customers and their indigenous consumer groups into a broader array of products that are both sold and underwritten by the banking organization.

The first step in this strategy is the use of the bank's franchise to cross-sell insurance products on a brokerage basis. The feasibility of this portion of the strategy relies on some form of value added, and banks have correctly centered attention on their ability to achieve substantial **economy in the distribution** of these products. Here, the key factor that is being exploited is the customer relationship and the distribution system already in place. The first has resulted in substantial gains in other products offered by banking institutions. The second is perhaps more important. To the extent that the distribution system is less costly than the independent broker mechanisms in place, it offers substantial cost savings to interested consumers. This has been done before in the financial product market in the discount brokerage area. In that case, low-cost producers, some of

---

[2]Representative of this view are S. Travis Pritchett, "Banking and Insurance," University of South Carolina, 1990; Steven D. Felgran, "Banks as Insurance Agencies: Legal Constraints and Competitive Advances," *New England Economic Review,* September/October 1985, pp. 119–128; and Sophie M. Korczwk, "Expanded Bank Powers: Implications for the Insurance Industry," Independent Insurance Agents of America, 1987.

whom were bank affiliated, took large market shares from full-cost brokers merely because of a lower cost of distribution.

In addition, the banking industry believes that substantial success can be achieved through not only production economies but also consumption economies, or **economies of scope in consumption.**[3] These economies may arise from a reduction in the search, information, and/or transaction costs borne by the end-user of financial products. In short, it comes down to ease and convenience of purchase, both of which may be substantially improved when several financial products are purchased from the same firm.

The banking industry argues that substantial market inroads are possible because of the combination of lower distribution costs and buyer receptivity to one-stop shopping for all financial products offered by one institution. Just as insurance firms expanded into securities products such as savings vehicles, mutual funds, commercial banks believe they can cross-sell their corporate and consumer customers from deposit and loan products into insurance coverage. (See Box 24.2.)

Beyond this, bankers also wish access to other aspects of the insurance business. The underwriting function offers the insurance industry a very substantial pool of assets under its management, currently worth in excess of $2 trillion. Banks have learned through their development of trust departments and their nonbank competitors' growing activity in investment management that these resources have substantial profit potential. Further, they view themselves as equally astute in the management and allocation of such assets. Accordingly, banks clearly wish to be in the underwriting business.

At the moment, however, legislation and regulation prohibit the clear integration of these industries. Banks in small communities have traditionally been allowed to sell insurance, but this has not been a permitted activity of larger institutions. In fact, attempts by banks located in towns under 5,000 to sell insurance outside their local communities have resulted in a string of legal actions centering on states' rights. However, in March of 1996, the Supreme Court ruled that the National Bank Act supersedes state laws, effectively knocking out bank insurance restrictions on nationally chartered institutions in the 21 states where their activity had been restricted by state statutes. This may, in fact, be the beginning of the end of restrictions at the state level, at least as they relate to permissible activity by banks in small communities. However, the implication of the ruling for large-scale bank entry into insurance sales is still unclear.

At the same time, bankers have met with some success in their attempts to expand allowable activity for state-chartered institutions. Currently, 27 states permit state-chartered institutions to sell insurance outright. However, moves at

---

[3]See Richard J. Herring and Anthony M. Santomero, "The Corporate Structure of Financial Conglomerates," *Journal of Financial Services Research,* December 1990, pp. 471–497.

Box 24.1

New Data Base Smarts: The Key to Bank Entry into Insurance

Willie Sutton had it wrong. The legendary thief said that he robbed banks because that was where the money was. Banks might have enough vault cash to interest those of Sutton's ilk, but they receive a surprisingly modest share of the cash earmarked by the consumer to financial services. Compare the bank's share with that of the insurance industry.

A representative household generates about $750 in annual net revenue—interest and fees received less interest paid—for the retail part of its bank. This includes the revenue on both the deposit and loan balances. In contrast, that same household provides nearly $1,200 in net revenue for its insurance companies and their agents.

A bank will take to the bottom line about $300 pretax per typical household. Despite the much larger net revenue, the insurer and its agents will manage about the same figure.

Many banks eyeballing these numbers are asking whether they can cut in on the insurance action. Since most banks do not and cannot choose the role of risk underwriter (except in credit life), their interest naturally focuses on insurance distribution.

Given today's relatively inefficient product economics, the distribution share of the $300 in insurance net income is about $150. Thus, if banks can preempt the services of insurance agents, they have the potential of increasing their return per typical household by at least 50%.

To be sure, displacing insurance agents across the full spectrum of product and customer segments is unrealistic at best. But banks appear logically positioned to begin serving some segments effectively and profitably. This article is the first in a series that discusses the economic potential of insurance sales and how to realize that potential.

The insurance business logically segments into three parts based on their end-market dynamics: individual, commercial risk (e.g., workers' compensation), and employee benefits (e.g., group health). It is likely that banking institutions will focus at least initially on individual lines, linking this business in varying degrees to the activities of their retail banks.

In 1994, the individual insurance market generated some $400 billion in premiums and deposits. P&C accounted for about 30% of this total (nearly everyone has to get auto insurance), individual health about a quarter, annuities slightly over a fifth, and life another fifth.

Projected growth rates in individual insurance lines vary widely, but, on average, we anticipate that the growth rate of revenue in these lines will exceed that of deposits and consumer credit. Individual annuity sales are anticipated to maintain their velocity, increasing at a compound annual rate of 15% to 20% from now through the end of the decade. Individual health should grow by 10% and property and casualty by at least 5%.

---

the state level are not always successful, and attempts to move the national regulatory framework to increase bank insurance capabilities have traditionally been quite difficult. In fact, attempts to expand bank insurance sales capability resulted in explicit prohibitions in the 1982 Garn-St. Germain Act and scuttled the reform and deregulation efforts in 1996.

This leaves only state regulatory authorities as the potential area of regulatory debate. However, here, success is not at all certain. For example, Delaware passed legislation in 1990 permitting state-chartered banks to engage in both the

The outlook for life premiums is not as rosy: A leveling or even a decline in premiums is predicted. However, this forecast assumes business as usual, which in the life area means that the current distribution system will continue to underserve sizable market segments, such as modest-income families, age 25 through 34. Today it does not make economic sense for an agent to sell to this segment. However, it may make abundant sense for bank entrants into the business, given their potential capacity to mount more cost-effective sales campaigns.

Although banks are accustomed to berating themselves over the inefficiency of their product delivery systems, in point of fact these systems, however flawed, are much more efficient than those of most insurance agencies. One source of the agency problem is the personnel turnover rate. On average, agencies experience a 25% to 35% annual turnover among sales professionals. Within three to four years, about 80% to 85% of agents who start in the business will leave. Imagine the performance impact if banks saw that level of turnover on the platform.

In addition, agencies typically lack the sophisticated marketing data base, decision support systems, and modeling capabilities that many banks have put into place to pinpoint prospects for discrete insurance and other product sales appeals. Not having the operations scale necessary to develop an adequate marketing infrastructure, most agencies are relegated to labor-intensive, and therefore higher-cost, sales initiatives.

Banks can not only reduce the high cost of prospecting for customers, a few have already taken steps to simplify the sales process itself. They are reengineering the complicated life insurance application and acceptance process that has traditionally slowed the selling effort. For example, one insurer, in association with bank marketers, has substituted a one-page "short form" for the usual multi-page application, while at the same time greatly simplifying the requirements for medical underwriting.

Together, more focused marketing and reduced application complexity can conceivably pare distribution costs enough to enable banks to serve life market segments that the agencies have not been able to serve. The upshot is that the future growth in life premiums may prove far more expansive than is currently estimated.

The maturation of bank marketing skills also might serve to expand sales of other insurance products, especially annuities. Bank marketing is increasingly geared to financial life-cycle planning. The more advanced banks see themselves as ministering in a unified fashion to all five consumer financial needs—transactions, credit, investments, insurance, and financial planning. As they develop the capacity to optimize the asset allocation choices of given customer segments, these banks will be advising some who are now too heavily into deposits to shift resources into investments, including bank annuities. This is not some future scenario. Depending on whose figures you believe, banks today sell between 20% and 30% of all annuities in the U.S.

Source: Dave Kaytes, "New Data Base Smarts: The Key to Bank Entry Into Insurance," *The American Banker,* December 12, 1995, p. 8.

underwriting and distribution of insurance. Insurance industry advocates vehemently protested the expansion of bank powers associated with this legislation and proceeded with a court challenge. The Supreme Court ruling upheld the legislation, but so far, it has not resulted in much activity even within that state because of the restrictions in state law.

In the end, we may well approach the European model of full-service financial firms, but it may be a long way off. In the meantime, their banks can offer customers a much wider array of products than their U.S. counterparts. European

Box 24.2

Why Banks Will Be Great in Insurance

Imagine this scenario.

A customer walks into his local bank branch to sign the final papers for his mortgage. At the same time, he purchases homeowner's insurance and makes arrangements for his insurance and mortgage payments to be bundled into one monthly fee.

The bank's customer service representative pulls up this customer's profile on a screen, and then suggests several competitively priced life insurance products he and his family might also consider.

Scenarios like this are common in Europe. But in the United States, stringent and non-uniform regulatory requirements prevent banks from offering a full spectrum of insurance products to their customers.

Yet as banks and consumer groups aggressively challenge these rules in courtrooms across the country, it's clear that the scenario is going to change.

Banks are ideally suited to become major distributors of insurance products for a number of reasons.

First, a bank's sales infrastructure, including branches, telephone centers, and other points of delivery, offers a cost-efficient means to sell insurance products.

Second, banks have accumulated massive amounts of information on customers and their purchasing habits. Banks have the information resources that can support the marketing and sales of insurance along with other financial services products.

Third, when banks sell insurance products, consumers benefit by having access to competitively priced products and services.

Currently, thousands of U.S. banks already sell insurance in one form or another. For example, just under half the states permit state-chartered banks to run insurance brokerages and almost all the states allow banks to lease lobby space to insurers.

Approximately 134 million Americans, or 53% of the population, can legally meet their insurance needs through bank insurance agencies.

In the coming years, as the regulatory environment becomes more uniform and even less restrictive throughout the country, the relationship between banks and insurance companies is going to become a lot closer.

Insurance companies, for example, will "manufacture" products that will be sold through outlets including bank branches and ATMs.

An individual bank will sell a range of life insurance products from multiple companies through its various delivery channels, giving consumers the broadest range of choice based on features and competitive pricing. Similarly, a bank may be able to offer its products through the insurance company's distribution channels. Each institution will leverage the other's strengths.

In effect, the traditional bank will shed its primary role as a lender and assume a new role as a seller of commodity products and services.

Capturing and harnessing the huge amounts of information that reside in banking institutions' information systems is no simple task. Entirely new classes of information solutions will have to be deployed, using technology that can sort, analyze, and integrate information into meaningful patterns so that it can be used most effectively.

Information management—the way a bank uses information to compete more effectively and fuel strategic growth—will be key to the operations of an integrated financial services company.

At the hub of the new integrated financial services company will be customer information and powerful new data base tools. Such tools will allow banks to pull together customer information from any set of disparate sources and then deliver the information "outward" to service representatives, private bankers, personal financial advisers, and others who will need more unified portraits of their customers.

If banks are to compete effectively in insurance sales, they must be prepared to institutionally reinvent themselves from lenders to relationship marketers. In this new marketplace, information resources are a bank's most important strategic asset.

Source: Glenn F. Santmire, "Why Banks Will Be Great in Insurance," *The American Banker,* August 10, 1995.

banks, most notably German institutions, have long been capable of offering both commercial banking and investment banking products through institutions known as **universal banks.**[4] At the same time, there are institutions in that very market that offer both banking and insurance products, taking the full-service institution one step further to an industry form known as **allfinanz.** U.S. institutions that wish to offer their customers such a wide array of products must either offer these services outside the United States or be prepared to wait a long time for regulatory relief. (See Box 24.3.)

The Stability Effects of Joint Activity

From a public-policy perspective, one of the key issues surrounding the expansion of banking firms into other areas of the financial service industry is the effect of such expansion on both bank and financial stability. A number of studies on the issue lend support to the argument that expanded bank powers will increase the financial stability of the resultant broad financial service firm.[5] Taken as a whole, the data suggest that conglomeration of banking and insurance adds to, rather than subtracts from, the stability of the financial service sector. An expansion of the interrelationships between different parts of the financial service industry would seem to add stability through standard diversification arguments. The results relating to public policy are clear. Congress, concerned about the savings and loan debacle and the continued poor performance of the banking industry, would find this stability result a forceful argument in favor of merged activities.

---

[4]Readers interested in the operations of a universal bank should see Anthony Saunders and Ingo Walter, *Universal Banking in the U.S.* (New York: Oxford University Press, 1993).

[5]See, for example, Anthony M. Santomero and E. C. Chung, "Evidence in Support of Broader Bank Powers," *Journal of Financial Markets, Institutions and Instruments* 1 (1992).

Box 24.3

Prudential Sets Sights on U.K. Banking Sector

A wave of competition appears set to force consolidation in Britain's life insurance industry as Prudential Corp. PLC prepares to muscle its way into the banking business, according to market experts.

Prudential said it applied to the Bank of England for a banking license to open a "branchless" deposit and mortgage-lending operation by the end of 1996.

The operation, which would rely on telephone and mail delivery and wouldn't offer checking-account services, would nevertheless compete head-on with building societies and, to a lesser extent, the clearing banks for mortgage customers—an area which is already seeing heated competition from a range of other participants.

"With banks beginning to spill into the insurance sector, there's been complementary pressure the other way," said Patrick Wolridge Gordon, analyst with S.G.S.T. Securities.

Prudential would be the first listed life insurance company to enter banking, though Scottish Widows' Fund, a nonlisted insurance company, recently opened a bank with the type of license Prudential is pursuing.

Widening the Gap

Experts say the move significantly widens the gap between Prudential and other insurers such as Legal & General Group PLC, which lack the clout that Prudential already has through its large capital and customer base.

Now, with Prudential setting the stage for one-stop shopping for banking, insurance and mortgage customers, other insurance competitors may be forced to rethink their strategies, experts note.

Because of the limited service, particulary the absence of checking accounts, Prudential's move isn't seen as a direct threat to U.K. retail banks, which already are struggling with overcapacity. But it hastens the push into the rapidly expanding market of "branchless" telephone banking, according to analysts.

Prudential, with six million customers and a well-known name, would have an instant edge in direct, telephone banking, which some say is slowly usurping the prevalence of branch banking in Britain. Telephone banking, while limited in service, compensates by offering bank drafts instead of checks and 24-hour convenience.

Prudential also appears serious, naming Michael Harris to head its planned banking operation. Mr. Harris had a key role in launching Midland Bank's telephone banking unit, First Direct, in 1989, which now has 560,000 customers.

The other U.K. clearing banks are all working on their own direct telephone banking systems, with some, like TSB Group PLC, already up and running.

"The idea that the branch network is critical (to a bank's business) is doubtful," said Wolridge Gordon of S.G.S.T. "Banks themselves are moving into direct banking, and Prudential's existing infrastructure is what many banks would regard as ideal."

New Competition

On the insurance side, Prudential's move could force other big insurance concerns to buy up their smaller rivals and building societies in a bid to keep up.

"The gap is widening between Prudential and the other life companies," said Andrew Pitt, analyst with Barclays de Zoete Wedd in London. "Prudential has already attempted to enter the retail-services sector and this leaves (those like) Legal & General miles behind."

There are about 80 mutually-owned life insurance companies in the U.K.—groups, which could be vulnerable to takeovers by the nine larger, listed companies, including Prudential. Some of the larger ones, such as Legal & General, probably will consider buying building societies, which perform similar functions to savings and loans in the U.S., as a way of catching up to Prudential's preemptive move, experts say.

Prudential said it has been planning a foray into the banking industry for some time. It makes sense, the company noted, because Prudential already handles some £700 million ($1.1 billion) of mortgages for its customers each year through building societies and banks. The insurer also says it pays £1 billion a year in maturing policies—money which is usually placed on deposit with building societies and banks.

One major shareholder, who asked not to be named, said Prudential's move "would seem to be a sensible broadening of their product range," and that "it may be a way of keeping money in house when things mature."

The shareholder expressed some concern about the £70 million Prudential will spend to set up a banking operation. "The one concern is, is it costing them a lot of money in the beginning. The main concern is what kind of payback they will get," the shareholder said.

For now, Prudential isn't offering any hints. Mr. Harris said the group isn't releasing any estimates yet of when they plan to break even. Some analysts estimate, however, that the banking operation could turn a profit by 1997.

EXHIBIT 24.1

Product offerings by financial institutions

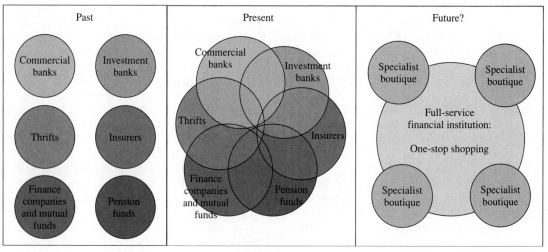

Past	Present	Future?

EXHIBIT 24.2

Geographical constraints

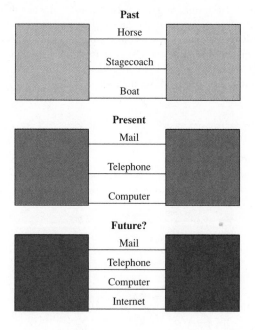

Past
Horse
Stagecoach
Boat

Present
Mail
Telephone
Computer

Future?
Mail
Telephone
Computer
Internet

Summary

It has often been said that a picture is worth a thousand words. If that is true, then a diagram ought to be worth at least a hundred. We will summarize this chapter with two sets of diagrams. In each diagram, we characterize the market of the past for financial services as segmented, either by institutional type or by geography (see Exhibits 24.1 and 24.2). The passage of time has caused a convergence. Institutions are looking more alike. Allowable activity for these institutions has begun to overlap. Geography has been connected with wires and mail, reducing the isolation of the past. Our vision of the future is a complete convergence of the financial sector, with

institution type and geographic location having little or no meaning.

Does this mean that all institutions of the future will provide all products to all customers? Assuredly not! While charters will allow a wide array of product offerings, each institution is likely to be competitive in only a few of these markets. There may be a few full-service providers, but most will be forced to find their niche on their own, without the "help" of a constraining regulatory authority restricting the firm's products or location of operation. It is a future of greater flexibility and diversity, but it is also one of greater responsibility for the managers of these institutions.

Key Concepts

allfinanz,   619
Bank Holding Company Act of 1956,   607
Bank Merger Act of 1960,   609
Douglas Amendment,   609
economy of scope and economy of
  distribution,   614–615
Garn-St. Germain Act of 1982,   609
Glass-Steagall Banking Act of 1933,   606
holding company form,   607

Interstate Banking and Branching Efficiency Act
  of 1994,   610
McCarran-Ferguson Act of 1945,   606
McFadden Act of 1927,   609
Northeast Bancorp case,   610
one-bank and multibank holding companies,   607
regulatory dialectic,   613
Section 20 subsidiaries,   608
universal banks,   619

Review Questions

1. Discuss the benefits and drawbacks to reduced government regulation of financial institutions.
2. The financial service sector has been subdivided by government legislation. Discuss the role that individual pieces of legislation play in this division. If you were rewriting this legislation, how would you divide the industry? Would you permit universal banking? Discuss the way you would approach the cost-benefit analysis of various structures.

3. The drive toward allfinanz can be seen as coming from two directions. Discuss and weigh the economic rationale of both sides in this movement toward the consolidation of the financial sector.
4. The 1927 McFadden Act reaffirmed states' rights over allowable geographic expansion of banks. The 1994 legislation overturned states' rights on this issue. Why would a state want to prevent intrusion and expansion by

commercial banks? Are these reasons economic? Are they reasonable? Are they persuasive?

5. The movement characterized in this chapter has been fostered by a laissez faire view of the financial structure. Are there social issues that should be weighed in determining appropriate allowable activity of financial institutions? Are they being missed in the debate?

References

Benston, G. J.; G. A. Henweck; and D. B. Humphrey. *The Separation of Commercial and Investment Banking: The Glass-Steagall Act Revisited and Reconsidered.* New York: St. Martin's Press, 1989.

Campbell, Tim S. *Money and Capital Markets.* Glenview, Ill.: Scott Foresman & Co., 1988.

Corrigan, Gerald E. "Reforming the U.S. Financial System: An International Perspective." *Quarterly Review.* Federal Reserve Bank of New York, Spring 1989.

Felgran, Steven D. "Banks as Insurance Agencies: Legal Constraints and Competitive Advances." *New England Economic Review,* September/October 1985.

Gorton, Gary, and Richard Rosen. "Corporate Control, Portfolio Choice, and the Decline of Banking." *Journal of Finance,* December 1995.

Herring, Richard J., and Anthony M. Santomero. "The Corporate Structure of Financial Conglomerates." *Journal of Financial Services Research,* December 1990.

Litan, Robert E. "Taking the Dangers Out of Banking Deregulation." *The Brookings Review,* Fall 1986.

Mishkin, Frederic. *The Economics of Money, Banking and Financial Markets.* 2nd ed. Glenview, Ill.: Scott Foresman & Co., 1989.

Pritchett, S. Travis. "Banking and Insurance." University of South Carolina, 1990.

Remolona, E. M., and K. C. Wulfekuhler. "Finance Companies, Bank Competition and Niche Markets." *Quarterly Review.* Federal Reserve Bank of New York, Summer 1992.

Santomero, Anthony M. "The Changing Structure of Financial Institutions: A Review Essay." *Journal of Monetary Economics,* September 1989.

———. "Banking and Insurance: A Banking Industry Perspective." In *S. S. Huebner Financial Management of Insurers,* edited by J. David Cummins and Joan Lamm-Tennant. Boston: Kluwer, 1993.

Santomero, Anthony M., and E. C. Chung. "Evidence in Support of Broader Bank Powers." *Journal of Financial Markets, Institutions and Instruments* 1 (1992).

Saunders, Anthony. "Conflicts of Interest: An Economic View." In *Deregulating Wall Street,* edited by Ingo Walter. New York: John Wiley & Sons, 1985.

Saunders, Anthony, and Ingo Walter. *Universal Banking in The U.S.* New York: Oxford University Press, 1993.

———. *Universal Banking: Financial System Design Reconsidered.* Burr Ridge, Ill.: Irwin Professional Publishing, 1996.

Chapter 25

Managing Financial Institutions

Financial institutions of every type face substantial management challenges in the current financial markets. This chapter reviews the management techniques employed by these institutions in their effort to operate profitably and to reduce the risks associated with default, interest rates, foreign exchange rates, and liquidity needs. It also reviews the special challenges facing each type of institution in light of the services that it performs.

If everything goes according to plan, it can be very profitable to own and operate a financial institution. As long as you are able to earn more on your assets than it costs to fund them—the cost of incurring and servicing liabilities—you have the potential for making profits. Because financial institutions generally operate with high leverage, the profits to equityholders can be substantial. Consider a finance company with $100 in assets, $95 in liabilities, and $5 in equity. Suppose the company earns 11 percent on assets, or $11, and pays 8 percent for its debt, or $7.60. It then earns $3.40 (= $11 – $7.60) on the equity of $5. This is an incredible return of 68 percent on equity.

Unfortunately, it is incredible. This spread between lending and borrowing rates has to be used for more than just profit. People must be paid; landlords require attention, and the ordinary costs of business must be covered. These expenses can be offset somewhat by fees and service charges, but the bulk of the company's spread will still go to covering these operating expenses. For our finance company, these costs would amount to about $2.50, leaving the shareholder with a mere 90¢ in return.[1] However, remember that equity is only 5 percent of total assets. Thus, a spread of only 0.9 percent on assets versus liabilities translates into an 18 percent return on equity. This is not a bad return for the services rendered to borrowers and investors in our hypothetical finance company.

However, many things can and do go wrong when one runs a financial institution. These events have the potential to wreak havoc upon the institution and perhaps even result in its demise. Because financial institutions are, by and large, highly levered, it does not take much of a miscalculation or wrong judgment about the returns on assets or the costs of liabilities before the entire equity capital or net worth of the institution can be depleted. Consider again our hypothetical financial institution with $100 in assets, $95 in liabilities, and $5 in equity capital. If assets decline in value by 5 percent, to $95, while liabilities remain unchanged, the entire $5, or 100 percent, of equity capital is depleted.

Indeed, this sensitivity of capital to small changes in the values of assets and/or liabilities (as well as changes in the spread between returns on assets and cost of funds) is one of the reasons that financial institutions are so highly regulated. But complying with regulations is no guarantee of profitability or even survival, nor can one absolve imprudent behavior with the excuse that all regulations were obeyed. While it is necessary to comply with regulations, such compliance is not sufficient to ensure profitability. Prudence dictates that managers take all necessary actions and develop necessary systems to promote the financial well-being of the institution.

In Chapters 8 through 10, we examined a number of risks—credit or default risk, interest rate risk, foreign exchange risk, and liquidity risk—but we have not described how these risks threaten financial institutions. The purposes of this chapter are to probe how these risks affect financial institutions and to review the risk management techniques that they employ in an effort to mitigate the risks associated with default, volatile interest and foreign exchange rates, and liquidity needs.

---

[1] We also forgot to mention taxes in our example. If we forget, Uncle Sam will not. In our case, however, assume that the 90 b.p. return is, in fact, after-tax net income.

While many of the risk management techniques are employed by the gamut of financial institutions, certain risks, and the risk management techniques they elicit, are more applicable to one kind of financial institution than another. Accordingly, we will conclude with a sketch of the differences between the various financial institutions insofar as they relate to the risks and risk management techniques discussed in this chapter.

Performance and Risk in Financial Institutions

As can be seen in the example above, financial institutions of all types must actively manage their organizations to obtain an adequate return on equity capital. Management achieves this goal by focusing on two features of performance—return and risk. The financial performance of the firm is dependent on its ability to achieve a positive return on capital while, at the same time, limiting the institution's exposure to risks that can destroy it.

Return is managed through the judicious setting of prices on loans and deposits and the control of operating expenses. On the asset side of the firm's balance sheet, loans must be priced at interest rates that incorporate expected portfolio losses and still offer an adequate return. Investments in securities can only be justified if their yields are equally adequate. On the liability side, the interest payments offered to depositors, or policy-, or bondholders, as the case may be, must be sufficient to attract needed resources but not so high as to waste them. In the end, the **spread** between revenue and expense must be adequate to absorb expected credit losses and all net operating costs. At the same time, credit processing, screening, and enforcement must be sufficiently efficient to keep **default rates** to manageable levels. And the **cost of operations,** including wages, rent, data processing, and miscellaneous operating expenses, must be kept both within bounds and under the net interest margin or spread alluded to above. For taxable institutions, such as commercial banks and stock insurance and thrift institutions, the effects of taxation must also be considered before the firm's profit flow can go to either retained earnings or stockholder dividends.

The two measures most often used to report the firm's resultant performance are the **return on assets** (ROA) and the **return on equity** (ROE). The first of these is the net income per dollar of average assets, while the second is expressed in terms of balance sheet equity. As institutions change their activities, expand their products, and, at times, create assets only to sell them, the return on assets measurement is declining in importance. Accordingly, most analysts following any of the institutions discussed here tend to focus on return on stockholders equity or, for mutual organizations, surplus. This return must be adequate to justify the owners' investment in the firm, and therefore, it must be competitive with returns obtainable elsewhere in the capital market.

The second challenge facing the manager is the control of risk. Here, there are many different risks to consider, measure, and control, with each particular institution dependent on some of these to a greater extent than others. Nonetheless, each and every institution must consider five specific kinds of risk:

1. Credit risk
2. Interest rate risk
3. Liquidity risk
4. Foreign exchange risk
5. Operating risk

There are clearly others, such as actuarial risk, off-balance-sheet risk, reputation risk, and environmental risk, to name just a few. However, the five risks listed here form the core of any list offered by industry pundits,[2] and accordingly, they will be the only ones we address here.

Credit risk is the risk associated with the repayment of a credit advance made by the institution. For direct loans, it is the risk that the borrower will not repay, will repay late, or otherwise will not make payments in accord with terms set forth in a credit agreement, and that recoveries will be insufficient to compensate the institution for the resources invested. For securities, likewise, credit risk represents the risk of formal default or bankruptcy and insufficient recovery to recoup the initial investment plus interest. As you will recall from Chapter 9, variations in the market's required break-even yield will cause investment losses due to credit risk even in the absence of formal default or bankruptcy. The risk here is that a deterioration in the condition of the borrower results in an investment loss.

Interest rate risk refers to the change in the value of a financial asset or liability occasioned by a change in the general level of interest rates. For an institution as a whole, it represents the net change in the value of the financial institution's equity as a result of interest rate movements. Interest rate risk also entails reinvestment risk—the risk that the firm will not be able to reinvest its interim cash flows at interest rates that are necessary to meet its liabilities. Each segment of the industry will have a unique way of measuring interest rate risk and reporting its exposure to variations in the values of assets and liabilities. Nonetheless, the risk is present in all segments of the industry, as no one portion of the industry is immune to interest rate variation.

Liquidity risk, however, is a coat of a different color. This is the risk to the institution that there will be a sudden call upon its resources that will strain its financial capacity. Liquidity risk is most often thought of as a sudden liability shortfall that is associated with a deposit withdrawal for depository institutions, or with a decline in borrowing capacity for institutions like finance companies. It may also be experienced by insurance firms, pension funds, or mutual funds as a sudden outflow to their customers. Sometimes, this risk is exacerbated when perceived

---

[2]For a longer list and a more general discussion of the issues facing firms in risk management, see G. Oldfield and A. Santomero, "The Place of Risk Management in Financial Institutions," working paper, Wharton Financial Institutions Center, 1994.

liquidity problems lead to a "run" on the financial institution, much like that described in Chapter 21. Too much liquidity can also be a liquidity risk if the excess liquidity arises at a time when investment opportunities are unattractive.

Foreign exchange risk is analogous to interest rate risk in that it measures the change in equity value due to variations in the level of the exchange rate. As institutions invest and borrow globally, the currency of a transaction need not be the same as the currency of the institution's home market. Therefore, when there is a mismatch between assets and liabilities that are denominated in a particular currency, the institution's value will change with currency fluctuations.

Finally, we have **operating risk.** Here, the concern is that system failures or human error will result in losses to the institution that could substantially affect its viability. These failures could be sudden, such as a computer breakdown, or cumulative, such as the inability to bring on-line a new computer application. But, these failures need not be machine-made. A failure to encode a check properly can be as costly as a computer breakdown.

Relevant to operating risk are such things as organizational structure, role of the board of directors, delegation of authority and responsibility, dual control, internal and external audits, performance evaluation, budgeting and planning, capital adequacy, and the regulatory agencies' examination and supervision. Our goal here is not to explain fully how managers of financial institutions manage these operations. This is best left to our colleagues in financial institution management texts, where an entire book can be devoted to the subject.[3] Rather, this chapter will center upon how the financial techniques developed here can be employed to manage the key financial risks enumerated above—namely, credit, interest rate, liquidity, and foreign exchange rate risks. We will now address each risk in turn.

Managing Credit Risk

As noted above, credit risk has a direct influence on financial institutions, and it is therefore an appropriate place to begin. Since the financial institution itself is responsible for satisfying its own liabilities, the usual focus, insofar as credit risk is concerned, is on the asset side of the balance sheet. Commercial banks, savings banks, savings and loan associations, and credit unions worry about deterioration in the creditworthiness of their borrowers, whose borrowings are listed as assets (loans) on the balance sheets of these institutions. Pension funds, insurance companies, and other financial institutions are concerned about a change in credit quality among the issuers of the securities in which they invest. Obviously, the investors in the liabilities of financial institutions—savers, depositors, policyowners, pensioners, lenders, deposit insurers, insolvency guarantors, and regulators— are also concerned about the credit quality of financial institutions' assets

---

[3]See A. Saunders, *Financial Institutions Management: A Modern Perspective,* second edition, (Burr Ridge, Ill.: Richard D. Irwin, 1997).

because, ultimately, the performance of the assets determines the ability of financial institutions to meet the obligations of their liabilities.

There are two types of risks imposed on financial institutions by credit risks. First, there is the possibility that default rates will rise above current or expected levels, thereby impairing the asset portfolio and eroding the equity of the financial institution. When a debtor defaults, only a portion of the borrowed amount is usually recovered. In the case of bonds that were originally issued in the subinvestment grade category, below S&P's BBB– or Moody's Baa3 ratings, often dubbed "high-yield bonds" by the salespersons and "junk bonds" by the holders, only around 35 percent of face value is recovered on average. For bonds of all ratings, the percentage rises to approximately 40–45 percent.

The second risk is related to the market price of the asset. Even if the borrower does not ultimately default, the market price of the credit instrument can fall substantially and remain at the depressed level for years. This decline in market price may be accompanied by similar declines in other related low-quality securities, or it may simply be a reflection of the change in credit quality of a particular issue. In either case, the lower market price may be inadequate to satisfy the demands placed upon a financial institution by its creditors, who may be writing checks, withdrawing savings, cashing in insurance policies, and so forth.

To demonstrate the effect of overexposure to low-quality credit, refer to Exhibit 25.1. Here we show the credit exposure of three financial institutions, all of which had sizable exposure to credit loss in their fixed-income portfolios in 1988. For each of these three institutions, we calculated the loss to market value of equity by taking the percentage of assets invested in junk bonds and multiplying it by the decline in market value, or the loss to default, after factoring in the recovery value of junk bonds. The loss in asset value was then subtracted from equity to arrive at the reduction in market value of equity. At one institution, an increase in default rates, or a decrease in the market prices of the low-quality bonds it held, left the institution with plenty of equity to remain financially healthy. The second institution, which held more of such bonds relative to its equity, was more susceptible to either an increase in default rates or a decline in the market prices of these bonds due to a perceived deterioration in credit or an increase in market aversion to credit risk. The third institution, which held very little equity and a large low-quality bond portfolio, showed extreme exposure to either manifestation of credit risk. (In fact, the latter two of these institutions became insolvent during a recent downturn in low-quality bond prices and a concomitant increase in default rates.)[4]

Institutions use several ways to reduce the credit risk in their asset portfolios. One way is to diversify their holdings of assets, particularly among those most likely to default. For example, an insurance company may have a portfolio

---

[4]Our analysis assumes that 50 percent of the face value is recovered by the investor in junk bonds. In reality, it is more likely that only around 35 percent would be recovered, on average, so the institutions depicted in Exhibit 25.1 probably would actually exhibit greater susceptibility to an increase in default rates.

EXHIBIT 25.1

Sensitivity of market value of equity to declining junk bond values and default risk

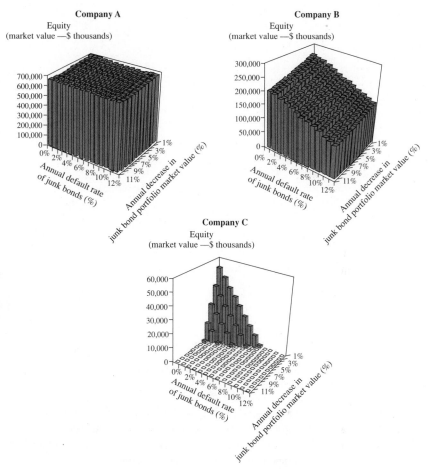

Note: All figures assume 50 percent redemption value in the event of default.

investment policy in place such that it (1) will not invest more than a certain percentage, say 1 1/2 percent, of its total portfolio in any one issue of a low-grade bond issuer; (2) will not invest more than another somewhat larger percentage, say 3 percent, in all the debt issues of any investment grade issuer; (3) will limit its percentage to perhaps 10 percent of any publicly traded issue; and (4) will not buy more than a certain percentage, say 25 percent, or a certain dollar amount of any private placement. Other financial institutions have similar criteria, and regulatory bodies impose their own minimal diversification standards.

The purpose of these **diversification guidelines** is to ensure that an individual company portfolio's default experience does not diverge too far from the experience of a broadly diversified portfolio of similar holdings. For instance, suppose a company chose to invest only in one or two bonds, both with a low probability of default, say 1 percent per year. Thus, during most years the

Exhibit 25.2

*Average one-year
default rates
(1970–1995)*

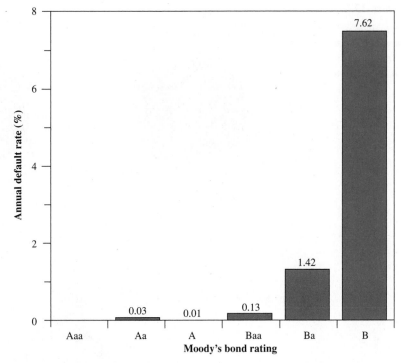

Source: "Corporate Bond Defaults and Default Rates 1938–1995," *Moody's Special Report,* January 1996.

company is unlikely to experience any defaults in its portfolio. But if during any particular year, one or both bonds go into default, it could devastate the company. This adverse experience may not happen for a hundred or more years, but it could happen the very first year, before sufficient reserves and surplus have been amassed to offset the potential problem. By diversifying broadly, it is less likely that all, or even a substantial portion, of the bonds held by the company will default during any given year. The company's experience is more likely to approach that of the broader population of bonds.

Diversifying among credit risks is insufficient to eliminate credit risk, however. It may be that an institution invests in a broadly diversified set of bonds that have, on average, a 7.62 percent rate of default in any given year. (This corresponds to a B-rated bond portfolio, according to Exhibit 25.2.) But the default rate may range from 0 percent in some years to higher than 20 percent in other years. (Indeed, the actual one-year default rates from 1970 to 1995 ranged from 0 percent to 21.74 percent.) This can be inferred from Exhibit 25.3, which shows an annual standard deviation of 4.8 percent for B-rated bonds. Two standard deviations above the mean default rate of 7.62 percent will give approximately 17 percent. However, the distribution of default rates is not symmetric but skewed to the right, so it would be possible to get much higher default rates during any given year. Thus, even if an institution has diversified broadly among all bonds within a

EXHIBIT 25.3

Standard deviations of one-year default rates (1970–1995)

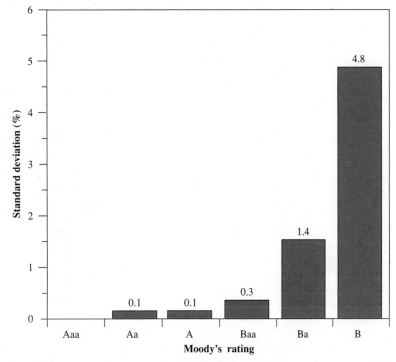

Source: "Corporate Bond Defaults and Default Rates 1938–1995," *Moody's Special Report,* January 1996.

given credit rating (say B), it may still suffer drastic experience during any given year. Indeed, this suffering may occur even if the default rate for a year does not change appreciably. Market prices of the bonds may decline for other reasons, such as a perception that default rates may increase at some time in the future, or because of a change in the supply and demand for the bonds due to changing taxation, regulatory policy, and so forth.

This latter sort of credit risk may be referred to as **systematic credit risk,** as opposed to **specific credit risk,** because it pervades the debt market in varying degrees over time. A financial institution can hedge against this kind of risk by undertaking a highly disciplined approach to investing. The investment strategy, which is described in detail elsewhere,[5] involves diversifying across broad sectors as well as across ratings or issuing firms. In this way, if it chooses judiciously, the institution takes investment positions in assets whose values tend to increase at times when credit risk elsewhere increases. Thus, at the time that losses are occurring in the bond or loan portfolio due to bad credit experience, profits are being made on the hedge portfolio that offset the losses. The hedge portfolio can

---

[5]See David F. Babbel, "Insuring Banks Against Systematic Credit Risk," *The Journal of Futures Markets* 9, no. 6 (December 1989); "Insuring Sovereign Debt Against Default," World Bank Discussion Paper no. 328, Washington D. C.: The World Bank, June 1996.

be altered to reduce the systematic component of credit risk to whatever levels are deemed acceptable.[6]

Two other approaches are taken to reduce the effects of exposure to credit risk, both of which involve reducing risk and return. One approach is for the financial institution to have strong reserves and sufficient equity capital so that it is able to withstand any adverse experience in credit risk. Another approach is to strictly limit the exposure to credit risk by investing only small amounts in risky credits while investing the remainder in high-grade credits. Both approaches have the effect of limiting credit risk and have a clear place in the market. Investors seeking quality may well find the conservative return adequate for their investment objectives. It is also common for the financial institution to monitor over time the credit quality of loans and investments it has made so that it can attempt to make a hasty exit or take loss mitigation measures when problems arise. While this tactic does not strictly limit exposure to credit risk, it is aimed at reducing large losses when credit deteriorates.

An altogether different approach is also possible, however. This approach involves "passing through" to the liability side of the balance sheet the risks assumed on the asset side of the balance sheet. For example, a mutual fund may invest heavily in junk bonds, but the liability of the fund fluctuates directly in response to the investment performance of the assets. The investor in the mutual fund, in effect, bears the risk of poor performance. Another example is an insurance company that establishes a "separate account" for a variable life insurance policy or defined-contribution pension plan, whose payoffs ultimately depend on the value and performance of some underlying asset portfolio. Here, rather than reducing risk, the institution is transferring it to a (hopefully) willing third party.

Of the five methods described above for managing credit risk—diversifying, hedging, reserving, limiting exposure, and passing through the risk to investors—none ultimately alters the global incidence of credit risk. Rather, these methods redistribute the risk among investors in a way that suits investors' tastes. Some investors like to hold debt of financially distressed enterprises because of the higher returns they expect to achieve.[7] To the extent that financial institutions and other investors eschew credit risk, however, the global demand for it will be reduced, which will drive up the interest rate spread investors will demand to hold low-quality debt instruments.

Managing Interest Rate Risk

With the increased interest rate volatility of recent years, it has become increasingly important to address the effects of this volatility on financial institutions and to manage the risks it presents. Interest rate risk management has assumed such

---

[6]It is even possible to create a similar hedge portfolio to reduce the credit risk of a single bond or a loan.

[7]See Eugene Fama and Kenneth French, "Multifactor Explanations of Asset Pricing Anomalies," *Journal of Finance*, March 1996.

importance during the past decade that a "cottage industry," which goes by the name **asset/liability management** (hereafter ALM), has proliferated and is directed exclusively toward managing interest rate risks. Clearly, ALM could denote a far more encompassing focus than interest rate risk management, yet today, the term is usually applied in that narrower context.

Interest rate risk has been defined as the effect of unanticipated changes in interest rates on the market value of an individual financial instrument or of portfolios of financial instruments, whether they be assets or liabilities. In the context of a financial institution, the risk is that the value of the liability portfolio will rise more rapidly if interest rates decline, or fall more slowly if interest rates increase, than will the market value of the asset portfolio. Such relative movements in portfolio values could shrink the financial institution's economic equity.[8]

Let us take an example to illustrate this point. Suppose a financial institution has $100 million in assets with an effective duration of 10 and $95 million in liabilities with an effective duration of 4.[9] To make the numbers simple, let us assume that assets are earning a 1 percent net spread over the cost of liabilities. Next, suppose that general interest rate levels rise suddenly by 300 basis points. The market value of assets will then decline by roughly $31.5 million (= −Effective duration × Change in interest rates × Initial value = −10 × .03 × $100 million), to $70 million. The cost of what it will take to fund liabilities (i.e., the present value of liabilities) will also fall in response to the 300 b.p. rise in the general level of interest rates. Considering the liability duration is 4, the decline in present value will be approximately $11.4 million (= −4 × .03 × $95 million), to $83.6 million. Even if, under the new interest rate environment, the financial institution is able to continue earning a consistently positive 1 percent spread, it will take nearly 14 years for the assets' value to catch up with the value of liabilities, and much longer to restore the 5 percent surplus position that existed prior to the change in interest rates.

Using the tools of "duration" from Chapter 8 as a measure of the price elasticity of an asset or liability with respect to a movement in interest rates, however, we can do much better. By matching the dollar duration of the portfolio of assets to the dollar duration of the related liabilities, one can **immunize** the firm's equity (surplus) from the effects of changing interest rates.[10] In effect, with matched dollar durations, a change in the value of assets occasioned by a movement in interest rates will be offset (approximately) by a like change in the present value of liabilities, regardless of the direction of change in interest rates.

---

[8]The economic equity of a financial institution is defined as the difference between the market value of assets and the present value of liabilities. In a regulatory context, book values are used to define equity.

[9]Recall from Chapter 8 that the measure called "effective duration" gives the approximate change in value, scaled in percentage terms, for a 100 b.p. change in interest rates. A brief review of Chapter 8 might prove helpful to better understand this section on interest rate risk.

[10]Recall that the effective dollar duration is equal to the effective duration multiplied by the initial dollar value; this measure relates the change in dollar price to a change in interest rates.

When the market value of the assets exceeds the value of the liabilities, it is useful to calculate how the resulting value of equity changes with movements in interest rates. The dollar duration of equity equals the dollar duration of assets minus the dollar duration of liabilities.

$$DD_{Equity} = DD_{Assets} - DD_{Liabilities}$$

To use the example above, suppose a firm has assets of $100 and liabilities of $95, so that surplus is $5. Assume further that the dollar duration of assets is $10 and the dollar duration of liabilities is also $10. Then, a 100 basis points move in interest would be accompanied by a change in assets of $10 and a like change in liabilities of $10, leaving surplus intact at $5.

Even a small asset/liability dollar duration mismatch can result in a relatively large interest rate sensitivity of the equity. This is because the value of the equity is typically small relative to that of the asset and liability portfolios.

Notice that we referred to the remedy to interest rate risk as matching dollar durations, not matching effective durations. When dollar durations are matched, the dollar amounts of changes in the values of assets and liabilities are roughly equal to each other. However, when effective durations are matched, the percentage changes in asset and liability values in response to movements in interest rates are approximately the same; however, the dollar amounts of the changes are not the same. The sensitivity of equity to interest rate moves, expressed in percentage terms, that is, effective duration, is given by the following formula:[11]

$$D_{Equity} = (D_{Assets} - D_{Liabilities})\frac{A}{E} + D_{Liabilities}$$

where D signifies effective duration, and A and E represent the market values of assets and equity, respectively. In words, this formula says:

$$\text{Interest sensitivity of equity} = (\text{Mismatch} \times \text{Leverage}) + \text{Interest sensitivity of liabilities}$$

In examining this formula, it is apparent that if the leverage is high, a small mismatch in effective durations between assets and liabilities can impart a high interest rate sensitivity to equity.

---

[11]This equation can be derived from the prior one by substituting the definitions for effective dollar duration into the formulas wherever DD appears. We then have:

$$(A \times D_A) - (L \times D_L) = E \times D_E$$

$$\left(\frac{A}{E}D_A\right) - \left(\frac{L}{E}D_L\right) = D_E$$

and substituting $A - E$ for L, we obtain:

$$\left(\frac{A}{E}D_A\right) - \left(\frac{A - E}{E}D_L\right) = D_E$$

which, when simplified, gives us our result.

In light of this significant risk, why would financial institutions deliberately mismatch the interest rate sensitivities of assets and liabilities? One reason for this is that they may expect that higher returns can be earned in some segments of the term structure over others. Perhaps these institutions believe that this additional anticipated return will compensate them for the additional risk they incur. As we said in earlier chapters, this is a dubious proposition. Alternatively, these institutions may wish to speculate on the direction of interest rate movements, and by deliberately mismatching durations of assets and liabilities, they can profit handsomely, provided that they correctly forecast the direction of interest rate movements. This, too, is a dubious proposition.

Let us consider another example—this one taken from an actual financial institution. We found the liabilities of this institution to aggregate to an effective duration of 5.6, whereas the assets aggregated to an effective duration of 3.8. Thus, the mismatch was −1.8. (Note that in the previous example, the mismatch was positive.) This particular institution had assets of around $4 billion and an equity value of $180 million. Therefore, its leverage ratio was 22.2. The equity effective duration was computed as follows:

$$D_{Equity} = [(3.8 - 5.6) \times 22.2] + 5.6 = -34.4$$

This means that for every 1 percent change in interest rates, the market value of equity will change in the same direction, because in this case equity duration happens to be negative, by over 34 percent.

To demonstrate the effect of interest rate changes over the years on this institution, purged of any extraneous responses to other economic events, we modeled the company over a seven-year period. Assets and liabilities were frozen at April 1987 levels, and the market values of these were changed only to reflect the effects of what happened to interest rates over the seven-year period from 1980–1987. Throughout the period, we maintained a constant duration mismatch of 1.8.[12]

Exhibit 25.4 shows the evolution in values over time that would have been caused by interest rate changes alone. The difference between the asset and liability value paths, plotted in Exhibit 25.5, portrays the evolution of economic value of equity over the same time period. Note that in April 1987, the value of equity was around $184 million and its duration was −34.4, just as we calculated above. Earlier, the equity was worth closer to $500 million, but a secular decline in interest rates over the period produced the erosion in equity value. We have noted that the equity duration at the outset was −12.2 but that later it was −34.4. How could this change occur if we held the duration mismatch constant at 1.8? The reason was that the leverage increased during the period as

---

[12]We use the term "mismatch" loosely here. In the case of dollar durations, a match is sought to minimize interest rate risk. In the case of effective durations, a mismatch is required, if there is positive equity, to minimize interest rate risk. The size of the mismatch needed can be determined by setting equity duration equal to zero and solving for the mismatch. In this case, the desired mismatch is −0.252, which can be obtained by shortening the asset portfolio duration.

EXHIBIT 25.4

*The effects of a 1.8
year duration
mismatch over time on
assets and liabilities*

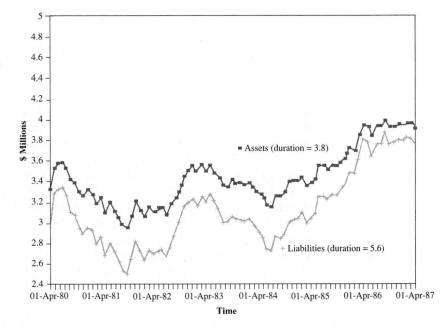

equity was eroded. The increased leverage translated into the more severe duration figure.[13]

In addition to engineering a proper match between the effective dollar durations (*DD*) of assets and liabilities, immunization against interest rate risk entails that the convexities of assets and liabilities be in proper balance. If, in addition to a dollar duration match between assets and liabilities, the convexity of the assets is greater than the convexity of the liabilities, the economic equity of the entity will be enhanced whether interest rates move up or down.[14] Such a portfolio is said to be immunized.

To illustrate the concept of asset/liability matching across the dimensions of both duration and convexity, we must examine liabilities and assets in turn. In Exhibit 25.6 we have illustrated the value profile of an insurance company liability—a single-premium deferred annuity (SPDA) block of business that is currently in force. Note the strong positive convexity apparent in the value profile of this liability. Then, in Exhibit 25.7, we have shown the value profiles for a seven-year noncallable 9 percent bond and a combination of a seven-year bond with a

---

[13]It happened that the institution in question undertook a massive portfolio restructuring in May 1987, so that further changes in interest rates would have little impact on economic equity. Had they not done so, the subsequent decline in interest rates may have eliminated the institution's remaining economic equity.

[14]These remarks assume parallel shifts in the term structure of interest rates. To manage against nonparallel shifts in the term structure, attention must be paid to elements of interest rate sensitivity in addition to those captured by duration and convexity measures.

EXHIBIT 25.5

Impact of interest rate movements over time on the market value of surplus

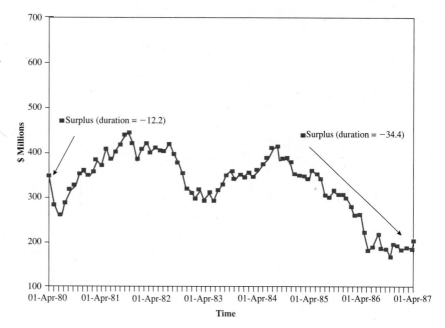

EXHIBIT 25.6

Price behavior of option-adjusted value

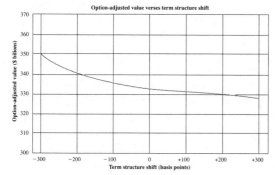

	Single-Premium Deferred Annuities		
Market Value ($ millions)	*Term Structure Shift (bp)*	*Option- Adjusted Duration*	*Option- Adjusted Convexity*
349.4	−300	2.49	n/a
340.9	−200	1.50	91.52
335.5	−100	0.73	87.92
333.1	0	0.45	28.52
331.6	+100	0.39	5.43
330.3	+200	0.53	(13.32)
328.6	+300	n/a	n/a

seven-year, 10 percent strike level interest rate cap. The combination of the bond and cap demonstrates what is called "financial engineering." Actually, we have purchased only 96 percent as much of the bond and used the remaining 4 percent of our funds to purchase the cap. Note how we have changed the value profile of the bond to a less steep, more convex profile by adding the cap to the portfolio. The new shape now more closely parallels the shape of the SPDA liability. Further efforts would be required to get an exact match, but the point here is that

Exhibit 25.7

Market value of bond and cap portfolio for a range of interest rates

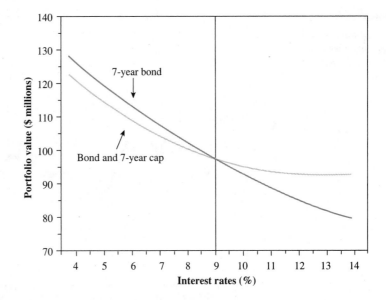

such financial engineering can be done to get the durations and convexities to match.[15]

As time passes and interest rates change, the dollar duration of assets and liabilities will tend to drift apart and convexities will change, resulting in a dollar duration mismatch and a convexity imbalance. To avoid this, the asset portfolio and/or liability mix must be rebalanced periodically; that is, steps must be taken to adjust the portfolio durations and convexities.

Managing Liquidity Risk

Liquidity risk was defined earlier as the risk to the institution that there will be a sudden need for resources that will put a strain upon the institution's ability to finance itself. This financial need may be caused by the usual ebb and flow of resources into the institution, or alternatively, it may result from an unexpected and unfortunate event that bears upon the financial soundness and viability of the institution.

The first type of liquidity concern was once a major risk affecting all financial institutions. Today, it is significantly less important due to money market instruments that are available to the financial institution, such as commercial paper and repos; as well as mechanisms that are in place in the capital markets that can provide rapid liquidity, such as federal funds and credit lines; and discount window loans from the Fed. Moreover, with the passage of time, many financial instruments

[15]For further details on this kind of financial engineering, see David F. Babbel, Peter Bouyoucos, and Rob Stricker, "Capping the Interest Rate Risk in Insurance Products," in *The Handbook of Fixed-Income Options,* edited by Frank J. Fabozzi (Burr Ridge, Ill.: Irwin Professional Publishing, 1996).

that were once illiquid have become more liquid so that it is easier for a financial institution to "undo" a position it may have in an asset. However, illiquidity risk can pose a problem, and financial institutions must be very careful to avoid it. Careful planning for seasonal liquidity needs is an important part of this activity.

However, liquidity concerns associated with questions surrounding the integrity of the asset portfolio are another matter. Conditions that can give rise to this type of need for liquidity may result from circumstances in which the asset portfolio is impaired by bad credit experience or from duration mismatch, when interest rates move in a direction opposite of that which would benefit the company. As creditors hear rumors of the impaired position of the institution, they may wish to withdraw their funds before it becomes common knowledge and they are caught waiting at the end of some line. Even if the asset portfolio is not fatally impaired, the inability to meet the liquidity requirements of a given moment may lead depositors and other creditors to suspect that it is impaired, thereby creating an increased need for liquidity. Such a financial institution may have a sound long-run investment philosophy and asset portfolio, but if its investments are illiquid, a sudden increase in withdrawals could require it to liquidate valuable assets at a loss due to their illiquid nature. The losses incurred thereby could place the institution in greater jeopardy.

This type of concern is usually expressed by depository institutions such as commercial banks because of their highly liquid liability structure and, at the same time, less liquid asset portfolio. However, this need for liquidity exists for other institutions, such as insurance companies, mutual funds, and finance companies. These institutions mitigate the potential for a cash need by constructing their asset portfolios in a manner that adds a greater degree of liquidity than would have been present in the absence of these concerns. In fact, depository institutions are generally characterized as holding a portion of their asset portfolios in somewhat more liquid, albeit lower-yielding, assets. These categories are sometimes referred to as **primary and secondary reserves** because of their relative position in providing necessary added liquidity. Primary reserves are highly liquid and include such items as cash in the vault and clearing account balances. They may also include other short-term highly liquid securities, but usually only those that have maturities of overnight duration, such as federal funds and repurchase agreements. Secondary reserves are somewhat less liquid and include short-term commercial paper, government securities, and other money market instruments. The relative size and composition of the primary and secondary reserves will depend, in part, on the costs of maintaining generally lower-earning reserves balanced against the need for liquidity through redemptions of the reserve accounts.

The lower the fluctuations in redemptions relative to inflows of new cash over time, the lower the liquidity requirements. This, in turn, is determined by the nature of the liabilities used to finance the institution and their maturity structure. Other things equal, the longer the term of the liabilities and the more local or retail the funding base, the more stable the liabilities and the less the institution needs to be concerned about underlying liquidity problems. Moreover, the capital (surplus) position of the bank will influence how much it must carry in these reserves. The less capital the bank maintains, the more asset liquidity it needs.

EXHIBIT 25.8   Net Foreign Exchange Exposure Report

	British pounds	*Japanese yen*	*Swiss francs*
Assets (in thousands)	10,000	30,000	4,000
Liabilities	15,000	20,000	10,000
Fx bought	65,000	100,000	50,000
Fx sold	50,000	125,000	55,000
Net position	+10,000	−15,000	−11,000

Managing Foreign Exchange Rate Risk

The highly levered structure of most financial institutions can magnify the effects of even small changes in exchange rates into large changes in their profitability and equity position. In this way, foreign exchange rate risk is similar to interest rate risk. The risk arises when a financial institution has assets and revenues denominated in one currency (or group of currencies) and liabilities and costs in another currency (or group of currencies). When the value of one currency changes relative to the other, the assets and liabilities also change in value, but in different directions; thus, the equity value also changes.

A financial institution must take care to manage its exposure to foreign exchange risk. It can do this by ensuring that assets and revenues are denominated in the same currency as liabilities and costs. Alternatively, the institution can undertake some off-balance-sheet actions such as currency swaps and forward rate agreements that restore the balance and reduce the exposure to foreign exchange rate risk.

The first step a financial institution must take is to map out its exposure to currency fluctuations. A simple table like that displayed in Exhibit 25.8 suffices. The **net foreign exchange (Fx) exposure** in any given currency, *i,* is calculated as follows:

$$\text{Net exposure}_i = (\text{Fx assets}_i - \text{Fx liabilities}_i) + (\text{Fx bought}_i - \text{Fx sold}_i)$$

As can be seen in Exhibit 25.8, the financial institution is "long" in sterling but "short" in yen and francs. Thus, it will be helped by an appreciation in the pound or a depreciation in yen and francs, relative to its domestic currency, which we will assume to be the U.S. dollar. On the other hand, it will be hurt if currencies move in the other direction. By examining its exposure, the institution can take corrective measures. For example, it may wish to undertake a currency swap or forward agreement to sell pounds for domestic currency or to acquire yen and francs.

Note also that the financial institution has exposures to several currencies. Thus, if the dollar experiences a general appreciation in value, this institution could be hurt by a depreciating pound, but at the same time, it would be helped by the depreciating yen and franc. These offsetting effects can lead to less currency exposure than would be indicated by a simplistic summing of net positions in foreign exchange. Therefore, a financial institution wishing to reduce its exposure to foreign exchange movements need not "zero out" its position in each currency. Rather, it may be able to reduce its exposure by considering the set of currencies and the institution's net exposure to these currencies individually and collectively. This, of course, is the same approach we have taken elsewhere, where we used covariance to reduce total risk. It works equally well here. In fact, recent advances in the management of foreign exchange exposure make extensive use of such covariation of currency positions in determining appropriate currency risk.[16]

Passing the Risks through to Investors

A trend that has been occurring in recent years is to shed the risks that challenge financial institutions rather than to manage them. In this case, the institution's role is reduced and the services rendered to its customers are decreased. This development of **risk transfer mechanisms** has occurred in two different ways. First, some assets that are created by the financial institution are not held by the originating firm. Rather, they are merely packaged and sold to investors who are willing to accept the returns associated with these assets in return for the risks they contain. In essence, the risks are transferred to the ultimate investors, and the financial institution acts as a conduit for the transfer of such risks. Mortgage-backed securities, auto loan-backed securities, and most other asset-backed securities, all of which were described in earlier chapters, are examples of this practice. The financial institution still retains the risks that transpire between the time of acquiring an asset on the balance sheet and then placing it to outsiders, but the risk does not pose a long-term exposure. The investor, on the other hand, accepts this risk in exchange for the higher return and the local servicing by the originating bank or its agent.

The second method used to transfer the risk inherent in the assets created or held by the institution is to correlate the returns to investors with the asset portfolio yield itself. The clearest cases in which this technique is used are the defined-contribution pension area, variable life insurance, and open-end mutual funds. In all of these instances, the return to investors is directly related to asset performance, net of a servicing and management fee for the value added by the financial institution operating as an agent for the investor. In exchange for this type of risk transfer, however, investors are often offered a wide range of investment options and a choice of investment strategies from which to choose. This is done to permit them some control of the risk-return profile of their investment and perhaps as a further mechanism for the institution to transfer the responsibility for investment outcome from the institution to the investor.

---

[16]For more detail on the techniques for foreign exchange risk management, see Anthony Saunders, *Financial Institutions Management: A Modern Perspective* (Burr Ridge, Ill.: Richard D. Irwin, 1994), chapters 11 and 18; and Tim Campbell and W. A. Kracaw, *Financial Risk Management: Fixed Income and Foreign Exchange* (New York: HarperCollins, 1993), chapter 11.

As was noted in Chapters 22 and 23, standard depository institutions have recently been losing market share to institutions and instruments such as those described here. Mortgage-backed securities, asset-based lending, and defined-contribution investment vehicles have been growing rapidly, at least partially at the expense of banks and other depository firms. Perhaps this is due to attempts by many standard institutions to reduce the risk that remains in their portfolios by transferring financial risk to investors. However, it is equally likely that investors, more knowledgeable about both the potential return to this type of risk absorption and the nature of the assets underlying these risks, have indicated their willingness to accept these investment risks.[17] In any case, the growth in this portion of the capital market is clearly evident from the data reported above and shows no sign of abating.

Differences among Financial Institutions

Every kind of financial institution is challenged by each of the risks addressed in this chapter to some degree or another, yet some institutions are more prone to suffer from some risks than others. Moreover, within a single category of financial institutions, the risks that predominate may differ, depending on the product mix of the particular company. With these caveats in mind, we will proceed to outline those risks that are most challenging to the various types of financial institutions studied here.

Open-End and Closed-End Mutual Funds

Open-end mutual funds are designed in such a way as to pass through to the investor any and all risks associated with their asset portfolios.[18] The concern over default risk rests upon the ability of these funds to evaluate the default premium embedded in the yield in corporate bonds. Likewise, the funds' performance in foreign securities must inevitably be associated with their exposure to foreign-denominated assets and their capability in foreign exchange rate analysis. Finally, interest rate risk embedded in long-term bond positions has the usual interest rate effects based upon the portfolio's duration and convexity. However, unlike other institutions that are financed through liabilities of various maturities, the interest rate risk of the fund is fully captured by its asset structure. Gains and losses associated with asset interest rate exposure flow directly to fund shareholders. In sum, therefore, the open-end mutual fund is a typical investor in financial assets with respect to credit, foreign exchange, and interest rate risk. However, mutual

---

[17]For a discussion of this issue, see Oldfield and Santomero, *op cit.*

[18]The only exception to this is money market mutual funds. In the case of some money market funds, returns are the result of accruing interest income with the proviso that the market value of underlying assets does not change substantially. This is sometimes referred to as the "break the buck" problem. See Marcia Stigum, *The Money Market,* 3rd ed. (Homewood, Ill.: Dow Jones-Irwin, 1990), chapter 26.

funds that are not merely index funds tend to favor certain securities with high volatility, high visibility, and low transaction costs.[19]

Illiquidity can pose a problem, however. There may be times of substantial withdrawal from these funds that can cause a serious cash drain and portfolio distortion. To satisfy the cash needs of withdrawing investors, these funds may need to liquidate huge amounts of securities at one time, perhaps at the same time that others are also trying to do so. At such times, there may be some difficulty in finding someone to absorb the large inventory of securities. Bid-ask spreads may widen precipitously at such times, particularly those of thinly traded securities, and it may be difficult to consummate transactions in a timely manner. A complication in tumultuous markets is that the closing price may reflect not the true market value but only the last trade.

To guard against this possibility, open-end mutual funds may maintain some of their assets in short-term, highly liquid securities that can be used to satisfy demands for immediate cash. But as cash and near-cash assets are often characterized by producing relatively low yields, the typical mutual fund does not like to hold any more of such instruments than necessary. Therefore, sometimes waiting periods may be imposed before an investor may cash out his position in a fund.

Closed-end funds, or investment companies, on the other hand, do not exhibit any of these risks. A closed-end fund has no need to liquidate its portfolio, as investors can merely trade its stock when cash is desired. Thus, it avoids the worst consequences of the risks that afflict financial institutions, as they are all passed along to the ultimate investors in the company. This is not to say that the securities in the portfolio do not exhibit duration, convexity, credit, and liquidity risks; rather, it is to say that these risks do not pose a severe problem for the company. Perhaps the worst thing that can happen to such a company is for its stock price to plummet and for its fixed costs to be spread over a smaller investment base.

Pension Plans

Pension funds, on the other hand, must recognize that the management of risk involves more than standard asset portfolio considerations. A typical defined-benefit plan has a very small surplus, if any, and liabilities that are of long duration. Indeed, many plans operate on an underfunded basis for years, which is equivalent to a negative surplus. Thus, interest rate risk management requires due consideration of the long duration of these liabilities, lest the resultant mismatch result in massive risk exposure to the plan sponsor and to its guarantor, the PBGC.

In such a circumstance as we noted above, prudence does not require a short-term investment portfolio. To see this point, let us relay the circumstances of a large defined-benefit pension plan. This fund management group was so risk averse that they placed most of the fund's $1 billion asset portfolio in default-free T-bills, which have a duration close to zero. The $1 billion in liabilities had a

---

[19]See Eric Falkenstein, "Preferences for Stock Characteristics as Revealed by Mutual Fund Portfolio Holdings," *Journal of Finance,* March 1996.

duration of 12. When interest rates declined in the late 1980s, the present value of the liabilities rose approximately $450 million, but the market value of the short-duration assets did not change appreciably. Thus, the economic position of the plan went from being fully funded to being underfunded by nearly half a billion dollars within the course of two years. This occurred merely because the management group had mismatched the asset and liability durations. What was deemed to be a secure, conservative investment strategy of buying T-bills turned out to be a very risky strategy indeed!

On the other hand, pension funds face little convexity risk and very little liquidity risk. As long-term providers of income, the outflow of resources to satisfy liability holders is both predictable and manageable. Unlike the open-end funds, little resources need to be devoted to a liquidity reserve. This feature also allows these institutions to take a longer view concerning credit risk and credit losses, whether they are derived from open market issues or private placements.

In the case of defined contribution pension plans, much if not all of the duration mismatch risk, convexity risk, and default risk is transferred to the pensioner. This is especially true if the investment policy is self-directed. On the other hand, some plans guarantee a certain rate of return over a period of time, such as one to five years, but do not guarantee any ultimate benefit. These plans would need to carefully manage the whole array of risks for this term, with specific concern devoted to the interest rate risk associated with the guarantee period.

Insurance Companies

By way of contrast, insurance companies, particularly life insurance companies, have complex interest rate risk in their balance sheets due to the collection of options embedded in both their assets and their liabilities. This results in a high degree of convexity in the value of the surplus of these companies. Let's look more closely into this case.

It is the nature of life insurance policy contracts to grant numerous options to policyholders, such as surrender options, withdrawal options, and policy loan privileges, which impart positive convexity to the liability value profile. At the same time, life insurance companies seek high-yielding assets, such as complex mortgage-backed securities and callable corporate bonds, that exhibit negative convexity. These debt issuers retain the option to prepay or call away the mortgages and bonds at some book value, in the case of mortgages, or at a prespecified premium over book value, in the case of bonds. This combination of assets and liabilities creates a surplus posture known as a **short straddle.** In a short straddle, the company has written options on the liability side of the balance sheet and has also effectively done so on the asset side of the balance sheet. For a company in a short straddle posture, a movement of interest rates in either direction can cause a depletion in economic surplus. (See Exhibit 25.9.) However, if interest rates remain relatively stable, it can reap large profits. The solution to a short straddle position is to restructure the assets and/or liabilities so that the convexities are better balanced. Such a restructuring of assets is shown in Exhibit 25.10. Note

Exhibit 25.9

A short straddle for interest rate movements

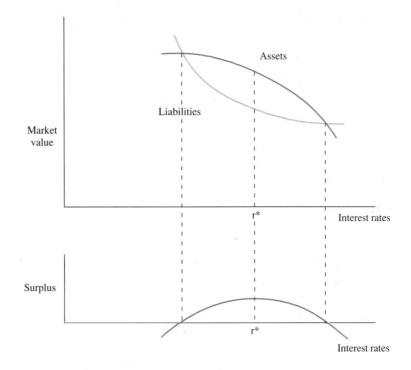

how the surplus profile after restructuring is flat; interest rate risk has been eliminated for the restructured institution.

Some insurance companies compound this interest rate risk by incurring duration mismatch risk along with the convexity imbalance. This duration mismatch risk is particularly dangerous for those companies with low surplus, as the effect of the mismatch is magnified by the leverage. (See Box 25.1.) With the recent announcement that measures of interest rate risk will be taken into account in the credit and claims-paying ratings of insurance companies, we expect that insurers will pay greater attention to this type of risk. (See Box 25.2.)

Credit risk is of less concern to most insurance companies because most invest strictly in high-grade securities. However, some companies have lost billions of dollars in junk bond portfolios, real estate, mortgages, and equities. The problem is compounded when these losses become known by consumers and sales agents. This may lead to a lack of confidence in an institution that depends upon its reputation of long-term stability to maintain its customer base. Rumors begin, and a "run on the bank" phenomenon can occur. Because there is no federal guarantor on insurance liabilities, and because most states do not have funded insurance insolvency guarantee programs, policyholders can get quite nervous when they perceive problems in the investment portfolio and can demand their money (in the form of account values) readily. While there are provisions in many policies that grant the company the right to delay making payment for up to six months, the exercise of this right usually worsens the run and ensures the demise of the company. The problems

EXHIBIT 25.10

Immunizing a short straddle

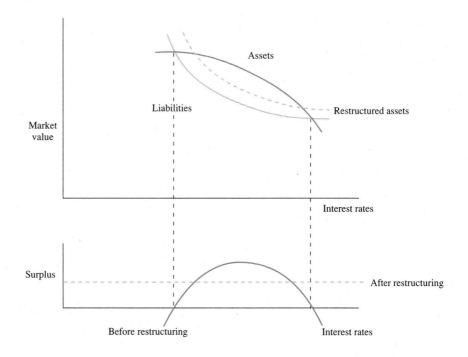

associated with a run can be more pronounced for life companies than for property/casualty companies because the former feature large consumer account values that are subject to withdrawal.

This, of course, suggests that insurers must recognize their vulnerability to a liquidity crisis when structuring their asset portfolio. When an insurer gets into trouble and needs to liquidate securities, it often cannot afford to sell its long-term and intermediate-term bonds, even though there may be liquid markets for them. This is because the demand for cash often arises in an increasing interest rate environment, and at such times, the bonds' market prices decline. If the bonds are sold, any capital losses are taken right out of statutory surplus, which will alarm regulators who are concerned about such things and may induce them to issue a cease and desist order and even take the company into receivership (both of which are fancy ways of saying that they could shut the company down). Thus, insurers typically maintain some short-term, cashlike instruments that will not decline in value as interest rates rise so that they will not be forced to take actions that will invite regulatory intervention at times when extra cash is needed to satisfy policy-holder demands.

Commercial Banks

The risks associated with managing a financial institution are all present in the case of commercial banks. First, they have a major portion of their portfolio in loans to consumers and commercial firms where credit risk has long been concentrated. Second, their depository structure depends upon demand deposits, discretionary

Box 25.1

The Duration of the Equitable

Equitable Assurance Society, one of the oldest life insurance companies in the United States, had a longer duration on its assets than on its liabilities as interest rates rose from the late 1970s through 1981. Therefore, the economic value of its assets fell more than the present value of its liabilities fell during this period, resulting in hundreds and hundreds of millions of dollars of loss in the economic value of surplus. Then, the Equitable shortened the duration of its asset portfolio in 1981 to avoid further erosion in its economic surplus, but it shortened the duration too much. As interest rates plummeted during the ensuing years, the Equitable's assets rose in value, but this rise did not match the rise in the cost required to fund the long-term liabilities that the company had assumed—

that is, the present value of the Equitable's liabilities rose more. As a result, the company lost hundreds of millions of dollars more in the economic value of its surplus.

Because insurers, including the Equitable, carried their bond portfolios at book values and their liabilities at actuarial values, the true magnitude of the losses, which were in the billions of dollars, did not show up in the income statement except over a period of several years. However, accounting results ultimately catch up with economic reality, and the dimensions of the problem were finally revealed. Lacking sufficient economic surplus, the company was forced to demutualize in 1992 so that surplus could be raised by the sale of stock.

savings deposits, and short-term wholesale borrowing, areas that have traditionally caused liquidity concerns. Third, their portfolio is rarely neutral with regard to interest rate effects. In fact, banks are traditionally seen as being relatively dependent upon short-run liabilities to finance long-term fixed-rate loans. Therefore, interest rate movements, particularly upward movements, are often seen as detrimental to bank equity value. Finally, banks have become increasingly global. Their funding and lending will be in multiple currencies, and their trading activity in the foreign exchange market exposes their balance sheet to potentially substantial foreign exchange risk.

Concerning the first of these, the banking industry is perceived to be faced with stiff challenges from credit risk. Profitable lending is the result of two functions: loan origination and loan collection. The unhappy history of lending institutions is that it has generally been easier to originate loans than it has been to collect them. While it is relatively easy to originate loans, it is not always easy to originate "good" loans. Much credit risk can be avoided through careful loan underwriting. For large commercial loans, the risk assessment process is similar to that which would be used by a credit rating specialist such as S&P or Moody's. For retail, individual loans, commercial banks rely on the "five Cs of credit," which are designed to assess the ability and willingness of a borrower to repay the debt. The five Cs include the following:[20]

---

[20]See J. F. Sinkey, *Commercial Bank Financial Management—In the Financial Services Industry,* 4th ed. (New York, Macmillan Publishing, 1992).

Box 25.2

Brace Yourself: A. M. Best's Interest Rate Risk Questionnaire Is Coming Soon!

Interest rate risk continues to come under the scrutiny of the rating agencies, including A. M. Best, the company that rates more insurers than any other.

Last year, S&P revealed the arbitrary use of a capital charge calculated by comparing how a mortgage-backed security would perform to how a corporate bond would perform, if interest rates were changed by 300 basis points. A. M. Best, realizing that the S&P approach is fraught with problems since it does not consider the interaction between assets and liabilities, has embarked on developing its own approach.

Starting this spring, Best will forward a special interest rate risk questionnaire to the top 200–300 writers of interest-sensitive life and pension products. This questionnaire will go well beyond the supplemental one now required as part of the annual rating process. Best's questionnaire is expected to be 8–10 pages in length, with an additional 15–20 pages possibly required, depending upon the company's business mix. The questionnaire will ask for detailed information about liabilities. Specifically, Best will want to know the company's product lines, additional detail about surrender charges, and the distribution source.

For example, Best will want to know the distribution source not only for new premiums but also for existing reserves. Some companies may find this type of information difficult to compile. However, Best believes that understanding interest rate risk must in-clude understanding the nature of liabilities. For example, business generated by certain distribution sources, like stock brokers, would be more subject to surrender during an upswing in interest rates than business generated by a career agency force. Thus, some types of premiums, and consequently reserves, would be more subject to liquidity and interest rate risk than others.

This questionnaire is another step Best is taking to understand the magnitude of interest rate risk taken by the industry. After the data are compiled and analyzed, Best is expected to add assets to the equation and devise some measure of interest rate and, potentially, liquidity risk. Importantly, Best believes that this will not change the overall capital requirement for the industry, but it may substantially change the capital requirement for any one company.

Before meeting with the rating agency, insurers must have a process in place that makes asset/liability management part of the overall financial management of the firm. That means understanding the risk to the company that results from a movement in interest rates. The company should be able to provide to the agency its modeling methodology and assumptions, and it should be able to support their reasonableness.

Source: *SAA Fax Alert*, Strategic Asset Alliance, Inc., Spokane, WA. March 1996.

1. Character—an assessment of the character of the borrower, aided by credit reports, job stability, and credit references.
2. Capacity—a ratio analysis of cash flow.
3. Capital—an investigation of the borrower's wealth.
4. Conditions—an analysis of the economic scenarios or conditions that could give rise to a default in an attempt to estimate the probability of default.
5. Collateral—a provision for recovery in the event of a loan default.

Of course, some of these same criteria find their way into the tools used in estimating credit risk in commercial loans. Once the loans are made, it is common for there to be periodic monitoring of the borrower's creditworthiness.

In recent years, massive losses have resulted from loans to the energy, real estate, and international sectors. These losses were the result of overconcentration, and large cyclical variations in the health of the sectors in which resources were invested. This has led many of these institutions to place more emphasis on diversification guidelines and to receive increased scrutiny by their regulators.

In the liquidity area, the industry has long recognized the need for primary and secondary reserves. In addition, it has developed a large and liquid interbank market. However, these liquidity mechanisms are generally not sufficient to stave off a run associated with a concern over bank solvency. In such cases, however, the presence of the Federal Reserve's discount window, coupled with deposit insurance, is generally perceived to be sufficient to assure stability.

In the area of interest rate risk, banks have a traditional method of reporting the interest rate structure of both assets and liabilities. This reporting mechanism is referred to as a **GAP report.** In this report, financial assets and liabilities are classified into two types: rate-sensitive and rate-insensitive. Rate-sensitive assets and liabilities are those that will be repriced within a specified interval (called the GAP interval or GAP maturity) and those that will be repriced later. Repricing occurs either when an asset or liability matures and must be reissued at a competitive rate or when its rate is reset periodically prior to maturity (as in the case of a floating-rate loan). The dollar amount of assets and liabilities that are mismatched is called the GAP. The GAP measures the volume of fixed-rate assets within a GAP interval that are financed with variable-rate liabilities, in the case of a negative GAP; in the case of a positive GAP, it measures the volume of variable-rate assets that are financed with fixed-rate liabilities within the same time interval.

Exhibit 25.11 shows the 1993 GAP report for Banc One, a super-regional commercial bank. The report refers to the "Core Bank" GAP because the bank is also active in adjusting the interest rate risk of its basic assets and liabilities through the use of derivative instruments such as swaps, caps, and so forth. This report illustrates the different quantities of assets and liabilities repriced over a given interval. Given that only a small fraction of the activity of commercial banks is conducted beyond five years, such reports tend to concentrate on the short end of the market, as can be observed in our exhibit.

Like many regional banks, Banc One tends to have a positive GAP. Asset repricings and maturities tend to be shorter than liabilities. This natural "asset-sensitive" mismatch reflects customer loan and deposit preferences. As a result, if interest rates are declining, margins will narrow as assets reprice downward faster than liabilities, with the reverse being true when rates are increasing. Banc One's one-year repricing GAP is a positive $14.4 billion, which is fairly high for a bank of its size. However, the Core Bank GAP report does not show what has been done to manage this interest rate risk exposure. This would be illustrated by combining the Core Bank report with the bank's activities in the wholesale and derivative markets. In the Banc One case, such a report would show that the core bank's

EXHIBIT 25.11   A GAP Analysis of Banc One's Interest Rate Risk Exposure

	Within Three Months	Four to Twelve Months	Total Year One	Two to Five Years	Over Five Years	Total
"Core Bank" GAP ($ millions)						
Assets						
Net loans and leases	$25,757	$ 7,605	$33,362	$16,154	$ 3,434	$52,950
Total investments*	18,340		18,340			18,340
Total earning assets	44,097	7,605	51,702	16,154	3,434	71,290
Nonearning assets	152		152		8,477	8,629
Total assets	$44,249	$ 7,605	$51,854	$16,154	$ 11,911	$79,919
Liabilities and equity						
Non-maturity deposits	$12,566	$ 2,528	$15,094	$ 5,645	$ 20,418	$41,157
CDs less than $100,000	4,153	5,927	10,080	5,299	360	15,739
CDs $100,000 and over	2,720	622	3,342	670	35	4,047
Borrowings	8,735	4	8,739	180	1,547	10,466
Nonpaying liabilities	199	12	211		1,265	1,476
Total liabilities	28,373	9,093	37,466	11,794	23,625	72,885
Equity					7,034	7,034
Total liabilities and equity	$28,373	$ 9,093	$37,466	$11,794	$ 30,659	$79,919
Total GAP	$15,876	$(1,488)	$14,388	$ 4,360	$(18,748)	
Cumulative GAP	$15,876	$14,388	$14,388	$18,748		

*Includes short-term investments and securities.
Source: *1993 Annual Statement*, Banc One.

mismatch was offset by activity in the wholesale time deposit and interest rate swap markets. The net effect was to reverse the GAP reported in Exhibit 25.11.

Only recently have commercial banks begun to use the more sophisticated approaches developed here. These techniques center on market values and the effect of interest rate movement on the value of bank equity through the use of duration methodology. Because much of the regulatory reporting requires historical or so-called book value accounting, however, the banking sector has tended to concentrate on GAP analysis rather than duration. But things are changing. There is increasing pressure to report balance sheets using market values rather than original purchase prices. As this unfolds, more institutions will be using the duration technology developed here.

In truth, commercial banks have less duration and convexity risk than one might expect. They tend to manage their GAP positions to substantially reduce their natural exposure to interest rate movement. With the development of derivative markets such as interest rate swaps, many have used this opportunity to match up assets and liabilities directly rather than to immunize the portfolio in aggregate using duration techniques.

In Exhibit 25.12, Banc One has applied the more sophisticated techniques and reported the effective durations of its assets and liabilities. Again, this is done not only for its core assets and liabilities but also for off-balance-sheet items such

EXHIBIT 25.12   A Duration Analysis of Banc One's Interest Rate Risk Exposure

As of December 31, 1993 ($ millions)	On Balance Sheet			Off Balance Sheet		Combined On & Off	
	Balance	Rate (%)	Effective Duration (years)	Notional Amount*	Net Spread (%)	Adjusted Rate (%)	Adjusted Effective Duration (years)
Assets							
Variable-rate prime loans	$16,179	6.75%	.29	$15,133	2.07%	8.73%	1.74
Other variable loans/investments	14,963	7.01	.19			7.01	.19
Total variable-rate assets	31,142	6.90	.24	15,133	2.07	7.91	1.00
Fixed-rate loans	27,889	9.64	2.19	58	(5.15)	9.63	2.19
Other fixed investments	12,259	6.82	2.95	1,205	(1.49)	6.67	2.82
Total fixed-rate assets	40,148	8.78	2.42	1,263	(1.66)	8.73	2.38
Other assets	8,629		1.34				1.34
Total assets	$79,919	7.10	1.45	$16,396	1.78	7.47	1.73
Liabilities							
Contractually repriceable	$27,479	2.41	2.08	$ 5,638	1.98	2.00	1.73
Variable deposits/borrowings	10,250	2.76	.05	198	(8.90)	2.93	.08
Total variable liabilities	37,729	2.51	1.53	5,836	1.61	2.26	1.28
Total fixed liabilities	20,003	4.61	1.49	8,624	2.33	3.61	.75
Non-interest-bearing DDA	13,677		3.42				3.42
Total deposits/borrowings	71,409	2.62	1.88	14,460	2.04	2.21	1.54
Other liabilities	1,476		.06				.06
Total liabilities	$72,885	2.57%	1.84	$14,460	2.04%	2.17%	1.51

*$5.6 billion of basic swaps are excluded from variable-rate prime notional amounts but are included in effective duration calculations.

Source: *1993 Annual Statement,* Banc One.

as swaps, which are used to adjust the interest rate risk exposure. Also reported is the effective duration of assets and liabilities for combined on- and off-balance-sheet items. Note that for on-balance-sheet items, Banc One was operating with a longer liability duration (1.84) than asset duration (1.45). However, when taking into account off-balance-sheet items, the combined liability duration shrinks to 1.51 and the asset duration extends to 1.73.

We have insufficient information to compute the equity duration from the data given in Exhibit 25.12 because many of the assets and liabilities are not reported at their market values. However, for pedagogical purposes, we will assume that the reported book values of the core assets and liabilities approximate their market values and that the market values of off-balance-sheet items are zero. We can then calculate equity effective duration as follows:

$$D_{Equity} = (D_{Assets} - D_{Liabilities}) \frac{A}{E} + D_{Liabilities}$$

$$D_{Equity} = (1.73 - 1.51) \times \frac{79.919}{(79.919 - 72.885)} + 1.51 = +4.01$$

If the calculation had been based on market values, the equity effective duration would likely have been even lower, as the bank was operating with less leverage than shown on a book value basis. Compare the apparently conservative +4.01 duration of this bank with the reckless −34.4 duration of the insurance company mentioned earlier.[21] While neither firm appears to be immunized from interest rate risk, the insurance company has almost nine time more exposure to interest rate risk than the bank. Moreover, they are exposed in different ways. Banc One appears to be positioned to benefit from a drop in interest rates, whereas the insurance company would benefit from an increase in interest rates.

Finally, commercial banks also have currency and foreign exchange risks. To a large degree, banks limit these risks through hedges in the forward and futures market, but many banks are dealers and traders in foreign exchange. Risks are limited here by tight controls on positions and **risk limits** on traders. The latter restrict currency exposure that a trader may take based upon the historical riskiness of the currency. Accordingly, losses and gains are generally smaller in the banking sector than in securities firms, where trading and risk tolerance tends to be higher.

Investment Banks

We have previously discussed investment banks at some length in Chapters 17, 18, and 20. Here, we will only touch upon the risks and operations of these institutions. Investment banks face virtually all of the financial risks faced by other financial institutions, but due to their high leverage, these risks are greatly magnified. (See Box 25.3.) Because investment banks are characterized by rapid turnover in their securities holdings, their focus is more on basis risk than on long-term credit risk. Basis risk is the risk that yields on different securities so they will not move in lock step. The divergence that typifies movements in various yields and prices is where the major risk lies. Therefore, investment banks do not focus simply on movements in interest rates, or even in changing shapes of the entire term structure of interest. Rather, they keep track of a plethora of yields, yield spreads, and security and commodity price movements. As some investment bank assets and liabilities are less liquid than others, they tend to use the liquid ones to hedge the price risk of the less liquid ones. It then becomes important to know how well the prices track each other.

Investment banking firms have developed financial risk management models that account for numerous variables. Unlike some financial institutions, whose risk management models focus mainly on the risks of a handful of factors,

---

[21]While the duration measures imply Banc One had a relatively conservative exposure to interest rate risk, this was actually not the case. Banc One suffered substantial losses in 1994 and 1995 occasioned by rising interest rates. Much of these losses were incurred in highly levered derivatives positions maintained by the bank. Obviously, our simplifying assumptions to use book values instead of market values for the core assets and liabilities and to impute a zero net value to its off-balance-sheet items masked the true interest rate risk of the institution. In practice, good analysts insist on using market values and also take into account the substantial impact of convexity.

investment bank models contain many more. For example, J. P. Morgan has over 500 factors in their "Risk Metrics" model, and Goldman Sachs has around 1,300, "although on any given day only around 650 risk factors are significant."[22] Small comfort! These risk factors include such seemingly obscure things as the basis risk in the contract prices of natural gas produced in Saskatchewan versus the North Slope in Alaska. But if you're short Saskatchewan and long North Slope, and levered 50 to 1, the basis risk could be significant.

Thrifts, Credit Unions, and Finance Companies

As noted in Chapters 22 and 23, other depository institutions are increasingly developing product lines in areas of activity that are similar to the commercial banking sector. By so doing, these institutions expose themselves to the same risks, and in general, they use the same techniques as commercial banks. Nonetheless, their historical markets present some unique challenges.

Finance companies, by their very nature, have substantial exposure to credit risk. These institutions have developed as direct competitors to banks for small- and middle-market commercial loans. Accordingly, their credit risk analysis must be first rate, and the spread must be sufficient to absorb the inherent risk of their market segment.

Savings banks and S&Ls, on the other hand, are faced with severe duration mismatch risk, which, in recent years, they have taken steps to reduce. Moreover, these institutions faced liquidity risks due to their depositors' (correct) perception of a relatively weak, underfunded federal deposit guarantee agency and a portfolio of relatively illiquid long-term mortgages. With the changeover to FDIC insurance, some of the consumer uneasiness has been alleviated.

Finally, credit unions, with their dependence upon the common bond, have often found their performance quite enviable. However, it should be recalled that management in these firms is generally nonprofessional and occasionally unskilled. This has led to regulatory oversight that has concentrated on the development of the skills outlined here. With generally short-term loans and a stable fund base, the risks are quite manageable. As the industry expands, it is essential that professionalism develops to ensure stability and service to its community.

---

[22]See Robert Litterman and Kurt Winkelmann, "Managing Market Exposure," *Risk Management Series,* Goldman, Sachs & Co., January 1996.

Box 25.3

Investment Banks Take on More Leverage . . . and Risk

There is a warning signal lost amid the hubbub of surging profit and trading activity on Wall Street: Investment banks are taking more risk than ever.

So says the Securities Industry Association. The trade group for Wall Street says investment banks are more steeply leveraged than at any time since statistics were compiled on the topic in 1980. The ratio of liabilities to equity capital at Wall Street's big investment banks hit 50-to-1 in 1995—a 43% jump from the ratio the prior two years.

Investment banks "are willing to take on greater leverage because they see opportunity—but they're exposing themselves to greater risk," says Jeffrey Schaefer, the SIA's research chief. Leverage involves investing borrowed money to achieve higher returns.

This is how it works:

Securities firms finance their stock and bond inventories with a "matched book"—having roughly an equal amount of borrowings and loans. This typically is done through repurchase agreements and reverse repurchase agreements. (In repurchase agreements, Wall Street firms finance customer purchases of securities and require the securities to be pledged as collateral. In a reverse repo, a customer sells securities and agrees to buy them back at a later date at a set interest rate.)

Investment banks profit if the loans are made at a higher interest rate than the borrowings.

But this matched-book business recently has become a bit unmatched. In 1995 alone, the amount of securities bought under agreements to resell grew 40% between the first and fourth quarters; securities firms earn interest on this asset. But securities sold under repurchase agreements—the industry's liability—ballooned more than 50% during the same time in 1995, the SIA says.

The net effect: Any sudden market pullback could hammer the securities holdings of investment banks more sharply than otherwise, according to some brokerage executives and analysts.

Some investment-banking executives throw cold water on the SIA conclusions. The net change in matched-book business "reflects growth in trading inventories—it doesn't necessarily indicate a gapping of the [matched] book," says John G. Macfarlane III, treasurer at Salomon Inc. "Net net, the Street's inventories have gone up."

For instance, Salomon's securities-trading inventory increased by about $20 billion, or 20%, during 1995, Mr. Macfarlane says.

And some Wall Street executives brush aside any one gauge to measure risk. "On the whole, measured that way, there's probably some increase in leverage over the past 10 years," says E. Gerald Corrigan, a member of the risk-management committee at Goldman, Sachs & Co. and formerly Federal Reserve Bank of New York president.

"But what you really need is a family of indicators that provide a high degree of assurance that you're not going to get blindsided," Mr. Corrigan says.

Nevertheless, the higher ratios the SIA cites are significant. For Wall Street's largest investment banks, matching assets and liabilities of their customers and their own financing needs plays, an ever more important role in hedging and investment strategies.

One reason investment banks are taking more risk is that their return on equity isn't keeping pace with surging profits. Though 1995 pretax profit of $7.4 billion was the second highest ever for Wall Street, return on equity and profit margins ranked just fourth, says the SIA's Mr. Schaefer.

To be sure, the lagging return on equity partly stems from declining volume in underwriting new stocks and bonds, a big Wall Street money-maker, which last year was down one-third from the 1993 record.

More fundamental, however, is that more businesses are operating with thinner margins. Thus, some investment banks, particularly those without a clear market niche or critical mass to compete worldwide, are poised for a shakeout, some investment bankers say.

Leveraging Up
The ratio of liabilities to equity capital at investment banks

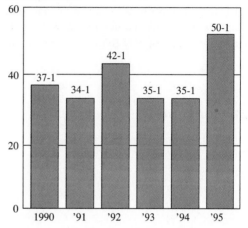

Source: Reprinted with permission of the Securities Industry Association.

Source: Siconolf, Michael, "Investment Banks Take on More Leverage . . . and Risk," *The Wall Street Journal,* March 8, 1996. Reprinted by permission of *The Wall Street Journal,* © 1996 Dow Jones & Company, Inc. All Rights Reserved Worldwide.

Summary

It takes great skill to manage a financial institution profitably. We have not touched on some of the skills required, such as personnel management, operations management, and marketing. However, we have focused on four major types of financial risk and on the management techniques that are employed to deal with these risks.

The increased competition among financial institutions within a given category, as well as the increased competition between one type of finan-

cial institution against another type, has meant that the financial risks must be better managed in order for an institution to survive. Much of modern finance theory has been directed toward providing techniques capable of improved risk management. Regulatory agencies are also giving increased emphasis to the proper utilization of such techniques, and we expect that those institutions that manage it best will be the ones that survive into the future editions of this textbook!

Key Concepts

asset/liability management,   635
credit risk,   628
default rates,   627
diversification guidelines,   631
foreign exchange risk,   629
GAP report,   651
immunization,   635
interest rate risk,   628
liquidity risk,   628
net foreign exchange exposure,   642
operating costs,   627

operating risk,   629
primary and secondary reserves,   641
return on assets,   627
return on equity,   627
risk limits,   654
risk transfer mechanisms,   643
short straddle,   646
specific credit risk,   633
spread,   627
systematic credit risk,   633

Review Questions

1. Consider a finance company with $30 in assets, $28 in liabilities, and $2 in equity. What does it earn on the equity if it pays 8 percent on its debt and receives 9.5 percent on its assets? What percentage must the assets decline in value for the equity to be erased?

2. A company has $25 in liabilities and $2 in equity. If it is paying 9 percent on its debt, what must it earn in order to maintain the current level of equity? What is the return on equity with a 9 percent return on assets?

3. What are the two types of credit risk faced by financial institutions? Discuss each and speculate which is generally of greater concern.

4. What methods can a financial institution employ to combat credit risk? What are some possible drawbacks to these methods?

5. Suppose that your firm possesses $50 million in assets with an effective duration of 8 years and $46 million in liabilities with an effective duration of 5 years. What are the new levels of assets and liabilities when interest rates rise 50 basis points? If the company consistently earns

a positive 2 percent spread, how long will it take to restore the original equity value?

6. Define what it means for a firm to "immunize" its portfolio. Why is effective dollar duration more useful than effective duration when immunizing?

7. Using the figures from Question 5, calculate the duration of equity.

8. In this chapter, it was stated that "insurers typically maintain some short-term, cashlike instruments." Describe the primary motivation for this reserve.

9. Using the wholesale time deposit market, how can the GAP reported in Exhibit 25.11 for the one-year period be eliminated? How would the action taken affect the return on assets calculation? How would it affect return on equity?

10. Evaluate the relative desirability of using core bank transactions, wholesale time deposits, or interest rate swaps to adjust interest rate risk exposure.

11. Prior to 1992, the European Monetary System required that currencies within the European Union fluctuate within narrow bands. What effect would such a central bank policy have on the management of foreign exchange risk and the willingness of institutions to accept an exposure to a particular currency?

12. In constructing a portfolio, attention must be paid to both duration and convexity. Explain why a highly levered firm must be even more careful in this process.

References

Altman, Edward I. "Managing the Commercial Lending Process." In *Handbook of Banking Strategy,* edited by R. C. Aspinwall and R. A. Eisenbeis. New York: John Wiley, 1985.

Babbel, David F. "Insuring Banks Against Systematic Credit Risk." *Journal of Futures Markets,* December 1989.

———. "Insuring Sovereign Debt Against Default." World Bank Discussion Paper no. 328. Washington, D. C.: The World Bank, June 1996.

Babbel, David F.; Peter Bouyoucos; and Rob Stricker. "Capping the Interest Rate Risk in Insurance Products." In *The Handbook of Fixed-Income Options,* edited by Frank J. Fabozzi. Burr Ridge, Ill.: Irwin Professional Publishing, 1996.

Beaver, W., and G. Parker. *Risk Management, Problems and Solutions.* New York: McGraw-Hill, 1995.

Brewer, E. "Bank Gap Management and the Use of Financial Futures." *Economic Perspectives.* Federal Reserve Bank of Chicago, March/April 1985.

Brewer, E.; D. Fortier; and C. Pavel. "Bank Risk from Nonbank Activities." *Economic Perspectives.* Federal Reserve Bank of Chicago, July/August 1988.

Brown, K. C., and D. J. Smith. "Recent Innovations in Interest Rate Risk Management and the Reintermediation of Commercial Banking." *Financial Management,* 1988.

Campbell, Tim S. *Money and Capital Markets.* Glenview, Ill.: Scott Foresman & Co., 1988.

Campbell, Tim S., and W. A. Kracaw. *Financial Risk Management: Fixed Income and Foreign Exchange.* New York: HarperCollins, 1993.

Cargill, Thomas, and Gillian G. Garcia. *Financial Reform in the 1980s.* Stanford, Ca.: Hoover Institution, Stanford University, 1985.

Cooper, Kerry, and Donald R. Fraser. *Banking Deregulation and the New Competition in Financial Services.* Cambridge, Mass.: Ballinger, 1986.

Falkenstein, Eric G. "Preferences for Stock Characteristics as Revealed by Mutual Fund Portfolio Holdings." *Journal of Finance,* March 1996.

Fama, Eugene F., and Kenneth R. French. "Multifactor Explanations of Asset Pricing Anomalies." *Journal of Finance,* March 1996.

Flannery, M. J., and C. M. James. "The Effect of Interest Rate Changes on the Common Stock Returns of Financial Institutions." *Journal of Finance,* 1984.

Hawawini, G. "Controlling the Interest Rate Risk of Bonds: An Introduction to Duration Analysis and

Immunization Strategies." *Finanzmarket and Portfolio Management,* 1986–1987.

Litterman, Robert, and Kurt Winkelmann. "Managing Market Exposure." *Risk Management Series.* Goldman, Sachs & Co., January 1996.

Oldfield, George, and Anthony M. Santomero. "The Place of Risk Management in Financial Institutions." Working paper, Wharton Financial Institutions Center, 1994.

Santomero, Anthony M. "Financial Risk Management: The Whys and Hows." *Journal of Financial Markets, Institutions and Investments,* 1995.

Saunders, Anthony. *Financial Institutions Management: A Modern Perspective,* second edition. Burr Ridge, Ill.: Richard D. Irwin, 1997.

Shaffer, Sherrill. "Interest Rate Risk: What's a Bank to Do?" *Business Review.* Federal Reserve Bank of Philadelphia, May/June 1991.

Sinkey, J. F. *Commercial Bank Financial Management—In the Financial Services Industry.* 4th ed. New York: Macmillan Publishing, 1992.

Smith C.; C. Smithson; and D. Wilford. *Strategic Risk Management.* New York: Harper and Row, 1990.

Stigum, Marcia. *The Money Market.* 3rd ed. Burr Ridge, Ill.: Irwin Profesional Publishing, 1990.

PART V

The Important Role of Banks

This chapter adds money to our discussion of the financial sector. Money is introduced into our analysis of the financial markets as the one security that is accepted in exchange for all other securities. Money facilitates trade and serves a number of useful purposes. Central to our treatment is the role of banks in the money supply process. The role of banks in multiple deposit expansion in both a simple and an extended model is presented to explain their role in the process and their pivotal role in the financial sector itself.

Up to this point, we have considered a large variety of financial securities and markets. However, all of the previous discussion depends on the existence and broad acceptance of the most important financial security—money. Every security we have discussed was denominated in terms of money. For example, in the United States, a stock price is stated in terms of the number of dollars that will be accepted in exchange for a share of stock. Likewise, the price of a bond is stated in terms of the expected dollar value of all of the bond's dollar-denominated cash flows through maturity. As such, money is central to our discussion of the financial markets, even though we have not explicitly dealt with it until this point in the book.

We will argue below that money is central to the financial sector because of its role as the medium of payment. **Money** is accepted in exchange for financial securities, goods, and services because the person who receives it is quite convinced that others will also accept it. He or she accepts money because it allows the transfer of one asset or good for a claim on others. It is this general acceptability of money that is key to its value as an exchange mechanism for today's large, complex economies.

The Role of Money in an Economy

The importance of money as a medium of exchange can be seen by considering a world where money does not exist. Imagine that your particular skill is building wooden chairs. While it is nice to have a place to sit, chairs are not a particularly healthy food. So, chair in hand, you head off to the market to buy bread. The first problem is finding someone who wants to buy a chair. The second one is finding that special someone who bakes bread that also needs a chair. Economists frequently refer to this as a **double coincidence of wants.** You want the baker's bread and he wants your chair. Once you have found such a person, a rate of exchange of bread for chairs must be determined. Most likely, the rate of exchange will be pretty high; that is, one chair ought to buy a lot of bread! As a consequence, you will be left with far more loaves of bread than you can eat before the bread gets moldy. This may lead you to decide to take the bread to the dairy and try to trade it for some milk or cheese. The same two problems face you here as in your previous exchange. However, if you are lucky, at the end of the day, that fine chair will have been traded for bread, milk, cheese, and possibly other goods. For your sake, we hope so, because your trading was both time-consuming and probably frustrating. Because you needed to **barter,** that is, trade one good for another, you probably spent a considerable amount of time and energy on the transactions.

This example highlights the traditional role that economists usually assign to money in a complex, decentralized economy. First, and foremost, money is viewed as a **medium of exchange,** facilitating the trading of goods. As such, it saves us all a lot of work. It could be argued that with the advent of credit cards and various kinds of charge accounts at major retailers, money is providing less and less of this service. However, remember that charging a purchase is not paying for it! It does not exchange value but merely defers the day of reckoning. We sometimes refer to money as a **means of payment** to make clear the distinction between facilitating exchange and payment. Credit cards, for example, are a medium of exchange but not payment. Money performs both roles, and with it, we no longer need an exact coincidence of wants in order for an exchange to take place. Instead, we can trade our produced good for money and proceed to use this to purchase desired consumption goods. In addition, money serves as a **standard of value** for all goods and services. Rather than needing to know the rate of exchange of chairs for bread, bread for milk, and so forth, one need only know the rate of exchange of money for each of the goods. In this way, a chair can be sold to anyone who needs it at its current market price in terms of exchangeable value, and the money, so received, can be used to purchase bread, milk, and cheese from other unrelated individuals.

Given that money performs these two essential roles, it also helps the economy in other ways. Since money can be used at any time to purchase goods, holding money allows us to **store value.** If we do not need a whole chair's worth of bread, milk, and cheese, we can save some of the money from the sale of the chair for use in the future. We can even denominate debts in terms of money. Individuals who receive a good or service today and promise to pay for the transaction in the future denominate their debt in monetary terms. Therefore, money is often said to perform the role of a **standard of deferred payment.** With the advent of inflation, this may be a costly way of keeping track of debts, but remember, the alternative may be even less attractive—sour milk or moldy bread. In essence, in most cases, money performs fairly well as a store of future purchasing power.

Money also has some things in common with the assets that have been the focus of this book. It is, in fact, a security itself. It represents a claim on some public or private institution. Consider a dollar bill. It is a Federal Reserve Note representing a debt obligation of the Federal Reserve System, our central bank. Just as with a bond, holders of these notes have claim on the Federal Reserve for the full face value of the note. This might not mean much, however. The claim against the central bank is discharged by printing more claims, so a demand for the repayment of a $50 bill will only lead to five $10 bills. The real value of money is its ability to cause others to give up real commodities or other financial assets in exchange for it. A check, which is another form of money, is a claim against the institution that holds the deposits of the checkwriter. Here, demands for repayment lead to an exchange of the bank's liability for central bank debt, or local currency. In fact, it is a testimony to the importance of money that payment for goods and financial assets is discharged by the use of currency or its surrogate, claims on your local bank.

Because of its centrality, it is important that anyone interested in financial markets and institutions understand how money enters the financial system and recognize who is responsible for changes in the quantity in circulation. Remember that all of the assets we have discussed are denominated in monetary terms! And as we noted in Chapter 10, the rate at which money is expanding affects inflation, the exchange rate, nominal interest rates, and, ultimately, the prices of financial assets. It is for this reason that financial institutions have whole departments devoted to analyzing the movement of the money supply and watching the Federal Reserve, the agency responsible for the amount of money in circulation. Indeed the chief economist at such institutions is often referred to as a "Fed watcher."

This and the following chapter will be devoted to a discussion of how money is created and how the money supply is managed. We will see how the value and quantity of money are determined and affected by the major players in the money supply process. As will become apparent, the major players in the money supply process are:

1. The central bank (the Federal Reserve in the United States)
2. The banking system
3. Depositors

The role of the banking system in the money supply process is perhaps the single most important factor, and this will be the focus of the present chapter. We will see how banks actually create money through holding fractional reserves against deposits from the public and by either buying or creating financial assets with the proceeds. This will be followed by Chapter 27, which will cover how the Federal Reserve affects the money supply process, its role in the financial sector, and the tools available to it for implementing its specific monetary goals.

A Simple Model of Banks in the Monetary System

A bank is an institution that accepts deposits from individuals or firms and then invests the proceeds in either open market securities or loans it originates for a variety of purposes. This was discussed at some length in the preceding chapters. What was not mentioned, however, was how this activity affects both the overall quantity of credit and the aggregate amount of money in the economy itself. In fact, this process has the ability to affect the quantities of both credit and money through variations in checkable deposits.

The key to the banking system's ability to create money is the **fractional reserve** system. Banks need to hold only a fraction of their deposits in the form of reserves on their balance sheet. The exact percentage is set by law or, where explicit laws don't exist, by the bank's need to provide liquidity for its depositors. In any case, our deposits are backed by a lot less than 100 percent reserves, and this is true throughout the world. The results of this are substantial.

As we know from previous chapters, there are various kinds of banks, including commercial banks, credit unions, savings and loans, and mutual savings banks. Each of these institutions does more than just take deposits and make loans, but for the purposes of this discussion, the other functions are irrelevant. Therefore, the generic term "bank" will be used throughout.

Suppose a depositor enters a bank to make a deposit. When she does so, let's suppose she arrives with currency. Given that the bank needs to hold only, say, 10 percent of these newly acquired funds in reserves, the remainder can be loaned out or used to purchase securities of various types in the market. This process of making new loans or purchasing securities from other investors creates liquidity in the economy and expands the total money supply. In fact, through this process, the banking system can create money equal to a multiple of the excess reserves in the system. Let's show how this process works through a series of examples.

Multiple Deposit Expansion in the Simple Model

We stated above that banks can create money by taking deposits and using the reserves beyond government-mandated reserve requirements to create loans. Consider a very simple example to illustrate this process. Assume the following:

1. *There is only one bank.* This is not necessary, but it does simplify the example.
2. *Banks hold only required reserves.* This just means that in this example, excess reserves will be converted immediately into loans. The required reserve ratio for this example will be 10 percent.
3. *The public holds no currency.* Any currency received by the public will be immediately deposited back into a bank.
4. *The Fed starts the process by increasing reserves by $100.* The actual process by which the Fed provides these reserves will be discussed later. For this example, this assumption means that our story begins with $100 of new deposits and $100 of new reserves for the banking system.

These assumptions provide the framework for a simple model of deposit creation. We can make it more complicated later.

The process of deposit creation can be seen by considering the bank's balance sheet and how it changes over time. Let's put assets on the left-hand side and liabilities on the right. Our balance sheet therefore looks like a "T," which is why this approach is generally referred to as T-account analysis. In this simple example, the bank's assets are reserves and loans; the bank's liabilities are deposits. Thus, after the Fed's action, the bank's balance sheet looks like the following:

The Only National Bank
Initial T-account

Assets		*Liabilities*	
Reserves	+$100	Deposits	+$100
Loans	$0		

However, because the required reserve ratio is 10 percent, the bank need only hold $10 to satisfy its **reserve requirement.** The rest, $90, can be defined as **excess reserves.** Because excess reserves make no money for the bank, it will not hold on to them. The bank will loan out the entire amount either by granting someone their request for a loan or by buying a security in the financial market. For argument's sake, assume that the bank grants a customer's request for a loan, thus exchanging the loan for excess reserves in the bank's T-account. With the loan made, the bank's T-account becomes:

The Only National Bank
First Stage: Make Loan

Assets		Liabilities	
Reserves	+$10	Deposits	+$100
Loans	+$90		

The recipient of the loan in this example uses the borrowed funds to purchase an automobile. The seller does not hold any currency. Therefore, the seller will deposit the money into the bank until it is needed. This will increase the deposits held by the bank and return the $90 in reserves. Therefore, the T-account becomes:

The Only National Bank
Second Stage: New Deposits

Assets		Liabilities	
Reserves	+$100	Deposits	+$190
Loans	+$90		

The bank now has $81 of excess reserves ($R_e$). This is found by subtracting required reserves (R_r) from total reserves (R). Required reserves in this example are 10 percent of deposits (D). Thus,

$$R_e = R - R_r$$

$$R_e = R - (0.10)D$$

$$\$81 = \$100 - (0.10) \times \$190$$

The bank will loan out this $81 of excess reserves. As before, the $81 will be deposited back in the bank, and the bank's resulting T-account will be:

The Only National Bank
Third Stage: Make Loan

Assets		Liabilities	
Reserves	+$100	Deposits	+$271
Loans	+$171		

The bank now has $72.90 of excess reserves to loan. The process will continue until the bank has loaned all excess reserves. At this point, the T-account will be:

The Only National Bank
Equilibrium Stage

Assets		Liabilities	
Reserves	+$100	Deposits	+$1,000
Loans	+$900		

This is an equilibrium because the bank has no more excess reserves with which to make loans, and the public is holding deposits only in National Bank. Remember, the public holds no currency in our example.

EXHIBIT 26.1   Deposit Expansion with One Bank

Stage	Deposit	Reserves	Required Reserves	Excess Reserves	Total Loans
1	$ 100.00	$100.00	$ 10.00	$ 90.00	$ 0.00
2	$ 190.00	$100.00	$ 19.00	$ 81.00	$ 90.00
3	$ 271.00	$100.00	$ 27.10	$ 72.90	$171.00
4	$ 343.90	$100.00	$ 34.40	$ 65.60	$243.90
5	$ 409.50	$100.00	$ 41.00	$ 59.00	$309.51
6	.	.	.	.	.
7	.	.	.	.	.
.	.	.	.	.	.
.	.	.	.	.	.
∞	$1,000.00	$100.00	$100.00	$1,000.00	$900.00

These equilibrium values could have been computed at the outset. The bank received $100 in reserves. Given a 10 percent required reserve ratio, R_r, these reserves can, and will, support $1,000 in deposits. We will show you how this number can be computed below. However, for now, it is important for you to understand how the process works. The point is that the system will expand until all reserves are required. The step-wise process is shown in Exhibit 26.1.

This process is pretty robust. It works the same way whether the bank makes loans or buys securities with its excess reserves. This is because the seller must deposit the revenue from the sale of the security into the banking system. Therefore, whether the bank uses the new reserves to make new loans, buy securities, or do some of each, the results are the same. One deposit associated with an increase in reserves expands into many deposits. For this reason, this process is often referred to as **multiple deposit expansion.**

Multiple Deposit Contraction in the Simple Model

The opposite process is called **multiple deposit contraction.** Consider changing the assumption that depositors wish to hold no currency. Instead, suppose depositors decide that they now need $50 of currency. They withdraw $50 from the bank depicted in the final T-account above. The bank's T-account then becomes:

The Only National Bank
$50 Currency Withdrawal

Assets		Liabilities	
Reserves	+$50	Deposits	+$950
Loans	+$900		

The bank now has only $50 of reserves, but its required reserves are 10 percent of deposits, or $95. Therefore, it has a deficiency in its reserves; that is, it has −$45 of excess reserves. The bank must raise its reserves by $45. The Fed, however, will not alter the reserves of the system merely because the bank finds itself in reserve deficiency. Therefore, the bank cannot turn to the Fed to get new reserves. On the other hand, the public is unwilling to deposit the $50 of currency that they now hold. Thus, the bank cannot increase its reserves.

The only option for the bank is to contract the size of its operation. This can be accomplished in two ways, namely, selling securities, if it has any, or reducing its loan portfolio. The latter is accomplished by calling in loans. Faced with such a call, people will use their deposits to repay their loans, causing a downward spiral analogous to the expansion described above. In the end, the bank calls in, or doesn't renew, $450 of loans. This act causes deposits to decline and the reserve shortage to be eliminated. The bank's T-account finally will become:

The Only National Bank
Equilibrium

Assets		Liabilities	
Reserves	+$50	Deposits	+$500
Loans	+$450		

The bank is now back in equilibrium; its reserves are all required reserves, and the bank has sufficient reserves to satisfy its mandatory reserve requirement.

Multiple Banks in the Simple Model

In the above example, there was only one bank. But even casual observation shows us that there is more than one bank in the world. In fact, the entire U.S. banking system has nearly 10,000 commercial banks in it, not to mention the other depository institutions we reviewed. How does this change the story? Interestingly, this fact does not change the impact of multiple deposit expansion or contraction on the economy. Consider the expansion example given above. The Only National Bank can be thought of as the entire U.S. banking system. Each step in the expansion process can be thought of as occurring at a different bank.

For example, in Exhibit 26.1, the first stage may occur at the First National Bank. This bank loans its excess reserve of $90 to the public. At the second stage, that $90 dollars is deposited into the Second National Bank. The Second National Bank now has excess reserves of $81, which it loans out. The process continues from bank to bank until the entire system has reached the equilibrium stage. In equilibrium, each bank in the system will hold some deposits, some loans, and just enough reserves to satisfy the 10 percent required reserve ratio. However, the total impact on the banking system of a $100 deposit will be the same as in the monopoly bank example.

The Formula for Multiple Deposit Expansion in the Simple Model

Finding the equilibrium level of deposits after a change in the level of reserves would appear to be quite difficult in the above examples. It seemed to require adding the deposit and loan stages until all reserves were used to satisfy the required reserve ratio. At that point, equilibrium is reached. However, using a little algebra, we can derive a simple formula for what is called the **reserve multiplier.**

Recall that the required reserves (R_r) are equal to the required reserve ratio (r) times deposits (D).

$$R_r = r \times D$$

We have also assumed that banks will hold no excess reserves in equilibrium. Therefore, required reserves will always equal total reserves (R) when the multiplier process is complete. In our notation, this can be stated as follows:

$$R_r = R$$

Substituting ($r \times D$) from the first equation for R_r in the second equation and dividing both sides by r gives us

$$D = (1/r) \times R$$

From this, it is apparent that deposits are a multiple ($1/r$) of reserves. If we want to know how a change in reserves is going to affect deposits, we could use this same equation. Using the symbol Δ to denote change in a variable, we can take the change in both sides of this equation to get

$$\Delta D = (1/r) \times \Delta R$$

This formula is fairly general. It applies when there is one bank in the system, and it applies equally to the whole system when there are many banks. This formula states that deposits will change by ($1/r$) times the change in total reserves.

Let's check this against the above examples. In the first example, reserves increased by $100. The required reserve ratio (r) was 10 percent. This formula says that for a $100 increase in reserves, deposits should increase by $1,000 [= ($1/.10$) × $100] in equilibrium. That is, in fact, what happened. The bank's reserves increased by $100. This led to the bank's deposits increasing by $1,000 by the time the system reached equilibrium. When reserves were decreased by $50, it led to a decrease in deposits of $500 [= ($1/.10$) × $50]. Again, this simple formula is correct. In fact, it gives the answer for the bank's equilibrium level of deposits under any circumstances outlined in our assumptions.

Extending the Simple Model of the Role of Banks

The simple model used above gives the basic intuition of how changes in reserves can cause multiple expansion or contraction of deposits. This model can be extended to show similar results for more complex but also more realistic views of the depository system. For example, suppose we allow the public to hold currency and two types of deposits. Also, let us allow banks to hold excess reserves. This more complex model of depository expansion will offer us some insight into how decisions made by the public and by banks can also affect the money supply.

First, let's add currency to the model. In the simple model, people were assumed to hold no currency. Yet, in the example of multiple deposit contraction, we saw how the decision of the public to hold currency could affect the level of deposits the system could sustain. In that example, as the public increased the level of currency held, the level of deposits decreased by a multiple of the change in currency. This was because reserves were taken out of the banking system.

Now assume that the public always holds some currency. The actual quantity of currency is determined by the public. It holds currency for making day-to-day transactions, such as purchasing a doughnut or going to a movie. However, whenever people vary the amounts they hold, it affects the level of reserves in the banking system.

Currency plus reserves in the banking system are often referred to by the title **monetary base** (B), or **high-powered money.** This title is descriptive, because both currency and reserves can be used to support bank deposit expansion. Thus, by definition:

$$B = C + R$$

We will argue in Chapter 27 that it is this quantity, not bank reserves, that the Federal Reserve controls.

Next, let's add some realism to the depository system. Assume that there are two types of deposits: checkable deposits (D_c) and time deposits (D_t). Checkable deposits, as the name would suggest, are deposits against which a check can be drawn. They are standard transactions accounts that can be used in place of currency for making purchases. For this reason, checkable deposits are sometimes referred to as demand deposits or transactions deposits. Time deposits, on the other hand, are deposits that are assumed to be left in place for a period of time in order to earn interest or for future needs. Total deposits (D) are just the sum of the two types of deposits:

$$D = D_c + D_t$$

Each type of deposit has its own required reserve ratio, r_c for checkable deposits and r_t for time deposits. Thus, required reserves are

$$R_r = r_c D_c + r_t D_t$$

Finally, as indicated above, let's assume that excess reserves can be held by the banking sector. Let's make these reserves constant at the fixed amount, R_e.

In this case, the monetary base is used for one of four purposes as represented by the four components on the right-hand side of the following expression for the monetary base:

$$B = r_c D_c + r_t D_t + R_e + C$$

We can use this equation to derive the analog to the reserve multiplier in this more complicated model by solving for D_c.

$$D_c = (1/r_c) \times (B - r_t D_t - R_e - C)$$

In our expanded model, the multiplier is now equal to the quotient of 1 divided by the required reserve ratio on checkable deposits, multiplied by the reserves available to support checkable deposits. The reserves available to support checkable deposits are no longer the entire monetary base as in the simple model. We must now subtract currency held by the public, excess reserves held by the bank, and required reserves being held against time deposits. As before, we can consider how a change in reserves will change the amount of checkable deposits in the system.

We can see that this formula in fact does work by returning to our multiple deposit contraction example. In that case, time deposits and excess reserves were both zero. The base was $100, currency was $50, and the required reserve ratio on checkable deposits was 10 percent. Using the formula, $D_c = (1/.10) \times (\$100 - \$50)$ = $500. This is the equilibrium level of checkable deposits in that example.

Money Supply Determination

It has long been argued that the quantity of money in an economy will affect the behavior of that economy. Those trained to worry about such things, referred to as macroeconomists, have long debated exactly why and how the variations in the quantity of money alter the workings of the economy. Some believe that increases in the money supply will naturally lead to an increase in output. According to this view, the increase in output stems from consumers having more money in their hands. Consumers desire to purchase goods and services with this money, and producers respond by hiring more workers and producing more output for the observed demand. Others stress the role that credit plays in the process. As reserves are increased to expand the money supply, credit is being expanded as well. This effect happens as banks find themselves with increased levels of excess reserves and decrease their interest rates in order to make more loans. Recipients of this credit demand a greater quantity of output and put pressure on current production. However, there is a limit to how much output can be increased. If demand exceeds the economy's ability to produce, prices will rise rather than output. Inflation is then a natural consequence of the increased level of spending induced by the increase in the money supply.[1]

In any case, to all of these experts, increases in the money supply will increase output, at least temporarily, and result in inflation beyond some point. The inflation, once started, becomes expected and embedded in all financial transactions. Nominal interest rates rise, and the prices of fixed-rate financial assets decline as a consequence. Accordingly, the quantity of money in circulation that is responsible for this cycle is of considerable importance. It will indicate the future direction of the economy and affect inflation, which will have an impact on the

---

[1]The issue of the role of money in macroeconomics can be found in every standard macroeconomics or money and banking textbook. Interested students should consult Abel and Bernanke, *Macroeconomics,* 2nd ed. (Reading, Mass.: Addison Wesley, 1995).

level of interest rates and the value of the myriad of financial assets that we have discussed in the course of this book.

With an understanding of multiple deposit expansion and reserve multipliers, we can turn our attention to money supply determination. The goal of this section is to understand how choices by banks and the public can affect both the money supply and its components. In order to do this, we will first provide a definition of the money supply and then derive the relevant money multiplier.

Definition of the Money Supply

Earlier in this chapter we argued that money was the medium of exchange. While it had other roles such as a standard and store of value, transactibility was a central feature. By this approach, the quantity of money in any economy should be equal to all of those things that can be and are used for transactions purposes. By this definition, currency clearly satisfies the criterion for inclusion; checkable deposits also qualify, notwithstanding our occasional difficulty with firms' willingness to accept them. However, should credit cards be counted as money? Are they money or credit? Should we use credit card purchases or unused credit card spending limits as a measure of their contribution to the money supply? This type of issue has been hotly debated for decades by economists, and it is also the reason that we introduced the notion of means of payment as a substitute definition of money. However, here we will avoid the issue by accepting the official definitions offered by the Federal Reserve; we will use the two most commonly referred to definitions of the money supply calculated by the Federal Reserve. A wider array of money supply definitions is contained in Box 26.1 for those of you who prefer greater ambiguity.

The first definition is a narrow one that includes only those items that can be used immediately to make transactions. This definition is called *M1*. *M1* includes currency, traveler's checks, demand deposits, and other checkable deposits. In terms that are consistent with our example above, *M1* is the sum of checkable deposits and currency.

$$M1 = D_c + C$$

In the first example of multiple expansion, equilibrium *M1* would have been $1,000. In the case of multiple contraction in the simple model, *M1* would have been the sum of checkable deposits ($500) and currency ($50), which was $550 in the final equilibrium.

While many economists prefer the narrower definition of money, others believe that a broader measure of money, called *M2,* is more appropriate. *M2* consists of *M1* plus small time deposits, savings deposits, money market deposit accounts, money market mutual fund balances, and overnight repurchase agreements. In terms of the expanded model developed above, *M2* is C plus D_c plus D_t , or

$$M2 = M1 + D_t$$

This definition of money includes items that have more limited spending capability, such as money market deposit accounts and money market mutual

---

Box 26.1

Definitions of the Money Supply

In addition to the two money supply definitions used in the text, monetary economists also have still broader definitions of the money supply. This table reports the definitions used for the full range of monetary aggregates as of December 1995. Notice that each definition is broader than the previous one.

Money Supply Measure	Composition of the Money Supply Measure
M1	1. Currency outside the U.S. Treasury, Federal Reserve Banks, and the vaults of depository institutions. 2. Traveler's checks of nonbank issuers. 3. Demand deposits at all commercial banks other than those owed to depository institutions, the U.S. government, and foreign banks and official institutions, less cash items in the process of collection and Federal Reserve float. 4. Other checkable deposits (OCDs), consisting of negotiable order of withdrawal (NOW) and automatic transfer service (ATS) accounts at depository institutions, credit union share draft accounts, and demand deposits at thrift institutions. Seasonally adjusted *M1* is computed by summing currency, traveler's checks, demand deposits, and OCDs, each seasonally adjusted separately.
M2	*M1* plus: 1. Overnight (and continuing-contract) repurchase agreements (RPs) issued by all depository institutions and overnight Eurodollars issued to U.S. residents by foreign branches of U.S. banks worldwide. 2. Savings (including MMDAs) and small time deposits (time deposits—including retail RPs in amounts of less than $100,000). 3. Balances in both taxable and tax-exempt general-purpose and broker-dealer money market funds. Excludes: 1. Individual retirement accounts (IRAs) and Keogh balances at depository institutions and money market funds. 2. All balances held by U.S. commercial banks, money market funds (general-purpose and broker-dealer), foreign governments, commercial banks, and the U.S. government.
M3	*M2* plus: 1. Large time deposits and term repurchase agreement liabilities (in amounts of $100,000 or more) issued by all depository institutions. 2. Term Eurodollars held by U.S. residents at foreign branches of U.S. banks worldwide and at all banking offices in the United Kingdom and Canada. 3. Balances in both taxable and tax-exempt, institution-only money market funds. Excludes: 1. All balances held by U.S. commercial banks, money market funds, and foreign banks and official institutions. 2. The estimates of overnight repurchase agreements and Eurodollars held by institution-only money market funds.
L	*M3* plus: 1. Nonbank public holdings of U.S. savings bonds, short-term Treasury securities, commercial paper, and bankers' acceptances, net of money market fund holdings of these assets.

Source: *Federal Reserve Bulletin.*

EXHIBIT 26.2

Ratio of currency relative to checkable deposits

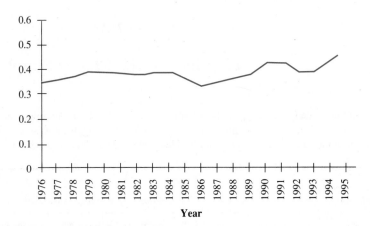

Source: *Federal Reserve Bulletin,* January 1996.

funds, as well as assets that cannot be spent directly but can be readily converted to a form that can be used in transactions. These assets are included because of their high degree of liquidity, which rivals, if not equals, that of the components of narrowly defined money. It is also true that they are all spendable to some degree by the holders of these assets.[2]

The Money Multiplier

In previous sections of this chapter, examples of multiple deposit expansion and contraction derived a relationship between changes in the monetary base and changes in the level of checkable deposits. Here, we would like to expand this analysis to consider how a change in the base will affect the *entire* money supply, not just checkable deposits. This will require us to return to the earlier models and to improve the analysis of the preferences of both the bank and the public. In particular, you will recall that bank excess reserves and consumer currency holdings were both assumed to be constant and independent of deposit balances. This seems too simplistic. Here, we will assume that currency, time deposits, and excess reserves all grow proportionally with checkable deposits. This is probably more realistic than the earlier assumption, but it is not entirely correct. Exhibit 26.2 reports the ratio of currency to checkable deposits over the last 20 years. Notice that the ratio has moved up somewhat over the period. Exhibit 26.3 reports a similar ratio for time deposits. Here, the ratio begins and ends at roughly the same point, although there is considerable variation over the 15-year period for which we have consistent data. Finally, Exhibit 26.4 examines the history of the excess reserve

---

[2]This statement is true for all *M2* components, with the exception of repurchase agreements. However, given their short-term nature, the Federal Reserve has chosen to include them in the *M2* statistics.

EXHIBIT 26.3

Ratio of time deposits to checkable deposits

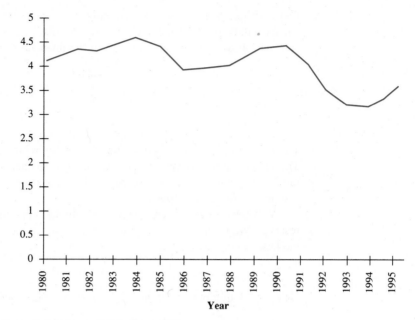

Source: *Federal Reserve Bulletin*, January 1996.

EXHIBIT 26.4

Ratio of excess reserve to checkable deposits

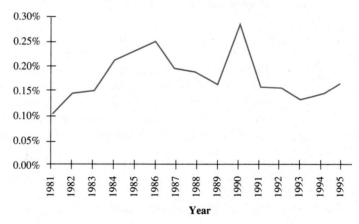

Source: *Federal Reserve Bulletin*, January 1996.

ratio. While this ratio is quite volatile, it should be noted that the range of the ratio is a fairly small number and moves only between 0.1 percent and 0.3 percent over the 15-year series. Therefore, while these assumptions are not exact, they can serve as a starting point for subsequent analysis.

The effect of this assumption is that every time checkable deposits change, the amount of currency and time deposits held by the public will also change.

Likewise, excess reserves in the banking system will vary, but in each case, the change will be proportional to checkable deposits. This is equivalent to assuming that the following ratios are constant in the financial sector:

$$c = C/D_c$$

$$t = D_t/D_c$$

$$e = R_e/D_c$$

The first ratio, c, represents the ratio of currency relative to checkable deposits. The second ratio, t, is the ratio of time deposits to checkable deposits. The third ratio, e, is the amount of excess reserves a bank chooses to hold relative to the amount of checkable deposits.

With these ratios, we can see how the money supply is affected by changes in reserves. We begin by revisiting the equation for the monetary base. Recall that the base is composed of all reserves plus currency, or

$$B = r_c D_c + r_t D_t + R_e + C$$

Using the definitions of c, t, and e given above, this equation can be rewritten as

$$B = r_c D_c + r_t t D_c + e D_c + c D_c$$

Solve this equation for D_c to get the following relationship between checkable deposits and the monetary base:

$$D_c = \frac{1}{r_c + r_t t + e + c} \times B$$

This equation is analogous to the deposit multiplier derived in the previous section. However, this time, variations in excess reserves and time deposits, with their effects on the monetary base available to support checkable deposits, are reflected within the multiplier directly rather than being subtracted from the base itself.[3]

Next, recall that by definition, $M1 = D_c + C$. Therefore, we can rewrite $M1$ as

$$M1 = D_c + c D_c$$

$$M1 = (1 + c) D_c$$

Then, by substituting the checkable deposit multiplier formula we just derived for D_c, we get

$$M1 = \frac{(1 + c)}{r_c + r_t t + e + c} \times B = m_1 B$$

---

[3] We can check this by once again using the numbers from the multiple deposit contraction example. In this case, we must calculate t, e, and c. Because there are no time deposits or excess reserves, t and e are both zero. The ratio of currency to checkable deposits in equilibrium is 10 percent, and as before, the required reserve ratio on checkable deposits is 10 percent. Thus, we get the correct answer of $D_c = [1/(0.10 + 0.10)] \times \$100 = \$500$.

Box 26.2

Money Stock and Liquid Asset Totals

Box 26.1 reported the actual definitions for the money supply aggregates used by the Federal Reserve. By way of realism, it might be useful to observe the aggregate totals and the actual multiplier for the United States. Toward this end, we report the money supply aggregates and reserves for the U.S. economy on December 31, 1995. (All units are in billions of dollars.)

M1	1,129
M2	3,780
M3	4,564
L	5,648
M1 components:	
Currency	373
Traveler's checks	9
Demand deposits	389
Other checkable deposits	353
Nontransaction components:	
In *M2*	2,658
In *M3*	783
Total reserves	56
Required reserves	55
Monetary base	434
M1 multiplier	2.601
M2 multiplier	8.710

Source: Federal Reserve System.

This formula is what we set out to derive. We now have $M1 = m_1 B$, where the **M1 money multiplier** is

$$m_1 = \frac{1 + c}{r_c + r_t t + e + c}$$

A similar multiplier can be derived for the *M2* definition of the money supply. Recall that $M2 = M1 + D_t = D_c + C + D_t$. We can replicate the derivation used for the *M1* money multiplier as follows.

$$M2 = M1 + D_t$$

$$M2 = D_c + cD_c + tD_c$$

$$M2 = (1 + c + t)D_c$$

$$M2 = \frac{1 + c + t}{r_c + r_t t + e + c} \times B = m_2 B$$

Therefore, the *M2* **money multiplier** is

$$m_2 = \frac{1 + c + t}{r_c + r_t t + e + c}$$

Thus, *M2* $= m_2 B$ gives the relationship between the monetary base and the *M2* **money supply.**

To confirm that the money multiplier formula works, let us return once again to the original examples. In the original example, the monetary base was $100, with no currency, excess reserves, or time deposits being held. In that case, *M1* = *M2*. In equilibrium, we had $e = t = c = 0$ and $r_c = 10$ percent. Thus, we get the correct answer that

$$M1 = (1/.10) \times \$100 = \$1,000$$

In the next example, currency increased to $50. In equilibrium, we now have

$$M1 = \frac{1 + 0.100}{.10 + .10} \times \$100 = \$550$$

This is, in fact, the right answer. *M1* is the sum of checkable deposits and currency. In that example, the equilibrium level of checkable deposits was $500 and currency was $50.

These two equations are of crucial importance. They link the reserve base and the money supply through the money multiplier, which in turn depends upon consumer and banking sector asset ratios. This approach allows us to see what effect changes in each of these ratios will have on the money supply. We could show you that for a given level of the monetary base:

1. An increase in either required reserve ratio will decrease *M1* and *M2*.
2. An increase in the currency to checkable deposits ratio will generally decrease *M1* and *M2*.
3. An increase in excess reserves will decrease *M1* and *M2*.
4. An increase in the time deposits ratio will decrease *M1* but will generally increase *M2*.

While we will not prove each of these statements, the intuition should be clear. Required reserves, excess reserves, and currency can each be thought of as a leakage from the process of multiple deposit creation. At each stage of the expansion process, each of these factors drains some of the reserves available for making loans. An increase in these factors makes for a larger leakage at each stage and thus a lower equilibrium money supply.

However, the main message offered by the money multiplier is the direct linkage between the reserve and the total money supply, given the values of these ratios. This relationship will prove important in the discussion of the Federal Reserve and monetary policy. Recall that the Fed can change the monetary base but not people's preferences. However, if the Fed knows the appropriate money multiplier, m_1 or m_2, then it will know what effect a change in the base will have on the money supply. In the next chapter, we discuss how the Fed goes about changing the monetary base, as well as what it is trying to accomplish in the process.

Summary

In this chapter, we have expanded our interest in the money and capital markets to investigate the role banks play in determining the total money supply. We have interest in this because variations in the money supply are closely linked to variations in inflation and economic activity, both of which have substantial implications for the financial markets. These two factors determine the nominal interest rate, equity returns, and the value of virtually every asset.

We saw how decisions about reserve levels and cash holdings have impacts on the money supply through the multiple deposit creation process, and how portfolio decisions by households change the total money supply in the economy as a whole. The key finding, however, is that the monetary base of the banking system is central to the determination of the money supply. This is determined by the Federal Reserve, as the ultimate provider of liquidity and reserves not only to the banking system but to the financial sector as a whole. It is to this part of the monetary system that we now turn.

Key Concepts

barter, 664
double coincidence of wants, 664
excess reserves, 667
fractional reserves, 666
high-powered money, 672
M1 and *M2*, 674
M1 and *M2* money multipliers, 679, 680
medium of exchange, means of payment, 664

monetary base, 672
money, 664
multiple deposit expansion and contraction, 669
reserve multiplier, 671
reserve requirement, 667
standard of value, standard of deferred payment, 665

Review Questions

1. Assume that the assumptions of the multiple deposit expansion model hold. The reserve ratio is 25 percent and the Fed increases reserves by $200. What are the equilibrium levels of assets and liabilities? What are the new levels under the multiple deposit contraction model with $50 held in currency?

2. Find the equilibrium levels of assets and liabilities under the multiple deposit expansion and contraction models when the reserve ratio is 15 percent, reserves are increased to $300, and you subsequently withdraw $75 for pocket change. What multiple is deposits of reserves?

3. What is the change in checkable deposits for a change in excess reserves? What is the change in checkable deposits for a change in time deposits? (Hint: It is not the reserve multiplier.)

4. Examine the money multiplier. Can it ever be less than 1? If so, what are the necessary conditions?

5. What types of transactions would affect *M1* and not *M2*? Is there any way of doing the reverse?

6. What would happen if the Fed set reserve requirements to zero? Is this a realistic scenario?

7. Explore what happens to the money multiplier with changes in the reserve requirements for both checking and savings accounts.

References

Abel, Andrew, and Ben Bernanke. *Macroeconomics.* 2nd ed. Reading, Mass.: Addison Wesley, 1995.

Burger, Albert E. *The Money Supply Process.* Belmont, Cal.: Wadsworth, 1971.

Federal Reserve Bank of Atlanta. *Fundamental Facts about United States Money.* Atlanta: Federal Reserve Bank of Alanta, 1989.

Gonczy, Anne Marie. *Modern Money Mechanics.* Chicago: Federal Reserve Bank of Chicago, 1992.

Goodfriend, M. "A Model of Money Stock Determination with Loan Demand and a Banking System Balance Sheet Constraint." *Economic Review.* Federal Reserve Bank of Richmond, January 1982.

Humphrey, Thomas M. "The Theory of Multiple Expansion of Deposits: What It Is and Whence It Came." *Economic Review.* Federal Reserve Bank of Richmond, March/April 1987.

Russell, Steven. "The U.S. Currency System: A Historical Perspective." *Review.* Federal Reserve Bank of St. Louis, September/October 1991.

Santomero, Anthony M., and Jeremy J. Siegel. "A General Equilibrium Money and Banking Paradigm." *Journal of Finance,* May 1982.

Tobin, James. "Commercial Banks as Creators of Money." In *Banking and Monetary Studies,* edited by Deane Carson. Burr Ridge, Ill.: Richard D. Irwin, 1963.

Walter, John R. "Monetary Aggregates: A User's Guide." *Economic Review.* Federal Reserve Bank of Richmond, January 1989.

CHAPTER 27

The Federal Reserve and the Money Supply Process

Chapter Outline

This chapter reviews the role of the central bank in an economy, including its goals and the tools at its disposal. It then outlines the origin and history of the Federal Reserve System, the U.S. central bank and primary monetary authority. Next, the structure of the system and the mechanisms by which it goes about

683

determining economic policy are outlined. The influences that help to determine the actions of the Fed are examined, and the chapter concludes with a discussion of the independence of the Fed.

In the previous chapter, it was pointed out that no discussion of the financial sector is complete without an understanding of the role that money plays within it. The value of all financial assets is stated in local currency, and variations in the supply of money affect the economy in a number of ways. Increases in the money supply will increase output, at least temporarily, and result in inflation beyond some point. The inflation is then embedded in nominal interest rates, forward exchange rates, and the value of future financial claims.

We then went on to present the process by which the money supply is determined. The complex interaction of the central bank, the banking sector, and public depositors, known as multiple deposit expansion, determines the money supply. In the process, reserves are lent over and over, leading to the notion of the money multiplier, which we discussed at some length.

Within the context of that discussion, the Federal Reserve quickly emerges as an important part of the money supply process. The Fed sets reserve requirements and can manipulate the monetary base of the United States. Because of the scope of the Federal Reserve's influence on financial markets, it is important to understand how it operates and how any central bank may operate. In this chapter, we will examine these questions. We begin with a brief outline of the goals of a central bank in any financial sector, and proceed to a description of the ways in which a central bank interacts with the financial sector to achieve these goals. The evolution of the Federal Reserve System from its origin as a decentralized body of regional Federal Reserve banks to its current status as the central guardian of the U.S. money supply and banking system is reviewed next. Here, in order to understand its pronouncements and behavior, we will examine both its procedures and the various types of pressures placed on the Fed.

It is hoped that we will have accomplished several things by the end of this discussion. First, you will have an understanding of how the central bank operates and precisely how difficult it is to achieve central bank objectives in the complexity of the modern financial sector. Second, you will learn enough about the central bank to watch its actions, anticipate its moves, and understand the implications of its decisions on the financial sector you have grown to know and love.

The Goals of Central Bank Policy

What is a **central bank**? How does it fit into the overall financial system? This is probably a good starting point to explain both the concept of a central bank and the American version, the Federal Reserve System. A central bank truly stands at the "center" of the financial system. It controls the monetary base of the economy, provides liquidity in times of crises, and, in various ways, ensures the integrity of the financial system. At times, the central bank also serves as a banker's bank and the government's bank as well.

The central bank can be either a government agency, a privately owned bank, or a combination of the two. It could have been established from the start as a government entity, as was the Federal Reserve, or it could evolve into its role, as the Bank of England did. However, whatever the ownership structure might be, the central bank is a governmental or quasi-governmental institution. As such, its goals and objectives extend beyond profit maximization to include broader social goals such as preventing financial crises and promoting both employment and growth in the economy. We begin our discussion of central banking by looking more closely at these goals in general terms. More will be said of the specifics in the U.S. context later in the chapter.

The central bank sees itself as the primary public policymaker in the financial sector. It sets its policies with the goal of assuring financial stability and maintaining a well-functioning macro economy. But what does a well-functioning economy mean, and how will you know one when you see it? This is the stuff of macroeconomics textbooks. There, our colleagues can go on for pages about the goals of policy and the problems one faces in trying to achieve them.

Nonetheless, policymakers continue to try to improve our lot through the use of monetary and fiscal policy. In each case, they seek to use the tools available to achieve a number of admirable **goals of central bank policy.** These goals include: (1) high employment, (2) high economic growth, (3) price stability, and occasionally (4) interest rate and exchange rate stability. Let's quickly look at each of these goals.

High Employment

Clearly, from the point of view of an individual who desires to work, it is better to be employed than unemployed. In addition, for the economy as a whole, an employed worker clearly produces more output than an unemployed worker. So, a high level of employment would seem to be desirable. In addition, as they are not able to provide for themselves or their dependents, unemployed workers represent not only lost productivity but also human suffering.

These arguments would seem to suggest that the employment of every individual who desires to work would be an admirable goal. However, this may not be the case. At any given time, there will be a number of workers that are moving for one reason or another. There may also be workers who are leaving the work force to get further education or to commit time to their families. Similarly, there are workers who are graduating from school or are returning from family care duties. Workers leaving jobs are creating vacancies that must be filled. Workers seeking jobs will fill those vacancies. This movement of workers between jobs is referred to as **frictional unemployment.** At any given time, this may be 5 or 6 percent of the work force. There is no clear consensus on the optimal level of frictional unemployment. However, there is a general belief that the level can be reduced through quicker retraining and better distribution of information about new jobs.

With frictional unemployment in mind, the goal of macroeconomic policy becomes reducing any **unintended unemployment.** Unintended unemployment is any amount beyond frictional unemployment. For example, the closing of a factory may force hundreds of workers into unemployment. These workers probably were not intending to switch jobs, but now they must do so. However, solving the problem of excessive unemployment is quite difficult for two reasons. First, at any moment, there is no clear consensus on how much unemployment is unintended and how much is frictional unemployment. While it is easy to say that 0 percent recorded unemployment is too little and that the 25 percent unemployment of the Great Depression is too much, the exact optimum is not so easy to find. The second problem is that measuring unemployment can be very difficult.

The first step in measuring unemployment is to define what it means to be unemployed. Then, you can just count everyone that satisfies the definition. This is easier said than done. For example, is the person that has been looking for a job for over a year and then gives up looking considered unemployed? Or are they then considered not in the work force and therefore not part of the unemployment calculation? Another example is the part-time employee. Is this person considered employed even if he or she is looking for a full-time job? Even when a definition is agreed upon, actually counting the number of unemployed workers is a monumental task.

Economic Growth

Economic growth is a social goal that is closely related to high employment. However, it is clearly not identical to it. In fact, at times, the goal of economic growth works against the employment goal. This is because growth is enhanced by firms that are incorporating technological advances into their production processes. Such capital investments, however, are often justified on the grounds that they will reduce the need for relatively expensive labor. In short, many may view the increase in technology as a threat to employment. However, such investment is more likely to occur when unemployment is low. When there are high levels of unemployment, it is cheaper for firms to hire unemployed labor for production than to invest in technology to enhance worker productivity. Therefore, in periods of low unemployment, firms are more likely to see new technology as a cost-effective way to enhance the productivity of the existing work force.

Another factor that influences economic growth is the level of saving in the economy. Savings are the funds that can be drawn upon for investment. As was discussed in Chapter 3, the level of saving is affected by interest rates, and as we shall explain, the Fed has some control over these rates. However, it should be remembered that growth is a long-term goal and it is too often sacrificed for short-term expediency.

Price Stability

A lack of stability in prices leads to real economic losses. For example, consider a person who borrows $100 today with a promise to pay back $105 in one year. Now, assume that over that year, prices rise by 5 percent. The real rate of interest earned by the lender is 0 percent. In essence, the borrower was able to use the money for one year free of charge. However, as we discussed at some length in Chapter 4, inflation only causes this problem if it is not anticipated. If the 5 percent inflation in prices had been anticipated, it would have been incorporated into the nominal interest rate.[1] In this case, a 10 percent interest rate would have been charged so that the lender would have earned a real return of 5 percent.

The point here is that it is the **unanticipated inflation** that leads to costs such as these. Unanticipated inflation imposes a cost on any party that receives payments specified in a **nominal contract.** Such a contract states the number of dollars to be delivered at a given time, regardless of the inflation rate. In our economy, most contracts are written in nominal terms. These include wage contracts as well as financial contracts. Therefore, a large segment of the economy can be affected by unexpected inflation. In addition, holding currency is costly when there is inflation, whether it is expected or not. Holding cash has a negative rate of return when there is inflation, that is, it loses value. For all of these reasons, one of the goals of economic policy is to maintain a steady and low rate of inflation. This allows nominal contracts to account for the expected inflation and reduces the losses from inflation to a minimum.

Interest Rate and Exchange Rate Stability

Another traditional goal of a central bank has been stability in financial asset prices. However, recently, both interest rates and exchange rates have fluctuated greatly. This fact notwithstanding, many would argue in favor of stability, other things equal. Stable interest rates are desirable because there are costs that must be borne by both lenders and borrowers when interest rates vary. When interest rates rise, investors that must sell securities for one reason or another lose money because of the lower prices resulting from higher interest rates. On the other hand, issuers of securities must try to forecast interest rates in order to then issue a security at the most favorable rate. Firms that must borrow money during a period of high interest rates will pay more in interest than if they could have waited for lower rates.

For similar reasons, it is often argued that fluctuating exchange rates can hurt international trade. In order to facilitate foreign investment, central governments have pursued a policy of stable exchange rates. To do this, they buy or sell foreign currency in order to stabilize the value of their currency relative to the foreign currency.

However, as above, most of these costs can be traced to unexpected and random rate changes rather than to change itself. Those that support stability often miss this distinction. To economists, however, the difference is fundamental.

---

[1]The text neglects both the cross-term and Mundell versus Darby controversy of Chapter 4. For ease of discussion, we simply assumed that the nominal rate increased by exactly the inflation rate. See Chapter 4 for a further discussion of these issues.

Conflicts among Goals

While many of these goals can be pursued simultaneously, some of them present difficult choices. For example, the goal of price stability and a stable financial system may conflict. After a stock market crash, the Fed may want to pump money into the system, but this can cause inflation and hurt price stability. Another example is the potential conflict between high unemployment and stable prices. In the early 1980s, central banks worldwide tightened monetary policy in order to curb inflation. This had the effect of raising unemployment. Unfortunately, central banks must ultimately weigh the cost associated with sacrificing one goal versus another goal and decide which goal should be pursued at any point in time.

The Role of the Central Bank in a Financial System

How does the central bank achieve these goals? We saw in the previous chapter that the central bank has control of the money supply through its ability to affect the monetary base and reserve requirements. However, a central bank does more than just this. It has a number of different roles within the financial sector that every financial expert needs to appreciate. We spotlight four here.

Control of the Money Supply

One of the first duties generally associated with a central bank is the **maintenance of a stable supply of money** to the economy. This would seem pretty simple. The central bank could just set the monetary base and required reserves at a fixed level. Through the money multiplier we would have a stable money supply. However, things are not that simple. As we saw in the previous chapter, the money supply is influenced by several behavioral choices that determine the value of the money multiplier. Depositors determine the amount of money they wish to hold as currency as well as the breakdown of their deposits between transaction accounts and savings balances. Therefore, without central bank action, the money multiplier would vary with these choices, and the money supply would expand and contract accordingly. For example, the money supply would decline every December as people withdraw money from their bank accounts to purchase gifts for the holidays. To prevent this, the central bank offsets these declines in the money multiplier with additional monetary base. In short, the central bank must be constantly monitoring the behavior of the economy in its efforts to maintain monetary stability.

The central bank acts proactively as well. During recessions, it attempts to expand the money supply to add funds to the financial market. During booms, it tries to slow the economy down. Last but not least, the central bank will intervene to ensure that the money supply is growing at the proper rate for strong economic growth over time without undue inflation. Much more will be said of this role and of the Federal Reserve's ability to carry it out in the following pages. However, we should not lose sight of the fact that this role is seen to be primary to the central bank's importance in the economy.

The Lender of Last Resort

A second function of a central bank is to act as the **lender of last resort.** Recall from the previous chapter that banks hold only a fraction of deposits in the form of reserves. If, for some reason, depositors desire to withdraw their money from the bank, the bank must use reserves to meet this demand. As reserves are depleted, the bank must recall loans to replenish reserves. However, this may take some time, while deposit withdrawal, particularly in the wholesale and interbank market, is very rapid. The central bank stands ready to provide the necessary liquidity in such cases, and it does so by replenishing reserves over the short term and restoring confidence in the system. After the crisis, the bank or banks involved can repay the loans and return to an adequate reserve level.

This mechanism serves as a protection against **bank panics.** These are situations in which depositors withdraw funds from depository institutions abruptly and in large volumes. While deposit insurance schemes exist worldwide in various forms, they, by themselves, are insufficient to ensure stability of the financial system. If a run were to start, the bank's reserves and any deposit insurance reserves could easily be exhausted. In such circumstances, there is no substitute for the central bank's intervention. As the lender of last resort, the central bank can provide reserves that will allow banks to weather a crisis.

Historically, this liquidity has been provided by the central bank making loans to the bank or banks in trouble. Banks requiring funds would produce collateral, such as loans or securities that they owned. These assets were discounted for the interest due over the term of the loan. As a result, this activity is frequently referred to as **discounting,** and it is said to take place at the central bank's **discount window.** Today, collateral requirements are generally gone, as is the physical teller window, but the activity itself remains.

While this function of a central bank is not a part of day-to-day operations, it is an important guarantee that adds to the stability of a banking system. We learned many hard lessons during the Great Depression about the importance of this function. In the 1930s, many central banks, including the Federal Reserve, failed to act effectively as a lender of last resort. However, in the years since then, they have performed this role well; some would argue too well!

Ensuring the Integrity of the Financial System

Beyond the explicit operations of the central bank to manage the money supply or to thwart a crisis, the central bank also affects the financial sector in a number of other ways that, collectively, are aimed at improving the overall operation of the financial system. In some countries, bank regulation falls within the purview of the central bank. Prudential regulation, on-site inspections, and policy setting may all come under central bank jurisdiction. This is true in the U.K. and Germany, for

Box 27.1

Settlement Risk Control

Major government central banks sent a stern message to commercial banks yesterday: Reduce settlement risk in the $1.2 trillion-a-day global foreign-exchange market, or we will force you.

Critical of many banks' risk-control practices and concerned they are moving too slowly in addressing the issue, the central banks warned that they are willing to impose new guidelines and back them up with tough supervisory measures that could hit banks' bottom lines.

The central banks also cautioned that problems arising from botched currency trades could extend beyond damaging individual institutions. Reducing settlement risk "is important for the safety and soundness of the world's financial systems," said William J. McDonough, president of the Federal Reserve Bank of New York.

Foreign-exchange settlement risk is the hazard that one party to a foreign-exchange trade will pay out the currency it sold but not receive the currency it purchased. Because each transaction involves two or more payments, bankers estimate that each day $3.2 trillion cascades through the world's foreign-exchange settlement systems.

In a report issued by the Bank for International Settlements, or BIS, central bankers from the world's 11 major industrial countries said many banks don't appreciate the size or complexity of settlement risk and that they lack formal mechanisms to measure and cope with their exposures. They also criticized banks for not devoting significant resources to efforts that have been shown to reduce settlement risk.

"Many banks do not recognize that they can routinely incur FX [foreign-exchange] settlement exposures equivalent to several days' trades, and that these exposures can persist overnight, and therefore over weekends and holidays," the report said. "The amount at risk to even a single counterparty [another bank] could easily exceed a bank's capital."

In preparing its report, the BIS studied about 80 major international banks. Surprisingly, some of them acknowledge that their senior executives "had never been fully briefed on the FX settlement process and the associated risks."

Collapses Cited

In the past five years currency-settlement problems have arisen during the collapses of Drexel Burnham Lambert Inc., BCCI SA and Barings PLC and the 1991 failed Soviet coup attempt. The BIS said that had the Barings mess not been handled successfully, more than $63 billion in European currency unit payments among 45 banks wouldn't have settled—even though less than 1 percent of the payments had anything to do with Barings.

Optimistically, the Fed's Mr. McDonough said that "this is something in which education can solve 98 percent of the problem."

However, the central banks threatened that in each country they might dictate guidelines for measuring individual bank settlement exposures, require they be publicly disclosed, impose risk-management guidelines and use examinations and audits to verify compliance.

example, but it is less so in the United States, where only certain institutions directly report to the Federal Reserve. Those institutions are, however, the largest ones! (See Chapter 21.)

Central banks may also be responsible for the smooth functioning of the government securities market and the regulation of its dealers and traders. They may set capital standards for market participants or help to qualify participants.

Possible Measures

If necessary, they also warned of "stronger supervisory measures," such as forcing individual banks to adopt specific mechanisms to control risks. These could include setting formal limits on how much settlement risk a bank can assume and making those risks subject to a bank's capital adequacy requirements. The BIS also is willing to consider imposing similar limits on nonbank financial institutions active in currency trading.

Bankers said that, if imposed, some of these measures could eat into their profits by raising their cost of capital. They said they know of only two banks—Swiss Bank Corp. and J.P. Morgan & Co.—that currently allocate capital to the assumed risk involved in settling trades or plan to do so.

The BIS recommended commercial banks "take immediate steps" to improve their credit-control procedures. It also told banks to bolster their back-office payments units, correspondent bank arrangements, risk-management controls and netting capabilities.

Commercial banks are further encouraged to "develop well-constructed multicurrency services" to reduce currency-settlement risk. These could include netting and other approaches, such as "payment vs. payment" systems where banks and a central clearing facility make simultaneous payments to one another.

Warning against Assumptions

What's more, the central bankers stressed that these risk-reduction services be financed by the private sector. They warned bankers against assuming that major banks are "too big to fail" or operating on the assumption that "authorities could always avoid closing down a major FX market participant unexpectedly."

One European banker said the central bankers "are in effect saying: 'If you want to have the casino, you pay for it.' "

Over the next two years, the central bankers said they will cooperate with bank industry groups to develop settlement mechanisms. But they are also prepared to get tough, if commercial banks drag their feet.

Why the concern? Central banks don't want their taxpayers to be left holding the bag if they are forced to bail out major banks. They also worry that failed currency trades could lead to liquidity problems in world financial markets, an upset in central banks' monetary policies and "global payments gridlock."

A particular systemic concern centers on the large impact messed-up trades could have on countries' domestic-payments systems. For instance, system operators estimate that foreign-exchange settlements account for 50 percent of the daily volume of the U.S. and British payment systems, 80 percent of the German and 90 percent of the Swiss systems.

These fears aren't new. They first arose when Bankhaus Herstatt collapsed in 1974 and U.S. banks didn't get the dollars they were due after they had already paid the marks they owed the German bank. But since then, central bankers have grown more concerned as currency trading volume has ballooned, become more complex and included new participants such as fast-trading hedge funds.

Source: Michael R. Sesit, "Central Banks Issue Warning on Trading," *The Wall Street Journal,* March 2, 1996. Reprinted by permission of *The Wall Street Journal,* © 1996 Dow Jones & Company, Inc. All Rights Reserved Worldwide.

Almost everywhere, however, central banks are deeply involved with the payment system itself. This, you will recall, is the clearing system among banks that processes massive amounts of both paper (e.g., drafts, checks, etc.) and money. Over time, the paper has been replaced by electronic impulses through worldwide computer networks. Nonetheless, central banks assure the integrity of the system, and they enter into multilateral agreements with their foreign counterparts. (See Box 27.1.)

The Banker's Bank

On top of all this, a central bank will also provide many of the functions of a standard bank. However, these services are provided only to other institutions and, at times, to the central government. First, the central bank serves as the bank that holds other banks' reserves. Second, as mentioned above, the central bank will make discount loans to other banks. Third, it can provide check-clearing services for banks. Beyond these functions, the central bank often plays the role of the government's bank. The government may keep balances and write checks against an account at the central bank. Further, the central bank often issues currency and may sell government securities on behalf of the national state.

These functions put the central bank in a good position to regulate the banking system in a country. It can easily monitor reserves and financial flows between banks, and it has unique access to the activities and financial condition of banks within the system.

The Origin and History of the Federal Reserve

The institution in the U.S. financial system that plays these roles is, of course, our **Federal Reserve.** The structure of the Federal Reserve differs from that of its counterparts in other countries; it is truly one of a kind. To understand the structure of the Federal Reserve System and how it functions in the current environment, we must consider its historical roots and the political climate within which it was created.

Our country was formed out of a deep mistrust of centralized authority. The Constitution of the United States spells out an elaborate set of checks and balances that are designed specifically to curb the authority of any one power. The two things that early Americans trusted least were a powerful executive branch and a powerful central bank. In fact, the public outcry against earlier attempts to establish a central bank led to the failure of the First Bank of the United States in 1811 and to Andrew Jackson's pledge to abolish the Second Bank of the United States in 1836. (For history buffs, this was followed by Jackson's famous "pet bank" period.) Both of these banks were originally intended to regulate the banking industry. However, the public mistrust of a strong central bank won out over the desire to regulate the banking industry.

As would be expected, however, without a central bank to act as the lender of last resort, a series of banking crises ensued. Panics, and losses to depositors, in 1873, 1884, 1893, and finally 1907 convinced the public that a central bank was necessary. However, in the spirit of the Constitution, the **Federal Reserve Act of 1913** provided for a system of checks and balances that divided power between 12 separate banks.

Originally, the Federal Reserve System was envisioned as a confederation of 12 regional banks that would serve as the local lenders of last resort. The sole tool of the Federal Reserve was to be the discount window. Each regional bank had the ability to set its own discount rate and policy, so this function was performed with varying degrees of sophistication. As a general rule, however, the system functioned under a "**real bills doctrine.**" If the banks would provide short-term corporate debt for discount, funds were generally made available.

At the time, little was understood of a central bank's ability to influence the money supply by directly affecting the bank's reserve base. Rather, the Fed was seen as passively providing the necessary money for the needs of commerce through its discounting mechanism. During the late 1920s, this role became evident and was seen by some as an important function of the Federal Reserve. However, fortune did not shine on the U.S. system. The strongest supporter of active monetary base control, Benjamin Strong, the president of the Federal Reserve Bank of New York, died in 1928. When liquidity was required and the money supply began to fall during the Great Stock Market Crash of 1929, there was little understanding of the potential role of the Federal Reserve and its ability to increase the money supply in response to the crisis. By the end of the decade, which was characterized by boom, bust, and financial collapse, the number of banking institutions fell by 50 percent! This failure in central bank policy led to economic collapse and opened the door to the New Deal of President Roosevelt in 1932.

The banking legislation that followed the crash, during the Great Depression, effectively centralized the Fed's power in the Board of Governors. The Banking Act of 1933 formally established a new body, the **Federal Open Market Committee** (FOMC), with the authority to control the money supply. The Banking Act of 1935 granted the Board of Governors the majority of votes on the FOMC. Next, the 1935 legislation also granted the Board of Governors the authority to change reserve requirements. Finally, the Board of Governors' power to "review and determine" the discount rate set by each of the regional banks soon made it the *de facto* power in this area as well. These legislative changes altered the Federal Reserve forever and have resulted in its current structure.

The Structure of the Federal Reserve System

As mentioned above, the intention of the Federal Reserve Act was to create a lender of last resort without creating a powerful central bank. The act provided for power to be diffused between the regional banks, the private banking sector, and the government. By 1935, this original format had evolved into the three major bodies of the Federal Reserve System: the Federal Reserve banks, the Board of Governors, and the Federal Open Market Committee. Other players in the Federal Reserve System as it exists today are the Federal Advisory Council and the member banks. The relationships between each of these bodies are portrayed in Exhibit 27.1.

Federal Reserve Banks

There are still only 12 **regional Federal Reserve banks,** though the geographic boundaries between districts have changed somewhat over the years. The locations of these banks and the boundaries of the districts are shown on the map in

Exhibit 27.1

*The organizational
structure of the
Federal Reserve
System*

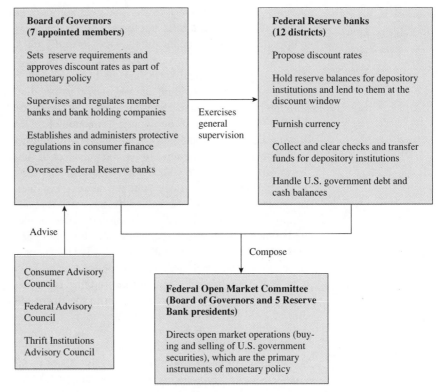

Source: Board of Governors of the Federal Reserve System, *The Federal Reserve System: Purposes and Functions.* Washington, D.C., 1984.

Exhibit 27.2. While all of these banks have the same authority within their respective districts, they differ greatly in size and power. The size of the districts relates somewhat to demographic differences between regions in the United States, at least at the turn of the century, when they were laid out. Their relative power relates to the commercial importance of the city. The three largest reserve banks, in terms of assets held, are New York, Chicago, and San Francisco. These three reserve banks hold over 50 percent of the combined assets in the Federal Reserve System. The New York bank alone holds about 30 percent of the assets. Because of the importance of New York as a financial center and the fact that its location puts it in direct contact with the largest commercial banks and financial markets in the country, the New York bank is referred to as "first among equals." It has become the bank that implements the Fed's policy to change the money supply, and it looms large in the financial markets. Further, the New York bank is often the contact point between the Fed and central banks of foreign countries.

Formally, each of the 12 banks is structured as a privately owned, incorporated institution. The member banks each hold the stock of the reserve bank in their district. However, legislation limits their influence and restricts their

EXHIBIT 27.2

Maps of the Federal Reserve System

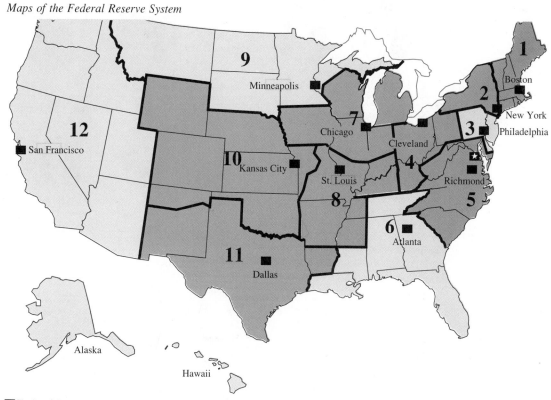

■ Federal Reserve Bank city
★ Board of Governors of the Federal
   Reserve System, Washington, D.C.

Note: The Federal Reserve officially identifies districts by number and Reserve Bank city (shown on both pages) and by letter (shown on the next page).
In the 12th District, the Seattle Branch serves Alaska, and the San Francisco Bank serves Hawaii.
The system serves commonwealths and territories as follows: the New York Bank serves the Commonwealth of Puerto Rico and the U.S. Virgin Islands; the San Francisco Bank serves American Samoa, Guam, and the Commonwealth of the Northern Mariana Islands. The Board of Governors revised the branch boundaries of the System most recently in December 1991.

Source: *Federal Reserve Bulletin.*

dividends to 6 percent annually. As is the case in all aspects of the Federal Reserve System, control of the banks is structured to limit the ability of any one group to take control of the system. Each bank is run by a board of nine directors. These directors are divided into three types, referred to as A, B, and C directors. The three A directors are professional bankers who are elected by the member banks. The three B directors are prominent businessmen in the area of industry, commerce, or agriculture, and they may not be officers, employees, or stockholders of banks. These B directors are also elected by the member banks. The three

Exhibit 27.2

(continued)

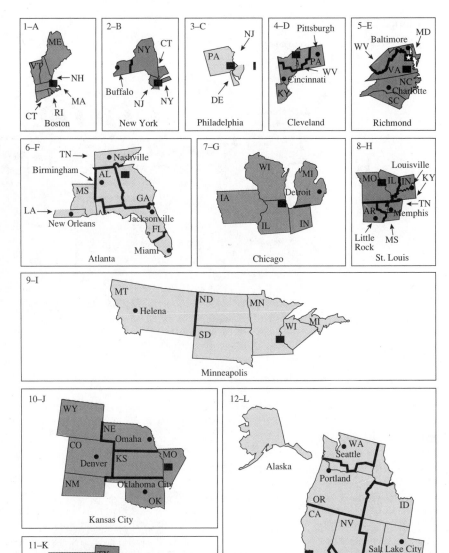

1–A Boston

2–B New York

3–C Philadelphia

4–D Cleveland

5–E Richmond

6–F Atlanta

7–G Chicago

8–H St. Louis

9–I Minneapolis

10–J Kansas City

11–K Dallas

12–L San Francisco

■ Federal Reserve Bank city
● Federal Reserve Branch city

★ Board of Governors of the Federal
Reserve System, Washington, D.C.

C directors are appointed by the Board of Governors to represent the broader public interest. These C directors are also not allowed to be officers, employees, or stockholders of banks. The Board of Directors, with approval of the Board of Governors, selects and advises the president and other officers for each bank.

The 12 Federal Reserve banks carry out a variety of duties. They make discount loans, examine member banks, clear checks, issue new currency, withdraw damaged currency from circulation, and evaluate merger applications. In addition, they perform more ceremonial roles such as maintaining local contact between the Federal Reserve System and the business community, collecting data on local business conditions, and maintaining a large staff of economists who research topics that relate to both monetary policy and local economic conditions.

But if the main function of the Federal Reserve System is to affect the money supply, what role do the banks play? The Federal Reserve banks are involved in monetary policy in three ways. First, but least important, they can "establish" the discount rate. However, the Board of Governors actually sets this rate through its power to review and determine the discount rate in each district. Second, and more importantly, they can decide which banks are granted discount loans. Here, too, if stakes are high, the Board is involved. Third, and most importantly, they are involved in the Fed's monetary policy role. Specifically, five of the presidents of the reserve banks serve on the Fed's monetary policy decision-making body, the FOMC. The president from New York is always on the FOMC, and the other four slots rotate between the remaining 11 banks.

The Board of Governors

The **Board of Governors of the Federal Reserve** is comprised of seven governors, who are appointed by the president of the United States with the advice and consent of Congress. Each governor serves a 14-year, nonrenewable term with one governor's term expiring every other January. This structure is intended to keep the governors free of political pressures. With nonrenewable terms, a governor does not need to defer to the president in order to win reappointment. Because only two terms expire during the four years of the president's term, no president should be able to unduly influence the Board of Governors through appointments. However, the custom of replacing resigning members for the remainder of their term somewhat mitigates this. While governors can be removed for "cause," none ever has been removed.

The **chairman of the Board of Governors,** on the other hand, serves a four-year term and is chosen from the members of the Board. Therefore, every president of the United States has the opportunity to appoint his own chairman, subject to this constraint. By tradition, every chairman has resigned his position as a governor following the end of his term as chairman. This allows some presidents to appoint more than two governors during a four-year term. The chairman presides at meetings of the Board, assigns each governor specific tasks, and is the main spokesman for the Federal Reserve. Nonetheless, Board decisions are made by majority vote, so the Board can override the chairman.

The primary duty of the Board of Governors is to conduct monetary policy. This is accomplished both by its control of the discount rate and its ability to set reserve requirements within certain limits. More importantly, however, the Board represents a clear majority on the monetary policy committee within the Fed. The Board members, together with five of the Federal Reserve bank presidents, form the Federal Open Market Committee. The FOMC controls the most important tool of monetary policy, open market operations, which will be discussed in detail below.

Beyond monetary policy, the chairman of the Board serves as an economic adviser to the president, testifies before Congress, and speaks to the media for the Federal Reserve. The chairman and the governors can serve as representatives of the United States in negotiations with foreign governments on economic matters. In addition, the Board of Governors sets the margin requirements for securities purchases. Its staff of professional economists provides economic analysis that the Board uses in decision making.

Federal Open Market Committee

The Federal Open Market Committee (FOMC) is comprised of 12 members: the 7 members of the Board of Governors, the president of the New York Federal Reserve Bank, and on a rotating basis, 4 presidents of the other 11 Federal Reserve banks. While only five presidents of the district banks are voting members of the FOMC at any one time, all attend the eight meetings that are held each year. Because the FOMC tends to make its decisions by consensus rather than by majority rule, the nonvoting presidents do have some influence on open market operations. The chairman of the Board of Governors serves as the chairman of the FOMC.

The eight meetings per year are the key decision points for monetary policy. At these meetings, the FOMC decides upon the size of the monetary base for the economy as a whole. It is presented with evidence on the state of the economy and the financial sector, all of which is prepared in relative secrecy by the Board staff. The Committee is then confronted with a clear decision: Should the monetary base be expanded to reduce the level of short-term interest rates in the financial markets, should the monetary base be reduced to increase overnight rates, or should it remain the same? Each choice has a forecasted effect on the money supply, interest rates, and economic output, which is tabulated by staff economists using state-of-the-art computer models. Each forecast, however, is only an estimate. After considerable debate, the FOMC decides upon a plan for monetary policy. This includes a target for fed funds, an estimate of the change in the monetary base, and projected growth in the monetary base until the next meeting—assuming no radical change in the economy.

These policy directives are carried out by the New York Federal Reserve bank under the direction of its president, who serves as vice chairman of the FOMC. The policies are usually implemented through the purchase or sale of securities by the New York Federal Reserve bank at its trading desk on Broad and Wall Streets in New York City. When securities are purchased, the seller, who is frequently a bank, or a securities dealer owned by a bank, receives payment from the New York Federal Reserve bank in the form of deposits on the Federal Reserve. This very act increases the monetary base of the economy and, in turn, leads to a multiple expansion of credit and the money supply. You can see now why this bank is such a central part of the system and its decision-making process.

The New York Fed trades on behalf of all of the accounts of the Federal Reserve System. The manager of this trading desk communicates regularly with the FOMC members regarding these trading activities. The FOMC even plays a role in both discount rate and required reserve rate policy. While it does not actually control either the discount rate or reserve requirements, the FOMC usually determines these levels.

Understanding How the Fed Sets Monetary Policy

Given all this information about the structure of the Fed, its goals, and its place within the financial sector, we are now in the position to explain the process by which the Fed actually implements monetary policy. Simply stated, monetary policy is achieved by the Fed through the use of three main quantitative tools and one qualitative tool. The first set includes open market operations, the discount window, and reserve requirements. The qualitative tool, sometimes referred to as **moral suasion,** includes a whole range of pressures that the Fed can bring to bear in an effort to control or influence decisions made by members of the banking sector. We will discuss each tool in turn, paying particular attention to how these tools affect the money supply.

Open Market Operations

Recall from Chapter 26 the examples given to illustrate the money multiplier. In that example, we simply said "assume the Fed provides $100 of monetary base," and we then saw the impact of that base on the money supply, either *M1* or *M2*, through the appropriate money multiplier. However, we did not explain how the monetary base was changed! The most direct way for the Fed to change the monetary base is through open market operations. In essence, the Fed enters the open market to buy or sell government securities.

There are two types of open market operations: dynamic and defensive. **Dynamic open market operations** are securities trades made to actively change the size or growth rate of the monetary base when, for example, the FOMC determines that the monetary base should be larger than it has been. **Defensive open market operations** are trades made to offset factors that affect the money supply but are outside the control of the Fed. For example, recall that when the public decides to hold more currency, the money multiplier changes. If the Fed wants to maintain a particular level of *M1*, then the monetary base will have to be changed to offset the new level of currency being held.

The actual day-to-day management of open market operations is carried out by the manager of the Federal Reserve System's open market account. The manager supervises the traders who work at a trading desk located in a room on the eighth floor of the Federal Reserve bank of New York. The manager is responsible for the daily trades of the Fed. Every day begins with the manager "taking the pulse" of the money markets. Sources of information include the daily estimates of reserves in the banking system, the current fed funds rate, and discussions with several government securities dealers. The current fed funds rate gives an indication of the level of excess reserves available in the system. A low fed funds rate would indicate that there is a large amount of reserves available to be loaned, while a high fed funds rate would indicate that banks do not have excess reserves to loan. The government securities dealers may be able to give an indication of the direction the market may take on any given day.

Next, the manager would receive reports from the research staff about the likely movements in other factors that influence the money supply. For example, if Treasury deposits in their account at the Federal Reserve are predicted to fall because the government is planning to make payments to social security recipients, a defensive sale of securities may be necessary to offset the expected increase in the monetary base. Other factors that would be forecast include currency holdings by the public and foreign deposits at the Fed.

The manager then combines all of the above information with the directive from the FOMC to determine the net open market operations that must be conducted that day. The combination of the dynamic operations necessary to carry out the FOMC directive and the defensive operations that are dictated by the predicted movements in the above factors lead to the net operations for the day. The manager will then call the members of the FOMC to get the "game plan" approved.

Typically, the plan is handed to the traders before noon. The traders then start contacting government securities traders at commercial and investment banks to get quotes for the desired securities. The Fed usually trades in Treasury bills because of the size and liquidity in this market. As noted in Chapter 11, any participant can trade large amounts of these securities without having a large effect on the price of these securities. Once the quotes have been collected, they are arranged in order from the most to the least favorable. Trades are then executed, starting with the best quote, until the day's goal has been achieved. This is all accomplished by about 12:30.

When open market operations are carried out through outright purchases or sales of securities, as in dynamic operations, trades are for cash delivery in the Federal Reserve's book entry clearing system. The trades transfer ownership, in the case of a Fed purchase, to the Fed and then transfer funds directly to the reserve account of the bank that sold the security. This has the immediate effect of increasing the reserves available to the banking system.

More often, though, the trading desk will engage in repurchase agreements or reverse repurchase agreements. The basics of these repos or reverse repos were discussed in a previous chapter. Essentially, a repo is the purchase of a security with the guarantee to sell it back at a specified date and price. The reverse repo would be the opposite. These are very desirable tools for carrying out defensive open market operations. Most defensive operations are intended to offset temporary changes in the money supply and must be reversed after a short period. A repo automates the reversal of a defensive operation and signals to the market the temporary nature of a particular operation.

Open market operations have several advantages. First, they can occur at any time the Fed desires. They can be quickly implemented, or they can be carried out slowly over a period of days or weeks. Second, the Fed can decide how much it wants to buy or sell and then execute that decision in the market. The Fed can control the size of the impact on the monetary base. Third, the effects of open market operations are reversible. If the Fed wants to undo a sale of securities, it can readily buy them back. Fourth and finally, they allow the Fed to make small adjustments without drawing a lot of public attention. You will see below that none of the other tools at their disposal are so flexible.

The Discount Window

The discount window is the popular name for the ability of the Fed to make loans to banks. Discount loans have two basic purposes. First, they provide reserves to a bank in a time of need. This is the lender-of-last-resort function of the Fed. Second, discount loans are a tool of monetary policy. This is because discount loans increase the monetary base.

Each reserve bank operates its own discount window. So, when we refer to the Fed operating the discount window, we are actually referring to each bank operating the discount window for its region. There are three types of discount loans: adjustment credit loans, seasonal credit loans, and extended credit loans.

Adjustment credit loans are very short-term loans that can be made based on a phone call from the bank. Typically, these loans are repaid by the end of the next business day. They are used to replenish reserves that have been depleted due to unanticipated levels of deposit withdrawal, and they allow the bank to maintain necessary reserve levels as they liquidate securities they hold. **Seasonal credit loans** are longer-term loans that give banks in agricultural or other seasonal markets the flexibility they need to make loans at different times of the year. **Extended credit loans** fall under the heading of lender of last resort. These loans must be applied for by submitting an application that states the amount of the loan and the repayment plan. These loans can be quite large and long-term relative to the other loans. Typically, extended credit loans are only made in cases of financial distress.

The **discount rate** is the interest rate charged on discount loans. This rate is set by each bank, subject to review by the Board of Governors. Several factors must be considered in setting the discount rate. The Fed must keep the federal funds rate in mind. If the discount rate falls below the federal funds rate, banks will have an incentive to make discount loans in order to make an arbitrage profit, because they could borrow at the discount rate, then lend that money at the federal funds rate. The Fed discourages discount borrowing for profit. Therefore, the frequency with which a bank takes discount loans is monitored. Further, the Fed

Exhibit 27.3

*Historical movement
of discount rate and
fed fund rate*

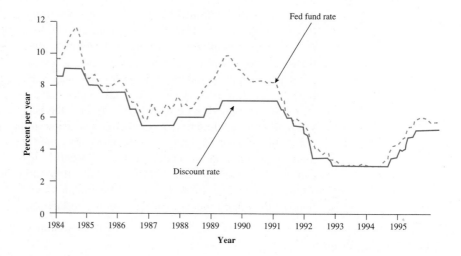

tries to observe what a bank does with its loans in order to determine whether need or profit motivated a bank's request for a discount loan. For this reason, one could argue that there is a cost beyond the discount rate that banks must consider. If a bank comes to the discount window too often, and for profit, it may not have access to the discount window in time of need. The Fed uses this credit rationing, sometimes referred to as a kind of moral suasion, to keep the discount window for the lender-of-last-resort function.

It is often argued that a change in the discount rate is a signal of Federal Reserve policy. For example, raising the discount rate is often interpreted as a signal of tighter monetary policy ahead, while reductions are seen as a signal of monetary ease. However, market participants must be cautious in their evaluation of this Fed signal. Sometimes, the discount rate is raised in response to an increase in the federal funds rate in order to remove profit opportunities from discount loans. In this case, there is no signal in the increase of the discount rate, though some may still interpret it as one. Therefore, as with open market operations, we must distinguish between dynamic and defensive moves in the discount rate. A dynamic change in the discount rate would in fact signal a change in Fed policy. On the other hand, defensive moves in the discount rate would simply be reactions to moves in the federal funds rate. Thus, the important number to watch is not the absolute level of the discount rate but rather the spread between the federal funds rate and the discount rate. Nonetheless, as can be seen from Exhibit 27.3, the discount rate historically has moved quite closely with the fed funds rate.

There are some disadvantages to using the discount window to conduct monetary policy. The biggest disadvantage is that the Fed cannot control the exact impact of discount policy on the monetary base. The Fed can only set the discount rate and then wait to see what happens. Raising or lowering the discount rate

---

Box 27.2

Success at the Discount Window

As discussed in this chapter, the Fed failed to use the discount window effectively during the Great Depression. However, since then, it has done an admirable job of using this tool to prevent panics. One recent example is the Black Monday crash of the stock market in October 1987. On Monday, October 19, 1987, the stock market experienced the largest single-day loss in its history. However, the biggest threat to the market was on Tuesday. As the market fell on Monday, banks withdrew lines of credit to securities specialists out of fear over the financial health of the securities firms. However, these securities firms were badly in need of funds to keep an orderly market and to maintain trading. Banks were withdrawing funds just as they were needed most. This could have led to a total collapse in the financial markets.

However, Alan Greenspan and E. Gerald Corrigan, Chairman of the Board of Governors and President of the New York Federal Reserve Bank respectively, announced before the market opened on Tuesday that the Fed stood ready "to serve as a source of liquidity to support the economic and financial system." Further, the Fed announced that it would make discount loans to any bank that would make loans to the securities industry. In essence, the Fed announced that it would do whatever was needed to support the financial industry. The outcome of this action was that markets did not fail, and in fact, the stock market rallied to a 100-point gain on Tuesday.

---

creates an incentive for banks to borrow less or more at the discount window. The Fed can only control the actual amount of borrowing through credit rationing. This is in contrast to open market operations, where the Fed can control the timing and size of the impact on the monetary base.

Another problem with discount policy is the confusion over what the Fed is signaling by a change in the discount rate. A defensive increase in the discount rate may by misinterpreted as a signal of a change in monetary policy. Therefore, the Fed is hesitant to increase the discount rate. On the other hand, the Fed may also be hesitant to decrease the discount rate because it will later have to increase the rate again. These factors make the discount window a much less favorable policy tool for the Fed.

Reserve Requirements

The two tools we discussed above are used to control the monetary base. Reserve requirements, on the other hand, impact the money multiplier directly. An increase in reserve requirements will decrease the money supply by decreasing the money multiplier. For this reason, small changes in reserve requirements can have a much larger effect on the money supply than can small changes in the other two tools.

Initially, the Fed set reserve requirements only for member banks. However, as of 1987, the Fed has control of the reserve requirements for all institutions

---

Box 27.3

Fed Watching—How It's Done

The policy-making Federal Open Market Committee is expected to leave short-term interest rates unchanged when it meets this morning.

Recent reports of surging employment and a solid gain in industrial output in February will be enough to stay the Fed's hand, economists said.

Concerns that the economy was turning sour spurred the Fed to cut the federal funds rate that banks charge each other for overnight loans one-quarter percentage point in both December and January.

The Fed's target for the funds rate is now 5.25%. The discount rate, which the Fed charges on loans to banks, was trimmed one-quarter point to 5% in January.

The Fed could stay on hold all year if the economy gathers steam, economists said. But some see the Fed shaving the federal funds rate again at a May 8 meeting.

"I don't think there is any reason for the Fed to cut rates right now with the economy perking up," said David Munro, chief U.S. economist at High Frequency Economics in Valhalla, N.Y.

But there's a good chance the Fed will trim rates again in May, he added.

Munro said that policymakers likely would prefer a "quiet" session today, since Greenspan will be appearing before the Senate Banking Committee after their meeting.

Normally the Fed enforces a "blackout" before and after Fed meetings. For about a week, policymakers do not publicly discuss monetary policy or the economy.

Greenspan's nomination by President Clinton is widely supported in Congress. His testimony is slated to start at noon. The FOMC meeting begins earlier than usual and is supposed to end by then.

Financial markets and Fed-watchers will be braced for any comments on the economy or interest rates.

News from the Labor Department earlier this month that the economy added 705,000 jobs in February rocked markets, sparking a massive sell-off of both stocks and Treasuries.

The bellwether 30-year Treasury bond tacked on one-quarter percentage point to its yield in the frenzied sell-off that followed the release of the report.

In January and February, bond prices suggested that traders saw a recession looming, said economist John Ryding of Bear, Stearns & Co. in New York. Now traders are looking for the economy to chug along at a modest clip.

Despite recent gyrations in financial markets, economists doubted that Greenspan's view of the

---

issuing transaction accounts. Currently, the Fed requires that all depository institutions hold reserves of 10 percent against transaction balances, except for those with balances below $52 million. The latter are subject to a 3 percent requirement. In addition, as of 1996, all other reserve ratios are set at zero, but they remain subject to review.

The principle advantage of reserve requirements as a tool of monetary policy is that they apply to all banks equally. However, reserve requirements have a multiplicative impact on the money supply. Therefore, it is often argued that it is difficult to make small changes in the money supply through this tool. While it is possible to specify small changes in reserve requirements, it is costly to implement changes. Therefore, reserve requirements are rarely used as an active tool of monetary policy.

economy has changed much since his semiannual Humphrey-Hawkins testimony on Feb. 20.

Then, he said the economy was moving through a "soft" spot. But he believed the economy would avoid a recession and perk up in the second half.

"The inflation numbers are good enough, and the economy is still sluggish enough" to warrant another rate cut in May, said Mark Zandi, chief economist at Regional Financial Associates in West Chester, Pa.

Not everyone believes the Fed would be wise to hold off on snipping interest rates.

Earlier this month the Shadow Open Market Committee, a private Fed-watching group, warned that the money supply is growing too slowly to keep the economy rolling.

A year before the last recession, the monetary base was expanding at a rate just below 4% from a year earlier. Yearly growth in the money base broke sharply last year and has fallen below 3%.

Economists generally agree that the economy firmed up a bit in February and March. But they note that the data have been tough to read lately because of some growth-dampening surprises that hit the economy in the first quarter.

"The statistics have been relatively muddied," said Zandi. "I don't think we're going to get a sense of where the economy really is going until May."

An impasse in talks over the federal budget shut down much of the government in early January.

Then, just as federal workers were about to get back on the job, a blizzard brought the Northeast to a near standstill.

By February, things seemed to return to normal. But in March, a 17-day strike against General Motors Corp. halted auto production.

The government shutdown, blizzard and strike each shaved one-quarter percentage point off gross domestic product growth in the first quarter, estimates David Wyss, chief financial economist at DRI-McGraw Hill Inc.

Stifled first-quarter growth almost guarantees a strong second-quarter rebound, economists say.

Even as the economy was being lashed, signs emerged that it was picking up from a meager 0.9% annual rate rise in fourth-quarter GDP.

The most stunning tidbit came from Labor: 705,000 jobs added to the economy in February.

But many analysts called the surge too good to be true. Skeptics predict that the February jobs total will be revised down sharply in the next employment report.

Despite the jump in employment, wage pressures stayed muted in February.

Source: *Investor's Business Daily,* March 26, 1996.

Understanding Monetary Policy Targets

Earlier in this chapter, we outlined the goals of the Fed. At the time, we mentioned that these goals are quite difficult to achieve because they are ill-defined in some cases and because they are sometimes in conflict with other goals. This has led some to suggest that "fine tuning" the economy to achieve macro-policy goals is all but impossible. They point out that there is a long and variable lag between the actions of the Fed and the impact of those actions on the level of economic activity or employment. If the Fed had to wait for a year to evaluate the effectiveness of its actions, it would never be able to keep up with the economy. If the action it took was too mild or too aggressive, it would be too late to fix it by the time the problem was manifest.

The best analogy we can offer for this view is the following one. To these skeptics, active monetary policy aimed at achieving the goals outlined above is like driving a car down a winding mountain road. However, this is no ordinary car. All of the controls, including the steering, brakes, and gas pedal, work with a somewhat random delay. For example, pressing the brake pedal will not begin to slow the car for between 5 and 10 seconds. Similarly, turning the steering wheel will turn the car, but not before the car has traveled another 100 or 200 feet down the road. With this rather bizarre vehicle, imagine that you have just negotiated a particularly tricky corner and want to accelerate to the next corner. You push down on the gas pedal and surprise, there is no effect. So, you push harder, and finally, you get a big burst of acceleration just as you arrive at the next corner. Successfully driving this car requires the driver to see a curve well down the road, apply the brakes and turn the wheel in advance, and then wait and hope that the random delays have been properly predicted. No one would be surprised to hear that the driver of this car has crashed into the mountain.

Generally, cars do not work like this. However, the Fed faces a challenge no less daunting than driving this imaginary car. The controls that the Fed uses are not steering wheels or brake and gas pedals; instead, they use tools outlined above—open market operations, discount window policy, and reserve requirements. Each of these controls is known to affect the economy in the ways we have already discussed. However, the delay before the effect is felt and the ultimate size of the effect, once it is felt, are difficult to predict. Therefore, like the driver of our imaginary car, the Fed must anticipate turns in the progress of our economy and apply just enough of the right control. With such a difficult task, it is no wonder that the success of their efforts is often questioned. The Fed has more than once been accused of driving right into the mountain or over the edge, so to speak.

Faced with this problem, the Fed has attempted to establish proximate goals for monetary policy. These targets are variables that are believed to lead to the desired outcome but are more directly observable or measurable. In terms of our analogy, these targets would be road signs indicating that we were still on the right road and going in the correct direction.

The targets actually used by the Fed have three properties. First, they are controllable. It would do no good for the Fed to choose a target over which it has no control. Second, they have a predictable effect on the goals. Third, they are measurable. This allows the Fed to quickly determine the impact of its policy actions.

The Fed uses two types of such targets: **operating targets** and **intermediate targets.** Operating targets, such as reserve levels or very short-term interest rates, are variables that are most responsive to its policy tools. Intermediate targets, such as monetary aggregates (*M1* or *M2*) or longer-term interest rates, are variables that are known to have a direct effect on employment or the price level. These targets work as a linkage between the tools of the Fed and its ultimate goals.

The Fed can use its tools to influence the operating targets. The impact of their action can be quickly measured and adjusted to achieve the desired result. The changes in the operating targets have an effect on the intermediate targets that can be predicted and evaluated over a slightly longer term. Finally, the changes in the intermediate targets have a predictable effect on the final goals of the Fed.

Summary

At the center of any financial system is a central bank. Historically, the role of the central bank was to ensure a stable monetary and financial system. Over time, central banks throughout the world have been asked to assist in achieving general public policy goals, such as full employment, sustainable growth, and price stability. Playing this important public policy role makes the central bank an even more important force in the financial community, one that must be watched and understood by every participant in the financial markets. Central bank actions affect the level of interest rates, expectations of future growth, and the value of virtually all financial assets.

For the U.S. market, the central bank is our Federal Reserve. As it currently exists, the Federal Reserve System stands as a truly unique government entity. It has roots in a system of regional Federal Reserve banks, but it functions now as a fairly centralized central bank. As such, the Fed controls the money supply, provides reserves to the financial markets, ensures stability, and serves as a banker's bank. We view the first of these as a cru-cial role, yet it is the one that was not granted to the Fed at its inception. Rather, the Fed grew up as the financial sector did. The Fed assumed its current role over time as it became clear that its actions had profound effects on the financial system and the overall economy. Inevitably the Fed's judgments will be scrutinized by all interested parties.

In this regard, market participants are truly interested parties. Decisions made by the Fed have profound effects on the markets, and its presence is always felt. Whether it is the Fed's daily intervention in the money market through the New York Federal Reserve bank, or its FOMC meetings setting short-term rates and plans for monetary growth, the Fed's actions are carefully scrutinized. In fact, many financial institutions have whole departments dedicated to examining Fed action and trying to forecast future moves. While most market participants don't devote all of their time to this activity, every investor needs to spend at least some time analyzing Fed actions and thinking about its future moves. The Fed looms large; it's probably not wise to ignore it.

Key Concepts

adjustment, seasonal, and extended credit
  loans, 701
bank panics, 689
Board of Governors of the Federal Reserve
  System, 697
central bank, 684
chairman of the Board of Governors, 697
discounting, 689
discount window, 689

dynamic versus defensive open market
  operations, 699
economic growth, 686
Federal Open Market Committee, 693
Federal Reserve Act of 1913, 692
Federal Reserve System, 692
frictional and unintended unemployment,
  685, 686
goals of central bank policy, 685
lender of last resort, 689

Review Questions

1. Briefly outline the four major functions of the American version of a central bank. At what policy goals are these functions aimed? Explain.
2. What roles do the Federal Reserve banks play in carrying out monetary policy? the Board of Governors? the FOMC?
3. Define and explain the tools used by the Fed to implement monetary policy. What entities are controlled by these tools?
4. If the Fed relaxes reserve requirements at the same time that it purchases bonds, what happens to the money supply?
5. When the Federal Reserve announces a change in the discount rate, the market inter-est rate may or may not change. Briefly explain the dynamics of this situation.
6. Once the FOMC determines an amenable level of monetary base, open market operations are executed. What is the procedure for execution?
7. The Fed appears to be more stringent in its regulation of large banks as opposed to smaller ones. Why do you think this is so? What would happen to the money supply if assets were transferred to the smaller banks on a large scale?
8. As reserve requirements increase, what happens to the Fed's monetary control?

References

Abel, Andrew, and Ben Bernanke. *Macroeconomics.* 2nd ed. Reading, Mass.: Addison Wesley, 1995.

Board of Governors of the Federal Reserve System. *The Federal Reserve System: Purposes and Functions.* 7th ed. Washington, D.C.: Board of Governors of the Federal Reserve System, 1984.

Board of Governors of the Federal Reserve System. *Annual Report.* Washington, D.C.: Board of Governors of the Federal Reserve System, 1995.

Burns, Arthur F. "The Independence of the Federal Reserve System." *Challenge,* July/August 1976.

Davis, R. G. "Intermediate Targets and Indicators for Monetary Policy: An Introduction to the Issues." *Quarterly Review.* Federal Reserve Bank of New York, Summer 1990.

Friedman, Milton. "The Case for Overhauling the Federal Reserve." *Challenge,* July/August 1985.

Friedman, Milton, and Anna Jacobson Schwartz. *A Monetary History of The United States 1867–1960.* Princeton, N.J.: Princeton University Press, 1963.

Greider, William. *Secrets of the Temple: How the Federal Reserve Runs the Country.* New York: Simon and Schuster, 1987.

Kane, Edward J. "External Pressure and the Operations of the Fed." In *Political Economy of International and Domestic Monetary Relations,* edited by Raymond E. Lombra and Willard E. Witte. Ames, Iowa: Iowa State University Press, 1982.

Maisel, Sherman. *Managing the Dollar.* New York: Norton, 1973.

McNees, S. K. "The Discount Window: The Other Tool of Monetary Policy." *New England Economic Review.* Federal Reserve Bank of Boston, July 1993.

Meek, Paul. *Open Market Operations.* New York: Federal Reserve Bank of New York, 1985.

Roth, Howard L. "Federal Reserve Open Market Techniques." *Economics Review.* Federal Reserve Bank of Kansas City, March 1986.

Werner, S. E. "The Changing Role of Reserve Requirements in Monetary Policy." *Economics Review.* Federal Reserve Bank of Kansas City, December 1992.

Name Index

Subject Index